DIGITAL SOUND & MUSIC

CONCEPTS, APPLICATIONS, AND SCIENCE

```
  . 1 0 1 0 1 0 .
 . 0 1 0 1 1 0 1 0
 0 1 1 1 1 0 0 0 1 0
 . 0 1 1 0 1 0 0 1 1 0
 0 1 0 0 1 0 1 1 1 1 0
 0 1 0 1 0 0 1 1 0 1 0
```

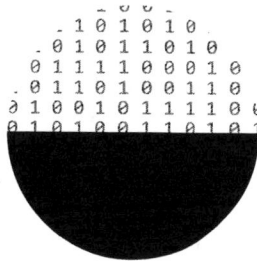

JENNIFER BURG
JASON ROMNEY
ERIC SCHWARTZ

Franklin, Beedle & Associates Inc.
Portland, Oregon
1/800-322-2665
https://fbeedle.com

CHAPTER TWO

SOUND WAVES • 55

CHAPTER THREE
MUSICAL SOUND • 121

CHAPTER FIVE

DIGITIZATION • 251

CHAPTER SIX
MIDI AND SOUND SYNTHESIS • 329

CHAPTER SEVEN
AUDIO PROCESSING • 405

CHAPTER EIGHT

GETTING TO WORK • 475

Preface

This book, originally developed under National Science Foundation grant support[*], was written to bridge academic disciplines and areas of practice that include music production, audio engineering for theatre and film, and computer science. Apart from the first and the last chapters, each chapter is divided into three sections. The first section covers general concepts, the second discusses applications, and the third delves into the mathematics and algorithms that underpin digital audio processing.

It is not intended that a single course would cover all the material in this book. Rather, portions of the book could be used in college-level courses such as the following:

  ⟩ Theatre or film sound design and production.
  ⟩ Digital music production.
  ⟩ A course covering sound in a New Media or Digital Media or Digital Arts program (particularly in programs that are interdisciplinary between computer science and music).
  ⟩ A computer science course introducing digital signal processing.
  ⟩ A computer science course which engages students in programming through audio applications.

The special value of this book is that it provides a broad context for students. In academic programs that emphasize applications, students are still able to "look under the hood" to gain a deeper understanding of audio processing at a lower level of abstraction. For students of computer science, physics, or mathematics, the relationship between science and applications provides interest and motivation.

The book also serves as a reference for anyone interested in digital audio processing. This includes hobbyists, those who are "self-taught" in music production, and

[*] Burg, Jennifer and Jason Romney, "Linking Science, Art, and Practice in Digital Sound," National Science Foundation Award Number 07177443.

even those already in the audio processing or music production industry who want a deeper understanding of their art and craft.

This book also has an online version, freely available along with a large number of learning supplements, at http://digitalsoundandmusic.com. The learning supplements include the following types:

  » Practical Exercises (suggestions for hands-on experiments or "pencil and paper" problems to solve).
  » Flash Tutorials (dynamic, interactive demonstrations of concepts).
  » MAX Demos (written in the MAX/MSP audio processing language).
  » MATLAB Exercises (which also can be done in the freeware equivalent, Octave).
  » Programming Exercises (C/C++ and Java).
  » Video Demos.

Icons in the margins of the book indicate that a learning supplement is available. The icons in the online version are live links that lead directly to the learning supplements. Solutions are available for instructors, on request, for learning supplements that entail problem-solving.

Portions of this book have been used in interdisciplinary, elective computer science/music courses that introduce students to the science of digital audio and MIDI and expose the students to simple programs that process sound. Sections of the book have likewise been used in a junior/senior level computer science course entitled Digital Media, where students apply their understanding of the science and mathematics of sound by implementing algorithms for digital audio processing. The book has also been used in New Media, Sound System Design, Sound System Engineering, Sound Design Technology, Applied Digital Projects, Sound Studio, and Production Audio and Ear training courses.

Jason has used the book in his Sound System Design, Sound System Engineering, Sound Design Technology, and Applied Digital Projects courses. He has also used the Flash and MAX demos in guest lectures in science and math classes at several elementary and secondary schools in North Carolina.

The authors hope that you enjoy applying your creativity to the marriage of science and sound. Feedback is welcome, including corrections, suggestions, example projects that have worked particularly well for instructors, and creative applications that bring to bear the principles covered in the book.

ACKNOWLEDGMENTS

In addition to the staff at our publisher, Franklin, Beedle & Associates, we would like to acknowledge the following for their help in the writing and editing of this book:

) Susan Reiser, for her use of the textbook in New Media courses at UNC Asheville and her valuable feedback.

) Michael Boger, for his eagle-eyed proofreading.

We also thank the following instructors who have corresponded with us about their work using the book in courses: Richard Thomas and his colleagues at Purdue University, Joe Pino at Carnegie Mellon University, and Phillip Conrad at University of California at Santa Barbara.

—JB, JR, ES

CHAPTER ONE
Getting Started

1.1 SOUNDS LIKE FUN!

We walk through this world wrapped in the vibrations of sound. Sounds are all around us all of the time, whether we pay attention to them or not. Most people love music. Its melodies, harmonies, rhythms, consonances, dissonances, reverberations, tonalities, and atonalities find resonance in our souls and echo in our minds. Those of us with an artistic calling may love the form, structure, beauty, and endless possibilities for creativity in music and sound. Those of us with a scientific bent may be fascinated by the intellectual intricacy of sound and music, endlessly moldable by mathematics, algorithms, and computers. Sounds can be maddeningly impossible to ignore, or surprisingly difficult to notice. If your neighbor decides to begin his deck construction project early on a Saturday morning, it's likely that you won't be able to tune out the pounding and sawing. But when your heart starts racing at a bullet-riddled chase scene in an action movie, you probably won't even notice how the movie's background score is manipulating your emotions. Music gets attached to events in our lives so that when we hear the same music again, the memories come wafting back into our thoughts. In short, sounds are a significant part of our experience of life.

So that's why we're here—we musicians, theatre and film sound designers, audio engineers, computer scientists, self-taught audiophiles, and generally curious folks. We're here to learn about what sound and music are, how they interact with the digital world, and what we can do with them when we apply our creativity, intellect, and computer-based tools. Let's get started!

1.2 HOW THIS BOOK IS ORGANIZED

What follows is a series of chapters and learning supplements that explore the science of digital sound with a concerted effort to link the scientific principles to "real life" practice. Each chapter is organized into three sections. The first section covers the basic principles being taught. The second section provides examples of where these principles are found in the professional practice of digital sound. The third section explores these principles further and allows for deeper experimentation with programming and computational tools. As you progress through each chapter, you'll come across demonstrations, exercises, and projects at varying levels of abstraction. Starting at the highest level of abstraction, you might begin with an off-the-shelf software tool like Logic Pro or Cakewalk Sonar, descend through tools like Max and MATLAB, and end at a low level of abstraction with C programming exercises. This book is intended to be useful to readers from different backgrounds—musicians, computer scientists, film sound designers, theatre sound designers, audio engineers, or anyone interested in sound. The book's structure should allow readers to explore the relationships among fundamental concepts, professional practice, and underlying science in the realm of digital sound, delving down to the level of abstraction that best fits their interests and needs.

1.3 A BRIEF HISTORY OF DIGITAL SOUND

It's difficult to measure the enormous impact that digital technology has had on sound design, engineering, and related arts. It was not that long ago that the ideas of sound designers and composers were severely limited by the capabilities of their tools. Magnetic tape, in its various forms, was king. Sound editing involved razor blades and bloody fingertips. Electronic music production required a wall full of equipment interconnected with scores of patch cables, all working together to play a single instrument's sound, live, one note at a time.

The concept of using digital technology to create sound has been around for a long time. The first documented instance of the idea was in 1842 when Ada Lovelace wrote about the analytical engine invented by Charles Babbage. Babbage was essentially making a digital calculator. Before the device was even built, Lovelace saw its potential applications beyond mere number crunching. She speculated that anything that could be expressed through and adapted to "the abstract science of operations"—for example, music—could then be placed under the creative influence of machine computation with amazing results. In Ada Lovelace's words:

> Supposing, for instance, that the fundamental relations of pitched sounds in the science of harmony and of musical composition were susceptible of such expression and adaptations, the engine might compose elaborate and scientific pieces of music of any degree of complexity or extent.

It took 140 years, however, before we began to see this idea realized in any practical format. In 1983, Yamaha released its DX-series keyboard synthesizers. The most popular of these was the DX7. What made these synthesizers significant from a historical perspective is that they employed digital circuits to make the instrument sounds and used an early version of the Musical Instrument Digital Interface (MIDI), later ratified in 1984, to handle the communication of the keyboard performance data in and out of the synthesizer.

The year 1982 saw the release of the digital audio compact disc (CD). The first commercially available compact disc was pressed on August 17, 1982, in Hannover, Germany. The disc contained a recording of Richard Strauss's *Eine Alpensinfonie*, played by the Berlin Philharmonic and conducted by Herbert von Karajan.

Today, digital sound and music are flourishing, and tools are available at a price that almost any aspiring sound artist can afford. This evolution in available tools has changed the way we approach sound. While current digital technology still has limitations, this isn't really what gets in the way when musicians, sound designers, and sound engineers set out to bring their ideas to life. It's the sound artists' *mastery* of their technical tools that is more often a bar to their creativity. Harnessing this technology in real practice often requires a deeper understanding of the underlying science being employed, a subject that artists traditionally avoid. However, the links that sound provides between science, art, and practice are now making interdisciplinary work more alluring and are encouraging musicians, sound designers, and audio engineers to cross these traditional boundaries. This book is aimed at a broad spectrum of readers who approach sound from various directions. Our hope is to help reinforce the interdisciplinary connections and to enable our readers to explore sound from their own perspective and at the depth they choose.

1.4 BASIC TERMINOLOGY

1.4.1 ANALOG VS. DIGITAL

With the evolution of computer technology in the past 50 years, sound processing has become largely digital. Understanding the difference between analog and digital processes and phenomena is fundamental to working with sound.

The difference between analog and digital processes runs parallel to the difference between continuous and discrete number systems. The set of real numbers constitutes a **continuous** system, which can be thought of abstractly as an infinite line of continuously increasing numbers in one direction and decreasing numbers in the other. For any two points on the line (i.e., real numbers), an infinite number of points exist between them. This is not the case with discrete number systems, like the set of integers. No integers exist between 1 and 2. Consecutive integers are completely separate and distinct, which is the basic meaning of **discrete**.

Analog processes and phenomena are similar to continuous number systems. In a time-based **analog** phenomenon, one moment of the phenomenon is perceived or measured as moving continuously into the next. Physical devices can be engineered to behave in a continuous, analog manner. For example, a volume dial on a radio can be turned left or right continuously. The diaphragm inside a microphone can move continuously in response to changing air pressure, and the voltage sent down a wire can change continuously as it records the sound level. However, communicating continuous data to a computer is a problem. Computers "speak digital," not analog. The word **digital** refers to things that are represented as discrete levels. In the case of computers, there are exactly two levels—like 0 and 1, or off and on. A two-level system is a binary system, encodable in a base-2 number system. In contrast to analog processes, digital processes measure a phenomenon as a sequence of discrete events encoded in binary.

It could be argued that sound is an inherently analog phenomenon, the result of waves of changing air pressure that continuously reach our ears. However, to be communicated to a computer, the changes in air pressure must be captured as discrete events and communicated digitally. When sound has been encoded in the language that computers understand, powerful computer-based processing can be brought to bear on the sound for manipulation of frequency, dynamic range, phase, and every imaginable audio property. Thus, we have the advent of digital signal processing (DSP).

> **ASIDE:** One might think, intuitively, that all physical phenomena are inherently continuous and thus analog. But the question of whether the universe is essentially analog or digital is actually quite controversial among physicists and philosophers, a debate stimulated by the development of quantum mechanics. Many now view the universe as operating under a wave-particle duality and Heisenberg's Uncertainty Principle. Related to this debate is the field of "string theory," which the reader may find interesting.

1.4.2 DIGITAL AUDIO VS. MIDI

This book covers both sampled digital audio and MIDI. **Sampled digital audio** (or simply digital audio) consists of streams of audio data that represent the amplitude of sound waves at discrete moments in time. In the digital recording process, a microphone detects the amplitude of a sound, thousands of times a second, and sends this information to an audio interface or sound card in a computer. Each amplitude value is called a **sample**. The rate at which the amplitude measurements are recorded by the sound card is called the **sampling rate**, measured in **Hertz** (samples/second). The sound being detected by the microphone is typically a combination of sound frequencies. The **frequency** of a sound is related to the pitch that we hear—the higher the frequency, the higher the pitch.

MIDI (**musical instrument digital interface**), on the other hand, doesn't contain data representing actual sound waves; instead, it consists of symbolic messages (according to a widely accepted industry standard) that represent instruments, notes, and velocity information, similar to the way music is notated on a score, encoded for computers. In other words, digital audio holds information corresponding to a physical sound, while MIDI data holds information corresponding to a musical performance.

In Chapter 5 we'll define these terms in greater depth. For now, a simple understanding of digital audio vs. MIDI should be enough to help you gather the audio hardware and software you need.

1.5 SETTING UP YOUR WORK ENVIRONMENT

1.5.1 OVERVIEW

There are three things you may want to set up in order to work with this book. It's possible that you'll need only one of the first two, depending on your focus. Everyone will probably need the third to work with the suggested exercises in this book:

⟩ a digital audio workstation.

⟩ a live sound reinforcement system.

⟩ software on your computer to do hands-on exercises.

First, we assume most readers will want their own digital audio workstation (DAW), consisting of a computer and the associated hardware and software for at-home or professional sound production (Figure 1.1 on the following page). Suggestions for particular components or component types are given in Section 1.5.2.

Secondly, it's possible that you'll also be using equipment for live performances. A live performance setup is pictured in Figure 1.2 on the following page. Much of the equipment and connectivity is the same as or similar to equipment in a DAW.

Thirdly, to use this book most effectively you'll need to gather some additional software so that you can view the book's learning supplements, complete some of the exercises, and even do your own experiments. The learning supplements include:

⟩ Flash interactive tutorials, accessible at our website and viewable within a standard web browser with the Flash plug-in installed (generally included and enabled by default).

⟩ Max demo patchers, which can be viewed with the Max run-time environment, freely downloadable from the Cycling '74 website. (If you wish to do the Max programming exercises you'll need to purchase Max, or use the free alternative, Pure Data.)

⟩ MATLAB exercises (with Octave as a freeware alternative).

⟩ audio and MIDI processing worksheets that can be done in Logic, Cakewalk Sonar, Reason, Audition, Audacity, or some other digital audio or MIDI processing program.

》 C and Java programs, for which you'll need C and/or Java compilers and IDEs if you wish to complete these assignments.

We don't expect that you'll want to go through all the learning supplements or do all the exercises. You should choose the types of learning supplements that are useful

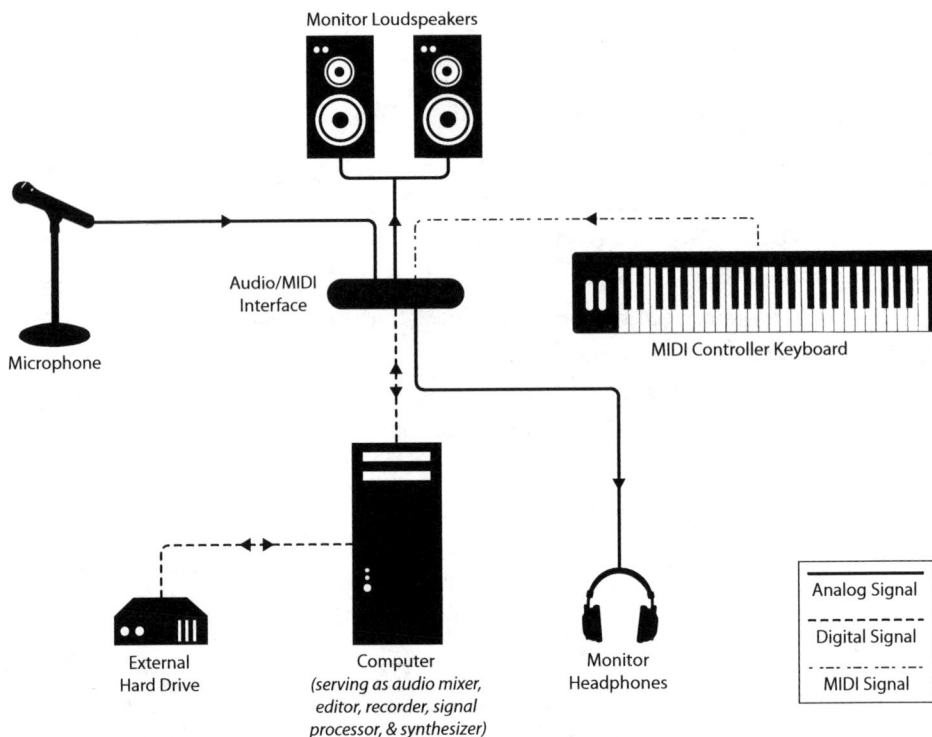

FIGURE 1.1: BASIC SETUP AND SIGNAL FLOW OF A DIGITAL AUDIO WORKSTATION

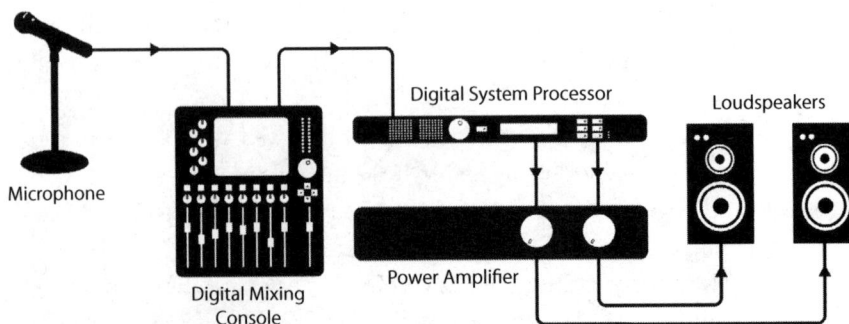

FIGURE 1.2: A SIMPLE LIVE SOUND REINFORCEMENT SYSTEM

to you and gather the necessary software accordingly. We give more information about the software for the learning supplements in 1.5.3.

In the sections that follow, we use a number of technical terms with only brief, if any, definitions, assuming that you have a basic computer vocabulary with regard to RAM, hard drives, sound cards, and so forth. Even if you don't fully understand all the terminology, when you're buying hardware and software to equip your DAW, you can refer your sales rep to this information to help you with your purchases. All terminology will be defined more completely as the book progresses.

1.5.2 HARDWARE FOR DIGITAL AUDIO AND MIDI PROCESSING

1.5.2.1 Computer System Requirements

Table 1.1 gives our recommendations for the components of an affordable DAW as well as equipment such as loudspeakers needed for live performances. Of course technology changes very quickly, so make sure to do your own research on the particular models of the components when you're ready to buy. The components listed in the table are a good starting point. Each category of components is explained in the sections that follow. We've omitted optional devices from the table, but include them in the discussion below.

Computer	Desktop or laptop with a fast processor, Mac or Windows operating system RAM—at least 2 GB Hard drive—a fast hard drive (separate and in addition to the operating system hard drive) dedicated to audio storage, at least 7200 RPM
Audio interface (i.e., sound card)	External audio interface with XLR connections. The audio interface may also serve as a MIDI interface
Microphone	Dynamic microphone with XLR connection. Possibly a condenser microphone as well
Cables and connectors	XLR cables for microphones, others as needed for peripheral devices

MIDI controller	A MIDI piano keyboard—may or may not include additional buttons and knobs. May have USB connectivity or require a MIDI interface. Possible all-in-one devices include both a keyboard and basic audio interface
Monitoring loudspeakers	Monitors with flat frequency response (so you hear an unaltered representation of the audio)
Studio headphones	Closed-back headphones (for better isolation)
Mixing console	Analog or digital mixer, as needed
Loudspeakers	Loudspeakers with amplifiers and directional/ frequency responses appropriate for the listening space

TABLE 1.1: BASIC HARDWARE COMPONENTS FOR A DAW AND LIVE PERFORMANCE SETUPS

A desktop or even a laptop computer with a fast processor is sufficient as the starting point for your DAW. Audio and MIDI processing make heavy demands on your computer's **RAM (random-access memory)**—the dynamic memory of a computer that holds data and programs while they're running. When you edit or play digital audio, a part of RAM called a **buffer** is set aside to hold the portion of audio data that you're going to need next. If your computer had to go all the way to the hard disk drive each time it needed to get the data, it wouldn't be able to play the audio in real-time. **Buffering** is a process of pulling data off permanent storage—the hard drive—and holding them in RAM so that the sound is immediately available to be played or processed. Audio is divided into streams, and often multiple audio streams are active at once, which implies that your computer has to set aside multiple buffers. MIDI instruments and samplers also make heavy demands on RAM. When a sampler is used, MIDI creates the sound of a chosen musical instrument by means of short audio clips called samples that are stored on the computer. All of these audio files have to be loaded into RAM so they can be instantly accessible to the MIDI keyboard. For these reasons, you'll probably need to upgrade the RAM capacity on your computer. A good place to begin is with 2 GB of RAM. RAM is easily upgradeable and can be increased later if needed. You can check the system requirements of your audio software for the specific RAM requirements of each application program.

You also need memory for permanent storage of your audio data—a large capacity **hard disk drive**. Most hard drives found in the standard configuration for desktop and laptop computers are not fast enough to keep up with real-time processing of digital audio. Your RAM buffers the audio playback streams to maintain the flow of data to your sound card, but your hard drive also needs to be fast enough to keep that buffer full of data. Digital audio processing requires at least a 7200-RPM hard drive hard that is dedicated to holding your audio files. That is, the hard drive needs to be a secondary one, in addition to your system hard drive. If you have a desktop computer, you might be able to install this second hard drive internally, but if you have a laptop or would simply like the ability to take your data with you, you'll need an external hard drive. The capacity of this hard drive should be as large as you can afford. At CD quality, digital audio files consume around ten megabytes per minute of sound. One minute of sound can easily consume one gigabyte of space on your hard drive. This is because you often work simultaneously with multiple tracks—sometimes even ten or more. In addition to these tracks, there are backup copies of the audio that are automatically created as you work.

> **ASIDE:** Early digital audio workstations utilized SCSI hard drives. These drives could be chained together in a combination of internal and external drives. Each hard drive could only hold enough data to accommodate a few tracks of audio, so the multitrack audio software at the time would perform a round-robin strategy of assigning audio data from different tracks to different SCSI hard drives in the chain. These SCSI hard drives, while small in size, provided impressive speed and performance and to this day, no external hard drive system can completely match the speed, performance, and reliability of external SCSI hard drives when used in digital audio.

New technologies are emerging that have the potential for eliminating the hard drive bottleneck. Mac computers now offer the Thunderbolt interface with bi-directional data transfer and a data rate of up to 10 GB/s. Solid state hard drives (SSDs)—distinguished by the fact that they have no moving parts—are fast and reliable. As these become more affordable, they may be the disk drives of choice for audio.

Before the advent of Thunderbolt and SSDs, the choice of external hard drives was between FireWire (IEEE 1394), USB interfaces, and eSATA. An advantage of FireWire over USB hard drives is that FireWire is not host-based. A host-based system like a USB drive does not get its own hardware address in the computer system. This means that the central processing unit (CPU) has to manage how the data move around on the USB bus. The data being transferred must first go through the CPU, which slows down the CPU by taking its attention away from its other tasks. FireWire devices, on the other hand, can transmit without running the data through the CPU first. FireWire also provides true bi-directional data transfers—simultaneously sending and receiving data. USB devices must alternate between sending and receiving.

For Mac computers, FireWire drives are preferable to USB for simultaneous real-time recording and playback of multiple digital audio streams. FireWire speeds of 400 or 800 are fine. These numbers refer to approximate MB/s half-duplex maximum data transfer rates. However, mixing 400 and 800 devices on the same bus is not a good idea. It's best just to pick one of the two speeds and make sure all your FireWire devices run at that speed.

The most important factor in choosing an external FireWire hard drive is the FireWire bridge chipset. This is the circuit that interfaces the IDE or SATA hard drive sitting in the box to the FireWire bus. There are a few chipsets out there, but the only chipsets that are reliable for digital audio are the Oxford FireWire chipsets. Make sure to confirm that the external FireWire hard drive you want to purchase uses an Oxford chipset.

Unfortunately, recent Windows operating systems have proven somewhat buggy for FireWire, so many Windows-based DAWs use USB interfaces, despite their short-comings. Alternatively, Windows computers could use eSATA hard drives, which perform just like internal SATA drives.

1.5.2.2 Digital Audio Interface

In order to work with digital sound, you need a device that can convert physical sound waves captured by microphones or other inputs into digital data for processing, and then convert the digital data back into analog form for your loudspeakers to reproduce as audible sound. **Audio interfaces** (or **sound cards**) provide this functionality.

Your computer probably came with a simple built-in sound card. This is suitable for basic playback or audio output, but to do recording with a high level of quality and control you need a more sophisticated, dedicated audio interface. There are many solutions out there. Leading manufacturers include AVID, M-Audio, MOTU, and Presonus. Things to look for when choosing an interface include how the box interfaces with the computer (USB, FireWire, PCI) and the number of inputs and outputs. You should have at least one low-impedance microphone input that uses an XLR connector. Some interfaces also come with instrument inputs that allow you to connect the output of an electric guitar directly into your computer. Figure 1.3 and Figure 1.4 show examples of appropriate audio interfaces.

FIGURE 1.3: M-AUDIO FASTTRACK PRO USB AUDIO INTERFACE

FIGURE 1.4: MOTU ULTRALITE MK3 FIREWIRE AUDIO INTERFACE

1.5.2.3 Drivers

A driver is a program that allows a peripheral device such as a printer or sound interface to communicate with your computer. When you attach an external sound interface to your computer, you have to be sure that the appropriate driver is installed. Generally you're given a driver installation disk with the sound interface, but it's better to go to the manufacturer's website and download the latest version of the driver. Be sure to download the version appropriate for your operating system. Drivers are pretty easy to install. You can look for instructions at the manufacturer's website and follow the steps in the windows that pop up as you do the installation. Remember that if you upgrade to a new operating system, you'll probably need to upgrade your driver as well. Some interfaces come with additional interface-related software that allows access to internal settings, controls, and DSP provided by the interface. This extra software may be packaged with the driver or it may be optional, but either way it is usually quite handy to install as well.

1.5.2.4 MIDI Keyboard

A MIDI keyboard is required to input MIDI performance data into your computer. A MIDI keyboard itself makes no instrument sounds. It simply sends the MIDI data to the computer communicating the keys pressed and other performance data collected, and the software handles the playback of instruments and sounds. Some MIDI keyboards are a combination MIDI input device and audio interface. These are called **audio interface keyboards**. Consolidating the MIDI keyboard and the audio interface into one component is convenient because it's easier to transport. The downside is that features and functionality may be more limited, and all the functionality is tied into one device, so if that one device breaks or becomes outdated, you lose both tools. Standalone MIDI controller keyboards connect either to your computer directly using USB, or to the MIDI input and output of a separate external audio interface. MIDI keyboards come in several sizes. Your choice of size depends on how many keys you need. Figure 1.5 and Figure 1.6 show examples of USB MIDI keyboard controllers.

FIGURE 1.5: M-AUDIO OXYGEN8 25-KEY MIDI KEYBOARD CONTROLLER
[IMAGE COURTESY OF M-AUDIO]

FIGURE 1.6: EDIROL PCR-M50 49-KEY MIDI KEYBOARD CONTROLLER

1.5.2.5 Recording Devices

Recording is one of the fundamental activities in working with sound. So what type of recording devices do you need? One possibility is to connect a microphone to your computer and use software on your computer as the recording interface. A computer-based digital audio workstation offers multiple channels of recording along with editing, mixing, and processing all in the same system. However, these workstations are not very portable or rugged, so they're often found in fixed recording studio setups.

Sometimes you may need to get out into the world to do your recording. Small portable recorders like the one shown in Figure 1.7 are available for field recordings. A disadvantage of such a device is that the number of inputs is usually limited to two to four channels. These recorders often have one or two built-in microphones with the added option of connecting external microphones as well.

Dedicated multitrack hardware recorders as shown in Figure 1.8 and Figure 1.9 are available for situations where portability and high channel counts are desirable. These recorders are generally very reliable but offer little opportunity for editing, mixing, and processing the recording. The recording needs to be transferred to another system afterwards for those tasks.

FIGURE 1.7: SMALL PORTABLE AUDIO RECORDER WITH BUILT-IN MICROPHONE

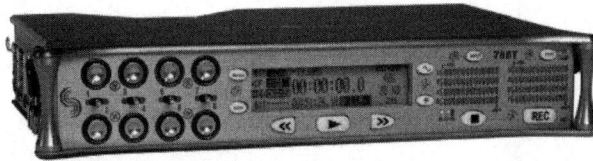

FIGURE 1.8: A DEDICATED 12-CHANNEL MULTITRACK RECORDER

FIGURE 1.9: A DEDICATED 48-CHANNEL MULTITRACK RECORDER

1.5.2.6 Microphones

Your computer may have come with a microphone suitable for gaming, voice recognition, or audio/video conferencing. However, that's not a suitable recording microphone. You need something that gives better quality and a wider frequency response. The audio interfaces we recommend in Section 1.5.2.2 include professional microphone inputs, and you need a professional microphone that's compatible with these inputs. Let's look at the basic types of microphones that you have to choose from.

The technology used inside a microphone has an impact on the quality of the sound it can capture. One common microphone technology uses a coil that moves inside a magnet, which happens to also be the reverse of how a loudspeaker works. These are called **dynamic microphones**. The coil is attached to a diaphragm that responds to the changing air pressure of a sound wave, and as the coil moves inside the magnet, an alternating current is generated on the microphone cable that is an electrical representation of the sound. Dynamic microphones are very durable and can be used reliably in any situation since they are **passive devices**, meaning that they require no external power source. Most dynamic microphones tend to come in a handheld size and are fairly inexpensive. Though durable, they're not as sensitive as other types of microphones. This lower sensitivity can be very effective in noisy environments when you're trying to capture isolated sounds. However, dynamic microphones are not very good at picking up transient sound—quick loud bursts like drum hits. They also may not pick up high frequencies as well as capacitance microphones do, which may compromise the clarity of certain kinds of sounds you'll want to record. In general, a dynamic microphone may come in handy during a high-energy live performance situation, yet it may not provide the same quality and fidelity as other types of microphones when used in a quiet, controlled recording environment.

Another type of microphone is a **capacitance** or **condenser microphone**. This type of microphone uses an electronic component called a capacitor as the transducer. The capacitor is made of two parallel conductive plates, physically separated by an air space. One of the plates requires a polarizing electrical charge, so condenser microphones require an external power supply. This is typically from a 48-volt DC power source called **phantom power**, but can sometimes be provided by a battery. The conductive plates are very thin, and when sound waves push against them, the distance between the plates changes, varying the charge accordingly and creating an electrical representation of the sound. Condenser microphones are much more sensitive than dynamic microphones. Consequently, they pick up much more detail in the sound, and even barely perceptible background sounds may end up being quite audible in the recording. This extra sensitivity results in a much better transient response and a much more uniform frequency response, reaching into very high frequencies. Because the transducers in condenser microphones are simple capacitors and don't require a weighty magnet, condenser microphones can be made quite large without becoming too heavy. They also can be made quite small, allowing them to be easily concealed. The smaller size also allows them to pick up high frequencies coming from various angles in a more uniform manner. A disadvantage of the capacitor microphone is that it requires external power, although this is often easily handled by most interfaces and mixing consoles. Also, capacitor elements can be quite delicate, and are much more easily damaged by excessive force or moisture. The features of a condenser microphone often result in a much higher quality signal, but this comes at a higher price. Top-of-the-line condenser microphones can cost thousands of dollars.

Electret condenser microphones are a type of condenser microphone in which the back plate of the capacitor is permanently charged at the factory. This means the microphone does not require a power supply to function, but it often requires an

extra powered preamplifier to boost the signal to a sufficient voltage. Easy to manufacture and often miniature in size, electret condenser microphones are used for the
vast majority of built-in microphones in phone, computer, and portable device technologies. While easy and economical to produce, electret microphones aren't necessarily of lower quality. In the field of professional audio they can be found in lavaliere
microphones attached to clothing or concealed for live performance. In these cases,
the small microphones are typically connected to a wireless transmitter with a battery
that powers the preamplifier as well as the radio frequency (RF) transmitter circuitry.

Generally speaking, you want to get the microphone as close as possible to the
sound source you want to capture. This improves your signal-to-noise ratio. When
getting the microphone close to the source is not practical—such as when you're recording a large choir, performing group, or conference meeting—a type of microphone called a **pressure zone microphone (PZM)** can be useful. A PZM, also called
a **boundary microphone**, is usually made of a small electret condenser microphone
attached to a metal plate with the microphone pointed at the plate rather than the
source itself. These microphones work best when attached to a large reflective surface
such as a hard stage floor or large conference table. The operating principle of the
pressure zone is that as a sound wave encounters a large reflective surface, the pressure
at the surface is much higher because it's a combination of the direct and reflected
energy. Essentially this extra pressure results in a captured amplitude boost, a benefit
normally available only by getting the microphone much closer to the sound source.
With a PZM, you can capture a sound at a sufficiently high volume even from a
significant distance. This can be quite useful for video teleconferencing when a large
group of people must be at a greater distance from the microphone, as well as in live
performance where microphones are placed at the edge of the stage. The downside to
a PZM is that the physical coupling to the boundary surface means that other sounds
such as foot noise, paper movement, and table bumps are picked up just as well as
the sound you're trying to capture. As a result, the signal-to-noise ratio tends to be
fairly low. In a live sound-reinforcement situation, you can also have acoustic gain
problems if you aren't careful about the physical relationship between the microphone
and the loudspeaker. Since the microphone is capturing the performer from a great
distance, the loudspeakers directly over the stage could easily be the same distance or
less distance from the microphone as the performer, resulting in the sound from the
loudspeaker arriving at the PZM at the same level or higher than the sound from the
performer, a perfect recipe for feedback. Feedback and acoustic gain are covered in
more detail in Chapter 4.

As part of a newer trend in this digital age, the prevalence of **USB digital microphones** is on the rise. Many manufacturers are offering a USB version of their popular microphones, both condenser and dynamic. These microphones output a digital

audio stream and are intended for direct recording into a computer software program, without the need for any additional preamplifier or audio interface equipment. You could even think of them as microphone-interface hybrids, essentially performing the duties of both. The benefits of these new digital microphones are of course simplicity, portability, and perhaps even cost if you consider not having to purchase the additional equipment and digital audio interface. However, while these USB microphones may be studio quality, there are some limitations that may influence your choice. Where traditional XLR cables can easily run over a hundred feet, USB cables have a maximum operable length of only 10 to 15 feet, which means you're pretty tied down to your computer workstation. Additionally, having only a USB connection means you won't be able to use the microphone in a live situation or plug it into an analog mixing console, portable recorder, or any other piece of audio gear. Finally, a dedicated audio interface allows you to plug in multiple microphones and instruments, provides a multitude of output connections, and provides onboard DSP and mixing tools to help you get the most out of your audio setup and workflow. Since you'll probably want to have a dedicated audio interface for these reasons anyway, you may be better off with a traditional microphone that interfaces with it, and is more flexible overall. That being said, a USB microphone could certainly be a handy addition to your everyday audio setup, particularly for situations when you're travelling and need a self-contained, portable solution.

If you buy only one microphone, it should be a dynamic one. The most popular professional dynamic microphone is the Shure SM58. Everyone working with sound should have at least one of these microphones. They sound good, they're inexpensive, and they're virtually indestructible. Figure 1.10 is a photo of an SM58. If you want to purchase a good-quality studio condenser microphone and you have a recording environment where you can control the noise floor, consider one like the AKG C414 microphone. This is a classic microphone with an impressive sound quality. However, it has a tendency to pick up more than you want it to, so you need to use it in a controlled recording room where it isn't going to pick up fan sounds, the hum from fluorescent lights, and the mosquitoes in the corner flapping their wings. Figure 1.11 is a photo of a C414 microphone.

Another way to classify microphones is by their directionality. The **directionality** of a microphone is its sensitivity to the range of audible frequencies coming from various angles, which can be depicted in a **polar plot** (also called a **polar pattern**). The three main categories of microphone directionality are **directional**, **bidirectional**, and **omnidirectional**.

You can think of the polar pattern essentially as a top-down view of the microphone. Around the edge circle are numbers in degrees, representing the direction at which sound is approaching the microphone. 0 degrees at the top of the circle is where the front of the microphone is pointing—often referred to as on-axis—and 180 degrees at the bottom of the circle is directly behind the microphone. The concentric rings with decreasing numbers are the sound levels in decibels, abbreviated dB, with the outer ring representing 0 dB, or no loss in level. The outermost line shows the decibel level at various angles.

We don't explain decibels in detail until Chapter 4, but for now it's sufficient to know that the more negative the dB value (closer to the center), the less the sound is picked up by the micro-

FIGURE 1.10: SHURE SM58 DYNAMIC MICROPHONE

FIGURE 1.11: AKG C414 CONDENSER MICROPHONE

phone at that angle. This may seem a bit counterintuitive, but remember the polar plot has nothing to with distance, so getting closer to the center doesn't mean getting closer to the microphone itself. The polar pattern for an omnidirectional microphone is given in Figure 1.12. As its name suggests, an omnidirectional microphone picks up sound equally from all directions. You can see that reflected in the polar pattern, where the sound level remains at 0 dB as you move around the circle regardless of the angle, as indicated by the black boldface outline.

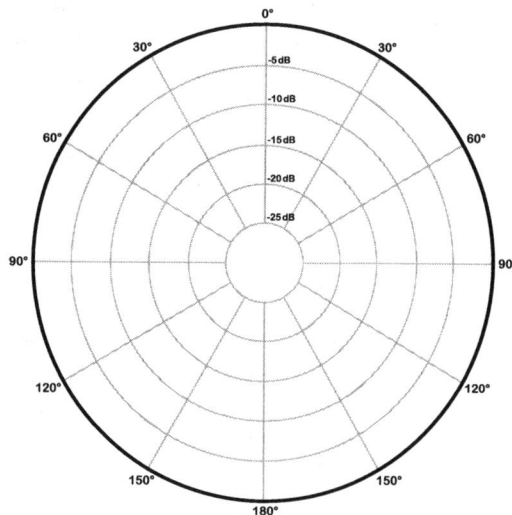

FIGURE 1.12: POLAR PLOT FOR AN OMNIDIRECTIONAL MICROPHONE

A **bidirectional** microphone is often referred to as a figure-eight microphone. It picks up sound with equal sensitivity at its front and back, but not at the sides. You can see this in Figure 1.13, where the sound level decreases as you move around the microphone away from the front (0°) or rear (180°), and at either side (90° and 270°) the sound picked up by the microphone is essentially none.

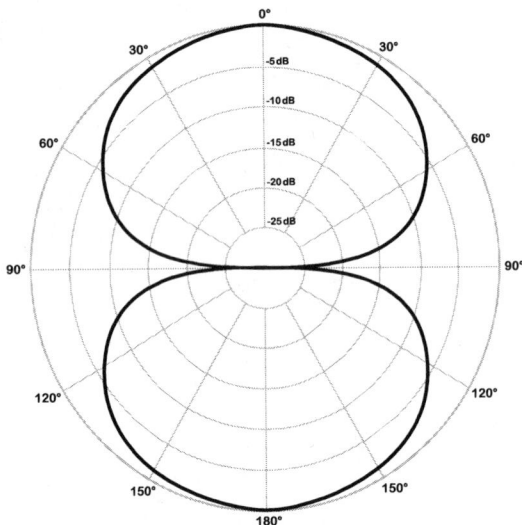

FIGURE 1.13: POLAR PLOT FOR A
BIDIRECTIONAL MICROPHONE

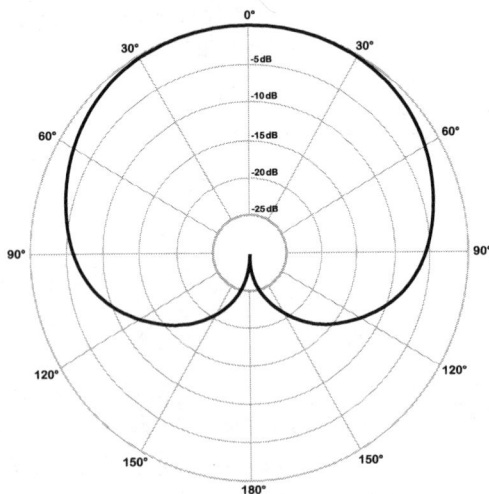

FIGURE 1.14: POLAR PLOT FOR
A CARDIOID MICROPHONE

Directional microphones can have a **cardioid** (Figure 1.14) a **supercardioid** (Figure 1.15), or a **hypercardioid** (Figure 1.16) pattern. You can see why they're called directional, as the cardioid microphone picks up sound in front but not behind the microphone. The super- and hypercardioid microphones behave similarly, offering a tighter frontal response with extra sound rejection at the sides. The lobe of extra sound pickup at the rear of these patterns is simply an unintended side effect of their focused design, but usually isn't a big issue in practical situations.

A special category of microphone called a **shotgun microphone** can be even more directional, depending on the length and design of the microphone (Figure 1.17). Shotgun microphones can be very useful in trying to pick up a specific sound from a noisy environment, often at a greater than the typical distance away from the source, without picking up the surrounding noise.

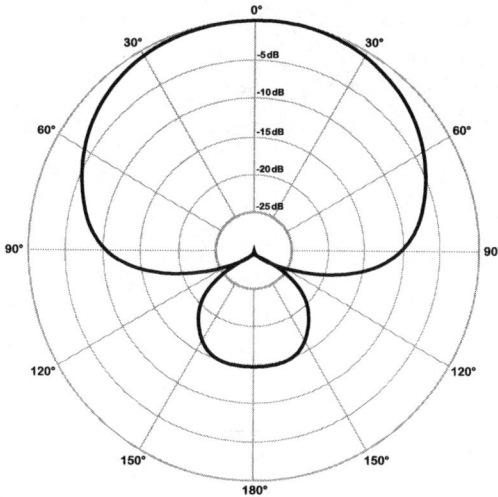

FIGURE 1.15: POLAR PLOT FOR A SUPERCARDIOID MICROPHONE

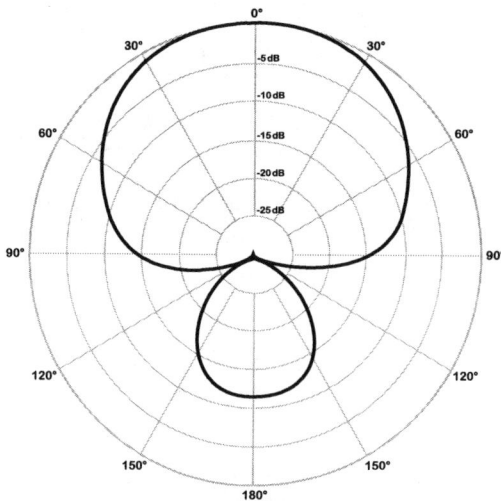

FIGURE 1.16: POLAR PLOT FOR A HYPERCARDIOID MICROPHONE

Some microphones offer the option of multiple, selectable polar patterns. This is true of the condenser microphone shown back in Figure 1.11. You can see five symbols on the front of the microphone representing the polar patterns from which you can choose, depending on the needs of what you're recording.

Polar plots can be even more detailed than the ones above, showing different patterns depending on the frequency. This is because microphones don't pick up all frequencies equally from all directions. The plots in Figure 1.18 show the pickup patterns of a particular cardioid microphone for individual frequencies from 125 Hz up to 16,000 Hz. You'll notice the polar pattern isn't as clean and consistent as you might expect. Even for a directional microphone, lower frequencies may often exhibit a more omnidirectional pattern, where higher frequencies can become even more directional.

The sensitivity that a microphone has to sounds at different frequencies is called its **frequency response** (a term also used to describe the behavior of filters in later chapters). If a microphone picks up all frequencies equally, it has a flat frequency response. However, a perfectly flat frequency response is not always desirable. The Shure SM58 microphone's popularity, for example, can be attributed in part to increased sensitivity at higher frequencies, which can make the human voice more clear and intelligible. Of course, you could achieve this same frequency response using an EQ (an equalization process that adjusts frequencies), but if you can get a microphone that naturally sounds good for the sound you're trying to capture, it can save you time, effort, and money.

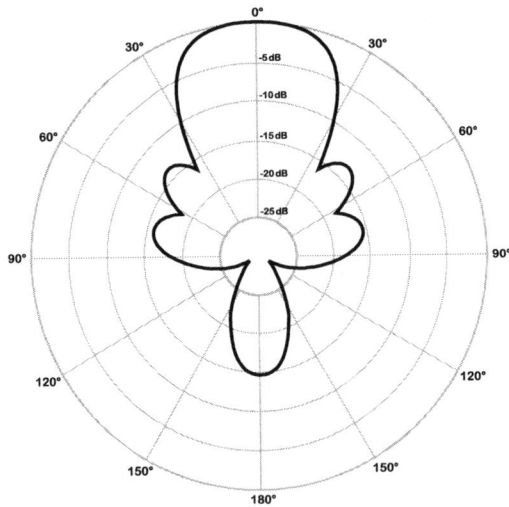

FIGURE 1.17: POLAR PLOT FOR A SHOTGUN MICROPHONE

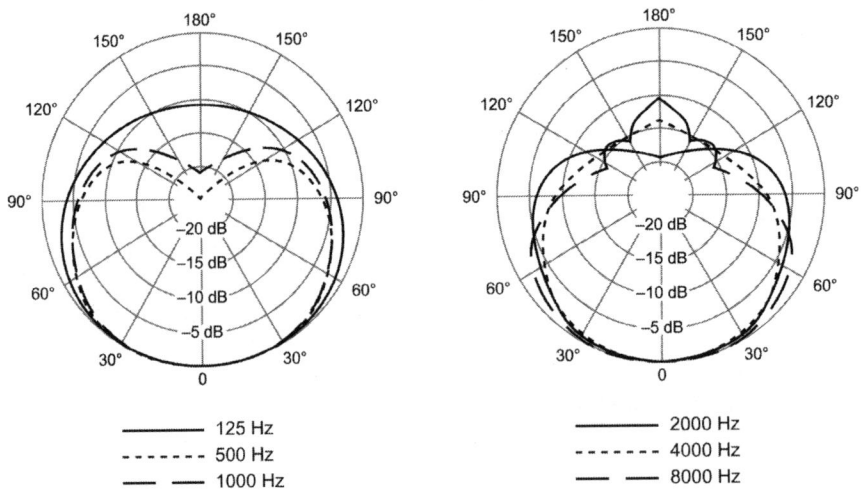

———— 125 Hz
- - - - 500 Hz
— — 1000 Hz

———— 2000 Hz
- - - - 4000 Hz
— — 8000 Hz

**FIGURE 1.18: POLAR PLOT OF A DYNAMIC CARDIOID MICROPHONE,
SHOWING PICKUP PATTERNS FOR VARIOUS FREQUENCIES**

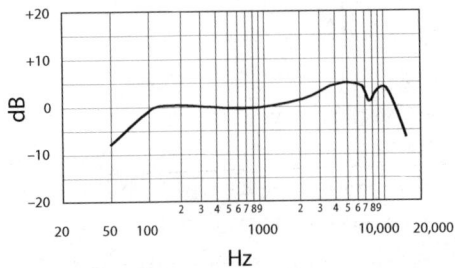

**FIGURE 1.19: ON-AXIS FREQUENCY RESPONSE
OF THE SHURE SM58 MICROPHONE**

Some microphones may have a very flat frequency response on-axis but due to the directional characteristics, that frequency response can become very uneven when off-axis. This is important to keep in mind when choosing a microphone. If the sound you're trying to record is stationary and you can get the microphone pointed directly at the sound, then a directional microphone can be very effective at capturing the sound you want without capturing the sounds you don't want. If the sound moves around or if you can't get the microphone pointed directly on-axis with the sound, you may need to use an omnidirectional microphone in order to keep the frequency response consistent. However, an omnidirectional microphone is very ineffective at rejecting other sounds in the environment. Of course, that's not always a bad thing, as with measuring and analyzing sounds in a room

ASIDE: Shure hosts an interactive tool on their website called the Shure Microphone Listening Lab where you can audition all the various microphones in their catalog. You can try it out yourself at http://www.shure.com/americas/buyers-guide/mic-listening-lab

when you want to make sure you're picking up everything that's happening in the environment, and as accurately and transparently as possible. In that case, an omnidirectional microphone with a flat frequency response is ideal.

FIGURE 1.20: A SMALL-DIAPHRAGM OMNIDIRECTIONAL MICROPHONE SPECIALIZED FOR MEASUREMENT USE

Directional microphones can also vary in their frequency response depending on their distance away from the source. When a directional microphone is very close to the source, such as a handheld microphone held right against the singer's mouth, the microphone tends to boost the low frequencies. This is known as the **proximity effect**. In some cases, this is desirable. Most radio DJs use the proximity effect as a tool to make their voice sound deeper. Getting the microphone closer to the source can also greatly improve acoustic gain in a live sound scenario. However, in some situations the extra low frequency from the proximity effect can muddy the sound and result in lower intelligibility. In that scenario, switching to an omnidirectional microphone may improve the intelligibility. Unfortunately, that switch can take also away some of your acoustic gain, negating the benefits of the closer microphone.

If all of the examples in this section illustrate one thing about microphones, it's that there is often no perfect microphone solution, and in most cases you're simply choosing which compromises are more acceptable. You can also start to see why there are so many different types of microphones available to choose from, and why many sound engineers have closets full of them to tackle any number of unique situations. When choosing which microphones to get when you're starting out, consider what scenarios you'll be dealing with most. Will you be working on more live gigs, or controlled studio recording? Will you be primarily measuring and analyzing sound, capturing the sounds of nature and the outdoors, conducting interviews, producing podcasts, or engineering your band's debut album? The answer to these questions will help you decide which types of microphones are best suited for your needs.

1.5.2.7 Direct Input Devices

Surprisingly, not all recording or performance situations require a separate microphone. In many cases, modern musical instruments have small microphones or magnetic pickups preinstalled inside of them. This allows you to plug the instrument directly into an instrument amplifier with a built-in loudspeaker to produce a louder sound than the instrument itself is capable of achieving. In a recording situation, you can often find great success connecting these instruments directly to your recording system. Since these instrument audio outputs usually have high output impedance, you need to run the signal through a transformer in order to convert the audio signal to a format that works with a professional microphone input. These transformers can be found inside devices called **direct injection** (**DI**) boxes like the one shown in Figure 1.21. A DI box has a ¼″ TS input jack that accepts the signal from an instrument and feeds it into the transformer. It also has a ¼″ TS output that allows you to connect the high impedance instrument signal to an instrument amplifier if desired. Coming out of the transformer is a low impedance, balanced microphone-level signal with an XLR connector. This can then be connected to a microphone input on your recording system. Some audio interfaces for a computer have instrument level inputs with the transformer included inside the interface. In that case, you can connect the instrument directly to the audio interface as long as you use a cable shorter than 15 feet. A longer cable results in too much loss in level due to the high output impedance of the instrument, as well as increase potential noise and interference picked up along the way by the unbalanced cable.

Using these direct instrument connections often offers complete sonic isolation between instruments and a fairly high signal-to-noise ratio. The downside is that you lose any sense of the instrument existing inside an acoustic space. For instruments like electric guitars, you may also lose some of the effects introduced on the instrument sound by the amplifier. If you have enough inputs on your recording system, you can always put a real microphone on the instrument or the amplifier in addition to the direct connection, and mix between the two signals later. This offers some additional flexibility, but comes

FIGURE 1.21: A DIRECT INJECTION BOX

at an additional cost of equipment and input channels. Alternatively, there are many microphone or amplifier simulation plug-ins that, when added to the direct instrument signal in your digital audio software, may be able to provide a more authentic live sound without the need for a physical amplifier and microphone.

1.5.2.8 Monitor Loudspeakers

Just like you use a video monitor on your computer to see the graphical elements you're working with, you need audio monitors to hear the sound you're working with on the computer. There are two main types of audio monitors, and you really need both. Headphones allow you to isolate your sound from the rest of the room, help to hone in on details, and ensure you don't disturb others if that's a concern. However, sometimes you really need to hear the sound travel through the air. In this case, professional reference monitor loudspeakers are needed.

Most inexpensive computer loudspeakers, or even high-end stereo systems, are not suitable sound monitors. This is because they're tuned for specific listening situations. The built-in loudspeaker on your computer is optimized to deliver system alerts and speech audio, and external computer loudspeakers or high-end stereo systems are optimized for consumer use to deliver finished music and soundtracks. This often involves a manipulation of the **frequency response**—that is, the way the loudspeakers selectively change the amplitudes of different frequencies, like boosting bass or treble to color the sound a certain way. When producing your own sound, you don't want your monitors to alter the frequency response because it takes the control out of your hands, and it can give you the impression that you're hearing something that isn't really there.

Professional reference monitor loudspeakers (which we call simply **monitors**) are tuned to deliver a flat frequency response at close proximity. That is, the frequencies are not artificially boosted or reduced, so you can trust what you hear from them.

Reference monitors are typically larger than standard computer loudspeakers, and you need to mount these up at the level of your ears in order to get the specified performance. You can purchase stands for them or just put them on top of a stack of books. Either way, the goal is to get them pointed on-axis to and equidistant from your ears. These monitors should be connected to the output of your audio interface. You can spend from $100 to several

FIGURE 1.22: EDIROL MA-15D REFERENCE MONITOR LOUDSPEAKERS

thousand dollars for monitor loudspeakers. Just get the best ones you can afford. Figure 1.22 shows some inexpensive monitors from Edirol and Figure 1.23 shows a mid-range monitor from Mackie.

1.5.2.9 Studio Headphones

Good-quality reference monitor loud-speakers are wonderful to work with, but if you're working in an environment where noise control is a concern you'll want to pick up some studio **headphones** as well. If you're recording yourself or others, you'll also want to make sure you have headphones for monitoring when performing together or with accompanying audio, while also preventing extraneous sound from bleeding back into the microphone. As a general rule, consumer grade headphones that come with your MP3 player aren't suitable

FIGURE 1.23: MACKIE MR8 REFERENCE
MONITOR LOUDSPEAKER

for sound production monitoring. You want something that isolates you from surrounding sounds and gives you a relatively flat frequency response. Of course, a danger with using any headphones lies in working with them for extended periods of time at an excessively high level, which can damage your hearing. Good headphone isolation (not to mention a quiet working environment) can minimize that risk. A set of closed-back studio headphones provides adequate isolation between your ears and the outside world and delivers a flat and accurate frequency response. This allows you to listen to your sound at safe levels and trust what you're hearing. However, in any final evaluation of your work, you should be sure to take off the headphones and listen to the sound through your monitor loudspeakers before sending it off as a finished mix. Things sound quite different when they travel through the air and in a room compared to when they're pumped straight into your ears.

Figure 1.24 shows some inexpensive studio headphones that cost less than $50. Figure 1.25 shows some more expensive studio headphones that cost over $200. You can compare the features of various headphones like these and get something that you can afford.

1.5.2.10 Cables and Connectors

In any audio system you'll have a wide assortment of cables using many different connectors. Some cables and connectors offer better signal transmission than others, and it's important to become familiar with the various options. When problems arise in an audio system, they're often the result of a bad connection or cable. Consequently, successful audio professionals purchase high-quality cables or often make the cables themselves to ensure quality. Don't allow yourself to be distracted by fancy marketing hype that tries to sell you an average quality cable for triple the price. Quality cables have more to do with the type of termination on the connector and appropriate shielding, jacketing, wire gauge, and conductive materials. Things like gold-plated contacts, de-oxygenated wire, and fancy packaging are less important.

FIGURE 1.24: AKG K77 CLOSED BACK STUDIO HEADPHONES

The XLR connectors shown in Figure 1.26 are widely used in professional audio systems. They are typically round connectors with three pins. Pin 1 is for the audio signal ground, pin 2 carries the positive polarity version of the signal, and pin 3 carries the inverted polarity version of the signal. The inverted polarity signal is the negative of the original. Informally, this means that a single-frequency sine wave that goes "up and down" is inverted by turning it into a sine wave of the same frequency and amplitude going "down and up," as shown in Figure 1.27.

FIGURE 1.25: SONY MDR 7509HD CLOSED BACK STUDIO HEADPHONES

XLR female 3-pin cable connector

XLR male 3-pin cable connector

XLR female 3-pin panel connector

XLR male 3-pin panel connector

FIGURE 1.26: XLR CONNECTORS

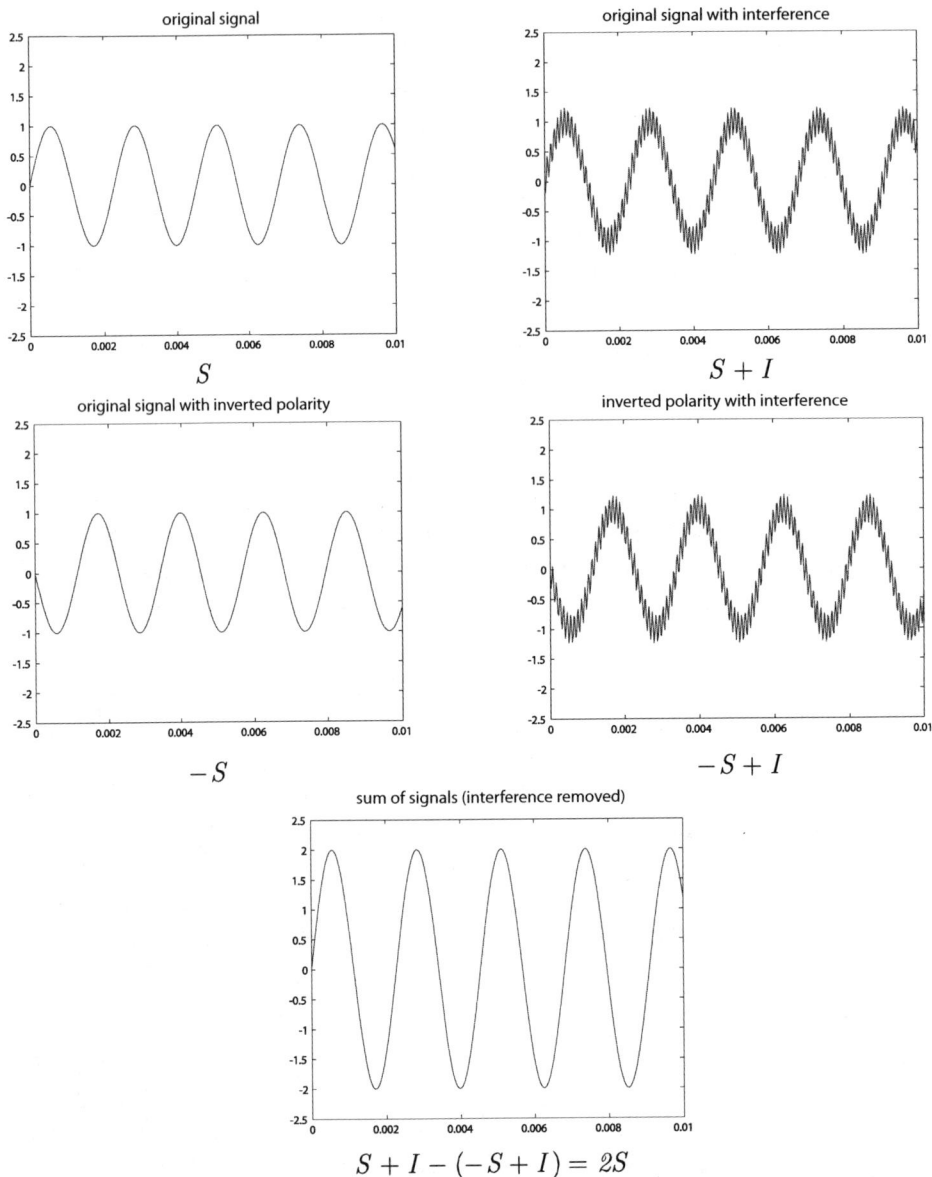

$$S$$

$$S + I$$

$$-S$$

$$-S + I$$

$$S + I - (-S + I) = 2S$$

The inverted signal containing interference is subtracted
from the original signal containing interference.

FIGURE 1.27: INTERFERENCE REMOVED ON BALANCE SIGNAL

Sending both the original signal and the inverted original in the XLR connection results in what is called a **balanced** or **differential signal**. The idea is that any interference that is collected on the cable is introduced equally to both signal lines. Thus, it's possible to get rid of the interference at the receiving end of the cable by subtracting the inverted signal from the original one (both now containing the interference as well). Let's call S the original signal and call I the interference collected when the signal is transmitted. Then:

$$S + I \text{ is the received signal plus interference}$$

$$-S + I \text{ is the received inverted signal plus interference}$$

If $-S + I$ is subtracted from $S + I$ at the receiving end, we get:

$$S + I - (-S + I) = S + I + S - I = 2S$$

That is, we erase the interference at the receiving end and end up with double the amplitude of the original signal, which is the same as giving the signal a 6 dB boost (explained in Chapter 4). This is illustrated in Figure 1.27. For the reasons just described, balanced audio signals, which run on two-conductor cables with XLR connectors, tend to be higher voltage and lower noise than unbalanced signals, which run on single-conductor or coaxial cables.

MAX DEMO:
Balanced Audio
http://bit.ly/29okyPg

Another important feature of the XLR connector is that it locks in place to prevent accidentally getting unplugged during your perfect take in the recording. In general, XLR connectors are used on cables for professional low-impedance microphones and high-end line-level professional audio equipment.

The ¼″ phone plug and its corresponding jack (Figure 1.28) are also widely used. The ¼″ plug comes in two basic configurations. The first is a tip/sleeve (TS) configuration. This would be used for unbalanced signals with the tip carrying the audio signal and the sleeve connecting to the shield of the cable. The TS version is used on musical instruments such as electric guitars that have electronic signal pick-ups. This is an unbalanced high-impedance signal. Consequently, you should not try to run this kind of signal on a cable that is longer than fifteen feet, or you risk picking up lots of noise along the way and get a significant reduction in signal amplitude. The second configuration is tip/ring/sleeve (TRS). This allows the connector to work with balanced audio signals using two-conductor cables. In that situation, the tip carries the positive polarity version of the signal, the ring carries the negative polarity version, and the sleeve connects to the signal ground via the cable shield. The advantages to using the ¼″ TRS connector over the XLR are that it is smaller, less expensive, and takes up less space on the physical equipment—so you can buy a less expensive interface. However, the trade-off here is that you lose the locking ability that you get with the XLR connector, making this connection more susceptible to accidental disconnection. The ¼″

TRS jack also wears out sooner than the XLR because the contact pins are spring-loaded inside the jack. There's also the possibility for a bit more noise to enter into the signal because, unlike the XLR connector, the ¼″ TRS connector doesn't keep the signal pins perfectly parallel throughout the entire connection. Thus it's possible that an interference signal could be introduced at the connection point that would not be equally distributed across both signal lines.

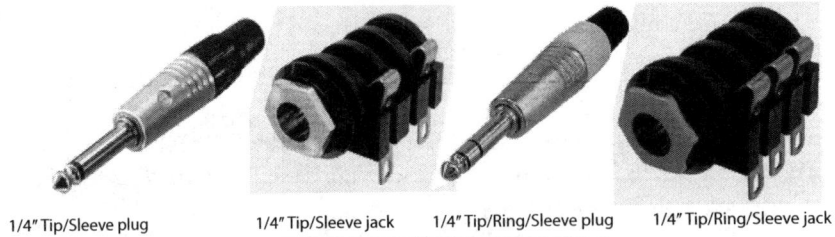

1/4″ Tip/Sleeve plug   1/4″ Tip/Sleeve jack   1/4″ Tip/Ring/Sleeve plug   1/4″ Tip/Ring/Sleeve jack

FIGURE 1.28: TS AND TRS CONNECTORS

The Neutrik connector company makes an XLR and ¼″ jack hybrid panel connector that accepts a male XLR connector or a ¼″ TRS plug, as shown in Figure 1.29. Depending on the equipment, the XLR connector could feed into a microphone preamplifier and the ¼″ jack would be configured to accept a high-impedance instrument signal. Other equipment may just feed both connector types into the same signal line, allowing flexibility in the connector type you use.

The ⅛″ or 3.5 mm phone plug shown in Figure 1.30 is very similar to the ¼″ plug, but it's used for different signals. Since it's so small, it can be easily used in portable audio devices and any other audio equipment that's too compact to accommodate a larger connector. It has all the same strengths and weaknesses of the ¼″ plug and is even more susceptible to damage and accidental disconnection. The most

FIGURE 1.29: NEUTRIK XLR AND
1/4″ COMBINATION CONNECTOR

common use of this connector is for headphone connections in small portable audio systems. The weaknesses of this connector far outweigh the strengths. Consequently, this connector is not widely used in professional applications but is quite common in consumer-grade equipment where reliability requirements are not as strict. Because of the proliferation of portable audio devices, even high-quality professional headphones now come with a ¼″ connector and an adapter that converts the connection to ⅛″.

This allows you to connect the headphones to consumer-grade and professional-grade equipment.

The RCA connector type shown in Figure 1.31 is used for unbalanced signals in consumer-grade equipment. It's commonly found in consumer CD and DVD players, home stereo receivers, televisions, and similar equipment for audio and video signals. It's an inexpensive connector but is not

FIGURE 1.30: 3.5 MM OR ⅛″ PLUG

recommended for professional analog equipment because it's unbalanced and not lockable. The RCA connector can be used for digital signals with acceptable reliability because digital signals are not susceptible to the same kind of interference problems as analog signals. Consequently, the RCA connector is used for S/PDIF digital audio, Dolby Digital, and other digital signals in many different kinds of equipment including professional-grade devices. When used for digital signals, the connector needs to use a 75-ohm coaxial type of cable.

RCA cable connector   RCA panel connector

FIGURE 1.31: RCA CONNECTORS

The DIN connector comes in many different configurations and is used for a variety of applications. In the digital audio environment, the DIN connector is used in a five-pin 180-degree arrangement for MIDI connections, as shown in Figure 1.32. In this configuration only three of the pins are used, so a five-conductor cable is not required. In fact, MIDI signals can use the same kind of cable as balanced microphones. In situations where MIDI signals need to be sent over long distances, it is often the case that adapters are made that have a five-pin, 180 degree DIN connector on one end and a three-pin XLR connector on the other. This allows MIDI to be transmitted on existing microphone lines that are run throughout most venues using professional audio systems.

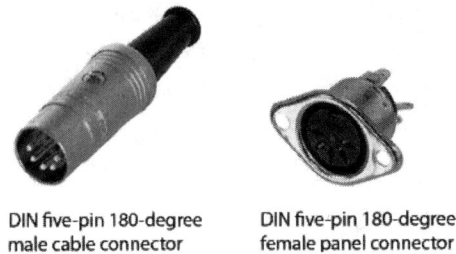

DIN five-pin 180-degree
male cable connector

DIN five-pin 180-degree
female panel connector

FIGURE 1.32: DIN CONNECTORS

The BNC connector type shown in Figure 1.33 is commonly used in video systems, but can be quite effective when used for digital audio signals. Most professional digital audio devices have a dedicated word clock connection that uses a BNC connector. (The word clock synchronizes data transfers between digital devices.) The BNC connector is able to accommodate a fairly low gauge (75-ohm) coaxial cable such as RG59 or RG6. The advantage of using this connector over other options is that it locks in place while still being able to be disconnected quickly. Also, the center pin is typically crimped to the copper conductor in the cable using crimping tools that are manufactured to very tight tolerances. This makes for a very stable connection that allows for high-bandwidth digital signals traveling on low-impedance cable to be transferred between equipment with minimal signal loss. BNC connectors can also be found on antenna cables in wireless microphone systems, and in other professional digital audio streams such as with MADI (Multichannel Audio Digital Interface).

BNC male cable connector

BNC female panel connector

FIGURE 1.33: BNC CONNECTORS

The D-subminiature connector is used for many different connections in computer equipment but is also used for audio systems when space is a premium (Figure 1.34). D-sub connections come in almost unlimited configurations. The D is often followed by a letter (A–E), indicating the size of the pins in the connector, followed by a number indicating the number of pins. It has become common practice to use a DB-25 connector on interface cards that would normally call for XLR or ¼″ connectors. A single DB-25 connector can carry eight balanced analog audio signals and can be converted to XLR using a fan-out cable. In other cases you might see a DE-9 connector used to collapse a combination of MIDI, S/PDIF, and word clock connections into a single connector on an audio interface. The interface would come with a special fan-out cable that would deliver the common connections for these signals.

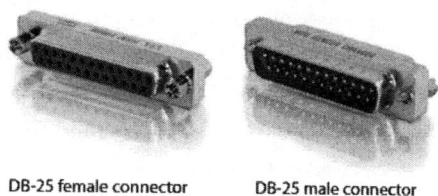

DB-25 female connector   DB-25 male connector

FIGURE 1.34: DBN CONNECTORS

The banana connector (Figure 1.35) is used for output connections on some power amplifiers that connect to loudspeakers. The advantage of this connector is that it is inexpensive and widely available. Most banana connectors also have a nesting feature that allows you to plug one banana connector into the back of another. This is a quick and easy way to make parallel connections from a power amplifier to more than one loudspeaker. The downside is that you have exposed pins on cables with fairly high-voltage signals, which is a safety concern. Usually, the safety issues can be avoided by making connections only when the system is powered off. The other potential problem with the banana connector is that it's very easy to insert the plug into the jack backwards. In fact, a backwards connection looks identical to the correct connection. Some banana connectors have a little notch on one side to help you tell the positive pin from the negative pin, but the more reliable way for verifying the connection is to pay attention to the colors of the wires. You're not going to break anything if you connect the cable backwards. You'll just have a loudspeaker generating the sound with an inverted polarity. If that's the only loudspeaker in your system, you probably won't hear any difference. But if that loudspeaker delivers sound to the same listening area as another loudspeaker, you'll hear some destructive interaction between the two sound waves that are working against each other. The banana connector is also used with electronics measurement equipment such as a digital multimeter.

FIGURE 1.35: BANANA PLUG CONNECTOR

The speakON connector was designed by the Neutrik connector company to attempt to solve all the problems with the other types of loudspeaker connections (Figure 1.36). The connector is round, and the panel-mount version fits in the same size hole as a panel-mount XLR connector. The pins carrying the electrical signal are not exposed on either the cable connector or the panel connector, and is also keyed in a way that allows it to connect only one way. This prevents the polarity inversion problem as long as the connector is wired up correctly. The connector also locks in place, preventing accidental disconnection. Making the connection is a little tricky if you've never done it before. The cable connector is inserted into the panel connector and then twisted to the right about ten degrees until it stops. Then, depending on the style of connector, a locking tab automatically engages, or you need to turn the outer ring clockwise to engage the lock. This connector is good in the way it solves the common problems with loudspeaker connections, but it is certainly more expensive than the other options.

Within the speakON family of connectors there are three varieties. The NL2 has only two signal pins, allowing it to carry a single audio signal. The NL4 has four signal pins, allowing it to carry two audio signals. This way you can carry the signal for the full-range loudspeaker and the signal for the subwoofer on a single cable, or you can use a single cable for a loudspeaker that does not use an internal passive crossover. In the latter case, the audio signal would be split into the high and low frequency bands at an earlier stage in the signal chain by an active crossover. Those two signals are then fed into two separate power amplifiers before coming together on a four-conductor cable with NL4 connectors. When the NL4 connector is put in place on the loudspeaker, the two signals are separated and routed to the appropriate loudspeaker drivers. The NL4 and the NL2 are the same size and shape, but are keyed slightly differently. An NL2 cable connector can plug into an NL4 panel connector and line up to the 1+/1– pins of the NL4. But the NL4 cable connector cannot connect to the NL2 panel connector. This helps you avoid a situation where you have two signals running on the cable with an NL4 connector where the second signal would not be used with the NL2 panel connector. The third type of speakON connector is the NL8, which has eight pins allowing four audio signals. The NL8 allows for even more flexible active-crossover solutions. Since it needs to accommodate eight conductors, the NL8 connector is significantly larger than the NL2 and NL4.

Because of these three different configurations, the term "speakON" is rarely used in conversations with audio professionals because the word could be describing any one of three very different connector configurations. Instead most people prefer to use the NL2, NL4, and NL8 model number when discussing the connections.

SpeakON NL2 cable connector   SpeakON NL2 panel connector

SpeakON NL4 cable connector   SpeakON NL4 panel connector

SpeakON NL8 cable connector   SpeakON NL8 panel connector

FIGURE 1.36: SPEAKON FAMILY OF CONNECTORS

The RJ45 connector is typically used with Category 5e (Cat 5e) ethernet cable (Figure 1.37). It has a locking tab that helps keep it in place when connected to a piece of equipment. This plastic locking tab breaks off very easily in an environment where the cable is being moved and connected several times. Once the tab breaks off, you can no longer rely on the connector to stay connected. The Neutrik connector company has designed a connector shell for the RJ45 called etherCON. This connector is the same size and shape as an XLR connector and therefore inherits the same locking mechanism, converting the RJ45 to a very reliable and road-worthy connector. Cat 5e cable is used for computer networking, but it is increasingly being used for digital audio signals on digital mixing consoles and processing devices.

The Toslink connector (Figure 1.38) differs from all the other connectors in this section in that it is used to transmit optical signals. There are many different fiber optic connection systems used in digital sound, but the Toslink series is by far the most common. Toslink was originally developed by Toshiba as a digital interconnect for their CD players. Now it is used for three main

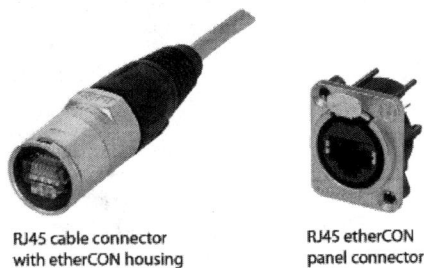

RJ45 cable connector
with etherCON housing

RJ45 etherCON
panel connector

FIGURE 1.37: RJ45 CONNECTORS

kinds of digital audio signals. One use is for transmitting two channels of digital audio using the Sony/Phillips Digital Interconnect Format (S/PDIF). S/PDIF signals can be transmitted either electronically using a coaxial cable on RCA connectors or optically using Toslink connectors.

Another signal is the Alcsis Digital Audio Technology (ADAT) Optical Interface. Originally developed by Alesis for their 8-track digital tape recorders as a way of transferring signals between two machines, ADAT is now widely used for transmitting up to eight channels of digital audio between various types of audio equipment. You also see the Toslink connector used in consumer audio home theatre systems to transmit digital audio in the Dolby Digital or DTS formats for surround sound systems. The standard Toslink connector is square-shaped with the round optical cable in the middle. There is also a miniature Toslink connector that is the same size as a 3.5 mm or ⅛" phone plug. This allows the connection system to take up less space on the equipment but also allows for some audio systems—mainly built-in sound cards on computers—to create a hybrid 3.5 mm jack that can accept both analog electrical connectors and digital optical miniature Toslink connectors.

The IEC connector (Figure 1.39) is used for a universal power connection on computers and most professional audio equipment. There are many different connector designs that technically fall under the IEC specification, but the one that we are referring to is the C13/C14 pair of connectors. Most computer and professional audio equipment now comes with power supplies that are able to adapt to the various power sources

Male Toslink cable connector

Female Toslink
panel connector

FIGURE 1.38: TOSLINK CONNECTORS

found in different countries. This helps the manufacturers because they no longer have to manufacture a different version of their product for each country. Instead, they put an IEC C14 inlet connector on their power supply, and then ship the equipment with a few different power cables that have an IEC C13 connector on one end and the common power connector for each country on the other end. The only significant problem is that this connector has no locking mechanism, which makes it very easy for the power cable to be accidentally disconnected. Some power supplies come with a simple wire bracket that goes down over the IEC connecter and attaches just behind the strain relief to keep the connector from falling out.

Neutrik decided to take what they learned from designing the speakON connector and apply it to the problems of the IEC connector. The powerCON connector (Figure 1.40) looks very similar to the speakON. The biggest difference is that it has three pins. Some professional audio equipment such as self-powered loudspeakers and power amplifiers have powerCON connectors instead of IEC. The advantage is that you get a locking connector with no exposed contacts. You can also create powerCON patch cables that allow you to daisy chain a power connection between several devices such as a stack of self-powered loudspeakers. PowerCON connectors are color-coded. A blue connector is used for a power input connection to a device. A white connector is used for a power output connection from a device.

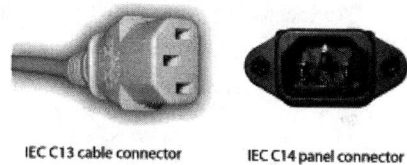

IEC C13 cable connector   IEC C14 panel connector

FIGURE 1.39: IEC CONNECTORS

1.5.2.11 Dedicated Hardware Processors

While the software and hardware tools available for working with digital audio on a modern personal computer have become quite powerful and sophisticated, they are still susceptible to all the weaknesses of crashes, bugs, and other unreliable behavior. In a well-tuned system, these problems are rare enough that the systems are reliable to use in most professional and home recording studios. In those cases when problems happen during a session, it's possible to reboot and get another take

powerCON power output cable connector (blue)   powerCON power input panel connector (blue)

powerCON power input cable connector (white)   powerCON power output panel connector (white)

FIGURE 1.40: POWERCON CONNECTORS

of the recording. In a live performance, however, the tolerance for failure is very low. You only get one chance to get it right and for many, the so-called "virtual sound systems" that can be operated on a personal computer are simply not reliable enough to be trusted for a multi-million dollar live event.

These productions tend to rely more on dedicated hardware solutions. In most cases these are still digital systems that essentially run on computers under the hood, but each device in the system is designed and optimized for only a single dedicated task—mixing the signals together, applying equalization (EQ), or playing a sound file, for example. When a computer-based digital audio workstation experiences a glitch, it's usually due to some other task the computer is trying to perform at the same time, such as checking for a software update, running a virus scan, or refreshing a Facebook page. Dedicated hardware solutions like the one shown in Figure 1.41 have only one task, and they can perform that task very reliably.

FIGURE 1.41: A DEDICATED DIGITAL SIGNAL PROCESSOR

Other hardware devices you might include with your system would be an analog or digital mixing console or dedicated hardware processing units such as equalizers, compressors, and reverberation processors. These dedicated processing units can be helpful in situations where you're working with live sound reinforcement and can't afford the latency that comes with completely software-based solutions. Some people simply prefer the sound of a particular analog processing unit and use it in place of more convenient software plug-ins. There may also be dedicated processing units that are calibrated in a way that's difficult to emulate in a software plug-in. One example of this is the Dolby LM100 Loudness Meter shown in Figure 1.42. Many television stations require programming that complies with certain loudness levels corresponding to this specific hardware device. Though some attempts have been made to emulate the functions of this device in a software plug-in, many audio engineers working in broadcasting still use this dedicated hardware device to ensure their programming is in compliance with regulations.

FIGURE 1.42: DOLBY LM100 LOUDNESS METER

1.5.2.12 Mixers

Mixers are an important part of any sound arsenal. **Audio mixing** is the process of combining multiple sounds, adjusting their levels and balance individually, dividing the sounds into one or more output channels, and either saving a permanent copy of the resulting sound or playing the sound live through loudspeakers. From this definition you can see that mixing can be done live, "on the fly" as sound is being produced, or it can be done off-line, as a post-production step applied to recorded sound or music.

Mixers can analog or digital. Digital mixers can be hardware or software. Picture first a live sound engineer working at an analog mixer like the one shown in Figure 1.43. His job is to use the vertical sliders (called **faders**) to adjust the amplitudes of the input channels, possibly turn other knobs to apply EQ, and send the resulting audio to the chosen output channels. He may also add dynamics processing and special effects by means of an external processor inserted in the processing chain.

A digital mixer is used in essentially the same way. In fact, the physical layout often looks remarkably similar as well. The controls of digital mixers tend to be modeled after analog mixers to make it easier for sound engineers to make the transition between devices. More detailed information on mixing consoles can be found in Chapter 8.

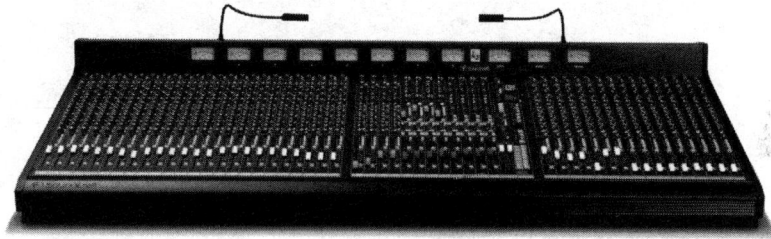

FIGURE 1.43: ANALOG MIXING CONSOLE

Music producers and sound designers for film and video do mixing as well. In the post-production phase, mixing is applied off-line to all of the recorded instrument, voice, or sound effects tracks captured during filming, foley, or tracking sessions. Some studios utilize large hardware mixing consoles for this mixing process as well, or the mixer may be part of a software program like Logic, ProTools, or Sonar. The graphical user interfaces of software mixers are often also made to look similar to hardware components. The purpose of the mixing process in post-production is, likewise, to make amplitude adjustments, and to add EQ, dynamics processing, and special effects to each track individually or in groups. Then the mixed-down sound is routed into a reduced number of channels for output, be it stereo, surround sound, or individual groups (often called "stems") in case they need to be edited or mixed further down the road.

If you're just starting out, you probably won't need a massive mixing console, many of which can cost thousands if not tens or hundreds of thousands of dollars. If you're doing live gigs, particularly where computer latency can be an issue, a small to mid-size mixing console may be necessary, such as a 16-channel board. In all other situations, current DAW software does a great job providing all the mixing power you'll need for just about any size project. For those who prefer hands-on mixing over a mouse and keyboard, mixer-like control surfaces are readily available that communicate directly with your software DAW. These control surfaces work much like MIDI keyboards, not ever touching any actual audio signals, but instead remotely controlling your software's parameters in a traditional mixer-like fashion while your computer does all the real work. These days, you can even do your mix on a touch-capable device like an iPad, communicating wirelessly with your DAW.

FIGURE 1.44: DAW HARDWARE CONTROL SURFACE

1.5.2.13 Loudspeakers

If you plan to work in sound for the theatre, then you'll also need some knowledge of loudspeakers. While the monitors we described in Section 1.5.2.8 are appropriate for studio work where you are often sitting very close, these aren't appropriate for distributing sound over long distances in a controlled way. For that you need loudspeakers which are specifically designed to maintain a controlled dispersion pattern and frequency response when radiating over long distances. These can include constant directivity horns and rugged cabinets with integrated rigging points for overhead suspension. Figure 1.46 shows an example of a popular loudspeaker for live performance.

These loudspeakers also require large power amplifiers. Most loudspeakers are specified with a sensitivity that defines how many dB SPL (sound pressure level in

FIGURE 1.45: TOUCH DEVICE CONTROL SURFACE APP

decibels) the loudspeaker can generate one meter away with only one watt of power. Using this specification along with the specification for the maximum power handling of the loudspeaker, you can figure out what kind of power amplifiers are needed to drive the loudspeakers, and how loud the loudspeakers can get. The process for aiming and calculating performance for loudspeakers is described in Chapters 4 and 8.

1.5.2.14 Analysis Hardware

When setting up sound systems for live sound, you need to make some acoustic measurements to help you configure the system for optimal use. There are dedicated hardware solutions available, but when you're just starting out, you can use software on your personal computer to analyze the measurements if you have the appropriate hardware interfaces for your computer. The audio interface you have for recording is sufficient as long as it can provide phantom power to the microphone inputs. The only other piece of hardware you need is at least one good analysis microphone.

FIGURE 1.46: MEYER UPA-1P LOUDSPEAKER

This is typically an omnidirectional condenser microphone with a very flat frequency response. High-quality analysis microphones such as the Earthworks M30 (shown previously in Figure 1.20) come with a calibration sheet showing the exact frequency response and sensitivity for that microphone.

Though the microphones are all manufactured together to the same specifications, there are still slight variations in each microphone even with the same model number. The calibration data can be very helpful when making measurements to account for any anomalies. In some cases, you can even get a digital calibration file for your microphone to load into your analysis software so it can make adjustments based on the imperfections in your microphone.

When looking for an analysis microphone, make sure it's an omnidirectional condenser microphone with a very small diaphragm like the one shown in Figure 1.47. The small diaphragm allows it to stay omnidirectional at high frequencies.

FIGURE 1.47: AN INEXPENSIVE ANALYSIS MICROPHONE FROM AUDIX

1.5.3   SOFTWARE FOR DIGITAL AUDIO AND MIDI PROCESSING

1.5.3.1 The Basics

Although the concepts in this book are general and basic, they are often illustrated in the context of specific application programs. The following sections include descriptions of the various programs that our examples and demonstrations use. The software shown can be used through two types of user interfaces: sample editors and multitrack editors.

A **sample editor**, as the name implies, allows you to edit down to the level of individual samples, as shown in Figure 1.48. Sample editors are based on the concept of destructive editing where you are making changes directly to a single audio file—for example, normalizing an audio file, converting the sampling rate or bit depth, adding metadata such as loop markers or root pitches, or performing any process that needs to directly and permanently alter the actual sample data in the audio file. Many sample editors also have batch processing capability, which allows you to perform a series of operations on several audio files at one time. For example, you could create a batch process in a sample editor that converts the sampling rate to 44.1 kHz, normalizes the amplitude values, and saves a copy of the file in AIFF format, applying these processes to an entire folder of 50 audio files. These kinds of operations would be impractical to accomplish with a multitrack editor.

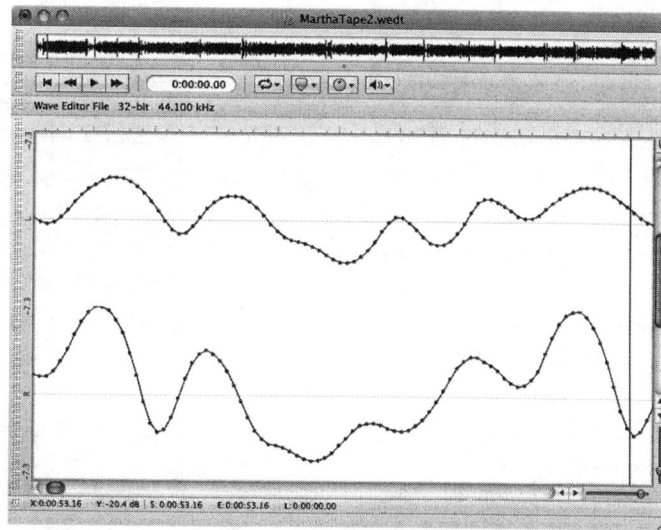

FIGURE 1.48: A SAMPLE EDITOR WINDOW ZOOMED DOWN TO THE LEVEL OF THE INDIVIDUAL SAMPLES (THE DOTS IN THE WAVEFORM INDICATE EACH SAMPLE)

Multitrack editors divide the interface into tracks. A **track** is an editable area on your audio arranging interface that corresponds to an individual input channel, which will eventually be mixed with others. One track might hold a singer's voice while another holds a guitar accompaniment, for example. Tracks can be of different types. For example, one might be an audio track and one a MIDI track. Each track has its own settings and routing capability, allowing for flexible, individual control. Within the tracks, the audio is represented by visual blocks, called regions, which are associated with specific locations in memory where the audio data corresponding to that region is stored. In other words, the regions are like little "windows" onto your hard disk where the audio data resides. When you move, extend, or delete a region, you're simply altering the reference "window" to the audio file. This type of interaction is known as non-destructive editing, where you can manipulate the behavior of the audio without physically altering the audio file itself, and is one of the most powerful aspects of multitrack editors. Multitrack editors are well-suited for music and post-production because they allow you to record sounds, voices, and multiple instruments separately, edit and manipulate them individually, layer them together, and eventually mix them down into a single file.

The software packages listed below handle digital audio, MIDI, or a combination of the two. Cakewalk, Logic, and Audition include both sample editors and multitrack editors, though they are primarily suited for one or the other. The list of software is not comprehensive, and versions of software change all the time, so you should compare our list with similar software that is currently available. There are many software options out there ranging from freeware to commercial applications that cost thousands of dollars. You generally get what you pay for with these programs, but everyone has to work within the constraints of a reasonable budget. This book shows you the power of working with professional-quality commercial software, but we also do our best to provide examples using software that is affordable for most students and educational institutions. Many of these software tools are available for academic licensing with reduced prices, so you may want to investigate that option as well. Keep in mind that some of these programs run on only one operating system, so be sure to buy something that runs on your preferred system.

1.5.3.2 Logic

Logic is developed by Apple and runs on the Mac operating system. This is a very comprehensive and powerful program that includes audio recording, editing, multitrack mixing, score notation, and a **MIDI sequencer**—a software interface for recording and editing MIDI. There are two versions of Logic: Logic Studio and Logic Express. Logic Studio is actually a suite of software that includes Logic Pro, Wave Burner, Soundtrack Pro, and a large library of music loops and software instruments. Logic Express is the core Logic program without all the extras, but it still comes with an impressive collection of audio and software instrument content. There is a significant price difference between the two, so if you're just starting out, try Logic Express. It's very affordable, especially when you consider all the features that are included. Figure 1.49 is a screenshot from the Logic Pro workspace.

FIGURE 1.49: LOGIC PRO WORKSPACE

1.5.3.3 Cakewalk Sonar and Music Creator

Cakewalk is a class of digital audio workstation software made by Roland. It features audio recording, editing, multitrack mixing, and MIDI sequencing. Cakewalk comes in different versions, all of which run only on the Windows operating system.

Cakewalk Sonar is the high-end version with the highest price tag. Cakewalk Music Creator is a scaled-back version of the software at a significantly lower price. Most beginners find the features that come with Music Creator to be more than adequate. Figure 1.50 is a screenshot of the Cakewalk Sonar workspace.

FIGURE 1.50: CAKEWALK SONAR WORKSPACE, MULTITRACK VIEW

1.5.3.4 Adobe Audition

Audition is DAW software made by Adobe. It was originally developed independently under the name "Cool Edit Pro," but was later purchased by Adobe and is now included in several of their software suites. The advantage to Audition is that you might already have it depending on which Adobe software suite you own. Audition runs on Windows or Mac operating systems and features audio recording, editing, and multitrack mixing. Traditionally, Audition hasn't included MIDI sequencing support. The latest version has begun to implement more advanced MIDI sequencing and software instrument support, but Audition's real power lies in its sample editing and audio manipulation tools.

1.5.3.5 Audacity

Audacity is a free, open-source audio editing program. It features audio recording, editing, and basic multitrack mixing. Audacity has no MIDI sequencing features. It's not nearly as powerful as programs like Logic, Cakewalk, and Audition. If you really want to do serious work with sound, it's worth the money to purchase a more advanced tool, but since it's free, Audacity is worth taking a look at if you're just starting out. Audacity runs on Windows, Mac, and Linux operating systems. Figure 1.51 is a screenshot of the Audacity workspace.

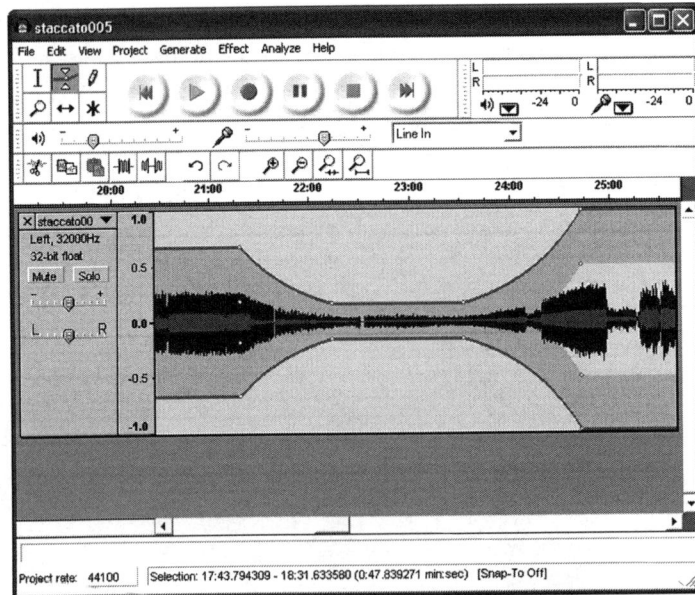

FIGURE 1.51: AUDACITY AUDIO EDITING SOFTWARE

1.5.3.6 Reason

Reason, a software synthesis program made by Propellerhead, is designed to emulate electronic musical instruments. The number of instruments you can load in the program is limited only by the speed and capacity of your computer. Reason comes with an impressive instrument library and includes a simple MIDI sequencer. Its real power lies is its ability to be integrated with other programs like Logic and Cakewalk, giving those programs access to great-sounding software instruments. Recent versions of Reason have added audio recording and editing features. Reason runs on both Mac and Windows operating systems. Figure 1.52 is a screenshot of the Reason workspace.

1.5.3.7 Software Plug-ins

Multitrack editors include the ability to use real-time software plug-ins to process the audio on specific tracks. The term *plug-in* likely grew out of the days of analog mixing consoles when you would physically plug in an external processing device to the signal chain on a specific channel of an analog mixing console. Most analog mixing consoles have specific connections labeled "Insert" on each channel of the mixing console to allow these external processors to be connected. In the world of digital multitrack editing software, a **plug-in** refers to an extra processing program that gets inserted to the signal chain of a channel in the software multitrack editor. For example, you might want to change the frequency response of the audio signal on Track 1 of your project. To do this, you'd insert an equalizer plug-in on Track 1 that performs this

FIGURE 1.52: REASON SOFTWARE INSTRUMENT RACK

kind of processing in real time as you play back the audio. Most DAW applications come with a variety of included plug-ins. Additionally, because plug-ins are treated as individual bits of software, it is possible to add third-party plug-ins to your computer that expand the processing options available for use in your projects, regardless of your specific DAW.

1.5.3.8 Music Composing and Notation Software

Musicians working with digital audio and MIDI often have need of software to help them compose and notate music. Examples of such software include Finale, Sibelius, and the free MuseScore. This software allows you to input notes via the mouse, keyboard, or external MIDI device. Some can also read and convert scanned sheet music or import various file types such as MIDI or MusicXML. Figure 1.53 shows a screen capture of Finale.

FIGURE 1.53: FINALE, A MUSIC COMPOSING AND NOTATION SOFTWARE ENVIRONMENT

1.5.3.9 Working in the Linux Environment

If you want to work with audio in the Linux environment, you can do so at different levels of abstraction.

Ardour is free digital audio processing software that operates on the Linux and OS X operating systems. Ardour has extensive features for audio processing, but it doesn't support MIDI sequencing. A screen capture of the Ardour environment is in Figure 1.54. Ardour allows you to work at the same high level of abstraction as Logic or Music Creator.

Ardour works in conjunction with Jack, an audio connection kit, and the GUI (graphical user interface) for Jack, QjackCtl. A screenshot of the Jack interface is in Figure 1.55. On the Linux platform, Jack can talk to the sound card through ALSA (Advanced Linux Sound Architecture).

If you want to work at a lower level of abstraction, you can also use functions of one of the Linux basic sound libraries. Two libraries in use at the time of the writing of this chapter are ALSA and OSS (Open Sound System), both illustrated in Chapter 2 examples.

1.5.3.10 Software for Live Performances

There are software packages that are used specifically for live sound. The first category is analysis software. This is software that you can run on your computer to analyze acoustic measurements taken through an analysis microphone connected to the audio interface. Current popular software solutions include Smaart from Rational Acoustics (Mac/Win), FuzzMeasure Pro (Mac), and EASERA (Win). Most of the impulse, frequency, and phase response figures you see in this book were created using

FIGURE 1.54: ARDOUR, FREE DIGITAL AUDIO PROCESSING SOFTWARE
FOR THE LINUX OR OS X OPERATING SYSTEMS

FIGURE 1.55: JACK AUDIO CONNECTION KIT

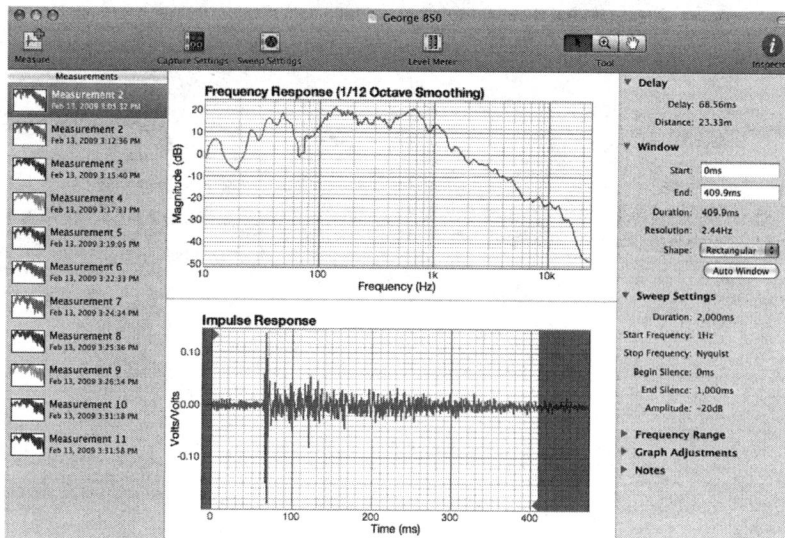

FIGURE 1.56: FUZZMEASURE PRO ANALYSIS SOFTWARE

FuzzMeasure Pro, shown in Figure 1.56. More information on these systems can be found in Chapter 2 and Chapter 8.

Another category of software used in live sound is sound playback software. Though it's possible to play sound cues from your DAW, the interface is really designed for recording and editing. A dedicated playback software application is much more reliable and easy to use for sound playback of a live show. Popular playback solutions include QLab from the company called Figure 53, shown in Figure 1.57. These systems allow you to create lists of cues that play and route the sound to multiple outputs on your audio interface. You can also automate the cues to fade in and out, layer sounds together, and even remotely trigger other systems such as lighting and projections.

FIGURE 1.57: QLAB PLAYBACK SOFTWARE FROM FIGURE 53

1.6 LEARNING SUPPLEMENTS

1.6.1 PRACTICAL EXERCISES

Throughout the book you'll see icons in the margins indicating learning supplements that are available for that section. If you're reading the book online, you can click on these links and go directly to the learning supplement on our website. If you're reading a printed version of the book, the learning supplements can be found by visiting

FIGURE 1.58: ICON FOR A PRACTICAL EXERCISE

our website and looking in the applicable section. The icon shown in Figure 1.58 indicates there is a supplement available in the form of a practical exercise. This could be a project you complete using the high-level sound production software described in earlier sections, a worksheet with practice math problems, or a hands-on exercise using tools in the world around you.

PRACTICAL EXERCISE:
Setting Up Your DAW
http://bit.ly/29okAGH

This brings us to our first practical exercise. As shown in the margin next to this paragraph, we have a learning supplement that walks you through setting up your digital audio workstation. Use this exercise to help you get all your new equipment and software up and running.

1.6.2 FLASH TUTORIALS

The icons shown in Figure 1.59 and Figure 1.60 indicate that supplements are available that require the Flash player web browser plug-in. The Flash tutorials are dynamic and interactive, helping to clarify concepts like longitudinal waves,

FIGURE 1.59: ICON FOR A FLASH TUTORIAL

FIGURE 1.60: ICON FOR A VIDEO TUTORIAL

musical notation, the playing of scales on a keyboard, EQ, and so forth. Questions at the ends of the Flash tutorials check your learning. The video tutorials use the Flash player to show a live action video demonstration of a concept. To play the tutorials, you need the Flash player plug-in to your web browser, which is standard and likely already installed. At most, you'll need to do an occasional upgrade of your Flash player, which on most computers is handled with automatic reminders of new versions and easy download and installation.

In addition to the software you need for actual audio recording and editing as described in the previous sections, you also may want some software for experimentation. The application programs listed below allow you to manipulate sound at descending levels of abstraction so that you can understand the operations in more depth. You can decide which of these software environments are useful to you as you learn more about digital audio.

1.6.3   MAX AND PURE DATA (Pd)

The icon shown in Figure 1.61 indicates there are supplements available that use the Max software. Max (formerly called Max/MSP/Jitter) is a real-time graphical programming environment for music, audio, and other media developed by Cycling '74. The core program, Max, provides the user interface, MIDI objects, timing for event-driven program-

FIGURE 1.61: ICON FOR MAX DEMO OR PROGRAMMING EXERCISE

ming, and inter-object communications. This functionality is extended with the MSP and Jitter modules. MSP supports real-time audio synthesis and digital signal processing. Jitter adds the ability to work with video. Max programs, called **patchers**, can be easily distributed and run by anyone who downloads the free Max runtime program. The runtime allows you to open the patchers and interact with them. If you want to be able to make your own patchers or make changes to existing ones, you need to purchase the full version. Max can also compile patchers into executable applications. In this book, Max demos are finished patchers that demonstrate a concept. Max programming exercises are projects that ask you to create or modify your own patcher from a given set of requirements. We provide example solutions for Max programming exercises in the solutions section of our website.

Max is powerful enough to be useful in real-world theatre, performance, music, and even video gaming productions, allowing sound designers to create sound systems and functionality not available in off-the-shelf software. On the Cycling '74 web page, you can find a list of interesting and creative applications.

Our Max demos require the Max runtime system, which can be downloaded free at the Cycling '74 website. Purchasing the full program is recommended for those who want to experiment with the demos more deeply or who want to complete the programming exercises. Figure 1.62 shows an example of a Max patcher windows.

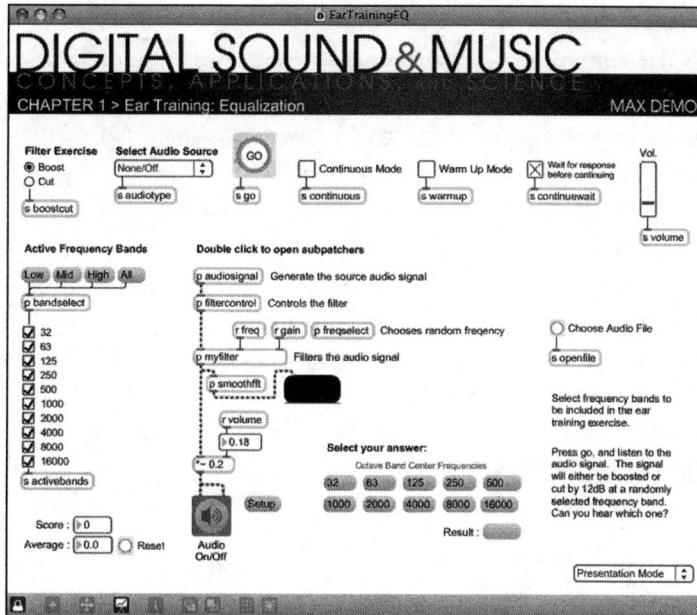

FIGURE 1.62: MAX GRAPHICAL PROGRAMMING ENVIRONMENT

If you can't afford Max, you might consider a free alternative, Pure Data (Pd), created by one of the originators of Max. Pure Data is open source software similar to Max in functionality and interface. For the Max programming exercises that involve audio programming, you might be able to use Pure Data and save yourself some money. However, Pure Data's documentation is not nearly as comprehensive as the documentation for Max.

1.6.4 MATLAB AND OCTAVE

The icon shown in Figure 1.63 indicates there is a MATLAB exercise available for that section of the book. MATLAB (Figure 1.64) is a commercial mathematical modeling tool that allows you to experiment with digital sound at a low level of abstraction. MATLAB, which stands for "matrix lab," is adept at manipulating matrices and arrays of data. Essentially, matrices

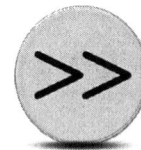

FIGURE 1.63: ICON FOR A MATLAB EXERCISE

are tables of information, and arrays are lists. Digital audio data related to a sound or piece of music is nothing more than an array of audio samples. The audio samples are generated in one of two basic ways in MATLAB. Sound can be recorded in an audio processing program like Adobe Audition, saved as an uncompressed PCM or a WAV file, and then input into MATLAB. Alternatively, it can be generated directly in MAT-LAB through the execution of sine functions. A sine function is given a frequency and amplitude related to the pitch and loudness of the desired sound. Executing a sine function at evenly spaced points produces numbers that constitute the audio data. Sine functions can also be added to each other to create complex sounds, the sound data can be plotted on a graph, and the sounds can be played in MATLAB. Operations on sine functions lay bare the mathematics of audio processing to give you a deeper understanding of filters, special effects, quantization errors, dithering, and the like. Although such operations are embedded at a high level of abstraction in tools like Logic and Audition, MATLAB allows you to create them "by hand" so that you really understand how they work.

MATLAB also has extra toolkits that provide higher-level functions. For example, the signal processing toolkit gives you access to functions such as specialized waveform generators, transforms, frequency responses, impulse responses, FIR (finite impulse response) filters, IIR (infinite impulse response) filters, and zero-pole diagram manipulations. The associated graphs help you to visualize how sound is changed when mathematical operations alter the properties of sound, amplitude, and phase.

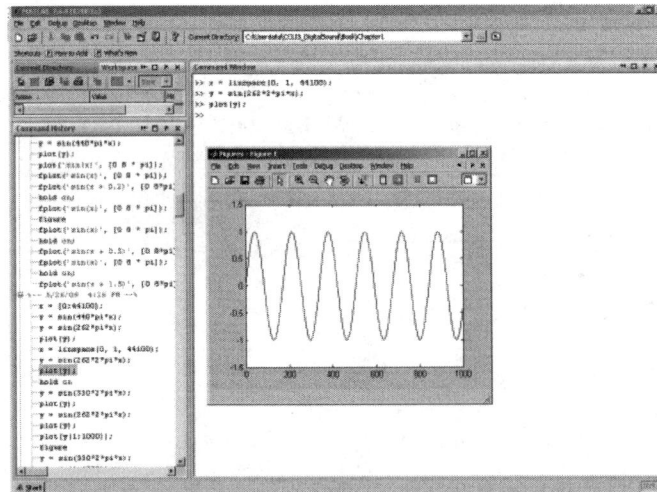

FIGURE 1.64: MATLAB MATHEMATICAL MODELING ENVIRONMENT

GNU Octave is an open source alternative to MATLAB that runs under the Linux, Unix, Mac OS X, or Windows operating systems. Like MATLAB, its specialty is array operations. Octave has most of the basic functionality of MATLAB, including the ability to read in or generate audio data, plot the data, perform basic array-based operations like adding or multiplying sine functions, and handle complex numbers. Octave doesn't have the extensive signal processing toolbox that MATLAB offers. However, third-party extensions to Octave are freely downloadable on the web, and at least one third-party signal processing toolkit has been developed with filtering, windowing, and display functions.

1.6.5 C++ AND JAVA PROGRAMMING EXERCISES

This book is intended to be useful not only to musicians, digital sound designers, and sound engineers, but also to computer scientists specializing in digital sound. Thus we include examples of sound processing done at a low level of abstraction, through C++ programs (Figure 1.65). The C++ programs that we use as examples are done on the Linux operating system. Linux is a good platform for audio programming be-

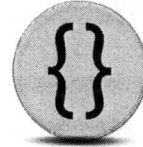

FIGURE 1.65: ICON FOR PROGRAMMING EXERCISES

cause it is open-source, allowing you to have direct access to the sound card and operating system. Windows, in contrast, is much more of a black box. Thus, low-level sound programming is harder to do in this environment.

If you have access to a computer running under Linux, you probably already have a C++ compiler installed. If not, you can download and install a GNU compiler. You can also try our examples under Unix, a relative of Linux. Your computer and operating system dictate what header files need to be included in your programs, so you may need to check the documentation on this.

Some Java programming exercises are also included with this book. Java allows you to handle sound at a higher level of abstraction with packages such as *java.sound.sampled* and *java.sound.midi*. You'll need a Java compiler and runtime to work with these programs.

1.7 WHERE TO GO FROM HERE

We've included a lot of information in this section. Don't worry if you don't completely understand everything yet. As you go through each chapter, you'll have the opportunity to experiment with all of these tools until you become confident with them. For now, start building up your workstation with the tools we've suggested, and enjoy the ride.

1.8 REFERENCES

Franz, David. *Recording and Producing in the Home Studio: A Complete Guide.* Boston, MA: Berklee Press, 2004.

Kirn, Peter. *Real World Digital Audio: Industrial-Strength Production Techniques.* Berkeley, CA: Peachpit Press, 2006.

Pohlmann, Ken C. *The Compact Disc Handbook.* Middleton, WI: A-R Editions, Inc., 1992.

Toole, Betty A. *Ada, The Enchantress of Numbers : A Selection from the Letters of Lord Byron's Daughter and Her Description of the First Computer.* Mill Valley, CA: Strawberry Press, 1992.

CHAPTER TWO

Sound Waves

2.1 CONCEPTS

2.1.1 SOUND WAVES, SINE WAVES, AND HARMONIC MOTION

Working with digital sound begins with an understanding of sound as a physical phenomenon. The sounds we hear are the result of vibrations of objects—for example, the human vocal cords, or the metal strings and wooden body of a guitar. In general, without the influence of a specific sound vibration, air molecules move around randomly. A vibrating object pushes against the randomly moving air molecules in the vicinity of the vibrating object, causing them first to crowd together and then to move apart. The alternate crowding together and moving apart of these molecules in turn affects the surrounding air pressure. The air pressure around the vibrating object rises and falls in a regular pattern, and this fluctuation of air pressure, propagated outward, is what we hear as sound.

Sound is often referred to as a wave, but we need to be careful with the commonly used term "sound wave," as it can lead to a misconception about the nature of sound as a physical phenomenon. On the one hand, there's the physical wave of energy passed through a medium as sound travels from its source to a listener. (We'll assume for simplicity that the sound is traveling through air, although it can travel through other media.) Related to this is the graphical view of sound, a plot of air pressure amplitude at a particular position in space as it changes over time. For single-frequency sounds, this graph takes the shape of a "wave," as shown in Figure 2.1. More precisely, a single-frequency sound can be expressed as a sine function and graphed as a sine wave (as we'll describe in more detail later). Let's see how these two things are related.

First, consider a very simple vibrating object—a tuning fork. When the tuning fork is struck, it begins to move back and forth. As the prong of the tuning fork vibrates outward (in Figure 2.2), it pushes the air molecules right next to it, which results in a rise in air pressure corresponding to a local increase in air density. This is called **compression**. Now, consider what happens when the prong vibrates inward. The air molecules have more room to spread out again, so the air pressure beside the tuning fork falls. The spreading out of the molecules is called **decompression** or **rarefaction**. A wave of rising and falling air pressure is transmitted to the listener's ear. This is the physical phenomenon of sound, the actual sound wave.

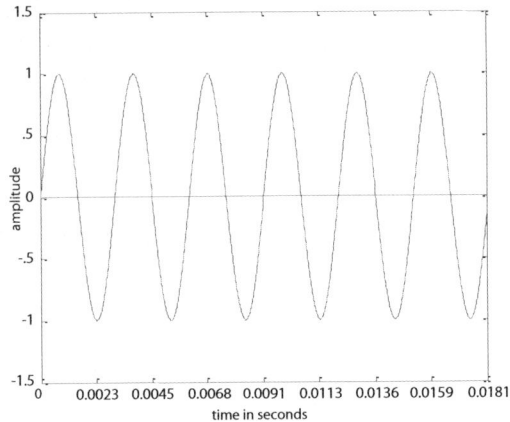

FIGURE 2.1: SINE WAVE REPRESENTING A SINGLE-FREQUENCY SOUND

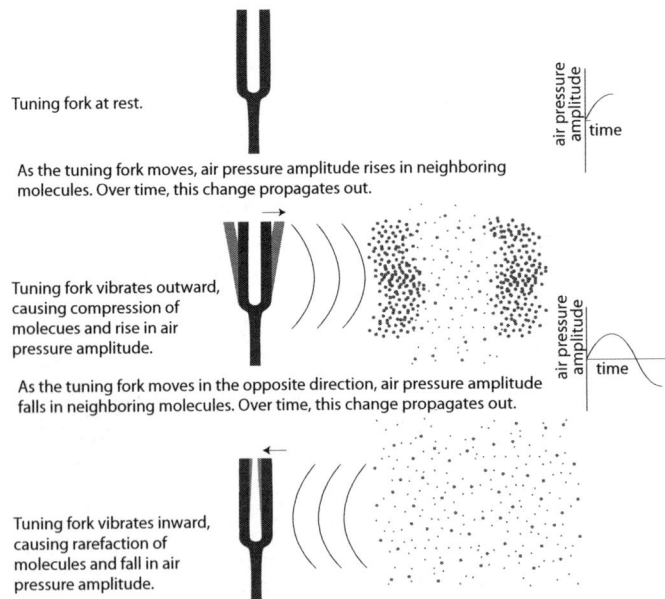

FIGURE 2.2: AIR PRESSURE AMPLITUDE AND SOUND WAVES

Assume that a tuning fork creates a single-frequency wave. Such a sound wave can be graphed as a sine wave, as illustrated in Figure 2.1. An incorrect understanding of this graph would be to picture air molecules going up and down as they travel across space from the place in which the sound originates to the place in which it is heard. This would be as if a particular molecule starts out where the sound originates and ends up in the listener's ear. This is *not* what is being pictured in a graph of a sound wave. It is the energy, not the air molecules themselves, that is being transmitted from the source of a sound to the listener's ear. If the wave in Figure 2.1 is intended to depict a single-frequency sound wave, then the graph has time on the *x*-axis (the horizontal axis) and air pressure amplitude on the *y*-axis. As described above, the air pressure rises and falls. For a single-frequency sound wave, the rate at which it does this is regular and continuous, taking the shape of a sine wave.

> **FLASH TUTORIAL:**
> Sound Waves and Harmonic Motion
> http://bit.ly/29rBNiX

Thus, the graph of a sound wave is a simple sine wave only if the sound has only one frequency component in it—that is, just one pitch. Most sounds are composed of multiple frequency components—multiple pitches. A sound with multiple frequency components also can be represented as a graph which plots amplitude over time; it's just a graph with a more complicated shape. For simplicity, we sometimes use the term "sound wave" rather than "graph of a sound wave" for such graphs, assuming that you understand the difference between the physical phenomenon and the graph representing it.

The regular pattern of compression and rarefaction described above is an example of **harmonic motion**, also called **harmonic oscillation**. Another example of harmonic motion is a spring dangling vertically. If you pull on the bottom of the spring, it will bounce up and down in a regular pattern. Its position—that is, its displacement from its natural resting position—can be graphed over time in the same way that a sound wave's air pressure amplitude can be graphed over time. The spring's position increases as the spring stretches downward, and it goes to negative values as it bounces upward. The speed of the spring's motion slows down as it reaches its maximum extension, and then it speeds up again as it bounces upward. This slowing down and speeding up as the spring bounces up and down can be modeled by the curve of a sine wave. In the ideal model, with no friction, the bouncing would go on forever. In reality, however, friction causes a **damping** effect such that the spring eventually comes to rest. We'll discuss damping more in a later chapter.

Now consider how sound travels from one location to another. The first molecules bump into the molecules beside them, and they bump into the next ones, and so forth as time goes on. It's something like a chain reaction of cars bumping into one another in a pile-up wreck. They don't all hit each other simultaneously. The first hits the second, the second hits the third, and so on. In the case of sound waves, this passing along of the change in air pressure is called **sound wave propagation**. The movement of the air molecules is different from the chain reaction pileup of cars, however, in that the molecules vibrate back and forth. When the molecules vibrate in the direction opposite of their original direction, the drop in air pressure amplitude is propagated through space in the same way that the increase was propagated.

Be careful not to confuse the speed at which a sound wave propagates and the rate at which the air pressure amplitude changes from highest to lowest. The speed at which the sound is transmitted from the source of the sound to the listener of the sound is the **speed of sound**. The rate at which the air pressure changes at a given point in space—i.e., vibrates back and forth—is the frequency of the sound wave. You may understand this better through the following analogy. Imagine that you're watching someone turn a flashlight on and off, repeatedly, at a certain fixed rate in order to communicate a sequence of numbers to you in binary code. The image of this person is transmitted to your eyes at the speed of light, analogous to the speed of sound. The rate at which the person is turning the flashlight on and off is the frequency of the communication, analogous to the frequency of a sound wave.

The above description of a sound wave implies that there must be a medium through which the changing pressure propagates. We've described sound traveling through air, but sound also can travel through liquids and solids. The speed at which the change in pressure propagates is the speed of sound. The speed of sound is different depending upon the medium in which sound is transmitted. It also varies by temperature and density. The speed of sound in air is approximately 1130 feet/second (ft/s) (or 344 meters/second (m/s)). Table 2.1 shows the approximate speed in other media.

Medium	Speed of sound in m/s	Speed of sound in ft/s
air (20° C, which is 68° F)	344	1130
water (just above 0° C, which is 32° F)	1410	4626
steel	5100	16,700
lead	1210	3970
glass	approximately 4000 (depending on type of glass)	approximately 13,200

TABLE 2.1: THE SPEED OF SOUND IN VARIOUS MEDIA

For clarity, we've thus far simplified the picture of how sound propagates. Figure 2.2 makes it look as though there's a single line of sound going straight out from the tuning fork and arriving at the listener's ear. In fact, sound radiates out from a source at all angles in a sphere. Figure 2.3 shows a top-view image of a real sound radiation pattern generated by software that uses sound dispersion data measured from an actual loudspeaker to predict how sound will propagate in a given three-dimensional space. In this case, we're looking at the horizontal dispersion of the loudspeaker. Shading is used to indicate the amplitude of sound. The figure shows that the amplitude of the sound is highest in front of the loudspeaker and lowest behind it. The simplification in Figure 2.2 suffices to give you a basic concept of sound as it emanates from a source and arrives at your ear. Later, when we begin to talk about acoustics, we'll consider a more complete picture of sound waves.

ASIDE:

Abbreviations:

feet   ft

seconds   s

meters   m

FIGURE 2.3: LOUDSPEAKER VIEWED FROM TOP WITH SOUND WAVES RADIATING AT MULTIPLE ANGLES

Sound waves are passed through the ear canal to the eardrum, causing vibrations which pass to little hairs in the inner ear. These hairs are connected to the auditory nerve, which sends the signal to the brain. The rate of a sound vibration—its frequency—is perceived as its pitch by the brain. The graph of a sound wave represents the changes in air pressure over time resulting from a vibrating source. To understand this better, let's look more closely at the concept of frequency and other properties of sine waves.

2.1.2 PROPERTIES OF SINE WAVES

We assume that you have some familiarity with sine waves from trigonometry, but even if you don't, you should be able to understand some basic concepts of this explanation.

A sine wave is a graph of a sine function $y = \sin(x)$. In the graph, the x-axis is the horizontal axis, and the y-axis is the vertical axis. A graph or phenomenon that takes the shape of a sine wave—oscillating up and down in a regular, continuous manner—is called a **sinusoid**.

In order to have the proper terminology to discuss sound waves and the corresponding sine functions, we need to take a little side trip into mathematics. We'll first give the sine function as it applies to sound, and then we'll explain the related terminology.

A single-frequency sound wave with frequency f, maximum
amplitude A, and phase θ is represented by the sine function

$$y = A \sin(2\pi f x + \theta)$$

where x is time and y is the amplitude of the sound wave at time x

---

EQUATION 2.1

Single-frequency sound waves are sinusoidal waves. Although pure single-frequency sound waves do not occur naturally, they can be created artificially by means of a computer. Naturally occurring sound waves are combinations of frequency components, as we'll discuss later in this chapter.

The graph of a sound wave is repeated Figure 2.4 with some of its parts labeled. The **amplitude** of a wave is its y value at some moment in time given by x. If we're talking about a pure sine wave, then the wave's amplitude, A, is the highest y value of the wave. We call this highest value the **crest** of the wave. The lowest value of the wave is called the **trough**. When we speak of the amplitude of the sine wave related to sound, we're referring essentially to the change in air pressure caused by the vibrations that created the sound. This air pressure, which changes over time, can be measured in Newtons/meter^2 or, more customarily, in decibels (abbreviated dB), a logarithmic unit explained in detail in Chapter 4. Amplitude is related to perceived loudness. The higher the amplitude of a sound wave, the louder it seems to the human ear.

In order to define frequency, we must first define a cycle. A **cycle** of a sine wave is a section of the wave from some starting position to the first moment at which it returns to that same position after having gone through its maximum and minimum amplitudes. Usually, we choose the starting position to be at some position where the wave crosses the *x*-axis, or zero crossing, so the cycle would be from that position to the next zero crossing where the wave starts to repeat, as shown in Figure 2.4.

The **frequency** of a wave, *f*, is the number of cycles per unit time, customarily the number of cycles per second. A unit that is used in speaking of sound frequency is **Hertz**, defined as 1 cycle/second, and abbreviated Hz. In Figure 2.4, the time units on the *x*-axis are seconds. Thus, the frequency of the wave is six cycles/0.0181 seconds ≈331 Hz. Henceforth, we'll use the abbreviation s for seconds and ms for milliseconds.

Frequency is related to pitch in human perception. A

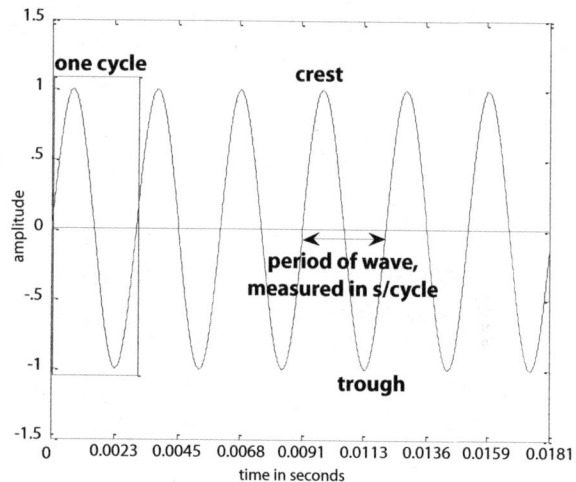

FIGURE 2.4: ONE CYCLE OF A SINE WAVE

single-frequency sound is perceived as a single pitch. For example, a sound wave of 440 Hz sounds like the note A on a piano (just above middle C). Humans hear in a frequency range of approximately 20 Hz to 20,000 Hz. The frequency ranges of most musical instruments fall between about 50 Hz and 5000 Hz. The range of frequencies that an individual can hear varies with age and other individual factors.

The period of a wave, *T*, is the time it takes for the wave to complete one cycle, measured in s/cycle. Frequency and period have an inverse relationship, given below.

Let the frequency of a sine wave be f and the period of a sine wave be T

Then

$$f = 1/T$$

and

$$T = 1/f$$

EQUATION 2.2

The period of the wave in Figure 2.4 is about three milliseconds per cycle. A 440 Hz wave (which has a frequency of 440 cycles/s) has a period of 1 s/440 cycles, which is about 0.00227 s/cycle. There are contexts in which it is more convenient to speak of period only in units of time, and in these contexts the "per cycle" can be omitted as long as units are handled consistently for a particular computation. With this in mind, a 440 Hz wave would simply be said to have a period of 2.27 milliseconds.

The **phase** of a wave, θ, is its offset from some specified starting position at $x = 0$. The sine of 0 is 0, so the blue wave in Figure 2.5 represents a sine function with no phase offset. However, consider a second sine wave with exactly the same frequency and amplitude, but displaced in the positive or negative direction on the x-axis relative to the first, as shown in Figure 2.5. The extent to which two waves have a phase offset relative to each other can be measured in degrees. If one sine wave is offset a full cycle from another, it has a 360 degree offset (denoted 360°); if it is offset a half cycle, is has a 180° offset; if it is offset a quarter cycle, it has a 90° offset, and so forth. In Figure 2.5, the red wave has a 90° offset from the blue. Equivalently, you could say it has a 270° offset, depending on whether you assume it is offset in the positive or negative x direction.

MAX DEMO: Phase and Polarity http://bit.ly/29m9rVc

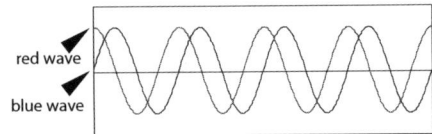

red wave
blue wave

FIGURE 2.5: TWO SINE WAVES WITH THE SAME FREQUENCY AND AMPLITUDE BUT DIFFERENT PHASES

Wavelength, λ, is the distance that a single-frequency wave propagates in space as it completes one cycle. Another way to say this is that wavelength is the distance between a place where the air pressure is at its maximum and a neighboring place where it is at its maximum. Distance is not represented on the graph of a sound wave, so we cannot directly observe the wavelength on such a graph. Instead, we have to consider the relationship between the speed of sound and a particular sound wave's period. Assume that the speed of sound is 1130 ft/s. If a 440 Hz wave takes 2.27 milliseconds to complete a cycle, then the position of maximum air pressure travels in 1 cycle × ((0.00227 s)/cycle) × ((1130 ft)/s) in one wavelength, which is 2.57 ft. This relationship is given more generally in the equation below.

Let the frequency of a sine wave representing a sound be f, the period be T, the wavelength be λ, and the speed of sound be c. Then

$$\lambda = cT$$

or equivalently

$$\lambda = c/f$$

EQUATION 2.3

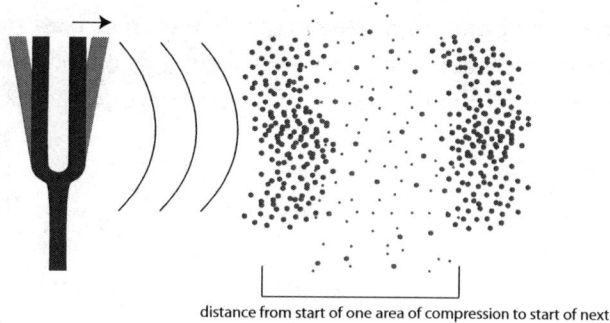

distance from start of one area of compression to start of next

FIGURE 2.6: WAVELENGTH

2.1.3 LONGITUDINAL AND TRANSVERSE WAVES

Sound waves are **longitudinal waves**. In a longitudinal wave, the displacement of the medium is parallel to the direction in which the wave propagates. For sound waves in air, air molecules are oscillating back and forth and propagating their energy in the same direction as their motion. You can picture a more concrete example if you remember the slinky toy of your childhood. If you and a friend lay a slinky along the floor and pull and push it back and forth, you create a longitudinal wave. The coils that make up the slinky are moving back and forth horizontally, in the same direction in which the wave propagates. The bouncing of a spring that is dangled vertically amounts to the same thing—a longitudinal wave.

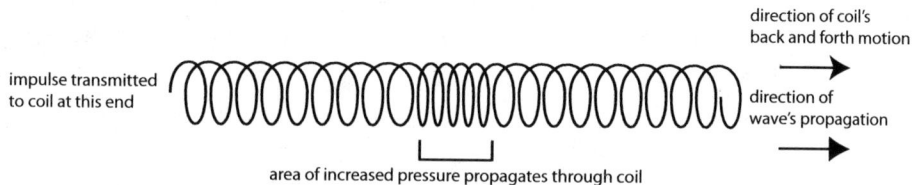

impulse transmitted to coil at this end

direction of coil's back and forth motion

direction of wave's propagation

area of increased pressure propagates through coil

FIGURE 2.7: LONGITUDINAL WAVE

In contrast, in a **transverse wave**, the displacement of the medium is perpendicular to the direction in which the wave propagates. A jump rope shaken up and down is an example of a transverse wave. We call the quick shake that you give to the jump rope an **impulse**—like imparting a "bump" to the rope that propagates to the opposite end.

The rope moves up and down, but the wave propagates from side to side, from one end of the rope to another. You could also use your slinky to create a transverse wave, flipping it up and down rather than pushing and pulling it horizontally.

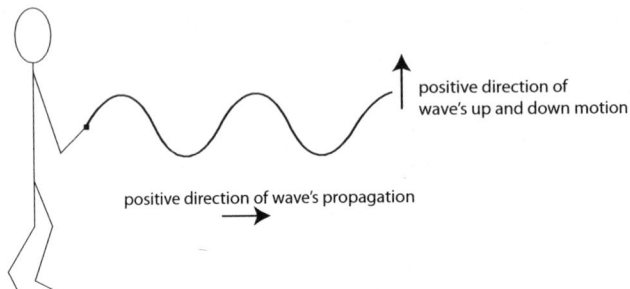

FLASH
TUTORIAL:
Longitudinal and
Transverse Waves
http://bit.ly/29nuMOi

VIDEO
TUTORIAL:
Longitudinal Waves
http://bit.ly/29jUarW

positive direction of
wave's up and down motion

positive direction of wave's propagation

FIGURE 2.8: TRANSVERSE WAVE

2.1.4 RESONANCE

2.1.4.1 Resonance as Harmonic Frequencies

Have you ever heard someone use the expression "That resonates with me"? A more informal version of this might be "That rings my bell." What they mean by these expressions is that an object or event stirs something essential in their nature. This is a metaphoric use of the concept of resonance.

Resonance is an object's tendency to vibrate or oscillate at a certain frequency that is basic to its nature. These vibrations can be excited in the presence of a stimulating force—like the ringing of a bell—or even in the presence of a frequency that sets it off—like glass shattering when just the right high-pitched note is sung. Musical instruments have natural resonant frequencies. When they are plucked, blown into, or struck, they vibrate at these resonant frequencies and resist others.

Resonance results from an object's shape, material, tension, and other physical properties. An object with resonance—for example, a musical instrument—vibrates at natural **resonant frequencies** consisting of a fundamental frequency and the related harmonic frequencies, all of which give an instrument its characteristic sound. The fundamental and harmonic frequencies are also referred to as the **partials**, since together they make up the full sound of the resonating object. The harmonic frequencies beyond the fundamental are called **overtones**. These terms can be slightly confusing.

The fundamental frequency is the **first harmonic** because this frequency is one times itself. The frequency that is twice the fundamental is called the **second harmonic** or, equivalently, the first overtone. The frequency that is three times the fundamental is called the **third harmonic** or second overtone, and so forth. The number of harmonic frequencies depends upon the properties of the vibrating object.

One simple way to understand the sense in which a frequency might be natural to an object is to picture pushing a child on a swing. If you push a swing when it is at the top of its arc, you're pushing it at its resonant frequency, and you'll get the best effect with your push. Imagine trying to push the swing at any other point in the arc. You would simply be fighting against the natural flow. Another way to illustrate resonance is by means of a simple transverse wave, as we'll show in the next section.

FLASH TUTORIAL:
Resonance as
Harmonic Frequencies
http://bit.ly/29uiSWs

2.1.4.2 Resonance of a Transverse Wave

We can observe resonance in the example of a simple transverse wave that results from sending an impulse along a rope that is fixed at both ends. Imagine that you're jerking the rope upward to create an impulse. The widest upward bump you could create in the rope would be the entire length of the rope. Since a wave consists of an upward movement followed by a downward movement, this impulse would represent half the total wavelength of the wave you're transmitting. The full wavelength, twice the length of the rope, is conceptualized in Figure 2.9. This is the **fundamental wavelength** of the fixed-end transverse wave. The fundamental wavelength (along with the speed at which the wave is propagated down the rope) defines the fundamental frequency at which the shaken rope resonates.

VIDEO TUTORIAL:
String Resonance
http://bit.ly/29f9yzX

If L is the length of a rope fixed at both ends, then λ is
the fundamental wavelength of the rope, given by

$$\lambda = 2L$$

EQUATION 2.4

Now imagine that you and a friend are holding a rope between you and shaking it up and down. It's possible to get the rope into a state of vibration where there are stationary points and other points between them where the rope vibrates up and down, as shown in Figure 2.10. This is called a **standing wave**. In order to get the rope into this state, you have to shake the rope at a resonant frequency. A rope can vibrate at more than one resonant frequency, each one giving rise to a specific **mode** –i.e., a pattern or shape of vibration. At its fundamental frequency, the whole rope is vibrating up and down (mode 1). Shaking at twice that rate excites the next resonant frequency of the rope, where one half of the rope is vibrating up while the other is vibrating down. This is the second harmonic (first overtone) of the vibrating rope (mode 2). In the third harmonic, the "up and down" vibrating areas each constitute one third of the rope's length (mode 3).

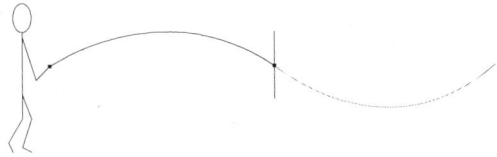

FIGURE 2.9: FULL WAVELENGTH OF IMPULSE SENT THROUGH FIXED-END ROPE

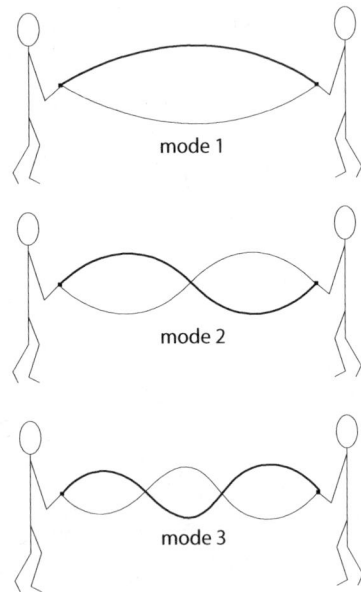

mode 1

mode 2

mode 3

FIGURE 2.10: VIBRATING A ROPE AT RESONANT FREQUENCIES

This phenomenon of a standing wave and resonant frequencies also manifests itself in a musical instrument. Suppose that instead of a rope, we have a guitar string fixed at both ends. Unlike the rope that is shaken at different rates of speed, guitar strings are plucked. This pluck, like an impulse, excites multiple resonant frequencies of the string at the same time, including the fundamental and any harmonics. The fundamental frequency of the guitar string results from the length of the string, the tension with which it is held between two fixed points, and the physical material of the string.

The harmonic modes of a string are depicted in Figure 2.11. The top picture in the figure illustrates the string vibrating according to its fundamental frequency. The wavelength λ of the fundamental frequency is two times the length of the string L. The second picture from the top in Figure 2.11 shows the second harmonic frequency of the string. Here, the wavelength is equal to the length of the string, and the corresponding frequency is twice the frequency of the fundamental. In the third harmonic frequency, the wavelength is ⅔ times the length of the string, and the corresponding frequency is three times the frequency of the fundamental. In the fourth harmonic frequency, the wavelength is ½ times the length of the string, and the corresponding frequency is four times the frequency of the fundamental. More harmonic frequencies could exist beyond this depending on the type of string.

Like a rope held at both ends, a guitar string fixed at both ends creates a standing wave as it vibrates according to its resonant frequencies. In a standing wave, there are points in the wave that don't move. These are called the **nodes**, as pictured in Figure 2.11. The **antinodes** are the high and low points between which the string vibrates. This is hard to illustrate in a still image, but you should imagine the wave as if it's anchored at the nodes and swinging back and forth between the nodes with high and low points at the antinodes.

It's important to note that this figure illustrates the physical movement of the string, *not* a graph of a sine wave representing the string's sound. The string's vibration is in the form of a **transverse wave**, where the string moves up and down while the tensile energy of the string propagates perpendicular to the vibration. Sound is a **longitudinal wave**.

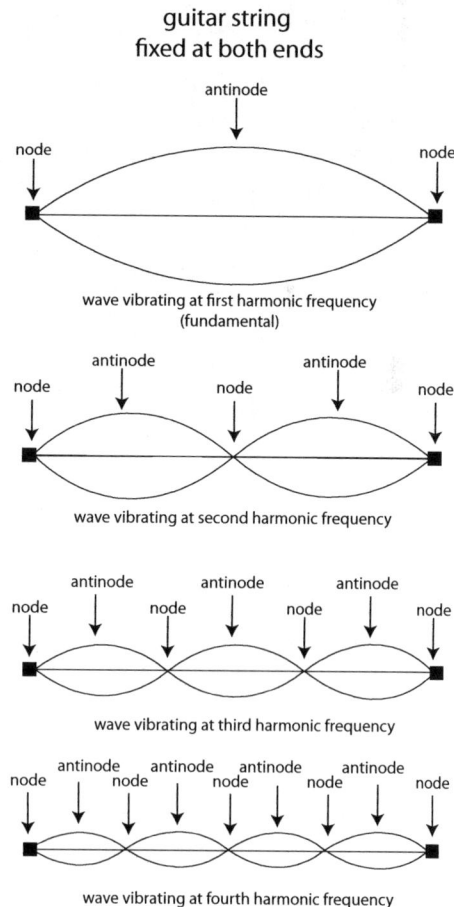

guitar string
fixed at both ends

wave vibrating at first harmonic frequency
(fundamental)

wave vibrating at second harmonic frequency

wave vibrating at third harmonic frequency

wave vibrating at fourth harmonic frequency

FIGURE 2.11: HARMONIC FREQUENCIES

The speed of the wave's propagation through the string is a function of the tension force on the string, the mass of the string, and the string's length. If you have two strings of the same length and mass and one is stretched more tightly than another, it will have a higher wave propagation speed and thus a higher frequency. The frequency arises from the properties of the string, including its fundamental wavelength, $2L$, and the extent to which it is stretched.

What is most significant is that you can *hear* the string as it vibrates at its resonant frequencies. These vibrations are transmitted to a resonant chamber, like a box, which in turn excites the neighboring air molecules. The excitation is propagated through the air as a transfer of energy in a longitudinal sound wave. The frequencies at which the string vibrates are translated into air pressure changes occurring with the same frequencies, and this creates the sound of the instrument. Figure 2.12 shows an example harmonic spectrum of a plucked guitar string. You can clearly see the resonant frequencies of the string, starting with the fundamental and increasing in integer multiples (twice the fundamental, three times the fundamental, etc.). It is interesting to note that not all the harmonics resonate with the same energy. Typically, the magnitude of the harmonics decreases as the frequency increases, where the fundamental is the most dominant. Also keep in mind that the harmonic spectrum and strength of the individual harmonics can vary somewhat depending on how the resonator is excited. How hard a string is plucked, or whether it is bowed or struck with a wooden stick or soft mallet, can have an effect on the way the object resonates and sounds.

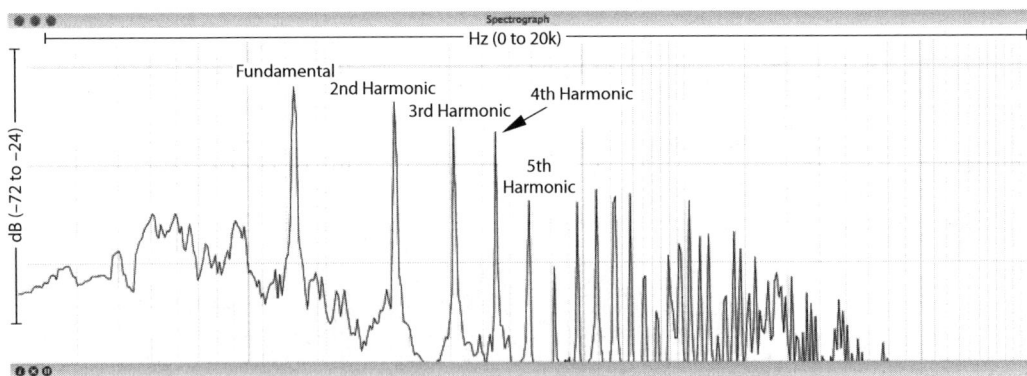

FIGURE 2.12: EXAMPLE HARMONIC SPECTRUM OF A PLUCKED GUITAR STRING

2.1.4.3 Resonance of a Longitudinal Wave

Not all musical instruments are made from strings. Many are constructed from cylindrical spaces of various types, like those found in clarinets, trombones, and trumpets. Let's think of these cylindrical spaces in the abstract as a pipe.

A significant difference between the type of wave created from blowing air into a pipe and a wave created by plucking a string is that the wave in the pipe is longitudinal while the wave on the string is transverse. When air is blown into the end of a pipe, air pressure changes are propagated through the pipe to the opposite end. The direction in which the air molecules vibrate is parallel to the direction in which the wave propagates.

VIDEO TUTORIAL: Pipe Resonance http://bit.ly/29Ix0Qf

Consider first a pipe that is open at both ends. Imagine that a sudden pulse of air is sent through one of the open ends of the pipe. The air is at atmospheric pressure at both open ends of the pipe. As the air is blown into the end, the air pressure rises, reaching its maximum at the middle and falling to its minimum again at the other open end. This is shown in the top part of Figure 2.13. The figure shows that the resulting fundamental wavelength of sound produced in the pipe is twice the length of the pipe (similar to the guitar string fixed at both ends).

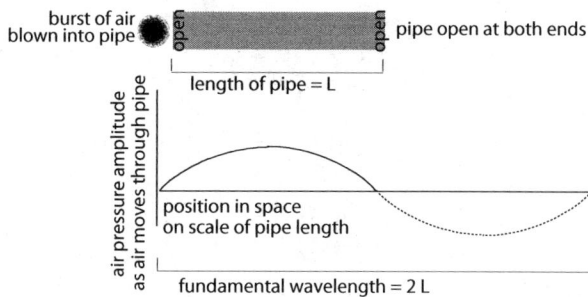

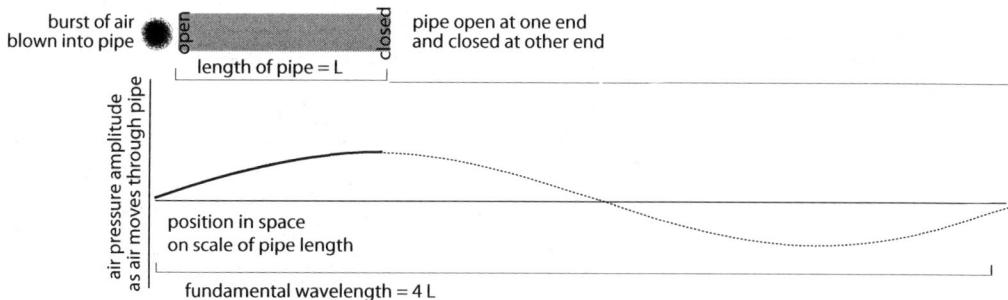

FIGURE 2.13: FUNDAMENTAL WAVELENGTH IN OPEN AND CLOSED PIPES

The situation is different if the pipe is closed at the end opposite to the one into which it is blown. In this case, air pressure rises to its maximum at the closed end. The bottom part of Figure 2.13 shows that in this situation, the closed end corresponds to the crest of the fundamental wavelength. Thus, the fundamental wavelength is four times the length of the pipe.

Because the wave in the pipe is traveling through air, it is simply a sound wave, and thus we know its speed—approximately 1130 ft/s. With this information, we can calculate the fundamental frequency of both closed and open pipes, given their length.

PRACTICAL EXERCISE:

Helmholtz Resonators
http://bit.ly/29nUAtH

Let L be the length of an open pipe, and let c be the speed of sound. Then the fundamental frequency of the pipe is

$$\frac{c}{2L}$$

EQUATION 2.5

Let L be the length of a closed pipe, and let c be the speed of sound. Then the fundamental frequency of the pipe is

$$\frac{c}{4L}$$

EQUATION 2.6

This explanation is intended to shed light on why each instrument has a characteristic sound, called its **timbre**. The timbre of an instrument is the sound that results from its fundamental frequency and the harmonic frequencies it produces, all of which are integer multiples of the fundamental. All the resonant frequencies of an instrument can be present simultaneously. They make up the frequency components of the sound emitted by the instrument. The components may be excited at a lower energy and fade out at different rates, however. Other frequencies contribute to the sound of an instrument as well, like the squeak of fingers moving across frets, the sound of a bow pulled across a string, or the frequencies produced by the resonant chamber of a guitar body. Instruments are also characterized by the way their amplitude changes over time when they are plucked, bowed, or blown into. The changes of amplitude are called the **amplitude envelope**, as we'll discuss in a later section.

Resonance is one of the phenomena that give musical instruments their characteristic sounds. Guitar strings alone do not make a very audible sound when plucked. However, when a guitar string is attached to a large wooden box with a shape and size that is proportional to the wavelengths of the frequencies generated by the string, the box resonates with the sound of the string in a way that makes it audible to a listener several feet away. Drumheads likewise do not make a very audible sound when hit with a stick. Attach the drumhead to a large box with a size and shape proportional to the diameter of the membrane, however, and the box resonates with the sound of that drumhead so it can be heard. Even wind instruments benefit from resonance. The wooden reed of a clarinet vibrating against a mouthpiece makes a fairly steady and quiet sound, but when that mouthpiece is attached to a tube, a frequency will resonate with a wavelength proportional to the length of the tube. Punching some holes in the tube that can be left open or covered in various combinations effectively changes the length of the tube and allows other frequencies to resonate.

2.1.5 DIGITIZING SOUND WAVES

In this chapter, we have been describing sound as continuous changes of air pressure amplitude. In this sense, sound is an **analog** phenomenon—a physical phenomenon that could be represented as continuously changing voltages. Computers require that we use a **discrete** representation of sound. In particular, when sound is captured as data in a computer, it is represented as a list of numbers. Capturing sound in a form that can be handled by a computer is a process called **analog-to-digital** conversion, whereby the amplitude of a sound wave is measured at evenly-spaced intervals in time—typically 44,100 times per second, or even more. Details of analog-to-digital conversion are covered in Chapter 5. For now, it suffices to think of digitized sound as a list of numbers. Once a computer has captured sound as a list of numbers, a whole host of mathematical operations can be performed on the sound to change its loudness, pitch, frequency balance, and so forth. We'll begin to see how this works in the following sections.

2.2 APPLICATIONS

2.2.1 ACOUSTICS

In each chapter, we begin with basic concepts in Section 1 and give applications of those concepts in Section 2. One main area where you can apply your understanding of sound waves is in the area of acoustics. Acoustics is a large topic, and thus we have devoted a whole chapter to it. Please refer to Chapter 4 for more on this topic.

2.2.2 SOUND SYNTHESIS

Naturally occurring sound waves almost always contain more than one frequency. The frequencies combined into one sound are called the sound's **frequency components**. A sound that has multiple frequency components is a **complex sound wave**. All the frequency components taken together constitute a sound's **frequency spectrum**. This is analogous to the way light is composed of a spectrum of colors. The frequency components of a sound are experienced by the listener as multiple pitches combined into one sound.

MAX DEMO:

Adding Sine Waves
http://bit.ly/29g3dV6

To understand frequency components of sound and how they might be manipulated, we can begin by synthesizing our own digital sound. Synthesis is a process of combining multiple elements to form something new. In sound synthesis, individual sound waves become one when their amplitude and frequency components interact and combine digitally, electrically, or acoustically. The most fundamental example of sound synthesis is when two sound waves travel through the same air space at the same time. Their amplitudes at each moment in time sum into a composite wave that contains the frequencies of both. Mathematically, this is a simple process of addition.

We can experiment with sound synthesis and understand it better by creating three single-frequency sounds using an audio editing program like Audacity or Adobe Audition. Using the "Generate Tone" feature in Audition, we've created three separate sound waves—the first at 262 Hz (middle C on a piano keyboard), the second at 330 Hz (the note E), and the third at 393 Hz (the note G). They're shown in Figure 2.14, each on a separate track. The three waves can be mixed down in the editing software—that is, combined into a single sound wave that has all three frequency components. The mixed down wave is shown on the bottom track.

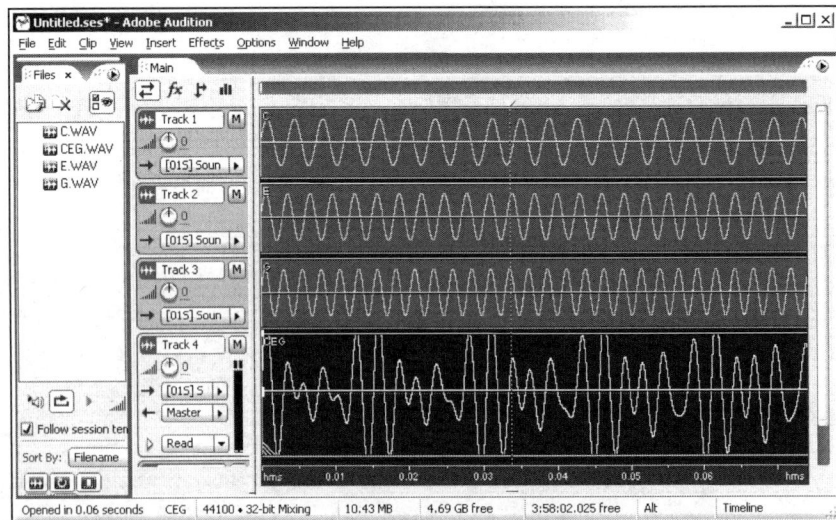

FIGURE 2.14: THREE WAVES MIXED DOWN INTO A WAVE WITH THREE FREQUENCY COMPONENTS

In a digital audio editing program like Audition, a sound wave is stored as a list of numbers, corresponding to the amplitude of the sound at each point in time. Thus, for the three audio tones generated, we have three lists of numbers. The mix-down procedure simply adds the corresponding values of the three waves at each point in time, as shown in Figure 2.15. Keep in mind that negative amplitudes (rarefactions) and positive amplitudes (compressions) can cancel each other out.

We're able to hear multiple sounds simultaneously in our environment because sound waves can be added. Another interesting consequence of the addition of sound waves results from the fact that waves have phases. Consider two sound waves that have exactly the same frequency and amplitude, but the second wave arrives exactly one half cycle after the first—that is, 180° out of phase, as shown in Figure 2.16. This could happen because the second sound wave is coming from a more distant loudspeaker than the first. The different arrival times result in phase cancellations as the two waves are summed when they reach the listener's ear. In this case, the amplitudes are exactly opposite each other, so they sum to 0.

Add the first three waves to get the fourth. To do so, add points at the same position along the x-axis.

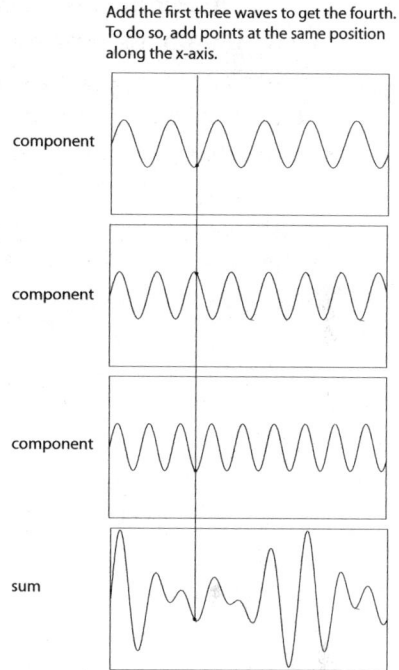

FIGURE 2.15: ADDING WAVES

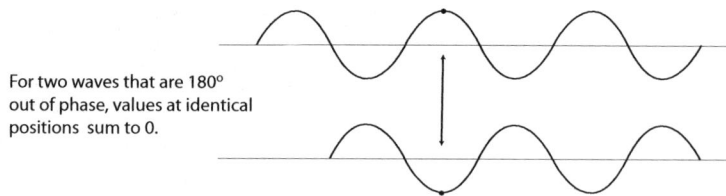

For two waves that are 180° out of phase, values at identical positions sum to 0.

FIGURE 2.16: COMBINING WAVES THAT ARE 180° OUT OF PHASE

2.2.3 SOUND ANALYSIS

We showed in the previous section how we can add frequency components to create a complex sound wave. The reverse of the sound synthesis process is **sound analysis**, which is the determination of the frequency components in a complex sound wave. In the 1800s, Joseph Fourier developed the mathematics that forms the basis of frequency analysis. He proved that any periodic sinusoidal function, regardless of its complexity, can be formulated as a sum of frequency components. These frequency components consist of a fundamental frequency and the harmonic frequencies related to this fundamental. Fourier's theorem says that no matter how complex a sound is, it's possible to break it down into its component frequencies—that is, to determine the different frequencies that are in that sound, and how much of each frequency component there is.

Fourier analysis begins with the **fundamental frequency** of the sound—the frequency of the longest repeated pattern of the sound. Then all the remaining frequency components that can be yielded by Fourier analysis (i.e., the **harmonic frequencies**) are integer multiples of the fundamental frequency. By "integer multiple" we mean that if the fundamental frequency is f_0, then each harmonic frequency f_n is equal to $(n+1)f_0$ for some non-negative integer n.

The **Fourier transform** is a mathematical operation used in digital filters and frequency analysis software to determine the frequency components of a sound. Figure 2.17 shows Adobe Audition's **waveform view** and a **frequency analysis view** for a sound with frequency components at 262 Hz, 330 Hz, and 393 Hz. The frequency analysis view is to the left of the waveform view. The graph in the frequency analysis view is called a **frequency response graph** or simply a **frequency response**. The waveform view has time on the x-axis and amplitude on the y-axis. The frequency analysis view has frequency on the x-axis and the magnitude of the frequency component on the y-axis (see Figure 2.18). In the frequency analysis view in Figure 2.17, we zoomed in on the portion of the x-axis between about 100 and 500 Hz to show that there are three spikes there, at approximately the positions of the three frequency components. You might expect that there would be three perfect vertical lines at 262, 330, and 393 Hz, but this is because digitizing and transforming sound introduces some error. Still, it is accurate enough to be the basis for filters and special effects with sounds.

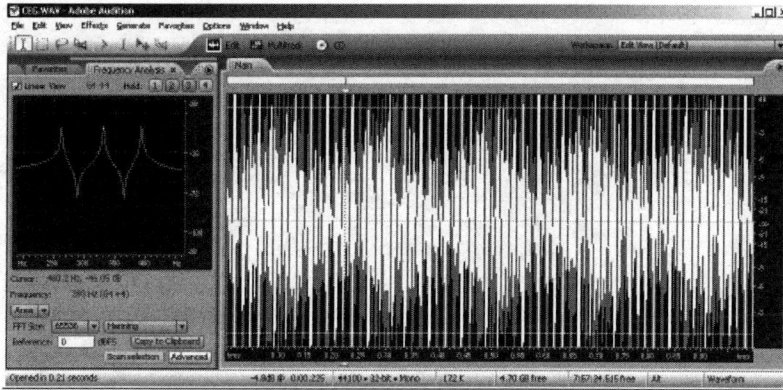

FIGURE 2.17: FREQUENCY ANALYSIS OF SOUND WITH THREE FREQUENCY COMPONENTS

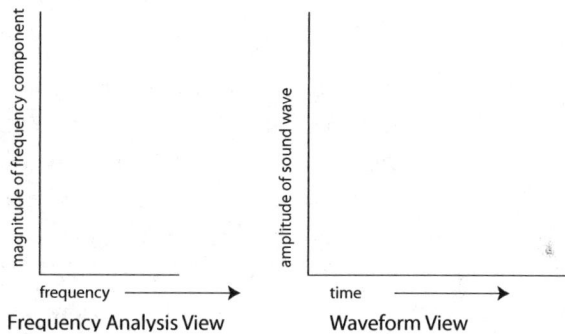

FIGURE 2.18: AXES OF FREQUENCY ANALYSIS AND WAVEFORM VIEWS

In the example just discussed, the frequencies that are combined in the composite sound never change. This is because of the way we constructed the sound, with three single-frequency waves that are held for one second. This sound, overall, is periodic because the pattern created from adding these three component frequencies is repeated over time, as you can see in the bottom of Figure 2.14.

Natural sounds, however, generally change in their frequency components as time passes. Consider something as simple as the word "information." When you say "information," your voice produces numerous frequency components, and these change over time. Figure 2.19 shows a recording and frequency analysis of the spoken word "information."

When you look at the frequency analysis view, don't be confused into thinking that the *x*-axis is time. The frequencies being analyzed are those that are present in the sound around the point in time marked by the dashed vertical line.

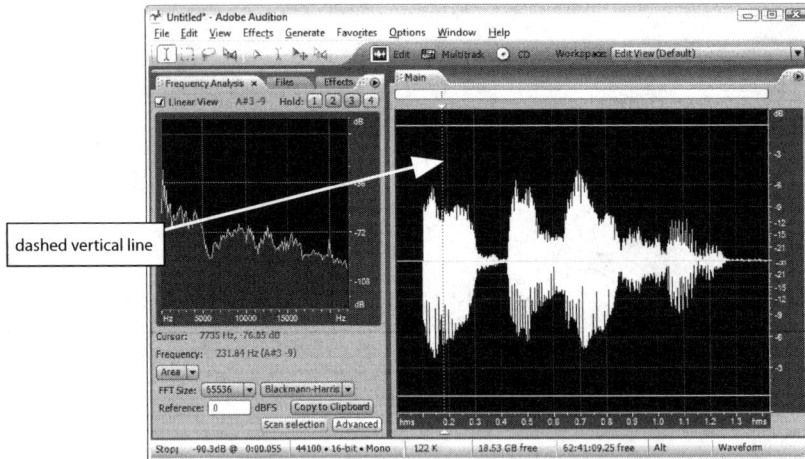

FIGURE 2.19: FREQUENCY ANALYSIS OF THE SPOKEN WORD "INFORMATION"

In music and other sounds, pitches (i.e., frequencies) change as time passes. Natural sounds are not periodic in the way that a one-chord sound is. The frequency components in the first second of such sounds are different from the frequency components in the next second. The upshot of this fact is that for complex non-periodic sounds, you have to analyze frequencies over a specified time period, called a **window**. When you ask your sound analysis software to provide a frequency analysis, you have to set the window size. The window size in Adobe Audition's frequency analysis view is called "FFT size." In the examples above, the window size is set to 65,536, indicating that the analysis is done over a span of 65,536 audio samples. The meaning of this window size is explained in more detail in Chapter 7. What is important to know at this point is that there's a tradeoff between choosing a large window and a small one. A larger window gives higher resolution across the frequency spectrum—breaking down the spectrum into smaller bands—but the disadvantage is that it "blurs" its analysis of the constantly changing frequencies across a larger span of time. A smaller window focuses on what the frequency components are in a more precise, short time frame, but it doesn't yield as many frequency bands in its analysis.

2.2.4 FREQUENCY COMPONENTS OF NON-SINUSOIDAL WAVES

In Section 2.1.3, we categorized waves by the relationship between the direction of the medium's movement and the direction of the wave's propagation. Another useful way to categorize waves is by their shape—square, sawtooth, and triangle, for example. These waves are easily described in

FLASH TUTORIAL:
Non-Sinusoidal
Waves
http://bit.ly/29ufD0L

mathematical terms and can be constructed artificially by adding certain harmonic frequency components in the right proportions. You may encounter square, sawtooth, and triangle waves in your work with software synthesizers. Although these waves are non-sinusoidal—i.e., they don't take the shape of a perfect sine wave—they still can be manipulated and played as sound waves, and they're useful in simulating the sounds of musical instruments.

A square wave rises and falls regularly between two levels (Figure 2.20, left). A sawtooth wave rises and falls at an angle, like the teeth of a saw (Figure 2.20, center). A triangle wave rises and falls in a slope in the shape of a triangle (Figure 2.20, right). Square waves create a hollow sound that can be adapted to resemble wind instruments. Sawtooth waves can be the basis for the synthesis of violin sounds. A triangle wave sounds very similar to a perfect sine wave, but with more body and depth, making it suitable for simulating a flute or trumpet. The suitability of these waves to simulate particular instruments varies according to the ways in which they are modulated and combined.

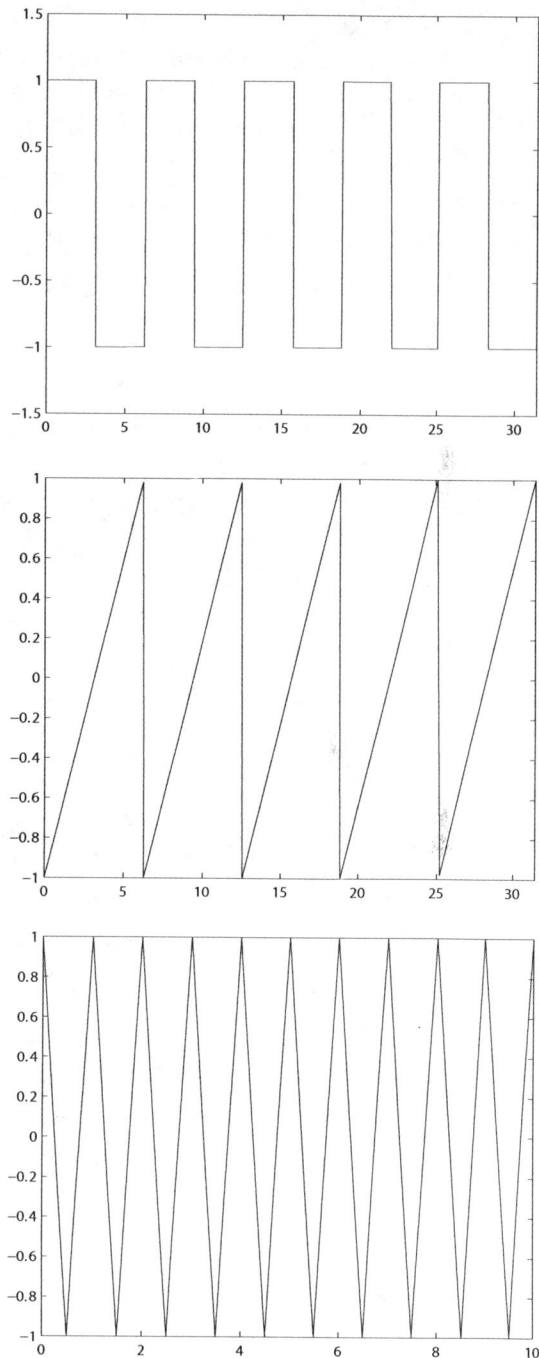

FIGURE 2.20: SQUARE, SAWTOOTH, AND TRIANGLE WAVES

PRACTICAL
EXERCISE:

Creating a

Sound Effect

http://bit.ly/29rQQZT

Non-sinusoidal waves can be generated by computer-based tools, such as Reason or Logic, which have built-in synthesizers for simulating musical instruments. Mathematically, non-sinusoidal waveforms are constructed by adding or subtracting harmonic frequencies in various patterns. A perfect square wave, for example, is formed by adding all the odd-numbered harmonics of a given fundamental frequency, with the amplitudes of these harmonics diminishing as their frequencies increase.

The odd-numbered harmonics are those with frequency nf where f is the fundamental frequency and n is a positive odd integer. A sawtooth wave is formed by adding *all* harmonic frequencies related to a fundamental, with the amplitude of each frequency component diminishing as the frequency increases. If you would like to look at the mathematics of non-sinusoidal waves more closely, see Section 2.3.3.

ASIDE: If you add the even numbered frequencies, you still get a sawtooth wave, but with double the frequency compared to the sawtooth wave with all frequency components.

2.2.5 FREQUENCY, IMPULSE, AND PHASE RESPONSE GRAPHS

Section 2.2.3 introduces frequency response graphs, showing one taken from Adobe Audition. In fact, there are three interrelated graphs that are often used in sound analysis. Since these are used in this and later chapters, this is a good time to introduce you to these types of graphs. The three types of graphs are impulse response, frequency response, and phase response.

Impulse, frequency, and phase response graphs are simply different ways of storing and graphing the same set of data related to an instance of sound. Each type of graph represents the information in a different mathematical domain. The domains and ranges of the three types of sound graphs are given in Table 2.2.

ASIDE: Although the term "impulse response" could technically be used for any instance of sound in the time domain, it is more often used to refer to instances of sound that are generated from a short burst of sound like a gun shot or balloon pop. In Chapter 7, you'll see how an impulse response can be used to simulate the effect of an acoustical space on a sound.

graph type	domain (x-axis)	range (y-axis)
impulse response	time	amplitude of sound at each moment in time
frequency response	frequency	magnitude of frequency across the audible spectrum of sound
phase response	frequency	phase of frequency across the audible spectrum of sound

TABLE 2.2: DOMAINS AND RANGES OF IMPULSE, FREQUENCY, AND PHASE RESPONSE GRAPHS

Let's look at examples of these three graphs, each associated with the same instance of sound. The graphs in the figures below were generated by sound analysis software called Fuzzmeasure Pro.

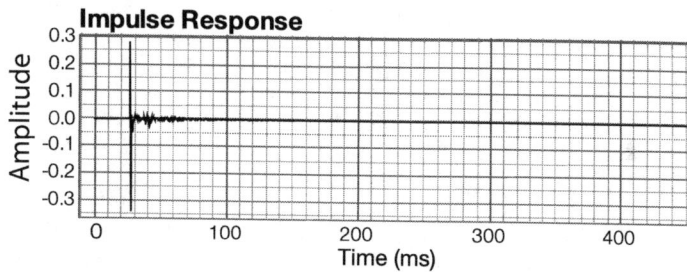

FIGURE 2.21: EXAMPLE IMPULSE RESPONSE GRAPH

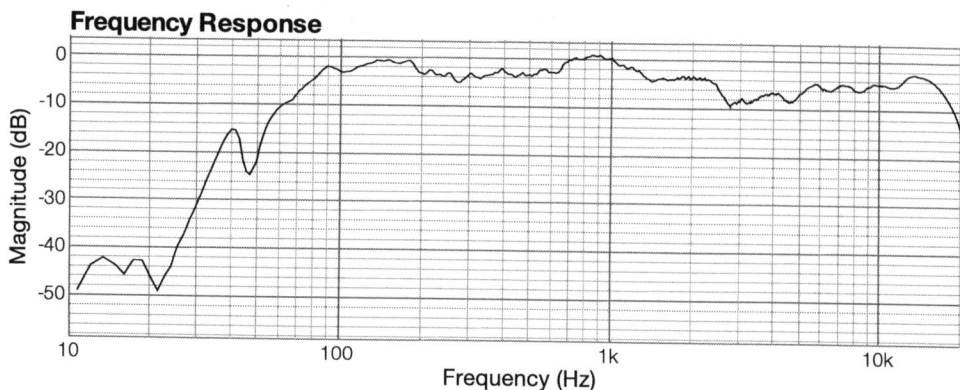

FIGURE 2.22: EXAMPLE FREQUENCY RESPONSE GRAPH

Phase Response

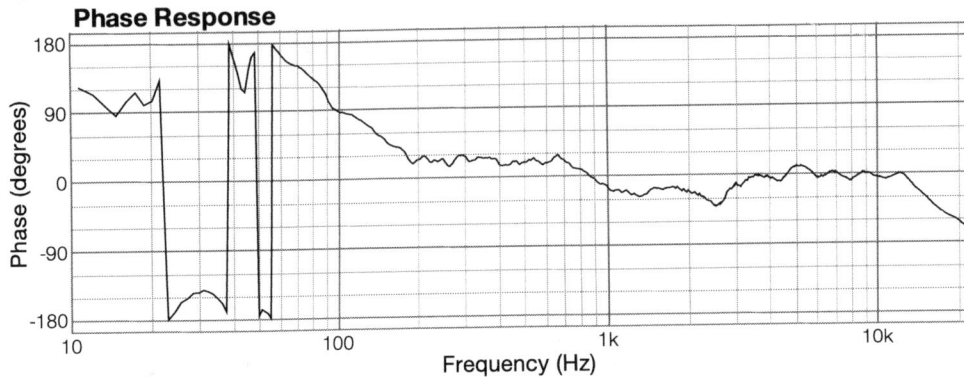

FIGURE 2.23: EXAMPLE PHASE RESPONSE GRAPH

The impulse response graph shows the amplitude of the sound wave over time. The data used to draw this graph are produced by a microphone (and associated digitization hardware and software), which samples the amplitude of sound at evenly-spaced intervals of time. The details of this sound sampling process are discussed in Chapter 5. For now, all you need to understand is that when sound is captured and put into a form that can be handled by a computer, it is nothing more than a list of numbers, each number representing the amplitude of sound at a moment in time.

Related to each impulse response graph are two other graphs—a frequency response graph that shows "how much" of each frequency is present in the instance of sound, and a phase response graph that shows the phase that each frequency component is in. Each of these two graphs covers the audible spectrum. In Section 3, you'll learn more about the mathematical process—the Fourier transform—that converts sound data from the time domain to the frequency and phase domain. Applying a Fourier transform to impulse response data—i.e., amplitude represented in the time domain—yields both frequency and phase information from which you can generate a frequency response graph and a phase response graph. The frequency response graph has the magnitude of the frequency on the *y*-axis on whatever scale is chosen for the graph. The phase response graph has phases ranging from −180° to 180° on the *y*-axis.

The main points to understand are these:

》 A graph is a visualization of data.

》 For any given instance of sound, you can analyze the data in terms of time, frequency, or phase, and you can graph the corresponding data.

》 These different ways of representing sound—as amplitude of sound over time or as frequency and phase over the audible spectrum—contain essentially the same information.

ASIDE: WAV and AIFF files store audio as amplitude information in the time domain, while MP3 files store audio as spectral data in the frequency domain. Both methods are able to capture the sonic information for playback later on.

⟩ The Fourier transform can be used to transform the sound data from one domain of representation to another. The Fourier transform is the basis for processes applied at the user level in sound measuring and editing software.

⟩ When you work with sound, you look at it and edit it in whatever domain or representation is most appropriate for your purposes at the time. You'll see this later in examples concerning frequency analysis of live performance spaces, room modes, precedence effect, and so forth.

2.2.6   EAR TESTING AND TRAINING

If you plan to work in sound, it's important to know the acuity of your own ears in three areas—the range of frequencies that you're able to hear, the differences in frequencies that you can detect, and the sensitivity of your hearing to relative time and direction of sounds. A good place to begin is to have your hearing tested by an audiologist to discover the natural frequency response of your ears. If you want to do your own test, you can use a sine wave generator in Logic, Audition, or similar software to step through the range of audible sound frequencies and determine the lowest and highest ones you can hear. The range of human hearing is about 20 Hz to 20,000 Hz, but this varies with individuals and changes as an individual ages.

MAX
DEMO:
Ear Training
for Frequencies
http://bit.ly/29kEL7U

You can not only test your ears for their current sensitivity; you can also train your ears to get better at identifying frequency and time differences in sound. Training your ears to recognize frequencies can be done by having someone boost frequency bands, one at a time, in a full-range noise or music signal while you guess which frequency is being boosted. In time, you'll start "guessing" correctly. Training your ears to recognize time or direction differences requires that someone create two sound waves with location or time offsets and then ask you to discriminate between the two. The ability to identify frequencies and hear subtle differences is very valuable when working with sound. The learning supplements for this section give sample exercises and worksheets related to ear training.

2.3 SCIENCE, MATHEMATICS, AND ALGORITHMS

2.3.1   MODELING SOUND IN MAX

Max (distributed by Cycling '74 and formerly called Max/MSP/Jitter) is a software environment for manipulating digital audio and MIDI data. The interface for Max is at a high level of abstraction, allowing you to patch together sound objects by dragging icons for them to a window and linking them with patch cords, similar to the way audio hardware is connected. If you aren't able to use Max, which is a commercial product, you can try substituting the freeware program Pure Data. We briefly discuss Pure Data in Section 2.3.2. In future chapters, we'll limit our examples to Max because of its highly developed functionality, but Pd is a viable free alternative that you might want to try.

MAX PROGRAMMING EXERCISE:

Adding Sine Waves with Phase Offsets
http://bit.ly/29f3HKR

Max can be used in two ways. First, it's an excellent environment for experimenting with sound simply to understand it better. As you synthesize and analyze sound through built-in Max objects and functions, you develop a better understanding of the event-driven nature of MIDI versus the streaming data nature of digital audio, and you see more closely how these kinds of data are manipulated through transforms, effects processors, and the like. Secondly, Max is actually used in the sound industry. When higher level audio processing programs like Logic, Pro Tools, Reason, or Sonar don't meet the specific needs of audio engineers, they can create specially-designed systems using Max.

Max is actually a combination of two components that can be made to work together. Max allows you to work with MIDI objects, and MSP is designed for digital audio objects. Since we won't go into depth in MIDI until Chapter 6, we'll just look at MSP for now.

Let's try a simple example of MSP to get you started. Figure 2.24 shows an MSP **patcher** for adding three pure sine waves. A patcher—whether it has Max objects, MSP objects, or both—is a visual representation of a program that operates on sound. The objects are connected by **patch cords**. These cords run between the **inlets** and **outlets** of objects.

One of the first things you'll probably want to do in MSP is create simple sine waves and listen to them. To be able to work on a patcher, you have to be in **edit mode**, as opposed to **lock mode**. You enter edit mode by clicking CTRL-E (or Apple-E) or by clicking the lock icon on the task bar. Once in edit mode, you can click on the + icon on the task bar, which gives you a menu of objects. (We refer you to the Max Help menu for details on inserting various objects.) The *cycle~* object creates a sine wave of whatever frequency you specify.

Notice that MSP objects are distinguished from Max objects by the tilde (~) at the end of their names. This reminds you that MSP objects send audio data streaming continuously through them, while Max objects typically are triggered by and trigger discrete events.

The speaker icon in Figure 2.24 represents the *ezdac~* object, which stands for "easy digital to analog conversion," and sends sound to the sound card to be played. A number object sends the desired frequency to each *cycle~* object, which in turn sends the sine wave to a *scope~* object (the sine wave graphs) for display. The three frequencies are summed with two consecutive +~ objects, and the resulting complex waveform is displayed.

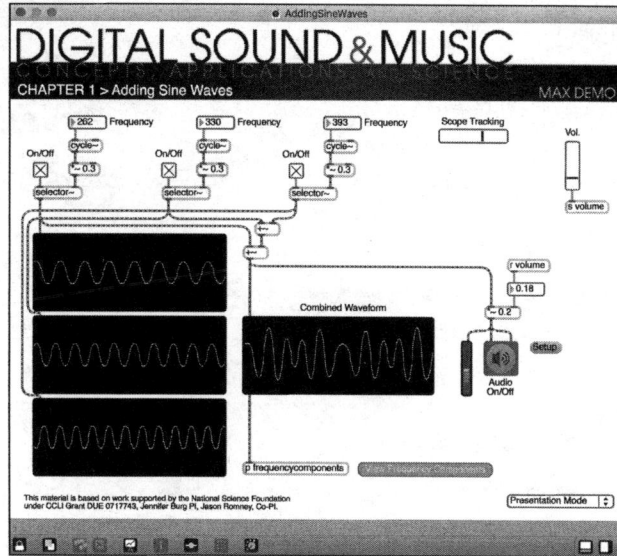

FIGURE 2.24: MSP PATCHER FOR ADDING THREE SINE WAVES

To understand these objects and functions in more detail, you can right click on them to get an Inspector window, which shows the parameters of the objects. Figure 2.25 shows the inspector for the *meter~* object, which looks like an LED and is to the left of the Audio On/Off switch in Figure 2.24. You can change the parameters in the Inspector as you wish. You also can right click on an object, go to the Help menu (Figure 2.26), and access an example patcher that helps you with the selected object. Figure 2.27 shows the Help patcher for the *ezdac~* object. The patchers in the Help can be run as programs, opened in Edit mode, and copied and pasted into your own patchers.

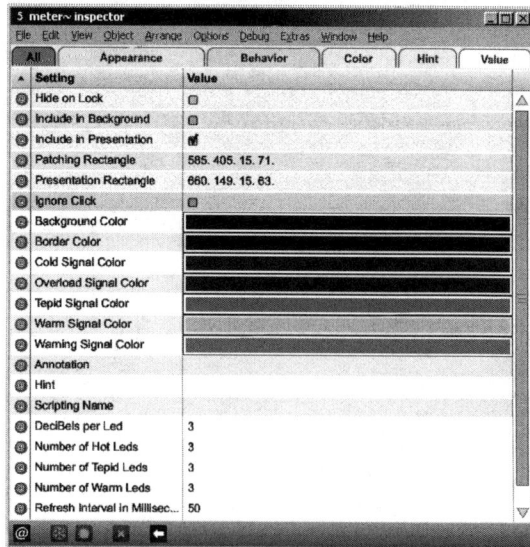

FIGURE 2.25: *METER~* INSPECTOR IN MAX

When you create a patcher, you may want to define how it looks to the user in what is called **presentation mode**, a view in which you can hide some of the implementation details of the patcher to make its essential functionality clearer. The example patcher's presentation mode is shown in Figure 2.28.

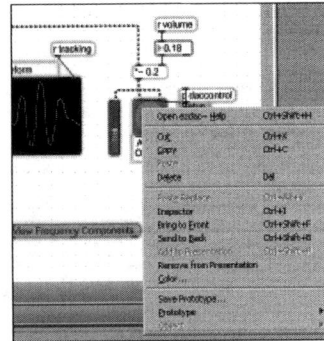

FIGURE 2.26: ACCESSING *EZDAC~* HELP IN MAX

2.3.2 MODELING SOUND WAVES IN PURE DATA (Pd)

Pure Data (Pd) is a free alternative to Max developed by one of the originators of Max, Miller Puckette, and his collaborators. Like Max, it is a graphical programming environment that links digital audio and MIDI.

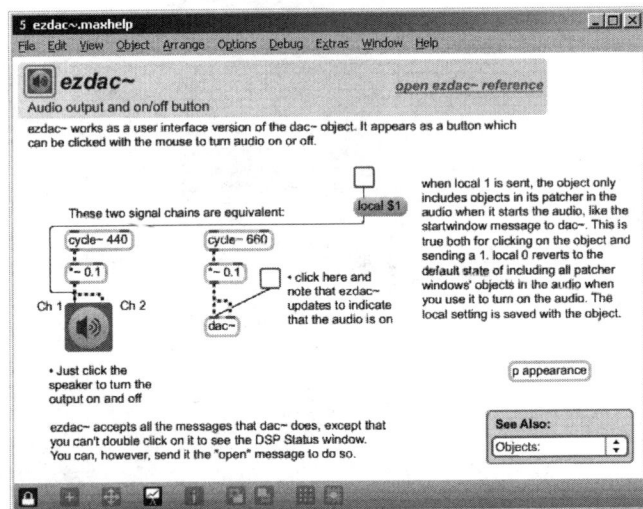

FIGURE 2.27: *EZDAC~* HELP PATCHER IN MAX

The Max program to add sine waves is implemented in Pd in Figure 2.29. You can see that the interface is very similar to Max's, although Pd has fewer GUI components and no presentation mode.

2.3.3 MODELING SOUND IN MATLAB

It's easy to model and manipulate sound waves in MATLAB, a mathematical modeling program. If you learn just a few of MATLAB's built-in functions, you can create sine waves that represent sounds of different frequencies, add them, plot the graphs, and listen to the resulting sounds. Working with sound in MATLAB helps you to understand the mathematics involved in digital audio processing. In this section, we'll introduce you to the basic functions that you can use for your work in digital sound.

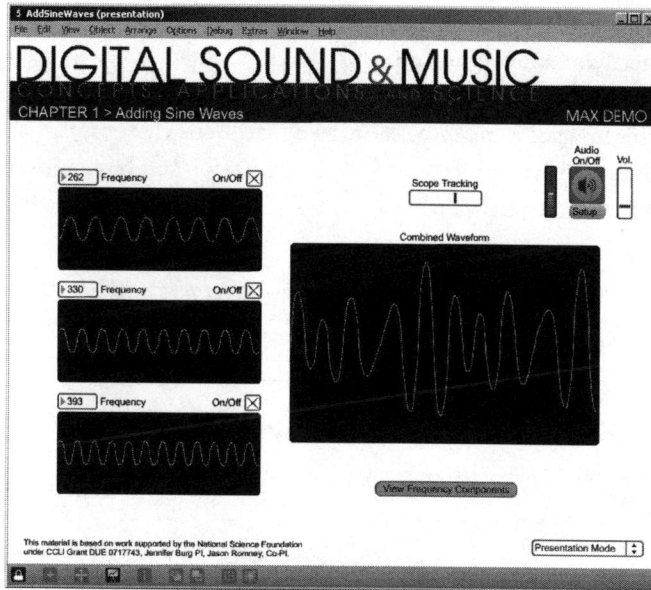

FIGURE 2.28: PRESENTATION MODE OF MAX PATCHER

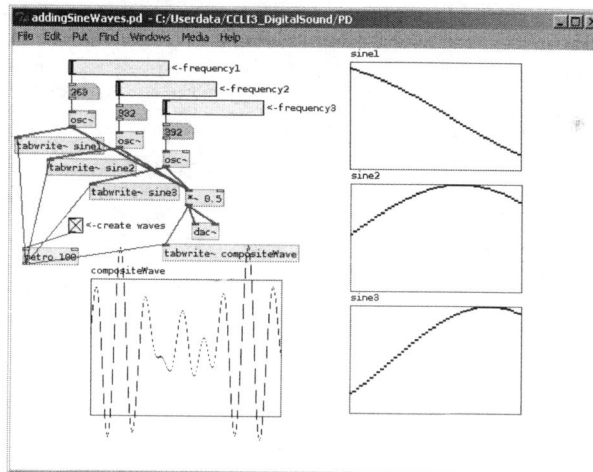

FIGURE 2.29: ADDING SOUND WAVES IN PURE DATA

This will get you started with MATLAB, and you can explore further on your own. If you aren't able to use MATLAB, which is a commercial product, you can try substituting the freeware program Octave. We introduce you briefly to Octave in Section 2.3.5. In future chapters, we'll limit our examples to MATLAB because it is widely used and has an extensive Signal Processing Toolbox that is extremely useful in sound processing. We suggest Octave as a free alternative that can accomplish some, but not all, of the examples in remaining chapters.

Before we begin working with MATLAB, let's review the basic sine functions used to represent sound. In the equation $y = A\sin(2\pi fx + \theta)$, frequency f is assumed to be measured in Hertz. An equivalent form of the sine function, and one that is often used, is expressed in terms of angular frequency, ω, measured in units of radians/s rather than Hertz. Since there are 2π radians in a cycle, and Hz is cycles/s, the relationship between frequency in Hertz and **angular frequency** in radians/s is as follows:

Let f be the frequency of a sine wave in Hertz. Then the angular frequency, ω, in radians/s, is given by

$$\omega = 2\pi f$$

EQUATION 2.7

We can now give an alternative form for the sine function.

A single-frequency sound wave with angular frequency ω, amplitude A, and phase θ is represented by the sine function

$$y = A\sin(\omega t + \theta)$$

EQUATION 2.8

In our examples below, we show the frequency in Hertz, but you should be aware of these two equivalent forms of the sine function. MATLAB's sine function expects angular frequency in Hertz, so f must be multiplied by 2π.

Now let's look at how we can model sounds with sine functions in MATLAB. Middle C on a piano keyboard has a frequency of approximately 262 Hz. To create a sine wave in MATLAB at this frequency and plot the graph, we can use the *fplot* function as follows:

```
fplot('sin(262*2*pi*t)', [0, 0.05, -1.5, 1.5]);
```

The graph in Figure 2.30 pops open when you type in the above command and hit Enter. Notice that the function you want to graph is enclosed in single quotes. Also, notice that the constant π is represented as *pi* in MATLAB. The portion in square brackets indicates the limits of the horizontal and vertical axes. The horizontal axis goes from 0 to 0.05, and the vertical axis goes from −1.5 to 1.5.

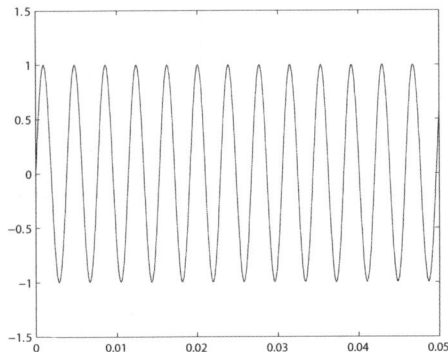

FIGURE 2.30: 262 HZ SINE WAVE IN MATLAB

If we want to change the amplitude of our sine wave, we can insert a value for *A*. If $A > 1$, we may have to alter the range of the vertical axis to accommodate the higher amplitude, as in

```
fplot('2*sin(262*2*pi*t)', [0, 0.05, -2.5, 2.5]);
```

After multiplying by $A = 2$ in the statement above, the top of the sine wave goes to 2 rather than 1.

To change the phase of the sine wave, we add a value θ. Phase is essentially a relationship between two sine waves with the same frequency. When we add θ to the sine wave, we are creating a sine wave with a phase offset of θ compared to a sine wave with phase offset of 0. We can show this by graphing both sine waves on the same graph. To do so, we graph the first function with the command

```
fplot('2*sin(262*2*pi*t)', [0, 0.05, -2.5, 2.5]);
```

We then type

```
hold on
```

This will cause all future graphs to be drawn on the currently open figure. Thus, if we type

```
fplot('2*sin(262*2*pi*t+pi)', [0, 0.05, -2.5, 2.5]);
```

we have two phase-offset graphs on the same plot. In Figure 2.31, the 0-phase-offset sine wave is labeled *red* and the 180° phase offset sine wave is labeled *blue*. Notice that the offset is given in units of radians rather than degrees, 180° being equal to π radians.

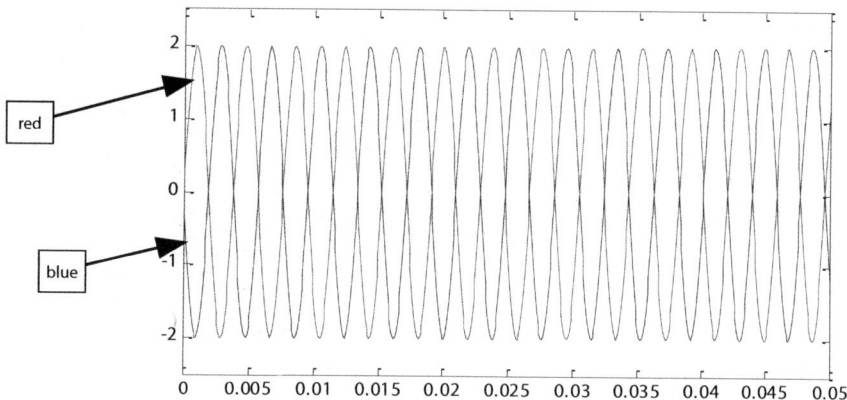

FIGURE 2.31: TWO SINE WAVES, ONE OFFSET 180° FROM THE OTHER

To change the frequency, we change ω. For example, changing ω to 440*2*pi gives us a graph of the note A above middle C on a keyboard.

```
fplot('sin(440*2*pi*t)', [0, 0.05, -1.5, 1.5]);
```

The above command gives the graph shown in Figure 2.32.

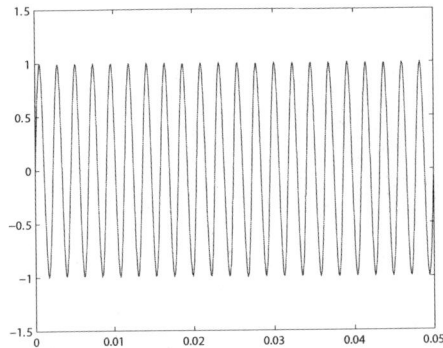

FIGURE 2.32: 440 HZ SINE WAVE

Then with

```
fplot('sin(262*2*pi*t)', [0, 0.05, -1.5, 1.5], 'red');
hold on
```

we get the graph shown in Figure 2.33.

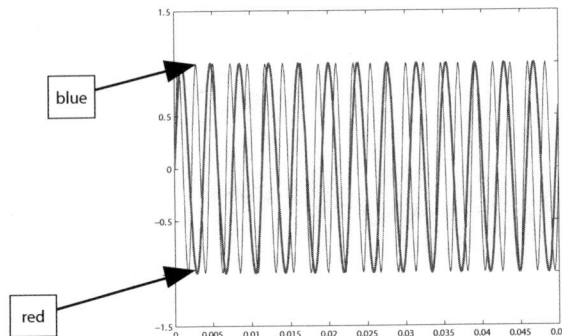

FIGURE 2.33: TWO SINE WAVES PLOTTED ON SAME GRAPH

The 262 Hz sine wave in the graph is labeled *red* to differentiate it from the blue 440 Hz wave. The last parameter in the *fplot* function causes the graph to be plotted in red. Changing the color or line width also can be done by choosing Edit/Figure Properties on the figure, selecting the sine wave, and changing its properties.

We also can add sine waves to create more complex waves, as we did using Adobe Audition in Section 2.2.2. This is a simple matter of adding the functions and graphing the sum, as shown below.

```
figure
fplot('sin(262*2*pi*t)+sin(440*2*pi*t)', [0, 0.05, -2.5, 2.5]);
```

First, we type *figure* to open a new empty figure (so that our new graph is not overlaid on the currently open figure). We then graph the sum of the sine waves for the notes C and A. The result is this:

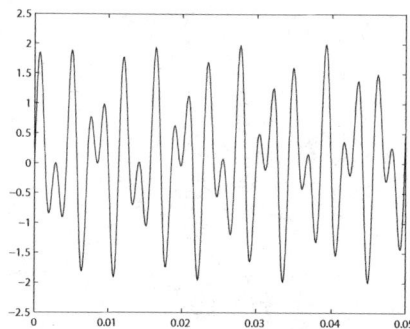

FIGURE 2.34: THE SUM OF TWO SINE WAVES

We've used the *fplot* function in these examples. This function makes it appear as if the graph of the sine function is continuous. Of course, MATLAB can't really graph a continuous list of numbers, which would be infinite in length. The name MATLAB, in fact, is an abbreviation of "matrix laboratory." MATLAB works with arrays and matrices. In Chapter 5, we'll explain how sound is digitized such that a sound file is just an array of numbers. The *plot* function is the best one to use in MATLAB to graph these values. Here's how this works.

First, you have to declare an array of values to use as input to a sine function. Let's say that you want one second of digital audio at a sampling rate of 44,100 Hz (i.e., samples/s), which is a standard sampling rate. Let's set the values of variables for sampling rate *sr* and number of seconds *s*, just to remind you for future reference of the relationship between the two.

```
sr = 44100;
s = 1;
```

Now, to give yourself an array of time values across which you can evaluate the sine function, you do the following:

```
t = linspace(0,s, sr*s);
```

This creates an array of *sr*s* values evenly spaced between and including the endpoints. Note that when you don't put a semi-colon after a command, the result of the command is displayed on the screen. Thus, without a semi-colon above, you'd see the

44,100 values scroll in front of you.

To evaluate the sine function across these values, you type

```
y = sin(2*pi*262*t);
```

One statement in MATLAB can cause an operation to be done on every element of an array. In this example, $y = sin(2*pi*262*t)$ takes the sine on each element of array t and stores the result in array y. To plot the sine wave, you type

```
plot(t,y);
```

Time is on the horizontal axis, between 0 and 1 second. Amplitude of the sound wave is on the vertical axis, scaled to values between −1 and 1. The graph is too dense for you to see the wave properly. There are three ways you can zoom in. One is by choosing Axes Properties from the graph's Edit menu and then resetting the range of the horizontal axis. The second way is to type an *axis* command like the following:

```
axis([0  0.1 -2 2]);
```

This displays only the first 1/10 of a second on the horizontal axis, with a range of −2 to 2 on the vertical axis so you can see the shape of the wave better. You can also ask for a plot of a subset of the points, as follows:

```
plot(t(1:1000),y(1:1000));
```

The above command plots only the first 1000 points from the sine function. Notice that the length of the two arrays must be the same for the *plot* function, and that numbers representing array indices must be positive integers. In general, if you have an array t of values and want to look at only the ith to the jth values, use $t(i:j)$.

An advantage of generating an array of sample values from the sine function is that with that array, you actually can hear the sound. When you send the array to the *wavplay* or *sound* function, you can verify that you've generated one second's worth of the frequency you wanted, middle C. You do this with

```
wavplay(y, sr);
```

(which works on Windows only) or, more generally,

```
sound(y, sr);
```

The first parameter is an array of sound samples. The second parameter is the sampling rate, which lets the system know how many samples to play per second.

MATLAB has other built-in functions for generating waves of special shapes. We'll go back to using *fplot* for these. For example, we can generate square, sawtooth, and triangular waves with the three commands given below:

```
fplot('square(t)',[0,10*pi,-1.5,1.5]);
```

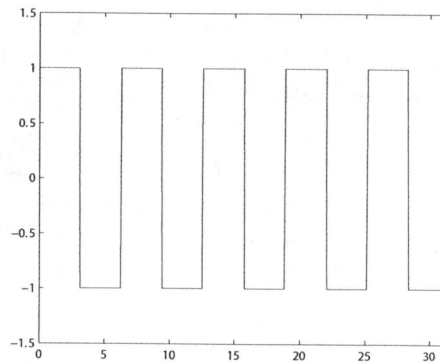

FIGURE 2.35: SQUARE WAVE

```
fplot('sawtooth(t)',[0,10*pi]);
```

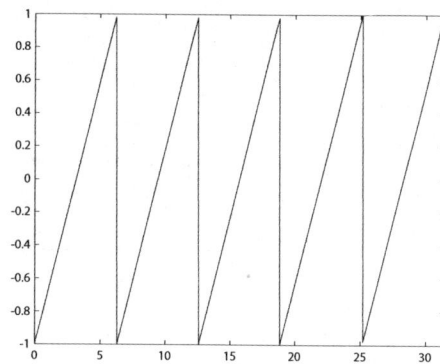

FIGURE 2.36: SAWTOOTH WAVE

```
fplot('2*pulstran(t,[0:10],''tripuls'')-1',[0,10]);
```
(Notice that the *tripuls* parameter is surrounded by two single quotes on each side.)

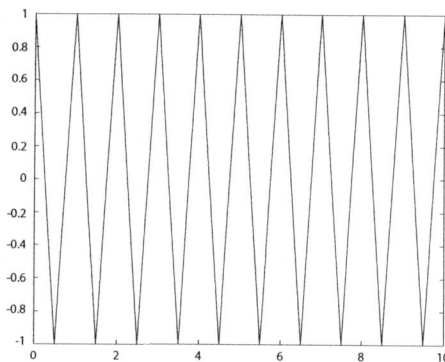

FIGURE 2.37: TRIANGLE WAVE

This section is intended only to introduce you to the basics of MATLAB for sound manipulation, and we leave it to you to investigate the above commands further. MATLAB has an extensive Help feature which gives you information on the built-in functions.

Each of the functions above can be created "from scratch" if you understand the nature of the non-sinusoidal waves. The ideal square wave is constructed from an infinite sum of odd-numbered harmonics of diminishing amplitude. More precisely, if f is the fundamental frequency of the non-sinusoidal wave to be created, then a square wave is constructed by the following infinite summation:

Let f be a fundamental frequency. Then a square wave created from this fundamental frequency is defined by the infinite summation

$$\sum_{n=0}^{\infty} \frac{1}{2n+1} \sin(2\pi(2n+1)ft)$$

EQUATION 2.9

Of course, we can't do an infinite summation in MATLAB, but we can observe how the graph of the function becomes increasingly square as we add more terms in the summation. To create the first four terms and plot the resulting sum, we can do

```
f1 = 'sin(2*pi*262*t) + sin(2*pi*262*3*t)/3 + sin(2*pi*262*5*t)/5 +
sin(2*pi*262*7*t)/7';
fplot(f1, [0 0.01 -1 1]);
```

This gives the wave in Figure 2.38.

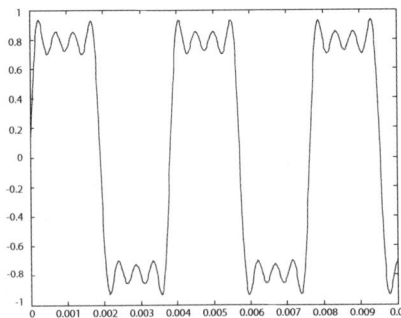

**FIGURE 2.38: CREATING A SQUARE WAVE
BY ADDING FOUR SINE FUNCTIONS**

You can see that it is beginning to get square but has many ripples on the top. Adding four more terms gives further refinement to the square wave, as illustrated in Figure 2.39.

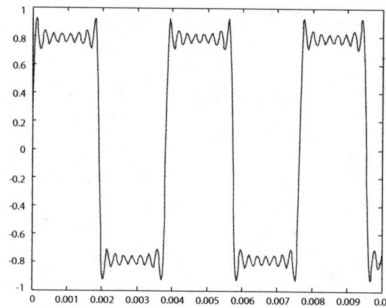

**FIGURE 2.39: CREATING A SQUARE WAVE
BY ADDING EIGHT SINE FUNCTIONS**

Creating the wave in this brute force manner is tedious. We can make it easier by using MATLAB's *sum* function and its ability to do operations on entire arrays. For example, you can plot a 262 Hz square wave using 51 terms with the following MATLAB command:

```
fplot('sum(sin(2*pi*262*([1:2:101])*t)./([1:2:101]))',[0 0.005 -1 1])
```

The array notation [1:2:101] creates an array of 51 points spaced two units apart—in effect, including the odd harmonic frequencies in the summation and dividing by the odd number. The *sum* function adds up these frequency components. The function is graphed over the points 0 to 0.005 on the horizontal axis and −1 to 1 on the vertical axis. The ./ operation causes the division to be executed element by element across the two arrays.

The sawtooth wave is an infinite sum of all harmonic frequencies with diminishing amplitudes, as in the following equation:

---

*Let f be a fundamental frequency. Then a sawtooth wave created from
this fundamental frequency is defined by the infinite summation*

$$\frac{2}{\pi} \sum_{n=1}^{\infty} \frac{\sin(2\pi n f t)}{n}$$

EQUATION 2.10

$2/\pi$ is a scaling factor to ensure that the result of the summation is in the range of −1 to 1.

The sawtooth wave can be plotted by the following MATLAB command:

```
fplot('-sum((sin(2*pi*262*([1:100])*t)./([1:100])))',[0 0.005 -2 2])
```

The triangle wave is an infinite sum of odd-numbered harmonics that alternate in their signs, as follows:

Let f be a fundamental frequency. Then a triangle wave created from this fundamental frequency is defined by the infinite summation

$$\frac{8}{\pi^2} \sum_{n=0}^{\infty} \left(\frac{\sin\left(2\pi(4n+1)ft\right)}{(4n+1)^2} \right) - \left(\frac{\sin\left(2\pi(4n+3)ft\right)}{(4n+3)^2} \right)$$

EQUATION 2.11

$8/\pi^2$ is a scaling factor to ensure that the result of the summation is in the range of -1 to 1. We leave the creation of the triangle wave as a MATLAB exercise.

If you actually want to hear one of these waves, you can generate the array of audio samples with

```
s = 1;
sr = 44100;
t = linspace(0, s, sr*s);
y = sawtooth(262*2*pi*t);
```

and then play the wave with

```
sound(y, sr);
```

>>
MATLAB EXERCISE:
Creating a
Triangle Wave
http://bit.ly/29o7Yj0

It's informative to create and listen to square, sawtooth, and triangle waves of various amplitudes and frequencies. This gives you some insight into how these waves can be used in sound synthesizers to mimic the sounds of various instruments. We'll cover this in more detail in Chapter 6.

In this chapter, all our MATLAB examples are done by means of expressions that are evaluated directly from MATLAB's command line. Another way to approach the problems is to write programs in MATLAB's scripting language. We leave it to the reader to explore MATLAB script programming, and we'll have examples in later chapters.

2.3.4 READING AND WRITING WAV FILES IN MATLAB

In the previous sections, we generated sine waves to generate sound data and manipulate it in various ways. This is useful for understanding basic concepts regarding sound. However, in practice you have real-world sounds that have been captured and stored in digital form. Let's look now at how we can read audio files in MATLAB and perform operations on them.

We've borrowed a short WAV file from Adobe Audition's demo files, reducing it to mono rather than stereo. MATLAB's *wavread* function imports WAV files, as follows:

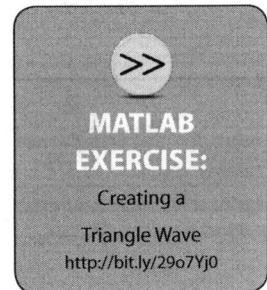

```
y = wavread('HornsE04Mono.wav');
```

This reads an array of audio samples into *y*, assuming that the file is in the current folder of MATLAB. (You can set this through the Current Folder window at the top of MATLAB.) If you want to know the sampling rate and bit depth (the number of bits per sample) of the audio file, you can get this information with

```
[y, sr, b] = wavread('HornsE04Mono.wav');
```

sr now contains the sampling rate and *b* contains the bit depth. The Workspace window shows you the values in these variables. Notice that *y*, which is the audio data, is represented in variables of type *double* (real numbers) ranging from –1 to 1.

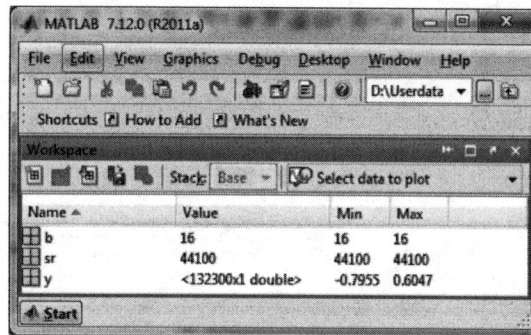

FIGURE 2.40: WORKSPACE IN MATLAB SHOWING
RESULTS OF *WAVREAD* FUNCTION

You can play the sound with

```
sound(y, sr);
```

Once you've read in a WAV file and have it stored in an array, you can easily do mathematical operations on it. For example, you can make it quieter by multiplying by a number less than 1, as in

```
y = y * 0.5;
```

You can also write out the new form of the sound file, as in

```
wavwrite(y, 'HornsNew.wav');
```

2.3.5 MODELING SOUND IN OCTAVE

Octave is a freeware, open-source version of MATLAB distributed by GNU. It has many but not all of the functions of MATLAB. There are versions of Octave for Linux, UNIX, Windows, and Mac OS X.

If you try to do the above exercise in Octave, most of the functions are the same. The *fplot* function is the same in Octave as in MATLAB except that for colors you must put a digit from 0 to 7 in single quotes rather than use the name of the color. The *linspace* function is the same in Octave as in MATLAB. To play the sound, you need to use the *playsound* function rather than *wavplay*. You also can use a *wavwrite* function (which exists in both MATLAB and Octave) to write the audio data to an external file. Then you can play the sound with your favorite media player.

There is no *square*, *sawtooth*, or *triangle* function in Octave. To create your own sawtooth, square, or triangle wave in Octave, you can use the Octave programs below. You might want to consider why the mathematical shortcuts in these programs produced the desired waveforms.

```
function saw = sawtooth(freq, samplerate)

x = [0:samplerate];
wavelength = samplerate/freq;
saw = 2*mod(x, wavelength)/wavelength-1;

end
```

PROGRAM 2.1: SAWTOOTH WAVE IN OCTAVE

```
function sqwave = squarewave(freq, samplerate)

x = [0:samplerate];
wavelength = samplerate/freq;
saw = 2*mod(x, wavelength)/wavelength-1; %start with sawtooth wave
sawzeros = (saw == zeros(size(saw))); %elminates division by zero in next step
sqwave = -abs(saw)./(saw+sawzeros);  %./ for element-by-element division

end
```

PROGRAM 2.2: SQUARE WAVE IN OCTAVE

```
function triwave = trianglewave(freq, samplerate)

x = [0:samplerate];
wavelength = samplerate/freq;
saw = 2*mod(x, wavelength)/wavelength-1; %start with sawtooth wave
tri = 2*abs(saw)-1;

end
```

PROGRAM 2.3: TRIANGLE WAVE IN OCTAVE

2.3.6   TRANSFORMING FROM ONE DOMAIN TO ANOTHER

In Section 2.2.3, we showed how sound can be represented graphically in two ways. In the waveform view, time is on the horizontal axis and amplitude of the sound wave is on the vertical axis. In the frequency analysis view, frequency is on the horizontal axis and the magnitude of the frequency component is on the vertical axis. The waveform view represents sound in the **time domain**. The frequency analysis view represents sound in the **frequency domain**. (See Figure 2.18 and Figure 2.19.) Whether sound is represented in the time or the frequency domain, it's just a list of numbers. The information is essentially the same—it's just that the way we look at it is different.

The one-dimensional Fourier transform is a function that maps real to the complex numbers, given by the equation below. It can be used to transform audio data from the time to the frequency domain.

$$F(n) = \int_{-\infty}^{\infty} f(k)e^{-i2\pi nk}dk \ \ where \ \ i = \sqrt{-1}$$

EQUATION 2.12: FOURIER TRANSFORM (CONTINUOUS)

Sometimes it's more convenient to represent sound data one way as opposed to another because it's easier to manipulate it in a certain domain. For example, in the time domain we can easily change the amplitude of the sound by multiplying each amplitude by a number. On the other hand, it may be easier to eliminate certain frequencies or change the relative magnitudes of frequencies if we have the data represented in the frequency domain.

2.3.7   THE DISCRETE FOURIER TRANSFORM (DFT) AND ITS INVERSE

To be applied to discrete audio data, the Fourier transform must be rendered in a discrete form. This is given in the equation for the discrete Fourier transform (DFT) below.

ASIDE: The second form of the discrete Fourier transform given in Equation 2.13, $1/N \sum_{k=0}^{N-1} f_k \ e^{-i2\pi kn/N}$, uses the constant e. It is derivable from the first by application of Euler's identify, $e^{i2\pi kn} = \cos(2\pi kn) + i\sin(2\pi kn)$. To see the derivation, see (Burg 2008).

$$F_n = \frac{1}{N}\left(\sum_{k=0}^{N-1} f_k \cos\frac{2\pi nk}{N} - if_k \sin\frac{2\pi nk}{N}\right) = \frac{1}{N}\left(\sum_{k=0}^{N-1} f_k e^{\frac{-i2\pi kn}{N}}\right) \ \ where \ \ i = \sqrt{-1}$$

EQUATION 2.13: DISCRETE FOURIER TRANSFORM

Notice that we've switched from the function notation used in Equation 2.12 ($F(n)$ and $f(k)$) to array index notation in Equation 2.13 (F_n and f_k) to emphasize that we are dealing with an array of discrete audio sample points in the time domain. Casting this equation as an algorithm (Algorithm 2.1) helps us to see how we could turn it into a computer program where the summation becomes a loop nested inside the outer *for* loop.

```
/*Input:
f, an array of digitized audio samples
N, the number of samples in the array
    Note: i=√(-1)
Output:
F, an array of complex numbers which give the
frequency components of the sound given by f */
    for (n=0 to N-1)
        Fₙ=1/N ∑ₖ₌₀ᴺ⁻¹ fₖcos(2πnk/N)-ifₖsin(2πnk/N)
```

ALGORITHM 2.1: DISCRETE FOURIER TRANSFORM

Each time through the loop, the magnitude and phase of the nth frequency component are computed, F_n. Each F_n is a complex number with a cosine and sine term, the sine term having the factor i in it.

We assume that you're familiar with complex numbers, but if not, a short introduction should be enough so that you can work with the Fourier algorithm.

A complex number takes the form $a + bi$, where $i = \sqrt{-1}$. Thus,

$$cos\left(\frac{2\pi nk}{N}\right) - if_k \sin\left(\frac{2\pi nk}{N}\right)$$

is a complex number. In this case, a is replaced with $\cos(2\pi nk/N)$ and b with $-f_k\sin(2\pi nk/N)$. Handling the complex numbers in an implementation of the Fourier transform is not difficult. Although i is an imaginary number, $\sqrt{-1}$, and you might wonder how you're supposed to do computation with it, you really don't have to do anything with it at all except assume it's there. The summation in the formula can be replaced by a loop that goes from 0 through $N-1$. Each time through that loop, you add another term from the summation into an accumulating total. You can do

>>

MATLAB EXERCISE:

Implementing the

DFT in MATLAB

http://bit.ly/29kDdLp

this separately for the cosine and sine parts, setting aside i. Also, in object-oriented programming languages, you may have a complex number class to do complex number calculations for you.

The result of the Fourier transform is an array of complex numbers F, each of the form $a + bi$, where the magnitude of the frequency component is equal to $\sqrt{a^2 + b^2}$.

The **inverse Fourier transform** transforms audio data from the frequency domain to the time domain. The inverse discrete Fourier transform is given in Algorithm 2.2.

C++
PROGRAMMING
EXERCISE:
Implementing the
DFT in C++
http://bit.ly/29nXDCj

```
/*Input:
F, an array of complex numbers representing audio data
in the frequency domain, the elements represented by the coefficients
of their real and imaginary parts, a and b respectively
N, the number of samples in the array
     Note: i=√(-1)
Output:  f, an array of audio samples in the time domain*/
   for (n=0 to N-1)
       f_k=∑_{n=0}^{N-1}(a_n cos(2πnk/N)+ib_n sin(2πnk/N)
```

ALGORITHM 2.2 INVERSE DISCRETE FOURIER TRANSFORM

2.3.8   THE FAST FOURIER TRANSFORM (FFT)

If you know how to program, it's not difficult to write your own discrete Fourier transform and its inverse through a literal implementation of the equations above. However, the "literal" implementation of the transform is computationally expensive. The equation in Algorithm 2.1 has to be applied N times, where N is the number of audio samples. The equation itself has a summation that goes over N elements. Thus, the discrete Fourier transform takes on the order of N^2 operations.

C++
PROGRAMMING
EXERCISE:
Comparison of DFT
and FFT in C++
http://bit.ly/29mcxbG

The **fast Fourier transform (FFT)** is a more efficient implementation of the Fourier transform that does so on the order of $N \times \log_2 N$ operations. The algorithm is made more efficient by eliminating duplicate mathematical operations. The FFT is the version of the Fourier transform that you'll often see in audio software and applications. For example, Adobe Audition uses the FFT to generate its frequency analysis view, as shown in Figure 2.41.

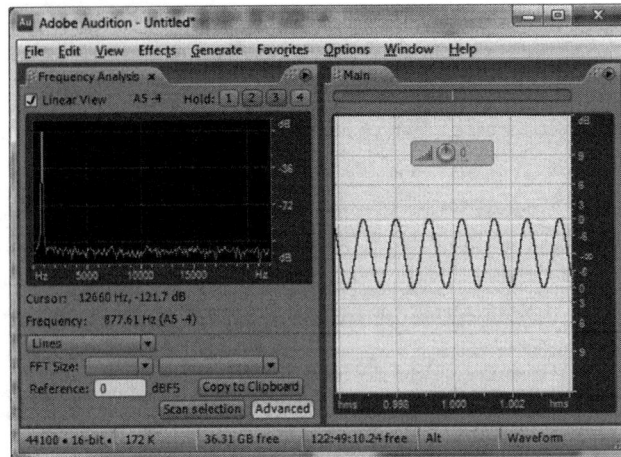

FIGURE 2.41: FREQUENCY ANALYSIS VIEW (LEFT) AND WAVEFORM VIEW (RIGHT) IN ADOBE AUDITION, SHOWING AUDIO DATA IN THE FREQUENCY DOMAIN AND TIME DOMAIN, RESPECTIVELY

2.3.9   APPLYING THE FOURIER TRANSFORM IN MATLAB

Generally when you work with digital audio, you don't have to implement your own FFT. Efficient implementations already exist in many programming language libraries. For example, MATLAB has FFT and inverse FFT functions, *fft* and *ifft*, respectively. We can use these to experiment and generate graphs of sound data in the frequency domain.

First, let's use sine functions to generate arrays of numbers that simulate single-pitch sounds. We'll make three one-second-long sounds using the standard sampling rate for CD quality audio, 44,100 samples per second. First, we generate an array of $sr*s$ numbers across which we can evaluate sine functions, putting this array in the variable t.

```
sr = 44100;   %sr is sampling rate
s = 1;        %s is number of seconds
t = linspace(0, s, sr*s);
```

Now we use the array t as input to sine functions at three different frequencies and phases, creating the note A at three different octaves (110 Hz, 220 Hz, and 440 Hz).

```
x = cos(2*pi*110*t);
y = cos(2*pi*220*t + pi/3);
z = cos(2*pi*440*t + pi/6);
```

x, *y*, and *z* are arrays of numbers that can be used as audio samples. *pi/3* and *pi/6* represent phase shifts for the 220 Hz and 440 Hz waves, to make our phase response graph more interesting. The figures can be displayed with the following:

```
figure;
plot(t,x);
axis([0 0.05 -1.5 1.5]);
title('x');
figure;
plot(t,y);
axis([0 0.05 -1.5 1.5]);
title('y');
figure;
plot(t,z);
axis([0 0.05 -1.5 1.5]);
title('z');
```

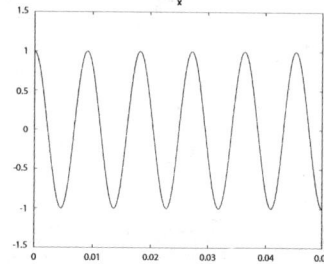

FIGURE 2.42: 110 HZ, NO PHASE OFFSET

We look at only the first 0.05 seconds of the waveforms in order to see their shape better. You can see the phase shifts in the figures below. The second and third waves don't start at 0 on the vertical axis.

Now we add the three sine waves to create a composite wave that has three frequency components at three different phases.

```
a = (x + y + z)/3;
```

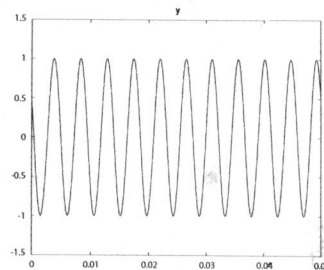

FIGURE 2.43: 220 HZ, π/3 PHASE OFFSET

Notice that we divide the summed sound waves by three so that the sound doesn't clip. You can graph the three-component sound wave with the following:

```
figure;
plot(t, a);
axis([0 0.05 -1.5 1.5]);
title('a = x + y + z');
```

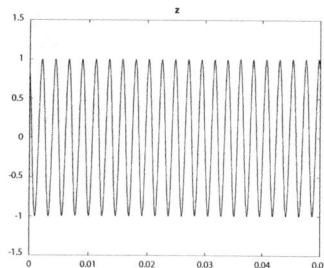

FIGURE 2.44: 440 HZ, π/6 PHASE OFFSET

Figure 2.45 is a graph of the sound wave in the
time domain. You could call it an impulse response graph, although when you're looking at a
sound file like this, you usually just think of it as
"sound data in the time domain." The term "impulse response" is used more commonly for time
domain filters, as we'll see in Chapter 7.

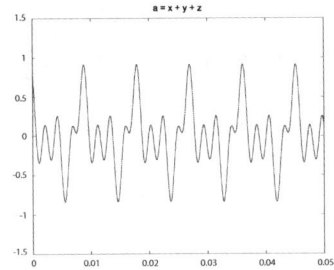

FIGURE 2.45: TIME DOMAIN DATA
FOR A 3-COMPONENT WAVEFORM

You might want to play the sound to be sure
you have what you think you have. The *sound*
function requires that you tell it the number of samples it should play per second,
which for our simulation is 44,100.

```
sound(a, sr);
```

When you play the sound file and listen carefully, you can hear that it has three tones.

MATLAB's Fourier transform (*fft*) returns an array of *double complex* values (dou-
ble-precision complex numbers) that represent the magnitudes and phases of the frequency components.

```
fftdata = fft(a);
```

In MATLAB's workspace window, *fftdata* values are labeled as type *double*, giving the
impression that they are real numbers, but this is not the case. In fact, the Fourier
transform produces complex numbers, which you can verify by trying to plot them in
MATLAB. The magnitudes of the complex numbers are given in the Min and Max
fields, which is computed by the *abs* function. For a complex number $a + bi$, the magnitude is computed as $\sqrt{a^2 + b^2}$.

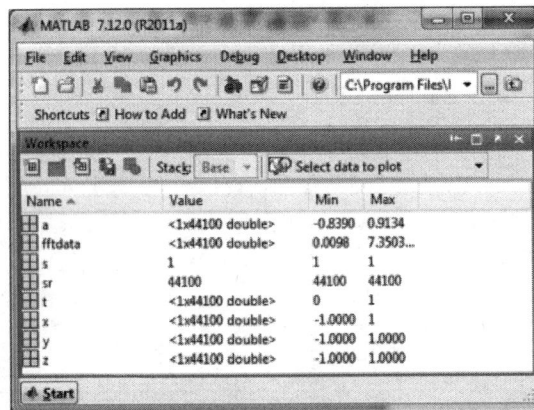

FIGURE 2.46: WORKSPACE IN MATLAB SHOWING VALUES AND
TYPES OF VARIABLES CURRENTLY IN MEMORY

To plot the results of the *fft* function such that the values represent the magnitudes of the frequency components, we first apply the *abs* function to *fftdata*.

```
fftmag = abs(fftdata);
```

Let's plot the frequency components to be sure we have what we think we have.

For a sampling rate of *sr* on an array of sample values of size *N*, the Fourier transform returns the magnitudes of *N*/2 frequency components, evenly spaced between 0 and *sr*/2 Hz. (We'll explain this completely in Chapter 5.) Thus, we want to display frequencies between 0 and *sr*/2 on the horizontal axis, and only the first *sr*/2 values from the *fftmag* vector.

```
figure;
freqs = [0: (sr/2)-1];
plot(freqs, fftmag(1:sr/2));
```

When you do this, you'll see that all the frequency components are way over on the left side of the graph. Since we know our frequency components should be 110 Hz, 220 Hz, and 440 Hz, we might as well look at only the first, say, 600 frequency components so that we can see the results better. One way to zoom in on the frequency response graph is to use the zoom tool in the graph window, or you can reset the axis properties in the command window, as follows.

ASIDE: If we zoomed in more closely at each of these spikes at frequencies 110, 220, and 440 Hz, we would see that they are not perfectly horizontal lines. The "imperfect" results of the FFT will be discussed later in the sections on FFT windows and windowing functions.

```
axis([0 600 0 8000]);
```

This yields the frequency response graph for our composite wave, which shows the three frequency components.

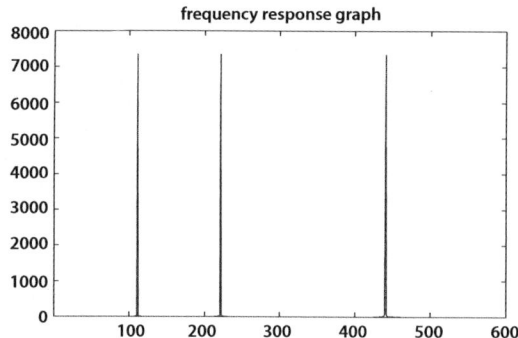

FIGURE 2.47: FREQUENCY RESPONSE GRAPH FOR A 3-COMPONENT WAVE

To get the phase response graph, we need to extract the phase information from the *fftdata*. This is done with the *angle* function. We leave that as an exercise.

Let's try the Fourier transform on a more complex sound wave—a sound file that we read in.

```
y = wavread('HornsE04Mono.wav');
```

As before, you can get the Fourier transform with the *fft* function.

```
fftdata = fft(y);
```

You can then get the magnitudes of the frequency components and generate a frequency response graph from this.

```
fftmag = abs(fftdata);
figure;
freqs = [0:(sr/2)-1];
plot(freqs, fftmag(1:sr/2));
axis([0 sr/2 0 4500]);
title('frequency response for HornsE04Mono.wav');
```

Let's zoom in on frequencies up to 5000 Hz.

```
axis([0 5000 0 4500]);
```

The graph below is generated.

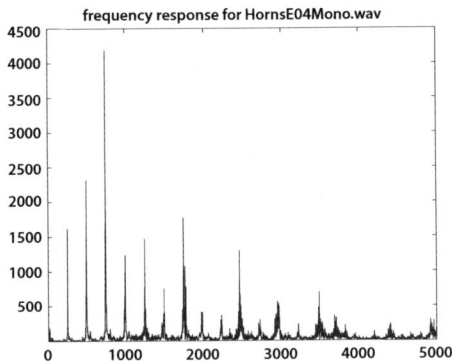

FIGURE 2.48: FREQUENCY RESPONSE
FOR *HORNSE04MONO.WAV*

The inverse Fourier transform gives us back our original sound data in the time domain.

```
ynew = ifft(fftdata);
```

If you compare *y* with *ynew*, you'll see that the inverse Fourier transform has recaptured the original sound data.

2.3.10 WINDOWING THE FFT

When we applied the Fourier transform in MATLAB in Section 2.3.9, we didn't specify a window size. Thus, we were applying the FFT to the entire piece of audio. If you listen to the WAV file *HornsE04Mono.wav*, a three-second clip, you'll first hear some low tubas and then some higher trumpets. Our graph of the FFT shows frequency components up to and beyond 5000 Hz, which reflects the sounds in the three seconds. What if we do the FFT on just the first second (44,100 samples) of this WAV file, as follows? The resulting frequency components are shown in Figure 2.49.

```
y = wavread('HornsE04Mono.wav');
sr = 44100;
freqs = [0:(sr/2)-1];
ybegin = y(1:44100);
fftdata2 = fft(ybegin);
fftdata2 = fftdata2(1:22050);
plot(freqs, abs(fftdata2));
axis([0 5000 0 4500]);
```

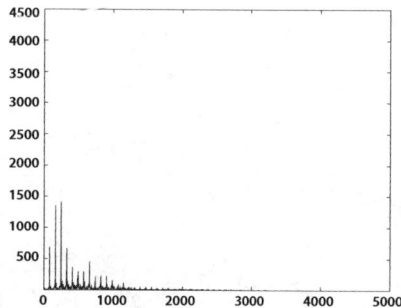

FIGURE 2.49: FREQUENCY COMPONENTS OF FIRST SECOND OF *HORNSE04MONO.WAV*

What we've done is focus on one short window of time in applying the FFT. An **FFT window** is a contiguous segment of audio samples on which the transform is applied. If you consider the nature of sound and music, you'll understand why applying the transform to relatively small windows makes sense. In many of our examples in this book, we generate segments of sound that consist of one or more frequency components that do not change over time, like a single pitch note or a single chord being played without change. These sounds are good for experimenting with the mathematics of digital audio, but they aren't representative of the music or sounds in our environment, in which the frequencies change constantly. The WAV file *HornsE04Mono.wav* serves as a good example. The clip is only three seconds long, but the first second is very different in frequencies (the pitches of tubas) from the last two seconds (the pitches of trumpets). When we do the FFT on the entire three seconds, we get a kind of "blurred" view of the frequency components, because the music actually changes over the three-second period. It makes more sense to look at small segments of time. This is the purpose of the FFT window.

Figure 2.50 shows an example of how FFT window sizes are used in audio processing programs. Notice the drop-down menu, which gives you a choice of FFT sizes ranging from 32 to 65,536 samples. The FFT window size is typically a power of 2. If your sampling rate is 44,100 samples per second, then a window size of 32 samples is about 0.0007 seconds, and a window size of 65,536 is about 1.486 seconds.

There's a tradeoff in the choice of window size. A small window focuses on the frequencies present in the sound over a short period of time. However, as mentioned earlier, the number of frequency components yielded by an FFT of size N is $N/2$. Thus, for a window size of, say, 128, only 64 frequency bands are output, and these bands spread over the frequencies from 0 Hz to $sr/2$ Hz where sr is the sampling rate (see Chapter 5.) For a window size of 65,536, 37,768 frequency bands are output, which seems like a good thing, except that with the large window size, the FFT is not isolating a short moment of time. A window size of around 2048 usually gives good results. If you set the size to 2048 and play a piece of music loaded into Audition, you'll see the frequencies in the frequency analysis view bounce up and down, reflecting the changing frequencies in the music as time passes.

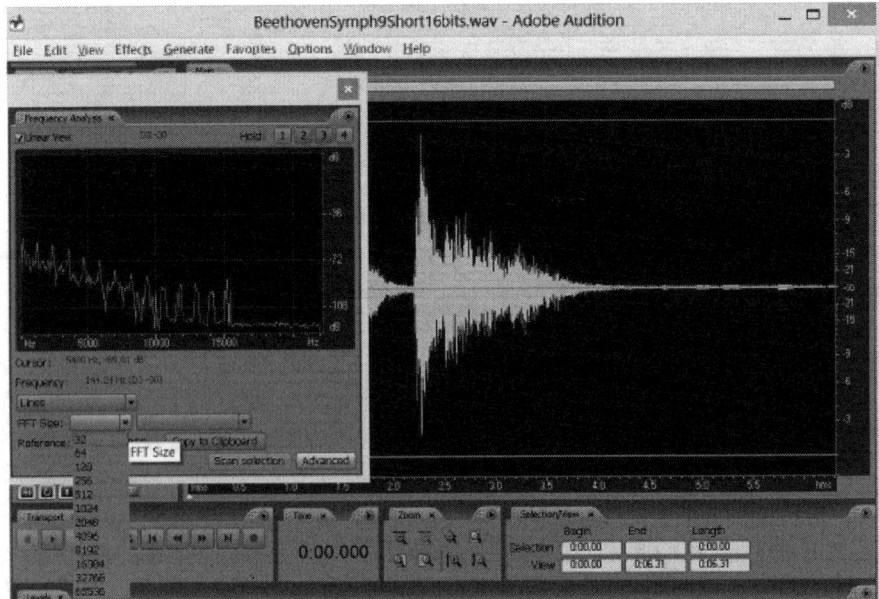

FIGURE 2.50: CHOICE OF FFT WINDOW SIZE IN ADOBE AUDITION

2.3.11 WINDOWING FUNCTIONS TO ELIMINATE SPECTRAL LEAKAGE

In addition to choosing the FFT window size, audio processing programs often let you choose from a number of windowing functions. The purpose of an FFT windowing function is to smooth out the discontinuities that result from applying the FFT to segments (i.e., windows) of audio data. A simplifying assumption for the FFT is that each windowed segment of audio data contains an integral number of cycles, which repeat throughout the audio. This, of course, is not generally the case. If it were the case—that is, if the window ended exactly where the cycle ended—then the end of the cycle would be at exactly the same amplitude as the beginning. The beginning and end would "match up." The actual discontinuity between the end of a window and its beginning is interpreted by the FFT as a jump from one level to another, as shown in Figure 2.51. (In this figure, we've cut and pasted a portion from the beginning of the window to its end to show that the ends don't match up.)

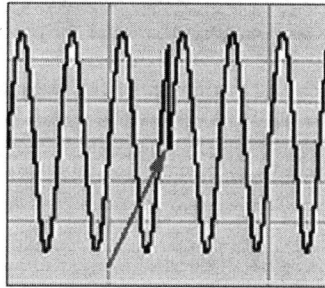

FIGURE 2.51: DISCONTINUITY BETWEEN THE END OF A WINDOW AND ITS BEGINNING

In the output of the FFT, the discontinuity between the ends and the beginnings of the windows manifests itself as frequency components that don't really exist in audio—called spurious frequencies, or **spectral leakage**. You can see the spectral leakage in Figure 2.51. Although the audio signal actually contains only one frequency at 880 Hz, the frequency analysis view indicates that there is a small number of other frequencies across the audible spectrum.

In order to smooth over this discontinuity and thereby reduce the amount of spectral leakage, the windowing functions effectively taper the ends of the segments to 0 so that they connect from beginning to end. The drop-down menu to the left of the FFT size menu in Audition is where you choose the windowing function. In Figure 2.50, the Hanning function is chosen. Four commonly used windowing functions are given in the table below.

$$u(t) = \begin{cases} \frac{2t}{T} \ for \ 0 \le t < \frac{T}{2} \\ 2 - \frac{2t}{T} \ for \ \frac{T}{2} \le t \le T \end{cases}$$

$$u(t) = \frac{1}{2}\left[1 - \cos\left(\frac{2\pi t}{T}\right)\right]$$
$$for \ 0 \le t \le T$$

triangular windowing function   **Hanning windowing function**

$$u(t) = 0.54 - 0.46 \cos\left(\frac{2\pi t}{T}\right)$$
$$for \ 0 \le t \le T$$

$$u(t) = 0.42 - 0.5 \cos\left(\frac{2\pi t}{T}\right)$$
$$+0.08 \cos\left(\frac{4\pi t}{T}\right)$$
$$for \ 0 \le t \le T$$

Hamming windowing function   **Blackman windowing function**

t is time.

T is length of period. If w is window size and sr is sampling rate, then $T = w/sr$.

FIGURE 2.52: WINDOWING FUNCTIONS

Windowing functions are easy to apply. The segment of audio data being transformed is simply multiplied by the windowing function before the transform is applied. In MATLAB, you can accomplish this with vector multiplication, as shown in the commands below.

```
y = wavread('HornsE04Mono.wav');
sr = 44100; %sampling rate
w = 2048;   %window size
T = w/sr;   %period
% t is an array of times at which the hamming function is evaluated
t = linspace(0, 1, 44100);
twindow = t(1:2048);   %first 2048 elements of t
% Create the values for the hamming function, stored in vector called hamming
hamming = 0.54 - 0.46 * cos((2 * pi * twindow)/T);
plot(hamming);
title('Hamming');
```

The Hamming function is shown as follows:

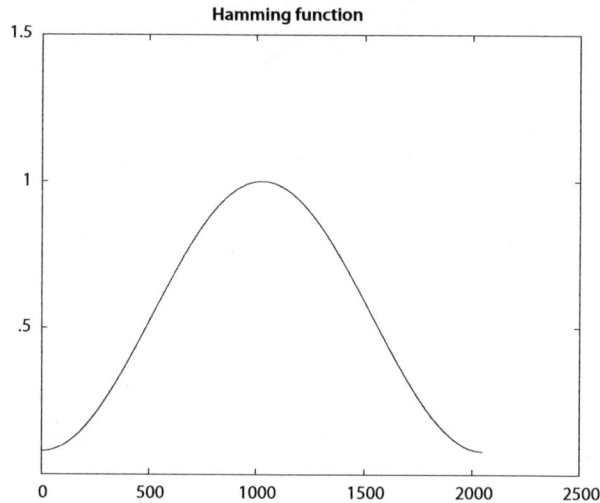

FIGURE 2.53: HAMMING WINDOWING FUNCTION

```
yshort = y(1:2048);   %first 2048 samples from sound file
%Multiply the audio values in the window by the Hamming function values,
% using element by element multiplication with .*.
% first convert hamming from a column vector to a row vector
ywindowed = hamming .* yshort;
figure;
plot(yshort);
title('First 2048 samples of audio data');
figure;
plot(ywindowed);
title('First 2048 samples of audio data, tapered by windowing function');
```

Before the Hamming function is applied, the first 2048 samples of audio data look like this:

First 2048 samples of audio data

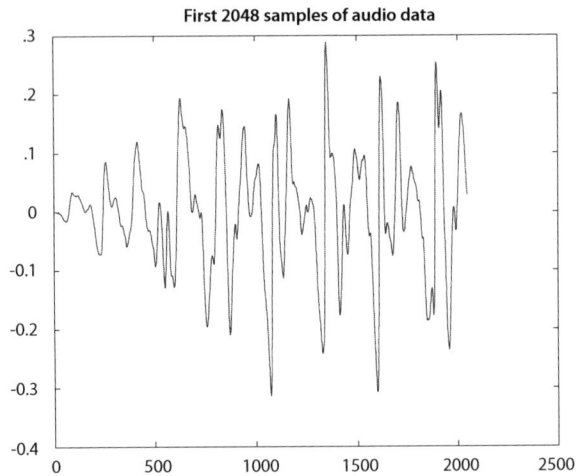

FIGURE 2.54: AUDIO DATA

After the Hamming function is applied, the audio data look like this:

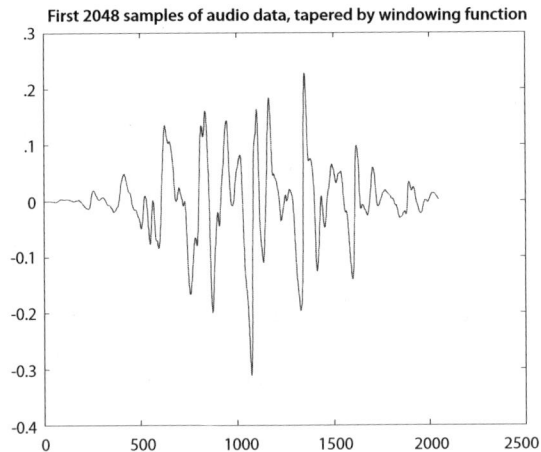

First 2048 samples of audio data, tapered by windowing function

FIGURE 2.55: AUDIO DATA AFTER APPLICATION
OF HAMMING WINDOWING FUNCTION

Notice that the ends of the segment are tapered toward 0.

Figure 2.56 compares the FFT results with no windowing function vs. with the Hamming windowing function applied. The windowing function eliminates some of the high frequency components that are caused by spectral leakage.

>>

MATLAB EXERCISE:

Windowing Functions

for the FFT
http://bit.ly/29gh2Y0

```
figure
plot(abs(fft(yshort)));
axis([0 300 0 60]);
hold on;
plot(abs(fft(ywindowed)),'r');
```

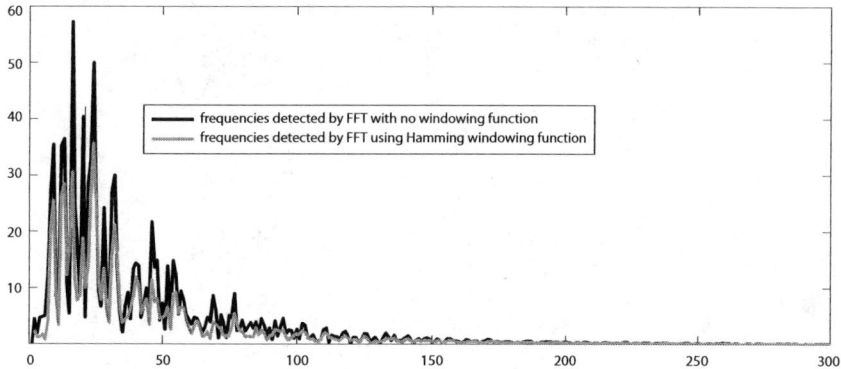

FIGURE 2.56: COMPARING FFT RESULTS WITH
AND WITHOUT WINDOWING FUNCTION

2.3.12 MODELING SOUND IN C++ UNDER LINUX

If you want to work at an even lower level of abstraction, a good environment for experimentation is the Linux operating system using "from scratch" programs written in C++. In our first example C++ sound program, we show you how to create sound waves of a given frequency, add frequency components to get a complex wave, and play the sounds via the sound device. This program is another implementation of the exercises in Max and MATLAB in Sections 2.3.1 and 2.3.3. The C++ program is given in Program 2.4.

ASIDE: In this example program, 8 bits are used to store each audio sample. That is, the bit depth is 8. The sound library also allows a bit depth of 16. The concept of bit depth will be explained in detail in Chapter 5.

```
//This program uses the OSS library.
#include <sys/ioctl.h> //for ioctl()
#include <math.h> //sin(), floor(), and pow()
#include <stdio.h> //perror
#include <fcntl.h> //open, O_WRONLY
#include <linux/soundcard.h> //SOUND_PCM*
#include <iostream>
#include <unistd.h>
using namespace std;
```

```
#define TYPE char
#define LENGTH 1 //number of seconds per frequency
#define RATE 44100 //sampling rate
#define SIZE sizeof(TYPE) //size of sample, in bytes
#define CHANNELS 1 //number of audio channels
#define PI 3.14159
#define NUM_FREQS 3 //total number of frequencies
#define BUFFSIZE (int) (NUM_FREQS*LENGTH*RATE*SIZE*CHANNELS)
                                        //bytes sent to audio device
#define ARRAYSIZE (int) (NUM_FREQS*LENGTH*RATE*CHANNELS)
                                        //total number of samples
#define SAMPLE_MAX (pow(2,SIZE*8 - 1) - 1)

void writeToSoundDevice(TYPE buf[], int deviceID) {
    int status;
    status = write(deviceID, buf, BUFFSIZE);
    if (status != BUFFSIZE)
        perror("Wrote wrong number of bytes\n");
    status = ioctl(deviceID, SNDCTL_DSP_SYNC, 0);
    if (status == -1)
        perror("SNDCTL_DSP_SYNC failed\n");
}

int main() {
    int deviceID, arg, status, f, t, a, i;
    TYPE buf[ARRAYSIZE];
    deviceID = open("/dev/dsp", O_WRONLY, 0);
    if (deviceID < 0)
        perror("Opening /dev/dsp failed\n");
// working
    arg = SIZE * 8;
    status = ioctl(deviceID, SNDCTL_DSP_SETFMT, &arg);
    if (status == -1)
        perror("Unable to set sample size\n");
    arg = CHANNELS;
    status = ioctl(deviceID, SNDCTL_DSP_CHANNELS, &arg);
    if (status == -1)
        perror("Unable to set number of channels\n");
    arg = RATE;
    status = ioctl(deviceID, SNDCTL_DSP_SPEED, &arg);
    if (status == -1)
        perror("Unable to set sampling rate\n");
    a = SAMPLE_MAX;
    for (i = 0; i < NUM_FREQS; ++i) {
        switch (i) {
            case 0:
                f = 262;
                break;
            case 1:
                f = 330;
                break;
            case 2:
                f = 392;
                break;
```

```
        }
        for (t = 0; t < ARRAYSIZE/NUM_FREQS; ++t) {
            buf[t + ((ARRAYSIZE / NUM_FREQS) * i)] = floor(a *
sin(2*PI*f*t/RATE));
        }
    }
    writeToSoundDevice(buf, deviceID);
}
```

PROGRAM 2.4: ADDING SINE WAVES AND SENDING SOUND TO SOUND DEVICE IN C++

To be able to compile and run a program such as this, you need to install a sound library in your Linux environment. At the time of the writing of this chapter, the two standard low-level sound libraries for Linux are the OSS (Open Sound System) and ALSA (Advanced Linux Sound Architecture). A sound library provides a software interface that allows your program to access the sound devices, sending and receiving sound data. ALSA is the newer of the two libraries and is preferred by most users. At a slightly higher level of abstraction are PulseAudio and Jack, applications which direct multiple sound streams from their inputs to their outputs. Ultimately, PulseAudio and Jack use lower-level libraries to communicate directly with the sound cards.

{}
C++
PROGRAMMING
EXERCISE:
Writing to an
Audio Device
http://bit.ly/29wruJ5

Program 2.4 uses the OSS library. In a program such as this, the sound device is opened, read from, and written to in a way similar to how files are handled. The sample program shows how you open */dev/dsp*, an interface to the sound card device, to ask this device to receive audio data. The variable *deviceID* serves as an ID of the sound device and is used as a parameter indicating the size of data to expect, the number of channels, and the data rate. We've set a size of eight bits (one byte) per audio sample, one channel, and a data rate of 44,100 samples per second. The significance of these numbers will be clearer when we talk about digitization in Chapter 5. The buffer size is a product of the sample size, data rate, and length of the recording (in this case, three seconds), yielding a buffer of 44,100 × 3 bytes.

{}
C++
PROGRAMMING
EXERCISE:
Creating
Sound Waves
http://bit.ly/29kHCxO

The sound wave is created by taking the sine of the appropriate frequency (262 Hz, for example) at 44,100 evenly-spaced intervals for one second of audio data. The value returned from the sine function is between −1 and 1. However, the sound card expects a value that is stored in one byte (i.e., 8 bits), ranging from −128 to 127. To put the value into this range, we multiply by 127 and, with the *floor* function, round down.

The three frequencies are created and concatenated into one array of audio values. The *write* function has the device ID, the name of the buffer for storing the sound data, and the size of the buffer as its parameters. This function sends the sound data to the sound card to be played. The three frequencies together produce a harmonious chord in the key of C. In Chapter 3, we'll explore what makes these frequencies harmonious.

The program requires some header files for definitions of constants like *O_WRONLY* (restricting access to the sound device to writing) and *SOUND_PCM_WRITE_BITS*. After you install the sound libraries, you'll need to locate the appropriate header files and adjust the *#include* statement accordingly. You'll also need to check the way your compiler handles the math and sound libraries. You may need to include the option *–lm* on the compile line to include the math library, or the *–lasound* option if you're using the ALSA library.

This program introduces you to the notion that sound must be converted to a numeric format that is communicable to a computer. The solution to the programming assignment given as a learning supplement has an explanation of the variables and constants in this program. A full understanding of the program requires that you know something about sampling and quantization, the two main steps in analog-to-digital conversion, a topic that we'll examine in depth in Chapter 5.

Also in Chapter 5, we give you an example of a C++ program that reads and writes raw audio data rather than having you dynamically create your own waveforms.

2.3.13 MODELING SOUND IN JAVA

The Java environment allows the programmer to take advantage of Java libraries for sound and to benefit from object-oriented programming features like encapsulation, inheritance, and interfaces. In this chapter, we are going to use the package *javax.sound.sampled*. This package provides functionality to capture, mix, and play sounds with classes such as *SourceDataLine*, *AudioFormat*, *AudioSystem*, and *LineUnavailableException*.

Program 2.5 uses a SourceDataLine object. This is the object to which we write audio data. Before doing that, we must set up the data line object with a specified audio format object. (See line 30.) The AudioFormat class specifies a certain arrangement of data in the sound stream, including the sampling rate, sample size in bits, and number of channels. A SourceDataLine object is created with the specified format, which in the example is 44,100 samples per second, eight bits per sample, and one channel for mono. With this setting, the line gets the required system resource and becomes operational. After the SourceDataLine is opened, data is written to the mixer using a buffer that contains data generated by a sine function. Notice that we don't directly access the sound device because we are using a SourceDataLine object to deliver data bytes to the mixer. The mixer mixes the samples and finally delivers the samples to an audio output device on a sound card.

```java
1 import javax.sound.sampled.AudioFormat;
2 import javax.sound.sampled.AudioSystem;
3 import javax.sound.sampled.SourceDataLine;
4 import javax.sound.sampled.LineUnavailableException;
5
6 public class ExampleTone1{
7
8   public static void main(String[] args){
9
10
11     try {
12         ExampleTone1.createTone(262, 100);
13     } catch (LineUnavailableException lue) {
14         System.out.println(lue);
15     }
16   }
17
18   /** parameters are frequency in Hertz and volume
20    **/
21   public static void createTone(int Hertz, int volume)
22     throws LineUnavailableException {
23     /** Exception is thrown when line cannot be opened */
24
25     float rate = 44100;
26     byte[] buf;
27     AudioFormat audioF;
28
29     buf = new byte[1];
30     audioF = new AudioFormat(rate,8,1,true,false);
31     //sampleRate, sampleSizeInBits,channels,signed,bigEndian
32
33     SourceDataLine sourceDL = AudioSystem.getSourceDataLine(audioF);
34     sourceDL = AudioSystem.getSourceDataLine(audioF);
35     sourceDL.open(audioF);
36     sourceDL.start();
37
38     for(int i=0; i<rate; i++){
39       double angle = (i/rate)*Hertz*2.0*Math.PI;
40       buf[0]=(byte)(Math.sin(angle)*volume);
41       sourceDL.write(buf,0,1);
42     }
43
44     sourceDL.drain();
45     sourceDL.stop();
46     sourceDL.close();
47   }
48 }
```

PROGRAM 2.5 : A SIMPLE SOUND-GENERATING PROGRAM IN JAVA

This program illustrates a simple of way of generating a sound by using a sine wave and the *javax.sound.sampled* library. If we change the values of the *createTone* procedure parameters, which are 262 Hz for frequency and 100 for volume, we can produce a different tone. The second parameter, *volume*, is used to change the amplitude of the sound. Notice that the sine function result is multiplied by the *volume* parameter in line 40.

Although the purpose of this section of the book is not to demonstrate how Java graphics classes are used, it may be helpful to use some basic plot features in Java to generate sine wave drawings. An advantage of Java is that it facilitates your control of windows and containers. We inherit this functionality from the *JPanel* class, which is a container where we are going to paint the sine wave generated. Program 2.6 is a variation of Program 2.5. It produces a Java window by using the procedure *paintComponent*. This sine wave generated again has a frequency of 262 Hz and a volume of 100.

```
 1 import javax.sound.sampled.AudioFormat;
 2 import javax.sound.sampled.AudioSystem;
 3 import javax.sound.sampled.SourceDataLine;
 4 import javax.sound.sampled.LineUnavailableException;
 5
 6 import java.awt.*;
 7 import java.awt.geom.*;
 8 import javax.swing.*;
 9
10 public class ExampleTone2 extends JPanel{
11
12   static double[] sines;
13   static int vol;
14
15   public static void main(String[] args){
16
17     try {
18         ExampleTone2.createTone(262, 100);
19     } catch (LineUnavailableException lue) {
20         System.out.println(lue);
21     }
22
23     //Frame object for drawing
24     JFrame frame = new JFrame();
25     frame.setDefaultCloseOperation(JFrame.EXIT_ON_CLOSE);
26     frame.add(new ExampleTone2());
27     frame.setSize(800,300);
28     frame.setLocation(200,200);29      frame.setVisible(true);
30   }
31
32   public static void createTone(int Hertz, int volume)
33     throws LineUnavailableException {
34
35     float rate = 44100;
36     byte[] buf;
```

```
37        buf = new byte[1];
38        sines = new double[(int)rate];
39        vol=volume;
40
41        AudioFormat audioF;
42        audioF = new AudioFormat(rate,8,1,true,false);
43
44        SourceDataLine sourceDL = AudioSystem.getSourceDataLine(audioF);
45        sourceDL = AudioSystem.getSourceDataLine(audioF);
46        sourceDL.open(audioF);
47        sourceDL.start();
48
49        for(int i=0; i<rate; i++){
50          double angle = (i/rate)*Hertz*2.0*Math.PI;
51          buf[0]=(byte)(Math.sin(angle)*vol);
52          sourceDL.write(buf,0,1);
53
54          sines[i]=(double)(Math.sin(angle)*vol);
55        }
56
57        sourceDL.drain();
58        sourceDL.stop();
59        sourceDL.close();
60     }
61
62     protected void paintComponent(Graphics g) {
63          super.paintComponent(g);
64          Graphics2D g2 = (Graphics2D)g;
65          g2.setRenderingHint(RenderingHints.KEY_ANTIALIASING,
66                              RenderingHints.VALUE_ANTIALIAS_ON);
67
68          int pointsToDraw=4000;
69          double max=sines[0];
70          for(int i=1;i<pointsToDraw;i++)  if (max<sines[i]) max=sines[i];
71          int border=10;
72          int w = getWidth();
73          int h = (2*border+(int)max);
74
75          double xInc = 0.5;
76
77          //Draw x and y axes
78          g2.draw(new Line2D.Double(border, border, border, 2*(max+border)));
79          g2.draw(new Line2D.Double(border, (h-sines[0]), w-border, (h-sines[0])));
80
81          g2.setPaint(Color.red);
82
83          for(int i = 0; i < pointsToDraw; i++) {
84              double x = border + i*xInc;
85              double y = (h-sines[i]);
86              g2.fill(new Ellipse2D.Double(x-2, y-2, 2, 2));
87          }
88      }
89 }
```

PROGRAM 2.6: VISUALIZING THE SOUND WAVES IN A JAVA PROGRAM

If we increase the value of the frequency in line 18 to 400 Hz, we can notice how the number of cycles increases, as shown in Figure 2.57. On the other hand, by increasing the volume, we obtain a higher amplitude for each frequency.

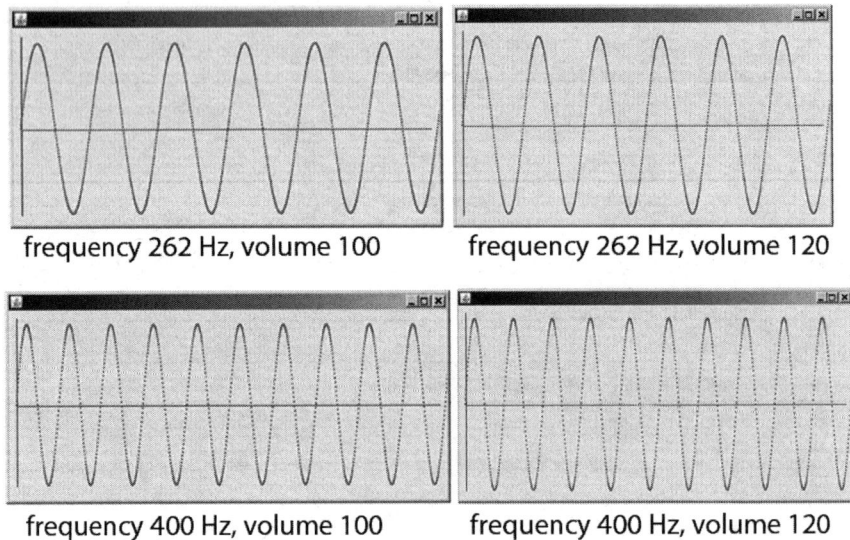

frequency 262 Hz, volume 100   frequency 262 Hz, volume 120

frequency 400 Hz, volume 100   frequency 400 Hz, volume 120

FIGURE 2.57: SOUND WAVES GENERATED IN A JAVA PROGRAM

We can also create square, triangle, and sawtooth waves in Java by modifying the *for* loop in lines 38 to 42. For example, to create a square wave, we may change the *for* loop to something like the following:

```
46      for(int i=0; i<rate; i++){
47        double angle1 = i/rate*Hertz*1.0*2.0*Math.PI;
48        double angle2 = i/rate*Hertz*3.0*2.0*Math.PI;
49        double angle3 = i/rate*Hertz*5.0*2.0*Math.PI;
50        double angle4 = i/rate*Hertz*7.0*2.0*Math.PI;
51
52        buf[0]=(byte)(Math.sin(angle1)*vol+
          Math.sin(angle2)*vol/3+Math.sin(angle3)*vol/5+
          Math.sin(angle4)*vol/7);
53        sdl.write(buf,0,1);
55        sines[i]=(double)(Math.sin(angle1)*vol+
          Math.sin(angle2)*vol/3+Math.sin(angle3)*vol/5+
          Math.sin(angle4)*vol/7);
57      }
```

This *for* loop produces the sine wave shown in Figure 2.58. This graph doesn't look like a perfect square wave, but the more harmonic frequencies we add, the closer we get to a square wave. (Note that you can create these waveforms more exactly by adapting the Octave programs above to Java.)

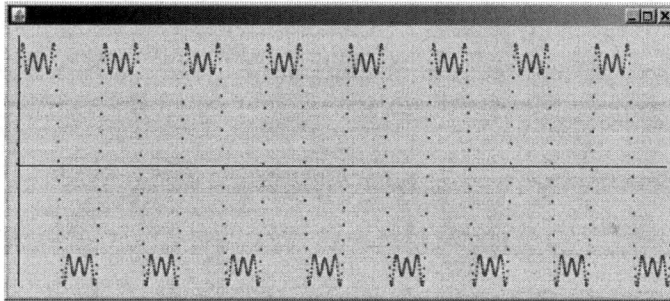

FIGURE 2.58: CREATING A SQUARE WAVE IN JAVA

2.4 REFERENCES

In addition to references cited in previous chapters:

Burg, Jennifer. *The Science of Digital Media.* Upper Saddle River, NJ: Prentice-Hall, 2009.

Everest, F. Alton. *Critical Listening Skills for Audio Professionals.* Boston: Course Technology, 2007.

Jaffee, D. "Spectrum Analysis Tutorial, Part 1: The Discrete Fourier Transform." *Computer Music Journal* 11, no. 2 (1987): 9–24.

————. "Spectrum Analysis Tutorial, Part 2: Properties and Applications of the Discrete Fourier Transform." *Computer Music Journal* 11, no. 3 (1987): 17–35.

Kientzle, Tim. *A Programmer's Guide to Sound*. Reading, MA: Addison-Wesley Developers Press, 1998.

Rossing, Thomas D., F. Richard Moore, and Paul A. Wheeler. *The Science of Sound*, 3rd ed. San Francisco: Addison-Wesley, 2002.

Smith, David M. *Engineering Computation with MATLAB*. Boston: Pearson Custom Publishing, 2008.

Steiglitz, K. *A Digital Signal Processing Primer*. Menlo Park, CA: Addison-Wesley, 1996.

CHAPTER THREE
Musical Sound

3.1 CONCEPTS

3.1.1 CONTEXT

Even if you're not a musician, if you plan to work in the realm of digital sound you'll benefit from an understanding of the basic concepts and vocabulary of music. The purpose of this chapter is to give you this foundation.

This chapter describes the vocabulary and musical notation of the Western music tradition—the music tradition that began with classical composers like Bach, Mozart, and Beethoven, and that continues as the historical and theoretic foundation of music in the United States, Europe, and Western culture. The major and minor scales and chords are taken from this context, which we refer to as Western music. Many other types of note progressions and intervals have been used in other cultures and time periods, leading to quite different characteristic sounds: the modes of ancient Greece, the Gregorian chants of the Middle Ages, the pentatonic scale of ancient music of Asia, the Hindu 22-note octave, or the whole tone scale of Debussy, for example. While we won't cover these, we encourage the reader to explore these other musical traditions.

To give us a common language for understanding music, we focus our discussion on the musical notation used for keyboards like the piano. Keyboard music expressed and notated in the Western tradition provides a good basic knowledge of music and gives us a common vocabulary when we start working with MIDI in Chapter 6.

3.1.2 TONES AND NOTES

Musicians learn to sing, play instruments, and compose music using a symbolic language of music notation. Before we can approach this symbolic notation, we need to establish a basic vocabulary.

In the vocabulary of music, a sound with a single fundamental frequency is called a **tone**. The **fundamental frequency** of a tone is the frequency that gives the tone its essential pitch. A piccolo plays tones with higher fundamental frequencies than the frequencies of a flute, and thus it is higher pitched.

A tone that has an onset and a duration is called a **note**. The **onset** of the note is the moment when it begins. The **duration** is the length of time that the note remains audible. Notes can be represented symbolically in musical notation, as we'll see in the next section. We will also use the word "note" interchangeably with "key" when referring to a key on a keyboard and the sound it makes when struck.

As described in Chapter 2, tones created by musical instruments, including the human voice, are not single-frequency. These tones have **overtones** at frequencies higher than the fundamental. Overtones add a special quality to the sound, but they don't change our overall perception of the pitch. When the frequency of an overtone is an integer multiple of the fundamental frequency, it is a **harmonic overtone**. Stated mathematically for frequencies f_1 and f_2, if $f_2 = nf_1$ and n is a positive integer, then f_2 is a harmonic frequency relative to fundamental frequency f_1. Notice that every frequency is a **harmonic frequency** relative to itself. It is called the first harmonic, since $n = 1$. The second harmonic is the frequency where $n = 2$. For example, the second harmonic of 440 Hz is 880 Hz; the third harmonic of 440 Hz is 3×440 Hz = 1320 Hz; the fourth harmonic of 440 Hz is 4×440 Hz = 1760 Hz; and so forth. Musical instruments like pianos and violins have harmonic overtones. Drums beats and other non-musical sounds have overtones that are not harmonic.

Another special relationship among frequencies is the **octave**. For frequencies f_1 and f_2, if $f_2 = 2nf_1$ where n is a positive integer, then f_1 and f_2 "sound the same," except that f_2 is higher pitched than f_1. Frequencies f_1 and f_2 are separated by n **octaves**. Another way to describe the octave relationship is to say that each time a frequency is moved up an octave, it is multiplied by two. A frequency of 880 Hz is one octave above 440 Hz; 1760 Hz is two octaves above 440 Hz; 3520 Hz is three octaves above 440 Hz; and so forth. Two notes separated by one or more octaves are considered equivalent in that one can replace the other in a musical composition without disturbing the harmony of the composition.

In Western music, an octave is separated into 12 frequencies corresponding to notes on a piano keyboard, named as shown in Figure 3.1. From C to B we have 12 notes, and then the next octave starts with another C, after which the sequence of letters repeats. An octave can start on any letter, as long as it ends on the same letter. (The sequence of notes is called an octave because there are eight notes in a diatonic scale, as is explained below.) The white keys are labeled with the letters. Each of the black keys can be called by one of two names. If it is named relative to the white key to its left, a **sharp** symbol is added to the name, denoted C♯, for example. If it is named relative to the white key to its right, a **flat** symbol is added to the name, denoted D♭, for example.

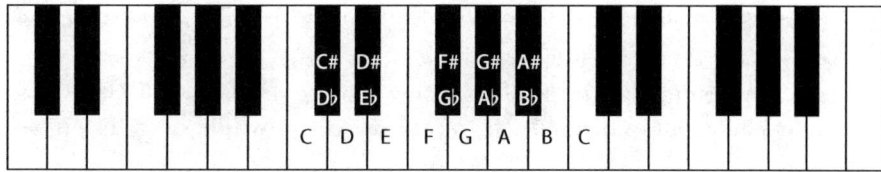

FIGURE 3.1: KEYBOARD SHOWING OCTAVE AND KEY LABELS

Each note on a piano keyboard corresponds to a physical key that can be played. There are 88 keys on a standard piano keyboard. MIDI keyboards are usually smaller. Since the notes from A through G are repeated on the keyboard, they are sometimes named by the number of the octave that they're in, as shown in Figure 3.2.

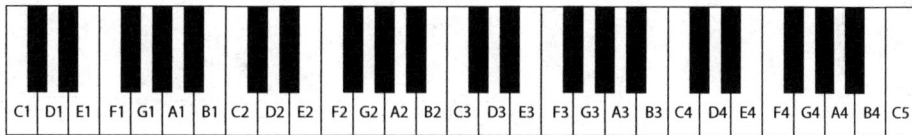

FIGURE 3.2: PIANO OR MIDI KEYBOARD

Middle C on a standard piano has a frequency of approximately 262 Hz. On a piano with 88 keys, middle C is the fourth C, so it is called C4. Middle C (C3 on the keyboard shown) is the central position for playing the piano, with regard to where the right and left hands of the pianist are placed. The standard reference point for tuning a piano is the A above middle C, which has a frequency of 440 Hz. This means that the next A going up the keys to the right has a frequency of 880 Hz. A note of 880 Hz is one octave away from 440 Hz, and both are called A on a piano keyboard.

The interval between two consecutive keys (also called notes) on a keyboard, whether the keys are black or white, is called a **semitone**. A semitone is the smallest frequency distance between any two notes. Neighboring notes on a piano keyboard (and equivalently, two neighboring notes on a chromatic scale) are separated by a frequency factor of $\sqrt[12]{2}$, which is approximately 1.05946. This relationship is described more precisely in the equation below.

Let f be the frequency of a note. Then the note one octave above f has a frequency of 2f. Given this octave relationship and the fact that there are 12 notes in an octave, the frequency of the note after the note with frequency f on a chromatic scale is $f\sqrt[12]{2} \approx 1.05946f$.

EQUATION 3.1

Thus, the factor 1.05946 defines a semitone. If two notes are divided by a semitone, then the frequency of the second is 1.05946 times the frequency of the first. The other frequencies between semitones are not used in Western music (except in pitch bending).

Two semitones constitute a **whole tone**, as illustrated in Figure 3.3. Semitones and whole tones can also be called **half steps** and **whole steps** (or just steps), respectively.

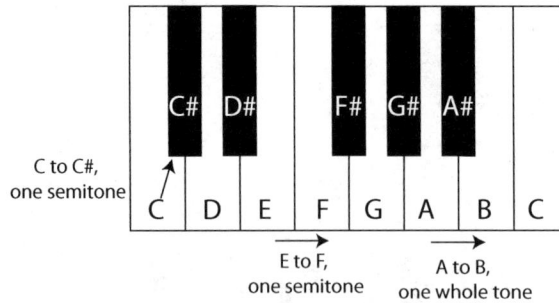

FIGURE 3.3: SEMITONES AND WHOLE TONES

The symbol ♯, called a **sharp**, denotes that a note is to be raised by a semitone. When you look at the keyboard in Figure 3.3, you can see that E♯ denotes the same note as F because raising E by a semitone takes you to the note F. Thus, this key on the keyboard has two names (although calling it F is more common). When two notes have different names but are the same pitch, they said to be **enharmonically equivalent**.

The symbol ♭, called a **flat**, denotes that a note is to be lowered by a semitone. C♭ is enharmonically equivalent to B. A natural symbol ♮ removes a sharp or flat from a note. Sharps, flats, and naturals are examples of **accidentals**, symbols that raise or lower a note by a semitone.

3.1.3   MUSIC VS. NOISE

It's fascinating to consider the way humans perceive sound, experiencing some sounds as musical and some as noise. Understanding frequency components and harmonics gives us some insight into why music is pleasing to our senses.

Consider the waveforms in Figure 3.4 and Figure 3.5. The first shows the notes C, E, and G played simultaneously. The second is a recording of scratching sounds. The first waveform has a regular pattern because the frequency components are pure sine waves with a harmonic relationship. The second sound has no pattern; the relationship of the frequency components is random at any moment in time and varies randomly over time. Sounds that are combinations of harmonic frequencies make patterns that are pleasing to hear. They're musical. Random patterns produce noise.

Musical instruments like violins, pianos, clarinets, and flutes naturally emit sounds with interesting harmonic components. Each instrument has an identifiable **timbre**—sometimes called its **tone color**—that results from its shape, the material of which it is made, its resonant structure, and the way it is played. These physical properties result in the instrument having a characteristic range of frequencies and harmonics. (See Figure 3.6.)

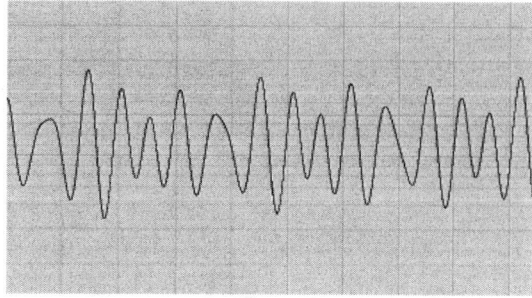

FIGURE 3.4: WAVEFORM OF MUSICAL SOUND

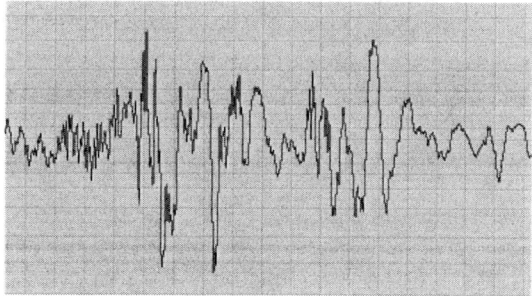

FIGURE 3.5: WAVEFORM OF NOISE

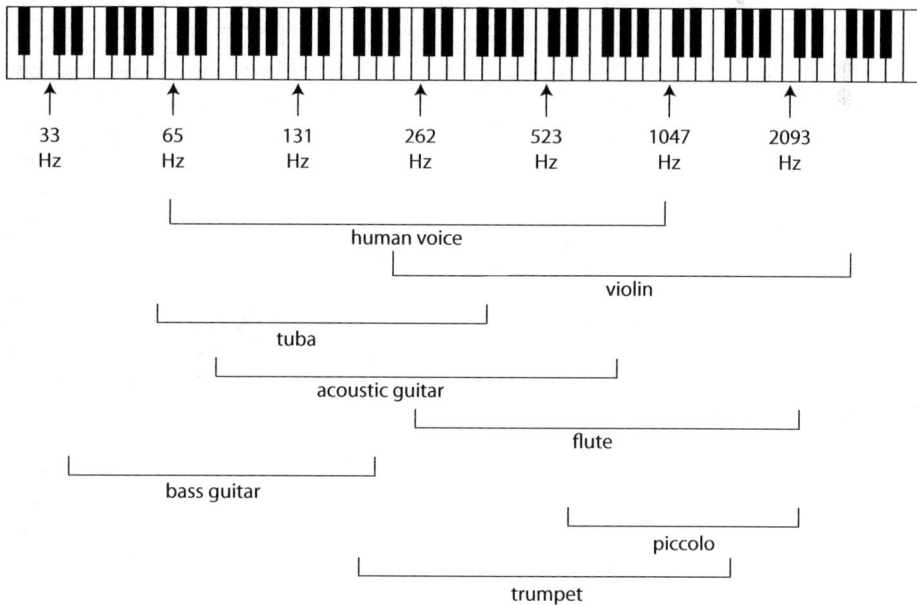

FIGURE 3.6: APPROXIMATE FREQUENCIES OF VARIOUS INSTRUMENTS

Instruments also are distinguished by the **amplitude envelope** for individual sounds created by the instrument. The amplitude envelope gives a sense of how the loudness of a single note changes over the short period of time when it is played. When you play a certain instrument, do you burst into the note or slide into it gently? Does the note linger or end abruptly? Imagine a single note played by a flute compared to the same note played by a piano. Although you don't always play a piano note the same way—for example, you can strike the key gently or briskly—it's still possible to get a picture of a typical amplitude envelope for each instrument and see how they differ.

The amplitude envelope consists of four components: **attack**, **decay**, **sustain**, and **release**, abbreviated **ADSR**, as illustrated in Figure 3.7. The attack is the time between when the sound is first audible and when it reaches its maximum loudness. The decay is the period of time when the amplitude decreases. Then the amplitude can level to a plateau in the sustain period. The release is when the sound dies away. The attack of a trumpet is relatively sudden, rising steeply to its maximum, because you have to blow pretty hard into a trumpet before the sound starts to come out. With a violin, on the other hand, you can stroke the bow across a string gently, creating a longer, less steep attack. The sustain of the violin note might be longer than that of the trumpet, also, as the bow continues to stroke across the string. Of course, these envelopes vary in individual performances depending on the nature of the music being played. Being aware of the amplitude envelope that is natural to an instrument helps in the synthesis of music. Tools exist for manipulating the envelopes of MIDI samples so that they sound more realistic or convey the spirit of the music better, as we'll see in Chapter 6.

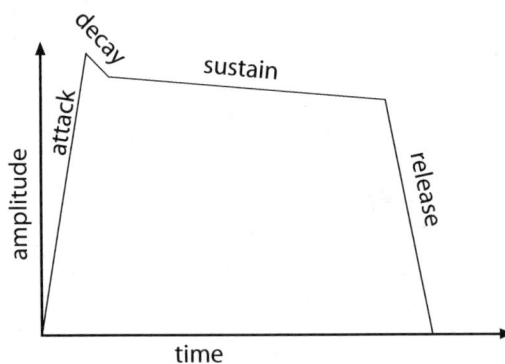

FIGURE 3.7: AMPLITUDE ENVELOPE

The combination of harmonic instruments in an orchestra gives rise to an amazingly complex and aesthetically pleasing pattern of frequencies that taken together are perceived as beautiful music. Non-harmonic instruments—e.g., percussion instruments—can contribute to this beauty as well. Drums, gongs, cymbals, and maracas are not musical in the same sense that flutes and violins are. The partials (frequency components) emitted by percussion instruments are not integer multiples of a fundamental, and thus these instruments don't have a distinct pitch with harmonic overtones. However, percussion instruments contribute accents to music, called **transients**. Transients are sounds that come in short bursts. Their attacks are quite sharp, their sustains are short, and their releases are steep. These percussive sounds are called "transient" because they come and go quickly. Because of this, we have to be careful not to edit them out with noise gates and other processors that react to sudden changes of amplitude. Even with their non-harmonic nature, transients add flavor to an overall musical performance, and we wouldn't want to do without them.

3.1.4 SCALES

Let's return now to a bit more music theory as we establish a working vocabulary and an understanding of musical notation.

Playing consecutive notes in an octave (but not necessarily all of them) is called playing a **scale**. There are different types of scales defined in Western music, which vary in the notes played within an octave. These different types of scales are referred to as **intonations**.

MAX DEMO:
Scale Generator
http://bit.ly/29f4wn6

Table 3.1 lists seven types of scales divided into three general categories—chromatic, diatonic, and pentatonic. A list of 1s and 2s is a convenient way to represent the notes that are played in each. Moving by a semitone is represented by the number 1, meaning "move over one note from the previous one." Moving by a whole tone is represented by the number 2, meaning "move over two notes from the previous one."

In a **chromatic scale**, 13 consecutive notes are played, each separated from the previous one by a semitone. A chromatic scale starts on any key and ends on the key which is an octave higher than the first. This is represented simply by the list 1–1–1–1–1–1–1–1–1–1–1–1. Note that while 13 notes are played, there are only 12 numbers on the list. The first note is played, and then the list represents how many semitones to move over to play the following notes.

Eight notes are played in a **diatonic scale**. As with a chromatic scale, a diatonic scale starts on any key and ends on the key which is an octave higher than the first. In a **major diatonic scale**, the pattern is 2–2–1–2–2–2–1. This means, "start on the first note, move over by a tone, a tone, a semitone, a tone, a tone, a tone, and a semitone." A major diatonic scale beginning on D3 is depicted in Figure 3.8. Those who grow up

in the tradition of Western music become accustomed to the sequence of sounds in a diatonic scale as the familiar do–re–mi–fa–so–la–ti–do. A diatonic scale can start on any note, but all diatonic scales have the same pattern of sound; one scale is just higher or lower than another. Diatonic scales sound the same because the differences in the frequencies between consecutive notes on the scale follow the same pattern, regardless of the note you start on.

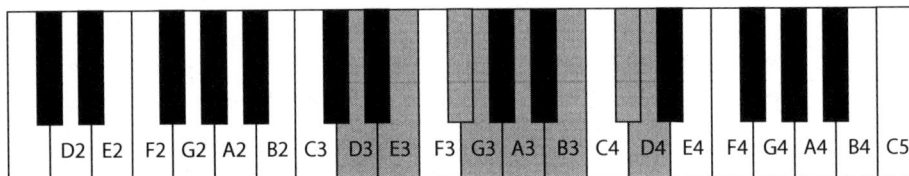

FIGURE 3.8: THE KEY OF D

A **minor diatonic scale** is played in the pattern 2–1–2–2–1–2–2. This pattern is also referred to as the **natural minor**. There are variations of minor scales as well. The **harmonic minor** scale follows the pattern 2–1–2–2–1–3–1, where 3 indicates a step and a half. The **melodic minor** follows the pattern 2–1–2–2–2–2–1 in the ascending scale, and 2–2–1–2–2–1–2 in the descending scale (played from highest to lowest note). The pattern of whole and half steps for major and minor scales are given in Table 3.1.

Type of scale	Pattern of whole steps (2) and half steps (1)
chromatic	1–1–1–1–1–1–1–1–1–1–1
major diatonic	2–2–1–2–2–2–1
natural minor diatonic	2–1–2–2–1–2–2
harmonic minor diatonic	2–1–2–2–1–3–1
melodic minor diatonic	2–1–2–2–2–2–1 ascending 2–2–1–2–2–1–2 descending
pentatonic major	2–3–2–2–3 or 2–2–3–2–3
pentatonic minor	3–2–3–2–2 or 3–2–2–3–2

TABLE 3.1: PATTERN OF WHOLE AND HALF STEPS FOR VARIOUS SCALES

Two final scale types ought to be mentioned because of their prevalence in music of many different cultures. These are the pentatonic scales, created from just five notes. An example of a **pentatonic major scale** results from playing only black notes beginning with F♯. This is the interval pattern 2–2–3–2–3, which yields the scale F♯– G♯–A♯–C♯–D♯–F♯. If you play these notes, you might recognize them as the opening strain from the Temptations' "My Girl," a pop song from the 1960s. Another variant of the pentatonic scale has the interval pattern 2–3–2–2–3, as in the notes C–D–F– G–A–C. These notes are the ones used in the song "Ol' Man River" from the musical Showboat (Figure 3.9).

Ol' man river,
C C D F
Dat ol' man river
D C C D F
He mus'know sumpin'
G A A G F
But don't say nuthin',
G   A C D C
He jes' keeps rollin'
D C C   A G
He keeps on rollin' along.
A C   C A G A F

FIGURE 3.9: PENTATONIC SCALE USED IN "OL' MAN RIVER"
[MUSIC BY JEROME KERN, LYRICS BY OSCAR HAMMERSTEIN II]

To create a minor pentatonic scale from a major one, begin three semitones lower than the major scale and play the same notes. Thus, the **pentatonic minor scale** relative to F♯–G♯–A♯–C♯–D♯–F♯ would be D♯–F♯–G♯–A♯–C♯–D♯, which is a D♯ pentatonic minor scale. The minor relative to C–D–F–G–A–C would be A–C–D–F–G–A, which is an A pentatonic minor scale. As with diatonic scales, pentatonic scales can be set in different keys.

It's significant that a chromatic scale really has no pattern to the sequence of notes played. We simply move up by semitone steps of 1–1–1–1–1–1–1–1–1–1–1–1. The distance between neighboring notes is always the same. In a diatonic scale, on the other hand, there is a pattern of varying half steps and whole steps between notes. A diatonic scale is more interesting. It has color. The pattern gives notes different importance to the ear. This difference in the roles that notes play in a diatonic scale is captured in the names given to these notes, listed in Table 3.2. Roman numerals are conventionally used for the positions of these notes. These names will become more significant when we discuss chords later in this chapter.

Position	Name for note
I	tonic
II	supertonic
III	mediant
IV	subdominant
V	dominant
VI	submediant
VII	leading note

TABLE 3.2: TECHNICAL NAMES FOR NOTES ON A DIATONIC SCALE

3.1.5   MUSICAL NOTATION

3.1.5.1   Score

In the tradition of Western music, a system of symbols has been devised to communicate and preserve musical compositions. This system includes symbols for notes, timing, amplitude, and keys. A musical composition is notated on a **score**. There are scores of different types, depending on the instrument being played. The score we describe is a standard piano or keyboard score.

A piano score consists of two **staves**, each of which consists of five horizontal lines. The staves are drawn one above the other. The top staff is called the **treble clef**, representing the notes that are played by the right hand. The symbol for the treble clef is placed at the far left of the top staff. (The word "clef" is French for "key.") The bottom staff is the **bass clef**, representing what is played with the left hand. The symbol for the bass clef is placed at the far left of the bottom staff. A blank score with no notes on it is pictured in Figure 3.10.

FIGURE 3.10: TREBLE AND BASS CLEF STAVES

Each line and space on the treble and bass clef staves corresponds to a note on the keyboard to be played, as shown in Figure 3.11 and Figure 3.12. A whole note (defined below) is indicated by an oval like those shown. The letter for the corresponding note is given in the figures. The letters are ordinarily not shown on a musical score. We have them here for information only. The treble clef is sometimes called the G clef because the symbol's bottom portion curls around the line on the staff corresponding to the note G. The bass clef is sometimes called the F clef because the symbol curls around the line on the staff corresponding to the note F.

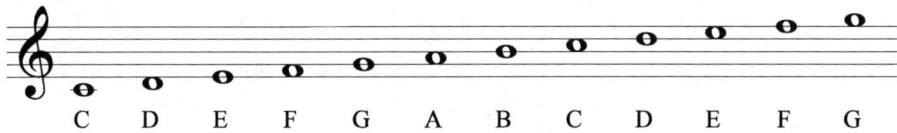

FIGURE 3.11: NOTES ON THE TREBLE CLEF STAFF

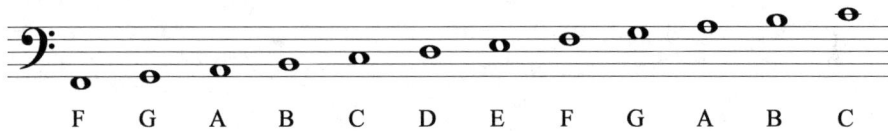

FIGURE 3.12: NOTES ON THE BASS CLEF STAFF

It's possible to place a note below or above one of the staves. The note's distance from the staff indicates what note it is. If it's a note that would fall on a line, a small line is placed through it, and if the note would fall on a space, a line is placed under or over it. The lines between the staff and the upper or lower note are displayed by a short line, also. The short lines that are used to extend the staff are called **ledger lines**. Examples of notes with ledger lines are shown in Figure 3.13 and Figure 3.14.

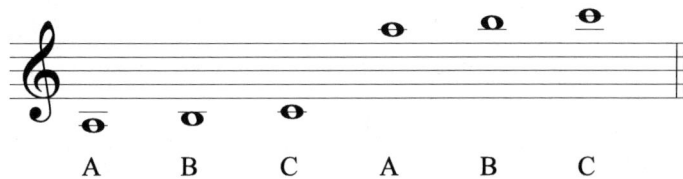

FIGURE 3.13: PLACING NOTES ABOVE OR BELOW THE TREBLE CLEF STAFF

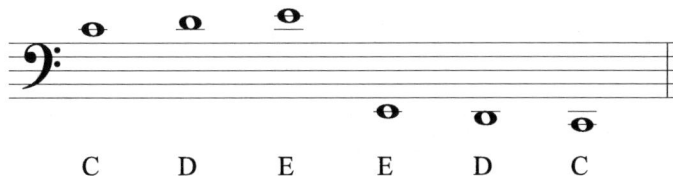

FIGURE 3.14: PLACING NOTES ABOVE OR BELOW THE BASS CLEF STAFF

Beginners who are learning to read music often use mnemonics to remember the notes corresponding to lines and spaces on a staff. For example, the lines on the treble clef staff, in ascending order, correspond to the notes E, G, B, D, and F, which can be memorized with the mnemonic "Every Good Boy Does Fine." The spaces on the treble clef staff, in ascending order, spell the word FACE. On the bass clef, the notes G, B, D, F, and A can be remembered as "Good Boys Deserve Favor Always," and the spaces A, C, E, G can be remembered as "A Cow Eats Grass" (or whatever mnemonics you like).

MAX DEMO:
Recognizing Notes
http://bit.ly/29ghA0i

3.1.5.2 Notes and their Durations

There are types of notes—whole notes, half notes, quarter notes, and so forth, as shown in Table 3.3. On the score, you can tell what type a note is by its shape and color (black or white) on the score. The durations of notes are defined relative to each other, as you can see in the table. The part of the note called the **flag** is shown in Figure 3.15. Each time we add a flag, we divide the duration of the previously defined note by two. We could continue to create smaller and smaller notes, beyond those listed in the table, by adding more flags to a note.

3.1.5.3 Rhythm, Tempo, and Meter

The timing of a musical composition and its performance is a matter of rhythm, tempo, and meter. **Rhythm** is a pattern in the length and accents of sounds. **Tempo** is the pace at which music is performed. We can sing "Yankee Doodle" in a fast, snappy pace or slowly, like a dirge. Obviously, most songs have tempos that seem more appropriate for them. **Meter** is the regular grouping of beats and placement of accents in notes. Let's consider meter in more detail.

FIGURE 3.15: FLAG ON NOTE

FLASH TUTORIAL:
Beats in a Measure
http://bit.ly/29LFPQL

Since the durations of different notes are defined relative to each other, we have to have some baseline. This is given in a score's **time signature**, which indicates which note gets one **beat**. Beats and notes are grouped into **measures**. Measures are sometimes called **bars** because they are separated from each other on the staff by a vertical line called a bar. A time signature of $\frac{x}{y}$, where x and y are integers, indicates that there are x beats to a measure, and a note of size $\frac{1}{y}$ gets one beat. (A half note is size ½, a quarter note is size ¼, and so forth.) A time signature of $\frac{4}{4}$ time is shown in Figure 3.16, indicating four beats to a measure with a quarter note getting one beat. A time signature of $\frac{3}{4}$

Note	Name	Duration
♪ (thirty-second note symbol)	thirty-second note	♪ ♪
♪ (sixteenth note symbol)	sixteenth note	♪ ♪
♪	eighth note	♪ ♪
♩	quarter note	♪ ♪
𝅗𝅥	half note	𝅗𝅥 𝅗𝅥
𝅝	whole note	𝅗𝅥 𝅗𝅥

TABLE 3.3: NOTES AND THEIR DURATION

indicates three beats to a measure with a quarter note getting one beat. $\frac{3}{4}$ is the meter for a waltz.

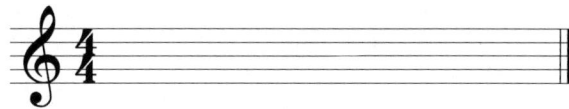

FIGURE 3.16: TIME SIGNATURE SHOWING TIME

If the time signature of a piece is $\frac{4}{4}$, then there are four beats to a measure and each quarter note gets a beat. Consider the score in Figure 3.17, which shows you how to play "Twinkle, Twinkle, Little Star" in $\frac{4}{4}$ time in the key of C. Each of the six syllables in "Twin-kle Twin-kle Lit-tle" corresponds to a quarter note, and each is given equal time—one beat—in the first measure. Then the note corresponding to the word "star" is held for two beats in the second measure. Measures three and four are similar to measures one and two.

FIGURE 3.17: SCORE FOR RIGHT HAND OF "TWINKLE, TWINKLE, LITTLE STAR"

Directions for tempo and rhythm are part of musical notation. As we've already seen, a musical score begins with an indication of how rhythm is to be handled in the form of a time signature that tells how many beats there are to a measure and which type of note gets one beat. The most common time signatures are $\frac{4}{4}$, $\frac{3}{4}$, and $\frac{6}{8}$, but other timings are possible. $\frac{4}{4}$ time is so common that it is sometimes abbreviated on the time signature as C for "common time." Exactly how long it takes to play a measure depends on the tempo of the overall piece.

The **tempo** of a musical piece depends on which type of note is given one beat and how many beats there are per minute. Tempo can be expressed at the beginning of the score explicitly, in terms of **beats per minute (BPM)**. For example, a marking such as θ = 72 placed above a measure indicates that a tempo of 72 beats per minute is recommend from this point on, with a quarter note getting one beat. Alternatively, an Italian key word like *allegro* or *andante* can be used to indicate the beats per minute in a way that can be interpreted more subjectively. A list of some of these tempo markings is given in Table 3.4.

Tempo marking	Meaning
prestissimo	extremely fast (more than 200 BPM)
presto	very fast (168–200 BPM)
allegro	fast (120–168 BPM)
moderato	moderately (108–120 BPM)
andante	"at a walking pace" (76–108 BPM)
adagio	slowly (66–76 BPM)
lento or largo	very slowly (40–60 BPM)

TABLE 3.4: TEMPO MARKINGS

Students learning to play the piano sometimes use a device called a **metronome** to tick out the beats per minute while they practice. Metronomes are also usually built into MIDI sequencers and keyboards.

3.1.5.4 Rests and their Durations

Rhythm is determined not only by the duration of notes but also by how much silence there is between notes. The duration of silence between notes is indicated by a **rest**. The symbols for rests are given in Table 3.5. The length of a rest corresponds to the length of a note of the same name.

VIDEO TUTORIAL:
Music with Rests
http://bit.ly/29wuh4Z

Rest	Name
𝄿	thirty-second rest
𝄾	sixteenth rest
𝄿	eighth rest
𝄽	quarter rest
▬	half rest
▬	whole rest

TABLE 3.5: RESTS AND THEIR DURATIONS

A dot placed after a note or rest increases its duration by one-half of its original value. This is shown in Table 3.6. Figure 3.18 shows a fragment of Mozart's "A Little Night Music," which contains eighth rests in the second, third, and fourth measures. Since this piece is in $\frac{6}{8}$ time, the eighth rest gets one beat.

Dotted note equivalence	Dotted rest equivalence
𝅗𝅥. = 𝅗𝅥 + ♩	▬. = ▬ + 𝄽
♩. = ♩ + ♪	𝄽. = 𝄽 + 𝄾
♪. = ♪ + ♬	𝄾. = 𝄾 + 𝄿

TABLE 3.6: DOTTED NOTES AND RESTS

FIGURE 3.18: EXAMPLE OF MUSIC WITH RESTS

3.1.5.5 Key Signature

Many words in the field of music and sound are overloaded—that is, they have different meanings in different contexts. The word "key" is one of these overloaded terms. Thus far, we have been using the word "key" to denote a physical key on the piano keyboard. (For the discussion that follows, we'll call this kind of key a "piano key.") There's another denotation for "key" that relates to diatonic scales, both major and minor. In this usage of the word, a **key** is a group of notes that constitute a diatonic scale, whether major or minor.

Each key is named by the note on which it begins. The beginning note is called the **key note** or **tonic note**. If we start a major diatonic scale on the piano key of C, then following the pattern 2–2–1–2–2–2–1, only white keys are played. This group of notes defines the key of C major. Now consider what happens if we start on the note D. If you look at the keyboard and consider playing only white keys starting with D, you can see that the pattern would be 2–1–2–2–2–1–2, not the 2–2–1–2–2–2–1 pattern we want for a major scale. Raising F and C each by a semitone—that is, making them F♯ and C♯—changes the pattern to 2–2–1–2–2–2–1. Thus the notes D, E, F♯, G, A, B, C♯ and D define the key of D. By this analysis, we see that the key of D requires two sharps—F♯ and C♯. Similarly, if we start on D and follow the pattern for a minor diatonic scale—2 1 2 2 1 2 2—we play the notes D, E, F, G, A, B♭, and D. This is the key of D minor.

Each beginning note determines the number of sharps or flats that are played in the 2–2–1–2–2–2–1 scale for a major key or in the 2–1–2–2–1–2–2 sequence for a minor key. Beginning an octave on the piano key C implies you're playing in the key of C and play no sharps or flats for C major. Beginning a scale on the piano key D implies that you're playing in the key of D and play two sharps for D major.

Let's try a similar analysis on the key of F. If you play a major scale starting on F using all white keys, you don't get the pattern 2–2–1–2–2–2–1. The only way to get that pattern is to lower the fourth note, B, to B♭. Thus, the key of F major has one flat. The key of F minor has four flats—A♭, B♭, D♭, and E♭, as you can verify by following the sequence 2–1–2–2–1–2–2 starting on F.

Like meter, the key of a musical composition is indicated at the beginning of each staff, in the key signature. The key signature indicates which notes are to be played as sharps or flats. The key signatures for all the major keys with sharps are given in Table 3.7. The key signatures for all the major keys with flats are given in Table 3.8.

You may have noticed that the keys of F major and D minor have the same key signature, each having one flat, B♭. So when you see the key signature for a musical composition and it has one flat in it, how do you know if the composition is written in F major or D minor, and what difference does it make? One difference lies in which note feels like the "home" note, the note to which the music wants to return to be at rest. A composition in the key of F tends to end in a chord that is rooted in F, as we'll see in the section on intervals and chords. A second difference is a subjective response to major and minor keys. Minor keys generally sound more somber, sad, or serious, while major keys are bright and happy to most listeners.

You can see in tables 3.7 and 3.8 that each major key has a relative minor key, as indicated by the keys being in the same row in the table and sharing a key signature. Given a major key k, the relative minor is named by the note that is three semitones below k. For example, A is three semitones below C, and thus A is the relative minor key with respect to C major. When keys are described, if the words "major" and "minor" are not given, then the key is assumed to be a major key.

You've seen how, given the key note, you can determine the key signature for both major and minor keys. So how do you work in reverse? If you see the key signature, how can you tell what key this represents? A trick for major keys is to name the note that is one semitone above the last sharp in the key signature. For example, the last sharp in the second key signature (G major/E minor) in Table 3.7 is F♯. One semitone above F♯ is G, and thus this is the key of G major. For minor keys, you name the note that is two semitones below the last sharp in the key signature. For the second key signature in Table 3.7, the last sharp is F♯. Two semitones below this is the note E. Thus, this is also the key signature for E minor.

To determine a major key based on a key signature with flats, you name the note that is five semitones below the last flat. In the key that has three flats, the last flat is A♭. Five semitones below that is E♭, so this is the key of E♭ major. (This turns out to be the next-to-last flat in each key with at least two flats.) To determine a minor key based on a key signature with flats, you name the note that is four semitones above the last flat. Thus, the key with three flats is the key of C minor. (You could also have gotten this by going three semitones down from the relative major key.)

Major key	Sharps	Minor key
C		A
G		E
D		B
A		F#
E		C#
B		G#
F#		D#
C#		A#

TABLE 3.7: RELATIVE MAJOR AND MINOR KEYS WITH SHARPS

Major key	Flats	Minor key
C		A
F		D
B♭		G
E♭		C
A♭		F
D♭		B♭
G♭		E♭
C♭		A♭

TABLE 3.8: RELATIVE MAJOR AND MINOR KEYS WITH FLATS

The key signature for a **harmonic minor key** is the same as the natural minor. What turns it into a harmonic minor key is the use of sharps or naturals on individual notes to create the desired pattern of whole tones and semitones. To create the pattern 2–1–2–2–1–3–1 (harmonic minor) from 2–1–2–2–1–2–2 (natural minor), it suffices to raise the seventh note a semitone. Thus, the scale for a harmonic minor is notated as shown in Figure 3.19. (In this section and following ones, we won't include measures and time signatures when they are not important to the point being explained.)

FIGURE 3.19: A-MINOR HARMONIC SCALE

Similarly, the **melodic minor** uses the key signature of the natural minor. Then adjustments have to be made in both the ascending and descending scales to create the melodic minor. To create the ascending pattern 2–1–2–2–2–2–1 (melodic minor) from 2–1–2–2–1–2–2 (natural minor), it suffices to raise both the sixth and seventh notes by a semitone. This is done by adding sharps, flats, or naturals as necessary, depending on the key signature. The descending pattern for a melodic minor is the same as for the natural minor—2–2–1–2–2–1–2. Thus, the notes that are raised in the ascending scale have to be returned to their normal position for the key by adding sharps, flats, or naturals, as necessary. This is because once an accidental is added in a measure, it applies to the note to which it was added for the remainder of the measure.

F-minor melodic is notated as shown in Figure 3.20. In F-minor melodic, since D and E are normally flat for that key, a natural sign is added to each to remove the flat and thus move them up one semitone. Then in the descending scale, the D and E must explicitly be made flat again with the flat sign.

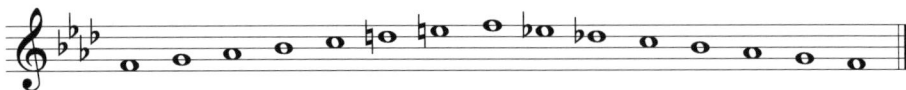

FIGURE 3.20: F-MINOR MELODIC SCALE

In E-minor melodic, a sharp is added to the sixth and seventh notes—C and D—to raise them each a semitone. Then in the descending scale, the D and E must explicitly be made natural again with the sign, as shown in Figure 3.21.

FIGURE 3.21: E-MINOR MELODIC SCALE

3.1.5.6 The Circle of Fifths

In Section 3.1.5, we showed how keys are distinguished by the sharps and flats they contain. One way to remember the keys is by means of the **circle of fifths**, a visual representation of the relationship among keys. The circle is shown in Figure 3.22. The outside of the circle indicates a certain key. The inner circle tells you how many sharps or flats are in the key.

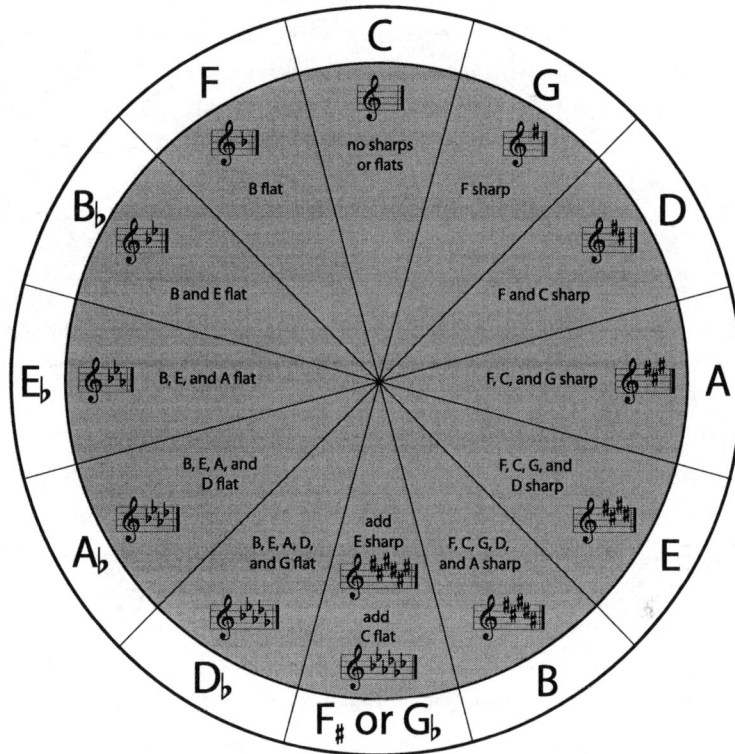

FIGURE 3.22: CIRCLE OF FIFTHS

A **fifth** is a type of interval. We'll discuss intervals in more detail in Section 3.1.6.2, but for now all you need to know is that a fifth is a span of notes that includes five lettered notes. For example, the notes A, B, C, D, and E comprise a fifth, as do C, D, E, F, and G.

If you start with the key of C and move clockwise by intervals of fifths (which we call "counting up"), you reach successive keys each of which has one more sharp than the

FLASH TUTORIAL:
Key Signatures
http://bit.ly/29lhaW1

previous one—the keys of G, D, A, and so forth. For example, starting on C and count up a fifth, you move through C, D, E, F, and G, five lettered notes comprising a fifth. Counting up a fifth consists of moving up seven semitones—C to C♯, C♯ to D, D to D♯, D♯ to E, E to F, F to F♯, and F♯ to G. Notice that on the circle, moving clockwise, you're shown G as the next key up from the key of C. The key of G has one sharp. The next key up, moving by fifths, is the key of D, which has two sharps. You can continue counting up through the circle in this manner to find successive keys, each of which has one more sharp than the previous one.

Starting with the key of C and moving *counterclockwise* by intervals of fifths ("counting down"), you reach successive keys each of which has one more flat than the previous one—the keys of F, B♭, E♭, and so forth. Counting down a fifth from C takes you through C, B, A, G, and F—five lettered notes taking you through seven semitones. Counting down a fifth from F takes you through F, E, D, C, and B. However, since we again want to move seven semitones, the B is actually B♭. The seven semitones are F to E, E to E♭, E♭ to D, D to D♭, D♭ to C, C to B, and B to B♭. Thus, the key with two flats is the key of B♭.

The keys shown in the circle of fifths are the same keys shown in Table 3.7 and Table 3.8. Theoretically, Table 3.7 could continue with keys that have seven sharps, eight sharps, and on infinitely. Moving the other direction, you could have keys with seven flats, eight flats, and on infinitely. These keys with an increasing number of sharps would continue to have equivalent keys with flats. We've shown in Figure 3.22 that the key of F♯, with six sharps, is equivalent to the key of G♭, with six flats. We could have continued in this manner, showing that the key of C♯, with seven sharps, is equivalent to the key of D♭, with five flats. Because the equivalent keys go on infinitely, the circle of fifths is sometimes represented as a spiral. Practically speaking, however, there's little point in going beyond a key with six sharps or flats because such keys are harmonically the same as keys that could be represented with fewer accidentals. We leave it as an exercise for you to demonstrate to yourself the continued key equivalences.

FLASH TUTORIAL: Circle of Fifths http://bit.ly/29LFHAU

FLASH TUTORIAL: Transposing Keys http://bit.ly/29rCJDP

3.1.5.7 Key Transposition

All major keys have a similar sound in that the distance between neighboring notes on the scale follows the same pattern. One key is simply higher or lower than another. The same can be said for the similarity of minor keys. Thus, a musical piece can be **transposed** from one major (or minor) key to another without changing its composition. A singer might prefer one key over another because it is in the range of his or her voice.

Figure 3.23 shows the first seven notes of "Twinkle, Twinkle, Little Star," right-hand part only, transposed from the key of C major to the keys of E major and C minor. If you play these on a keyboard, you'll hear that C major and E major sound the same, except that the second is higher than the first. The one in C minor sounds different because the fifth and sixth notes (A) are lowered by a semitone in the minor key, giving a more somber sound to the sequence of notes. It doesn't "twinkle" as much.

FIGURE 3.23: TRANSPOSITION FROM KEY OF C MAJOR TO E MAJOR AND C MINOR

3.1.6 MUSICAL COMPOSITION

3.1.6.1 Historical Context

For as far back in history as we can see, we find evidence that human beings have made music. We know this from ancient drawings of lutes and harps, Biblical references to David playing the lyre for King Saul, and the Greek philosopher Pythagoras's calculation of harmonic intervals. The history of music and musical styles is a fascinating evolution of classical forms, prescriptive styles, breaks from tradition, and individual creativity. An important thread woven through this evolution is the mathematical basis of music and its relationship with beauty.

In the 6th century BC, the Greek philosopher Pythagoras recognized the mathematical basis of harmony, noting how the sound of a plucked string changes in proportion to the length of the string. However, harmony was not the dominant element of music composition as it developed through the Middle Ages. The chanting of medieval monks consisted of a single strand of notes, rather unmelodic, with no instrumental accompaniment and, by modern standards, a free-form rhythm. Madrigals of the Middle Ages were composed of single solo lines with simple instrumental accompaniment. In the Baroque period, multiple strands became interwoven in a style called polyphony, exemplified in the fugues, canons, and contrapuntal compositions of Johann Sebastian Bach. Although we have come to think of harmony as an essential element of music, its music-theoretical development and its central position in music composition didn't begin in earnest until the eighteenth century, spurred by Jean-Philippe Rameau's *Treatise on Harmony*.

In this chapter, we emphasize the importance of harmony in musical composition because it is an essential feature of modern Western music. However, we acknowledge that perceptions of what is musical vary from era to era and culture to culture, and we can give only a small part of the picture here. We encourage the reader to explore other references on the subject of music history and theory for a more complete picture.

3.1.6.2 Intervals

An understanding of melody and harmony in Western music composition begins with intervals. An **interval** is the distance between two notes, measured by the number of lettered notes it contains. If the notes are played at the same time, the interval is a **harmonic interval**. If the notes are played one after the other, it is a **melodic interval**. If there are at least three notes played simultaneously, they constitute a **chord**. When notes are played at the same time, they are stacked up vertically on the staff. Figure 3.24 shows a harmonic interval, a melodic interval, and a chord.

FIGURE 3.24: INTERVALS AND CHORDS

Intervals are named by the number of lettered notes from the lowest to highest, inclusive. The name of the interval can be expressed as an ordinal number. For example, if the interval begins at F and ends in D, there are six lettered notes in the interval, F, G, A, B, C, and D. Thus, this interval is called a sixth. If the interval begins with C and ends in E, it is called a third, as shown in Figure 3.25. Note that in this regard the presence of sharps or flats isn't significant. The interval between F and D is a sixth, as is the interval between F and D♯.

FIGURE 3.25: INTERVALS OF DIFFERENT SIZES: A SIXTH AND A THIRD

Because there are eight notes in an octave, with the last letter repeated, there are eight intervals in an octave. These are shown in Figure 3.26, in the key of C. Each interval is constructed in turn by starting on the key note and moving up by zero lettered notes, one lettered note, two lettered notes, and on up to eight lettered notes. Moving up one lettered note means moving up to the next line or space on the staff.

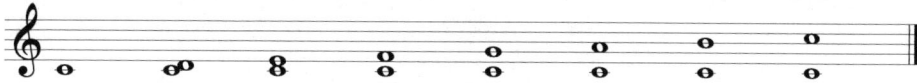

FIGURE 3.26: INTERVALS IN AN OCTAVE, KEY OF C MAJOR

The same intervals can be created in any key. For example, to create them in the key of D, all we have to do is move the bottom note of each interval to the key note D and move up zero notes from D for unison, one note for a major second, two notes for a major third, and so forth, as shown in Figure 3.27. Note, however, that F and C are implicitly sharp in this key.

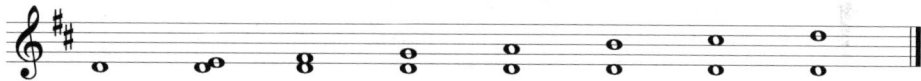

FIGURE 3.27: INTERVALS IN KEY OF D MAJOR

A major interval can be converted to a minor interval by lowering the higher note one semitone. For example, in the key of C, the minor intervals are C to D♭ (minor second), C to E♭ (minor third), C to A♭ (minor sixth), and C to B♭ (minor seventh). It isn't possible to turn a fourth or fifth into a minor interval. This is because if you lower the higher note by one semitone, you've change the interval to a smaller one because you've lost one of the lettered notes in the interval. For example, in the key of C if you shorten a fourth by one semitone, the top note is an E rather than F, so the interval is no longer a fourth. There's no black key to use between E and F. A third, on the other hand, can be shortened so that instead of being from C to E, it's from C to E♭. There are still three lettered notes in the interval—C, D, and E—but now we have a minor third instead of a major third.

The intervals that cannot be made minor are called **perfect**. These are the perfect unison, perfect fourth, perfect fifth, and perfect eighth.

Two other types of intervals exist: diminished and augmented. A **diminished interval** is one semitone smaller than a perfect interval or two semitones smaller than a major interval. An **augmented interval** is one semitone larger than a perfect or major interval. All the intervals for the key of C are shown in Figure 3.28. The intervals for other keys could be illustrated similarly.

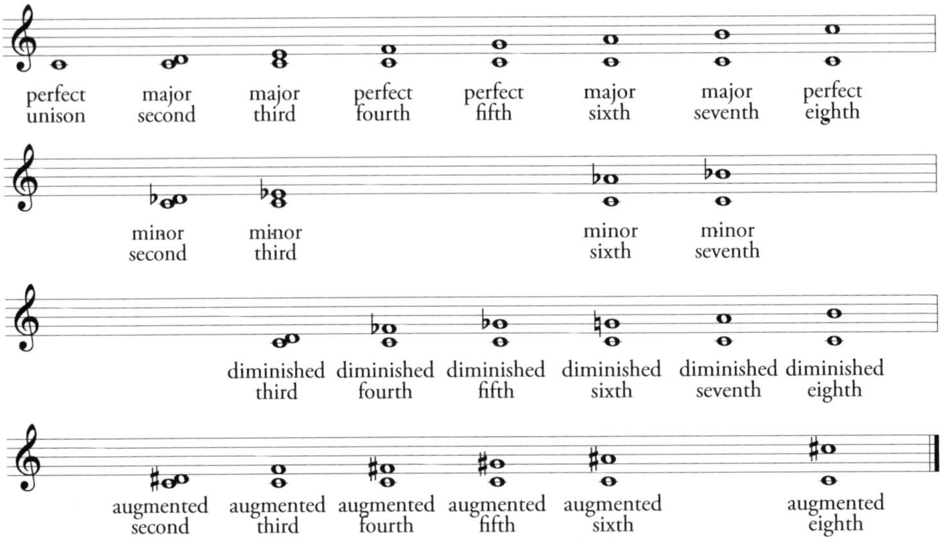

FIGURE 3.28: ALL INTERVALS FOR THE KEY OF C

You can create a **compound interval** by taking any of the interval types defined above and moving the upper note up by one or more octaves. If you're trying to identify intervals in a score, you can count the number of lettered notes from the beginning to the end of the interval and "mod" that number by 7. The result gives you the type of interval. For example, if the remainder is 3, then the interval is a third. The *mod* operation divides by an integer and gives the remainder. This is the same as repeatedly subtracting 7 (the number of notes in an octave, not counting the repeat of the first note an octave higher) until you reach a number that is less than 7. Figure 3.29 shows examples of two compound intervals. The first goes from C4 to G5, a span of 12 notes. 12 mod 7 = 5, so this is a compound perfect fifth. The second interval goes from E4 to G5♯, a span of 10 notes. 10 mod 7 = 3, so this is a compound third. However, because the G is raised to G♯, this is, more precisely, a compound *augmented* third.

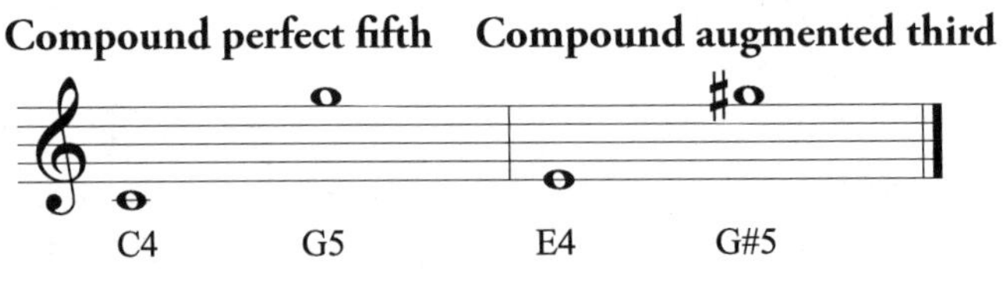

FIGURE 3.29: COMPOUND INTERVALS

Intervals can be characterized as either consonant or dissonant. Giving an oversimplified definition, we can say that sounds that are pleasing to the ear are called **consonant**, and those that are not are called **dissonant**. Of course, these qualities are subjective. Throughout the history of music, the terms consonant and dissonant have undergone much discussion. Some music theorists would define consonance as a state when things are in accord with each other, and dissonance as a state of instability or tension that calls for resolution. In Section 3.3, we'll look more closely at a physical and mathematical explanation for the subjective perception of consonance as it relates to harmony.

Intervals help us to characterize the patterns of notes in a musical composition. The musical conventions from different cultures vary not only in their basic scales but also in the intervals that are agreed upon as pleasing to the ear. In Western music the perfect intervals, major and minor thirds, and major and minor sixths are generally considered consonant, while the seconds, sevenths, augmented, and diminished intervals are considered dissonant. The consonant intervals come to be used frequently in musical compositions of a culture, and the listener's enjoyment is enhanced by a sense of recognition. This is not to say that dissonant intervals are simply ugly and never used. It is the combination of intervals that makes a composition. The combination of consonant and dissonant intervals gives the listener an alternating sense of tension and resolution, expectation and completion in a musical composition.

MAX DEMO:
Ear Training for Music
http://bit.ly/29m9FM3

3.1.6.3 Chords

A chord is three or more notes played at the same time. We will look at the most basic chords here—**triads**, which consist of three notes.

Triads can be major, minor, diminished, or augmented. The lowest note of a triad is its **root**. In a **major triad**, the second note is a major third above the root, and the third note is a perfect fifth above the root. In the **root position** of a triad in a given key, the tonic note of the key is the root of the triad. (Refer to Table 3.2 for the names of the notes in a diatonic scale.) The major triads for the keys of C, F, and A are shown in root position in Figure 3.30.

FIGURE 3.30: MAJOR TRIADS IN ROOT POSITION

In a **minor triad**, the second note is a diatonic minor third above the root, and the third note is a diatonic perfect fifth above the root. The minor triads for the keys of C, F, and A are shown in root position in Figure 3.31.

Key of C   **Key of F**   **Key of A**

FIGURE 3.31: MINOR TRIADS IN ROOT POSITION

Chords can be inverted by changing the root note. In the first inversion, the root note is moved up an octave. In the **second inversion**, the mediant of the key becomes the root and the tonic is moved up an octave. In the **third inversion**, the dominant of the key becomes the root, and both the mediant and tonic are moved up an octave. The first and second inversions are shown in Figure 3.32.

Root position   **First inversion**   **Second inversion**

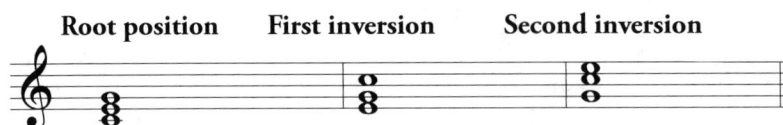

FIGURE 3.32: INVERSIONS FOR MAJOR TRIAD IN KEY OF C

A **diminished triad** has a root note followed by a minor third and a diminished fifth. An **augmented triad** has a root note followed by a major third and an augmented fifth. The diminished and augmented triads for the key of C are shown in Figure 3.33.

Diminished   **Augmented**

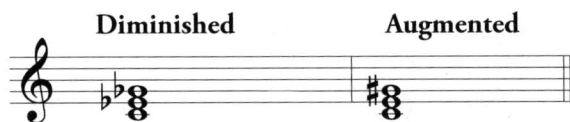

FIGURE 3.33: DIMINISHED AND AUGMENTED TRIADS IN KEY OF C

We've looked only at triads so far. However, chords with four notes are also used, including the major, minor, and dominant sevenths. The **major seventh** chord consists of the root, major third, perfect fifth, and major seventh. The **minor seventh** chord consists of the root, minor third, perfect fifth, and minor seventh. The **dominant seventh** chord consists of the root, major third, perfect fifth, and minor seventh. Dominant chords have three inversions. The dominant seventh chord for the key of C is shown with its inversions in Figure 3.34. (Note that B is flat in all the inversions.)

Root position   **1st inversion**   **2nd inversion**   **3rd inversion**

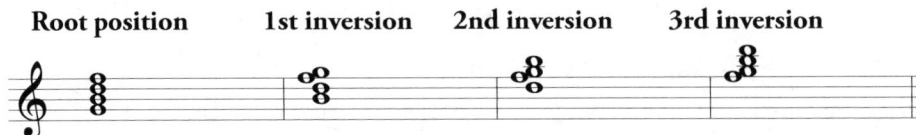

FIGURE 3.34: DOMINANT SEVENTH CHORDS FOR THE KEY OF C

Thus we have seven basic chords that are used in musical compositions. These are summarized in Table 3.9.

Name	Chord	Notes
major triad		root, major third, perfect fifth
minor triad		root, minor third, perfect fifth
diminished triad		root, minor third, diminished fifth
augmented triad		root, major third, augmented fifth
major seventh		root, major third, perfect fifth, major seventh
minor seventh		root, minor third, perfect fifth, minor seventh
dominant seventh		root, major third, perfect fifth, minor seventh

TABLE 3.9: TYPES OF CHORDS

All major keys give rise to a sequence of triads following the same pattern. To see this, consider the sequence you get in the key of C major by playing a triad starting on each of the piano keys in the scale. These triads are shown in Figure 3.35. Each is named with the name of its root note.

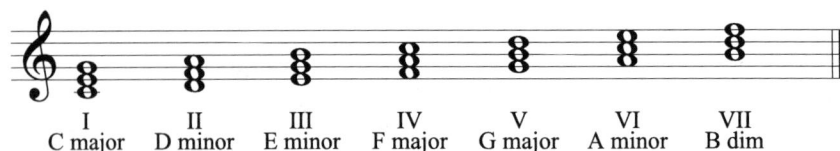

FIGURE 3.35: TRIADS IN C MAJOR

Each of the chords in this sequence can be characterized based on its root note. Triad I is easy to see. The first note is C and it's a major triad, so it's C major. Triad II starts on D, so consider what kind of triad this would be in the key of D. It has the notes D, F, and A. However, in the key of D, F should be sharp. D is not sharp in the triad II shown, so this is a minor triad from the key of D. Triad III has the notes E, G, and B. In the key of E, G is sharp, but in the triad III shown, it is not. Thus, the third triad in the key of C is E minor. Let's skip to triad VII, which has the notes B, D, and F. In the key of B, the notes D and F are sharp, but they're not in triad VII. This makes triad VII a B diminished. By this analysis, we can determine that the sequence of chords in C major is C major, D minor, E minor, F major, G major, A minor, and B diminished.

All major keys have this same sequence of chord types—major, minor, minor, major, major, minor, and diminished. For example, the key of D has the chords D major, E minor, F minor, G major, A major, B minor and C diminished. If we do a similar analysis for the minor keys, we find that they follow the pattern minor, diminished, augmented, minor, major, major, and diminished, as summarized in Table 3.10.

> **FLASH TUTORIAL:**
> Chords
> http://bit.ly/29uggY7

> **FLASH TUTORIAL:**
> Identifying Chords in a Key
> http://bit.ly/29w8Ot7

Chord number	Chord type if the triad sequence comes from a major key	Chord type if the triad sequence comes from a minor key
I	major	minor
II	minor	diminished
III	minor	augmented
IV	major	minor
V	major	major
VI	minor	major
VII	diminished	diminished

TABLE 3.10: TYPES OF TRIAD CHORDS IN MAJOR AND MINOR KEYS

3.1.6.4 Chord Progressions

So what is the point of identifying and giving names to intervals and chords? The point is that this gives us a way to analyze music and compose it in a way that yields a logical order and an aesthetically pleasing form. When chords follow one another in certain progressions, they provoke feelings of tension and release, expectation and satisfaction, conflict and resolution. This emotional rhythm is basic to music composition.

Let's look again at the chords playable in the key of C, as shown in Figure 3.35. Chord progressions can be represented by a sequence of Roman numerals. For example, the right-hand part of "Twinkle, Twinkle, Little Star" in the key of C major, shown in Figure 3.23, could be accompanied by the chords I–IV–I–IV–I–V–I in the left hand, as shown in Figure 3.36. This chord progression is in fact a very common pattern.

FIGURE 3.36: "TWINKLE, TWINKLE, LITTLE STAR" WITH CHORDS AS ROMAN NUMERALS

You can play this yourself with reference to the triads from the key of C major, shown in Figure 3.35. However, to make the chords easier to play, you'll want to invert them so that the root note is either C or the B below C, making it easier for your hand to move from one note to the next. Thus, chord I can be played as C–E–G; chord IV as C–F–A (2nd inversion); and chord V as B–D–G (1st inversion), as shown in Figure 3.37.

FIGURE 3.37: "TWINKLE, TWINKLE, LITTLE STAR" WITH CHORDS IN BASS CLEF

A simple way of looking at chord progressions is based on **tonality**—a system for defining the relationships of chords based on the tonic note for a given key. Recall that the tonic note is the note that begins the scale for a key. In fact, the key's name is derived from the tonic note. In the key of C, the tonic note is C. Triad I is the tonic triad because it begins on the tonic note. You can think of this as the home chord, the chord where a song begins and to which it wants to return. Triad V is called the dominant chord. It has this name because chord progressions in a sense pull toward the dominant chord, but then tend to return to the home chord, chord I. Returning to chord I gives a sense of completion in a chord progression, called a **cadence**. The progression from I to V and back to I again is called a **perfect cadence** because it is the clearest example of tension and release in a chord progression. It is the most commonly used chord progression in modern popular music, and probably in Western music as a whole.

Another frequently used progression moves from I to IV and back to I. IV is the subdominant chord, named because it serves as a counterbalance to the dominant. The I–IV–I progression is called the **plagal cadence**. Churchgoers may recognize it as the sound of the closing "amen" to a hymn. Together, the tonic, subdominant, and dominant chords and their cadences serve as foundational chord progressions. You can see this in "Twinkle, Twinkle, Little Star," a tune for which Wolfgang Amadeus Mozart wrote twelve variations.

The perfect and plagal cadences are commonly used chord progressions, but they're only the tip of the iceberg of possibilities. "Over the Rainbow" from *The Wizard of Oz*, with music written by Harold Arlen, is an example of how a small variation from the chord progression of "Twinkle, Twinkle, Little Star" can yield beautiful results. If you speed up the tempo of "Over the Rainbow," you can play it with the same chords as are used for "Twinkle, Twinkle, Little Star," as shown in Figure 3.38. The only one that sounds a bit "off" is the first IV.

VIDEO TUTORIAL: "Over the Rainbow" in the Key of C http://bit.ly/29wu2XP

VIDEO TUTORIAL: "Over the Rainbow" in the Key of E-flat http://bit.ly/29LZFM1

FIGURE 3.38: "OVER THE RAINBOW" PLAYED IN C WITH CHORDS OF "TWINKLE, TWINKLE, LITTLE STAR"

It's remarkable how the color of a melody can shift when the accompanying chords are changed only slightly. Figure 3.39 shows "Over the Rainbow" played in the key of E♭ with the chord sequence I–III–IV–I–IV–I–III–V–I For the key of E♭, these chords are E♭–G minor–A♭–E♭–A♭–E♭–G minor–B♭–E♭. The use of G minor adds a melancholy tone which fits the song's theme. We could also change the fourth chord, currently an E♭ major, to a G minor and add to this effect.

FIGURE 3.39: "OVER THE RAINBOW" IN THE KEY OF E♭
[ORIGINAL LYRICS BY E.Y. HARBURG ADAPTED BY ISRAEL KAMAKAWIWO'OLE]

3.1.7 DYNAMICS AND ARTICULATION

Dynamics symbols tell how loudly or quietly music should be played. These terms were brought into usage by Italian composers, and we still use the Italian terms and symbols. The terms are summarized in Table 3.11 along with the signs used to denote them on the staff. Additional *p*s and *f*s can be added to emphasize the loudness or quietness, but four *p*s or *f*s is usually the limit. The symbols are displayed below the staff in the area to which they are applied.

Term	Sign	Meaning
piano	*p*	quiet
mezzo piano	*mp*	moderately quiet
pianissimo	*pp*	very quiet
forte	*f*	loud
mezzo forte	*mf*	moderately loud

fortissimo	*ff*	very loud
subito forte	*sf*	suddenly loud
subito forte piano	*sfp*	suddenly loud and soft
sforzando	*sfz*	forceful sudden accent

TABLE 3.11: DYNAMICS TERMS AND SYMBOLS

Gradual changes in dynamics are indicated by **crescendo** and **decrescendo** symbols (Figure 3.40). The **decrescendo** can also be called a **diminuendo**. The crescendo indicates that the music should gradually grow louder. The decrescendo is the opposite. These symbols can be made longer or shorter depending on the time over which the change should occur. They are usually placed below the staff, but occasionally above.

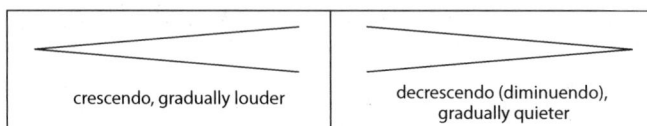

crescendo, gradually louder   decrescendo (diminuendo), gradually quieter

FIGURE 3.40: SYMBOLS FOR GRADUAL CHANGES IN DYNAMICS

Articulation marks (Table 3.12) indicate the manner in which a note is to be performed. A little dot above or below a note (depending on the direction of the note's stem) indicates that it is to be played **staccato**—that is, played as a short note not held down, and thus not linked directly in sound to the next note. A "greater than" sign above or below a note, called an **accent**, indicates that the note should be played louder, with special emphasis. A straight line above or below a note, called a **tenuto**, emphasizes that a note is to be held for its full value. A dot with a semicircle above it, called a **fermata**, means that a note is to be held longer than its normal value. The articulation marks and dynamics symbols help a composer to guide the style and technique applied to the performance of a composition.

| **Term** | **Symbol** | **Meaning** |
| staccato | | Play the note with a quick key strike, not holding the note to blend with the next |

accent		Accent the note
tenuto		Hold the note for its full length
fermata		Hold the note longer than its full length

TABLE 3.12: ARTICULATION MARKS

3.2 APPLICATIONS

3.2.1 PIANO ROLL AND EVENT LIST VIEWS

Learning to read music on a staff is important for anyone working with music. However, for non-musicians working on computer-based music, there are other, perhaps more intuitive ways to picture musical notes. Some software programs—MIDI sequencers, for example—provide two other views that you may find helpful—the piano roll view and the event list view. We'll talk more about MIDI sequencers in Chapter 6, but this will give you a preview of their graphical user interfaces.

A **piano roll view** is essentially a graph with the vertical axis representing the notes on a piano and the horizontal axis showing time. In Figure 3.41 you can see a graphical representation of a piano keyboard flipped vertically and placed on the left side of the window. On the horizontal row at the top of the window you can see a number representing each new measure. This graph forms a grid where notes can be placed at the intersection of the note and beat where the note should occur. Notes can also be adjusted to any duration. In this case, you can see each note starting on a quarter beat. Some notes are longer than others. The quarter notes are shown using bars that start on a quarter beat but don't extend beyond the neighboring quarter beat. The half notes start on a quarter beat and extend beyond the neighboring quarter beat. In most cases you can grab note events using your mouse pointer and move them to different notes on the vertical scale as well as move them to a different beat on the grid. You can even extend or shorten the notes after they've been entered. You can also usually draw new notes directly into the piano roll.

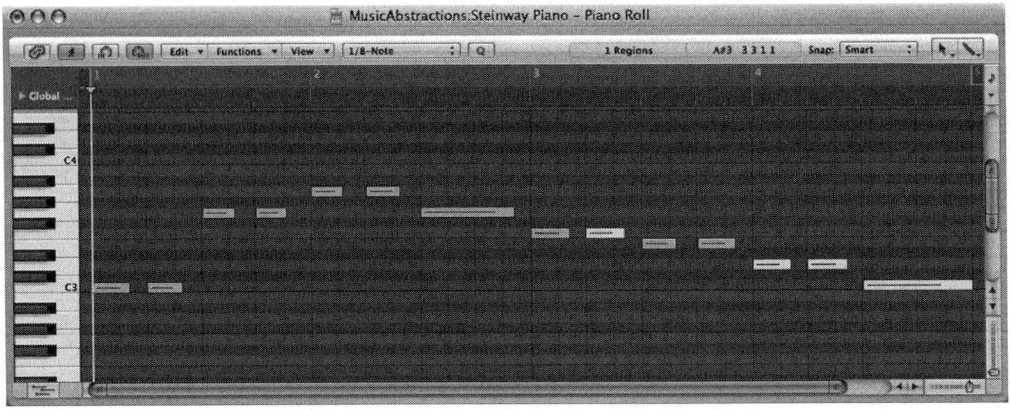

FIGURE 3.41: PIANO ROLL VIEW OF MELODY OF "TWINKLE, TWINKLE, LITTLE STAR"

Another way you might see the musical data is in an **event list view**, as shown in Figure 3.42. This is a list showing information about every musical event that occurs for a given song. Each event usually includes the position in time that the event occurs, the type of event, and any pertinent details about the event such as note

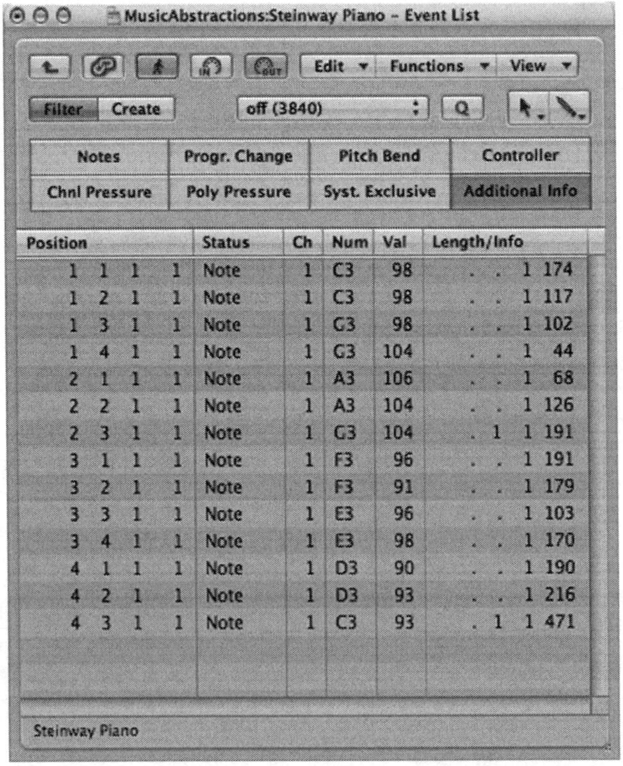

FIGURE 3.42: EVENT LIST VIEW OF MELODY OF "TWINKLE, TWINKLE, LITTLE STAR"

number, duration, etc. The event position value is divided into four columns. These are Bars:Beats:Divisions:Ticks. You should already be familiar with bars and beats. Divisions are some division of a beat. This is usually an eighth or a sixteenth and can be user-defined. Ticks are a miniscule value. You can think of these like frames or milliseconds. The manual for your specific software will give you its specific time value of ticks.

You can edit events in an event list by changing the properties, and you can add and delete events in this view. The event list is useful for fixing problems that you can't see in the other views. Sometimes data gets captured from your MIDI keyboard that shouldn't be part of your sequence. In the event list, you can select the specific events that shouldn't be there (like a MIDI volume change or program change).

3.2.2 TABLATURE

Tablature (tab) is a common way of notating music when played on plucked string instruments. Basic guitar tablature requires that the player be somewhat familiar with the song already. As shown in Figure 3.43, guitar tabs use six lines like the regular music staff, but in this case, each line represents one of the six guitar strings. The top line represents the high E string and the bottom line represents the low E string. Numbers are then drawn on each line representing the fret number to use for that note on that string. To play the song, every time you see a number, you put your finger on that string at the fret number indicated and pluck that string. Simple tablature doesn't give any indication of how long to play each note, so you need to be familiar with the song already. In some cases, the spacing of the numbers can give some indication of rhythm and duration.

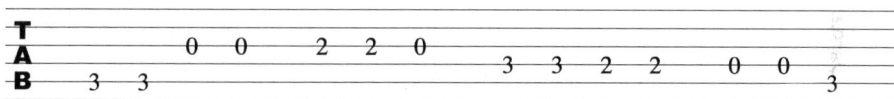

FIGURE 3.43: GUITAR TABLATURE FOR MELODY OF "TWINKLE, TWINKLE, LITTLE STAR"

3.2.3 CHORD PROGRESSION

The most abstract method of encoding musical data is probably the chord progression. Consider the following chord progression for "Twinkle, Twinkle, Little Star":

```
C              F   C
Twinkle, twinkle, little star,

F    C    G     C
How I wonder what you are.
```

```
C    F        C       G
Up above the world so high,
C    F        C    G
Like a diamond in the sky,
C                    F    C
Twinkle, twinkle, little star,
F    C    G        C
How I wonder what you are.
```

A trained musician who is already somewhat familiar with the tune should be able to extract the entire song from this chord progression, as shown in Figure 3.37. You may have witnessed an example of this if you've ever seen a live band that seemed able to play anything requested on the spur of the moment. Most good "gigging" bands can do this. Certainly, their ability to do this comes in part from a good familiarity with popular music, but that doesn't mean they've memorized all those songs ahead of time. Musicians call this approach "faking it" and at most bookstores you can purchase "fake books" that contain hundreds of chord progressions for songs. With the musical data so highly compressed, it is not unheard of for a fake book to have well over a thousand songs in a size that can fit quite comfortably in a small backpack.

In Section 3.1.6.2 we learned about intervals and in Section 3.1.6.3 we learned about chords. **Chord progressions** are a repeating sequence of chords at musical intervals. Music is built with chord progressions. If you know what chord is being used at any given time in the song, you should also know which notes you could play for that part of the song. In the case of the chord progression for "Twinkle, Twinkle, Little Star," we begin with the tonic C major chord. Then we move to the perfect fourth, an F major chord. Occasionally, we use the perfect fifth, a G major chord. This is called a **I–IV–V** chord progression. Many popular songs are built from this chord progression. In the simplest form, you could play these chords on the keyboard as you sing the melody and you should have something that sounds respectable. From there you could improvise bass lines, solos, and arrangements by playing notes that fit with the key signature and chord currently in use.

MAX DEMO: Music Improvisation http://bit.ly/29ma4hy

In addition to using fake books, you can train your ears to recognize chord progressions and then fake the songs by ear. See the learning supplements for this section to start training your ears and try experimenting with improvising along with a chord progression.

3.2.4   GUITAR CHORD GRID

Figure 3.44 shows a guitar chord grid for the accompaniment. The chord grid corresponds to the guitar fret board with the vertical lines represented as six strings, and the horizontal lines represented as frets. A black dot represents a place on the fret board where you put one of your fingers. When all your fingers are in the indicated locations, you can strum the strings to play the chord. Keep in mind that the chord grid shows you one way to play the chord, but there are always other fingering combinations that result in the same chord. If the grid you're looking at looks too hard to play, you might be able to find a grid showing an alternate fingering that is easier.

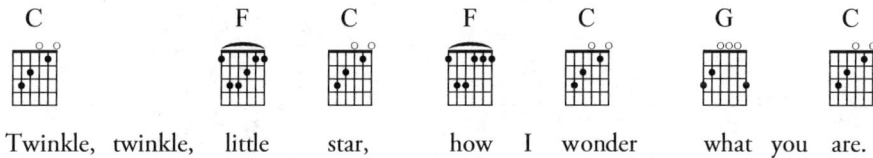

FIGURE 3.44: GUITAR CHORD GRIDS FOR "TWINKLE, TWINKLE, LITTLE STAR"

3.3 SCIENCE, MATHEMATICS, AND ALGORITHMS

3.3.1   EQUAL TEMPERED VS. JUST TEMPERED INTERVALS

In Section 3.1.4 we described the diatonic scales that are commonly used in Western music. These scales are built by making the frequency of each successive note $\sqrt[12]{2}$ times the frequency of the previous one. This is just one example of a **temperament**, a system for selecting the intervals between tones used in musical composition. In particular, it is called **equal temperament** or **equal tempered intonation**, and it produces **equal tempered** scales and intervals. While this is the intonation our ears have gotten accustomed to in Western music, it isn't the only one, nor even the earliest. In this section we'll look at an alternative method for constructing scales that dates back to Pythagoras in the sixth century BC—**just tempered intonation**—a tuning in which frequency intervals are chosen based upon their harmonic relationships.

First let's look more closely and the equal tempered scales as a point of comparison. The diatonic scales described in Section 3.1.4 are called equal tempered because the factor by which the frequencies get larger remains equal across the scale. Table 3.13 shows the frequencies of the notes from C4 to C5, assuming that A4 is 440 Hz. Each successive frequency is $\sqrt[12]{2}$ times the frequency of the previous one.

Note	Frequency
C4	261.63 Hz
C4♯ (B4♭)	277.18 Hz
D4	293.66 Hz
D4♯ (E4♭)	311.13 Hz
E4	329.63 Hz
F4	349.23 Hz
F4♯ (G4♭)	369.99 Hz
G4	392.00 Hz
G4♯ (A4♭)	415.30 Hz
A4	440.00 Hz
A4♯ (B4♭)	466.16 Hz
B4	493.88 Hz
C5	523.25 Hz

TABLE 3.13: FREQUENCIES OF NOTES FROM C4 TO C5

It's interesting to note how the ratio of two frequencies in an interval affects our perception of the interval's consonance or dissonance. Consider the ratios of the frequencies for each interval type, as shown in Table 3.14. Some of these ratios reduce very closely to fractions with small integers in the numerator and denominator. For example, the frequencies of G and C, a perfect fifth, reduce to approximately 3:2; and the frequencies of E and C, a major third, reduce to approximately 5:4. Pairs of frequencies that reduce to fractions such as these are the ones that sound more consonant, as indicated in the last column of the table.

Interval	Notes in interval	Ratio of frequencies	Common perception of interval
perfect unison	C	$261.63/261.63 = 1/1$	consonant
minor second	C C♯	$277.18/261.63 \approx 1.059/1$	dissonant
major second	C D	$293.66/261.63 \approx 1.122/1$	dissonant
minor third	C D E♭	$311.13/261.63 \approx 1.189/1 \approx 6/5$	consonant
major third	C D E	$329.63/261.63 \approx 1.260/1 \approx 5/4$	consonant

perfect fourth	C D E F	349.23/261.63 ≈ 1.335/1 ≈ 4/3	strongly consonant
augmented fourth	C D E F♯	369.99/261.63 ≈ 1.414/1	dissonant
perfect fifth	C D E F G	392.00/261.63 ≈ 1.498/1 ≈ 3/2	strongly consonant
minor sixth	C D E F G A♭	415.30/261.63 ≈ 1.587/1 ≈ 8/5	consonant
major sixth	C D E F G A	440.00/261.63 ≈ 1.681/1 ≈ 5/3	consonant
minor seventh	C D E F G A B♭	466.16/261.63 ≈ 1.781/1	dissonant
major seventh	C D E F G A B	493.88/261.63 ≈ 1.887/1	dissonant
perfect octave	C C	523.26/261.63 = 1/1	consonant

TABLE 3.14: RATIO OF BEGINNING AND ENDING FREQUENCIES IN INTERVALS

There's a physical and mathematical explanation for this consonance. The fact that the frequencies of G and C have approximately a 3/2 ratio is visible in a graph of their sine waves. Figure 3.45 shows that three cycles of G fit almost exactly into two cycles of C. The sound waves fit together in an orderly pattern, and the human ear notices this agreement. But notice that we said the waves fit together *almost* exactly. The ratio of 392/261.63 is actually closer to 1.4983, not exactly 3/2, which is 1.5. Wouldn't the intervals be even more harmonious if they were built upon the frequency relationships of natural harmonics?

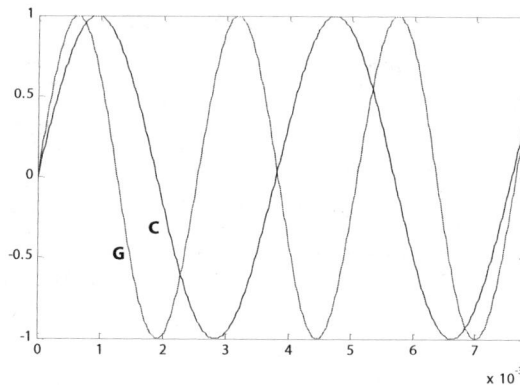

FIGURE 3.45: HOW CYCLES MATCH FOR PAIRS OF FREQUENCIES

To consider how and why this might make sense, recall the definition of harmonic frequencies from Chapter 2. For a fundamental frequency f, the harmonic frequencies are $1f$, $2f$, $3f$, $4f$, and so forth. These are frequencies whose cycles *do* fit together exactly. As depicted in Figure 3.46, the ratio of the third to the second harmonic is $(3f)/(2f) = 3/2$. This corresponds very closely, but not precisely, to what we have called a perfect fifth in equal tempered intonation—for example, the relationship between G and C in the key of C, or between D and G in the key of G. Similarly, the ratio of the fifth harmonic to the fourth is $(5f)/(4f) = 5/4$, which corresponds to the interval we have referred to as a major third.

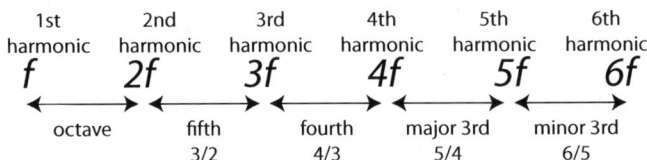

1st harmonic	2nd harmonic	3rd harmonic	4th harmonic	5th harmonic	6th harmonic
f	$2f$	$3f$	$4f$	$5f$	$6f$

octave	fifth 3/2	fourth 4/3	major 3rd 5/4	minor 3rd 6/5

FIGURE 3.46: RATIO OF FREQUENCIES IN HARMONIC INTERVALS

Just tempered intonations use frequencies that have these harmonic relationships. The Pythagorian diatonic scale is built entirely from fifths. The just tempered scale shown in Table 3.15 is a modern variant of the Pythagorian scale. By comparing columns three and four, you can see how far the equal tempered tones are from the harmonic intervals. An interesting exercise would be to play a note in equal tempered frequency and then in just tempered frequency and see if you can notice the difference.

Interval	Notes in interval	Ratio of frequencies in equal temperament	Ratio of frequencies in just temperament
perfect unison	C	261.63/261.63 = 1.000	1/1 = 1.000
minor second	C–C♯	277.18/261.63 ≈ 1.059	16/15 ≈ 1.067
major second	C–D	293.66/261.63 ≈ 1.122	9/8 = 1.125
minor third	C–D–E♭	311.13/261.63 ≈ 1.189	6/5 = 1.200
major third	C–D–E	329.63/261.63 ≈ 1.260	5/4 ≈ 1.250
perfect fourth	C–D–E–F	349.23/261.63 ≈ 1.335	4/3 ≈ 1.333
augmented fourth	C–D–E–F♯	369.99/261.63 ≈ 1.414	7/5 = 1.400
perfect fifth	C–D–E–F–G	392.00/261.63 ≈ 1.498	3/2 = 1.500
minor sixth	C–D–E–F–G–A♭	415.30/261.63 ≈ 1.587	8/5 = 1.600

major sixth	C–D–E–F–G–A	440.00/261.63 ≈ 1.682	5/3 ≈ 1.667
minor seventh	C–D–E–F–G–A–B♭	466.16/261.63 ≈ 1.782	7/4 = 1.750
major seventh	C–D–E–F–G–A–B	493.88/261.63 ≈ 1.888	15/8 = 1.875
perfect octave	C–C	523.26/261.63 = 2.000	2/1 = 2.000

TABLE 3.15: EQUAL TEMPERED VS. JUST TEMPERED SCALES

3.3.2   EXPERIMENTING WITH MUSIC IN MAX

Max (and its open source counterpart, PD) is a powerful environment for experimenting with sound and music. We use one of our own learning supplements, a Max patcher for generating scales (see Section 3.1.4), as an example of the kinds of programs you can write.

> **MAX PROGRAMMING EXERCISE:**
> Transposing Notes
> http://bit.ly/29m9eRZ

When you open this patcher, it is in presentation mode (Figure 3.47), as indicated by the drop-down menu in the bottom-right corner. In presentation mode, the patcher is laid out in a user-friendly format, showing only the parts of the interface that you need in order to run the tutorial, which in this case allows you to generate major and minor scales in any key you choose. You can change to programming mode (Figure 3.48) by choosing this option from the drop-down menu.

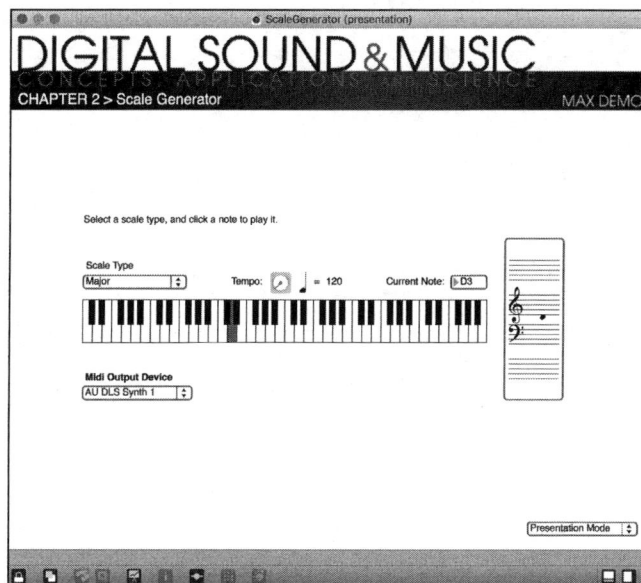

FIGURE 3.47: MAX PATCHER IN PRESENTATION MODE

Programming mode reveals more of the Max objects used in the program. You can now see that the scale-type menu is connected to a list object. This list changes in accordance with the selection, each time giving the number of semitones between consecutive notes on the chosen type of scale. You can also see that the program is implemented with a number of send, receive, and patcher objects. Send and receive objects pass data between them, as the names imply. Objects named *s* followed by an argument, as in *s notepitch*, are the send objects. Objects named *r* followed by an argument, as in *r notepitch*, are the receive objects. Patcher objects are "subpatchers" within the main program, their details hidden so that the main patcher is more readable. You can open a patcher object in programming mode by double-clicking on it. The *metronome*, *handlescale*, and *handlenote* patcher objects are open in Figure 3.49, Figure 3.50, and Figure 3.51, respectively.

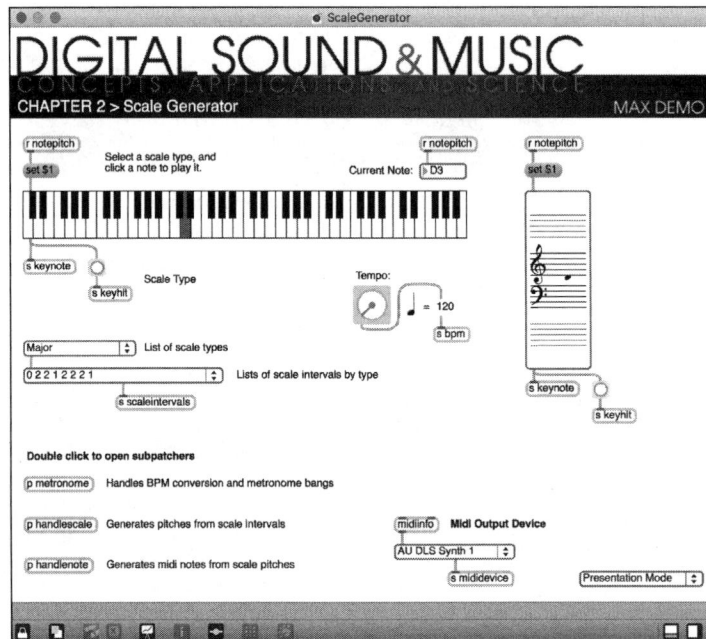

FIGURE 3.48: MAX PATCHER IN PROGRAMMING MODE

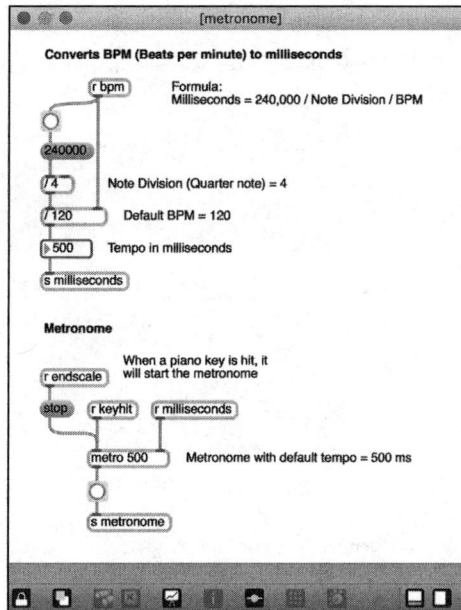

FIGURE 3.49: METRONOME PATCHER OBJECT

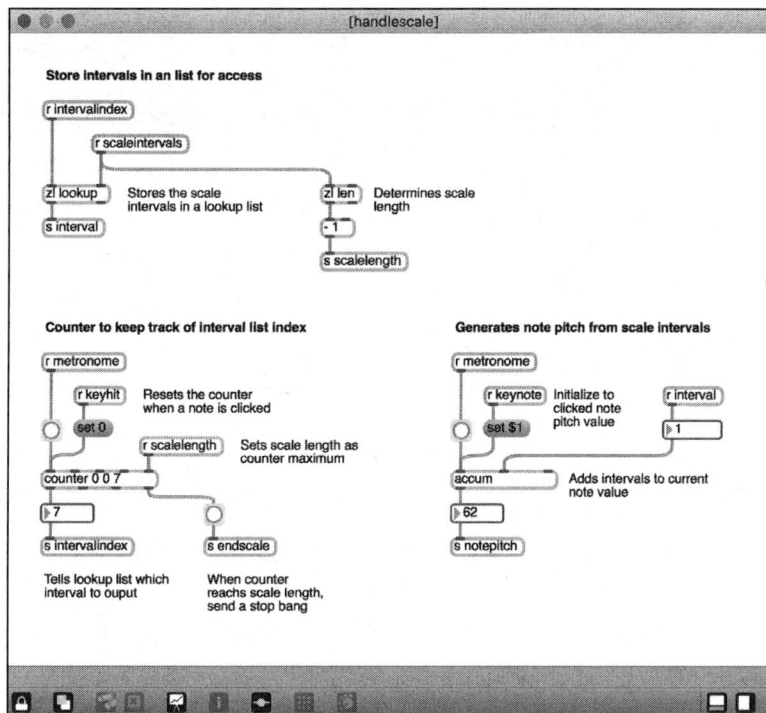

FIGURE 3.50: HANDLESCALE PATCHER OBJECT

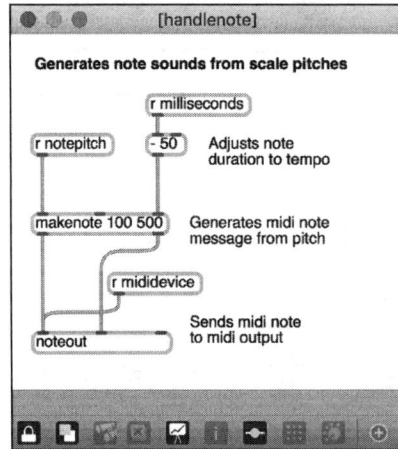

FIGURE 3.51: HANDLENOTE PATCHER OBJECT

In this example, you still can't see the details of how messages are being received and processed. To do so, you have to unlock the main patcher window by clicking the lock icon in the bottom-left corner. This puts you in a mode where you can inspect and even edit objects. The main patcher is unlocked in Figure 3.52. You must have the full Max application, not just the runtime, to go into full programming mode.

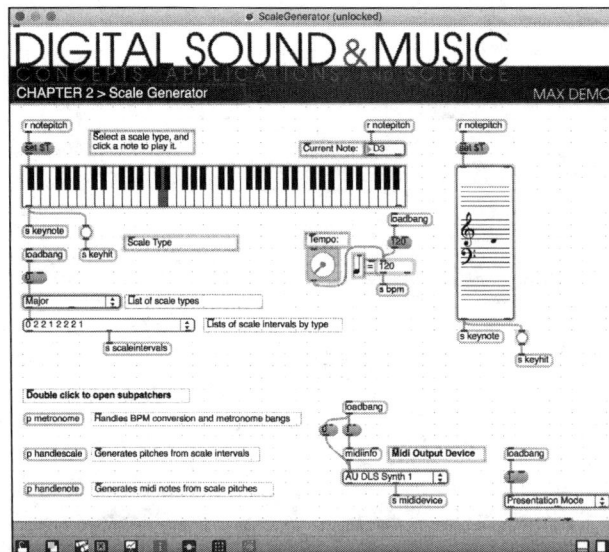

FIGURE 3.52: MAX PATCHER UNLOCKED, ACCESSIBLE TO THE PROGRAMMER

With all the patcher objects exposed and the main patcher unlocked, you can now see how the program is initialized and how the user is able to trigger the sending and receiving of messages by selecting from a menu, turning the dial to set a tempo, and clicking the mouse on the keyboard display. Here's how the program runs:

> The *loadbang* object is triggered when the program begins. It is used to initialize the tempo to 120 bpm and to set the default MIDI output device. Both of these can be changed by the user.

> The user can select a type of scale from a menu. The list of intervals is set accordingly and sent in the variable *scaleintervals*, to be received by the *handlescale* patcher object.

> The user can select a tempo through the *dial* object. The input value is sent to the *metronome* patcher object to determine the timing of the notes played in the scale.

> The user can click a key on the *keyboard* object. This initiates the playing of a scale by sending a *keyhit* message to both the *metronome* and the *handlescale* patcher.

> When the *metronome* patcher receives the *keyhit* message, it begins sending a tick every *n* milliseconds. The value of *n* is calculated based on the *bpm* value. Each tick of the metronome is what Max calls a *bang* message, which is used to trigger buttons and set actions in motion. In this case, the *bang* sets off a counter in the *handlescale* patcher, which counts out the correct number of notes as it plays a scale. The number of notes to play for a given type of scale is determined by a lookup list in the *zl* object, a multipurpose list processing object.

> The pitch of the note is initially determined by the clicked *keyboard* key value, and then is subsequently calculated by accumulating each of the provided interval offsets from the *scaleintervals* list. As the correct *notepitch* is set for each successive note, it is sent to the *handlenote* patcher, which makes a MIDI message from this information and outputs the MIDI note. To understand this part of the patcher completely, you need to know a little bit about MIDI messages, which we don't cover in detail until Chapter 6. It suffices for now to understand that middle C is sent as a number message with the value 60. Thus, a C major scale starting on middle C is created from the MIDI notes 60, 62, 64, 65, 67, 69, 71, and 72.

Max has many types of built-in objects with specialized functions. We've given you a quick overview of some of them in this example. However, as a beginning Max programmer, you can't always tell from looking at an object in programming mode just what type of object it is and how it functions. To determine the types of objects and look more closely at the implementation, you need to unlock the patcher, as shown in Figure 3.52. Then if you select an object and right click on it, you get a menu that tells the type of object at the top. In the example in Figure 3.53, the object is a *kslider*. From the context menu, you can choose to see the Help or an Inspector associated with the object. To see the full array of Max built-in objects, go to Max Help from the main Help menu, and from there to Object by Function.

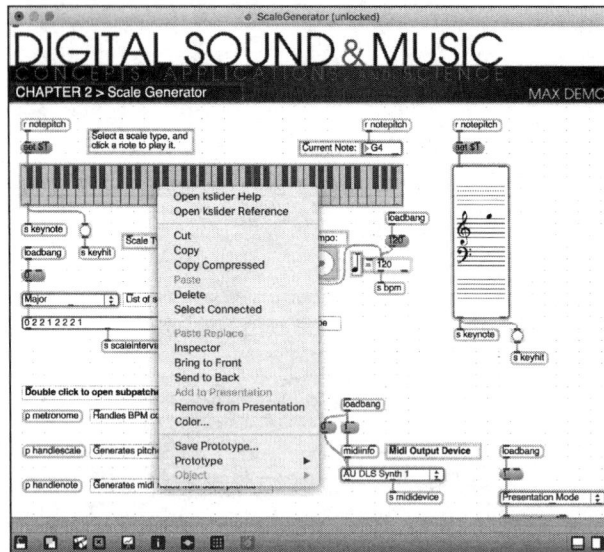

FIGURE 3.53: CONTEXT MENU FOR A KSLIDER OBJECT

3.3.3 EXPERIMENTING WITH MUSIC IN MATLAB

Chapter 2 introduces some command line arguments for evaluating sine waves, playing sounds, and plotting graphs in MATLAB. For this chapter, you may find it more convenient to write functions in an external program. Files that contain code in the MATLAB language are called M-files, ending in the .m suffix. Here's how you proceed when working with M-files:

> Create an M-file using MATLAB's built-in text editor (or any text editor).
> Write a function in the M-file.
> Name the M-file *fun1.m* where *fun1* is the name of the function in the file.
> Place the M-file in your current MATLAB directory.
> Call the function from the command line, giving input arguments as appropriate and accepting the output by assigning it to a variable if necessary.

> **MATLAB EXERCISE:**
> Chords in MATLAB
> http://bit.ly/29gfvkN

The M-file can contain internal functions that are called from the main function. We refer you to MATLAB's Help for details of syntax and program structure, but offer the program in Algorithm 3.1 to get you started. This program allows the user to create major and minor scales beginning with a start note. The start note is represented as a number of semitones offset from middle C. The function plays eight seconds of sound at a sampling rate of 44,100 samples per second and returns the raw data to the user, where it can be assigned to a variable on the command line if desired.

```
function outarray = MakeScale(startnoteoffset, isminor)
%outarray is an array of sound samples on the scale of (-1,1)
%outarray contains the 8 notes of a diatonic musical scale
%each note is played for one second
%the sampling rate is 44100 samples/s
%startnoteoffset is the number of semitones up or down from middle C at
%which the scale should start.
%If isminor == 0, a major scale is played; otherwise a minor scale is played.
sr = 44100;
s = 8;
outarray = zeros(1,sr*s);
majors=[0 2 4 5 7 9 11 12];
minors=[0 2 3 5 7 8 10 12];
if(isminor == 0)
    scale = majors;
else
    scale = minors;
end
scale = scale/12;
scale = 2.^scale;
%.^ is element-by-element exponentiation
t = [1:sr]/sr;
%the statement above is equivalent to
startnote = 220*(2^((startnoteoffset+3)/12))
scale = startnote * scale;
%Yes, ^ is exponentiation in MATLAB, rather than bitwise XOR as in C++
for i = 1:8
    outarray(1+(i-1)*sr:sr*i) = sin((2*pi*scale(i))*t);
end
 sound(outarray,sr);
```

ALGORITHM 3.1: GENERATING SCALES

The variables *majors* and *minors* hold arrays of integers, which can be created in MATLAB by placing the integers between square brackets with no commas separating them. This is useful for defining, for each note in a diatonic scale, the number of semitones that the note is away from the key note.

The variable *scale* is also an array, the same length as *majors* and *minors* (eight elements, because eight notes are played for the diatonic scale). Say that a major scale is to be created. Each element in the scale is set to $2^{majors[i]/12}$, where *majors*[*i*] is the original value of element *i* in the array *majors*. (Note that arrays are

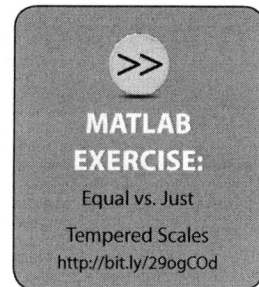

>>

MATLAB EXERCISE:

Equal vs. Just

Tempered Scales
http://bit.ly/29ogCOd

numbered beginning at 1 in MATLAB.) This sets the *scale* equal to $[1, 2^{2/12}, 2^{4/12}, 2^{5/12},$ $2^{7/12}, 2^{9/12}, 2^{11/12}, 2]$. When the start note is multiplied by each of these numbers, one at a time, the frequencies of the notes in a scale are produced.

The line

```
x = [1:sr]/sr;
```

creates an array of 44,100 points between 0 and 1, at which the sine function is evaluated. (This is essentially equivalent to $x = linspace(0, 1, sr)$, which we used in previous examples.)

A3, with a frequency of 220 Hz, is used as a reference point from which all other frequencies are built. Thus

```
startnote = 220*(2^((startnoteoffset+3)/12));
```

sets the start note to be middle C plus the user-defined offset.

In the *for* loop that repeats for eight seconds, the statement

```
outarray(1+(i-1)*sr:sr*i) = sin((2*pi*scale(i))*t);
```

writes the sound data into the appropriate section of *outarray*. It generates these samples by evaluating a sine function of the appropriate frequency across the 44,100-element array *x*. This statement is an example of how conveniently MATLAB handles array operations. A single call to a sine function can be used to evaluate the function over an entire array of values. The statement

```
scale = scale/12;
```

works similarly, dividing each element in the array *scale* by 12. The statement

```
scale = 2.^scale;
```

is also an element-by-element array operation, but in this case a dot has to be added to the exponentiation operator since ^ alone is matrix exponentiation, which can have only an integer exponent.

3.3.4   EXPERIMENTING WITH MUSIC IN C++

Algorithm 3.2 below is a C++ program analogous to the MATLAB program for generating scales. It uses the same functions for writing to the sound device as used in

{}

C++ PROGRAMMING EXERCISE:

Chords in C++
http://bit.ly/29gjUo4

{}

C++ PROGRAMMING EXERCISE:

Playing with Music
http://bit.ly/29gky4S

{}

C++ PROGRAMMING EXERCISE:

Equal vs. Just
Tempered Scales in C++
http://bit.ly/29wrHwa

the last section of Chapter 2. You can try your hand at a similar program by doing one of the suggested programming exercises. The first exercise has you generate (or recognize) chords of seven types in different keys. The second exercise has you generate equal tempered and just tempered scales and listen to the result to see if your ears can detect the small differences in frequencies. Both of these programs can be done in either MATLAB or C++.

```cpp
//This program works under the OSS library
#include <sys/ioctl.h> //for ioctl()
#include <math.h> //sin(), floor()
#include <stdio.h> //perror
#include <fcntl.h> //open, O_WRONLY
#include <linux/soundcard.h> //SOUND_PCM*
#include <iostream>
#include <stdlib.h>
using namespace std;
#define LENGTH 1 //number of seconds
#define RATE 44100 //sampling rate
#define SIZE sizeof(short) //size of sample, in bytes
#define CHANNELS 1 // number of stereo channels
#define PI 3.14159
#define SAMPLE_MAX 32767 // should this end in 8?
#define MIDDLE_C 262
#define SEMITONE 1.05946
enum types {BACK = 0, MAJOR, MINOR};
double getFreq(int index){
    return MIDDLE_C * pow(SEMITONE, index-1);
}
int getInput(){
    char c;
    string str;
    int i;
    while ((c = getchar()) != '\n' && c != EOF)
        str += c;
    for (i = 0; i < str.length(); ++i)
        str.at(i) = tolower(str.at(i));
    if (c == EOF || str == "quit")
        exit(0);
    return atoi(str.c_str());
}
int getIndex()
{
    int input;
    cout
        << "Choose one of the following:\n"
        << "\t1) C\n"
        << "\t2) C sharp/D flat\n"
        << "\t3) D\n"
        << "\t4) D sharp/E flat\n"
        << "\t5) E\n"
        << "\t6) F\n"
```

```
            << "\t7) F sharp/G flat\n"
            << "\t8) G\n"
            << "\t9) G sharp/A flat\n"
            << "\t10) A\n"
            << "\t11) A sharp/B flat\n"
            << "\t12) B\n"
            << "\tor type quit to quit\n";
    input = getInput();
    if (! (input >= BACK && input <= 12))
        return -1;
    return input;
}
void writeToSoundDevice(short buf[], int buffSize, int deviceID) {
    int status;
    status = write(deviceID, buf, buffSize);
    if (status != buffSize)
        perror("Wrote wrong number of bytes\n");
    status = ioctl(deviceID, SOUND_PCM_SYNC, 0);
    if (status == -1)
        perror("SOUND_PCM_SYNC failed\n");
}
int getScaleType(){
    int inp ut;
    cout
        << "Choose one of the following:\n"
        << "\t" << MAJOR << ") for major\n"
        << "\t" << MINOR << ") for minor\n"
        << "\t" << BACK << ") to back up\n"
        << "\tor type quit to quit\n";
    input = getInput();
    return input;
}
void playScale(int deviceID){
    int arraySize, note, steps, index, scaleType;
    int break1; // only one half step to here
    int break2; // only one half step to here
    int t, off;
    double f;
    short *buf;
    arraySize = 8 * LENGTH * RATE * CHANNELS;
    buf = new short[arraySize];
    while ((index = getIndex()) < 0)
        cout << "Input out of bounds. Please try again.\n";
    f = getFreq(index);
    while ((scaleType = getScaleType()) < 0)
        cout << "Input out of bounds. Please try again.\n";
    switch (scaleType) {
        case MAJOR :
            break1 = 3;
            break2 = 7;
            break;
        case MINOR :
            break1 = 2;
            break2 = 5;
```

```
                  break;
              case BACK :
                  return;
              default :
                  playScale(deviceID);
      }
      arraySize = LENGTH * RATE * CHANNELS;
      for (note = off = 0; note < 8; ++note, off += t) {
          if (note == 0)
              steps = 0;
          else if (note == break1 || note == break2)
              steps = 1;
          else steps = 2;
          f *= pow(SEMITONE, steps);
          for (t = 0; t < arraySize; ++t)
              buf[t + off] = floor(SAMPLE_MAX*sin(2*PI*f*t/RATE));
      }
      arraySize = 8 * LENGTH * RATE * SIZE * CHANNELS;
      writeToSoundDevice(buf, arraySize, deviceID);
      delete buf;
      return;
}
int main(){
    int deviceID, arg, status, index;
    deviceID = open("/dev/dsp", O_WRONLY, 0);
    if (deviceID < 0)
        perror("Opening /dev/dsp failed\n");
    arg = SIZE * 8;
    status = ioctl(deviceID, SOUND_PCM_WRITE_BITS, &arg);
    if (status == -1)
        perror("Unable to set sample size\n");
    arg = CHANNELS;
    status = ioctl(deviceID, SOUND_PCM_WRITE_CHANNELS, &arg);
    if (status == -1)
        perror("Unable to set number of channels\n");
    arg = RATE;
    status = ioctl(deviceID, SOUND_PCM_WRITE_RATE, &arg);
    if (status == -1)
        perror("Unable to set sampling rate\n");
    while (true)
            playScale(deviceID);
}
```

ALGORITHM 3.2: GENERATING SCALES IN C++

3.3.5   EXPERIMENTING WITH MUSIC IN JAVA

Let's try making chords in Java as we did in C++. We'll give you the code for this first exercise to get you started, and then you can try some exercises on your own. The Chords in Java program plays a chord selected from the list shown in Figure 3.54. The program contains two Java class files, one called Chord and the other called

ChordApp. The top-level class (i.e., the one that includes the *main* function) is the ChordApp class. The
ChordApp class is a subclass of the JPanel, which
is a generic window container. The JPanel provides
functionality to display a window as a user interface.
The constructor of the ChordApp class creates a list
of radio buttons and displays the window with these
options (Figure 3.54). When the user selects a type of
chord, the method *playChord()* is called through the
Chord class shown in Algorithm 3.4 (line 138).

The ChordApp class contains the method *play-
Chord* (line 7), which is a variation of the code shown
in the MATLAB section. In the *playChord* method,
the ChordApp object creates a Chord object, initial-
izing it with the array *scale*, which contains the list
of notes to be played in the chord. These notes are
summed in the Chord class in lines 46 to 48.

JAVA
PROGRAMMING
EXERCISE:
Chords in Java
http://bit.ly/29hbBoe

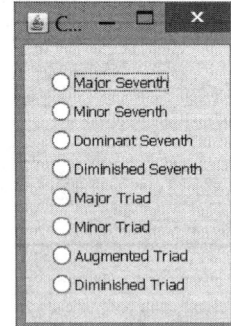

FIGURE 3.54: INTERFACE FOR
JAVA CHORD-PLAYING PROGRAM

```
1  import java.awt.*;
2  import java.awt.event.*;
3  import javax.swing.*;
4
5  public class ChordApp extends JPanel implements ActionListener {
6
7      public static void playChord(String command)
8      {/**Method that decides which Chord to play */
9          float[] major7th = {0, 4, 7, 11};
10         float[] minor7th = {0, 3, 7, 10};
11         float[] domin7th = {0, 4, 7, 10};
12         float[] dimin7th = {0, 3, 6, 10};
13         float[] majorTri = {0, 4, 7};
14         float[] minorTri = {0, 3, 7};
15         float[] augmeTri = {0, 4, 8};
16         float[] diminTri = {0, 3, 6};
17
18         float[] scale;
19
20         if      (command == "major7th")
21             scale = major7th;
22         else if (command == "minor7th")
23             scale = minor7th;
24         else if (command == "domin7th")
25             scale = domin7th;
26         else if (command == "dimin7th")
27             scale = dimin7th;
28         else if (command == "majorTri")
29             scale = majorTri;
```

```
30              else if (command == "minorTri")
31                  scale = minorTri;
32              else if (command == "augmeTri")
33                  scale = augmeTri;
34              else
35                  scale = diminTri;
36
37              float startnote = 220*(2^((2+3)/12));
38
39              for(int i=0;i<scale.length;i++){
40                  scale[i] = scale[i]/12;
41                  scale[i] = (float)Math.pow(2,scale[i]);
42                  scale[i] = startnote * scale[i];
43              }
44
45              //once we know which Chord to play, we call the Chord function
46              Chord chord = new Chord(scale);
47              chord.play();
48          }
49
50      public ChordApp() {
51              super(new BorderLayout());
52
53              try {
54      UIManager.setLookAndFeel(UIManager.getSystemLookAndFeelClassName());
55                  SwingUtilities.updateComponentTreeUI(this);
56              } catch (Exception e) {
57                  System.err.println(e);
58              }
59
60              JRadioButton maj7thButton = new JRadioButton("Major Seventh");
61              maj7thButton.setActionCommand("major7th");
62
63              JRadioButton min7thButton = new JRadioButton("Minor Seventh");
64              min7thButton.setActionCommand("minor7th");
65
66              JRadioButton dom7thButton = new JRadioButton("Dominant Seventh");
67              dom7thButton.setActionCommand("domin7th");
68
69          JRadioButton dim7thButton = new JRadioButton("Diminished Seventh");
70              dim7thButton.setActionCommand("dimin7th");
71
72              JRadioButton majTriButton = new JRadioButton("Major Triad");
73              majTriButton.setActionCommand("majorTri");
74
75              JRadioButton minTriButton = new JRadioButton("Minor Triad");
76              minTriButton.setActionCommand("minorTri");
77
78              JRadioButton augTriButton = new JRadioButton("Augmented Triad");
79              augTriButton.setActionCommand("augmeTri");
80
81          JRadioButton dimTriButton = new JRadioButton("Diminished Triad");
82              dimTriButton.setActionCommand("diminTri");
83
```

```
84              ButtonGroup group = new ButtonGroup();
85              group.add(maj7thButton);
86              group.add(min7thButton);
87              group.add(dom7thButton);
88              group.add(dim7thButton);
89              group.add(majTriButton);
90              group.add(minTriButton);
91              group.add(augTriButton);
92              group.add(dimTriButton);
93
94              maj7thButton.addActionListener(this);
95              min7thButton.addActionListener(this);
96              dom7thButton.addActionListener(this);
97              dim7thButton.addActionListener(this);
98              majTriButton.addActionListener(this);
99              minTriButton.addActionListener(this);
100             augTriButton.addActionListener(this);
101             dimTriButton.addActionListener(this);
102
103             JPanel radioPanel = new JPanel(new GridLayout(0, 1));
104             radioPanel.add(maj7thButton);
105             radioPanel.add(min7thButton);
106             radioPanel.add(dom7thButton);
107             radioPanel.add(dim7thButton);
108             radioPanel.add(majTriButton);
109             radioPanel.add(minTriButton);
110             radioPanel.add(augTriButton);
111             radioPanel.add(dimTriButton);
112
113             add(radioPanel, BorderLayout.LINE_START);
114             setBorder(BorderFactory.createEmptyBorder(20,20,20,20));
115         }
116
117     public static void main(String[] args) {
118         javax.swing.SwingUtilities.invokeLater(new Runnable() {
119             public void run() {
120                 ShowWindow();
121             }
122         });
123     }
124
125     private static void ShowWindow() {
126         JFrame frame = new JFrame("Chords App");
127         frame.setDefaultCloseOperation(JFrame.EXIT_ON_CLOSE);
128
129         JComponent newContentPane = new ChordApp();
130         newContentPane.setOpaque(true); //content panes must be opaque
131         frame.setContentPane(newContentPane);
132
133         frame.pack();
134         frame.setVisible(true);
135     }
136     /** Listens to the radio buttons. */
137     public void actionPerformed(ActionEvent e) {
```

```
138            ChordApp.playChord(e.getActionCommand());
139        }
140 }
```

ALGORITHM 3.3: CHORDAPP CLASS

```
1
2
3 import javax.sound.sampled.AudioFormat;
4 import javax.sound.sampled.AudioSystem;
5 import javax.sound.sampled.SourceDataLine;
6 import javax.sound.sampled.LineUnavailableException;
7
8 public class Chord {
9     float[] Scale;
10
11    public Chord(float[] scale) {
12        Scale=scale;
13    }
14
15    public void play() {
16        try {
17            makeChord(Scale);
18        } catch (LineUnavailableException lue) {
19            System.out.println(lue);
20        }
21    }
22
23    private void makeChord(float[] scale)
24    throws LineUnavailableException
25    {
26        int freq = 44100;
27        float[] x=new float[(int)(freq)];
28
29        byte[] buf;
30        AudioFormat audioF;
31
32        for(int i=0;i<x.length;i++){
33            x[i]=(float)(i+1)/freq;
34        }
35
36        buf = new byte[1];
37        audioF = new AudioFormat(freq,8,1,true,false);
38
39        SourceDataLine sourceDL = AudioSystem.getSourceDataLine(audioF);
40        sourceDL = AudioSystem.getSourceDataLine(audioF);
41        sourceDL.open(audioF);
42        sourceDL.start();
43
44        for (int j=0;j<x.length;j++){
45            buf[0]= 0;
46            for(int i=0;i<scale.length;i++){
47            buf[0]=(byte)(buf[0]+(Math.sin((2*Math.PI*scale[i])*x[j])*10.0))
48            }
```

```
49              sourceDL.write(buf,0,1);
50          }
51
52          sourceDL.drain();
53          sourceDL.stop();
54          sourceDL.close();
55      }
56  }
```

ALGORITHM 3.4: CHORD CLASS

As another exercise, you can try to play and compare equal vs. just tempered scales, the same program exercise from Section 3.3.5.

In the last exercise associated with this section, you're asked to create a metronome-type object that creates a beat sound according to the user's specifications for tempo. You may want to borrow something similar to the code in the ChordApp class to create the graphical user interface.

{}

JAVA PROGRAMMING EXERCISE:

Equal vs. Just Tempered Scales

in Java
http://bit.ly/29mbU1V

{}

JAVA PROGRAMMING EXERCISE:

Creating a Metronome

in Java
http://bit.ly/29kHY7C

3.4 REFERENCES

In addition to references listed in previous chapters:

Barzun, Jacques, ed. *Pleasures of Music: A Reader's Choice of Great Writing about Music and Musicians from Cellini to Bernard Shaw*. New York: Viking Press, 1951.

Hewitt, Michael. *Music Theory for Computer Musicians*. Boston: Course Technology, 2008.

Loy, Gareth. *Musimathics: The Mathematical Foundations of Music*. 2 vols. Cambridge, MA: The MIT Press, 2006–07.

Roads, Curtis, John Strawn, Curtis Abbott, John Gordon and Philip Greenspun. *The Computer Music Tutorial*. Cambridge, MA: The MIT Press, 1996.

Swafford, Jan. *The Vintage Guide to Classical Music*. New York: Vintage Books, 1992.

Wharram, Barbara. *Elementary Rudiments of Music*. Mississauga, Ontario: The Frederick Harris Music Company, 1969.

CHAPTER FOUR

Sound Perception and Acoustics

4.1 CONCEPTS

4.1.1 ACOUSTICS

The word **acoustics** has multiple definitions, all of them interrelated. In the most general sense, acoustics is the scientific study of sound, covering how sound is generated, transmitted, and received. Acoustics can also refer more specifically to the properties of a room that cause it to reflect, refract, and absorb sound. We can also use the term *acoustics* as the study of particular recordings or particular instances of sound and the analysis of their sonic characteristics. We'll touch on all these meanings in this chapter.

4.1.2 PSYCHOACOUSTICS

Human hearing is a wondrous creation that in some ways we understand very well, and in other ways we don't understand at all. We can look at anatomy of the human ear and analyze—down to the level of tiny little hairs in the basilar membrane—how vibrations are received and transmitted through the nervous system. But how this communication is translated by the brain into the subjective experience of sound and music remains a mystery. (See Levitin 2007.)

We'll probably never know how vibrations of air pressure are transformed into our marvelous experience of music and speech. Still, a great deal has been learned from an analysis of the interplay among physics, the human anatomy, and perception. This interplay is the realm of **psychoacoustics**, the scientific study of sound perception. Any number of sources can give you the details of the anatomy of the human ear and how it receives and processes sound waves. Pohlman (2005), Rossing, Moore, and Wheeler (2002), and Everest and Pohlmann (2009) are good sources, for example. In this chapter, we want to focus on the elements that shed light on best practices in recording, encoding, processing, compressing, and playing digital sound. Most important for our purposes is an examination of how humans subjectively perceive the frequencies, amplitude, and direction of sound. A concept that appears repeatedly in this context is the *non-linear* nature of human sound perception. Understanding this concept leads to a mathematical representation of sound that is modeled after the way we humans experience it, a representation well-suited for digital analysis and processing of sound, as we'll see in what follows. First, we need to be clear about the language we use in describing sound.

4.1.3   OBJECTIVE AND SUBJECTIVE MEASURES OF SOUND

In speaking of sound perception, it's important to distinguish between words which describe objective measurements and those that describe subjective experience. The terms *intensity* and *pressure* denote objective measurements that relate to our subjective experience of the *loudness* of sound. **Intensity**, as it relates to sound, is defined as the power carried by a sound wave per unit of area, expressed in watts per square meter (**W/m²**). **Power** is defined as energy per unit of time, measured in **watts (W)**. Power can also be defined as the rate at which work is performed or energy converted. Watts are used to measure the output of power amplifiers and the power handling levels of loudspeakers. **Pressure** is defined as force divided by the area over which it is distributed, measured in newtons per square meter (**N/m²**) or more simply, **pascals (Pa)**. In relation to sound, we speak specifically of **air pressure amplitude** and measure it in pascals. Air pressure amplitude caused by sound waves is measured as a displacement above or below equilibrium atmospheric pressure. During audio recording, a microphone measures this constantly changing air pressure amplitude and converts it to electrical units of **volts (V)**, sending the voltages to the sound card for analog-to-digital conversion. We'll see below how and why all these units are converted to decibels.

The objective measures of intensity and air pressure amplitude relate to our subjective experience of the loudness of sound. Generally, the greater the intensity or pressure created by the sound waves, the louder this sounds to us. However, loudness can be measured only by subjective experience—that is, by an individual saying how loud the sound *seems* to him or her. The relationship between air pressure amplitude and loudness is *not* linear. That is, you can't assume that if the pressure is doubled, the sound seems twice as loud. In fact, it takes about ten times the pressure for a sound to seem twice as loud. Further, our sensitivity to amplitude differences varies with frequencies, as we'll discuss in more detail in Section 4.1.6.3.

When we speak of the amplitude of a sound, we're speaking of the sound pressure displacement as compared to equilibratory atmospheric pressure. The range of the quietest to the loudest sounds in our comfortable hearing range is actually quite large. The loudest sounds are on the order of 20 Pa. The quietest are on the order of 20 μPa, which is 20×10^{-6} Pa. (These values vary by the frequencies that are heard.) Thus, the loudest has about 1,000,000 times more air pressure amplitude than the quietest.

Since intensity is proportional to the square of pressure, the loudest sound we listen to (at the verge of hearing damage) is $(10^6)^2 = 10^{12} = 1,000,000,000,000$ times more intense than the quietest. (Some sources even claim a factor of 10 trillion between loudest and quietest intensities. It depends on what you consider the threshold of pain and hearing damage.) This is a wide dynamic range for human hearing.

Another subjective perception of sound is **pitch**. As you learned in the previous chapters, the pitch of a note is how high or low the note seems to you. The related objective measure is **frequency**. In general, the higher the frequency, the higher the perceived pitch. But once again, the relationship between pitch and frequency is not linear, as you'll see below. Also, our sensitivity to frequency differences varies across the spectrum, and our perception of the pitch depends partly on how loud the sound is. A high pitch can seem to get higher when its loudness is increased, whereas a low pitch can seem to get lower. Context matters as well in that the pitch of a frequency may seem to shift when it is combined with other frequencies in a complex tone.

Let's look at these elements of sound perception more closely.

4.1.4   UNITS FOR MEASURING ELECTRICITY AND SOUND

In order to define decibels, which are used to measure sound loudness, we need to define some units that are used to measure electricity as well as acoustical power, intensity, and pressure.

Both analog and digital sound devices use electricity to represent and transmit sound. Electricity is the flow of electrons through wires and circuits. There are four interrelated components in electricity that are important to understand:

) potential energy (in electricity called *voltage* or *electrical pressure*, measured in volts, abbreviated V),

) intensity (in electricity called *current*, measured in amperes or amps, abbreviated A),

) resistance (measured in ohms, abbreviated Ω),

) power (measured in watts, abbreviated W).

Electricity can be understood through an analogy to the flow of water (borrowed from Thompson 2005). Picture two tanks connected by a pipe. One tank has water in it; the other is empty. Potential energy is created by the presence of water in the first tank. The water flows through the pipe from the first tank to the second with some intensity. The pipe has a certain amount of resistance to the flow of water as a result of its physical properties, like its size. The potential energy provided by the full tank, reduced somewhat by the resistance of the pipe, results in the power of the water flowing through the pipe.

By analogy, in an electrical circuit we have two voltages connected by a conductor. Analogous to the full tank of water, we have a voltage—an excess of electrons—at one end of the circuit. Let's say that at other end of the circuit we have 0 voltage, also called **ground** or **ground potential**. The voltage at the first end of the circuit causes pressure, or potential energy, as the excess electrons want to move toward ground. This flow of electricity is called the **current**. The physical connection between the two halves of the circuit provides resistance to the flow. The connection might be a copper wire, which offers little resistance and is thus called a good conductor. On the other hand, something could intentionally be inserted into the circuit to reduce the current—a resistor for example. The power in the circuit is determined by a combination of the voltage and the resistance.

The relationship among potential energy, intensity, resistance, and power are captured in Ohm's law, which states that intensity (or current) is equal to potential energy (or voltage) divided by resistance:

$$I = \frac{V}{R} \quad \textit{where I is intensity, V is potential energy, and R is resistance}$$

EQUATION 4.1: OHM'S LAW

Power is defined as intensity multiplied by potential energy.

$$P = IV$$

$$\textit{where P is power, I is intensity, and V is potential energy}$$

EQUATION 4.2: EQUATION FOR POWER

Combining the two equations above, we can represent power as follows:

$$P = \frac{V^2}{R} \quad \textit{where P is power, V is potential energy, and R is resistance}$$

EQUATION 4.3: EQUATION FOR POWER IN TERMS OF VOLTAGE AND RESISTANCE

Thus, if you know any two of these four values, you can get the other two from the equations above.

Volts, amps, ohms, and watts are convenient units to measure potential energy, current, resistance, and power in that they have the following relationship:

1 V across 1 Ω of resistance will generate 1 A of current and result in 1 W of power

The above discussion speaks of power (W), intensity (I), and potential energy (V) in the context of electricity. These words can also be used to describe acoustical power and intensity as well as the air pressure amplitude changes detected by microphones and translated to voltages. Power, intensity, and pressure are valid ways to measure sound as a physical phenomenon. However, decibels are more appropriate to represent the loudness of one sound relative to another, as well see in the next section.

4.1.5   DECIBELS

4.1.5.1 Why Decibels for Sound?

No doubt you're familiar with the use of decibels related to sound, but let's look more closely at the definition of decibels and why they are a good way to represent sound levels as perceived by human ears.

First consider Table 4.1. From column 3, you can see that the sound of a nearby jet engine has on the order of $10^7 = 10,000,000$ times greater air pressure amplitude than the threshold of hearing. That's quite a wide range. Imagine a graph of sound loudness that has perceived loudness on the horizontal axis and air pressure amplitude on the vertical axis. We would need numbers ranging from 0 to 10,000,000 on the vertical axis (Figure 4.1). This axis would have to be compressed to fit on a sheet of paper or a computer screen, and we wouldn't see much space between, say, 100 and 200. Thus, our ability to show small changes at low amplitude would not be great. Although we perceive a vacuum cleaner to be approximately twice as loud as normal conversation, we would hardly be able to see any difference between their respective air pressure amplitudes if we have to include such a wide range of numbers, spacing them evenly on what is called a *linear scale*. A linear scale turns out to be a very poor representation of human hearing. We humans can more easily distinguish the difference between two low amplitude sounds that are close in amplitude than we can distinguish between two high amplitude sounds that are close in amplitude. The linear scale for loudness doesn't provide sufficient resolution at low amplitudes to show changes that might actually be perceptible to the human ear.

Sound	Approximate air pressure amplitude in pascals	Ratio of air amplitude of sound to that of the threshold of hearing	Approximate loudness in dBSPL
1. Threshold of hearing	$0.00002 = 2 \times 10^{-5}$	1	0
2. Breathing	$0.00006325 = 6.325 \times 10^{-5}$	3.16	10
3. Rustling leaves	$0.0002 = 2 \times 10^{-4}$	10	20
4. Refrigerator humming	$0.002 = 2 \times 10^{-3}$	10^2	40
5. Normal conversation	$0.02 = 2 \times 10^{-2}$	10^3	60
6. Vacuum cleaner	$0.06325 = 6.325 \times 10^{-2}$	3.16×10^3	70
7. Dishwasher	$0.1125 = 1.125 \times 10^{-1}$	5.63×10^3	75
8. City traffic	$0.2 = 2 \times 10^{-1}$	10^4	80
9. Lawnmower	$0.3557 = 3.557 \times 10^{-1}$	1.78×10^4	85
10. Subway	$0.6325 = 6.325 \times 10^{-1}$	3.16×10^4	90
11. Symphony orchestra	6.325	3.16×10^5	110
12. Fireworks	$20 = 2 \times 10^1$	10^6	120
13. Rock concert	$20+ = 2 \times 10^1+$	10^6+	120+
14. Shotgun firing	$63.25 = 6.325 \times 10^1$	3.16×10^6	130
15. Jet engine close by	$200 = 2 \times 10^2$	2×10^7	140

TABLE 4.1: LOUDNESS OF COMMON SOUNDS MEASURED IN AIR PRESSURE AMPLITUDE AND IN DECIBELS

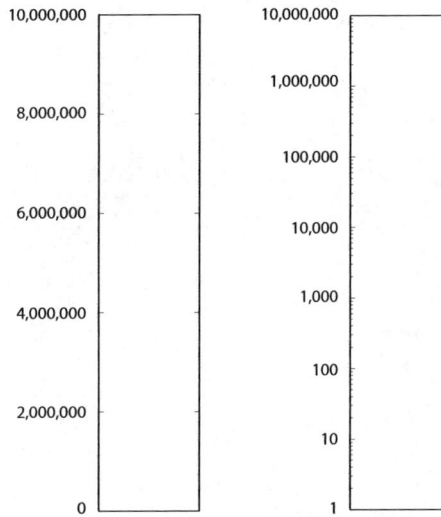

FIGURE 4.1: LINEAR VERSUS LOGARITHMIC SCALE

Now let's see how these observations begin to help us make sense of the decibel. A decibel is based on a ratio—that is, one value relative to another, as in X_1/X_0. Hypothetically, X_0 and X_1 could measure anything, as long as they measure the same type of thing in the same units—e.g., power, intensity, air pressure amplitude, noise on a computer network, loudspeaker efficiency, signal-to-noise ratio, etc. Because decibels are based on a ratio, they imply a comparison. Decibels can be a measure of

⟩ a change from level X_0 to level X_1
⟩ a range of values between X_0 and X_1
⟩ a level X_1 compared to some agreed upon reference point X_0.

What we're most interested in with regard to sound is some way of indicating how loud it seems to human ears. What if we were to measure relative loudness using the threshold of hearing as our point of comparison—the X_0, in the ratio X_1/X_0, as in column 3 of Table 4.1? That seems to make sense. But we already noted that the ratio of the loudest to the softest thing in our table is 10,000,000/1. A ratio alone isn't enough to turn the range of human hearing into manageable numbers, nor does it account for the non-linearity of our perception.

The discussion above is given to explain why it makes sense to use the *logarithm of the ratio of X_1/X_0* to express the loudness of sounds, as shown in Equation 4.4. Using the logarithm of the ratio, we don't have to use such widely-ranging numbers to represent sound amplitudes, and we "stretch out" the distance between the values corresponding to low amplitude sounds, providing better resolution in this area.

The values in column 4 of Table 4.1, measuring sound loudness in decibels, come from the following equation for **decibels-sound-pressure-level**, abbreviated **dBSPL**.

$$dBSPL = \Delta Voltage\ dB = 20 \log_{10} \left(\frac{V_1}{V_0} \right)$$

EQUATION 4.4: DEFINITION OF dBSPL, ALSO CALLED ΔVoltage dB

In this definition, V_0 is the air pressure amplitude at the threshold of hearing, and V_1 is the air pressure amplitude of the sound being measured.

Notice that in Equation 4.4, we use Δ *Voltage dB* as synonymous with dBSPL. This is because microphones measure sound as air pressure amplitudes, turn the measurements into voltage levels, and convey the voltage values to an audio interface for digitization. Thus, voltages are just another way of capturing air pressure amplitude.

Notice also that because the dimensions are the same in the numerator and denominator of V_1/V_0, the dimensions cancel in the ratio. This is always true for decibels. Because they are derived from a ratio, decibels are **dimensionless units**. Decibels aren't volts or watts or pascals or newtons; they're just the logarithm of a ratio.

Hypothetically, the decibel can be used to measure anything, but it's most appropriate for physical phenomena that have a wide range of levels where the values grow exponentially relative to our perception of them. Power, intensity, and air pressure amplitude are three physical phenomena related to sound that can be measured with decibels. The important thing in any usage of the term *decibels* is that you know the reference point—the level that is in the denominator of the ratio. Different usages of the term decibel sometimes add different letters to the dB abbreviation to clarify the context, as in dBPWL (decibels power level), dBSIL (decibels sound intensity level), and dBFS (decibels full scale), all of which are explained below.

Comparing the columns in Table 4.1, we now can see the advantages of decibels over air pressure amplitudes. If we had to graph loudness using Pa as our units, the scale would be so large that the first ten sound levels (from silence all the way up to subways) would not be distinguishable from 0 on the graph. With decibels, loudness levels that are easily distinguishable by the ear can be seen as such on the decibel scale.

Decibels are also more intuitively understandable than air pressure amplitudes as a way of talking about loudness changes. As you work with sound amplitudes measured in decibels, you'll become familiar with some easy-to-remember relationships summarized in Table 4.2. In an acoustically-insulated lab environment with virtually no background noise, a 1-dB change yields the smallest perceptible difference in loudness. However, in average real-world listening conditions, most people can't notice a loudness change less than 3 dB. A 10-dB change results in about a doubling of perceived loudness. It doesn't matter if you're going from 60 to 70 dBSPL or from 80 to 90 dBSPL. The increase still sounds approximately like a doubling of loudness. In contrast, going from 60 to 70 dBSPL is an increase of 43.24 mPa, while going from 80 to 90 dBSPL is an increase of 432.5 mPa. Here you can see that saying that you "turned up the volume" by a certain air pressure amplitude wouldn't give much information about how much louder it's going to sound. Talking about loudness changes in terms of decibels communicates more.

Change of sound amplitude	How it is perceived in human hearing
1 dB	Smallest perceptible difference in loudness, only perceptible in acoustically-insulated noiseless environments
3 dB	Smallest perceptible change in loudness for most people in real-world environments
+10 dB	An approximate doubling of loudness
–10 dB	An approximate halving of loudness

TABLE 4.2: HOW SOUND LEVEL CHANGES IN DB ARE PERCEIVED

You may have noticed that when we talk about a "decibel change," we refer to it as simply decibels or dB, whereas if we are referring to a sound loudness level relative to the threshold of hearing, we refer to it as dBSPL. This is correct usage. The difference between 90 and 80 dBSPL is 10 dB. The difference between any two decibel levels that have the same reference point is always measured in dimensionless dB. We'll return to this in a moment when we try some practice problems in Section 2.

4.1.5.2 Various Usages of Decibels

Now let's look at the origin of the definition of *decibel* and how the word can be used in a variety of contexts.

The **bel**, named for Alexander Graham Bell, was originally defined as a unit for measuring power. For clarity, we'll call this the **power difference bel**, also denoted *ΔPower B*:

$$1 \ power \ difference \ bel = \Delta Power \ B = \log_{10}\left(\frac{P_1}{P_0}\right)$$

EQUATION 4.5: ΔPower B, power difference bel

The decibel is 1/10 of a bel. The decibel turns out to be a more useful unit than the bel because it provides better resolution. A bel doesn't break measurements into small enough units for most purposes.

We can derive the **power difference decibel** (Δ***Power dB***) from the power difference bel simply by multiplying the log by 10. Another name for Δ*Power dB* is **dBPWL** (decibels power level).

$$\Delta Power\ dB = dBPWL = 10\log_{10}\left(\frac{P_1}{P_0}\right)$$

EQUATION 4.6: ΔPower dB, ABBREVIATED dBPWL

When this definition is applied to give a sense of the acoustic power of a sound, then P_0 is the power of sound at the threshold of hearing, which is $10^{-12}\,\text{W} = 1\,\text{pW}$ (picowatt).

Sound can also be measured in terms of intensity. Since intensity is defined as power per unit area, the units in the numerator and denominator of the decibel ratio are W/m^2, and the threshold of hearing intensity is $10^{-12}\ \text{W/m}^2$. This gives us the following definition of Δ***Intensity dB***, also commonly referred to as **dBSIL** (decibels-sound intensity level).

$$\Delta Intensity\ dB = dBSIL = 10\log_{10}\left(\frac{I_1}{I_0}\right)$$

EQUATION 4.7: ΔIntensity dB, ABBREVIATED dBSIL

Neither power nor intensity is a convenient way of measuring the loudness of sound. We give the definitions above primarily because they help to show how the definition of dBSPL was derived historically. The easiest way to measure sound loudness is by means of air pressure amplitude. When sound is transmitted, air pressure changes are detected by a microphone and converted to voltages. If we consider the relationship between voltage and power, we can see how the definition of Δ*Voltage dB* was derived from the definition of Δ*Power dB*. By Equation 4.3, we know that power varies with the square of voltage. From this we get

$$10\log_{10}\left(\frac{P_1}{P_0}\right) = 10\log_{10}\left(\left(\frac{V_1}{V_0}\right)^2\right) = 20\log_{10}\left(\frac{V_1}{V_0}\right)$$

The relationship between power and voltage explains why there is a factor of 20 is in Equation 4.4.

We can show how Equation 4.4 is applied to convert from air pressure amplitude to dBSPL and vice versa. Let's say we begin with the air pressure amplitude of a humming refrigerator, which is about 0.002 Pa.

ASIDE: $\log_b(y^x) = x\log_b y$

$$dBSPL = 20 \log_{10} \left(\frac{0.002\, Pa}{0.00002\, Pa} \right) = 20 \log_{10} (100) = 20 \times 2 = 40\, dBSPL$$

Working in the opposite direction, you can convert the decibel level of normal conversation (60 dBSPL) to air pressure amplitude:

$$60 = 20 \log_{10} \left(\frac{x}{0.00002\, Pa} \right) = 20 \log_{10} \left(\frac{50000x}{Pa} \right)$$

$$\frac{60}{20} = \log_{10} \left(\frac{50000x}{Pa} \right)$$

$$3 = \log_{10} \left(\frac{50000x}{Pa} \right)$$

$$10^3 = \frac{50000x}{Pa}$$

$$x = \frac{1000}{50000}\, Pa$$

$$x = 0.02\, Pa$$

Thus, 60 dBSPL corresponds to air pressure amplitude of 0.02 Pa.

Rarely would you be called upon to do these conversions yourself. You'll almost always work with sound intensity as decibels. But now you know the mathematics on which the dBSPL definition is based.

ASIDE: If $x = \log_b y$, then $b_x = y$

So when would you use these different ap-plications of decibels? Most commonly you use dBSPL to indicate how loud things seem relative to the threshold of hearing. In fact, you use this type of decibel so com-monly that the SPL is often dropped off and simply dB is used where the context is clear. You learn that human speech is about 60 dB, rock music is about 110 dB, and the loudest thing you can listen to without hearing damage is about 120 dB—all of these measurements implicitly being dBSPL.

The definition of intensity decibels, dBSIL, is mostly of interest to help us under-stand how the definition of dBSPL can be derived from dBPWL. We'll also use the definition of intensity decibels in an explanation of the inverse square law, a rule of thumb that helps us predict how sound loudness decreases as sound travels through space in a free field (Section 4.2.1.6).

There's another commonly used type of decibel that you'll encounter in digital au-dio software environments—the **decibels full scale (dBFS)**. You may not understand this type of decibel completely until you've read Chapter 5 because it's based on how audio signals are digitized at a certain bit depth (the number of bits used for each audio sample). We'll give the definition here for completeness and revisit it in Chapter 5. The definition of dBFS uses the largest-magnitude sample size for a given bit depth as its reference point. For a bit depth of n, this largest magnitude would be 2^{n-1}.

$$dBFS = 20 \log_{10} \left(\frac{|x|}{2^{n-1}} \right)$$

where n is a given bit depth and x is an integer sample value

between -2^{n-1} and $2^{n-1} - 1$

EQUATION 4.8: DECIBELS FULL SCALE, ABBREVIATED dBFS

Figure 4.2 shows an audio processing environment where a sound wave is measured in dBFS. Notice that since $|x|$ is never more than 2^{n-1}, $\log_{10}(|x|/ 2^{n-1})$ is never a positive number. When you first use dBFS it may seem strange because all sound levels are at most 0. With dBFS, 0 represents maximum amplitude for the system, and values move toward $-\infty$ as you move toward the horizontal axis (i.e., toward quieter sounds).

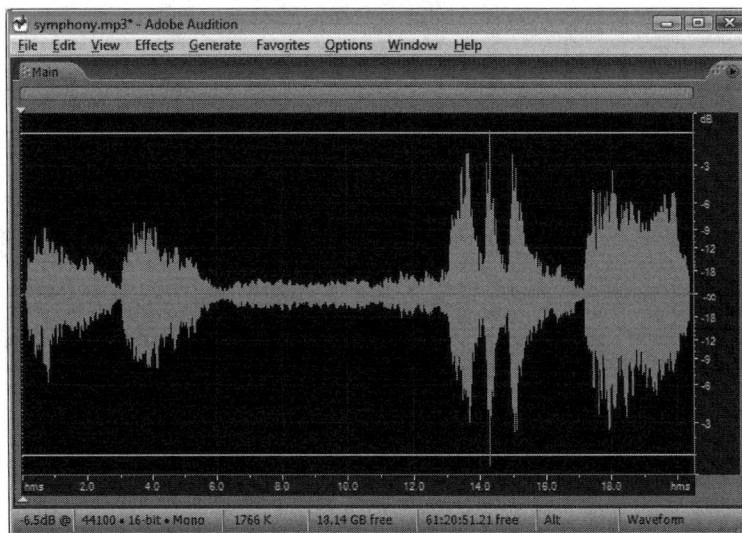

FIGURE 4.2: SOUND AMPLITUDE MEASURED IN DBFS

The discussion above has considered decibels primarily as they measure sound loudness. Decibels can also be used to measure relative electrical power or voltage. For example, dBV measures voltage using 1 V as a reference level, dBu measures voltage using 0.775 V as a reference level, and dBm measures power using 0.001 W as a reference level. These applications come into play when you're considering loudspeaker or amplifier power or wireless transmission signals. In Section 4.2, we'll give you some practical applications and problems where these different types of decibels come into play.

The reference levels for different types of decibels are listed in Table 4.3. Notice that decibels are used in reference to the power of loudspeakers or the input voltage to audio devices. We'll look at these applications more closely in Section 4.2. Of course, there are many other common usages of decibels outside of the realm of sound.

What is being measured	Abbreviations in common usage	Common reference point	Equation for conversion to decibels
Acoustical			
Sound power	dBPWL or $\Delta Power$ dB	$P_0 = 10^{-12}\,W$ $= 1\,pW$ (picowatt)	$10\log_{10}(P_1/P_0)$
Sound intensity	dBSIL or $\Delta Intensity\ dB$	threshold of hearing, $I_0 = 10^{-12}\,W/m^2$	$10\log_{10}(I_1/I_0)$
Sound air pressure amplitude	dBSPL or $\Delta Voltage$ dB	threshold of hearing, $P_0 = 0.00002\,N/m^2$ $= 2 \times 10^{-5}\,Pa$	$20\log_{10}(V_1/V_0)$
Sound amplitude	dBFS	2^{n-1} where n is a given bit depth x is a sample value, $-2^{n-1} \le x \le 2^{n-1} - 1$	dBFS $= 20\log_{10}$ $(|x|/2^{n-1})$
Electrical			
Radio frequency transmission power	dBm	$P_0 = 1\,mW = 10^{-3}\,W$	$10\log_{10}(P_1/P_0)$
Loudspeaker acoustical power	dBW	$P_0 = 1\,W$	$10\log_{10}(P_1/P_0)$

Input voltage from micro-phone, loudspeaker voltage, consumer-level audio voltage	dBV	$V_0 = 1\,\text{V}$	$20\log_{10}\,(V_1/V_0)$
Professional-level audio voltage	dBu	$V_0 = 0.775\,\text{V}$	$20\log_{10}\,(V_1/V_0)$

TABLE 4.3: USAGES OF THE TERM DECIBELS WITH DIFFERENT REFERENCE POINTS

4.1.5.3 Peak Amplitude vs. RMS Amplitude

Microphones and sound level meters measure the amplitude of sound waves over time. There are situations in which you may want to know the largest amplitude over a time period. This "largest" can be measured in one of two ways: as peak amplitude or as RMS amplitude.

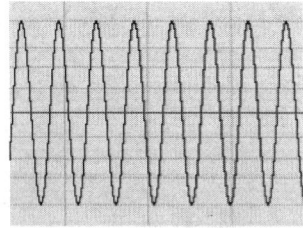

FIGURE 4.3: SINE WAVE REPRESENTING SOUND

Let's assume that the microphone or sound level meter is measuring sound amplitude. The sound pressure level of greatest magnitude over a given time period is called the peak amplitude. For a single-frequency sound representable by a sine wave, this would be the level at the peak of the sine wave. The sound represented by Figure 4.4 would obviously be perceived as louder than the same-frequency sound represented by Figure 4.3. However, how would the loudness of a sine-wave-shaped sound compare to the loudness of a square-wave-shaped sound with the same peak amplitude (Figure 4.3 versus Figure 4.5)? The square wave would actually sound louder. This is because the square wave is at its peak level more of the time as compared to the sine wave. To account for this difference in perceived loudness, RMS amplitude (root-mean-square amplitude) can be used as an

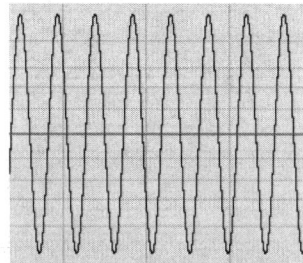

FIGURE 4.4: SINE WAVE REPRESENTING A HIGHER AMPLITUDE SOUND

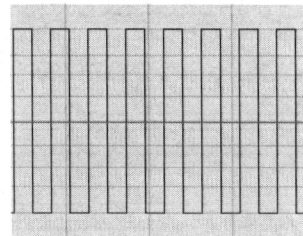

FIGURE 4.5: SQUARE WAVE REPRESENTING SOUND

alternative to peak amplitude, providing a better match for the way we perceive the loudness of the sound.

Rather than being an instantaneous peak level, RMS amplitude is similar to a standard deviation, a kind of average of the deviation from 0 over time. RMS amplitude is defined as follows:

$$V_{RMS} = \sqrt{\frac{\sum_{i=1}^{n}(S_i)^2}{n}}$$

where n is the number of samples taken and S_i is the ith sample

EQUATION 4.9: EQUATION FOR RMS AMPLITUDE, V$_{RMS}$

Notice that squaring each sample makes all the values in the summation positive. If this were not the case, the summation would be 0 (assuming an equal number of positive and negative crests) since the sine wave is perfectly symmetrical.

The definition in Equation 4.9 could be applied using whatever units are appropriate for the context. If the samples are being measured as voltages, then RMS amplitude is also called RMS voltage. The samples could also be quantized as values in the range determined by the bit depth, or the samples could also be measured in dimensionless decibels, as shown for Adobe Audition in Figure 4.6.

ASIDE: In some sources, the term RMS power is used interchangeably with RMS amplitude or RMS voltage. This isn't very good usage. To be consistent with the definition of power, RMS power ought to mean "RMS voltage multiplied by RMS current." Nevertheless, you sometimes see the term **RMS power** used as a synonym of RMS amplitude as defined in Equation 4.9.

For a pure sine wave, there is a simple relationship between RMS amplitude and peak amplitude.

$$\text{for pure sine waves}$$
$$V_{RMS} = \frac{V_{peak}}{\sqrt{2}} = 0.707 \times V_{peak}$$
$$\text{and}$$
$$V_{peak} = 1.414 \times V_{RMS}$$

EQUATION 4.10: RELATIONSHIP BETWEEN V_RMS AND V_PEAK FOR PURE SINE WAVES

Of course most of the sounds we hear are not simple waveforms like those shown; natural and musical sounds contain many frequency components that vary over time.

In any case, the RMS amplitude is a better model for our perception of the loudness of complex sounds than is peak amplitude.

Sound processing programs often give amplitude statistics as either peak or RMS amplitude or both. Notice that RMS amplitude has to be defined over a particular window of samples, labeled as Window Width in Figure 4.6. This is because the sound wave changes over time. In the figure, the window width is 1000 milliseconds (ms).

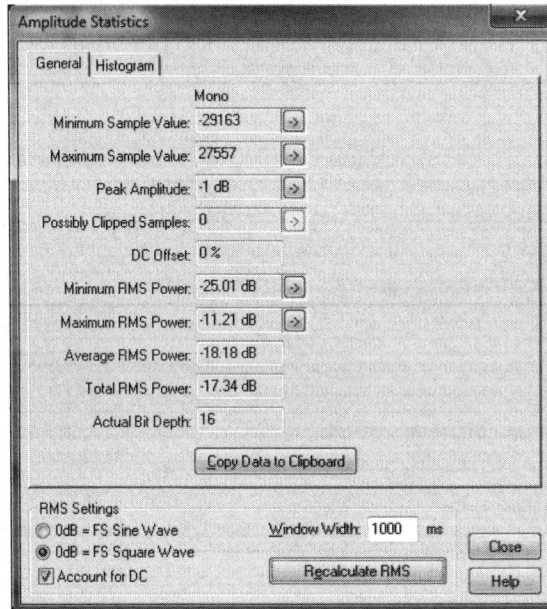

FIGURE 4.6: AMPLITUDE STATISTICS WINDOW FROM ADOBE AUDITION

You need to be careful with some usages of the term *peak amplitude*. For example, VU meters, which measure signal levels in audio equipment, use the word *peak* in their displays, where RMS amplitude would be more accurate. Knowing this is important when you're setting levels for a live performance, as the actual peak amplitude is higher than RMS. Transients like sudden percussive noises should be kept well below what is marked as "peak" on a VU meter. If you allow the level to go too high, the signal will be clipped.

4.1.6   SOUND PERCEPTION

4.1.6.1 Frequency Perception

In Chapter 3, we discussed the non-linear nature of pitch perception when we looked at octaves as defined in traditional Western music. The A above middle C (call it A4) on a piano keyboard sounds very much like the note that is 12 semitones above it, A5, except that A5 has a higher pitch. A5 is one octave higher than A4. A6 sounds like A5 and A4, but it's an octave higher than A5. The progression between octaves is not linear with respect to frequency. The frequency of A2 is twice the frequency of A1. The frequency of A3 is twice the frequency of A2, and so forth. A simple way to think of this is that as the frequencies increase by multiplication, the perception of the pitch change increases by addition. In any case, the relationship is non-linear, as you can clearly see if you plot frequencies against octaves, as shown in Figure 4.7.

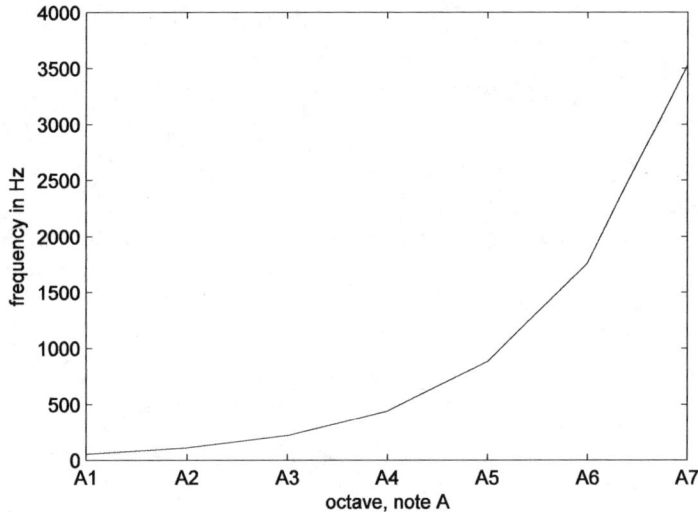

FIGURE 4.7: NON-LINEAR NATURE OF PITCH PERCEPTION

The fact that this is a non-linear relationship implies that the higher up you go in frequencies, the bigger the difference in frequency between neighboring octaves. The difference between A2 and A1 is 110 – 55 = 55 Hz, while the difference between A7 and A6 is 3520 – 1760 = 1760 Hz. Because of the non-linearity of our perception, frequency response graphs often show the frequency axis on a logarithmic scale, or you're given a choice between a linear and a logarithmic scale, as shown in Figure 4.8. Notice that you can select or deselect "linear" in the upper left-hand corner. In the figure on the right, the distance between 10 and 100 Hz on the horizontal axis is the same as the distance between 100 and 1000, which is the same as 1000 and 10,000. This is more in keeping with how our perception of the pitch changes as the frequencies get higher. You should always pay attention to the scale of the frequency axis in graphs such as this.

linear frequency response

logorithmic frequency response

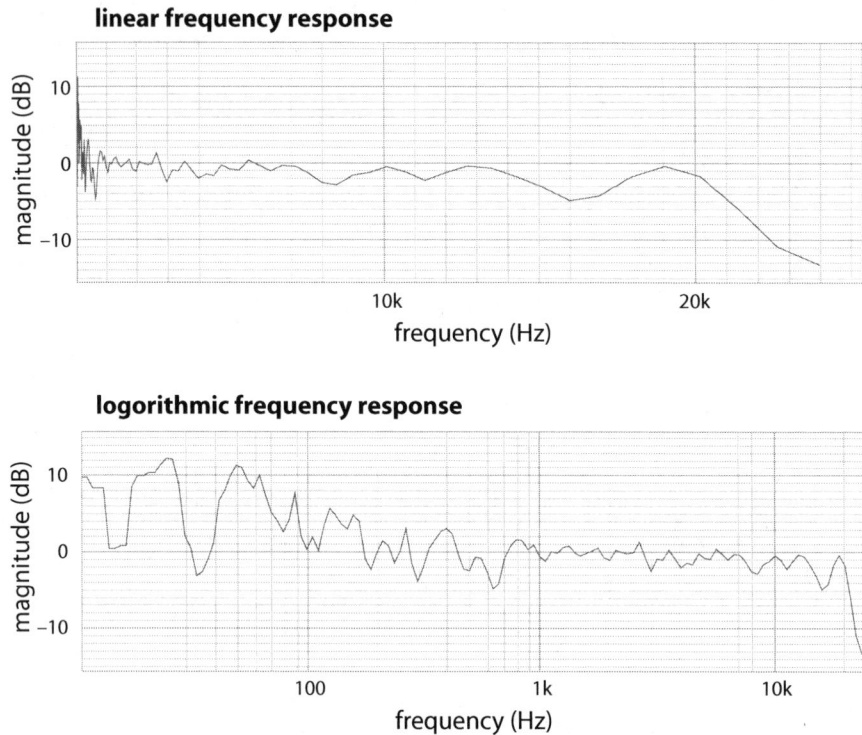

FIGURE 4.8: FREQUENCY RESPONSE GRAPHS WITH LINEAR AND NONLINEAR SCALES FOR FREQUENCY

The range of frequencies within human hearing is, at best, 20 Hz to 20,000 Hz. The range varies with individuals and diminishes with age, especially for high frequencies. Our hearing is less sensitive to low frequencies than to high; that is, low frequencies have to be more intense for us to hear them than high frequencies.

Frequency resolution (also called frequency discrimination) is our ability to distinguish between two close frequencies. Frequency resolution varies by frequency, loudness, the duration of the sound, the suddenness of the frequency change, and the acuity and training of the listener's ears. The smallest frequency change that can be noticed as a pitch change is referred to as a just-noticeable difference (JND). At low frequencies, it's possible to notice a difference between frequencies that are separated by just a few Hertz. Within the 1000 Hz to 4000 Hz range, it's possible for a person to hear a JND of as little as 1/12 of a semitone. (But 1/12 a semitone step from 1000 Hz is about 88 Hz, while 1/12 a semitone step from 4000 Hz is about 353 Hz.) At low frequencies, tones that are separated by just a few Hertz can be distinguished as separate pitches, while at high frequencies, two tones must be separated by hundreds of Hertz before a difference is noticed.

You can test your own frequency range and discrimination with a sound processing program like Audacity or Audition, generating and listening to pure tones, as shown in Figure 4.9. Be aware, however, that the monitors or headphones you use have an impact on your ability to hear the frequencies.

4.1.6.2 Critical Bands

One part of the ear's anatomy that is helpful to consider more closely is the area in the inner ear called the basilar membrane. It is here that sound vibrations are detected, separated by frequencies, and transformed from mechanical energy to electrical impulses sent to the brain. The basilar membrane is lined with rows of hair cells and thousands of tiny hairs emanating from them. The hairs move when stimulated by vibrations, sending signals to their base cells and the attached nerve fibers, which pass electrical impulses to the brain. In his pioneering work on

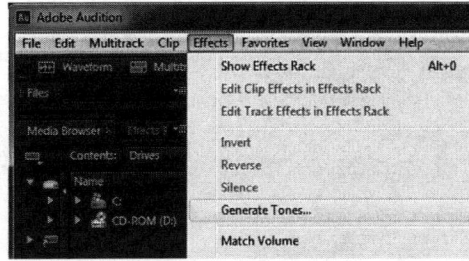

Select Generate/Tone

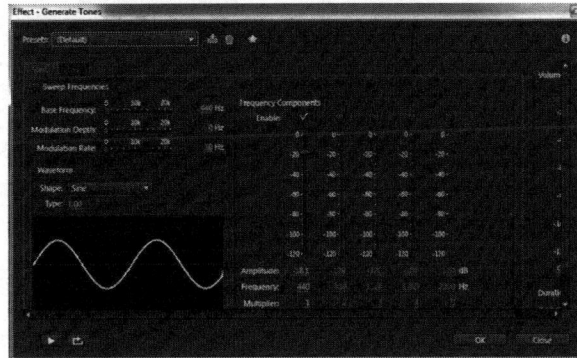

Choose the frequency

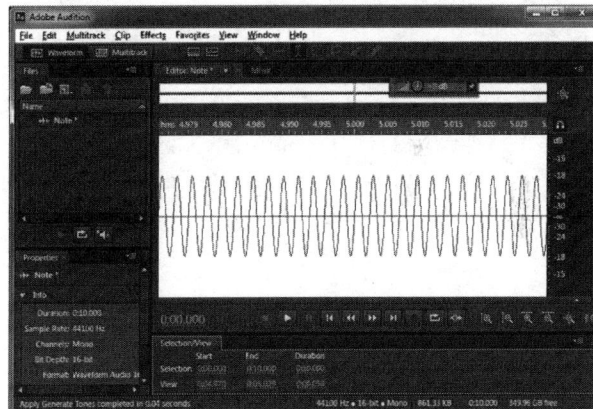

Listen to the sound to test your hearing

FIGURE 4.9: CREATING A SINGLE-FREQUENCY TONE IN ADOBE AUDITION

frequency perception, Harvey Fletcher discovered that different parts of the basilar membrane resonate more strongly to different frequencies. Thus, the membrane can be divided into frequency bands, commonly called critical bands. Each critical band of hair cells is sensitive to vibrations within a certain band of frequencies. Continued research on critical bands has shown that they play an important role in many aspects of human hearing, affecting our perception of loudness, frequency, timbre, and dissonance versus consonance. Experiments with critical bands have also led to an understanding of frequency masking, a phenomenon that can be put to good use in audio compression.

Critical bands can be measured by the band of frequencies that they cover. Fletcher discovered the existence of critical bands in his pioneering work on the cochlear response. Critical bands are the source of our ability to distinguish one frequency from another. When a complex sound arrives at the basilar membrane, each critical band acts as a kind of bandpass filter, responding only to vibrations within its frequency spectrum. In this

> **ASIDE:** A bandpass filter allows only the frequencies in a defined band to pass through, filtering out all other frequencies. Bandpass filters are studied in Chapter 7.

way, the sound is divided into frequency components. If two frequencies are received within the same band, the louder frequency can overpower the quieter one. This is the phenomenon of masking, first observed in Fletcher's original experiments.

Critical bands within the ear are not fixed areas, but instead are created during the experience of sound. Any audible sound can create a critical band centered on it. However, experimental analyses of critical bands have arrived at approximations that are useful guidelines in designing audio processing tools. Table 4.4 is one model taken after Fletcher, Zwicker, and Barkhausen's independent experiments (Tobias 1970). Here, the basilar membrane is divided into 25 overlapping bands, each with a center frequency and with variable bandwidths across the audible spectrum. The width of each band is given in Hertz, semitones, and octaves. (The widths in semitones and octaves were derived from the widths in Hertz, as explained in Section 4.3.2.) The center frequencies are graphed against the critical bands in Hertz in Figure 4.10.

You can see from the table and figure that, measured in Hertz, the critical bands are wider for higher frequencies than for lower. This implies that there is better frequency resolution at lower frequencies because a narrower band results in less masking of frequencies in a local area.

Table 4.4 shows that critical bands are generally in the range of two to four semitones wide, mostly less than four. This observation is significant as it relates to our experience of consonance versus dissonance. Recall from Chapter 3 that a major third consists of four semitones. For example, the third from C to E is separated by

Critical band	Center frequency in hertz	Range of frequencies in hertz	Bandwidth in hertz	Bandwidth in semitones relative to start*	Bandwidth in octaves relative to start*
1	50	1–100	100		–
2	150	100–200	100	12	1
3	250	200–300	100	7	0.59
4	350	300–400	100	5	0.42
5	450	400–510	110	4	0.31
6	570	510–630	120	4	0.30
7	700	630–770	140	3	0.29
8	840	770–920	150	3	0.26
9	1000	920–1080	160	3	0.23
10	1170	1080–1270	190	3	0.23
11	1370	1270–1480	210	3	0.22
12	1600	1480–1720	240	3	0.22
13	1850	1720–2000	280	3	0.22
14	2150	2000–2320	320	3	0.21
15	2500	2320–2700	380	3	0.22
16	2900	2700–3150	450	3	0.22
17	3400	3150–3700	550	3	0.23
18	4000	3700–4400	700	3	0.25
19	4800	4400–5300	900	3	0.27
20	5800	5300–6400	1100	3	0.27
21	7000	6400–7700	1300	3	0.27
22	8500	7700–9500	1800	4	0.30
23	10500	9500–12000	2500	4	0.34
24	13500	12000–15500	3500	4	0.37
25	18775	15500–22050	6550	6	0.5

*See Section 4.3.2 for an explanation of how the last two columns of this table were derived.

TABLE 4.4: AN ESTIMATE OF CRITICAL BANDS USING THE BARK SCALE

four semitones (stepping from C to C#, C# to D, D to D#, and D# to E.) Thus, the notes that are played simultaneously in a third generally occupy separate critical bands. This helps to explain why thirds are generally considered consonant—each of the notes having its own critical band. Seconds, which exist in the same critical band, are considered dissonant. At very low and very high frequencies, thirds begin to lose their consonance for most listeners. This is consistent with the fact that the critical bands at the low frequencies (100–200 and 200–300 Hz) and high frequencies (over 12,000 Hz) span more than a third, so that at these frequencies, a third lies within a single critical band.

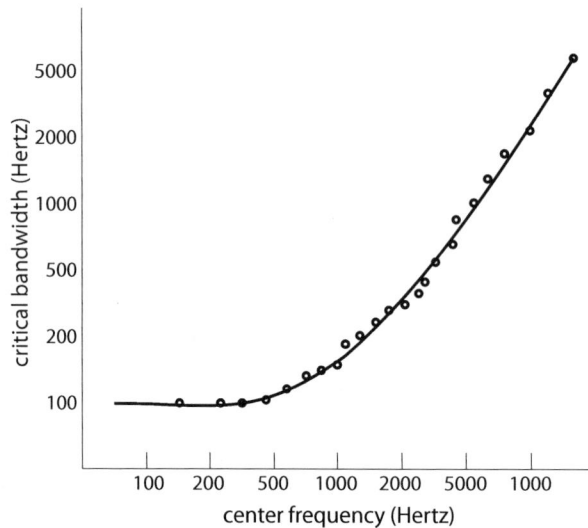

FIGURE 4.10: CRITICAL BANDS GRAPHED FROM TABLE 4.4

4.1.6.3 Amplitude Perception

In the early 1930s at Bell Laboratories, groundbreaking experiments by Fletcher and Munson clarified the extent to which our perception of loudness varies with frequency (Fletcher and Munson 1933). Their results—refined by later researchers (Robinson and Dadson 1956) and adopted as ISO 226 by the International Organization for Standardization—are illustrated in a graph of equal-loudness contours shown in Figure 4.11. In general, the graph shows how much you have to "turn up" or "turn down" a single frequency tone to make it sound equally loud to a 1000 Hz tone. Each curve on the graph represents an *n*-phon contour. One **phon** is defined as a 1000 Hz sound wave at a loudness of 1 dBSPL. An ***n*-phon contour** is created as follows:

» Frequency is on the horizontal axis and loudness in decibels is on the vertical axis.

» *n* curves are drawn.

» Each curve, from 1 to *n*, represents the intensity levels necessary in order to make each frequency, across the audible spectrum, sound equal in loudness to a 1000 Hz wave at *n* dBSPL.

Let's consider, for example, the 10-phon contour. This contour was created by playing a 1000 Hz pure tone at a loudness level of 10 dBSPL, and then asking groups of listeners to say when they thought pure tones at other frequencies matched the loudness of the 1000 Hz tone. Notice that low-frequency tones had to be increased by 60 or 75 dB to sound equally loud. Some of the higher-frequency tones—in the vicinity of 3000 Hz—actually had to be turned down in volume to sound equally loud to the 10 dBSPL, 1000 Hz tone. Also notice that the louder the 1000 Hz tone is, the less lower-frequency tones have to be turned up to sound equal in loudness. For example, the 90-phon contour goes up only about 30 dB to make the lowest frequencies sound equal in loudness to 1000 Hz at 90 dBSPL, whereas the 10-phon contour has to be turned up about 75 dB.

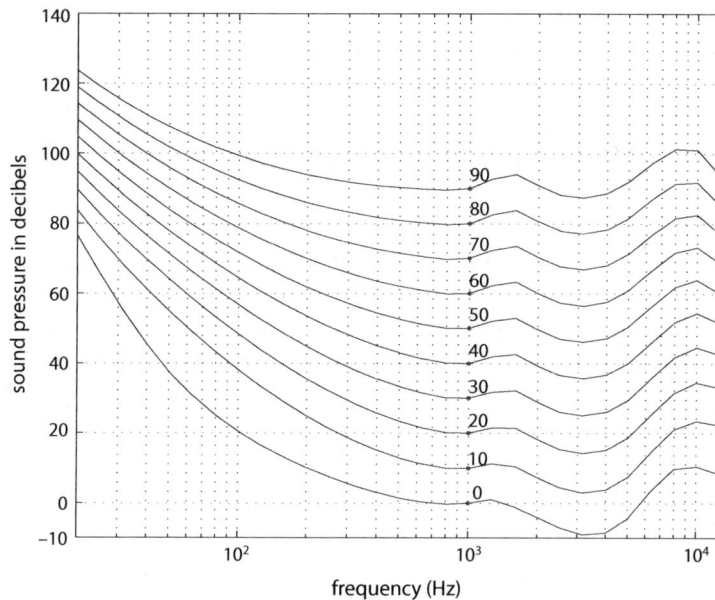

FIGURE 4.11: EQUAL-LOUDNESS CONTOURS
(FIGURE DERIVED FROM A PROGRAM BY JEFF TACKET,
POSTED AT THE MATLAB CENTRAL FILE EXCHANGE)

With the information captured in the equal-loudness contours, devices that measure the loudness of sounds—for example, SPL meters (sound pressure level meters)—can be designed so that they compensate for the fact that low-frequency sounds seem less loud than high-frequency sounds at the same amplitude. This compensation is called "weighting." Figure 4.12 graphs three weighting functions—A, B, and C. The A-, B-, and C-weighting functions are approximately inversions of the 40-phon, 70-phon, and 100-phon loudness contours, respectively. This implies that applying A-weighting in an SPL meter causes the meter to measure loudness in a way that matches our differences in loudness perception at 40 phons.

To understand how this works, think of the graphs of the weighting as frequency filters—also called frequency response graphs. When a weighting function is applied by an SPL meter, the meter uses a filter to reduce the influence of frequencies to which our ears are less sensitive, and conversely to increase the weight of frequencies that our ears *are* sensitive to. The fact that the A-weighting graph is lower on the left side than on the right means that an A-weighted SPL meter reduces the influence of low-frequency sounds as it takes its overall loudness measurement. On the other hand, it boosts the amplitude of frequencies around 3000 Hz, as seen by the bump above 0 dB around 3000 Hz. It doesn't matter that the SPL meter meddles with frequency components as it measures loudness. After all, it isn't measuring frequencies. It's measuring how loud the sounds seem to our ears. The use of weighted SPL meters is discussed further in Section 4.2.2.2.

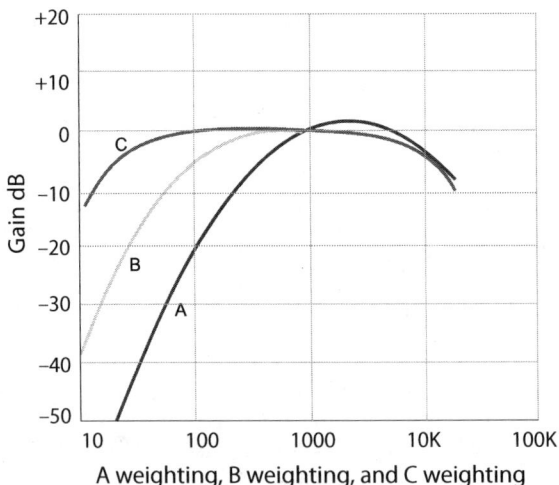

FIGURE 4.12: GRAPHS OF A-, B-, AND C-WEIGHTING FUNCTIONS
(FIGURE DERIVED FROM A PROGRAM BY JEFF TACKETT,
POSTED AT THE MATLAB CENTRAL FILE EXCHANGE)

4.1.7   THE INTERACTION OF SOUND WITH ITS ENVIRONMENT

Sometimes it's convenient to simplify our understanding of sound by considering how it behaves when there is nothing in the environment to impede it. An environment with no physical influences to absorb, reflect, diffract, refract, reverberate, resonate, or diffuse sound is called a **free field**. A free field is an idealization of real world conditions that facilitates our analysis of how sound behaves. Sound in a free field can be pictured as radiating out from a point source, diminishing in intensity as it gets farther from the source. A free field is partially illustrated in Figure 4.13. In this figure, sound is radiating out from a loudspeaker, with the gray shading indicating highest to lowest intensity sound as it emanates outward. The area in front of the loudspeaker might be considered a free field. However, because the loudspeaker partially blocks the sound from going behind itself, the sound is lower in amplitude there. You can see that there is *some* sound behind the loudspeaker, resulting from reflection and diffraction.

FIGURE 4.13: SOUND RADIATION FROM A LOUDSPEAKER, VIEWED FROM TOP

4.1.7.1 Absorption, Reflection, Refraction, and Diffraction

In the real world, there are any number of things that can get in the way of sound, changing its direction, amplitude, and frequency components. In enclosed spaces, absorption plays an important role. **Sound absorption** is the conversion of sound's energy into heat, thereby diminishing the intensity of the sound. The diminishing of sound intensity is called **attenuation**. A general mathematical formulation for the way sound attenuates as it moves through the air is captured in the inverse square law, which shows that sound decreases in intensity in proportion to the square of the distance from the source. (See Section 4.2.1.6.)

The attenuation of sound in the air is due to the air molecules themselves absorbing and converting some of the energy to heat. The amount of attenuation depends in part on the air temperature and relative humidity. Thick, porous materials can absorb and attenuate the sound even further, and they're often used in architectural treatments to modify and control the acoustics of a room. Even hard, solid surfaces absorb some of the sound energy, although most of it is reflected back. The material of walls and ceilings, the number and material of seats, the number of people in an audience, and all solid objects have to be taken into consideration acoustically in sound setups for live performance spaces.

Sound that is not absorbed by objects is instead reflected from, diffracted around, or refracted into the object. Hard surfaces reflect sound more than soft ones, which are more absorbent. The **law of reflection** states that the angle of incidence of a wave is equal to the angle of reflection. This means that if a wave were to propagate in a straight line from its source, it would reflect in the way pictured in Figure 4.14. In reality, however, sound radiates out spherically from its source. Thus, a wavefront of sound approaches objects and surfaces from various angles. Imagine a cross-section of the moving wavefront approaching a straight wall, as seen from above. Its reflection would be as pictured in Figure 4.15, like a mirror reflection.

ASIDE: Diffraction also has a lot to do with microphone and loudspeaker directivity. Consider how microphones often have different polar patterns at different frequencies. Even with a directional mic, you'll often see lower frequencies behave more omnidirectionally, and sometimes an omnidirectional mic may be more directional at high frequencies. That's largely because of the size of the wavelength compared to the size of the microphone diaphragm. It's hard for high frequencies to diffract around a larger object, so for a mic to have a truly omnidirectional pattern, the diaphragm has to be very small.

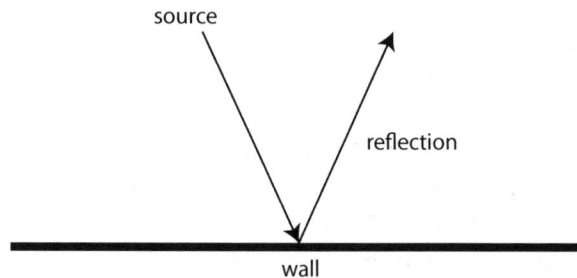

FIGURE 4.14: ANGLE OF INCIDENCE EQUALS ANGLE OF REFLECTION

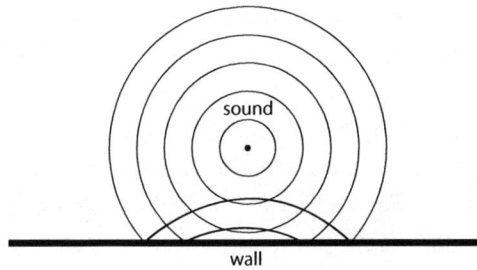

FIGURE 4.15: SOUND RADIATING FROM SOURCE AND REFLECTING OFF FLAT WALL, AS SEEN FROM ABOVE

In a special case, if the wavefront were to approach a concave curved solid surface, it would be reflected back to converge at one point in the room, the location of that point depending on the angle of the curve. This is how whispering rooms are constructed, such that two people whispering in the room can hear each other perfectly if they're positioned at the sound's focal points, even though the focal points may be at the far opposite ends of the room. A person positioned elsewhere in the room cannot hear their whispers at all. A common shape found with whispering rooms is an ellipse, as seen in Figure 4.16. The shape and curve of these walls cause any and all sound emanating from one focal point to reflect directly to the other.

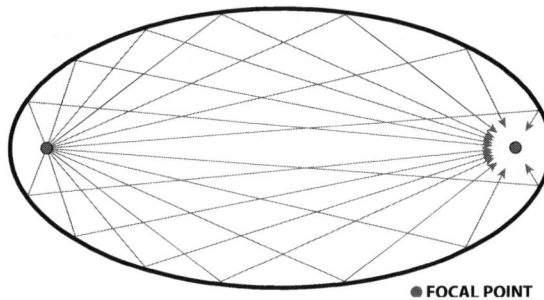

● **FOCAL POINT**

FIGURE 4.16: SOUND REFLECTS DIRECTLY BETWEEN FOCAL POINTS IN A WHISPERING ROOM

Diffraction is the bending of a sound wave as it moves past an obstacle or through a narrow opening. The phenomenon of diffraction allows us to hear sounds from sources that are not in the direct line of sight, such as a person standing around a corner or on the other side of a partially-obstructing object. The amount of diffraction is dependent on the relationship between the size of the obstacle and the size of the sound's wavelength. Low-frequency sounds (i.e., long-wavelength sounds) are diffracted more than high frequencies (i.e., short wavelengths) around the same obstacle. In other words, low-frequency sounds are better able to travel around obstacles. In fact, if the wavelength of a sound is significantly larger than an obstacle that the sound encounters, the sound wave continues as if the obstacle isn't even there. For example, your stereo speaker drivers are probably protected behind a plastic or metal grill, yet the sound passes through it intact and without noticeable coloration. The obstacle presented by the wire mesh of the grill (perhaps a millimeter or two in diameter) is even smaller than the smallest wavelength we can hear (about two centimeters for 20 kHz, 10 to 20 times larger than the wire), so the sound diffracts easily around it.

Refraction is the bending of a sound wave as it moves through different media. Typically we think of refraction with light waves, as when we look at something through glass or underwater. In acoustics, the refraction of sound waves tends to be more gradual, as the properties of the air change subtly over longer distances. This causes a bending in sound waves over a long distance, primarily due to temperature, humidity, and in some cases, wind gradients, over distance and altitude. This bending can result in noticeable differences in sound levels, either as a boost or an attenuation, also referred to as a **shadow zone**.

4.1.7.2 Reverberation, Echo, Diffusion, and Resonance

Reverberation is the result of sound waves reflecting off of many objects or surfaces in the environment. Imagine an indoor room in which you make a sudden burst of sound. Some of that sound is transmitted through or absorbed by the walls or objects, and the rest is reflected back, bouncing off the walls, ceilings, and other surfaces in the room. The sound wave that travels straight from the sound source to your ears is called the **direct signal**. The first few instances of reflected sound are called **primary** or **early reflections**. Early reflections arrive at your ears about 60 ms or sooner after the direct sound, and play a large part in imparting a sense of space and room size to the human ear. Early reflections may be followed by a handful of secondary and higher-order reflections. At this point, the sound waves have had plenty of opportunity to bounce off of multiple surfaces, multiple times. As a result, the reflections that are arriving now are more numerous, closer together in time, and quieter. Much of the initial energy of the reflections has been absorbed by surfaces or expended in the distance traveled through the air. This dense collection of reflections is **reverberation**, illustrated in Figure 4.17. Assuming that the sound source is only momentary, the generated sound eventually decays as the waves lose energy, the reverberation becoming less and less loud until the sound is no longer discernable. Typically, **reverberation time** is defined as the time it takes for the sound to decay in level by 60 dB from its direct signal.

impulse response

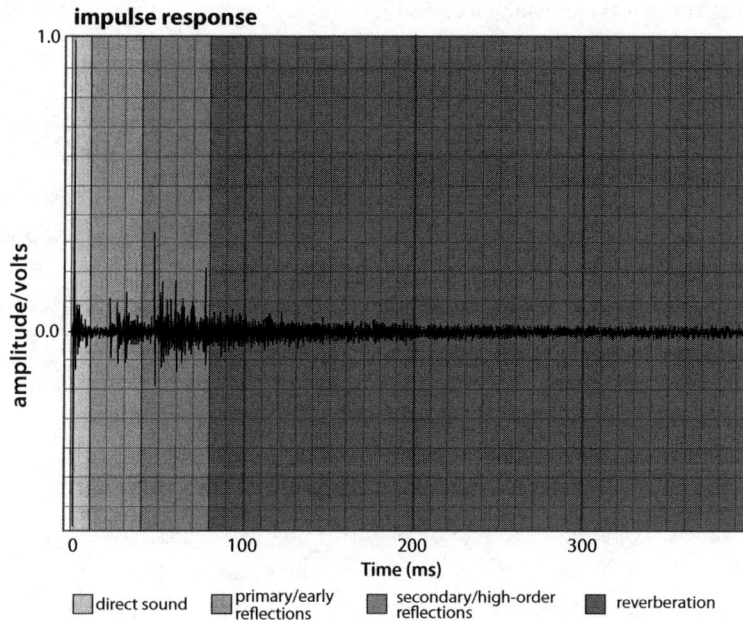

FIGURE 4.17: SOUND REFLECTIONS AND REVERBERATION

Single, strong reflections that reach the ear in a significant amount of time (about 100 ms) after the direct signal can be perceived as an echo, essentially a separate recurrence of the original sound. Even reflections as little as 50 ms apart can cause an audible echo, depending on the type of sound and room acoustics. While echo is often employed artistically in music recordings, echoes tend to be detrimental and distracting in a live setting and are usually avoided or require remediation in performance and listening spaces.

Diffusion is another property that interacts with reflections and reverberation. **Diffusion** relates to the ability to distribute sound energy more evenly in a listening space. While a flat, even surface reflects sounds strongly in a predictable direction, uneven or curved surfaces diffuse sound more randomly and evenly. Like absorption, diffusion is often used to treat a space acoustically to help break up harsh reflections that interfere with the natural sound. Unlike absorption, however, which attempts to eliminate the unwanted sound waves by reducing the sound energy, diffusion attempts to redirect the sound waves in a more natural manner. A room with lots of absorption has less overall reverberation, while diffusion maintains the sound's intensity and helps turn harsh reflections into more pleasant reverberation. Usually a combination of absorption and diffusion is employed to achieve the optimal result. There are many unique types of diffusing surfaces and panels that are manufactured based on mathematical algorithms to provide the most random, diffuse reflections possible.

Putting these concepts together, we can say that the amount of time it takes for a particular sound to decay depends on the size and shape of the room, its diffusive properties, and the absorptive properties of the walls, ceilings, and objects in the room. In short, all the aforementioned properties determine how sound reverberates in a space, giving the listener a "sense of place."

Reverberation in an auditorium can enhance the listener's experience, particularly in the case of a music hall where it gives the individual sounds a richer quality and helps them blend together. Excessive reverberation, however, can reduce intelligibility and make it difficult to understand speech. In Chapter 7, you'll see how artificial reverberation is applied in audio processing.

A final important acoustical property to be considered is resonance. In Chapter 2, we defined resonance as an object's tendency to vibrate or oscillate at a certain frequency that is basic to its nature. Like a musical instrument, a room has a set of resonant frequencies, called its **room modes**. Room modes result in locations in a room where certain frequencies are boosted or attenuated, making it difficult to give all listeners the same audio experience. We'll talk more about how to deal with room modes in Section 4.2.2.5.

4.2 APPLICATIONS

4.2.1 WORKING WITH DECIBELS

4.2.1.1 Real-world Considerations

We now turn to practical considerations related to the concepts introduced in Section 1. We first return to the concept of decibels.

An important part of working with decibel values is learning to recognize and estimate decibel differences. If a sound isn't loud enough, how much louder does it need to be? Until you can answer that question in a decibel value, you will have a hard time figuring out what to do. It's also important to understand the kind of decibel differences that are audible. The average listener cannot distinguish a difference in sound pressure level that is less than 3 dB. With training, you can learn to recognize differences in sound pressure level of 1 dB, but differences that are less than 1 dB are indistiguishable even to well-trained listeners.

Understanding the limitations to human hearing is very important when working with sound. For example, when investigating changes you can make to your sound equipment to get higher sound pressure levels, you should be aware that unless the change amounts to 3 dB or more, most of your listeners will probably not notice. This concept also applies when processing audio signals. When manipulating the frequency response of an audio signal using an equalizer, unless you're making a difference of 3 dB with one of your filters, the change will be imperceptible to most listeners.

Having a reference to use when creating audio material or sound systems is also helpful. For example, there are usually loudness requirements imposed by the television network for television content. If these requirements are not met, there will be level inconsistencies between the various programs on the television station that can be very annoying to the audience. These requirements could be as simple as limiting peak levels to –10 dBFS or as strict as meeting a specified dBFS average across the duration of the show.

You might also be putting together equipment that delivers sound to a live audience in an acoustic space. In that situation you need to know how loud in dBSPL the system needs to perform at the distance of the audience. There is a minimum dBSPL level you need to achieve in order to get the signal above the noise floor of the room, but there is also a maximum dBSPL level you need to stay under in order to avoid damaging people's hearing or violating laws or policies of the venue. Once you know these requirements, you can begin to evaluate the performance of the equipment to verify that it can meet these requirements.

4.2.1.2 Rules of Thumb

Table 4.2 gives you some rules of thumb for how changes in decibels are perceived as changes in loudness. Turn a sound up by 10 dB and it sounds about twice as loud. Turn it up by 3 dB, and you'll hardly notice any difference.

Similarly, Table 4.5 gives you some rules of thumb regarding power, voltage, and distance changes. These rules give you a quick sense of how boosts in power and voltage affect sound levels.

Change in power, voltage, or distance	Approximate change in dB
power × 2	3 dB increase
power ÷ 2	3 dB decrease
power × 10	10 dB increase
power ÷ 10	10 dB decrease
voltage × 2	6 dB increase
voltage ÷ 2	6 dB decrease
voltage × 10	20 dB increase
voltage ÷ 10	20 dB decrease
distance away from source × 2	6 dB decrease

TABLE 4.5: RULES OF THUMB FOR CHANGES IN POWER, VOLTAGE, OR DISTANCE IN DB

In the following sections, we'll give examples of how these rules of thumb come into practice. A mathematical justification of these rules is given in Section 4.3.

4.2.1.3 Determining Power and Voltage Differences and Desired Changes in Power Levels

Decibels are also commonly used to compare the power levels of loudspeakers and amplifiers. For power, Equation 4.6 applies:

$$\Delta Power\ dB = 10\log_{10}\left(\frac{P_1}{P_0}\right)$$

Based on this equation, how much more powerful is an 800 W amplifier than a 200 W amplifier, in decibels?

$$10\log_{10}\left(\frac{800\ W}{200\ W}\right) = 10\log_{10}4 = 6\ dB\ increase\ in\ power$$

For voltages, Equation 4.4 is used:

$$\Delta Voltage\ dB = 20\log_{10}\left(\frac{V_1}{V_0}\right)$$

If you increase a voltage level from 100 V to 1000 V, what is the increase in decibels?

$$20\log_{10}\left(\frac{100\ V}{10\ V}\right) = 20\log_{10} = 20\ dB\ increase\ in\ voltage$$

It's worth pointing out here that because the definition of decibels sound pressure level was derived from the power decibel definition, then if there's a 3 dB increase in the power of an amplifier, there is a corresponding 3 dB increase in the sound pressure level it produces. We know that a 3 dB increase in sound pressure level is barely detectable, so the implication is that doubling the power of an amplifier doesn't increase the loudness of the sounds it produces very much. You have to multiply the power of the amplifier by ten in order to get sounds that are approximately twice as loud.

The fact that doubling the power gives about a 3 dB increase in sound pressure level has implications with regard to how many speakers you ought to use for a given situation. If you double the speakers (assuming identical speakers), you double the power, but you get only a 3 dB increase in sound level. If you quadruple the speakers, you get a 6 dB increase in sound because each time you double, you go up by 3 dB. If you double the speakers again

> **ASIDE:** Multiplying power times two corresponds to multiplying voltage times $\sqrt{2}$ because power is proportional to voltage squared.
>
> $$P \propto V^2$$
>
> Thus
>
> $$10\log_{10}((2 \times P_0)/P_0) =$$
> $$10\log_{10}((\sqrt{2} \times V_0)/V_0)^2 =$$
>
> 3 dB increase.

(eight speakers now), you hypothetically get a 9 dB increase, not taking into account other acoustical factors that may affect the sound level.

Often, your real world problem begins with a decibel increase you'd like to achieve in your live sound setup. What if you want to increase the level by ΔdB? You can figure out how to do this with the power ratio formula, derived in Equation 4.11.

$$\Delta dB = 10 \log_{10} \left(\frac{P_1}{P_0} \right)$$

$$\frac{\Delta dB}{10} = \log_{10} \left(\frac{P_1}{P_0} \right)$$

Thus

$$\frac{P_1}{P_0} = 10^{\frac{\Delta dB}{10}}$$

where P_0 is the starting power, P_1 is the new power level,
and ΔdB is the desired change in decibels

EQUATION 4.11: DERIVATION OF POWER RATIO FORMULA

It may help to recast the equation to clarify that for the problem we've described, the desired decibel change and the beginning power level are known, and we wish to compute the new power level needed to get this decibel change.

$$P_1 = P_0 \times 10^{\frac{\Delta dB}{10}}$$

where P_0 is the starting power, P_1 is the new power level,
and ΔdB is the desired change in decibels

EQUATION 4.12: POWER RATIO FORMULA

Applying this formula, what if you start with a 300 W amplifier and want to get one that is 15 dB louder?

$$P_1 = 300\ W \times 10^{\frac{15}{10}} = 9486\ W$$

You can see that it takes quite an increase in wattage to increase the power by 15 dB. Instead of trying to get more watts, a better strategy would be to choose different loudspeakers that have a higher sensitivity. The sensitivity of a loudspeaker is defined as the sound pressure level that is produced by the loudspeaker with one watt of power when measured one meter away. Also, because the voltage gain in a power amplifier is fixed, before you go buy a bunch of new loudspeakers, you may also want to make sure that you're feeding the highest possible voltage signal into the power amplifier. It's quite possible that the 15 dB increase you're looking for is hiding somewhere in the signal chain of your sound system due to inefficient gain structure between devices. If you can get 15 dB more voltage into the amplifier by optimizing your gain structure, the power amplifier quite happily amplifies that higher voltage signal assuming you haven't exceeded the maximum input voltage for the power amplifier. Chapter 8 includes a Max demo on gain structure that may help you with this concept.

4.2.1.4 Converting from One Type of Decibel to Another

A similar problem arises when you have two pieces of sound equipment whose nominal output levels are measured in decibels of different types. For example, you may want to connect two devices where the nominal voltage output of one is given in dBV, and the nominal voltage output of the other is given in dBu. You first want to know if the two voltage levels are the same. If they are not, you want to know how much you have to boost the one of lower voltage to match the higher one.

The way to do this is to convert both dBV and dBu back to voltage. You can then compare the two voltage levels in decibels. From this you know how much the lower voltage hardware needs to be boosted. Consider an example where one device has an output level of –10 dBv and the other operates at 4 dBu. Convert –10 dBV to voltage:

$$-10 = 20 \log_{10} \left(\frac{v}{1} \right)$$

$$\frac{-10}{20} = \log_{10} v$$

$$-0.5 = \log_{10} v$$

$$10^{-0.5} = v \approx 0.316$$

Thus, –10 dBV converts to 0.316 V.

By a similar computation, we get the voltage corresponding to 4 dBu, this time using 0.775 V as the reference value in the denominator. Convert 4 dBu to voltage:

$$4 = 20 \log_{10} \left(\frac{v}{0.775} \right)$$

$$\frac{4}{20} = log_{10} \left(\frac{v}{0.775} \right)$$

$$0.2 = \log_{10} \left(\frac{v}{0.775} \right)$$

$$10^{0.2} \times 0.775 = v \approx 1.228$$

Thus, 4 dBu converts to 1.228 V.

Now that we have the two voltages, we can compute the decibel difference between them. Compute the voltage difference between 0.316 V and 1.228 V:

$$\Delta dB = 20 \log_{10} \left(\frac{1.228}{0.316} \right) \approx 12 \, dB$$

From this you see that the lower-voltage device needs to be boosted by 12 dB in order to match the other device.

4.2.1.5 Combining Sound Levels from Multiple Sources

In the last few sections, we've mostly been discussing power and voltage decibels. These decibel computations are relevant to our work because power levels and voltages produce sounds. But we can't hear volts and watts. Ultimately, what we want to know is how loud things sound. Let's return now to decibels as they measure audible sound levels.

Think about what happens when you add one sound to another in the air or on a wire and want to know how loud the combined sound is in decibels. In this situation, you can't just add the two decibel levels. For example, if you add an 85 dBSPL lawnmower on top of a 110 dBSPL symphony orchestra, how loud is the sound? It *isn't* 85 dBSPL + 110 dBSPL = 195 dBSPL. Instead, we derive the sum of decibels d_1 and d_2 as follows:

Convert d_1 to air pressure:

$$85 = 20 \log_{10} \left(\frac{x}{0.00002} \right)$$

$$x = 10^{\frac{85}{20}} \times (0.00002) \approx 0.36 \, Pa$$

Convert d_2 to air pressure:

$$110 = 20 \log_{10} \left(\frac{x}{0.00002} \right)$$

$$x = 10^{\frac{110}{20}} \times (0.00002) \approx 6.32 \, Pa$$

Sum the air pressure amplitudes and and convert back to dBSPL:

$$dBSPL = 20 \log_{10} \left(\frac{0.36 + 6.32}{0.00002} \right)$$

$$dBSPL \approx 110.5 \, dB$$

The combined sounds in this case are not perceptibly louder than the louder of the two original sounds being combined.

4.2.1.6 Inverse Square Law

The last row of Table 4.5 is known as the **inverse square law**, which states that *the intensity of sound from a point source is proportional to the inverse of the square of the* *distance r from the source.* Perhaps of more practical use is the related rule of thumb that *for every doubling of distance from a sound source, you get a decrease in sound level of 6 dB.* We can informally prove the inverse square law by the following argument.

For simplification, imagine a sound as coming from a point source. This sound radiates spherically (equally in all directions) from the source. Sound intensity is defined as sound power passing through a unit area. The fact that intensity is measured per unit area is what is significant here. You can picture the sound spreading out as it moves away from the source. The farther the sound gets away from the source, the more it has "spread out," and thus its intensity lessens per unit area as the sphere representing the radiating sound gets larger. This is illustrated in Figure 4.18.

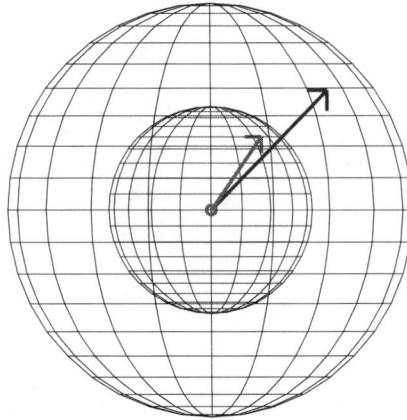

FIGURE 4.18: SPHERE REPRESENTING SOUND RADIATING FROM A POINT SOURCE; RADII REPRESENTING TWO DIFFERENT DISTANCES FROM THIS SOUND

This phenomenon of sound attenuation as sound moves from a source is captured in the inverse square law, illustrated in Figure 4.19:

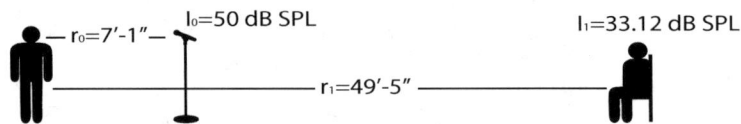

I_0=50 dB SPL r_0=7'-1" I_1=33.12 dB SPL r_1=49'-5"

FIGURE 4.19: APPLYING THE INVERSE SQUARE LAW

$$I_1 - I_0 = 10 \log_{10} \left(\frac{r_0{}^2}{r_1{}^2} \right) = 20 \log_{10} \left(\frac{r_0}{r_1} \right) \ dB$$

where r_0 is the initial distance from the sound, r_1 is the new distance from the sound, I_0 is the intensity of the sound at the microphone in decibels, and I_1 is the intensity of the sound at the listener location in decibels

EQUATION 4.13: INVERSE SQUARE LAW

What this means in practical terms is the following. Say you have a sound source, a singer, who is a distance $r_0 = 7'1''$ from the microphone, as shown in Figure 4.19. The microphone detects her voice at a level of $I_0 = 50$ dBSPL. The listener is a distance $r_1 = 49'5''$ from the singer. Then the sound reaching the listener from the singer has an intensity of

$$I_1 - I_0 = 20 \log_{10} \left(\frac{r_0}{r_1} \right)$$

$$I_1 = I_0 + 20 \log_{10} \left(\frac{r_0}{r_1} \right) = 50 + 20 \log_{10} \left(\frac{7.0833}{49.4167} \right)$$

$$= 50 - 16.8728 = 33.12 \; dBSPL$$

Notice that when $r_1 < r_0$ the logarithm gives a negative number, which makes sense because the sound is less intense as you move away from the source.

The inverse square law is a handy rule of thumb. Each time we double the distance from our source, we decrease the sound level by 6 dB. The first doubling of distance is a perceptible but not dramatic decrease in sound level. Another doubling of distance (which would be four times the original distance from the source) yields a 12 dB decrease, which makes the source sound less than half as loud as it did from the initial distance. These numbers are only approximations for ideal free-field conditions. Many other factors intervene in real-world acoustics. But the inverse square law gives a general idea of sound attenuation that is useful in many situations.

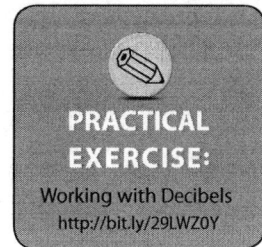

> **PRACTICAL EXERCISE:**
> Working with Decibels
> http://bit.ly/29LWZ0Y

4.2.2 ACOUSTIC CONSIDERATIONS FOR LIVE PERFORMANCES

4.2.2.1 Potential Acoustic Gain (PAG)

When setting up for a live performance, an important function of the sound engineer operating the amplification/mixing system is to set the initial sound levels.

The **acoustic gain** of an amplification system is the difference between the loudness as perceived by the listener when the sound system is turned on as compared to when the sound system is turned off. One goal of the sound engineer is to achieve a high **potential acoustic gain**, or **PAG**—the gain in decibels that can be added to the original sound without causing feedback. This potential acoustic gain is the entire reason the sound system is installed and the sound engineer is hired. If you can't make the sound louder and more intelligible, you fail as a sound engineer. The word *potential* is used here because the PAG represents

> **FLASH TUTORIAL:**
> Potential Acoustic Gain
> http://bit.ly/29g6Cbe

the maximum gain possible without causing feedback. **Feedback** can occur when the loudspeaker sends an audio signal back through the air to the microphone at the same level or louder than the source. In this situation, the two similar sounds arrive at the microphone at the same level but at a different phase. The first frequency from the loudspeaker to combine with the source at a 360 degree phase relationship is reinforced by 6 dB. The 6 dB reinforcement at that frequency happens over and over in an infinite loop. This sounds like a single sine wave that gets louder and louder. Without intervention on the part of the sound engineer, this sound continues to get louder until the loudspeaker is overloaded. To stop a feedback loop, you need to interrupt the electro-acoustical path that the sound is traveling either by muting the microphone on the mixing console or by turning off the amplifier that is driving the loudspeaker. If feedback happens too many times, you'll likely not be hired again.

The equation for PAG is given below.

$$PAG = 20 \log_{10} \left(\frac{D_1 \times D_0}{D_s \times D_2} \right)$$

where D_s is the distance from the sound source to the microphone,
D_0 is the distance from the sound source to the listener,
D_1 is the distance from the microphone to the loudspeaker, and
D_2 is the distance from the loudspeaker to the listener

EQUATION 4.14: POTENTIAL ACOUSTIC GAIN (PAG)

PAG is the limit. The amount of gain added to the signal by the sound engineer in the sound booth must be less than this. Otherwise, there will be feedback.

In typical practice, you should stay 6 dB below this limit in order to avoid the initial sounds of the onset of feedback. This is sometimes described as sounding "ringy" because the sound system is in a situation where it is trying to cause feedback but hasn't quite found a frequency at exactly a 360° phase offset. This 6 dB safety factor should be applied to the result of the PAG equation. The amount of acoustic gain needed for any situation varies, but as a rule of thumb, if your PAG is less than 12 dB, you need to make some adjustments to the physical locations of the various elements of the sound system in order to increase the acoustic gain. In the planning stages of your sound system design, you'll be making guesses on how much gain you need. Generally you want the highest possible PAG, but in your efforts to increase the PAG you will eventually get to a point where the compromises required to increase the gain are unacceptable. These compromises could include financial cost and visual aesthetics. Once the sound system has been purchased and installed, you'll be able to test the system to see how close your PAG predictions are to reality. If you find that the system causes feedback before you're able to turn the volume up to the desired level, you don't have enough PAG in your system. You need to make adjustments to your sound system in order to increase your gain before feedback.

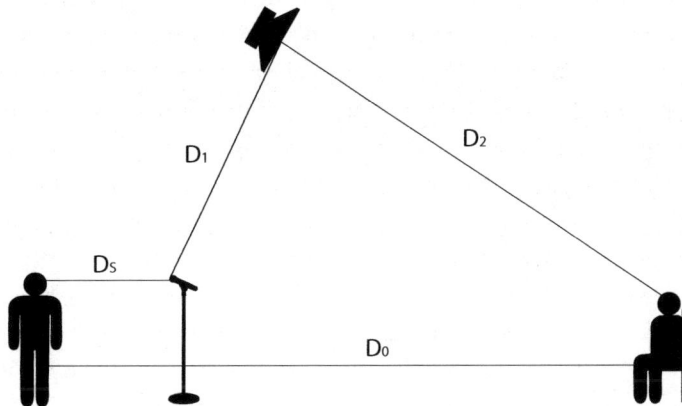

FIGURE 4.20: POTENTIAL ACOUSTIC GAIN, $PAG = 20\log_{10}((D_1 \times D_0)/(D_s \times D_2))$

Increasing the PAG can be achieved by a number of means, including:
) moving the source closer to the microphone
) moving the loudspeaker farther from the microphone
) moving the loudspeaker closer to the listener.

It's also possible to use directional microphones and loudspeakers or to apply filters or equalization, although these methods do not yield the same level of success as physically moving the various sound system components. These issues are illustrated in the interactive Flash tutorial associated with this section.

Note that PAG is the "potential" gain. Not all aspects of the sound need to be amplified by this much. The gain just gives you "room to play." Faders in the mixer can still bring down specific microphones or frequency bands in the signal. But the potential acoustic gain lets you know how much louder than the natural sound you will be able to achieve.

The Flash tutorial associated with this section also helps you to visualize how acoustic gain works and what its consequences are.

4.2.2.2 Checking and Setting Sound Levels

One fundamental part of analyzing an acoustic space is checking sound levels at various locations in the listening area. In the ideal situation, you want everything to sound similar at various listening locations. A realistic goal is to have each listening location be within 6 dB of the other locations. If you find locations that are outside that 6 dB range, you may need to reposition some loudspeakers, add loudspeakers, or apply acoustic treatment to the room. With the knowledge of decibels and acoustics that you gained in Section 4.1, you should have a better understanding now of how this works.

There are two types of sound pressure level (SPL) meters for measuring sound levels in the air. The most common is a dedicated handheld SPL meter like the one shown in Figure 4.21. These meters have a built-in microphone and operate on battery power. They have been specifically calibrated to convert the voltage level coming from the microphone into a value in dBSPL.

There are some options to configure that can make your measurements more meaningful. One option is the response time of the meter. A fast response allows you to see level changes that are short, such as peaks in the sound wave. A slow response shows you more of an average SPL. Another option is the weighting of the meter. The concept of SPL weighting comes from the equal-loudness contours explained in Section 4.1.6.3. Since the frequency response of the human hearing system changes with the SPL, a number of weighting contours are offered, each modeling the human frequency response with a slightly different emphasis. A-weighting has a rather steep roll-off at low frequencies. This means that the low frequencies are attenuated more than they are in B or C-weighting. B-weighting has less roll off at low frequencies. C-weighting is almost a flat frequency response except for a little attenuation at low frequencies. The rule of thumb is that if you're measuring levels of 90 dBSPL or lower, A-weighting gives you the most accurate representation of what you're hearing. For levels between 90 dBSPL and 110 dBSPL, B-weighting gives you the most accurate indication of what you hear. Levels in excess of 110 dBSPL should use C-weighting. If your SPL meter doesn't have an option for B-weighting, you should use C-weighting for all measurements higher than 90 dBSPL.

The other type of SPL meter is one that is part of a larger acoustic analysis system. As described in Chapter 2, these systems can consist of a computer, audio interface, analysis microphone, and specialized audio analysis software. When using this analysis software to make SPL measurements, you need to calibrate the software. The issue here is that because the software has no knowledge or control over the microphone sensitivity and the preamplifier on the audio interface, it has no way of knowing which analog voltage levels and corresponding digital sample values represent actual SPL levels. To

FIGURE 4.21: HANDHELD SPL METER

solve this problem, an SPL calibrator is used. An SPL calibrator is a device that generates a 1 kHz sine wave at a known SPL level (typically 94 dBSPL) at the transducer. The analysis microphone is inserted into the round opening on the calibrator, creating a tight seal. At this point, the tip of the microphone is up against the transducer in the calibrator, and the microphone is receiving a known SPL level. Now you can tell the analysis software to interpret the current signal level as a specific SPL level. As long as you don't change microphones and you don't change the level of the preamplifier, the calibrator can then be removed from the microphone, and the software is able to interpret other varying sound levels relative to the known calibration level. Figure 4.22 shows an SPL calibrator and the calibration window in the Smaart analysis software.

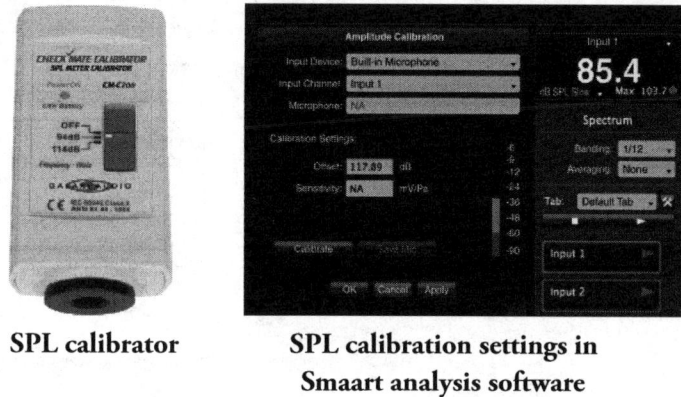

SPL calibrator   **SPL calibration settings in Smaart analysis software**

FIGURE 4.22: ANALYSIS SOFTWARE NEEDS TO BE CALIBRATED FOR SPL

4.2.2.3 Impulse Responses and Reverberation Time

In addition to sound amplitude levels, it's important to consider frequency levels in a live sound system. Frequency measurements are taken to set up the loudspeakers and levels so that the audience experiences the sound and balance of frequencies in the way intended by the sound designer.

One way to do frequency analysis is to have an audio device generate a sudden burst or "impulse" of sound and then use appropriate software to graph the audio signal in the form of a frequency response. The frequency response graph, with frequency on the *x*-axis and the magnitude of the frequency component on the *y*-axis, shows the amount of each frequency in the audio signal in one window of time. An impulse response graph is generated in the same way that a frequency response graph is generated, using the same hardware and software. The **impulse response graph** (or simply **impulse response**) has time on the *x*-axis and amplitude of the audio signal on the *y*-axis. It is this graph that helps us to analyze the reverberations in an acoustic space.

An impulse response measured in a small chamber music hall is shown in Figure 4.23. Essentially what you are seeing is the occurrences of the stimulus signal arriving at the measurement microphone over a period of time. The first big spike at around 48 milliseconds is the arrival of the direct sound from the loudspeaker. In other words, it took 48 milliseconds for the sound to arrive back at the microphone after the analysis software sent out the stimulus audio signal. The delay results primarily from the time it takes for sound to travel through the air from the loudspeaker to the measurement microphone, with a small amount of additional latency resulting from the various digital and analog conversions along the way. The next tallest spike at 93 milliseconds represents a reflection of the stimulus signal from some surface in the room. There are a few small reflections that arrive before that, but they're not large enough to be of much concern. The reflection at 93 milliseconds arrives 45 milliseconds after the direct sound and is approximately 9 dB quieter than the direct sound. This is an audible reflection that is outside the precedence zone and may be perceived by the listener as an audible echo. (The precedence effect is explained in Section 4.2.2.6.) If this reflection is problematic, you can try to absorb it. You can also diffuse it and convert it into the reverberant energy shown in the rest of the graph.

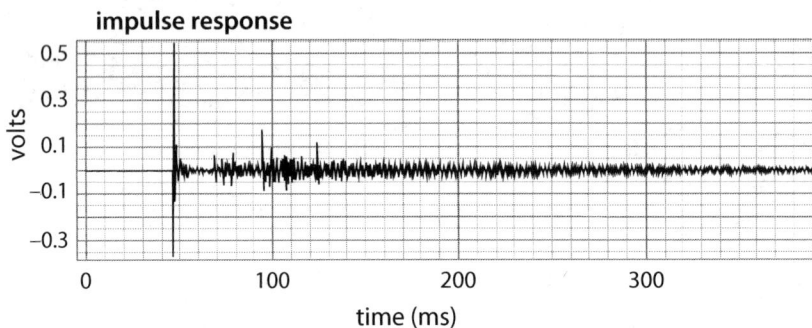

FIGURE 4.23: IMPULSE RESPONSE OF SMALL CHAMBER MUSIC HALL

Before you can take any corrective action, you need to identify the surface in the room causing the reflection. The detective work can be tricky, but it helps to consider that you're looking for a surface that is visible to both the loudspeaker and the microphone. The surface should be at a distance 50 feet longer than the direct distance between the loudspeaker and the microphone. In this case, the loudspeaker is up on the stage and the microphone out in the audience seats. More than likely, the reflection is coming from the upstage wall behind the loudspeaker. If you measure approximately 25 feet between the loudspeaker and that wall, you've probably found the culprit. To see if this is indeed the problem, you can put some absorptive material on that wall and take another measurement. If you've guess correctly, you should see that spike disappear or get significantly smaller. If you wanted to give a speech or perform percussion instruments in this space, this reflection would probably cause intelligibility problems. However, in this particular scenario, where the room is primarily used for chamber music, this reflection is not of much concern. In fact, it might even be desirable, as it makes the room sound larger.

As you can see in Figure 4.23, the overall sound energy decays very slowly over time. Some of that sound energy can be defined as reverberant sound. In a chamber music hall like this, a longer reverberation time might be desirable. In a lecture hall, a shorter reverberation time is better. You can use this impulse response data to determine the RT60 reverberation time of the room as shown in Figure 4.24. **RT60** is the time it takes for reflections of a sound to decay by 60 dB. In the figure, RT60 is determined for eight separate frequency bands. As you can see, the reverberation time (also called early decay time, EDT) varies for different frequency bands. This is due to the varying absorption rates of high versus low frequencies. Because high frequencies are more easily absorbed, the reverberation time of high frequencies tends to be lower. On average, the reverberation time of this room is around 1.3 seconds.

ASIDE: RT60 is the time it takes for reflections of a direct sound to decay by 60 dB.

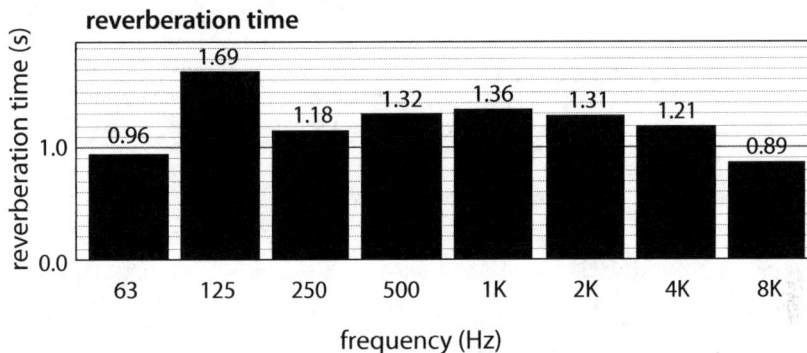

FIGURE 4.24: RT60 REVERBERATION TIME OF SMALL CHAMBER MUSIC HALL

The music hall in this example is equipped with curtains on the wall that can be lowered to absorb more sound and reduce the reverberation time. Figure 4.25 shows the impulse response measurement taken with the curtains in place. At first glance, this data doesn't look very different from Figure 4.23, when the curtains were absent. There is a slight difference, however, in the rate of decay for the reverberant energy. The resulting reverberation time is shown in Figure 4.26. Adding the curtains reduces the average reverberation time by around 0.2 seconds.

impulse response

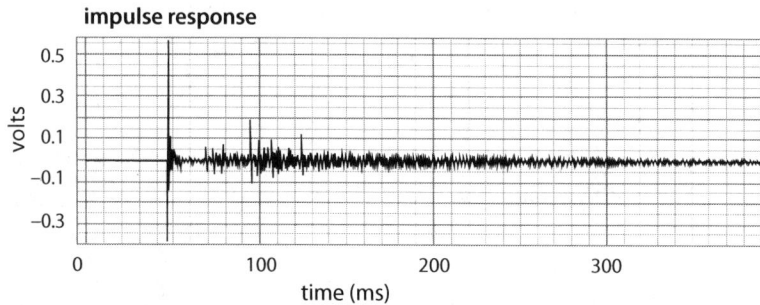

FIGURE 4.25: IMPULSE RESPONSE OF SMALL CHAMBER MUSIC
HALL WITH CURTAINS ON SOME OF THE WALLS

reverberation time

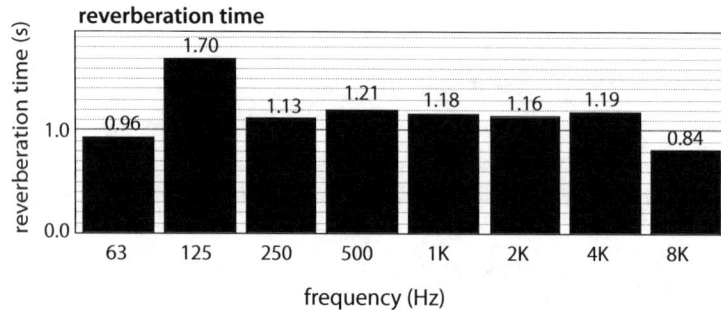

FIGURE 4.26: RT60 REVERBERATION TIME OF SMALL CHAMBER
MUSIC HALL WITH CURTAINS ON SOME OF THE WALLS

4.2.2.4 Frequency Levels and Comb Filtering

When working with sound in acoustic space, you discover that there is a lot of potential for sound waves to interact with each other. If the waves are allowed to interact destructively—causing frequency cancelations—the result can be detrimental to the sound quality perceived by the audience.

Destructive sound wave interactions can happen when two loudspeakers generate identical sounds that are directed to the same acoustic space. They can also occur when a sound wave combines in the air with its own reflection from a surface in the room.

Let's say there are two loudspeakers aimed at you, both generating the same sound. Loudspeaker A is 10 feet away from you, and Loudspeaker B is 11 feet away. Because sound travels at a speed of approximately one foot per millisecond, the sound from Loudspeaker B arrives at your ears one millisecond after the sound from Loudspeaker A, as shown in Figure 4.27. That one millisecond of difference doesn't seem like much. How much damage can it really inflict on your sound? Let's again assume that both sounds arrive at the same amplitude. Since the position of your ears to the two loud-speakers is directly related to the timing difference, let's also assume that your head is stationary, as if you are sitting relatively still in your seat at a theater. In this case, a one millisecond difference causes the two sounds to interact destructively. In Chapter 2 you read about what happens when two identical sounds combine out of phase. In real life, phase differences can occur as a result of an offset in time. That extra one millisecond that it takes for the sound from Loudspeaker B to arrive at your ears results in a phase difference relative to the sound from Loudspeaker A. The audible result of this depends on the type of sound being generated by the loudspeakers.

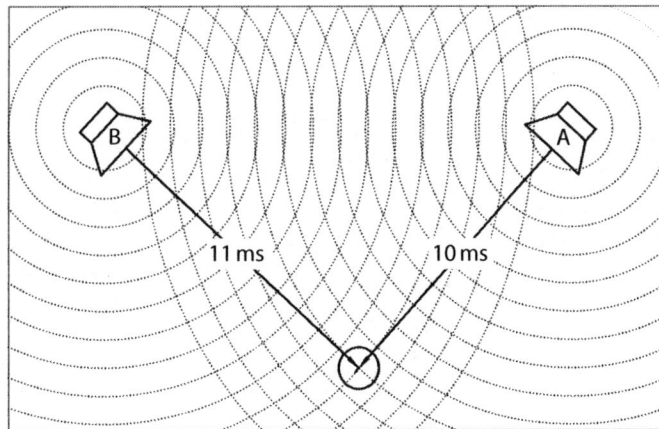

FIGURE 4.27: TWO LOUDSPEAKERS ARRIVING AT A LISTENER ONE MILLISECOND APART

Let's assume, for the sake of simplicity, that both loudspeakers are generating a 500 Hz sine wave, and the speed of sound is 1000 ft/s. (As stated in Section 2.1.1, the speed of sound in air varies depending upon temperature and air pressure so you don't always get a perfect 1130 ft/s.) Recall that wavelength equals velocity multiplied by period ($\pi = cT$). Then with this speed of sound, a 500 Hz sine wave has a wavelength λ of two feet.

$$\pi = cT = \left(\frac{1000\ ft}{s} \right) \left(\frac{1\ s}{500\ cycles} \right) = \frac{2\ ft}{cycle}$$

At a speed of 1000 ft/s, sound travels one foot each millisecond, which implies that with a one millisecond delay, a sound wave is delayed by one foot. For 500 Hz, this is half the frequency's wavelength. If you remember from Chapter 2, half a wavelength is the same thing as a 180° phase offset. In sum, a one millisecond delay between Loudspeaker A and Loudspeaker B results in a 180° phase difference between the two 500 Hz sine waves. In a free-field environment with your head stationary, this results in a cancellation of the 500 Hz frequency when the two sine waves arrive at your ear. This phase relationship is illustrated in Figure 4.28.

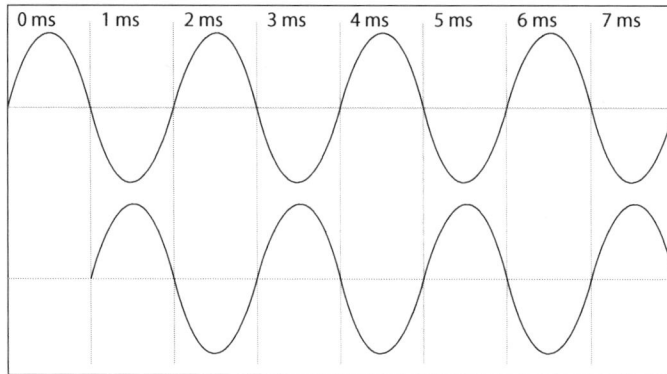

FIGURE 4.28: PHASE RELATIONSHIP BETWEEN TWO 500 HZ SINE WAVES ONE MILLISECOND APART

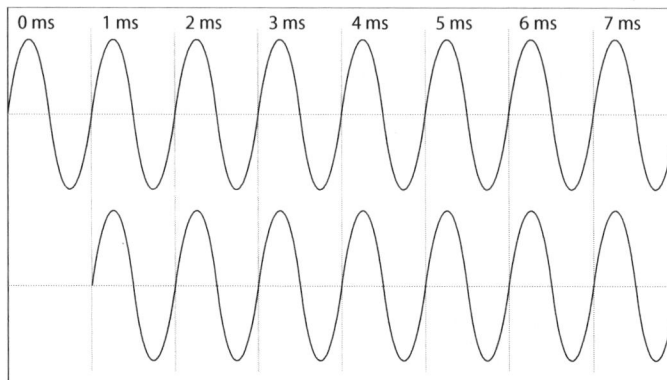

FIGURE 4.29: PHASE RELATIONSHIP BETWEEN TWO 1000 HZ SINE WAVES ONE MILLISECOND APART

If we switch the frequency to 1000 Hz, we're now dealing with a wavelength of one foot. An analysis similar to the one above shows that the one millisecond delay results in a 360° phase difference between the two sounds. For sine waves, two sounds combining at a 360° phase difference behave the same as a 0° phase difference. For all intents and purposes, these two sounds are coherent, which means when they combine at your ear, they reinforce each other, which is perceived as an increase in amplitude. In other words, the totally in-phase frequencies get louder. This phase relationship is illustrated in Figure 4.29.

Simple sine waves serve as convenient examples for how sound works, but they are rarely encountered in practice. Almost all sounds you hear are complex sounds made up of multiple frequencies. Continuing our example of the one millisecond offset between two loudspeakers, consider the implications of sending two identical sine wave sweeps through two loudspeakers. A **sine wave sweep** contains all frequencies in the audible spectrum. When those two identical complex sounds arrive at your ear one millisecond apart, each of the matching pairs of frequency components combines at a different phase relationship. Some frequencies combine with a phase relationship that is a multiple of 180°, causing cancellations. Some frequencies combine with a phase relationship that is a multiple of 360°, causing reinforcements. All the other frequencies combine in phase relationships that vary between multiples of 0° and 360°, resulting in amplitude changes somewhere between complete cancellation and perfect reinforcement. This phenomenon is called **comb filtering**, which can be defined as a regularly repeating pattern of frequencies being attenuated or boosted as you move through the frequency spectrum. (See Figure 4.32.)

To understand comb filtering, let's look at how we detect and analyze it in an acoustic space. First, consider what the frequency response of the sine wave sweep would look like if we measured it coming from one loudspeaker that is 10 feet away from the listener. This is the black line in Figure 4.30. As you can see, the line in the audible spectrum (20 to 20,000 Hz) is relatively flat, indicating that all frequencies are present, at an amplitude level just over 100 dBSPL. The gray line shows the frequency response for an identical sine sweep, but measured at a distance of 11 feet from the one loudspeaker. This frequency response is a little bumpier than the first. Neither frequency response is perfect because environmental conditions affect the sound as it passes through the air. Keep in mind that these two frequency responses, represented by the black and gray lines on the graph, were measured at different times, each from a single loudspeaker, and at distances from the loudspeaker that varied by one foot—the equivalent of offsetting them by one millisecond. Since the two sounds happened at different moments in time, there is of course no comb filtering.

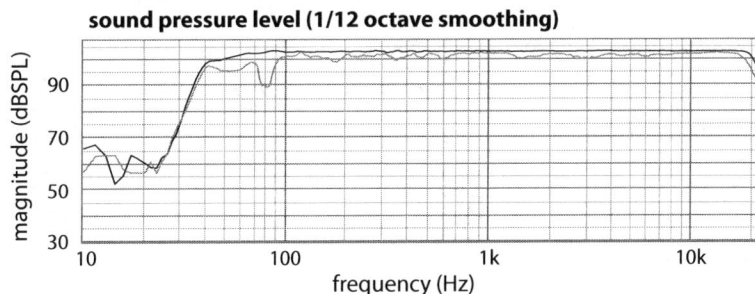

sound pressure level (1/12 octave smoothing)

FIGURE 4.30: FREQUENCY RESPONSE OF TWO SOUND SOURCES ONE MILLISECOND APART

The situation is different when the sound waves are played at the same time through the two loudspeakers not equidistant from the listener, such that the frequency components arrive at the listener in different phases. Figure 4.31 is a graph of frequency versus phase for this situation. You can understand the graph in this way: For each frequency on the x-axis, consider a pair of frequency components of the sound being analyzed, the first belonging to the sound coming from the closer speaker and the second belonging to the sound coming from the farther speaker. The graph shows that degree to which these pairs of frequency components are out of phase, which ranges between −180° and 180°.

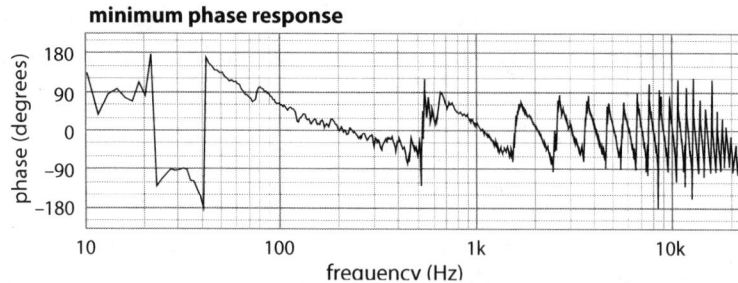

minimum phase response

FIGURE 4.31: PHASE RELATIONSHIP PER FREQUENCY FOR
TWO SOUND SOURCES ONE MILLISECOND APART

Figure 4.32 shows the resulting frequency response when these two sounds are combined. Notice that the frequencies that have a 0° relationship are now louder, at approximately 110 dB. On the other hand, frequencies that are out of phase are now substantially quieter, some by as much as 50 dB depending on the extent of the phase offset. You can see in the graph why the effect is called "comb filtering." The scalloped effect in the graph is how comb filtering appears in frequency response graphs—a regularly repeated pattern of frequencies being attenuated or boosted as you move through the frequency spectrum.

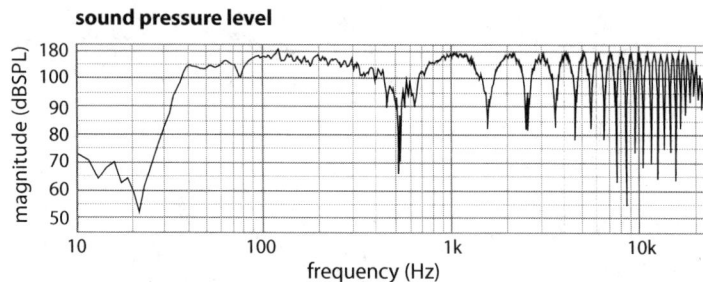

sound pressure level

FIGURE 4.32: COMB FILTERING FREQUENCY RESPONSE OF
TWO SOUND SOURCES ONE MILLISECOND APART

We can try a similar experiment to try to hear the phenomenon of comb filtering using just noise as our sound source. Recall that **noise** consists of random combinations of sound frequencies, usually sound that is not wanted as part of a signal. Two types of noise that a sound processing or analysis system can generate artificially are **white noise** and **pink noise** (and there are others). In white noise, there's an approximately equal number of each of the frequency components across the range of frequencies within the signal. In pink noise, there's an approximately equal number of the frequencies in each octave of frequen-

MAX
DEMO:
Comb Filtering
http://bit.ly/29h8xlH

cies. (Octaves, as defined in Chapter 3, are spaced such that the beginning frequency of one octave is ½ the beginning frequency of the next octave. Although each octave is twice as wide as the previous one—in the distance between its upper and lower frequencies—octaves sound like they are about the same width to human hearing.) The learning supplements to this chapter include a demo of comb filtering using white and pink noise.

Comb filtering in the air is very audible, but it is also very inconsistent. In a comb-filtered environment of sound, if you move your head just slightly to the right or left, you find that the timing difference between the two sounds arriving at your ear changes. With a change in timing comes a change in phase differences per frequency, resulting in comb filtering of some frequencies but not others. Add to this the fact that the source sound is constantly changing, and, all things considered, comb filtering in the air becomes something that is very difficult to control.

One way to tackle comb filtering in the air is to increase the delay between the two sound sources. This may seem counterintuitive since the difference in time is what caused this problem in the first place. However, a larger delay results in comb filtering that starts at lower frequencies, and as you move up the frequency scale, the cancellations and reinforcements get close enough together that they happen within critical bands. The sum of cancellations and reinforcements within a critical band essentially results in the same overall amplitude as would have been there had there been no comb filtering. Since all frequencies within a critical band are perceived as the same frequency, your brain glosses over the anomalies, and you end up not noticing the destructive interference. (This is an oversimplification of the complex perceptual influence of critical bands, but it gives you a basic understanding for our purposes.) In most cases, once you get a timing difference that is larger than five milliseconds on a complex sound that is constantly changing, the comb filtering in the air is not heard anymore. We explain this point mathematically in Section 4.3.2.

The other strategy to fix comb filtering is to simply prevent identical sound waves from interacting. In a perfect world, loudspeakers would have shutter cuts that would let you put the sound into a confined portion of the room. This way the coverage pattern for each loudspeaker would never overlap with another. In the real world, loudspeaker coverage is very difficult to control. We discuss this further and demonstrate how to compensate for comb filtering in the video tutorial entitled "Loudspeaker Interaction" in Chapter 8, Section 8.2.4.4.

Comb filtering in the air is not always the result of two loudspeakers. The same thing can happen when a sound reflects from a wall in the room and arrives in the same place as the direct sound. Because the reflection takes a longer trip to arrive at that spot in the room, it is slightly behind the direct sound. If the reflection is strong enough, the amplitudes between the direct and reflected sound are close enough to cause comb filtering. In really large rooms, the timing difference between the direct and reflected sound is large enough that the comb filtering is not very problematic. Our hearing system is quite good at compensating for any anomalies that result in this kind of sound interaction. In smaller rooms, such as recording studios and control rooms, it's quite possible for reflections to cause audible comb filtering. In those situations, you need to either absorb the reflection or diffuse the reflection at the wall.

The worst kind of comb filtering isn't the kind that occurs in the air but the kind that occurs on a wire. Let's reverse our scenario and instead of having two sound sources, let's switch to a single sound source such as a singer and use two microphones to pick up that singer. Microphone A is one foot away from the singer, and Microphone B is two feet away. In this case, Microphone B catches the sound from the singer one millisecond after Microphone A. When you mix the sounds from those two microphones (which happens all the time), you now have a one millisecond comb filter imposed on an electronic signal that then gets delivered in that condition to all the loudspeakers in the room and from there to all the listeners in the room equally. Now your problem can be heard no matter where you sit, and no matter how much you move your head around. Just one millisecond delay causes a very audible problem that no one can mask or hide from. The best way to avoid this kind of problem is never to allow two microphones to pick up the same signal at the same time. A good sound engineer at a mixing console ensures that only one microphone is on at a time, thereby avoiding this kind of destructive interaction. If you must have more than one microphone, you need to keep those microphones far away from each other. If this is not possible, you can achieve modest success fixing the problem by adding some extra delay to one of the microphones. This changes the phase effect of the two microphones combining, but doesn't mimic the difference in level that would come if they were physically farther apart.

4.2.2.5 Resonance and Room Modes

In Chapter 2, we discussed the concept of resonance. Now we consider how resonance comes into play in real, hands-on applications.

Resonance plays a role in sound perception in a room. One practical example of this is the standing wave phenomenon, which in an acoustic space produces the phenomenon of room modes. **Room modes** are collections of resonances that result from sound waves reflecting from the surfaces of an acoustical space, producing places where sounds are amplified or attenuated. Places where the reflections of a particular frequency reinforce each other, amplifying that frequency, are the frequency's **antinodes**. Places where the

frequency's reflections cancel each other are the frequency's **nodes**. Consider this simplified example—a 10-foot-wide room with parallel walls that are good sound reflectors. Let's assume again that the speed of sound is 1000 ft/s. Imagine a sound wave emanating from the center of the room. The sound waves reflecting off the walls either constructively or destructively interfere with each other at any given location in the room, depending on the relative phase of the sound waves at that point in time and space. If the sound wave has a wavelength that is *exactly* twice the width of the room, then the sound waves reflecting off opposite walls cancel each other in the center of the room but reinforce each other at the walls. Thus, the center of the room is a node for this sound wavelength and the walls are antinodes.

We can again apply the wavelength equation, $\pi = c/f$, to find a frequency f that corresponds to a wavelength λ that is exactly twice the width of the room, $2 \times 10 = 20$ ft.

$$\lambda = \frac{c}{f}$$

$$20\frac{ft}{cycle} = \frac{1000\frac{ft}{s}}{f}$$

$$f = \frac{50\ cycles}{s}$$

At the antinodes, the signals are reinforced by their reflections, so that the 50 Hz sound is unnaturally loud at the walls. At the node in the center, the signals reflecting off the walls cancel out the signal from the loudspeaker. Similar cancellations and reinforcements occur with harmonic frequencies at 100 Hz, 150 Hz, 200 Hz, and so forth, whose wavelengths fit evenly between the two parallel walls. If listeners are scattered around the room, standing closer to either the nodes or antinodes, some hear the harmonic frequencies very well and others do not. Figure 4.33 illustrates the node and antinode positions for room modes when the frequency of the sound wave is 50 Hz, 100 Hz, 150 Hz, and 200 Hz. Table 4.6 shows the relationships among frequency, wavelength, number of nodes and antinodes, and number of harmonics.

Cancelling and reinforcement of frequencies in the room mode phenomenon is also an example of comb filtering.

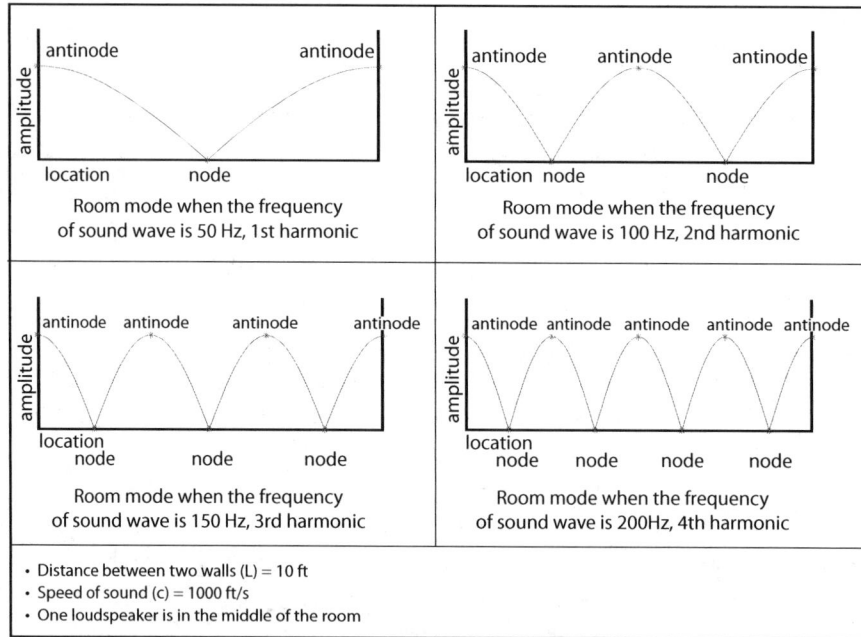

FIGURE 4.33: ROOM MODE

Frequency	Antinodes	Nodes	Wavelength	Harmonics
$f_0 = c/(2L)$	2	1	$\lambda = 2L$	1st harmonic
$f_1 = c/L$	3	2	$\lambda = L$	2nd harmonic
$f_2 = (3c)/(2L)$	4	3	$\lambda = (2L)/3$	3rd harmonic
$f_k = (kc)/(2L)$	$k+1$	k	$\lambda = (2L)/k$	kth harmonic

TABLE 4.6: ROOM MODE, NODES, ANTINODES, AND HARMONICS

This example is actually more complicated than shown because there are multiple parallel walls in a room. Room modes can exist that involve all four walls of a room plus the floor and ceiling. This problem can be minimized by eliminating parallel walls whenever possible in the building design. Often the simplest solution is to hang material on the walls at selected locations to absorb or diffuse the sound.

The standing wave phenomenon can be illustrated with a concrete example that also relates to instrument vibrations and resonances. Figure 4.34 shows an example of a standing wave pattern on a vibrating plate. In this case, the flat plate is resonating at 95 Hz, which represents a frequency that fits evenly with the size of the plate. As the plate bounces up and down, the sand on the plate keeps moving until it finds a place that isn't bouncing. In this case, the sand collects in the nodes of the standing wave. (These are called Chladni patterns, after the German scientist who originated the experiments in the early 1800s.) If a similar resonance occurred in a room, the sound would get noticeably quieter in the areas corresponding to the pattern of sand because those would be the places in the room where air molecules simply aren't moving (neither compression nor rarefaction). For a more complete demonstration of this example, see the video demo called Plate Resonance linked in this section.

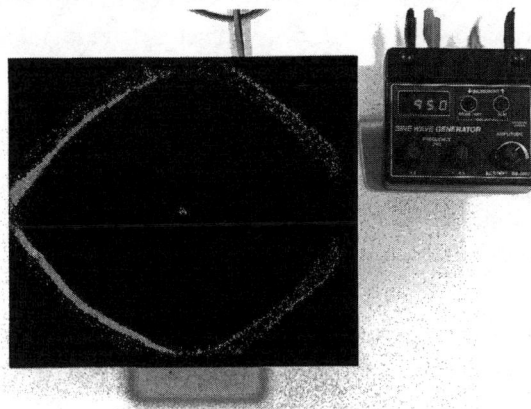

FIGURE 4.34: RESONANT FREQUENCY ON A FLAT PLATE

4.2.2.6 The Precedence Effect

When two or more similar sound waves interact in the air, not only does the perceived frequency response change, but your perception of the location of the sound source can change as well. This phenomenon is called the **precedence effect**. The precedence effect occurs when two similar sound sources arrive at a listener at different times from different directions, causing the listener to perceive both sounds as if they were coming from the direction of the sound that arrived first.

The precedence effect is sometimes intentionally created within a sound space. For example, it might be used to reinforce the live sound of a singer on stage without making it sound as if some of the singer's voice is coming from a loudspeaker. However, there are conditions that must be in place for the precedence effect to occur. First is that the difference in time arrival at the listener between the two sound sources needs to be more than one millisecond. Also, depending on the type of sound, the difference in time needs to be less

MAX
DEMO:
Delay Panner
http://bit.ly/29f4VG8

than 20 to 30 milliseconds, or the listener will perceive an audible echo. Short transient sounds starts to echo around 20 milliseconds, but longer sustained sounds don't start to echo until around 30 milliseconds. The required condition is that the two sounds cannot be more than 10 dB different in level. If the second arrival is more than 10 dB louder than the first, even if the timing is right, the listener begins to perceive the two sounds to be coming from the direction of the louder sound.

When you intentionally apply the precedence effect, you have to keep in mind that comb filtering still applies in this scenario. For this reason, it's usually best to keep the arrival differences to more than five milliseconds because our hearing system is able to more easily compensate for the comb filtering at longer time differences.

The advantage to the precedence effect is that although you perceive the direction of both sounds as arriving from the direction of the first arrival, you also perceive an increase in loudness as a result of the sum of the two sound waves. This effect has been around for a long time and is a big part of what gives a room "good acoustics." There are rooms where sound seems to propagate well over long distances, but this isn't because the inverse square law is magically being broken. The real magic is the result of reflected sound. If sound is reflecting from the room surfaces and arriving at the listener within the precedence time window, the listener perceives an increase in sound level without noticing the direction of the reflected sound. One goal of an acoustician is to maximize the good reflections and minimize the reflections that would arrive at the listener outside of the precedence time window, causing an audible echo.

The fascinating part of the precedence effect is that multiple arrivals can be daisy-chained, and the effect still works. There could be three or more distinct arrivals at the listener, and as long as each arrival is within the precedence time window of the previous arrival, all the arrivals sound like they're coming from the direction of the first arrival. From the perspective of acoustics, this is equivalent to having several early reflections arrive at the listener. For example, a listener might hear a reflection 20 milliseconds after the direct sound arrives. This reflection would image back to the first arrival of the direct sound, but the listener would perceive an increase in sound level. A second reflection could also arrive 40 milliseconds later. Alone, this 40 millisecond reflection would cause an audible echo, but when it's paired with the first 20 millisecond reflection, no echo is perceived by the listener because the second reflection is arriving within the precedence time window of the first reflection. Because the first reflection arrives within the precedence time window of the direct sound, the sound of both reflections image back to the direct sound. The result is that the listener perceives an overall increase in level along with a summation of the frequency response of the three sounds.

The precedence effect can be replicated in sound reinforcement systems. It is common practice now in live performance venues to put a microphone on a performer and relay that sound out to the audience through a loudspeaker system in an effort to increase the overall sound pressure level and intelligibility perceived by the audience.

Without some careful attention to detail, this process can lead to a very unnatural sound. Sometimes this is fine, but in some cases the goal might be to improve the level and intelligibility while still allowing the audience to perceive all the sound as coming from the actual performer. Using the concept of the precedence effect, a loudspeaker system could be designed that has the sound of multiple loudspeakers arriving at the listener from various distances and directions. As long as each loudspeaker arrives at the listener within 5 to 30 milliseconds and within 10 dB of the previous sound with the natural sound of the performer arriving first, all the sound from the loudspeaker system images in the listener's mind back to the location of the actual performer. When the precedence effect is handled well, it simply sounds to the listener like the performer is naturally loud and clear, and that the room has good acoustics.

As you can imagine from the issues discussed above, designing and setting up a sound system for a live performance is a complicated process. A good knowledge of digital signal processing is required to manipulate the delay, level, and frequency response of each loudspeaker in the system, and to properly line up all the listening points in the room. The details of this process are beyond the scope of this book. For more information, see (Davis and Patronis 2006) and (McCarthy 2009).

4.2.2.7 Effects of Temperature

In addition to the physical obstructions with which sound interacts, the air through which sound travels can have an effect on the listener's experience. As discussed in Chapter 2, the speed of sound increases with higher air temperatures. It seems fairly simple to say that if you can measure the temperature of the air you're working in, you should be able to figure out the speed of sound in that space. In actual practice, however, air temperature is rarely uniform throughout an acoustic space. When sound is played outdoors, in particular, the wave front encounters varying temperatures as it propagates through the air.

Consider the scenario where the sun has been shining down on the ground all day. The sun warms up the ground. When the sun sets at the end of the day (which is usually when you start an outdoor performance), the air cools down. The ground is still warm, however, and affects the temperature of the air near the ground. The result is a temperature gradient that gets warmer the closer you get to the ground. When a sound wave front tries to propagate through this temperature gradient, the portion of the wave front that is closer to the ground travels faster than the portion that is higher up in the air. This causes the wave front to curve upwards towards the cooler air. Usually, the listeners are sitting on the ground, and therefore the sound is traveling away from them. The result is a quieter sound for those listeners. So if you spent the afternoon setting your sound system volume to a comfortable listening level, when the performance begins at sundown, you'll have to increase the volume to maintain those levels because the sound is being refracted up towards the cooler air.

Figure 4.35 shows a diagram representing this refraction. Recall that sound is a longitudinal wave where the air pressure amplitude increases and decreases, vibrating the air molecules back and forth in the same direction in which the energy is propagating. The vertical lines represent the wave fronts of the air pressure propagation. Because the sound travels faster in warmer air, the propagation of the air pressure is faster as you get closer to the ground. This means that the wave fronts closer to the ground are ahead of those farther from the ground, causing the sound wave to refract upwards.

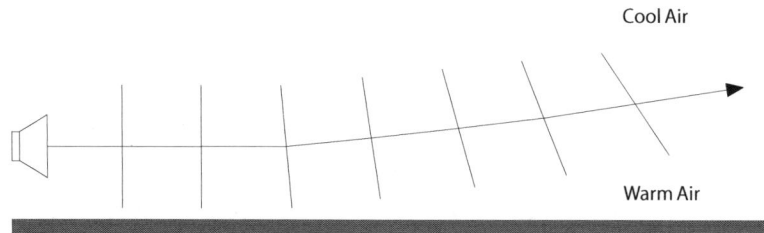

FIGURE 4.35: SOUND REFRACTED TOWARD COOLER AIR

A similar thing can happen indoors in a movie theater or other live performance hall. Usually, sound levels are set when the space is empty prior to an audience arriving. When an audience arrives and fills all the seats, things suddenly get a lot quieter, as any sound engineer will tell you. Most attribute this to sound absorption in the sense that a human body absorbs sound much better than an empty chair. Absorption does play a role, but it doesn't entirely explain the loss of perceived sound level. Even if human bodies are absorbing some of the sound, the sound arriving at the ears directly from the loudspeaker, with no intervening obstructions, arrives without having been dampened by absorption. It's the reflected sound that gets quieter. Also, most theater seats are designed with padding and perforation on the underside of the seat so that they absorb sound at a similar rate to a human body. This way, when you're setting sound levels in an empty theatre, you should be able to hear sound being absorbed the way it will be absorbed when people are sitting in those seats, allowing you to set the sound properly. Thus, absorption can't be the only reason for the sudden drop in sound level when the listeners fill the audience. Temperature is also a factor here. Not only is the human body a good absorber of acoustic energy, but it is also very warm. Fill a previously empty audience area with several hundred warm bodies, turn on the air conditioning that vents out from the ceiling, and you're creating a temperature gradient that is even more dramatic than the one that is created outdoors at sundown. As the sound wave front travels toward the listeners, the air nearest to the listeners allows the sound to travel faster while the air up near the air conditioning vents slows the propagation of that portion of the wave front. Just as in the outdoor example, the wave front is refracted upward toward the cooler air, and there may be a loss in sound level perceived by the listeners.

There isn't anything that can be done about the temperature effects. Eventually the temperature will even out as the air conditioning does its job. The important thing to remember is to listen for a while before you try to fix the sound levels. The change in sound level as a result of temperature will likely fix itself over time.

4.2.2.8 Modifying and Adapting to the Acoustical Space

An additional factor to consider when you're working with indoor sound is the architecture of the room, which greatly affects the way sound propagates. When a sound wave encounters a surface (walls, floors, etc.) several things can happen. The sound can reflect off the surface and begin traveling another direction, it can be absorbed by the surface, it can be transmitted by the surface into a room on the opposite side, or it can be diffracted around the surface if the surface is small relative to the wavelength of the sound.

Typically some combination of all four of these things happens each time a sound wave encounters a surface. Reflection and absorption are the two most important issues in room acoustics. A room that is too acoustically **reflective** is not very good at propagating sound intelligibly. This is usually described as the room being too "live." A room that is too acoustically **absorptive** is not very good at propagating sound with sufficient amplitude. This is usually described as the room being too "dead." The ideal situation is a good balance between reflection and absorption to allow the sound to propagate through the space loudly and clearly.

The kinds of reflections that can help you are called **early reflections**, which arrive at the listener within 30 milliseconds of the **direct sound**. The direct sound arrives at the listener directly from the source. An early reflection can help with the perceived loudness of the sound because the two sounds combine at the listener's ear in a way that reinforces, creating a precedence effect. Because the reflection sounds like the direct sound and arrives shortly after the direct sound, the listener assumes both sounds come from the source and perceives the result to be louder as a result of the combined amplitudes. If you have early reflections, it's important that you don't do anything to the room that would stop those early reflections such as modifying the material of the surface with absorptive material. You can create more early reflections by adding reflective surfaces to the room that are angled in such a way that the sound hitting that surface is reflected to the listener.

If you have reflections that arrive at the listener more than 30 milliseconds after the direct sound, you'll want to fix that because these reflections sound like echoes and destroy the intelligibility of the sound. You have two options when dealing with late reflections. The first is simply to absorb them by attaching to the reflective surface something absorptive like a thick curtain or acoustic absorption tile (Figure 4.36). The other option is to diffuse the reflection.

When reflections get close enough together, they cause **reverberation**. Reverberant sound can be a very nice addition to the sound as long as the reverberant sound is quieter than the direct sound. The relationship between the direct and reverberant sound is called the **direct to reverberant ratio**. If that ratio is too low, you'll have intelligibility problems. Diffusing a late reflection using diffusion tiles (Figure 4.37) generates several random reflections instead of a single one. If done correctly, diffusion converts

FIGURE 4.36: ACOUSTIC ABSORPTION TILE

FIGURE 4.37: ACOUSTIC DIFFUSION TILE

the late reflection into reverberation. If the reverberant sound in the room is already at a sufficient level and duration, then absorbing the late reflection is probably the best route. For more information on identifying reflections in the room, see Section 4.2.2.3.

If you've exhausted all the reasonable steps you can take to improve the acoustics of the room, the only thing that remains is to increase the level of the direct sound in a way that doesn't increase the reflected sound. This is where sound reinforcement systems come in. If you can use a microphone to pick up the direct sound very close to the source, you can then play that sound out of a loudspeaker that is closer to the listener in a way that sounds louder to the listener. If you can do this without directing too much of the sound from the loudspeaker at the room surfaces, you can increase the direct to reverberant ratio, thereby increasing the intelligibility of the sound.

4.2.3   ACOUSTICAL CONSIDERATIONS FOR THE RECORDING STUDIO

In a recording studio, all the same acoustic behaviors exist that are described in 4.2.2.8. The goals and concerns are somewhat different, however. At the most basic level, your main acoustic concern in a recording studio is to accurately record a specific sound without capturing other sounds at the same time.

These other sounds can include noise from the outside; sound bleed from other instruments; noise inside the room from air handlers, lights, or other noise-generating devices; and reflections of the sound you're recording that are coming back to the microphone from the room surfaces.

The term **isolation** is used often in the context of recording studios. Isolation refers to acoustically isolating the recording studio from the outside world. It also refers to acoustically isolating one sound from another within the room. When isolating the studio from the sounds outside, the basic strategy is to build really thick walls. The thicker and more solid the wall, the less likely it is that a sound wave can travel through the wall. Any seams in the wall or openings such as doors and windows have to be completely sealed off. Even a small crack under a door can result in a significant amount of sound coming in from the outside. In most cases, the number of doors and windows in a recording studio is limited because of isolation concerns. Imagine that you have a great musician playing in the studio, and he plays a perfect sequence that he has so far been unable to achieve. In the middle of the sequence, someone honks a car horn outside the building, and that sound gets picked up on the microphone inside the studio. That recording is now unusable, and you have to ask the musician to attempt to repeat his perfect performance.

One strategy for allowing appropriate windows and doors into the building without compromising the acoustic isolation of the studio is to build a room inside of a room. This can be as small as a freestanding booth inside of a room, or you can build an entire recording studio as a room within a larger room within a building. The booth or studio needs to be isolated as much as possible from any vibrations of the larger room. This is sometimes called **floating** the room in a way that no surface of the booth or the studio physically touches any of the surfaces of the larger room that come in contact with the outside world. For a small recording booth, floating can be as simple as putting the booth on large wheel casters. Floating an entire studio involves a complicated system of floor supports that can absorb vibration. Figure 4.38 shows an example of a floating isolation booth that can be used for recording within a larger room.

FIGURE 4.38: A SMALL FLOATING ISOLATION BOOTH
(PHOTO COURTESY OF WHISPERROOM INC.)

The other isolation concern when recording is isolating the microphones from one another and from the room acoustics. For example, if you're recording two musicians, each playing a guitar, you want to record in a way that allows you to mix the balance between the two instruments later. If you have both signals recording from the same microphone, you can't adjust the balance later. Using two microphones can help, but then you have to figure out how to get one microphone to pick up only the first guitar and another microphone to pick up only the second. This perfect isolation is really possible only if you record each sound separately, which is a common practice. However, if both sounds must be recorded simultaneously, you'll need to seek as much isolation as possible. This can be achieved by getting the microphones closer to the thing you want to pick up the loudest. You can also put acoustic baffles between the microphones. These baffles are simple moveable partitions that acoustically absorb sound. You can also put each musician in an isolation booth and allow them to hear each other through closed-backed headphones.

If you need to isolate the microphone from the reflections in the room without resorting to an isolation booth, you can achieve modest success by enclosing the microphone with a small acoustic baffle on the microphone stand like the one shown in Figure 4.39. This helps isolate the microphone from sounds coming from behind or from the sides, but provides no isolation from sounds arriving at the front of the microphone. This kind of baffle has no impact on the ambient noise level picked up by the microphone. It only serves to isolate the microphone from certain reflections coming from the studio walls.

**FIGURE 4.39: ACOUSTIC BAFFLE
FOR A MICROPHONE STAND**

Room ventilation is a notorious contributor to room noise in a recording studio. Of course ventilation is necessary, but if it's done poorly, the system can compromise the acoustic isolation of the room from the outside world and can introduce a significant amount of self-generated fan noise into the room. The commercially available portable isolation booths typically have ventilation systems available that do not compromise the isolation and noise level for the booth. If you're putting in a ventilation system for a large studio, be prepared to spend a lot of money and hire an expert to design a system that meets your requirements. In the worst-case scenario, you may need to shut off the ventilation system while recording if the system is creating too much noise in the room.

There are differing opinions on acoustical treatment for the studio. In the room where the actual performing happens, some like a completely acoustically dead room, while others want to have a little bit of natural reverberation. Most studios have some combination of acoustic absorption treatment and some diffusion treatment on the room surfaces. The best approach is to have flexible acoustic treatment on the walls. This can take the form of reversible panels on the wall that have absorption material on one side and diffusion panels on the other side. This way you can customize the acoustics of the room as needed for each recording.

In the control room where the mixing happens, you don't necessarily want a completely dead room. You do want a quiet room, and you want to remove any destructive early reflections that arrive at the mixing position. Other than that, you generally want to try to mimic the environment in which the listener will ultimately experience the sound. For film, you would want to mimic the acoustics of a screening room. For music, you may want to mimic the acoustics of a living room or similar listening space. This way, you're mixing the sound in an acoustic environment that allows you to hear the problems that will be audible by the consumer. As a rule of thumb, you should design the acoustics of the room for the best-case listening scenario for the consumer. Then test your mix in less desirable listening environments once you have something that sounds good in the studio.

4.3 SCIENCE, MATHEMATICS, AND ALGORITHMS

4.3.1 DERIVING POWER AND VOLTAGE CHANGES IN DECIBELS

Let's turn now to explore more of the mathematics of concepts related to acoustics.

In Section 4.1.5.1, Table 4.2 lists some general guidelines regarding sound perception, and in Section 4.2.1.2, Table 4.5 gives some rules of thumb regarding power or voltage changes converted to decibels. We can't mathematically prove the relationships in Table 4.2 because they're based on subjective human perception, but we can prove the relationships in Table 4.5.

First, let's prove that if we double the power in watts, we get a 3 dB increase. As you work through this example, you see that you don't always use decibels related to the reference points in Table 4.3. (That is, the standard reference point is not always the value in the denominator.) Sometimes you compare one wattage level to another, or one voltage level to another, or one sound pressure level to another, wanting to know the difference between the two in decibels. In those cases, the answer represents a difference in two wattage, voltage, or sound pressure levels, and it is measured in dB.

In general, to compare two power levels, we use the following:

$$\text{The difference in decibels between power } P_0 \text{ and power } P_1 = 10 \log_{10}\left(\frac{P_0}{P_1}\right)$$

EQUATION 4.15

If $P_1 = 2P_0$ then we have

$$10 \log_{10}\left(\frac{2P_0}{P_0}\right) = 10 \log_{10} 2 \approx 3 \, dB \, increase$$

You can illustrate this rule of thumb with two specific wattage levels—for example 1000 W and 500 W. First, convert watts to dBm. Table 4.3 gives the reference point for the definitions of dBm, dBW, dBV, and dBu. The table shows that dBM uses 0.001 W as the reference point, which means that it is in the denominator inside the log.

$$10 \log_{10}\left(\frac{1000}{0.001}\right) = 60 \, dBm$$

Thus, 1000 W is 60 dBm.

What is 500 W in dBM? The standard reference point for dBm is 0.001 W. This yields

$$10 \log_{10}\left(\frac{500}{0.001}\right) \approx 57 \, dBm$$

We see that 500 W is about 57 dBm, confirming that doubling the wattage results in a 3 dB increase, just as we predicted. We get the same result if we compute the increase in decibels based on dBW. dBW uses a reference point of 1 W in the denominator.

$$10 \log_{10} \left(\frac{1000}{1} \right) = 30 \, dBW$$

1000 W is about 30 dBW.

$$10 \log_{10} \left(\frac{500}{1} \right) \approx 27 \, dBW$$

500 W is about 27 dBW. Again, doubling the wattage results in a 3 dB increase, as predicted.

Continuing with Table 4.5, we can show that if we multiply the power by 10, we have a 10 dB increase in power.

$$10 \log_{10} 10 = 10 \, dB \ increase \ in \ power$$

If we divide the power by 10, we get a 10 dB decrease in power.

$$10 \log_{10} \left(\frac{1}{10} \right) = -10 \, dB. \ This \ is \ a \ 10 \, dB \ decrease \ in \ power$$

For voltage, we use the formula $20\log_{10}(V_1/V_0)$, as shown in Table 4.3. From this we can show that if we double the voltage, we have a 6 dB increase.

$$20 \log_{10} 2 \approx 6 \, dB \ increase \ in \ voltage$$

If we multiply the voltage times 10, we get a 20 dB increase.

$$20 \log_{10} 10 = 20 \, dB \ increase \ in \ voltage$$

Don't be fooled into thinking that if we multiply the voltage by 5, we'll get a 10 dB increase. Instead, multiplying voltage times 5 yields about 14 dB increase in voltage.

$$20 \log_{10} 5 \approx 14 \, dB \ increase \ in \ voltage$$

The rest of the rows in Table 4.3 related to voltage can be proven similarly.

4.3.2 WORKING WITH CRITICAL BANDS

Recall from Section 4.1 that critical bands are areas in the human ear that are sensitive to certain bandwidths of frequencies. The presence of critical bands in our ears is responsible for the masking of frequencies that are close to other louder ones that are received by the same critical band.

In most sources, tables that estimate the widths of critical bands in human hearing give the bandwidths only in Hertz. In Table 4.4 in Section 4.1.6.2, we added two additional columns. Column 5 of Table 4.4 derives the number of semitones n in a critical band based on the beginning and ending frequencies in the band. Column 6 is the approximate size of the critical band in octaves. Let's look at how we derived these two columns.

First, consider column 5, which gives the critical bandwidth in semitones. Chapter 3 explains that there are 12 semitones in an octave. The note at the high end of an octave has twice the frequency of a note at the low end. Thus, for frequency f_2 that is n semitones higher than f_1,

$$f_2 = \sqrt[12]{2}^n \times f_1$$

To derive column 5 for each row, let b be the beginning frequency of the band, and let e be the end frequency of the band in that row. We want to find n such that

$$e = b \times \left(\sqrt[12]{2} \right)^n$$

This equation can be simplified to find n.

$$e = b \times 2^{\frac{n}{12}}$$

$$\frac{e}{b} = 2^{\frac{n}{12}}$$

Table 4.7 is included to give an idea of the twelfth root of two and powers of it.

$\sqrt[12]{2}^1 = 2^{\frac{1}{12}}$	1.0595
$\sqrt[12]{2}^2 = 2^{\frac{2}{12}}$	1.1225
$\sqrt[12]{2}^3 = 2^{\frac{3}{12}}$	1.1892
$\sqrt[12]{2}^4 = 2^{\frac{4}{12}}$	1.2599
$\sqrt[12]{2}^5 = 2^{\frac{5}{12}}$	1.3348
$\sqrt[12]{2}^6 = 2^{\frac{6}{12}}$	1.4142
$\sqrt[12]{2}^7 = 2^{\frac{7}{12}}$	1.4983
$\sqrt[12]{2}^8 = 2^{\frac{8}{12}}$	1.5874
$\sqrt[12]{2}^9 = 2^{\frac{9}{12}}$	1.6818
$\sqrt[12]{2}^{10} = 2^{\frac{10}{12}}$	1.7818
$\sqrt[12]{2}^{11} = 2^{\frac{11}{12}}$	1.8877
$\sqrt[12]{2}^{12} = 2^{\frac{12}{12}}$	2

TABLE 4.7: POWERS OF THE TWELFTH ROOT OF TWO

In Table 4.4, Column 5 is an estimate for n rounded to the nearest integer, which is the approximate number of semitone steps from the beginning to the end of the band.

Column 6 is derived based on the n computed for column 5. If n is the number of semitones in a critical band and there are 12 semitones in an octave, then $n/12$ is the size of the critical band in octaves. Column 6 is $n/12$.

4.3.3   A MATLAB PROGRAM FOR EQUAL-LOUDNESS CONTOURS

You may be interested in seeing how Figure 4.11 was created with a MATLAB program. The MATLAB program below is included with permission from its creator, Jeff Tackett. The program relies on data available in ISO 226. The data is given in a comment in the program. ISO is The International Organization for Standardization (www.iso.org).

```
figure;
[spl,freq_base] = iso226(10);
semilogx(freq_base,spl)
hold on;
for phon = 0:10:90
[spl,freq] = iso226(phon);%equal-loudness data
plot(1000,phon,'.r');
text(1000,phon+3,num2str(phon));
plot(freq_base,spl);%equal-loudness curve
end
axis([0 13000 0 140]);
grid on % draw grid
xlabel('Frequency (Hz)');
ylabel('Sound Pressure in Decibels');
hold off;

function [spl, freq] = iso226(phon)
% Generates an Equal-Loudness Contour as described in ISO 226
% Usage:  [SPL FREQ] = ISO226(PHON);
%            PHON is the phon value in dB SPL that you want the equal
%              loudness curve to represent. (1phon = 1dB @ 1kHz)
%            SPL is the Sound Pressure Level amplitude returned for
%              each of the 29 frequencies evaluated by ISO226.
%            FREQ is the returned vector of frequencies that ISO226
%              evaluates to generate the contour.
%
% Desc:    This function will return the equal-loudness contour for
%            your desired phon level. The frequencies evaluated in this
%            function only span from 20Hz - 12.5kHz, and only 29 selective
%            frequencies are covered. This is the limitation of the ISO
%            standard.
%
%            In addition the valid phon range should be 0 - 90 dB SPL.
%            Values outside this range do not have experimental values
%            and their contours should be treated as inaccurate.
%
```

```
%               If more samples are required you should be able to easily
%               interpolate these values using spline().
%
% Author: Jeff Tackett 03/01/05
%               /----------------------------------------\
%%%%%%%%%%%%%%%%%             TABLES FROM ISO226             %%%%%%%%%%%%%%%%%
%               \----------------------------------------/
f = [20 25 31.5 40 50 63 80 100 125 160 200 250 315 400 500 630 800 ...
1000 1250 1600 2000 2500 3150 4000 5000 6300 8000 10000 12500];

af = [0.532 0.506 0.480 0.455 0.432 0.409 0.387 0.367 0.349 0.330 0.315 ...
0.301 0.288 0.276 0.267 0.259 0.253 0.250 0.246 0.244 0.243 0.243 ...
0.243 0.242 0.242 0.245 0.254 0.271 0.301];

Lu = [-31.6 -27.2 -23.0 -19.1 -15.9 -13.0 -10.3 -8.1 -6.2 -4.5 -3.1 ...
-2.0  -1.1  -0.4   0.0   0.3   0.5   0.0 -2.7 -4.1 -1.0  1.7 ...
2.5   1.2  -2.1  -7.1 -11.2 -10.7  -3.1];

Tf = [ 78.5  68.7  59.5  51.1  44.0  37.5  31.5  26.5  22.1  17.9  14.4 ...
11.4   8.6   6.2   4.4   3.0   2.2   2.4   3.5   1.7  -1.3  -4.2 ...
-6.0  -5.4  -1.5   6.0  12.6  13.9  12.3];
%%%%%%%%%%%%%%%%%%%%%%%%%%%%%%%%%%%%%%%%%%%%%%%%%%%%%%%%%%%%%%%%%%%%%%%%%%%%%%%

%Error Trapping
if((phon < 0) || (phon > 90))
disp('Phon value out of bounds!')
spl = 0;
freq = 0;
else
%Setup user-defined values for equation
Ln = phon;

%Deriving sound pressure level from loudness level (iso226 sect 4.1)
Af=4.47E-3 * (10.^(0.025*Ln) - 1.15) + (0.4*10.^(((Tf+Lu)/10)-9 )).^af;
Lp=((10./af).*log10(Af)) - Lu + 94;

%Return user data
spl = Lp;
freq = f;
end
```

PROGRAM 4.1: MATLAB PROGRAM FOR GRAPHING EQUAL-LOUDNESS CONTOURS

4.3.4 THE MATHEMATICS OF THE INVERSE SQUARE LAW AND PAG EQUATIONS

The inverse square law says, in essence, that for two points at distance r_0 and r_1 from a point sound source, where $r_1 > r_0$, the sound intensity diminishes by $20\log_{10}(r_0/r_1)$dB. To derive the inverse square law mathematically, we can use the formula for the surface area of a sphere, $4\pi r^2$, where r is the radius of the sphere. Notice that in Figure 4.18, the radius of the sphere is also the distance from the sound source to the surface of that sphere. Recall that intensity is defined as power per unit area—that is, power proportional to the area over which it is spread. As the sound gets farther from the source, it spreads out over a larger area. At any distance r from the source, $I = P/(4\pi r^2)$ where I is intensity and P is the power at the source. Notice that if you increase the radius of the sphere by a factor of n, I gets smaller by a factor of n^2. Thus, I is proportional to the inverse of r^2, which can be stated mathematically as $I \propto 1/r^2$. We can state this more completely as

$$I_1 = I_0 \times \left(\frac{r_0}{r_1}\right)^2$$

where I_0 is the intensity of the sound at the first location,
I_1 is the intensity of the sound at the second location,
r_0 is the initial distance from the sound,
and r_1 is the distance from the sound

EQUATION 4.16: RATIO OF SOUND INTENSITY COMPARING ONE LOCATION TO ANOTHER

We usually represent intensities in decibels, so let's convert to decibels applying the definition of dBSIL.

$$10 \log_{10} I_1 = 10 \log_{10}\left(I_0 \times \left(\frac{r_0}{r_1}\right)^2\right)$$

$$10 \log_{10} I_1 = 10 \log_{10} I_0 + 10 \log_{10}\left(\frac{r_0}{r_1}\right)^2$$

Thus

$$I_{1_{dBSIL}} - I_{0_{dBSIL}} = 20 \log_{10}\left(\frac{r_0}{r_1}\right) \, dB$$

where $I_{0_{dBSIL}}$ is the intensity of the sound at the first location in decibels,
$I_{1_{dBSIL}}$ is the intensity of the sound at the second location in decibels,
r_0 is the initial distance from the sound,
and r_1 is the new distance from the sound

EQUATION 4.17: DIFFERENCE IN SOUND INTENSITY FROM ONE LOCATION TO A NEW LOCATION

Recall that when you subtract dBSIL from dBSIL, you get dB.

Based on the inverse square law, it is easy to prove that if you double the distance from the sound, you get about a 6 dB decrease (as listed in Table 4.5).

$$Distance\ \Delta dB = 10 \log_{10}\left(\frac{r_0{}^2}{(2 \times r_0)^2}\right) = 10 \log_{10}\left(\frac{1}{4}\right) \approx -6\,dB$$

In Section 4.2.2.1, we looked at how the PAG is determined so that a sound engineer can know the limits of the gain he can apply to the sound without getting feedback. You can understand why feedback happens and how it can be prevented by applying the inverse square law.

First, we can derive an equation for the sound level that comes from the singer arriving at the microphone at intensity I_M versus arriving at the listener at intensity I_L, without sound reinforcement. All sound levels are in decibels. By the inverse square law, the relationship between I_L and I_M is this:

$$I_L - I_M = 20 \log_{10}\left(\frac{D_s}{D_0}\right)$$

EQUATION 4.18: DIFFERENCE IN SOUND INTENSITY AT THE LISTENER VS. AT THE MICROPHONE

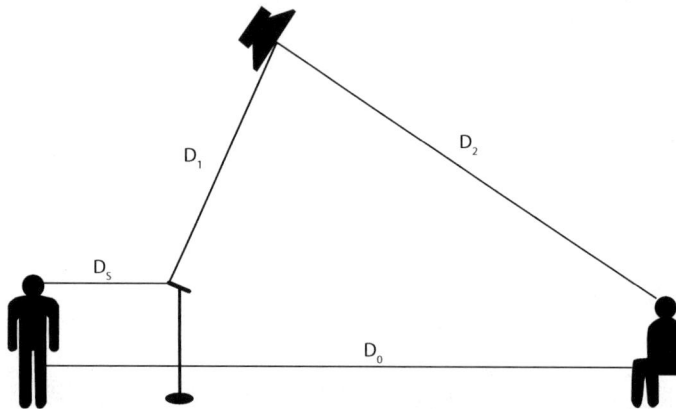

FIGURE 4.40: COMPUTING THE PAG

We can also apply the inverse square law to the sound coming from the loud-speaker and arriving at microphone at intensity $I_{M'}$ versus arriving the listener at intensity $I_{L'}$, with reinforcement. Feedback occurs where $I_M = I_{M'}$. Thus we have

$$I_{L'} - I_{M'} =$$

$$I_{L'} - I_M = 20 \log_{10}\left(\frac{D_1}{D_2}\right)$$

EQUATION 4.19: DIFFERENCE IN REINFORCED SOUND INTENSITY AT THE LISTENER VS. THE MIC

Subtracting Equation 4.18 from Equation 4.19, we get

$$I_{L'} - I_L = 20 \log_{10} \left(\frac{D_1}{D_2} \right) - 20 \log_{10} \left(\frac{D_s}{D_0} \right)$$

$$I_{L'} - I_L = 20 \log_{10} \left(\frac{\frac{D_1}{D_2}}{\frac{D_s}{D_0}} \right)$$

$$I_{L'} - I_L = 20 \log_{10} \left(\frac{D_1 \times D_0}{D_s \times D_2} \right)$$

$I_{L'} = I_L$ represents the PAG, the maximum amount by which the original sound can be boosted without feedback.

$$PAG = 20 \log_{10} \left(\frac{D_1 \times D_0}{D_s \times D_2} \right)$$

This was Equation 4.14 originally discussed in Section 4.2.2.1.

4.3.5   THE MATHEMATICS OF DELAYS, COMB FILTERING, AND ROOM MODES

In Section 4.2.2.4, we showed what happens when two copies of the same sound arrive at a listener at different times. For each of the frequencies in the sound, the copy of the frequency coming from Loudspeaker B is in a different phase relative to the copy coming from Loudspeaker A (Figure 4.27). In the case of frequencies that are offset by exactly one half of a cycle, the two copies of the sound are completely out of phase, and those frequencies are lost for the listener in that location. This is an example of comb filtering caused by delay.

To generalize this mathematically, let's assume that loudspeaker B is d feet farther away from a listener than loudspeaker A. The speed of sound is c. Then the delay t, in seconds, is

{}

PROGRAMMING EXERCISE:

Creating Comb
Filtering in C++
http://bit.ly/29ib84M

$$t = \frac{d\ ft}{c\ ft/s}$$

EQUATION 4.20: DELAY T FOR OFFSET D BETWEEN TWO LOUDSPEAKERS

Assume for simplicity that the speed of sound is 1000 ft/s. Thus, for an offset of 20 feet, you get a delay of 0.020 seconds.

$$t = \frac{20\ ft}{1000\ ft/s}$$

$$t = 0.02\ s = 20\ ms$$

What if you want to know the frequencies of the sound waves that will be combed out by a delay of t? The fundamental frequency to be combed, f_0, is the one that is delayed by half of the period, since this delay will offset the phase of the wave by 180°. We know that the period is the inverse of the frequency, which gives us

$$t = \frac{1}{2 \times f_0}$$

$$f_0 = \frac{1}{2 \times t}$$

Additionally, all integer multiples of f_0 will also be combed out, since they also will be 180° offset from the other copy of the sound. Thus, we can use this formula for the frequencies combed out by delay t.

>>

MATLAB EXERCISE:

Creating Comb

Filtering in MATLAB
http://bit.ly/29f27lX

PRACTICAL EXERCISE:

Delay and

Comb Filtering
http://bit.ly/29ialkj

Given a delay t between two identical copies of a sound,
then the frequencies f_i that will be combed out are

$$f_i = \frac{i + 1}{2t}\ for\ all\ integers\ i \geq 0$$

EQUATION 4.21: COMB FILTERING

For a 20 foot separation in distance, which creates a delay of 0.02 seconds, the combed frequencies are 25 Hz, 50 Hz, 75 Hz, and so forth.

In Section 4.2.2.4, we made the point that comb filtering in the air can be handled by increasing the delay between the two sound sources. A 40 foot distance between two identical sound sources results in a 0.04 seconds delay, which then combs out 12.5 Hz, 25 Hz, 37.5 Hz, 50 Hz, and so forth. The larger delay, the lower the frequency at which combing begins, and the closer the combed frequencies are to one another. You can see this in Figure 4.41 below. In the first graph, a delay of 0.5682 milliseconds combs out integer multiples of 880 Hz. In the second graph, a delay of 2.2727 milliseconds combs out integer multiples of 220 Hz.

If the delay is long enough, frequencies that are combed out are within the same critical band as frequencies that are amplified. Recall that all frequencies in a critical band are perceived as the same frequency. If one frequency is combed out and another is amplified within the same critical band, the resulting perceived amplitude of the frequency in that band is the same as would be heard without comb filtering. Thus, a long enough delay mitigates the effect of comb filtering. The exercise associated with this section has you verify this point.

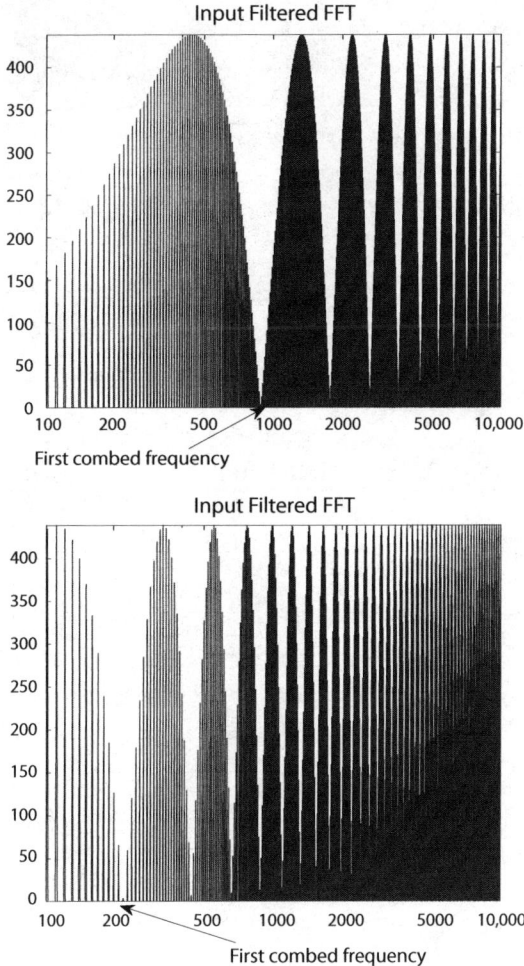

Input Filtered FFT

First combed frequency

Input Filtered FFT

First combed frequency

FIGURE 4.41: COMPARISON OF DELAYS, 0.5682 MS (TOP) AND 2.2727 MS (BOTTOM)

Room mode operates by the same principle as comb filtering. Picture a sound being sent from the center of a room. If the speed of sound in the room is 1000 ft/s and the room has parallel walls that are 10 feet apart, how long will it take the sound to travel from the center of the room, bounce off one of the walls, and come back to the center? Since the sound is traveling $5 + 5 = 10$ ft, we get a delay of $t = (10 \text{ ft})/(1000 \text{ ft/s}) = 0.01$ seconds. This implies that a sound wave of frequency $f_0 = 1/(2 \times 0.01 = 50$ Hz will be combed out in the center of the room. The center of the room is a node with regard to a frequency of 50 Hz.

For the second harmonic, 100 Hz, the nodes are 2.5 feet from the wall. The time it takes for sound to move from a point 2.5 feet from the wall and bounce back to that same point is $2.5 + 2.5 = 5$ ft, yielding a delay of $t = (5 \text{ ft})/(1000 \text{ ft/s}) = 0.005$ s. This is half the period of the 100 Hz wave, meaning a frequency of 100 Hz will be combed out at those points. However, in the center of the room, we still have a delay of $t = (10 \text{ ft})/(1000 \text{ ft/s}) = 0.01$ s which is the full period of the 100 Hz wave, meaning the 100 Hz wave gets *amplified* at the center of the room.

The other harmonic frequencies can be explained similarly.

4.4 REFERENCES

In addition to references cited in previous chapters:

Davis, Don and Eugene Patronis, Jr. *Sound System Engineering,* 3rd ed. Burlington, MA: Focal Press, 2006.

Everest, F. Alton and Ken C. Pohlmann. *Master Handbook of Acoustics,* 5th ed. New York: McGraw-Hill, 2009.

Fletcher, H., and W.A. Munson. "Loudness, Its Definition, Measurement, and Calculations." *Journal of the American Statistical Association* 5 (1933): 82–108.

Levitin , Daniel J. *This Is Your Brain on Music: The Science of a Human Obsession.* New York: Plume, 2007.

MCCarthy, Bob. *Sound Systems: Design and Optimization; Modern Techniques and Tools for Sound System Design and Alignment,* 2nd ed. Burlington, MA: Focal Press, 2009.

Pohlmann, Ken C. *Principles of Digital Audio,* 5th ed. New York: McGraw-Hill, 2005.

Robinson, D.W. and R.S. Dadson. "A Re-determination of the Equal-Loudness Relations for Pure Tones." *British Journal of Applied Physics* 7 (1956): 166–181.

Rossing, Thomas, F. Richard Moore, and Paul A. Wheeler. *The Science of Sound,* 3rd ed. San Francisco: Addison-Wesley Developers Press, 2002.

Thompson, Daniel M. *Understanding Audio: Getting the Most Out of Your Project or Professional Recording Studio.* Boston: Berklee Press, 2005.

Tobias, Jerry V., ed. *Foundations of Modern Auditory Theory,* vol. 1. New York: Academic Press, 1970.

>>

MATLAB EXERCISE:

Creating Room Modes

in MATLAB

http://bit.ly/29f22VJ

CHAPTER FIVE
Digitization

5.1 CONCEPTS

5.1.1 ANALOG VS. DIGITAL

Today's world of sound processing is quite different from what it was just a few decades ago. A large portion of sound processing is now done by digital devices and software—mixers, dynamics processors, equalizers, and a whole host of tools that previously existed only as analog hardware. This is not to say, however, that in all stages—from capturing to playing—sound is now treated digitally. As it is captured, processed, and played back, an audio signal can be transformed numerous times from analog to digital or digital to analog. A typical scenario for live sound reinforcement is pictured in Figure 5.1. In this setup, a microphone—an analog device—detects continuously changing air pressure, records this as analog voltage, and sends the information down a wire to a digital mixing console. Although the mixing console is a digital device, the first circuit within the console that the audio signal encounters is an analog preamplifier. The preamplifier amplifies the voltage of the audio signal from the microphone before passing it on to an **analog-to-digital converter (ADC)**. The ADC performs a process called **digitization** and then passes the signal into one of many digital audio streams in the mixing console. The mixing console applies signal-specific processing such as equalization and reverberation, and then it mixes and routes the signal together with other incoming signals to an output connector. Usually this output is analog, so the signal passes through a **digital-to-analog converter (DAC)** before being sent out. That signal might then be sent to a digital system processor responsible for applying frequency, delay, and dynamics processing for the entire sound system and distributing that signal to several outputs. The signal is similarly converted to digital on the way into this processor via an ADC, and then back through a DAC to analog on the way out. The analog signals are then sent to analog power amplifiers before they are sent to a loudspeaker, which converts the audio signal back into a sound wave in the air.

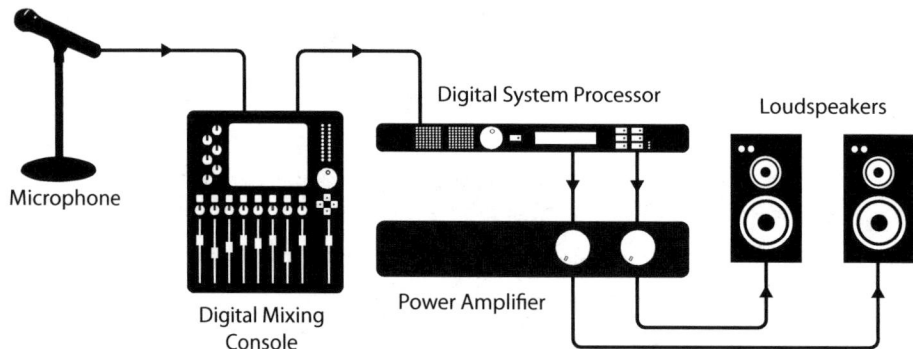

FIGURE 5.1: EXAMPLE OF A SIMPLE LIVE SOUND REINFORCEMENT SYSTEM

A sound system like the one pictured can be a mix of analog and digital devices, and it is not always safe to assume a particular piece of gear can, will, or should be one type or the other. Even some power amplifiers nowadays have a digital signal stage that may require conversion from an analog input signal. Of course, with the prevalence of digital equipment and computerized systems, it is likely that an audio signal will exist digitally at some point in its lifetime. In systems using multiple digital devices, there are also ways of interfacing two pieces of equipment using digital signal connections that can maintain the audio in its digital form and eliminate unnecessary analog-to-digital and digital-to-analog conversions. Specific types of digital signal connections and related issues in connecting digital devices are discussed later in this chapter.

The previous figure shows a live sound system setup. A typical setup of a computer-based audio recording and editing system is pictured in Figure 5.2. While this workstation is essentially digital, the DAW, like the live sound system, includes analog components such as microphones and loudspeakers.

Understanding the digitization process paves the way for understanding the many ways that digitized sound can be manipulated. Let's look at this more closely.

5.1.2 DIGITIZATION

5.1.2.1 Two Steps: Sampling and Quantization

In the realm of sound, the digitization process takes an analog occurrence of sound, records it as a sequence of discrete events, and encodes it in the binary language of computers. Digitization involves two main steps, sampling and quantization.

Sampling is a matter of measuring air pressure amplitude at equally-spaced moments in time, where each measurement constitutes a **sample**. The number of samples taken per second (samples/s) is the **sampling rate**. Units of samples/s are also referred to as **Hertz** (Hz). (Recall that Hertz is also used to mean cycles/s with regard

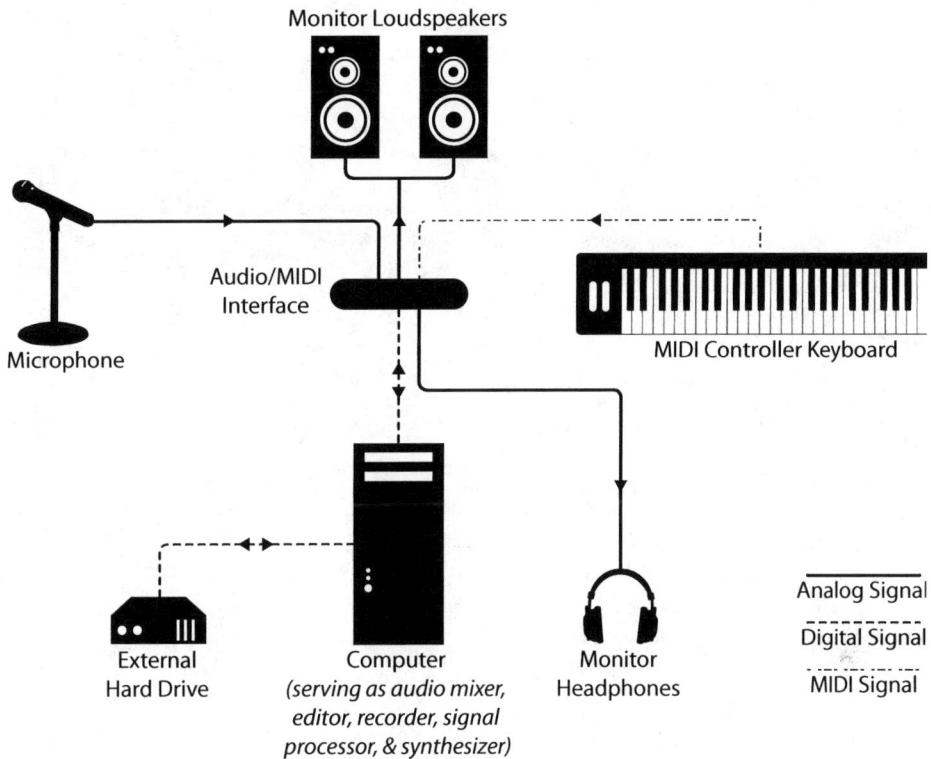

FIGURE 5.2: ANALOG AND DIGITAL COMPONENTS IN A DAW

to a frequency component of sound. Hertz is an overloaded term, having different meanings depending on where it is used, but the context makes the meaning clear.)

Quantization is a matter of representing the amplitude of individual samples as integers expressed in binary. The fact that integers are used forces the samples to be measured in a finite number of discrete levels. The range of the integers possible is determined by the **bit depth**, the number of bits used per sample. A sample's amplitude must be rounded to the nearest of the allowable discrete levels, which introduces error in the digitization process.

ASIDE: It's possible to use real numbers instead of integers to represent sample values in the computer, but that doesn't get rid of the basic problem of quantization. Although a wide range of samples values can be represented with real numbers, there is still only a finite number of them, so rounding is still necessary with real numbers.

When sound is recorded in digital format, a sampling rate and a bit depth are specified. Often there are default audio settings in your computing environment, or you may be prompted for initial settings, as shown in Figure 5.3. The number of channels must also be specified—mono for one channel and stereo for two. More channels are possible in the final production (e.g., 5.1 surround).

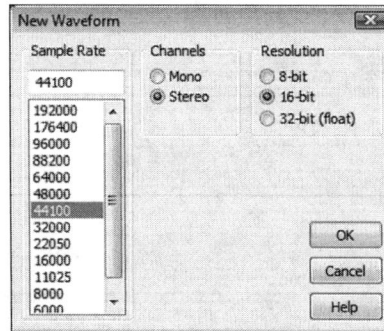

FIGURE 5.3: PROMPTING FOR SAMPLING RATE, BIT DEPTH, AND NUMBER OF CHANNELS

A common default setting is designated **CD quality audio**, with a sampling rate of 44,100 Hz, a bit depth of 16 bits (two bytes) per channel, with two channels. Sampling rate and bit depth have an impact on the quality of a recording. To understand how this works, let's look at sampling and quantization more closely.

5.1.2.2 Sampling and Aliasing

Recall from Chapter 2 that the continuously changing air pressure of a single-frequency sound can be represented by a sine function, as shown in Figure 5.4. One cycle of the sine wave represents one cycle of compression and rarefaction of the sound wave. In digitization, a microphone detects changes in air pressure, sends corresponding voltage changes down a wire to an ADC, and the ADC regularly samples the values. The physical process of measuring the changing air pressure amplitude over time can be modeled by the mathematical process of evaluating a sine function at particular points across the horizontal axis.

> **FLASH TUTORIAL:**
> Sampling
> and Aliasing
> http://bit.ly/29LFUE8

Figure 5.4 shows eight samples being taken for each cycle of the sound wave. The samples are represented as circles along the waveform. The sound wave has a frequency of 440 cycles/s (440 Hz), and the sampling rate has a frequency of 3520 samples/s (3520 Hz). The samples are stored as binary numbers. From these stored values, the amplitude of the digitized sound can be recreated and turned into analog voltage changes by the DAC.

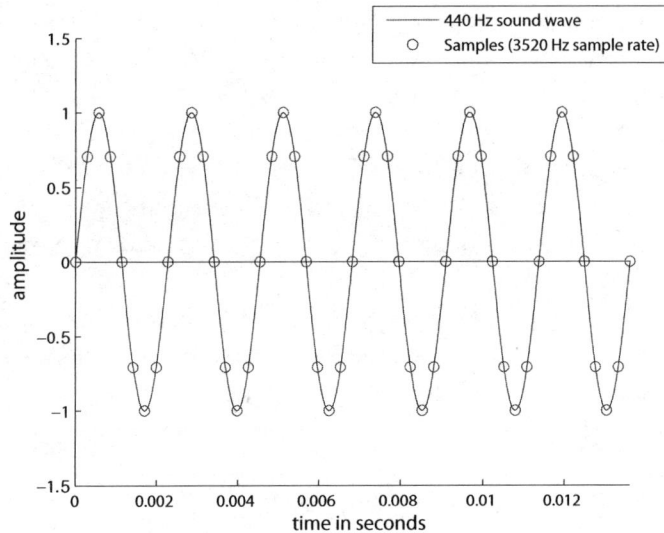

FIGURE 5.4: GRAPH OF SINE FUNCTION MODELING A 440 HZ SOUND WAVE

The quantity of these stored values that exists within a given amount of time, as defined by the sampling rate, is important to capturing and recreating the frequency content of the audio signal. The higher the frequency content of the audio signal, the more samples per second (higher sampling rate) are needed to accurately represent it in the digital domain. Consider what would happen if only one sample was taken for every one-and-a-quarter cycles of the sound wave, as pictured in Figure 5.5.

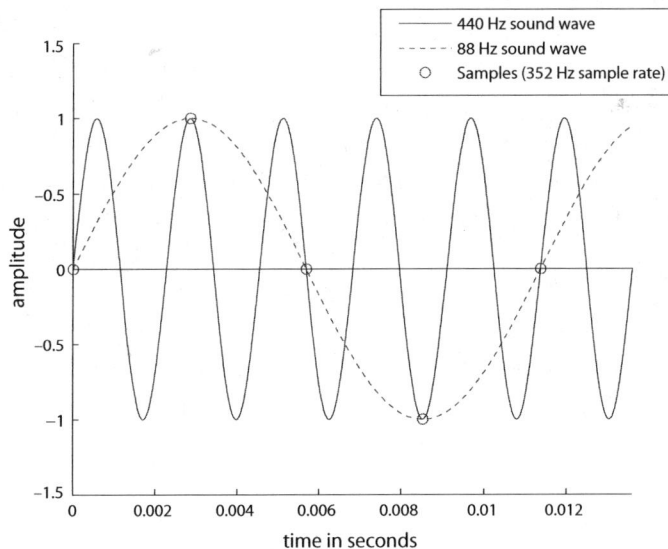

FIGURE 5.5: 440 HZ WAVE UNDERSAMPLED

This would not be enough information for the DAC to correctly reconstruct the sound wave. Some cycles have been "jumped over" by the sampling process. In the figure, the higher-frequency wave is the original analog 440 Hz wave.

When the sampling rate is too low, the reconstructed sound wave appears to be lower frequency than the original sound (or have an incorrect frequency component, in the case of a complex sound wave). This is a phenomenon called **aliasing**—the incorrect digitization of a sound frequency component resulting from an insufficient sampling rate.

For a single-frequency sound wave to be correctly digitized, the sampling rate must be at least twice the frequency of the sound wave. More generally, for a sound with multiple frequency components, the sampling rate must be at least twice the frequency of the highest frequency component. This is known as the **Nyquist theorem**.

The Nyquist Theorem

*Given a sound with a maximum frequency component of f Hz, a sampling rate of at least 2f is required to avoid aliasing. The minimum acceptable sampling rate (2f in this context) is called the **Nyquist rate**.*

*Given a sampling rate of f, the highest-frequency sound component that can be correctly sampled is f/2. The highest-frequency component that can be correctly sampled is called the **Nyquist frequency**.*

In practice, aliasing is generally not a problem. Standard sampling rates in digital audio recording environments are high enough to capture all frequencies in the range audible to humans. The highest audible frequency is about 20,000 Hz. In fact, most people don't hear frequencies this high, as our ability to hear high frequencies diminishes with age. The **CD-quality sampling rate** is 44,100 Hz (44.1 kHz), which is acceptable as it is more than twice the highest audible component. In other words, with CD-quality audio, the highest frequency we care about capturing (20 kHz for audibility purposes) is less than the Nyquist frequency for that sampling rate, so this is fine. A sampling rate of 48 kHz is also widely supported, and sampling rates go up as high as 192 kHz.

Even if a sound contains frequency components that are above the Nyquist frequency, to avoid aliasing the ADC generally filters them out before digitization.

Section 5.3.1 gives more detail about the mathematics of aliasing and an algorithm for determining the frequency of the aliased wave in cases where aliasing occurs.

5.1.2.3 Bit Depth and Quantization Error

When samples are taken, the amplitude at that moment in time must be converted to integers in binary representation. The number of bits used for each sample, called the **bit depth**, determines the precision with which you can represent the sample amplitudes. For this discussion, we assume that you know that basics of binary representation, but let's review briefly.

Binary representation, the fundamental language of computers, is a base-2 number system. Each *bit* in a binary number holds either a 1 or a 0. Eight bits together constitute one *byte*. The bit positions in a binary number are numbered from right to left starting at 0, as shown in Figure 5.6. The rightmost bit is called the **least significant bit**, and the leftmost is called the **most significant bit**. The ith bit is called $b[i]$.

b[7]	b[6]	b[5]	b[4]	b[3]	b[2]	b[1]	b[0]
1	0	1	1	0	0	1	1
$2^7=128$	$2^6=64$	$2^5=32$	$2^4=16$	$2^3=8$	$2^2=4$	$2^1=2$	$2^0=1$

$$1\,0\,1\,1\,0\,0\,1\,1_2 = 128 + 0 + 32 + 16 + 0 + 0 + 2 + 1 = 179_{10}$$

FIGURE 5.6: AN 8-BIT BINARY NUMBER CONVERTED TO DECIMAL

The value of an n-bit binary number is equal to

$$\sum_{i=0}^{n-1} b[i] \times 2^i$$

EQUATION 5.1

Notice that doing the summation from $i=0$ to $n-1$ causes the terms in the sum to be in the reverse order from that shown in Figure 5.6. The summation for our example is

$$10110011_2 = (1\times1)+(1\times2)+(0\times4)+(0\times8)+(1\times16)+(1\times32)+(0\times64)+(1\times128) = 179_{10}$$

Thus, 10110011 in base 2 is equal to 179 in base 10. (Base 10 is also called **decimal**.) We leave off the subscript 2 in binary numbers and the subscript 10 in decimal numbers when the base is clear from the context.

From the definition of binary numbers, it can be seen that the largest decimal number that can be represented with an n-bit binary number is 2^n-1, and the number of different values that can be represented is 2^n. For example, the decimal values that can be represented with an 8-bit binary number range from 0 to 255, so there are 256 different values.

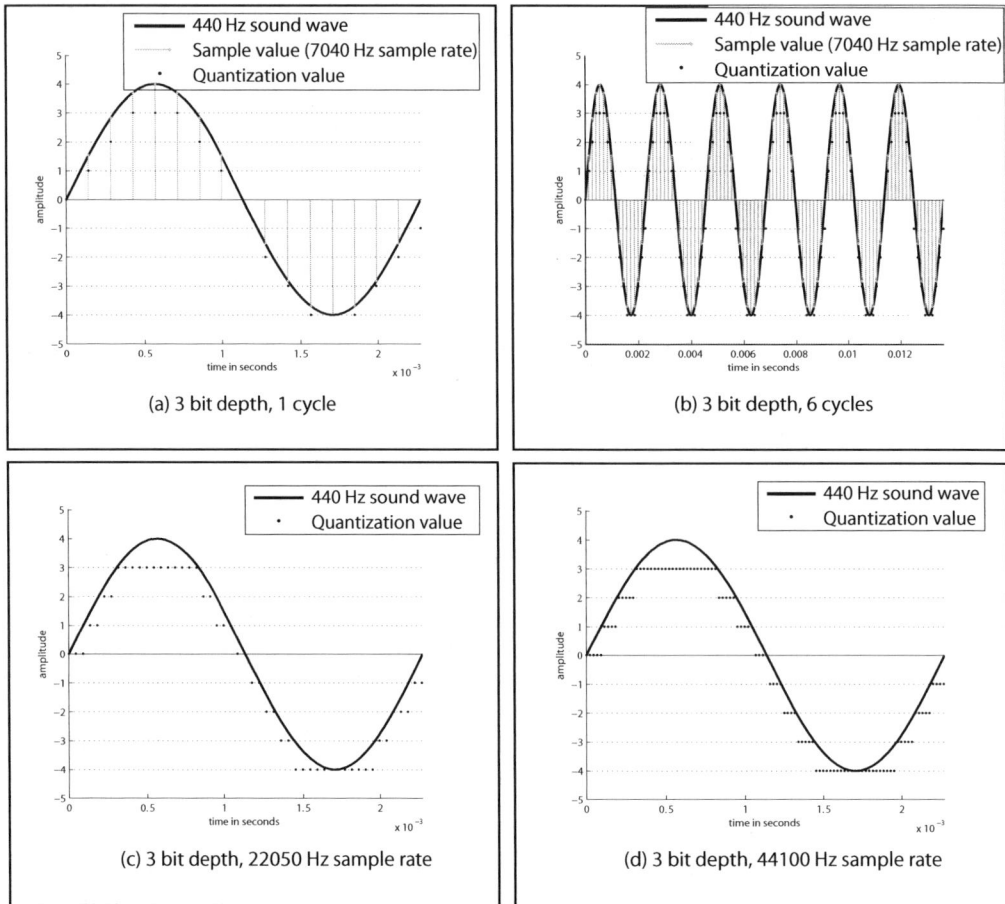

FIGURE 5.7: QUANTIZATION OF A SAMPLED SOUND WAVE

These observations have significance with regard to the bit depth of a digital audio recording. A bit depth of 8 allows 256 different discrete levels at which samples can be recorded. A bit depth of 16 allows $2^{16} = 65,536$ discrete levels, which in turn provides much higher precision than a bit depth of 8.

The process of quantization is illustrated Figure 5.7. Again, we model a single-frequency sound wave as a sine function, centering the sine wave on the horizontal axis. We use a bit depth of 3 to simplify the example, although this is far lower than any bit depth that would be used in practice. With a bit depth of 3, $2^3 = 8$ quantization levels are possible. By convention, half of the quantization levels are below the horizontal axis (that is, 2^{n-1} of the quantization levels). One level is the horizontal axis itself (level 0), and $2^{n-1} - 1$ levels are above the horizontal axis. These levels are labeled in the figure, ranging from -4 to 3. When a sound is sampled, each sample must be scaled to one of 2^n discrete levels. However, the samples in reality might not fall neatly

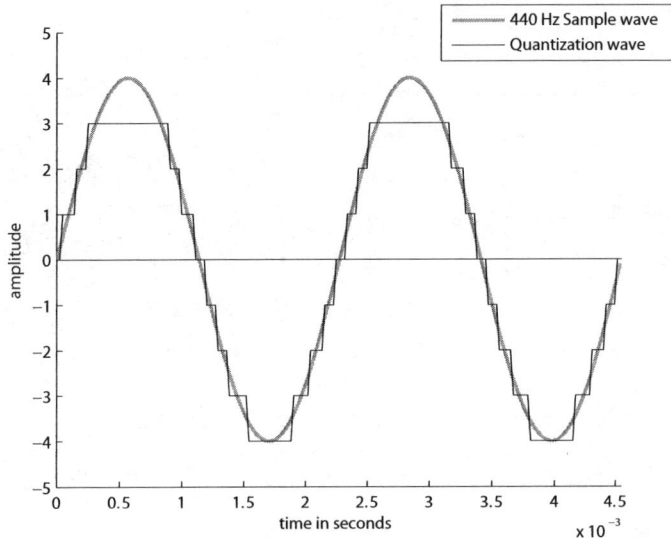

FIGURE 5.8: QUANTIZED WAVE

onto these levels. They have to be rounded up or down by some consistent convention. We round to the nearest integer, with the exception that values at 3.5 and above are rounded down to 3. The original sample values are represented by gray dots on the graphs. The quantized values are represented as black dots. The difference between the original samples and the quantized samples constitutes rounding error. The lower the bit depth, the more values potentially must be rounded, resulting in greater quantization error. Figure 5.8 shows a simple view of the original wave vs. the quantized wave.

    Quantization error is sometimes referred to as noise. **Noise** can be broadly defined as part of an audio signal that isn't supposed to be there. However, some sources would argue that a better term for quantization error is **distortion**, defining distortion as an unwanted part of an audio signal that is related to the true signal. If you subtract the stair-step wave from the true sine wave in Figure 5.8, you get the dark gray part of the graphs in Figure 5.9. This is precisely the error—i.e., the distortion—resulting from quantization. Notice that the error follows a regular pattern that changes in tandem with the original "correct" sound wave. This makes the distortion sound more noticeable in human perception, as opposed to completely random noise. The error wave constitutes sound itself. If you take the sample values that create the error wave graph in Figure 5.9, you can actually play them as sound. You can compare and listen to the effects of various bit depths and the resulting quantization error in the Max Demo "Bit Depth" on page 264.

FLASH TUTORIAL:
Quantization
http://bit.ly/29uha6R

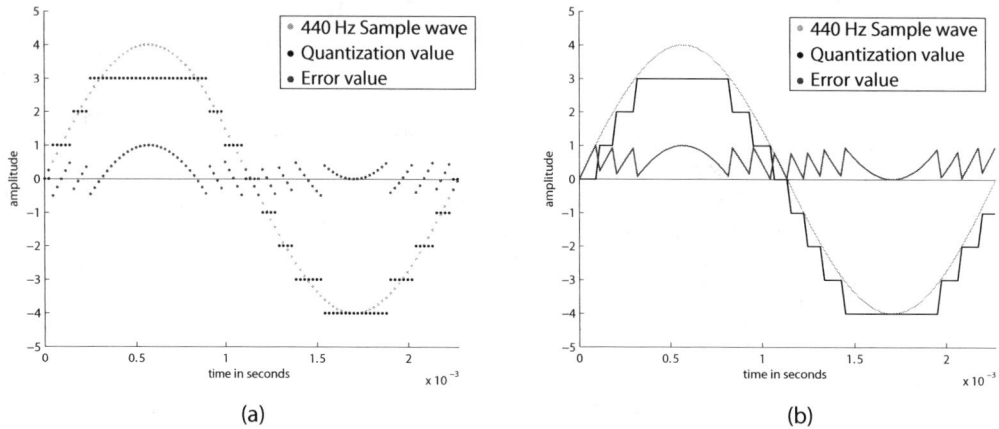

FIGURE 5.9: ERROR WAVE RESULTING FROM QUANTIZATION

For those who prefer to distinguish between noise and distortion, noise is defined as an unwanted part of an audible signal arising from environmental interference—like background noise in a room where a recording is being made, or noise from the transmission of an audio signal along wires. This type of noise is more random than the distortion caused by quantization error. Section 5.3 shows you how you can experiment with sampling and quantization in MATLAB and C++ to understand the concepts in more detail.

5.1.2.4 Dynamic Range

Another way to view the implications of bit depth and quantization error is in terms of dynamic range. The term **dynamic range** has two main usages with regard to sound. First, an occurrence of sound that takes place over time has a dynamic range, defined as the range between the highest- and lowest-amplitude moments of the sound. This is best illustrated by music. Classical symphonic music generally has a wide dynamic range. For example, Beethoven's Fifth Symphony begins with a high-amplitude "Bump bump bump baaaaaaaa" and continues with a low-amplitude string section. The difference between the loud and quiet parts is intentionally dramatic and is what gives the piece a wide dynamic range. You can see this in the short clip of the symphony graphed in Figure 5.10. The dynamic range of this clip is a function of the ratio betwee the largest sample value and the smallest. Notice that you don't measure the range across the horizontal axis but from the highest-magnitude sample either above or below the axis to the lowest-magnitude sample on the same side of the axis.

A sound clip with a narrow dynamic range has a much smaller difference between the loud and quiet parts. In this second usage of the term *dynamic range*, we're focusing on the dynamic range of a particular occurrence of sound or music.

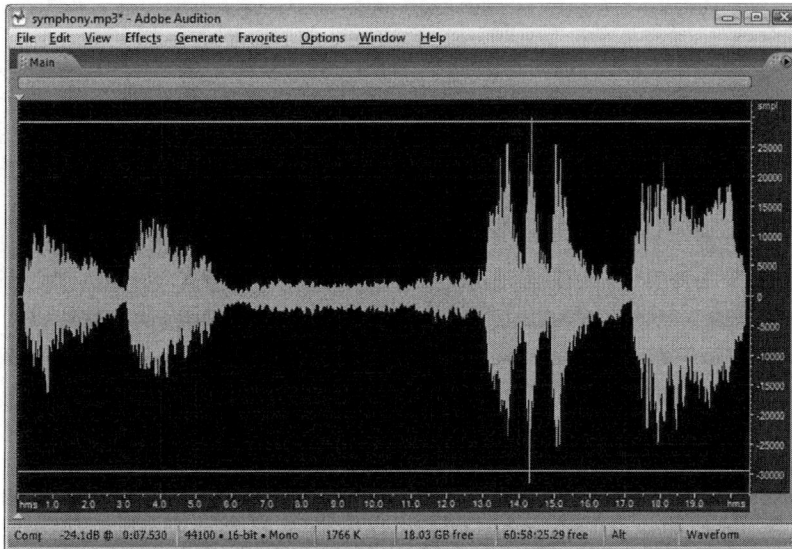

FIGURE 5.10: MUSIC WITH A WIDE DYNAMIC RANGE (BEETHOVEN'S FIFTH SYMPHONY)

In yet another usage of the term, the **potential dynamic range of a digital recording** refers to the possible range of high- and low-amplitude samples as a function of the bit depth. Choosing the bit depth for a digital recording automatically constrains the dynamic range, a higher bit depth allowing for a wider dynamic range.

Consider how this works. A digital recording environment has a maximum amplitude level that it

```
ASIDE: MATLAB Code for Figure 5.11 and Figure 5.12:
hold on;
f = 440;T = 1/f;
Bdepth = 3; bit depth
Drange = 2^(Bdepth-1); dynamic range
axis = [0 2*T -(Drange+1) Drange+1];
SRate = 44100; %sample rate
sample_x = (0:2*T*SRate)./SRate;
sample_y = Drange*sin(2*pi*f*sample_x);
plot(sample_x,sample_y,'r-');
q_y = round(sample_y); %quantization value
for i = 1:length(q_y)
    if q_y(i) == Drange
        q_y(i) = Drange-1;
    end
end
plot(sample_x,q_y,'-')
for i = -Drange:Drange-1 %quantization level
    y = num2str(i); fplot(y,axis,'k:')
end
legend('Sample wave','Quantization
wave','Quantization level')
y = '0'; fplot(y,axis,'k-')
ylabel('amplitude');xlabel('time in seconds');
hold off;
```

can record. On the scale of *n*-bit samples, the maximum amplitude (in magnitude) would be 2^{n-1}. The question is this: How far, relatively, can the audio signal fall below the maximum level before it is rounded down to silence? The figures below show the dynamic range at a bit depth of 3 (Figure 5.11) compared to the dynamic range at a bit depth of 4 (Figure 5.12). Again, these are non-practical bit depths chosen for simplicity of illustration. The higher bit depth gives a wider range of sound amplitudes that can be recorded. The smaller bit depth loses more of the quiet sounds when they are rounded down to zero or overpowered by the quantization noise. You can see this in the right hand view of Figure 5.13, where a portion of Beethoven's Ninth Symphony has been reduced to four bits per sample. Quantization error for various bit depths is compared in Figure 5.14.

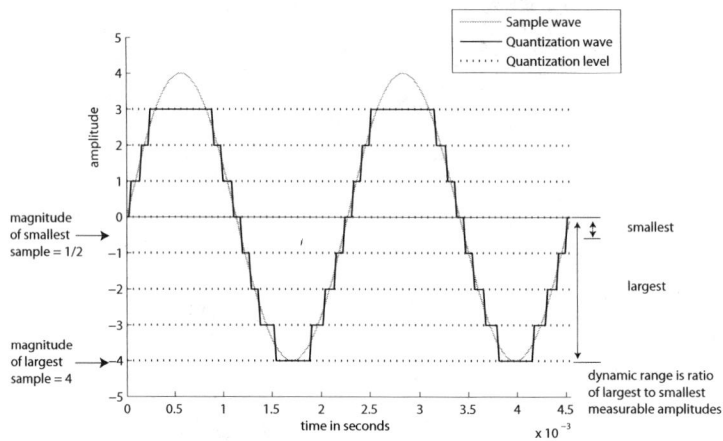

FIGURE 5.11: DYNAMIC RANGE FOR WAVE QUANTIZED AT 3 BITS

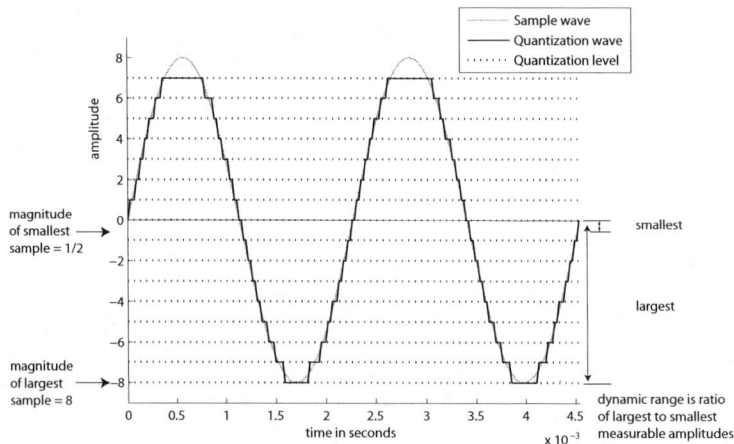

FIGURE 5.12: DYNAMIC RANGE FOR WAVE QUANTIZED AT 4 BITS

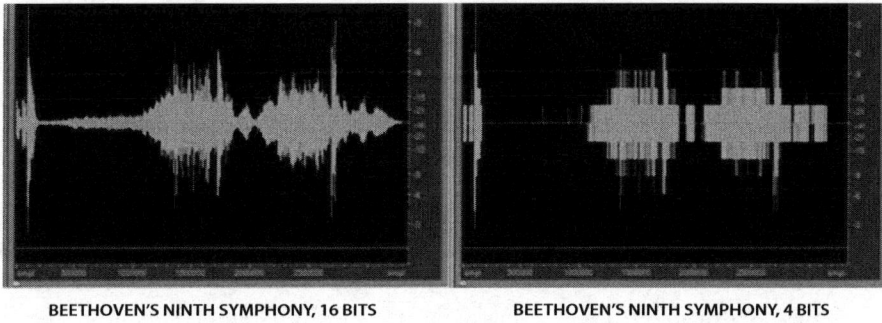

BEETHOVEN'S NINTH SYMPHONY, 16 BITS   BEETHOVEN'S NINTH SYMPHONY, 4 BITS

FIGURE 5.13: SAMPLE VALUES FALLING TO 0 DUE TO INSUFFICIENT BIT DEPTH

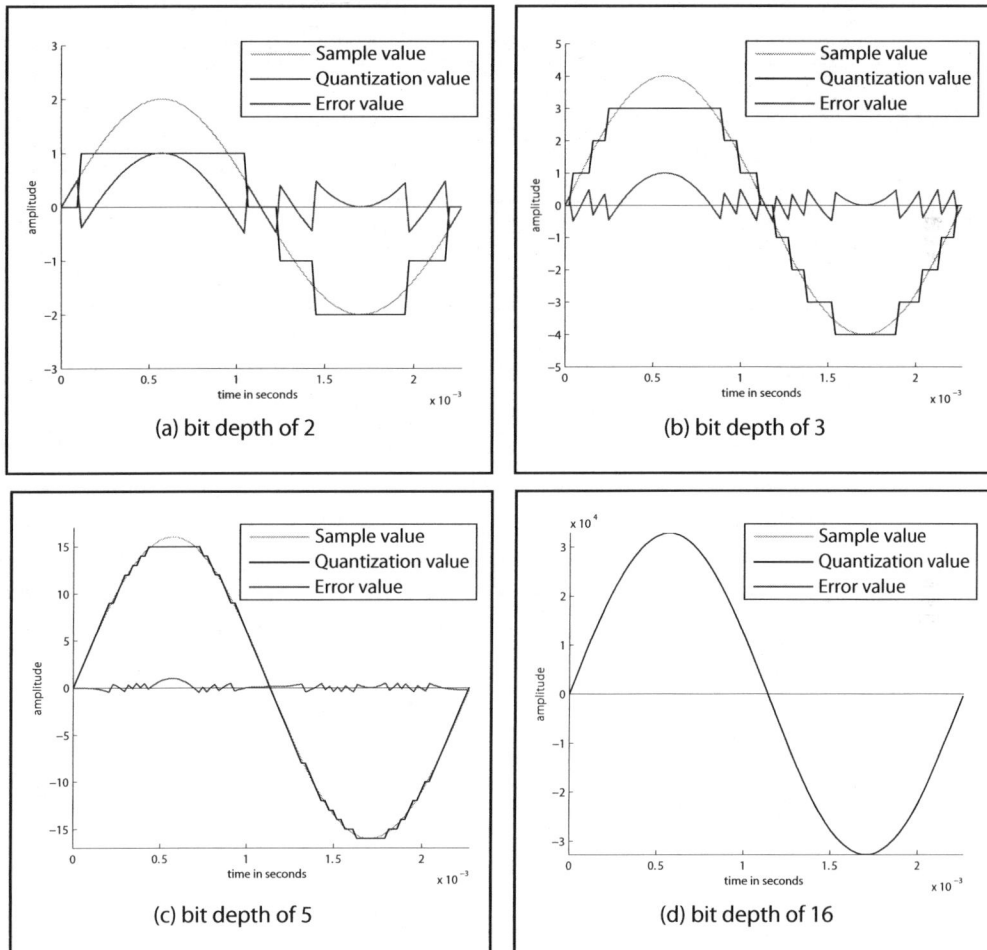

(a) bit depth of 2

(b) bit depth of 3

(c) bit depth of 5

(d) bit depth of 16

FIGURE 5.14: WAVE QUANTIZED AT DIFFERENT BIT DEPTHS

The term *dynamic range* has a precise mathematical definition that relates back to quantization error. In the context of music, we encountered dynamic range based on the ratio between the loudest and quietest musical passages of a song or performance. Digitally, the loudest potential passage of the music (or other audio signal) that could be represented would have full amplitude (all bits on). The quietest possible passage is the quantization noise itself. Any sound quieter than that would simply be masked by the noise or rounded down to silence. The ratio between the loudest and quietest parts is therefore the highest (possible) amplitude of the audio signal compared to the amplitude of the quantization noise, or the ratio between the signal level to the noise level. This is what is known as signal-to-quantization-noise ratio (SQNR), and in this context, dynamic range is the same thing. This definition is given in Equation 5.2.

Given a bit depth of n, the dynamic range of a digital audio recording is equal to

$$20 \log_{10} \left(\frac{2^{n-1}}{1/2} \right) \, dB$$

EQUATION 5.2

You can see from the equation that dynamic range as SQNR is measured in decibels. Decibels are a dimensionless unit derived from the logarithm of the ratio between two values. For sound, decibels are based on the ratio between the air pressure amplitude of a given sound and the air pressure amplitude of the threshold of hearing. For dynamic range, decibels are derived from the ratio between the maximum and minimum amplitudes of an analog waveform quantized with n bits. The maximum magnitude amplitude is 2^{n-1}. The minimum amplitude of an analog wave that would be converted to a non-zero value when it is quantized is ½. Signal-to-quantization-noise is based on the ratio between these maximum and minimum values for a given bit depth. It turns out that this is exactly the same value as the dynamic range.

Equation 5.2 can be simplified as shown in Equation 5.3.

$$20 \log_{10} \left(\frac{2^{n-1}}{1/2} \right) = 20 \log_{10}(2^n) = 20n \log_{10}(2) \approx 6.04n$$

EQUATION 5.3

Equation 5.3 gives us a method for determining the possible dynamic range of a digital recording as a function of the bit depth. For bit depth n, the possible dynamic range is approximately *6n* dB. A bit depth of 8 gives a dynamic range of approximately 48 dB, a bit depth of 16 gives a dynamic range of about 96 dB, and so forth.

When we introduced this section, we added the adjective *potential* to *dynamic range* to emphasize that it is the maximum possible range that can be used as a function of the bit depth. But not all of this dynamic range is used if the amplitude of a digital recording is relatively low, never reaching its maximum. Thus, it is important to consider the **actual dynamic range** (or **actual SQNR**) as opposed to the **potential dynamic range** (or **potential SQNR**, just defined). Take, for example, the situation illustrated in Figure 5.15. A bit depth of 7 has been chosen. The amplitude of the wave is 24 dB below the maximum possible. Because the sound uses so little of its potential dynamic range, the actual dynamic range is small. We've used just a simple sine wave in this example so that you can easily see the error wave in proportion to the sine wave, but you can imagine a music recording that has a low actual dynamic range because the recording was done at a low level

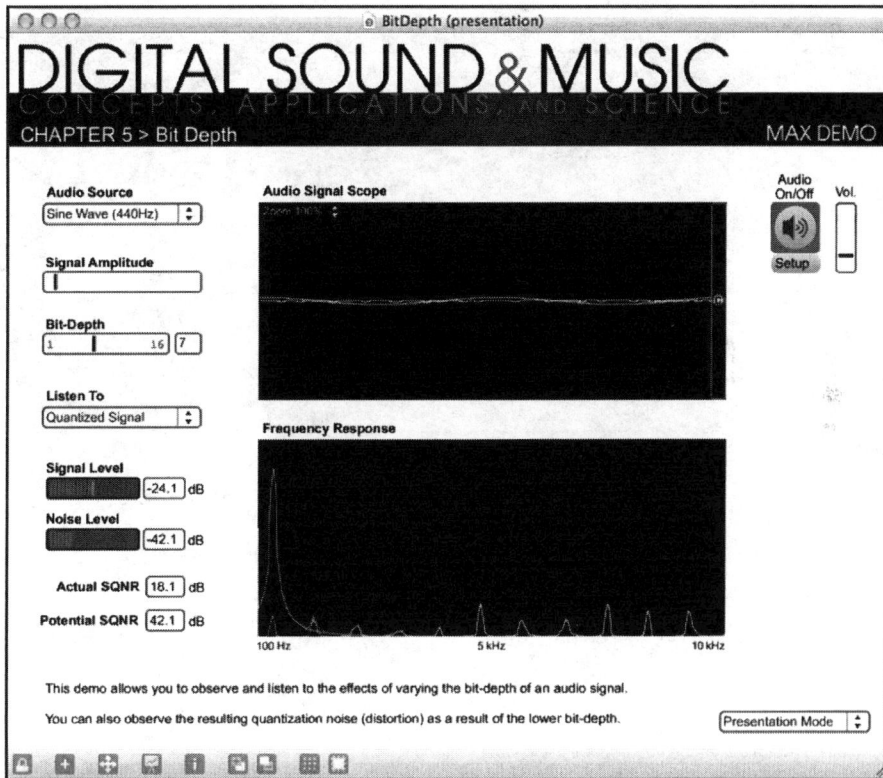

FIGURE 5.15: POTENTIAL SQNR COMPARED TO ACTUAL SQNR

of amplitude. The difference between potential dynamic range and actual dynamic range is illustrated in detail in the interactive Max Demo associated with this section. This demo shows that, in addition to choosing a bit depth appropriately to provide sufficient dynamic range for a sound recording, it's important that you use the available dynamic range optimally. This entails setting microphone input voltage levels so that the loudest sound produced is as close as possible to the maximum recordable level. These practical considerations are discussed further in Section 5.2.2.

We have one more related usage of decibels to define in this section. In the interface of many software digital audio recording environments, you'll find that **decibels relative to full scale (dBFS)** is used. (In fact, it is used in the Signal Level and Noise Level meters in Figure 5.15.) As you can see in Figure 5.16, which shows amplitude in dBFS, the maximum amplitude is 0 dBFS, at equidistant positions above and below the horizontal axis. As you move toward the horizontal axis (from either above or below) through decreasing amplitudes, the dBFS values become increasingly negative.

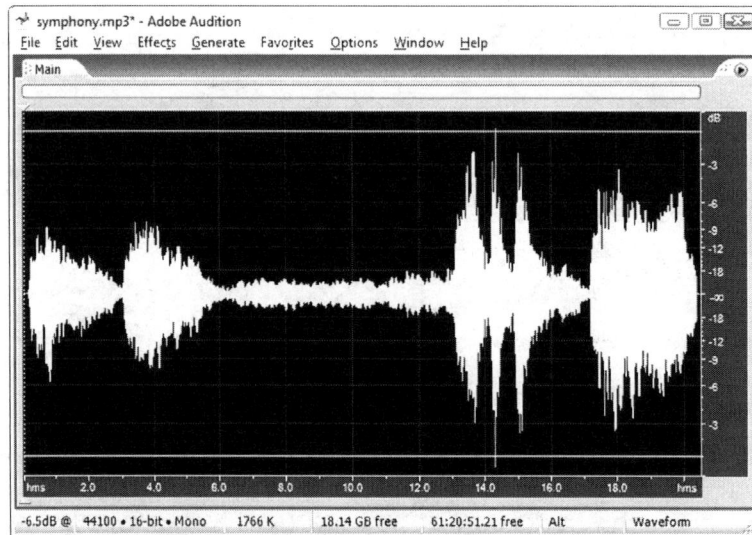

FIGURE 5.16: DYNAMIC RANGE SHOWN IN DBFS

The equation for converting between dB and dBFS is given in Equation 5.4.

For n-bit samples, **decibels full scale (dBFS)** is defined as follows:

$$dBFS = 20 \log_{10} \left(\frac{x}{2^{n-1}} \right)$$

where x is an integer sample value between 0 and 2^{n-1}

EQUATION 5.4

Generally, computer-based sample editors allow you to select how you want the vertical axis labeled, with choices including sample values, percentage, values normalized between −1 and 1, and dBFS. Chapter 7 goes into more depth about dynamics processing and the adjustment of dynamic range of an already-digitized sound clip.

5.1.2.5 Audio Dithering and Noise Shaping

It's possible to take an already-recorded audio file and reduce its bit depth. In fact, this is commonly done. Many audio engineers keep their audio files at 24 bits while they're working on them, and reduce the bit depth to 16 bits when they're finished processing the files or ready to burn to an audio CD. The advantage of this method is that when the bit depth is higher, less error is introduced by processing steps like normalization or adjustment of dynamics. Because of this advantage, even if you choose a bit depth of 16 from the start, your audio processing system may be using 24 bits (or an even higher bit depth) behind the scenes anyway during processing, as is the case with Pro Tools.

Audio dithering is a method to reduce the quantization error introduced by a low bit depth. Audio dithering can be used by an ADC when quantization is initially done, or it can be used on an already-quantized audio file when bit depth is being reduced. Oddly enough, dithering works by adding a small amount of random noise to each sample. You can understand the advantage of doing this if you consider a situation where a number of consecutive samples would all round down to 0 (silence), causing breaks in the sound. If a small random amount is added to each of these samples, some round up instead of down, smoothing over those breaks. In general, dithering reduces the perceptibility of the distortion because it causes the distortion to no longer follow exactly in tandem with the pattern of the true signal. In this situation, low-amplitude noise is a good trade-off for distortion.

Noise shaping is a method that can be used in conjunction with audio dithering to further compensate for bit-depth reduction. It works by raising the frequency range of the rounding error after dithering, putting it into a range where human hearing is less sensitive. When you reduce the bit depth of an audio file in an audio processing environment, you are often given an option of applying dithering and noise shaping, as shown in Figure 5.17. Dithering can be done without noise shaping, but noise shaping is applied only after dithering. Also note that dithering and noise shaping cannot be done apart from the requantization step because they are embedded into the way the requantization is done. A popular algorithm for dithering and noise shaping is the proprietary POW-r (Psychoacoustically Optimized Wordlength Reduction), which is built into Pro Tools, Logic Pro, Sonar, and Ableton Live.

Dithering and noise shaping are discussed in more detail in Section 5.3.7.

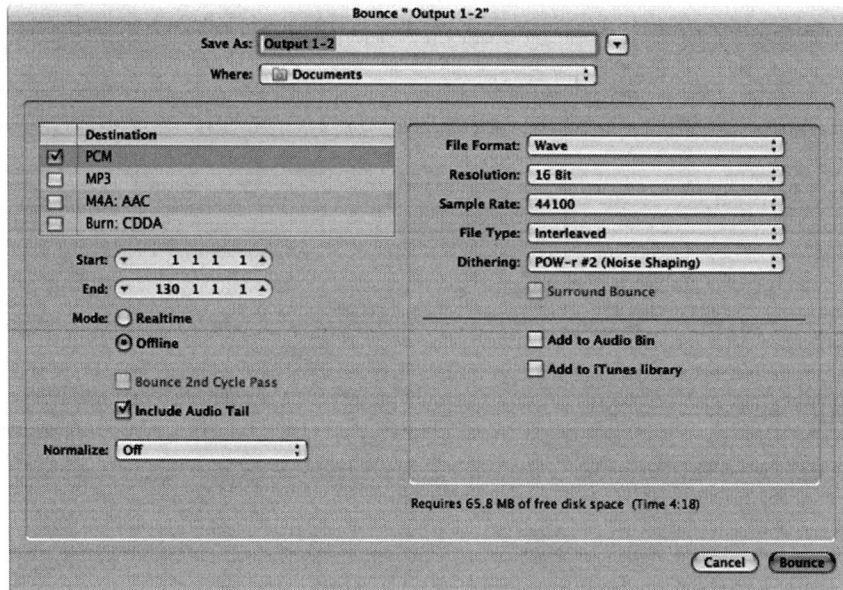

FIGURE 5.17: CHANGING BIT DEPTH WITH DITHER IN LOGIC

5.1.3   AUDIO DATA STREAMS AND TRANSMISSION PROTOCOLS

Audio data passed from one device to another is referred to as a **stream**. There are several different formats for transmitting a digital audio stream between devices. In some cases, you might want to interconnect two pieces of equipment digitally, but they don't offer a compatible transmission protocol. The best thing to do is make sure you purchase equipment that is compatible with the equipment you already have. In order to succeed at this, you'll need to understand and be able to identify the various options for digital audio transmission.

The most common transmission protocol, particularly in consumer-grade equipment is the Sony/Phillips Digital Interconnect Format (**S/PDIF**). With S/PDIF you can transmit two channels on a single wire. Typically this means you can transmit both the left and right channels of a stereo pair using a single cable instead of two cables required for analog transmission. S/PDIF can be transmitted electrically or optically. Electrical transmission involves **RCA** (Radio Corporation of America) connectors and a low loss, high bandwidth coaxial cable. This cable is different from the cable you would use for analog transmission. For S/PDIF you need a cable like what is used for video. S/PDIF transmits the digital data electrically in a stream of square wave pulses. Using a cheap, low bandwidth cable can result in a loss of high frequency content that can ultimately lose the square wave form, resulting in data loss. When looking for a cable for electrical S/PDIF transmission, look for something with RCA connectors on each end and an impedance of 75 Ω (ohms).

S/PDIF can also be transmitted optically using an optical cable with **TOSLINK** (TOShiba-LINK) connectors. Optical transmission has the advantage of being able to run longer distances without the risk of signal loss, and it is not susceptible to electromagnetic interference like an electrical signal. Optical cables are more easily broken, so if you plan to move your equipment around, you should invest in an optical cable that has good insulation.

S/PDIF is considered a consumer grade transmission protocol. S/PDIF has a professional grade cousin called **AES3**, more commonly known as **AES/EBU** (Audio Engineering Society/European Broadcasting Union). The actual format of the digital stream is almost identical. The main differences are the type of cable and connectors used and the maximum distance you can reliably transmit the signal. AES/EBU can be run electrically as a balanced signal using three-pin XLR connectors with a 110 Ω twisted pair cable, or as an unbalanced signal using BNC connectors a with a 75 Ω coaxial cable. The unbalanced version has a maximum trans-

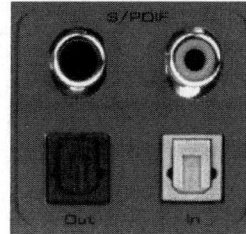

FIGURE 5.18: S/PDIF CONNECTIONS USING RCA AND TOSLINK CONNECTORS

FIGURE 5.19: AES/EBU CONNECTIONS USING XLR CONNECTORS

mission distance of 1000 meters as opposed to the 100 meters maximum for the balanced version. The balanced signal, as shown in Figure 5.19, is by far the most common implementation.

If you need to transmit more than two channels of digital audio between devices, there are several options available. The most common is the **ADAT Optical Interface** (Alesis Digital Audio Tape). Alesis developed the system to allow signal transfer between their eight-track digital audio tape recorders, but the system has since been widely adopted for multi-channel digital signal transmission between devices at short distances. ADAT can transmit eight channels of audio at sampling rates up to 48 kHz, or four channels at sampling rates up to 96 kHz. ADAT uses the same optical TOSLINK cable used for S/PDIF. This makes it relatively inexpensive for the consumer. However, the protocol must be licensed from Alesis if a manufacturer wants to implement it in their equipment.

There are several other emerging standards for multi-channel digital audio transmission, more than we can cover in the scope of this chapter. What is important to know is that most protocols allow digital transmission of 64 channels or more of digital audio over long distances using fiber optic, or Cat 5e cable. Examples of this kind of transmission include MADI, AVB, CobraNet, A-Net, and mLAN. If you need this level of functionality, you will likely be able to purchase interface cards that use these protocols for most computers and digital mixing consoles.

5.1.4   SIGNAL PATH IN AN AUDIO RECORDING SYSTEM

In Section 5.1.1, we illustrated a typical setup for a computer-based digital audio recording and editing system. Let's look at this more closely now, with special attention to the signal path and conversions of the audio stream between analog and digital forms.

Figure 5.20 illustrates a recording session where a singer is singing into a microphone and monitoring the recording session with headphones. As the audio stream makes its way along the signal path, it passes through a variety of hardware and software, including the microphone, audio interface, audio driver, CPU, input and output buffers (which could be hardware or software), and hard drive. The **CPU (central processing unit)** is the main hardware workhorse of a computer, doing the actual computation that is required for tasks like accepting audio streams, running application programs, sending data to the hard drive, sending files to the printer, and so forth. The CPU works hand-in-hand with the **operating system**, which is the software program that manages which task is currently being worked on, like a conductor conducting an orchestra. Under the direction of the operating system, the CPU can give little slots of times to various processes, swapping among these processes very quickly so that it looks like each one is advancing normally. This way, multiple processes can appear to be running simultaneously.

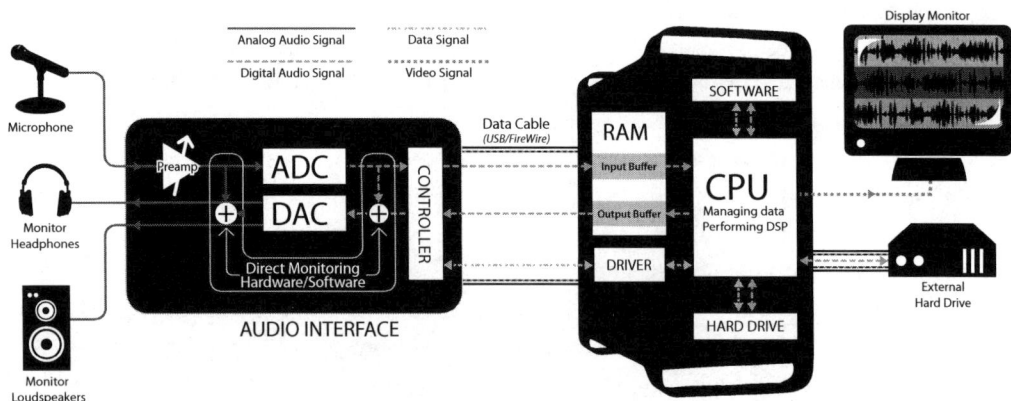

FIGURE 5.20: SIGNAL PATH IN DIGITAL AUDIO RECORDING

Now let's get back to how a recording session works. During the recording session, the microphone, an analog device, receives the audio signal and sends it to the audio interface in analog form. The audio interface could be an external device or an internal sound card. The audio interface performs analog-to-digital conversion and passes the digital signal to the computer. The audio signal is received by the computer in a digital stream that is interpreted by a driver, a piece of software that allows two hardware devices to communicate. When an audio interface is connected to a computer, an appropriate driver must be installed in the computer so that the digital audio stream generated by the audio interface can be understood and located by the computer.

The driver interprets the audio stream and sends it to an audio input buffer in RAM. Saying that the audio buffer is in RAM implies that this is a software buffer. (The audio interface has a small hardware buffer as well, but we don't need to go to this level of detail.) The **audio input buffer** provides a place where the audio data can be held until the CPU is ready to process it. Buffering of audio input is necessary because the CPU may not be able to process the audio stream as soon as it comes into the computer. The CPU has to handle other processes (monitor displays, operating system tasks, etc.) at the same time. It also has to make a copy of the audio data on the hard disk because the digitizing and recording process generates too much data to fit in RAM. Moving back and forth to the hard drive is time consuming. The input buffer provides a holding place for the data until the CPU is ready for it.

Let's follow the audio signal now to its output. In Figure 5.20, we're assuming that you're working on the audio in a program like Sonar or Logic. These audio processing programs serve as the user interface for the recording process. Here you can specify effects to be applied to tracks, start and stop the recording, and decide when and how to save the recording in permanent storage. The CPU performs any digital signal processing (DSP) called for by the audio processing software. For example, you might want reverb added to the singer's voice. The CPU applies the reverb and then sends the processed data to the **software output buffer**. From here, the audio data go back to the audio interface to be converted back to analog format and sent to the singer's headphones or a set of connected loudspeakers. Possibly, the track of the singer's voice could be mixed with a previously recorded instrumental track before it is sent to the audio interface and then to the headphones.

For this recording process to run smoothly—without delays or breaks in the audio—you must choose and configure your drivers and hard drives appropriately. These practical issues are discussed further in section 5.2.3.

Figure 5.20 gives an overview of the audio signal path in one scenario, but there are many details and variations that have not been discussed here. We're assuming a software system such as Logic or Sonar is providing the mixer and DSP, but it's possible for additional hardware to play these roles—a hardware mixing console, equalizer, or dynamics compressor, for example. Some professional grade software applications may even have additional external DSP processors to help offload some of the work from the CPU itself, such as with Pro Tools HD. This external gear could be analog or digital, so additional DAC/ADC conversions might be necessary. We also haven't considered details like microphone pre-amps, loudspeakers and loudspeaker amps, data buses, and multiple channels. We refer the reader to the references at the end of the chapter for more information.

> **FLASH TUTORIAL:**
> Audio Signal Path
> http://bit.ly/29LG52r

5.1.5 CPU AND HARD DRIVE CONSIDERATIONS

As you work with digital audio, it's important that you have some understanding of the demands on your computer's CPU and hard drive.

In general, the CPU is responsible for running all active processes on your computer. Processes take turns getting slices of time from the CPU so that they can all be making progress in their execution at the same time. You might have processes running on your computer at the same time you're recording and not even be aware of it. For example, you may have automatic software updates activated. What if an automatic update tries to run while audio capture is in progress? The CPU is going to have to take some time to deal with that. If it's dealing with a software update, it isn't dealing with your audio stream.

Even if you make your best effort to turn off all other processes during recording, the CPU still has other important work to do that keeps it from returning immediately to the audio buffer. One of the CPU's most important responsibilities during audio recording is writing audio data out to the hard drive. To understand how this works, it may be helpful to review briefly the different roles of RAM and hard disk memory with regard to a running program.

Ordinarily, we think of software programs operating according to the following scenario. Data is loaded into RAM, which is a space in memory temporarily allocated to a certain program. The program does computation on the data, changing it in some way. Since the RAM allocated to the program is released when the program finishes its computation, the data must be written out to the hard disk if you want a permanent copy. In this sense, RAM is considered volatile memory. For all intents and purposes, the data in RAM disappear when the program finishes execution.

But what if the program you're running is an audio processing program like Logic or Sonar through which you're recording audio? The recording process causes audio data to be read into RAM. Why can't Sonar or Logic just store all the audio data in RAM until you're done working on it and write it out to the hard disk when you've finished? The problem is that a very large amount of data is generated as the recording is being done—176,400 bytes per second for CD-quality audio. For a recording of any significant length, it isn't feasible to store all the audio data in RAM. Thus, audio samples are constantly pulled from the RAM buffer by the CPU and placed on a hard drive. This takes a significant amount of the CPU's time.

In order to keep up efficiently with the constant stream of data, the hard drive needs a dedicated space in which to write the audio data. Most audio recording programs automatically claim a large portion of hard drive space when you start recording. The size of this hard drive allocation is usually controllable in the preferences of your audio software. For example, if your software is configured to allocate 500 MB of hard drive space for each audio stream, 500 MB is immediately claimed on the hard drive when you start recording, and no other software may write to that space. If your recording uses 100 MB, the operating system returns the remaining 400 MB of space to be available to other programs. It's important to make sure you configure the software to claim an appropriate amount of space. If your recording ends up needing more than 500 MB, the software begins dynamically finding new chunks of space on the hard drive to put the extra data. In this situation, it's possible for dropouts to happen if sufficient space cannot be found fast enough. The problem is compounded by multitrack recording. Imagine what happens if you're recording 24 tracks of audio at one time. The software has to find 24 blocks of space on the hard drive that are 500 MB in size. That's 12 GB of free space that needs to be immediately and exclusively available.

One way to avoid problems is to dedicate a separate hard drive other than your startup drive for audio capture and data storage. That way you know that no other program will attempt to use the space on that drive. You also need to have a hard drive that is large enough and fast enough to handle this amount of sustained data being written, and often read back. In today's technology, at least a 7200 RPM, one terabyte dedicated external hard drive with a high-speed connection should be sufficient.

5.1.6 DIGITAL AUDIO FILE TYPES

You saw in the previous section that the digital audio stream moves through various pieces of software and hardware during a recording session, but eventually you're going to want to save the stream as a file in permanent storage. At this point you have to

ASIDE: In our discussion of file types, we'll use capital letters like AIFF and WAV to refer to different formats. Generally there is a corresponding suffix, called a file extension, used on file names (e.g., .aiff or .wav). However, in some cases, more than one suffix can refer to the same basic file type. For example, .aif, .aif, and .aifc are all variants of the AIFF format.

decide the format in which to save the file. Your choice depends on how and where you're going to use the recording.

Audio file formats differ in a number of aspects. They can be free or proprietary, platform-restricted or cross-platform, compressed or uncompressed, container files or simple audio files, and copy-protected or unprotected. (Copy protection is more commonly referred to as **digital rights management** or **DRM**.)

Proprietary file formats are controlled by a company or an organization. The particulars of a proprietary format and how the format is produced are not made public and their use is subject to patents. Some proprietary files formats are associated with commercial software for audio processing. Such files can be opened and used only in the software with which they're associated. Some examples are CWP files for Cakewalk Sonar, SES for Adobe Audition multitrack sessions, AUP projects for Audacity, and PTF for Pro Tools. These are project file formats that include meta-information about the overall organization of an audio project. Other proprietary formats—MP3, for example—may have patent restrictions on their use, but they have openly documented standards and can be licensed for use on a variety of platforms. As an alternative, there exist some free, open source audio file formats, including Ogg and FLAC.

Platform-restricted files can be used only under certain operating systems. For example, WMA files run under Windows, AIFF files run under Apple OS, and AU files run under Unix and Linux. The MP3 format is cross-platform. AAC is a cross-platform format that has become widely popular from its use on phones, pad computers, digital radio, and video game consoles.

The basic format for uncompressed audio data is called **PCM (pulse code modulation)**. The term *pulse code modulation* is derived from the way in which raw audio data is generated and communicated. That is, it is generated by the process of sampling and quantization described in section 5.1 and communicated as binary data by electronic pulses representing 0s and 1s. WAV, AIFF, AU, RAW, and PCM files can store uncompressed audio data. RAW files contain only the audio data, without even a header on the file.

You can't tell from the file extension whether or not a file is compressed, and if it is compressed, you can't necessarily tell what compression algorithm (called a **codec**) was used. There are both compressed and uncompressed versions of WAV, AIFF, and AU files. When you save an audio file, you can choose which type you want.

> **ASIDE:** Pulse code modulation was introduced by British scientist A. Reeves in the 1930s. Reeves patented PCM as a way of transmitting messages in "amplitude-dichotomized, time-quantized" form—what we now call "digital."

One basic reason that WAV and AIFF files come in compressed and uncompressed versions is that, in reality, these are **container**

file formats rather than simple audio files. A container file wraps a simple audio file in a meta-format which specifies blocks of information that should be included in the header along with the size and position of chunks of data following the header. The container file may allow options for the format of the actual audio data, including whether or not it is compressed. If the audio is compressed, the system that tries to open and play the container file must have the appropriate codec in order to decompress and play it. AIFF files are container files based on a standardized format called IFF. WAV files are based on the RIFF format. MP3 is a container format that is part of the more general MPEG standard for audio and video. WMA is a Windows container format. Ogg is an open source, cross-platform alternative.

In addition to audio data, container files can include information like the names of songs, artists, song genres, album names, copyrights, and other annotations. The metadata may itself be in a standardized format. For example, MP3 files use the **ID3** format for metadata.

Compression is inherent in some container file types and optional in others. MP3, AAC, and WMA files are always compressed. Compression is important if one of your main considerations is the ability to store lots of files. Consider the size of a CD quality audio file, which consists of two channels of 44,100 samples per second with two bytes per sample. This gives

$$2 \times \frac{44,100 \, samples}{sec} \times \frac{2 \, bytes}{sample} \times 60 \, \frac{sec}{min} \times 5 \, min = 52,920,000 \, bytes \approx 50.5 \, MB$$

A five minute piece of music, uncompressed, takes up over 50 MB of memory. MP3 and AAC compression can reduce this to less than a tenth of the original size. Thus, MP3 files are popular for portable music players, since compression makes it possible to store many more songs.

Compression algorithms are of two basic types: lossless or lossy. In the case of a **lossless compression algorithm**, no audio information is lost from compression to decompression. The audio information is compressed, making the file smaller for storage and transmission. When it is played or processed, it is decompressed, and the exact data that was originally recorded is restored. Examples of lossless compression algorithms include FLAC (Free Lossless Audio Codec), Apple Lossless, MPEG-4 ALS (Audio Lossless Coding), Monkey's Audio, and TTA (True Audio). In the case of a **lossy compression algorithm**, it's impossible to get back exactly the original data upon decompression. Examples of lossy compression formats are MP3, AAC, Ogg Vorbis, and the μ-law and A-law compression used in AU files. More details of audio codecs are given in section 5.3.8.4.

With the introduction of portable music players, copy-protected audio files became more prevalent. Apple introduced iTunes in 2001, allowing users to purchase and download music from their online store. The audio files, encoded in a proprietary version of the AAC format and using the *.m4p* file extension, were protected with Apple's FairPlay DRM (digital rights management) system. DRM enforces limits on where the file can be played and whether it can be shared or copied. In 2009, Apple lifted restrictions on music sold from its iTunes store, offering an unprotected *.m4a* file as an alternative to *.m4p*. Copy protection is generally embedded within container file formats like MP3. WMA (Windows Media Audio) files are another example, based on the Advanced Systems Format (ASF) and providing DRM support.

Common audio file types are summarized in Table 5.1.

AIFF and WAV have been the most commonly used file types in recent years. CAF files are an extension of AIFF files without AIFF's 4 GB size limit. This additional file size was needed for all the looping and other metadata used in GarageBand and Logic.

All along the way as you work with digital audio, you'll have to make choices about the format in which you save your files. A general strategy is this:

》 When you're processing the audio in a software environment such as Audition, Logic, or Pro Tools, save your work in the software's proprietary format until you're finished working on it. These formats retain meta-information about non-destructive processes—filters, EQ, etc.—applied to the audio as it plays. Non-destructive processes do not change the original audio samples. Thus, they are easily undone, and you can always go back and edit the audio data in other ways for other purposes if needed.

》 The originally recorded audio is the best information you have, so it's always good to keep an uncompressed copy of this. Generally, you should keep as much data as possible as you edit an audio file, retaining the highest bit depth and sampling rate appropriate for the work.

> **ASIDE:** Why are 52,920,000 bytes equal to about 50.5 MB? You might expect a megabyte to be 1,000,000 bytes, but in the realm of computers, things are generally done in powers of 2. Thus, we use the following definitions:
>
> kilo = 2^{10} = 1024
> mega = 2^{20} = 1,048,576
>
> You should become familiar with the following abbreviations:
>
> | kilobits | kb | 2^{10} bits |
> |---|---|---|
> | kilobytes | kB | 2^{10} bytes |
> | megabits | Mb | 2^{20} bits |
> | megabytes | MB | 2^{20} bytes |
>
> Based on these definitions, 52,920,000 bytes is converted to megabytes by dividing by 1,048,576 bytes.
>
> Unfortunately, usage is not entirely consistent. You'll sometimes see *kilo* assumed to be 1000 and *mega* assumed to be 1,000,000 (e.g., in the specification of the storage capacity of a CD).

File Type	Platform	File Extensions	Compression	Container	Proprietary	DRM
PCM	cross	.pcm	no	no	no	no
RAW	cross	.raw	no	no	no	no
WAV	cross	.wav	optional (lossy)	yes, RIFF format	no	no
AIFF	Mac	.aif .aiff	no	yes, IFF format	no	no
AIFF-C	Mac	.aifc	yes, with various codecs (lossy)	yes, IFF format	no	
CAF	Mac	.caf	yes	yes	no	no
AU	Unix/Linux	.au .snd	optional μ-law (lossy)	yes	no	no
MP3	cross	.mp3	MPEG (lossy)	yes	license required for distribution or sale of codec but not for use	optional
AAC	cross	.m4a .m4b .m4p .m4v .m4r .3gp .mp4 .aac	AAC (lossy)	more of a compression standard than a container; ADIF is a container	license required for distribution or sale of codec but not for use	
WMA	Windows	.wma	WMA (lossy)	yes	yes	optional
Ogg Vorbis	cross	.ogg .oga	Vorbis (lossy)	yes	no, open source	optional
FLAC	cross	.flac	FLAC (lossless)	yes	no, open source	optional

TABLE 5.1: COMMON AUDIO FILE TYPES

⟩ At the end of processing, save the file in the format suitable for your platform of distribution (e.g., CD, DVD, web, or live performance). This may be compressed or uncompressed, depending on your purposes.

5.2 APPLICATIONS

5.2.1 CHOOSING AN APPROPRIATE SAMPLING RATE

Before you start working on a project, you should decide what sampling rate you're going to be working with. This can be a complicated decision. One thing to consider is the final delivery of your sound. If, for example, you plan to publish this content only as an audio CD, then you might choose to work with a 44,100 Hz sampling rate to begin with since that's the required sampling rate for an audio CD. If you plan to publish your content to multiple formats, you might choose to work at a higher sampling rate and then convert down to the rate required by each different output format.

> **PRACTICAL EXERCISE:**
> Audio File
> Compression
> http://bit.ly/29jQOoW

The sampling rate you use is directly related to the range of frequencies you can sample. With a sampling rate of 44,100 Hz, the highest frequency you can sample is 22,050 Hz. But if 20,000 Hz is the upper limit of human hearing, why would you ever need to sample a frequency higher than that? And why do we have digital systems able to work at sampling rates as high as 192,000 Hz?

First of all, the 20,000 Hz upper limit of human hearing is an average statistic. Some people can hear frequencies higher than 20 kHz, and others stop hearing frequencies after 16 kHz. The people who can actually hear 22 kHz might appreciate having that frequency included in the recording. It is, however, a fact that there isn't a human being alive who can hear 96 kHz, so why would you need a 192 kHz sampling rate?

Perhaps we're not always interested in the range of human hearing. A scientist who is studying bats, for example, may not be able to hear the high frequency sounds the bats make but may need to capture those sounds digitally to analyze them. We also know that musical instruments generate harmonic frequencies much higher than 20 kHz. Even though you can't consciously hear those harmonics, their presence may have some impact on the harmonics you can hear. This might explain why someone with well-trained ears can hear the difference between a recording sampled at 44.1 kHz and the same recording sampled at 192 kHz.

The catch with recording at those higher sampling rates is that you need equipment capable of capturing frequencies that high. Most microphones don't pick up much above 22 kHz, so running the signal from one of those microphones into a 96 kHz ADC isn't going to give you any of the frequency benefits of that higher sampling rate. If you're willing to spend more money, you can get a microphone that can handle frequencies as high as 140 kHz. Then you need to make sure that every further device handling the audio signal is capable of working with and delivering frequencies that high.

If you don't need the benefits of sampling higher frequencies, the other reason you might choose a higher sampling rate is to reduce the latency of your digital audio system, as is discussed in section 5.2.3.

A disadvantage to consider is that higher sampling rates mean more audio data, and therefore larger file sizes. Whatever your reasons for choosing a sampling rate, the important thing to remember is that you need to stick to that sampling rate for every audio file and every piece of equipment in your signal chain. Working with multiple sampling rates at the same time can cause a lot of problems.

5.2.2   INPUT LEVELS, OUTPUT LEVELS, AND DYNAMIC RANGE

In this section, we consider how to set input and output levels properly and how these settings affect dynamic range.

When you get ready to make a digital audio recording or set sound levels for a live performance, you typically test the input level and set it so that your loudest inputs don't clip. **Clipping** occurs when the sound level is beyond the maximum input or output voltage level. It manifests itself as unwanted distortion or breaks in the sound. When capturing vocals, you can set the sound levels by asking a singer to sing the loudest note he thinks he's going to sing in the whole piece, and make sure that the level meter doesn't hit the limit. Figure 5.21 shows this situation in a software interface. The level meter at the bottom of the figure has hit the right-hand side and thus has turned red, indicating that the input level is too high and clipping has occurred. In this case, you need to turn down the input level and test again before recording an actual take. The input level can be changed by a knob on your audio interface or, in the case of some advanced interfaces with digitally controlled analog preamplifiers, by a software interface accessible through your operating system. Figure 5.22 shows the input gain knob on an audio interface.

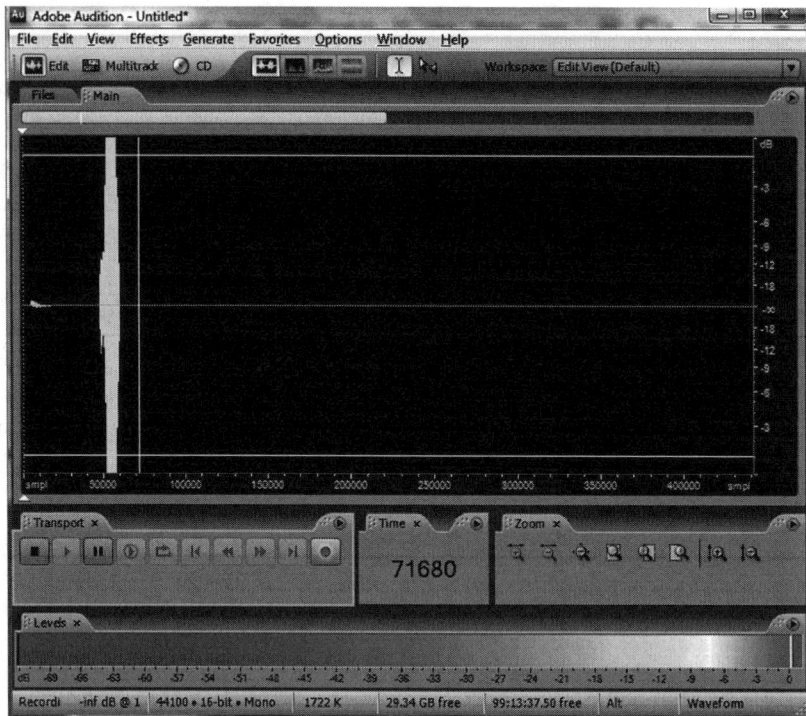

FIGURE 5.21: CLIPPED INPUT LEVEL

FIGURE 5.22: INPUT GAIN KNOB ON AUDIO INTERFACE

Let's look more closely at what's going on when you set the input level. Any hardware system has a maximum input voltage. When you set the input level for a recording session or live performance, you're actually adjusting the analog input amplifier for the purpose of ensuring that the loudest sound you intend to capture does not generate a voltage higher than the maximum allowed by the system. However, when you set input levels, there's no guarantee that the singer won't sing louder than expected. Also, depending on the kind of sound you're capturing, you might have **transients**— short loud bursts of sound like cymbal claps or drum beats—to account for. When setting the input level, you need to save some headroom for these occasional loud sounds. **Headroom** is loosely defined as the distance between your "usual" maximum amplitude and the amplitude of the loudest sound that can be captured without clipping. Allowing for sufficient headroom obviously involves some guesswork. There's no guarantee that the singer won't sing louder than expected, or some unexpectedly loud transients may occur as you record, but you make your best estimate for the input level and adjust later if necessary, though you might lose a good take to clipping if you're not careful.

Let's consider the impact that the initial input level setting has on the dynamic range of a recording. Recall from section 5.1.2.4 that the quietest sound you can capture is relative to the loudest as a function of the bit depth. A 16-bit system provides a dynamic range of approximately 96 dB. This implies that, in the absence of environmental noise, the quietest sounds that you can capture are about 96 dB below the loudest sounds you can capture. That 96 dB value is also assuming that you're able to capture the loudest sound at the exact maximum input amplitude without clipping, but as we know leaving some headroom is a good idea. The quietest sounds that you can capture lie at

> **ASIDE:** Why is the smallest value for a 16-bit sample −90.3 dB? Because $20 \log_{10} (1/32768) = 90.3$ dB.

what is called the **noise floor**. We could look at the noise floor from two directions, defining it as either the minimum amplitude level that can be captured or the maximum amplitude level of the noise in the system. With no environmental or system noise, the noise floor is determined entirely by the bit depth, the only noise being quantization error.

In the software interface shown in Figure 5.21, input levels are displayed in decibels-full-scale (dBFS). The audio file shown is a sine wave that starts at maximum amplitude, 0 dBFS, and fades all the way out. (The sine wave is at a high enough frequency that the display of the full timeline renders it as a solid shape, but if you zoom in you see the sine wave shape.) Recall that with dBFS, the maximum amplitude of sound for the given system is 0 dBFS, and increasingly negative numbers refer to increasingly quiet sounds. If you zoom in on this waveform and look at the last few samples (as shown in the bottom portion of Figure 5.23), you can see that the lowest sample values—the ones at the end of the fade—are −90.3 dBFS. This is the noise floor resulting from quantization error for a bit depth of 16 bits. A noise floor of −90.3 dBFS implies that any sound sample that is more than 90.3 dB below the maximum recordable amplitude is recorded as silence.

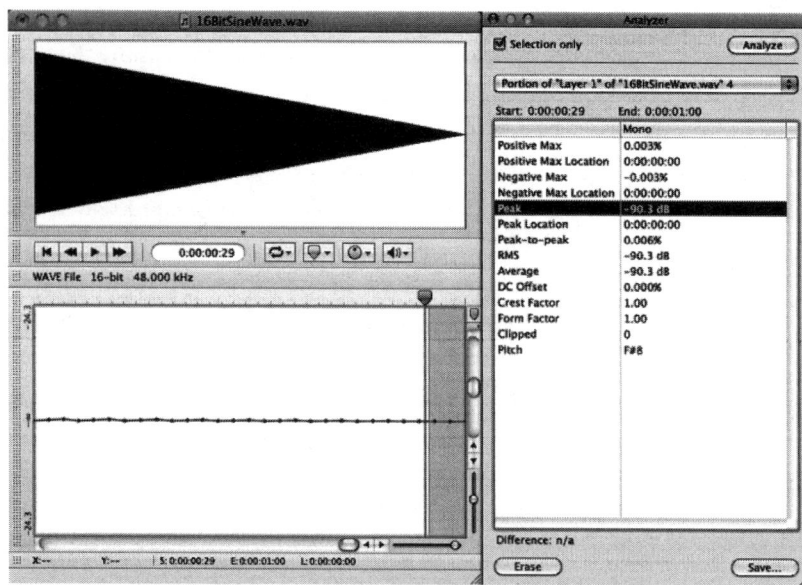

FIGURE 5.23: FINDING THE SMALLEST POSSIBLE SAMPLES IN A DIGITAL AUDIO RECORDING

In reality, there is almost always some real-world noise in a sound capturing system. Every piece of audio hardware makes noise. For example, noise can arise from electrical interference on long audio cables or from less-than-perfect audio detection in microphones. Also, the environment in which you're capturing the sound will have some level of background noise such as from the air conditioning system. The maximum amplitude of the noise in the environment or the sound-capturing system constitutes the real noise floor. Sounds below this level are masked by the noise. This means that either they're muddied up with the noise, or you can't distinguish them at all as part of the desired audio signal. In the presence of significant environmental or system noise during recording, the available dynamic range of a 16-bit recording is the difference between 0 dBFS and the noise floor caused by the environmental and system noise. For example, if the noise floor is −70 dBFS, then the dynamic range is 70 dB. (Remember that when you subtract dBFS from dBFS, you get dB.)

So we've seen that the bit depth of a recorded audio file puts a fixed limit on the available dynamic range, and that this potential dynamic range can be made smaller by environmental noise. Another thing to be aware of is that you can waste some of the available dynamic range by setting your input levels in a way that leaves more headroom than you need. If you have 96 dB of dynamic range available but it turns out that you use only half of it, you're squeezing your actual sound levels into a smaller dynamic range than necessary. This results in less accurate quantization than you could have had, and it puts more sounds below the noise floor than would have been there if you had used a greater part of your available dynamic range. Also, if you underuse your available dynamic range, you might run into problems when you try to run any long fades or other processes affecting amplitude, as demonstrated in the practical exercise "Bit Depth and Dynamic Range" in this section.

It should be clarified that increasing the input levels also increases any background environmental noise levels captured by a microphone, but can still benefit the signal by boosting it higher above any electronic or quantization noise that occurs downstream in the system. The only way to get a better dynamic range over your air conditioner hum is to turn it off or get the microphone closer to the sound you want to record. This increases the level of the sound you want without increasing the level of the background noise.

So let's say you're recording with a bit depth of 16 and you've set your input level just about perfectly to use all of that dynamic range possible in your recording. Will you actually be able to get the benefit of this dynamic range when the sound is listened to, considering the range of human hearing, the range of the sound you want to hear, and the background noise level in a likely listening environment? Let's consider the dynamic range of human hearing first and the dynamic range of the types of things we might want to listen to. Though the human ear can technically handle a sound as loud as 120 dBSPL, such high amplitudes certainly aren't comfortable to listen to, and if you're exposed to sound at that level for more than a few minutes, you'll damage your hearing. The sound in a live concert or dance club rarely exceeds 100 dBSPL, which is pretty loud to most ears. Generally, you can listen to a sound comfortably up to about 85 dBSPL. The quietest thing the human ear can ear is just above 0 dBSPL. The dynamic range between 85 dBSPL and 0 dBSPL is 85 dB. Thus, the 96 dB dynamic range provided by a 16-bit recording effectively pushes the noise floor below the threshold of human hearing at a typical listening level.

> **PRACTICAL EXERCISE:**
> Bit Depth and
> Dynamic Range
> http://bit.ly/29nUYIE

We haven't yet considered the noise floor of the listening environment, which is defined as the maximum amplitude of the unwanted background noise in the listening environment. The average home listening environment has a noise floor of around 50 dBSPL. With the dishwasher running and the air conditioner going, that noise floor could get up to 60 dBSPL. In a car (perhaps the most hostile listening environment) you could have a noise floor of 70 dBSPL or higher. Because of this high noise floor, car radio music doesn't require more than about 25 dB of dynamic range. Does this imply that the recording bit depth should be dropped down to eight bits or even lower for music intended to be listened to on the car radio? No, not at all.

Here's the bottom line. You'll almost always want to do your recordings in 16 bit sample sizes, and sometimes 24 bits or 32 bits are even better, even though there's no

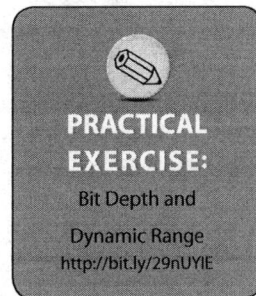

listening environment on earth (other than maybe an anechoic chamber) that allows you the benefit of the dynamic range these bit depths provide. The reason for the large bit depths has to do with the processing you do on the audio before you put it into its final form. Unfortunately, you don't always know how loud things will be when you capture them. If you guess low when setting your input level, you could easily get into a situation where most of the audio signal you care about is at the extreme quiet end of your available dynamic range, and fadeouts don't work well because the signal too quickly fades below the noise floor. In most cases, a simple sound check and a bit of preamp tweaking can get you lined up to a place where 16 bits are more than enough. But if you don't have the time, if you'll be doing lots of layering and audio processing, or if you just can't be bothered to figure things out ahead of time, you'll probably want to use 24 bits. Just keep in mind that the higher the bit depth, the larger the audio files are on your computer.

An issue we're not considering in this section is applying dynamic range compression as one of the final steps in audio processing. We mentioned that the dynamic range of car radio music's listening environment is about 25 dB. If you play music that covers a wider dynamic range than 25 dB on a car radio, a lot of the soft parts are going to be drowned out by the noise caused by tire vibrations, air currents, etc. Turning up the volume on the radio isn't a good solution, because it's likely that you'll have to make the loud parts uncomfortably loud in order to hear the quiet parts. In fact, the dynamic range of music prepared for radio play is often compressed after it has been recorded, as one of the last steps in processing. It might also be further compressed by the radio broadcaster. The dynamic range of sound produced for theatre can be handled in the same way, its dynamic range compressed as appropriate for the dynamic range of the theatre listening environment. Dynamic range compression is covered in Chapter 7.

5.2.3   LATENCY AND BUFFERS

In Section 5.1.4, we looked at the digital audio signal path during recording. A close look at this signal path shows how delays can occur in between input and output of the audio signal, and how such delays can be minimized.

Latency is the period of time between when an audio signal enters a system and when the sound is output and can be heard. Digital audio systems introduce latency problems not present in analog systems. It takes time for a piece of digital equipment to process audio data, time that isn't required in fully analog systems where sound travels along wires as electric current at nearly the speed of light. An im-

FLASH TUTORIAL:

Reducing Latency
http://bit.ly/29uk642

mediate source of latency in a digital audio system arises from analog-to-digital and digital-to-analog conversions. Each conversion adds latency on the order of milliseconds to your system. Another factor influencing latency is buffer size. The input buffer must fill up before the digitized audio data is sent along the audio stream to output. Buffer sizes vary by your driver and system, but a size of 1024 samples would not be unusual, so let's use that as an estimate. At a sampling rate of 44.1 kHz , it would take about 23 ms to fill a buffer with 1024 samples, as shown below.

$$\frac{1\ sec}{44,100\ samples} \times 1024\ samples \approx 0.023\ sec = 23\ ms$$

Thus, total latency including the time for ADC, DAC, and buffer filling is on the order of milliseconds. A few milliseconds of delay may not seem very much, but when multiple sounds are expected to be synchronized when they arrive at the listener, this amount of latency can be a problem, resulting in phase offsets and echoes.

Let's consider a couple of scenarios in which latency can be a problem, and then look at how the problem can be dealt with. Imagine a situation where a singer is singing live on stage. Her voice is taken in by the microphone and undergoes digital processing before it comes out the loudspeakers. In this case, the sound is not being recorded, but there's latency nonetheless. Any ADC/DAC conversions and audio processing along the signal path can result in an audible delay between when a singer sings into a microphone and when the sound from the microphone radiates out of a loudspeaker. In this situation, the processed sound arrives at the audience's ears after the live sound of the singer's voice, resulting in an audible echo. The simplest way to reduce the latency here is to avoid analog-to-digital and digital-to-analog conversions whenever possible. If you can connect two pieces of digital sound equipment using a digital signal transmission instead of an analog transmission, you can cut your latency down by at least two milliseconds because you'll have eliminated two signal conversions.

Buffer size contributes to latency as well. Consider a scenario in which a singer's voice is being digitally recorded (Figure 5.20). When an audio stream is captured in a digital device like a computer, it passes through an input buffer. This input buffer must be large enough to hold the audio samples that are coming in while the CPU is off somewhere else doing other work. When a singer is singing into a microphone, audio samples are being collected at a fixed rate—say 44,100 samples per second. The singer isn't going to pause her singing and the sound card isn't going to slow down the number of samples it takes per second just because the CPU is busy. If the input buffer is too small, samples have to be dropped or overwritten because the CPU isn't there in time to process them. If the input buffer is sufficiently large, it can hold the samples that accumulate while the CPU is busy, but the amount of time it takes to fill up the buffer is added to the latency.

The singer herself will be affected by this latency if she's listening to her voice through headphones as her voice is being digitally recorded (called **live sound monitoring**). If the system is set up to use **software monitoring**, the sound of the singer's voice enters the microphone, undergoes ADC and then some processing, is converted back to analog, and reaches the singer's ears through the headphones. Software monitoring requires one analog-to-digital and one digital-to-analog conversion. Depending on the buffer size and amount of processing done, the singer may not hear herself back in the headphones until 50 to 100 milliseconds after she sings. Even an untrained ear will perceive this latency as an audible echo, making it extremely difficult to sing on beat. If the singer is also listening to a backing track played directly from the computer, the computer will deliver that backing track to the headphones sooner than it can deliver the audio coming in live to the computer. (A *backing track* is a track that has already been recorded and is being played while the singer sings.)

Latency in live sound monitoring can be avoided by **hardware monitoring** (also called **direct monitoring**). Hardware monitoring splits the newly digitized signal before sending it into the computer, mixing it directly into the output and eliminating the longer latencies caused by analog-to-digital conversion and input buffers (Figure 5.25). The disadvantage of hardware monitoring is that the singer cannot hear her voice with processing such as reverb applied. (Audio interfaces that offer direct hardware monitoring with zero latency generally let you control the mix of what's coming directly from the microphone and what's coming from the computer. That's the purpose of the **monitor mix knob**, circled in Figure 5.24.) When the mix knob is turned fully counterclockwise, only the direct input signals (e.g., from the microphone) are heard. When the mix knob is turned fully counterclockwise, only the signal from the DAW software is heard.

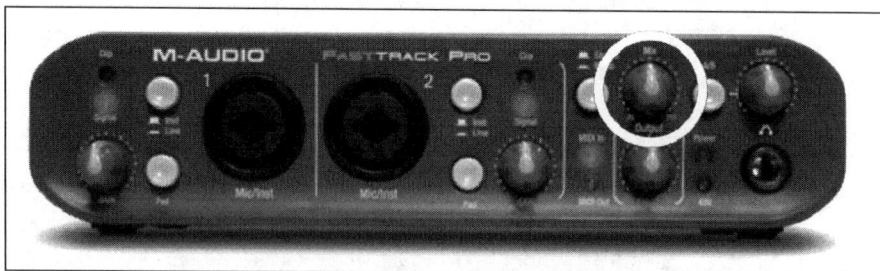

FLASH TUTORIAL:
Direct Monitoring
http://bit.ly/29hYgeY

FIGURE 5.24: MIX KNOB ON AUDIO INTERFACE

In general, the way to reduce latency caused by buffer size is to use the most efficient driver available for your system. In Windows systems, ASIO drivers are a good choice. ASIO drivers cut down on latency by allowing your audio application program to speak directly to the sound card, without having to go through the operating system. Once you have the best driver in place, you can check the interface to see if the driver gives you any control over the buffer size. If you're allowed to adjust the size, you can find the optimum size mostly by trial and error. If the buffer is too large, the latency will be bothersome. If it's too small, you'll hear breaks in the audio because the CPU may not be able to return quickly enough to empty the buffer, and thus audio samples are dropped out.

With dedicated hardware systems (digital audio equipment as opposed to a DAW based on your desktop or laptop computer) you don't usually have the ability to change the buffer size because those buffers have been fixed at the factory to perfectly match the performance of the specific components inside that device. In this situation, you can reduce the latency of the hardware by increasing your internal sampling rate. This may seem counterintuitive at first because a higher sampling rate means that you're processing more data per second. This is true, but remember that the buffer sizes have been specifically set to match the performance capabilities of that hardware, so if the hardware gives you an option to run at a higher sampling rate, you can be confident that the system is capable of handling that speed without errors or dropouts. For a buffer of 1024 samples, a sampling rate of 192 kHz has a latency of about 5.3 ms, as shown below.

$$1024 \; samples \times \frac{1 \; sec}{192,000 \; samples} \approx 5.3 \; ms$$

If you can increase your sampling rate, you won't necessarily get a better sound from your system, but the sound is delivered with less latency.

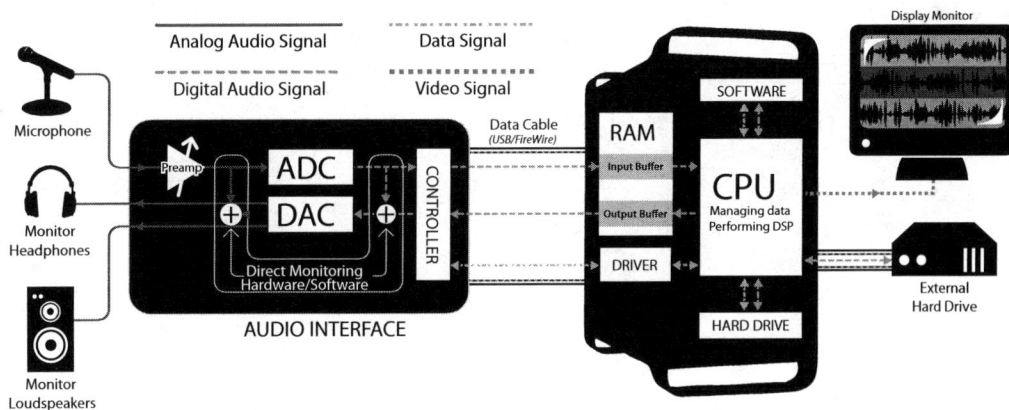

FIGURE 5.25: SIGNAL PATH IN DIGITAL AUDIO RECORDING WITH DIRECT MONITORING

5.2.4   WORD CLOCK

When transmitting audio signals between digital audio hardware devices, you need to decide whether to transmit in digital or analog format. Transmitting in analog involves performing analog-to-digital conversions coming into the devices and digital-to-analog conversions coming out of the devices. As described in Section 5.2.3, you pay for this strategy with increased latency in your audio system. You may also pay for this in a loss of quality in your audio signal as a result of multiple quantization errors and a loss of frequency range if each digital device is using a different sampling rate. If you practice good *gain structure* (essentially, controlling amplitude changes from one device to the next) and keep all your sampling rates consistent, the loss of quality is minimal, but it is still something to consider when using analog interconnects. (See Chapter 8 for more on setting gain structure.)

FLASH TUTORIAL: Word Clock http://bit.ly/29ktYKQ

Interconnecting these devices digitally can remove the latency and potential signal loss of analog interconnects, but digital transmission introduces a new set of problems, such as timing. There are several different digital audio transmission protocols, but all involve essentially the same basic process in handling data streams. The signal is transmitted as a stream of small blocks or frames of data containing the audio sample along with timing, channel information, and error correction bits. These data blocks are a constant stream of bits moving down a cable. The stream of bits is only meaningful when it gets split back up into the blocks containing the sample data in the same way it was sent out. If the stream is split up in the wrong place, the data block is invalid. To solve this problem, each digital device has a clock that runs at the speed of the sampling rate defined for the audio stream. This clock is called a **word clock**. Every time the clock ticks, the digital device grabs a new block of data—sometimes called an **audio word**—from the audio stream. If the device receiving the digital audio stream has a word clock that is running in sync with the word clock of the device sending the digital audio stream, each block that is transmitted is received and interpreted correctly. If the word clock of the receiving devices falls out of sync, it starts chopping up the blocks in the wrong place and the audio data will be invalid.

Even the most expensive word clock circuit is imperfect. This imperfection is measured in parts per million (ppm), and can be up to 50 ppm even in good quality equipment. At a sampling rate of 44.1 kHz, this equates to a potential drift of $44,100 \times (50 / 1,000,000) \approx 2.2$ samples per second. Even if two word clocks start at precisely the same time, they are likely to drift at different rates and thus will eventually be out of sync. To avoid the errors that result from word clock drift, you need to synchronize the word clocks of all your digital devices. There are three basic strategies for word clock synchronization. The strategy you choose depends on the capability of the equipment you are using.

The first word clock synchronization strategy is to slave all your digital devices to a dedicated word clock generator. Any time you can go with a dedicated hardware solution, chances are good that the hardware is going to be pretty reliable. If the box only has to do one thing, it will probably be able to do it well. A dedicated word clock generator has a very stable word clock signal and several output connectors to send that word clock signal to all the devices in your system. It may also have the ability to generate and sync to other synchronization signals such as MIDI Time Code (MTC), Linear Time Code (LTC), and video black burst (the word clock equivalent for video equipment). An example of a dedicated synchronization tool is shown in Figure 5.26.

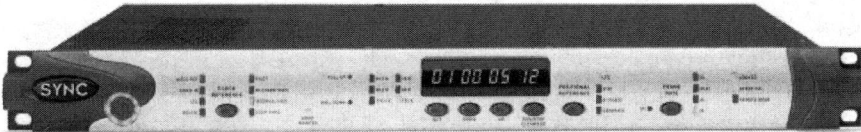

FIGURE 5.26: DEDICATED SYNCHRONIZATION TOOL FROM AVID

External word clock synchronization is typically accomplished using low impedance coaxial cable with BNC connectors. If your word clock generator has several outputs, you can connect each device directly to the clock master as shown in Figure 5.27. Otherwise you can connect the devices up in sequence from a single word clock output of your clock master, as shown in Figure 5.28.

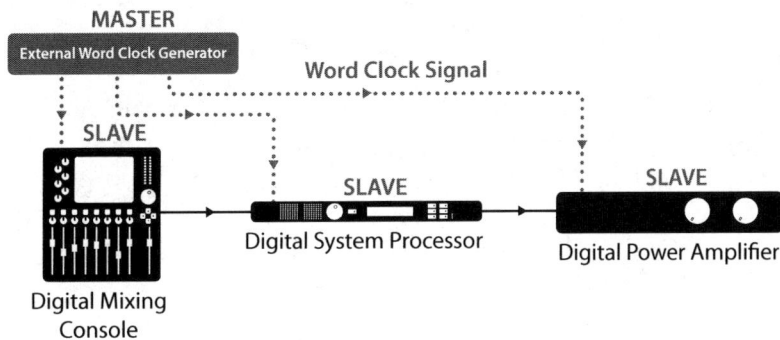

FIGURE 5.27: SYNCHRONIZING TO AN EXTERNAL WORD CLOCK GENERATOR WITH MULTIPLE OUTPUTS

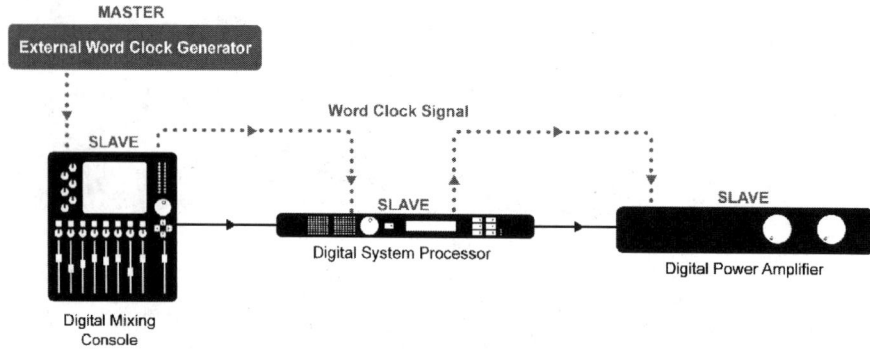

FIGURE 5.28: SYNCHRONIZING TO AN EXTERNAL WORD CLOCK GENERATOR WITH A SINGLE OUTPUT

If you don't have a dedicated word clock generator, you could choose one of the digital audio devices in your system to be the word clock master and slave all the other devices in your system to that clock using the external word clock connections as shown in Figure 5.29. The word clock of the device in your system is probably not as stable as a dedicated word clock generator (in that it may have a small amount of jitter), but as long as all the devices are following that clock, you will avoid any errors.

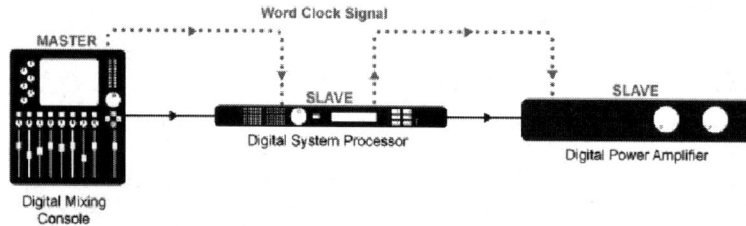

FIGURE 5.29: SYNCHRONIZING TO THE FIRST DIGITAL DEVICE IN YOUR SIGNAL CHAIN USING EXTERNAL WORD CLOCK CONNECTIONS

In some cases your equipment may not have external word clock inputs. This is common in less expensive equipment. In that situation you could go with a self-clocking solution where the first device in your signal chain is designated as the word clock master and each device in the signal chain is set to slave to the word clock signal embedded in the audio stream coming from the previous device in the signal chain, as shown in Figure 5.30.

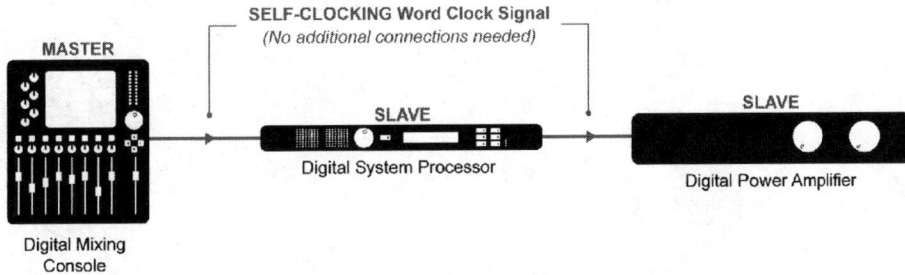

FIGURE 5.30: SYNCHRONIZING TO THE CLOCKING SIGNAL EMBEDDED IN THE DIGITAL AUDIO STREAM

Regardless of the synchronization strategy you use, the goal is to have one word clock master with every other digital device in your system set to slave to the master word clock. If you set this up correctly, you should have no problems maintaining a completely digital signal path through your audio system and benefit from the decreased latency from input to output.

5.3 SCIENCE, MATHEMATICS, AND ALGORITHMS

5.3.1 READING AND WRITING AUDIO FILES IN MATLAB

A number of exercises in this book ask that you experiment with audio processing by reading an audio file into MATLAB or a C++ program, manipulate it in some way, and either listen directly to the result or write the result back to a file. In Chapter 2 we introduced how to read in WAV files in MATLAB. Let's look at this in more detail now.

In some cases, you may want to work with raw audio data coming from an external source. One way to generate raw audio data is to take a clip of music or sound and, in Audacity or some other higher level tool, save or export the clip as an uncompressed or raw file. Audacity allows you to save in uncompressed WAV or AIFF formats (Figure 5.31).

FIGURE 5.31: EXPORTING AN UNCOMPRESSED AUDIO FILE IN AUDACITY

From the next input box that pops open, you can see that although this file is being saved as uncompressed PCM, it still has a WAV header on it containing metadata.

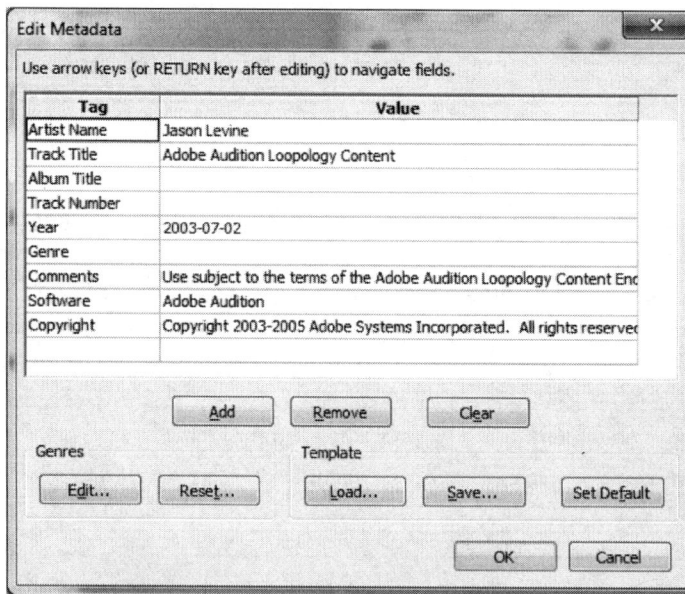

FIGURE 5.32: PROMPT FOR METADATA TO BE STORED IN HEADER OF UNCOMPRESSED WAV FILE

The WAV file can be read as an array in MATLAB with the following:

```
xWav = wavread('HornsE04Mono.wav');
```

The *wavread* function strips the header off and places the raw audio values into the array *x*. These values have a maximum range from −1 to 1. If you want to know the sampling rate *sr* and bit depth *b*, you can use this:

```
[xWav, sr, b] = wavread('HornsE04Mono.wav');
```

If the file is stereo, you'll get a two-dimensional array with the same number of samples in each channel.

Adobe Audition allows you to save an audio file as raw data with no header by deselecting the "Save extra non-audio information" box (Figure 5.33).

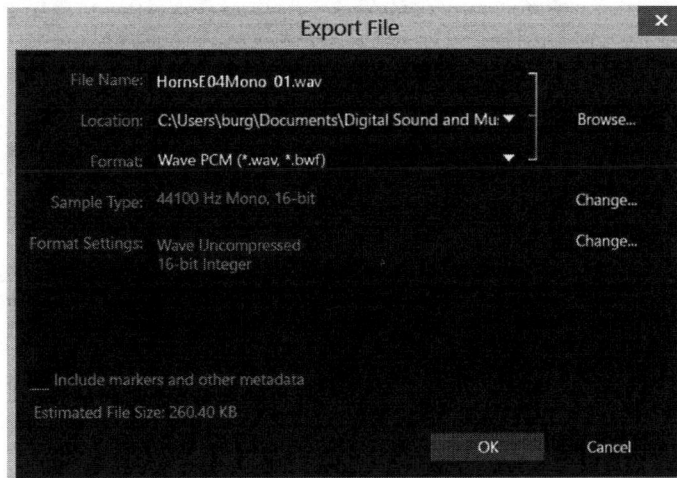

FIGURE 5.33: SAVING A RAW AUDIO FILE IN ADOBE AUDITION

When you save a file in this manner, you need to remember the sampling rate and bit depth. A raw audio file is read in MATLAB as follows:

```
fid = fopen('HornsE04Mono.raw', 'r');
xRaw16 = fread(fid, 'int16');
```

fid is the file handle, and the *r* in single quotes means that the file is being opened to be read. The type specifier *int16* is used in *fread* so that MATLAB knows to interpret the input as 16-bit signed integers. MATLAB's workspace window should show you that the values are in the maximum range of −32,768 to 32,767 (-2^{b-1} to $2^{b-1}-1$ where *b* is the bit depth). The values don't span the maximum range possible because they were at low amplitude to begin with.

For *HornsE04Mono_8bits.raw*, an 8-bit file, you can use

```
fid2 = fopen('HornsE04Mono_8bits.raw', 'r');
xRaw8 = fread(fid2, 'int8');
```

The values of *xRaw8* range from –128 to 127, as shown in Figure 5.34.

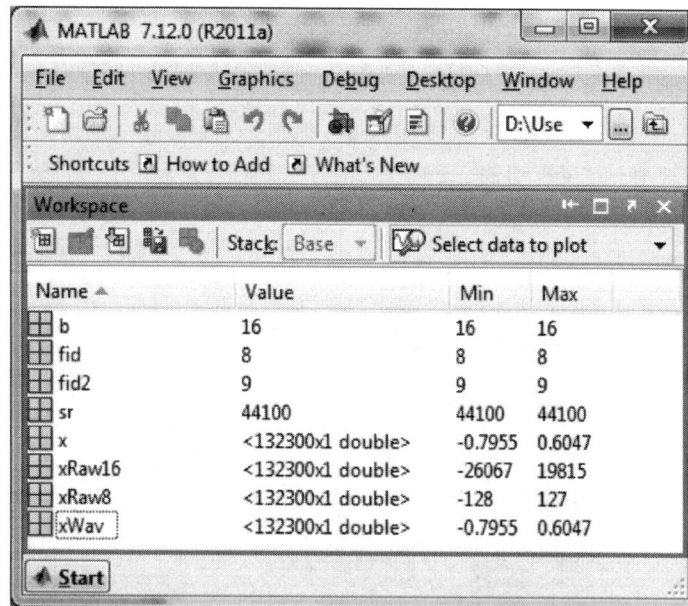

FIGURE 5.34: VALUES OF VARIABLES AFTER READING IN AUDIO FILES IN MATLAB

A stereo RAW file has twice as many samples as the corresponding mono file, with the samples for the two stereo channels interleaved.

You can use the *fwrite* function in MATLAB to write the file back out to permanent storage after you've manipulated the values.

5.3.2 RAW AUDIO DATA IN C++

In Chapters 2 and 3, we showed you how to generate sinusoidal waveforms as arrays of values that could be sent directly to the sound device and played. But what if you want to work with more complicated sounds and music in C++? In this case, you'll need to be able to read audio files into your programs in order to experiment with audio processing.

In C++, raw audio data in 8-bit or 16-bit format can be read into an array of characters (*char*) or short integers (*short*), respectively, assuming that characters are stored in 8 bits and short integers are 16 bits on your system. This

{}

C++
PROGRAMMING
EXERCISE:
Reading and Writing
Sound Files in C++
http://bit.ly/29omdnC

is demonstrated in Program 5.1. You can use this in the programming exercise on dithering and mu-law encoding.

```cpp
//This program runs under OSS
//The program expects an 8-bit raw sound file.
//You can alter it to read a 16-bit file into short ints
#include <sys/ioctl.h> //for ioctl()
#include <math.h> //sin(), floor()
#include <stdio.h> //perror
#include <fcntl.h> //open
#include <linux/soundcard.h> //SOUND_PCM*
#include <stdlib.h>
#include <unistd.h>

using namespace std;

#define TYPE char
#define RATE 44100 //sampling rate
#define SIZE sizeof(TYPE) //size of sample, in bytes
#define CHANNELS 1 //number of stereo channels
#define PI 3.14159
#define SAMPLE_MAX (pow(2,SIZE*8 - 1) - 1)

void writeToSoundDevice(TYPE* buf, int deviceID, int buffSize) {
  int status;
  status = write(deviceID, buf, buffSize);
  if (status != buffSize)
    perror("Wrote wrong number of bytes\n");
  status = ioctl(deviceID, SOUND_PCM_SYNC, 0);
  if (status == -1)
    perror("SOUND_PCM_SYNC failed\n");
}

int main(int argc, char* argv[])
{
  int deviceID, arg, status, i, numSamples;
  numSamples = atoi(argv[1]);

  TYPE* samples = (TYPE *) malloc((size_t) numSamples * sizeof(TYPE)* CHANNELS);
  FILE *inFile = fopen(argv[2], "rb");
  fread(samples, (size_t)sizeof(TYPE), numSamples*CHANNELS, inFile);
  fclose(inFile);

  deviceID = open("/dev/dsp", O_WRONLY, 0);
  if (deviceID < 0)
    perror("Opening /dev/dsp failed\n");
  arg = SIZE * 8;
  status = ioctl(deviceID, SOUND_PCM_WRITE_BITS, &arg);
  if (status == -1)
    perror("Unable to set sample size\n");
  arg = CHANNELS;
  status = ioctl(deviceID, SOUND_PCM_WRITE_CHANNELS, &arg);
  if (status == -1)
```

```
    perror("Unable to set number of channels\n");
  arg = RATE;
  status = ioctl(deviceID, SOUND_PCM_WRITE_RATE, &arg);
  if (status == -1)
    perror("Unable to set number of bits\n");

  writeToSoundDevice(samples, deviceID, numSamples * CHANNELS);
  FILE *outFile = fopen(argv[3], "wb");
  fwrite(samples, 1, numSamples*CHANNELS, outFile);
  fclose(outFile);
  close(deviceID);
}
```

PROGRAM 5.1: READING RAW DATA IN A C++ PROGRAM, OSS LIBRARY

When you write a low-level sound program such as this, you need to use a sound library such as OSS or ALSA. There's a lot of documentation online that will guide you through installation of the sound libraries into the Linux environment and show you how to program with the libraries. (See the websites cited in the references at the end of the chapter.) The ALSA version of Program 5.1 is given in Program 5.2. The solution to the exercise associated with this section shows you a couple of ways to create the raw audio files to use as input.

```
/*This program demonstrates how to read in a raw
  data file and write it to the sound device to be played.
  The program uses the ALSA library.
  Use option -lasound on compile line.*/

#include </usr/include/alsa/asoundlib.h>
#include <math.h>
#include <iostream>
using namespace std;

static char *device = "default";    /*default playback device */
int main(int argc, char* argv[])
{
  int err, numSamples;
  snd_pcm_t *handle;
  snd_pcm_sframes_t frames;
  numSamples = atoi(argv[1]);
  char* samples = (char*) malloc((size_t) numSamples);
  FILE *inFile = fopen(argv[2], "rb");
  int numRead = fread(samples, 1, numSamples, inFile);
  fclose(inFile);
  if ((err=snd_pcm_open(&handle, device, SND_PCM_STREAM_PLAYBACK, 0)) < 0){
      printf("Playback open error: %s\n", snd_strerror(err));
      exit(EXIT_FAILURE);
    }
  if ((err =
    snd_pcm_set_params(handle,SND_PCM_FORMAT_U8,
      SND_PCM_ACCESS_RW_INTERLEAVED,1,44100, 1, 100000) ) < 0 ){
          printf("Playback open error: %s\n", snd_strerror(err));
```

```
        exit(EXIT_FAILURE);
    }
  frames = snd_pcm_writei(handle, samples, numSamples);
  if (frames < 0)
    frames = snd_pcm_recover(handle, frames, 0);
  if (frames < 0) {
    printf("snd_pcm_writei failed: %s\n", snd_strerror(err));
  }
  snd_pcm_close(handle);
  return 0;
}
```

PROGRAM 5.2: READING RAW DATA IN A C++ PROGRAM, ALSA LIBRARY

5.3.3   READING AND WRITING FORMATTED AUDIO FILES IN C++

So far, we've worked only with raw audio data. However, most sound is handled in file types that store not only the raw data but also a header containing information about how the data is formatted. Two of the commonly used file formats are WAV and AIFF. If you want to read or write a WAV file without the help of an existing library of functions, you need to know the required format.

In WAV and AIFF, data are grouped in **chunks**. Let's look at the WAV format as an example. The format chunk always comes first, containing information about the encoding format, number of channels, sampling rate, data transfer rate, and byte alignment. The samples are stored in the data chunk. The way in which the data is stored depends on whether the file is compressed or not and the bit depth of the file. Optional chunks include the fact, cue, and playlist chunks. To see this format firsthand, you could try taking a RAW audio file, converting it to WAV or AIFF, and then see if it plays in an audio player.

More often, however, it is more to the point to use a higher level library that allows you to read and write WAV and AIFF audio files. The *libsndfile* library serves this purpose. If you install this library, you can read WAV or AIFF files into your C++ programs, manipulate them, and write them back to permanent storage as WAV or AIFF files without needing to know the detail of endianness or file formats. The website for *libsndfile* has example programs for you to follow (http://www.mega-nerd .com/libsndfile). Program 5.3 demonstrates the library with a simple program that opens a sound file (e.g., WAV), reads the contents, reduces the amplitude by half, and writes the result back in the same format.

```
//Give the input and output file names on the command line
#include <stdio.h>
#include <stdlib.h>
#include <string.h>
#include <math.h>
```

```
#include <sndfile.h>
#include <iostream>
using namespace std;

#define ARRAY_LEN(x)        ((int) (sizeof (x) / sizeof (x [0])))
#define MAX(x,y)    ((x) > (y) ? (x) : (y))
#define MIN(x,y)    ((x) < (y) ? (x) : (y))

void reduceAmplitude (SNDFILE *, SNDFILE *) ;
sf_count_t sfx_read_double (SNDFILE *, double *, sf_count_t);

int main (int argc, char ** argv) {
  SNDFILE *infile, *outfile ;
  SF_INFO sfinfo ;
  double buffer [1024] ;
  sf_count_t count ;

  if (argc != 3) {
    printf("\nUsage :\n\n    <executable name>  <input file> <output file>\n") ;
    exit(0);
  }

  memset (&sfinfo, 0, sizeof (sfinfo)) ;
  if ((infile = sf_open (argv [1], SFM_READ, &sfinfo)) == NULL) {
    printf ("Error : Not able to open input file '%s'\n", argv [1]);
    sf_close (infile);
    exit (1) ;
  }

  if ((outfile = sf_open (argv [2], SFM_WRITE, &sfinfo)) == NULL) {
    printf ("Error : Not able to open output file '%s'\n", argv [argc - 1]);
    sf_close (infile);
    exit (1);
  }

  while ((count = sf_read_double (infile, buffer, ARRAY_LEN (buffer))) > 0) {
    for (int i = 0; i < 1024; i++)
      buffer[i] *= 0.5;
    sf_write_double (outfile, buffer, count);
  }

  sf_close (infile) ;
  sf_close (outfile) ;
  return 0 ;
}
```

PROGRAM 5.3: READING A FORMATTED SOUND FILE USING THE LIBSNDFILE LIBRARY

5.3.4 MATHEMATICS AND ALGORITHMS FOR ALIASING

Many of the concepts introduced in Sections 5.1 and 5.2 may become clearer if you experiment with the mathematics, visualize or listen to the audio data in MATLAB, or write some of the algorithms to see the results first-hand. We'll try that in this section.

It's possible to predict the frequency of an aliased wave in cases where aliasing occurs. The algorithm for this is given in Algorithm 5.1. There are four cases to consider. We'll use a sampling rate of 1000 Hz to illustrate the algorithm. At this sampling rate, the Nyquist frequency is 500 Hz.

```
algorithm aliasing {
/*Input:
Frequency of a single-frequency sound wave to be sampled, f_act
    Sampling rate, f_samp
Output:
    Frequency of the digitized audio wave, f_obs*/
  f_nf = ½ * f_samp    //Nyquist frequency is ½ sampling rate
  if (f_act <= f_nf)                //Case 1, no aliasing
    f_obs = f_act
  else if (f_nf < f_act <= f_samp)  //Case 2
    f_obs = f_samp - f_act;
  else {
    p = f_act / f_nf   //integer division, drop remainder
    r = f_act mod f_nf    //remainder from integer division
      if (p is even) then          //Case 3
      f_obs = r;
    else if (p is odd) then        //Case 4
      f_obs = f_nf - r;
  }
}
```

ALGORITHM 5.1

In the first case, when the actual frequency is less than or equal to the Nyquist frequency, the sampling rate is sufficient and there is no aliasing. In the second case, when the actual frequency is between the Nyquist frequency and the sampling rate, the observed frequency is equal to the sampling rate minus the actual frequency. For example, a sampling rate of 1000 kHz causes an 880 kHz sound wave to alias to 120 kHz (Figure 5.35).

FLASH TUTORIAL:

Nyquist and Aliasing
http://bit.ly/29gYgMQ

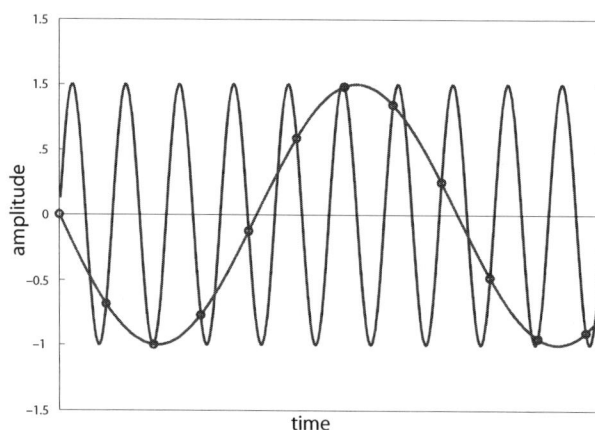

FIGURE 5.35: 880 HZ WAVE SAMPLED AT 1000 HZ

For an actual frequency that is above the sampling rate, like 1320 Hz, the calculations are as follows:

$$p = \frac{1320}{500} = 2$$
$$r = 1320 \bmod 500 = 320$$
$$p \text{ } is \text{ } even, \text{ } so$$
$$f_{obs} = 320$$

Thus, a 1320 Hz wave sampled at 1000 Hz aliases to 320 Hz (Figure 5.36).

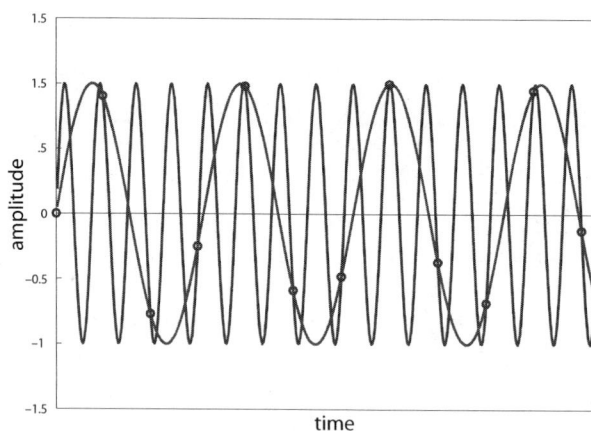

FIGURE 5.36: 1320 HZ WAVE SAMPLED AT 1000 HZ

For an actual frequency of 1760 Hz, we have

$$p = \frac{1760}{500} = 3$$

$$r = 1760 \bmod 500 = 260$$

$$p \text{ is odd, so}$$

$$f_{obs} = 500 - 260 = 240$$

Thus, a 1760 Hz wave sampled at 1000 Hz aliases to 240 Hz (Figure 5.37).

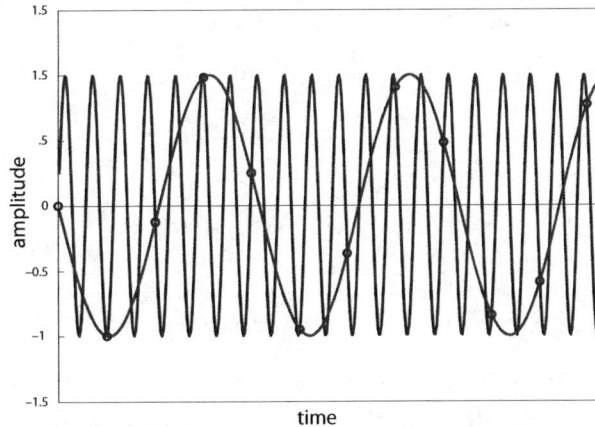

FIGURE 5.37: 1760 HZ WAVE SAMPLED AT 1000 HZ

The graph in Figure 5.38 shows *f_obs* as a function of *f_act* for a fixed sampling rate, in this case 1000 Hz. For a different sampling rate, the graph would still have the same basic repeated peak shape, but its peaks would be at different places. The first peak from the left is located at the Nyquist frequency on the horizontal axis, which is half the sampling rate. After the first peak, case 3 is always on the left side of a peak and case 4 is always on the right.

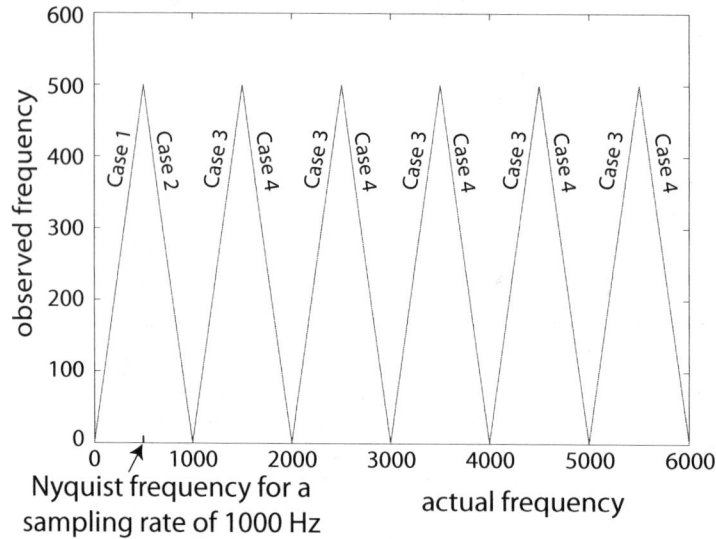

observed frequency (y-axis)
actual frequency (x-axis)

Nyquist frequency for a sampling rate of 1000 Hz

Case 1, Case 2, Case 3, Case 4, Case 3, Case 4, Case 3, Case 4, Case 3, Case 4, Case 3, Case 4, Case 3, Case 4

FIGURE 5.38: OBSERVED FREQUENCY PLOTTED AGAINST ACTUAL
FREQUENCY FOR A FIXED SAMPLING RATE OF 1000 HZ

5.3.5   SIMULATING SAMPLING AND QUANTIZATION IN MATLAB

Now that you've looked more closely at the process of sampling and quantization in this chapter, you should have a clearer understanding of the MATLAB and C++ examples in Chapters 2 and 3.

In MATLAB, you can generate samples from a sine wave of frequency f at a sampling rate r for s seconds in the following way:

```
f = 440;
sr = 44100;
s = 1;
t = linspace(0,s,sr * s);
y = sin(2*pi*f*t);
```

We've looked at statements like these in Chapter 2, but let's review. The statement *linspace(0, s, sr * s)* creates a one-dimensional array (which can also be called a *vector*) of *sr*s* values evenly spaced between 0 and *s*. These are the points at which the samples are to be taken. One statement in MATLAB can cause an operation to be done on every element of a

> **ASIDE:** An alternative way to get the points at which samples are taken is this:
>
> ```
> f = 440;
> sr = 44100;
> s = 1;
> t = [1:sr*s];
> y = sin(2*pi*f*(t/sr*s));
> ```
>
> Plugging in the numbers from this example, you get
>
> ```
> y = sin(2*pi*440*t/44100);
> ```

vector. For example, $y = sin(2*pi*f*t)$ takes the sine on each element of t and stores the result in vector y. Since t has 44,100 values in it, y does also. In this way, MATLAB simulates the sampling process for a single-frequency sound wave.

Quantization can also be simulated in MATLAB. Notice that from the above sequence of commands, all the elements of y are between -1 and 1. To quantize these values to a bit depth of b, you can do the following:

```
b = 8;
sample_max = 2^(b-1)-1;
y_quantized = floor(y*sample_max);
```

> **MATLAB EXERCISE:**
> Experimenting with Quantization Error
> http://bit.ly/29kCx8Q

The plot function graphs the result.

```
plot(t, y);
```

If we want to zoom in on the first, say, 500 values, we can do so with

```
plot(t(1:500), y(1:500));
```

With these basic commands, you can do the suggested exercise ("Experimenting with Quantization Error") in this section, which has you experiment with quantization error and dynamic range at various bit depths.

5.3.6 SIMULATING SAMPLING AND QUANTIZATION IN C++

You can simulate sampling and quantization in C++ just as you can in MATLAB. The difference is that you need loops to operate on arrays in C++, while one command in MATLAB can cause an operation to be performed on each element in an array. (You can also write loops in MATLAB, but it isn't necessary where array operations are available.) For example, the equivalent of the MATLAB lines above is given in C++ below. (We use mostly C syntax but, for simplicity, include some C++ features like dynamic allocation with *new* and the ability to declare variables anywhere in the program.)

> **C++ PROGRAMMING EXERCISE:**
> Simulating Sampling and Quantization in C++
> http://bit.ly/29LYpsh

```
int f = 440;
int r = 44100;
double s = 1;
int b = 8;
double* y = new double[r*s];
for (int t = 0; t < r * s; t++)
 y[t] = sin(2*PI*f*(t/(r*s)));
```

To quantize the samples in y to a bit depth of b, we do this:

```
int sample_max = pow(2, b-1) - 1;
short* y_quantized = new short[r*s];
```

```
for (int i = 0; i < r * s; i++)
    y_quantized[i] = floor(y * sample_max);
```

The suggested programming exercise in this section ("Experimenting with Quantization Error in C++") uses code such as this to implement Algorithm 5.1 for aliasing and to experiment with quantization error at various bit depths.

5.3.7 THE MATHEMATICS OF DITHERING AND NOISE SHAPING

Dithering is described in Section 5.1.2.5 as the addition of low-amplitude random noise to an audio signal as it is being quantized. The purpose of dithering is to prevent neighboring sample values from quantizing all to the same level, which can cause breaks or choppiness in the sound. Noise shaping can be performed in conjunction with dithering to raise the noise to a higher frequency where it is not noticed as much. Now let's look at the mathematics of dithering and noise shaping.

First, the amount of random noise to be added to each sample must be determined. A probability density function can be used for this purpose. We'll use the **triangular probability density function** graphed in Figure 5.39 as an example. This graph depicts the following:

》 There is 0 probability that an amount less than −1 or greater than 1 will be added to any given sample.
》 As x moves from −1 to 0 and as x moves from 1 to 0, there is an increasing probability that x will be added to any given sample.

Thus, it's most likely that some number close to 0 will be added as dither, and the highest magnitude value to be added or subtracted is 1. If you were to implement dithering yourself in MATLAB or a C++ program (as in the exercises associated with this section), you could create a triangular probability density function by getting a random number between −1 and 0 and another between 0 and 1 and summing them.

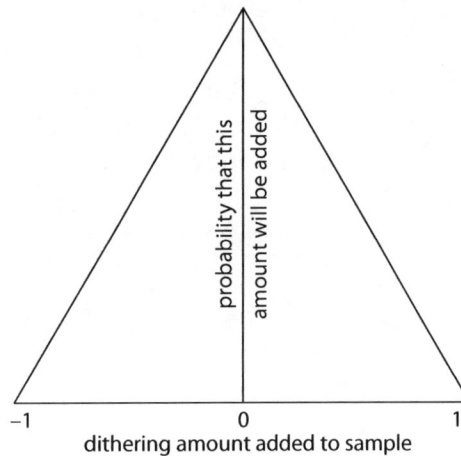

FIGURE 5.39: TRIANGULAR PROBABILITY DENSITY FUNCTION

Audio processing programs like Adobe Audition or Sound Forge offer a variety of probability functions for noise shaping, as shown in Figure 5.40. The rectangular probability density function gives equal probability for all numbers within a given range. The Gaussian function weighs the probabilities according to a Gaussian rather than a triangular shape, so it would look like Figure 5.39 except more bell-shaped. This creates noise that is more like common environmental noise, like tape hiss.

Requantization without dithering, with dithering, and with dithering and noise shaping are compared in Figure 5.41. A 16-bit audio file has been requantized to four bits (an unlikely scenario, but it makes the point). From these graphs, it may look like noise shaping adds additional noise. In fact, the reason the noise graph looks more dense when noise shaping is added is that the frequency components are higher.

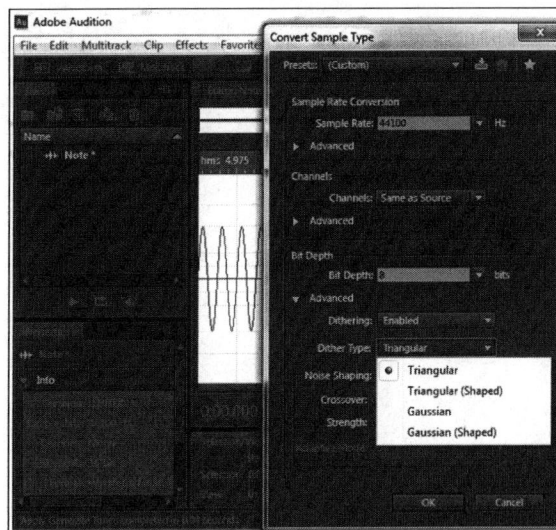

FIGURE 5.40: PROBABILITY FUNCTIONS FOR NOISE SHAPING

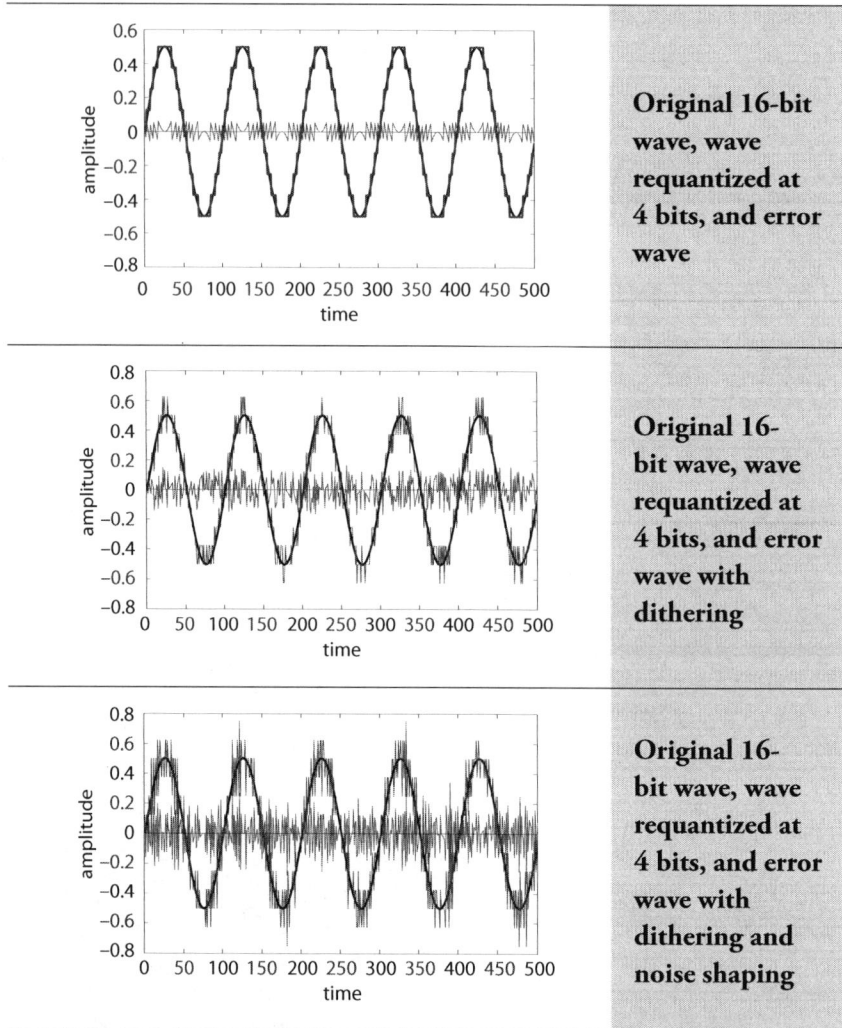

Original 16-bit wave, wave requantized at 4 bits, and error wave

Original 16-bit wave, wave requantized at 4 bits, and error wave with dithering

Original 16-bit wave, wave requantized at 4 bits, and error wave with dithering and noise shaping

FIGURE 5.41: COMPARISON OF REQUANTIZATION WITHOUT DITHERING, WITH DITHERING, AND WITH DITHERING AND NOISE SHAPING

To examine this more closely, we can extract the noise into a separate audio file by subtracting the original file from the requantized one. We've done this for both cases—noise from dither, and noise from dither and noise shaping. (The noise includes the quantization error.) Closeups of the noise graphs are shown in Figure 5.42. What you should notice is that dither-with-noise-shaping noise has higher frequency components than dither-only noise.

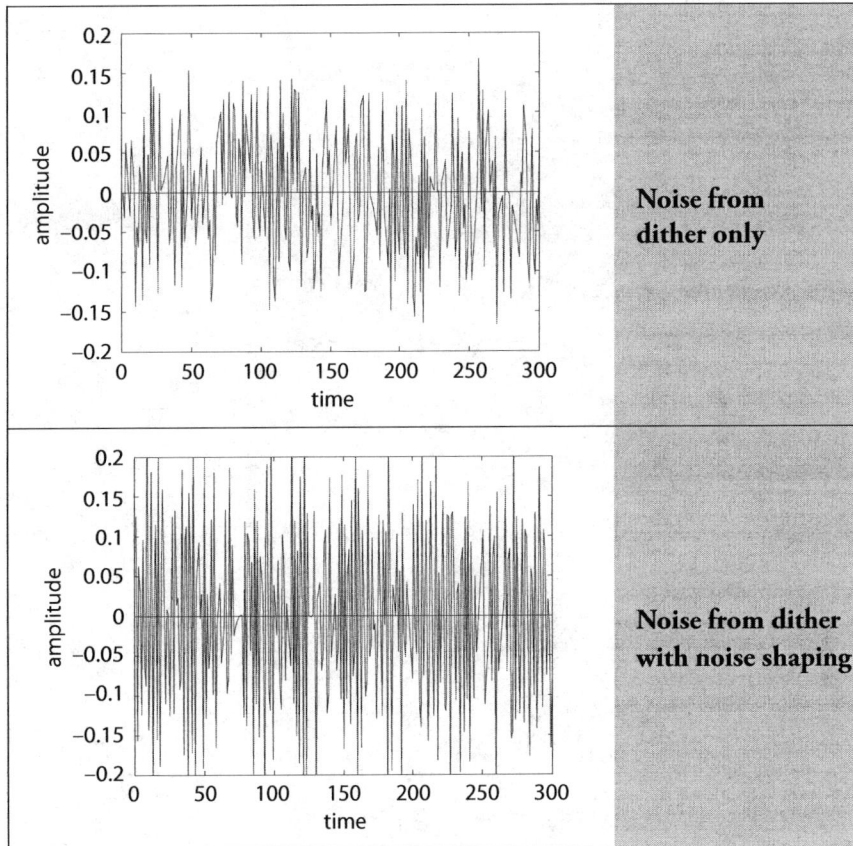

FIGURE 5.42: CLOSEUP OF NOISE FROM DITHER AND NOISE FROM DITHER WITH NOISE SHAPING (QUANTIZATION NOISE INCLUDED)

You can see this also in the spectral view of the noise files in Figure 5.43. In a **spectral view of an audio file**, time is on the x-axis, frequency is on the y-axis, and the amplitude of the frequency is represented by the color at each (x,y) point. The lowest amplitude is represented by blue, medium amplitudes move from red to orange, and the highest amplitudes move from yellow to white. You can see that when dithering alone is applied, the noise is spread out over all frequencies. When noise shaping is added to dithering, there is less noise at low frequency and more noise at high frequency. The effect is to pull more of the noise to high frequencies, where it is noticed less by human ears. (ADCs also can filter out the high frequency noise if it is above the Nyquist frequency.) (You can't see these colors in a black and white edition of this text but will see them if you try this yourself.)

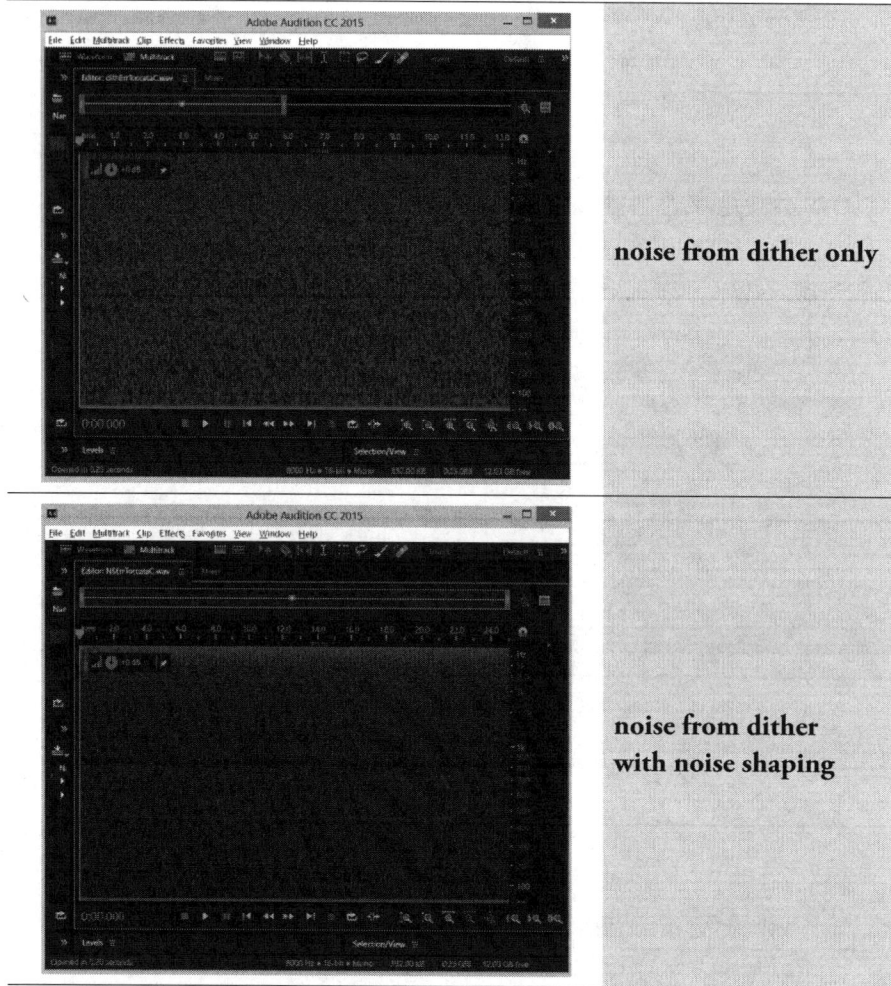

FIGURE 5.43: SPECTRAL VIEW OF NOISE FROM DITHERING AND NOISE FROM DITHERING WITH NOISE SHAPING (QUANTIZATION NOISE INCLUDED)

Noise shaping algorithms, first developed by C.C. Cutler in the 1950s (US Patent No. 2.927.962), operate by computing the error from quantizing a sample (including the error from dithering and noise shaping) and adding this error to the next sample before it is quantized. If the error from the ith sample is positive, then, by subtracting the error from the next sample, noise shaping makes it more likely that the error for the $i + 1^{st}$ sample will be negative. This causes the error wave to go up and down more frequently (i.e., the frequency of the error wave is increased). The algorithm is given in Algorithm 5.2. You can output your files as uncompressed RAW files, import the data into MATLAB, and graph the error waves, comparing the shape of the error with dither only and with noise shaping using various values for *c*, the scaling factor. The algorithm given is the most basic kind of noise shaping you can do. Many refinements and variations of this algorithm have been implemented and distributed commercially.

```
algorithm noise_shape {
/*Input:
     b_orig, the original bit depth
     b_new, the new bit depth to which samples are to be quantized
     F_in, an array of N digital audio samples that are to be
     quantized, dithered, and noise shaped. It's assumed that these are read
     in from a RAW file and are values between
     -2^b_orig-1 and (2^b_orig-1)-1.
     c, a scaling factor for the noise shaping
Output:
     F_out, an array of N digital audio samples quantized to bit
     depth b_new using dither and noise shaping*/

    s = (2^b_orig)/(2^b_new);
    c = 0.8;  //Other scaling factors can be tried.*/
    e = 0;
    for (i = 0; i < N; i++) {
/*Get a random number between -1 and 1 from some probability density function*/
        d = pdf();
        F_scaled  = F_in[i] / s;  //Integer division, discarding remainder
        F_scaled_plus_dith_and_error = F_scaled + d + c*e;
        F_out[i] =  floor(F_scaled_plus_dith_and_error);
        e = F_scaled - F_out[i];
    }
}
```

ALGORITHM 5.2

5.3.8   ALGORITHMS FOR AUDIO COMPANDING AND COMPRESSION

5.3.8.1 Mu-law Encoding

Mu-law encoding (also denoted μ-**law**) is a nonlinear companding method used in telecommunications. **Companding** is a method of compressing a digital signal by reducing the bit depth before it is transmitted, and then expanding it when it is received. The advantage of mu-law encoding is that it preserves some of the dynamic range that would be lost if a linear method of reducing the bit depth were used instead. Let's look more closely at the difference between linear and nonlinear methods of bit depth reduction.

Picture this scenario. A telephone audio signal is to be transmitted. It is originally 16 bits. To reduce the amount of data that has to be transmitted, the audio data is reduced to 8 bits. In a linear method of bit depth reduction, the amount of quantization error possible at low amplitudes is the same as the amount of error possible at high amplitudes. However, this means that the *ratio* of the error to the sample value is *greater* for low amplitude samples than for high. Let's assume that converting from 16 bits to 8 bits is done by dividing by the sample value by 256 and rounding down. Consider a 16-bit sample that is originally 32,767, the highest positive value possible. (16-bit samples range from –32,768 to 32,767.) Converted to 8 bits, the sample value becomes 127. (32767 / 256 = 127 with a remainder of 255.) The error from rounding is 255 / 32,768. This is an error of less than 1%. But compare this to the error for the lowest magnitude 16-bit samples, those between 0 and 255. They all round to 0 when reduced to a bit depth of 8, which is 100% error. The point is that with a linear bit depth reduction method, rounding down has a greater impact on low amplitude samples than on high amplitude ones.

In a nonlinear method such as mu-law encoding, when the bit depth is reduced, the effect is that not all samples are encoded with the same number of bits. Low amplitude samples are given more bits to protect them from quantization error.

Equation 5.5 (which is, more precisely, a function) effectively redistributes the sample values so that there are more quantization levels at lower amplitudes and fewer quantization levels at higher amplitudes. For requantization from 16 to 8 bits, $\mu = 255$.

Let x be a sample value, $-1 \leq x \leq 1$. Let $sign(x) = -1$ if x is negative and $sign(x) = 1$ otherwise. Then the **mu-law function** (also denoted μ-**law**) is defined by

$$mu(x) = sign(x)\left(\frac{\ln(1+\mu|x|)}{\ln(1+\mu)}\right) = sign(x)\left(\frac{\ln(1+255|x|)}{5.5452}\right) for\ \mu = 255$$

EQUATION 5.5

The graph of the mu-law function in Figure 5.44 has the original sample value (on a scale of –1 to 1) on the *x*-axis and the sample value after it is run through the mu-law function on the *y*-axis. Notice that the difference between, say, *mu*(0.001) and *mu*(0.002) is greater than the difference between *mu*(0.981) and *mu*(0.982).

mu(0.001) = 0.0410
mu(0.002) = 0.0743
mu(0.981) = 0.9966
mu(0.982) = 0.9967

The mu-law function has the effect of "spreading out" the quantization intervals more at lower amplitudes.

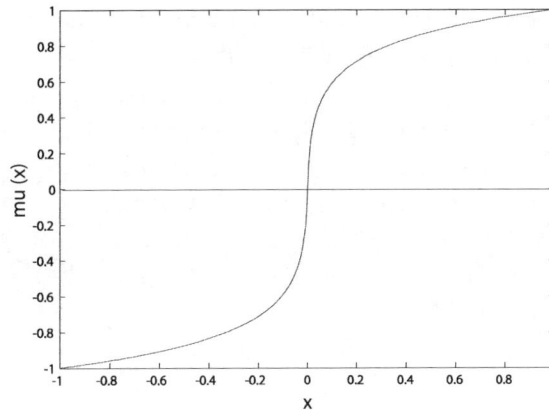

FIGURE 5.44: GRAPH OF μ-LAW FUNCTION

It may be easier to see how this works if we start with sample values on a 16-bit scale (i.e., between −32,768 and 32,767) and then scale the results of the mu-law function back to 8 bits. For example, what happens if we begin with sample values of 33, 66, 32,145, and 32,178? (Notice that these normalize to 0.001, 0.002, 0.981, and 0.982, respectively, on a −1 to 1 scale.)

$mu(33/32768) = 0.0412;$
$floor(128*0.0412) = 5;$
$mu(66/32768) = 0.0747;$
$floor(128* 0.0747) = 9;$
$mu(32145/32768) = 0.9966;$
$floor(128*0.9966) = 127;$
$mu(32178/32768) = 0.9967;$
$floor(128*0.9967) = 127;$

The sample values 33 and 66 on a 16-bit scale become 5 and 9, respectively, on an 8-bit scale. The sample values 32,145 and 32,178 both become 127 on an 8-bit scale. Even though the difference between 66 and 33 is the same as the difference between 32,178 and 32,145, 66 and 33 fall to different quantization levels when they are converted to 8 bits, but 32,178 and 32,145 fall to the same quantization level. There are more quantization levels at lower amplitudes after the mu-law function is applied.

The result is that there is less error at low amplitudes, after requantization to 16 bits, than there would have been

>>

MATLAB EXERCISE:
Mu-Law Encoding
in MATLAB
http://bit.ly/29wkgFb

{}

C++ PROGRAMMING EXERCISE:
Mu-Law Encoding
in C++
http://bit.ly/29gkmmf

if a linear quantization method had been used. Equation 5.6 shows the function for expanding back to the original bit depth.

Let x be a μ-law encoded sample value, $-1 \leq x \leq 1$.
Let $sign(x) = -1$ if x is negative and $sign(x) = 1$ otherwise.
*Then the **inverse μ-law function** is defined by*

$$mu\_inverse(x) = sign(x)\left(\frac{(\mu+1)^{|x|}-1}{\mu}\right) = sign(x)\left(\frac{256^{|x|}-1}{255}\right) for \mu = 255$$

EQUATION 5.6

Our original 16-bit values of 33 and 66 convert to 5 and 9, respectively, in 8 bits. We can convert them back to 16 bits using the inverse mu-law function as follows:

$mu\_inverse(5/128) = .00094846$
$ceil(32768* .00094846) = 32$
$mu\_inverse(9/128) = 0.0019$
$ceil(32768*0.0019) = 63$

The original value of 33 converts back to 32. The original value of 66 converts back to 63. On the other hand, look what happens to the higher amplitude values that were originally 32,145 and 32,178 and convert to 127 at 8 bits.

$mu\_inverse(127/128) = 0.9574$
$ceil(32768*0.9574) = 31373$

Both 32,145 and 32,178 convert back to 31,373.

With mu-law encoding, the results are better than they would have been if a linear method of bit reduction had been used. Let's look at the linear method. Again suppose we convert from 16 to 8 bits by dividing by 256 and rounding down. Then both 16-bit values of 33 and 66 would convert to 0 at 8 bits. To convert back up to 16 bits, we multiply by 256 again and still have 0. We've lost all the information in these samples. On the other hand, by a linear method, both 32,145 and 32,178 convert to 125 at 8 bits. When they're scaled back to 16 bits, they both become 32,000.

A comparison of percentage errors for all of these samples using the two conversion methods is shown in Table 5.2. You can see that mu-law encoding preserves information at low amplitudes that would have been lost by a linear method. The overall result is that with a bit depth of only 8 bits for transmitting the data, it is possible to retrieve a dynamic range of about 12 bits or 72 dB when the data is uncompressed to 16 bits (as opposed to the 48 dB expected from just 8 bits). The dynamic range is increased because fewer of the low amplitude samples fall below the noise floor.

Original sample at 16 bits	Sample after linear companding, 16 to 8 to 16	Percentage error	Sample after nonlinear companding, 16 to 8 to 16	Percentage error
33	0	100%	32	3%
66	0	100%	63	4.5%
32145	32,000	0.45%	31,373	2.4%
32178	32,000	0.55%	31,373	2.5%

TABLE 5.2: COMPARISON OF ERROR IN LINEAR AND NONLINEAR COMPANDING

Rather than applying the mu-law function directly, common implementations of mu-law encoding achieve an equivalent effect by dividing the 8-bit encoded sample into a sign bit, mantissa, and exponent, similar to the way floating point numbers are represented. An advantage of this implementation is that it can be performed with fast bit-shifting operations. The programming exercise associated with this section gives more information about this implementation, comparing it with a literal implementation of the mu-law and inverse mu-law functions based on logarithms.

Mu-law encoding (and its relative, A-law, which is used Europe) reduces the amount of data in an audio signal by quantizing low-amplitude signals with more precision than high amplitude ones. However, since this bit-depth reduction happens in conjunction with digitization, it might more properly be considered a conversion rather than a compression method.

Actual audio compression relies on an analysis of the frequency components of the audio signal coupled with a knowledge of how the human auditory system perceives sound—a field of study called **psychoacoustics**. Compression algorithms based on psychoacoustical models are grouped under the general category of **perceptual encoding**, as is explained in the following section.

5.3.8.2 Psychoacoustics and Perceptual Encoding

Psychoacoustics is the study of how the human ears and brain perceive sound. Psychoacoustical experiments have shown that human hearing is nonlinear in a number of ways, including perception of octaves, perception of loudness, and frequency resolution.

For a note C2 that is one octave higher than a note C1, the frequency of C2 is twice the frequency of C1. This implies that the frequency width of a lower octave is smaller than the frequency width of a higher octave. For example, the octave C5 to C6 is twice the width of C4 to C5. However, the octaves are perceived as being the same width in human hearing. In this sense, our perception of octaves is nonlinear.

Humans hear best (i.e., have the most sensitivity to amplitude) in the range of about 1000 to 5000 Hz, which is close to the range of the human voice. We hear less well at both ends of the frequency spectrum. This is illustrated in Figure 5.45, which shows the shape of the threshold of hearing plotted across frequencies.

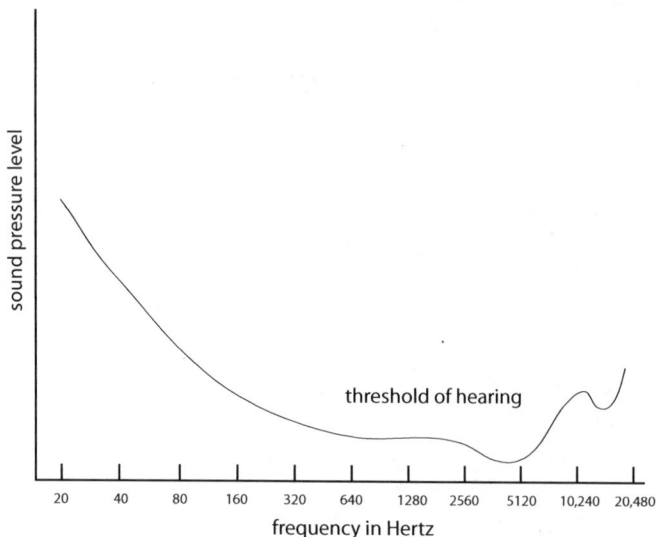

FIGURE 5.45: THRESHOLD OF HEARING PLOTTED OVER FREQUENCIES IN RANGE OF HUMAN HEARING

Human ability to distinguish between frequencies decreases nonlinearly from low to high frequencies. At the very lowest audible frequencies, we can tell the difference between pitches that are only a few Hz apart, while at high frequencies the pitches must be separated by more than 100 Hz before we notice a difference. This difference in frequency sensitivity arises from the fact that the inner ear is divided into **critical bands**. Each band is tuned to a range of frequencies. Critical bands for low frequencies are narrower than those for high ones. Between frequencies of 1 and 500 Hz, critical bands have a width of about 100 Hz or less, whereas the width of the critical band at the highest audible frequency is about 4000 Hz.

The goal of applying psychoacoustics to compression methods is to determine the components of sounds that human ears don't perceive very well, if at all. These are the parts that can be discarded, thereby decreasing the amount of data that must be stored in digitized sound. An understanding of critical bands within the human ear helps in this regard. Within a band, a phenomenon called **masking** can occur. Masking results when two frequencies are received by a critical band at about the same moment in time, one of the frequencies being significantly louder than the first so that it makes the first inaudible. The loud frequency is called the **masking tone**, and the quiet one is the **masked frequency**. Masking causes the threshold of hearing to be raised within a critical band in the presence of a masking tone. The new threshold of hearing is called the **masking threshold**, as depicted in Figure 5.46. Note that this graph represents the masking tone in one critical band in a narrow window of time. Audio compression algorithms look for places where masking occurs in all of the critical bands over each consecutive window of time for the duration of the audio signal.

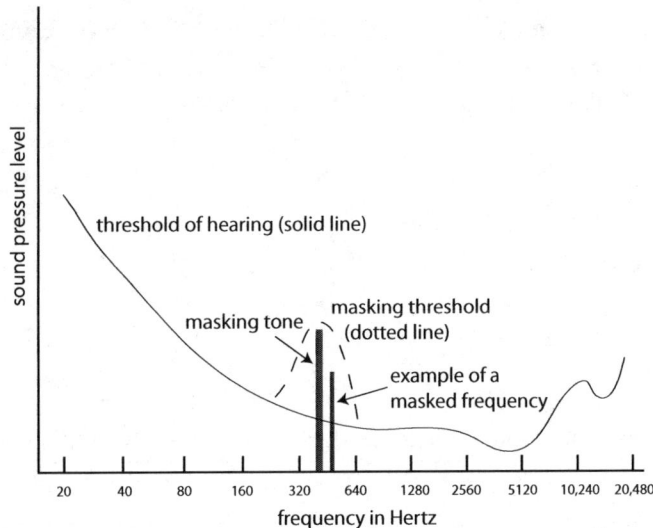

FIGURE 5.46: THRESHOLD OF HEARING ALTERED IN PRESENCE OF MASKING TONE

Another type of masking, called **temporal masking**, occurs with regard to transients. **Transients** are sudden bursts of sounds like drum beats, hand claps, finger snaps, and consonant sounds. When two transients occur close together in time, the louder one can mask the weaker one. Identifying instances of temporal masking is another important part of perceptual encoding.

5.3.8.3 MP3 and AAC Compression

Two of the best known compression methods that use perceptual encoding are MP3 and AAC. MP3 is actually a shortened name for MPEG-1 Audio Layer III. It was developed through a collaboration of scientists at Fraunhofer IIS, AT&T Bell Labs, Thomson-Brandt, CCETT, and others and was approved by ISO/IEC as part of the MPEG standard in 1993. MP3 was a landmark compression method in the way that it popularized the exchange of music by means of the web. Although MP3 is a lossy compression method in that it discards information that cannot be retrieved, music lovers were quick to accept the tradeoff between some loss of audio quality and the ability to store and exchange large numbers of music files.

AAC (Advanced Audio Coding) is the successor of MP3 compression, using similar perceptual encoding techniques but improving on these and supporting more channels, sampling rates, and bit rates. AAC is available within both the MPEG-2 and MPEG-4 standards and is the default audio compression method for iPhones, iPods, iPads, Android phones, and a variety of video game consoles. Table 5.1 shows the file name extensions associated with MP3 and AAC compression.

You may have read that MP3 offers a compression ratio of about 11 to 1. This number gives you a general idea, but exact compression ratios vary. Table 5.3 on page 277 shows ranges of bit rates available for different layers within the MPEG standard. Typically, an MP3 compressor offers a number of choices of bit rates, these varying with sampling rates, as shown in Figure 5.47 for Adobe Audition's MP3/mp3Pro encoder. The bit rate indicates how many bits of compressed data is generated per second. A constant bit rate of 128 kb/s for mono audio sampled at 44,100 Hz with 16 bits per sample gives a compression ratio of 5.5:1, as shown in the calculation below.

44100 samples/s*16=705600 b/s uncompressed

705600 uncompressed:128000 b/s compressed ≈5.5:1

For stereo (32 bits per sample) at a sampling rate of 44,100, compressed to 128 kb/s, the compression ratio is approximately 11:1. This is where the commonly-cited compression ratio comes from—the fact that frequently, MP3 compression is used on CD-quality stereo at a bit rate of 128 kb/s, which most listeners seem to think gives acceptable quality. For a given implementation of MP3 compression and a fixed sampling rate, bit depth, and number of channels, a higher bit rate yields better quality in the compressed audio than a lower bit rate. When fewer bits are produced per second of audio, more information must be thrown out.

The MPEG standard does not prescribe how compression is to be implemented. Instead, it prescribes the format of the encoded audio signal, which is a bit stream made up of frames with certain headers and data fields. The MPEG standard suggests two psychoacoustical models that could accomplish the encoding. The second model, used for MP3, is more complex and generally results in greater compression than the first.

ASIDE: MPEG is an acronym for Motion Picture Experts Group and refers to a family of compression methods for digital audio and video. MPEG standards were developed in phases and layers beginning in 1988, as outlined in Table 5.3. The phases are indicated by Arabic numerals and the layers by Roman numerals.

In reality, there can be great variability in the time efficiency and quality of MP3 encoders. The advantage to not dictating details of the compression algorithm is that implementers can compete with novel implementations and refinements. If the format of the bit stream is always the same, including what each part of the bit stream represents, then decoders can be implemented without having to know the details of the encoder's implementation.

Version	Bit rates*	Applications	Channels	Sampling rates supported
MPEG-1		CD, DAT, ISDN, video games, digital audio broadcasting, music shared on the web, portable music players	mono or stereo	32, 44.1, and 48 kHz (and 16, 22.05, and 24 kHz for MPEG-2 LSF, low sampling frequency)
Layer I	32–448 kb/s			
Layer II	32–384 kb/s			
Layer III	32–320 kb/s			
MPEG-2		multichannels, multilingual extensions	5.1 surround	32, 44.1, and 48 kHz
Layer I	32–448 kb/s			
Layer II	32–384 kb/s			
Layer III	32–320 kb/s			
AAC in MPEG-2 and MPEG-4 (Advanced Audio Coding)	8–384 kb/s	multichannels, music shared on the web, portable music players, cell phones	up to 48 channels	32, 44.1, and 48 kHz and other rates between 8 and 96 kHz

*Available bit rates vary with sampling rate.

TABLE 5.3: MPEG AUDIO

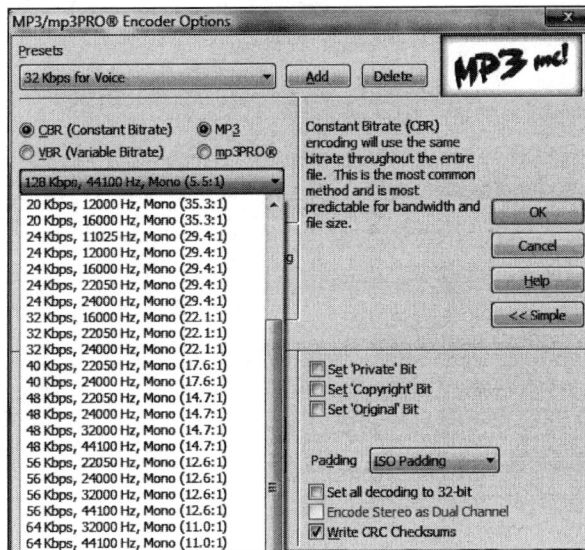

FIGURE 5.47: BIT RATE CHOICES IN ADOBE AUDITION'S MP3/MP3PRO ENCODER

An MP3 bit stream is divided into frames each of which represents the compression of 1152 samples. The size of the frame containing the compressed data is determined by the bit rate, a user option that is set prior to compression. As before, let's assume that a bit rate of 128 kb/s is chosen to compress an audio signal with a sampling rate of 44.1 kHz. This implies that the number of frames of compressed data that must be produced per second is 44,100 / 1152 ≈ 38.28. The chosen bit rate of 128 kb/s is equal to 16,000 bytes per second. Thus, the number of bytes allowed for each frame is 16,000 / 38.28 ≈ 418. You can see that if you vary the sampling rate or the bit rate, there will be a different number of bytes in each frame. This computation considers only the data part of each compressed frame. Actually, each frame consists of a 32-byte header followed by the appropriate number of data bytes, for a total of approximately 450 bytes in this example.

The format of the header is shown in Figure 5.48 and explained in Table 5.4.

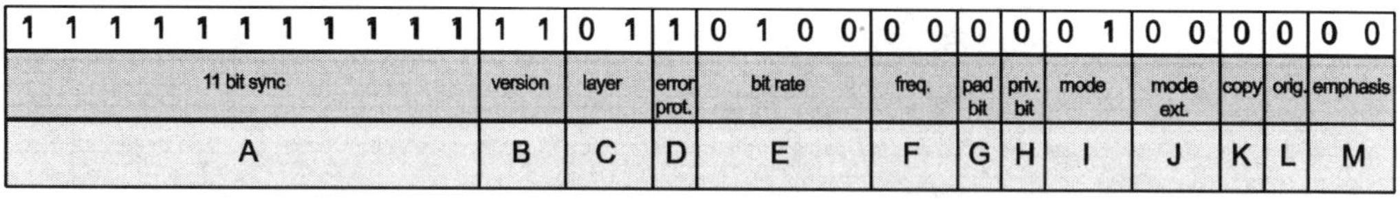

1 1 1 1 1 1 1 1 1 1 1	1 1	0 1	1	0 1 0 0	0 0	0	0	0 1	0 0	0	0	0
11 bit sync	version	layer	error prot.	bit rate	freq.	pad bit	priv. bit	mode	mode ext.	copy	orig.	emphasis
A	B	C	D	E	F	G	H	I	J	K	L	M

FIGURE 5.48: MP3 FRAME HEADER

MP3 supports both **constant bit rate (CBR)** and **variable bit rate (VBR)**. VBR makes it possible to vary the bit rate frame by frame, allocating more bits to frames that require greater frequency resolution because of the complexity of the sound in that part of the audio. This can be implemented by allowing the user to specify the maximum bit rate. An alternative is to allow the user to specify an average bit rate. Then the bit rate can vary frame by frame but is controlled so that it averages to the chosen rate.

A certain amount of variability is possible even within CBR. This is done by means of a **bit reservoir** in frames. A bit reservoir is created from bits that do not have to be used in a frame because the audio being encoded is relatively simple. The reservoir provides extra space in a subsequent frame that may be more complicated and requires more bits for encoding.

Field I in Table 5.4 makes reference to the **channel mode**. MP3 allows for one mono channel, two independent mono channels, two stereo channels, and **joint stereo mode**. Joint stereo mode takes advantage of the fact that human hearing is less sensitive to the location of sounds that are at the lowest and highest ends of the audible frequency ranges. In a stereo audio signal, low or high frequencies can be combined into a single mono channel without much perceptible difference to the listener. The joint stereo option can be specified by the user.

Field	Length in bits	Contents
A	11	all 1s to indicate start of frame
B	2	MPEG-1 indicated by bits 1 1
C	2	Layer III indicated by bits 0 1
D	1	0 means protected by CRC* (with 16-bit CRC following header) 1 means not protected
E	4	bit rate index 0000 free 0001 32 kb/s 0010 40 kb/s 0011 48 kb/s 0100 56 kb/s 0101 64 kb/s 0110 80 kb/s 0111 96 kb/s 1000 112 kb/s 1001 128 kb/s 1010 160 kb/s 1011 192 kb/s 1100 224 kb/s 1101 256 kb/s 1110 320 kb/s 1111 bad
F	2	frequency index 00 44,100 Hz 01 48,000 Hz 10 32,000 Hz 11 reserved
G	1	0 frame is not padded 1 frame is padded with an extra byte Padding is used so that bit rates are fitted exactly to frames. For example, a 44,100 Hz audio signal at 128 kb/s yields a frame of about 417.97 bytes
H	1	private bit, used as desired by implementer
I	2	channel mode 00 stereo 01 joint stereo 10 2 independent mono channels 11 1 mono channel
J	2	mode extension used with joint stereo mode
K	1	0 if not copyrighted 1 if copyrighted
L	1	0 if copy of original media 1 if not
M	2	indicates emphasized frequencies

*CRC stands for cyclical redundancy check, an error-correcting code that checks for errors in the transmission of data.

TABLE 5.4: CONTENTS OF MP3 FRAME HEADER

A sketch of the steps in MP3 compression is given in Algorithm 5.3 and the algorithm is diagrammed in Figure 5.49. This algorithm glosses over details that can vary by implementation but gives the basic concepts of the compression method.

```
algorithm MP3 {
/*Input: An audio signal in the time domain
  Output: The same audio signal, compressed
/*
Process the audio signal in frames
For each frame {
   Use the Fourier transform to transform the time domain data to
the frequency domain, sending
        the results to the psychoacoustical analyzer {
          Based on masking tones and masked frequencies, determine
the signal-to-masking noise
              ratios (SMR) in areas across the frequency spectrum
          Analyze the presence and interactions of transients
        }
   Divide the frame into 32 frequency bands
   For each frequency band {
       Use the modified discrete cosine transform (MDCT) to divide
each of the 32 frequency bands
           into 18 subbands, for a total of 576 frequency subbands
       Sort the subbands into 22 groups, called scale factor
bands, and based on the SMR, determine
           a scaling factor for each scale factor band
       Use nonuniform quantization combined with scaling factors
to quantize
       Encode side information
       Use Huffman encoding on the resulting 576 quantized MDCT
coefficients
       Put the encoded data into a properly formatted frame in the
bit stream
       }
}
```

ALGORITHM 5.3: MP3 COMPRESSION

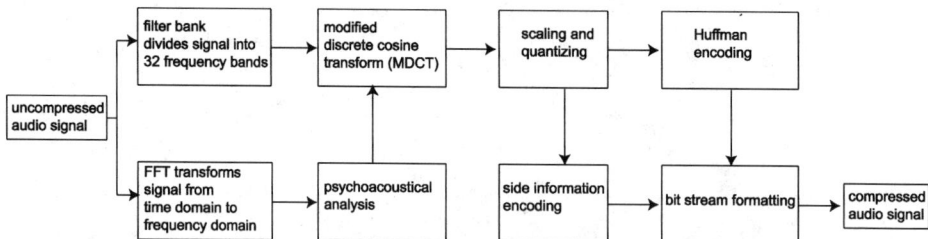

FIGURE 5.49: MP3 COMPRESSION

Let's look at the steps in this algorithm more closely.

1. Divide the audio signal in frames.

MP3 compression processes the original audio signal in frames of 1152 samples. Each frame is split into two granules of 576 samples each. Frames are encoded in a number of bytes consistent with the bit rate set for the compression at hand. In the example described above (with a sampling rate of 44.1 kHz and requested bit rate of 128 kb/s), 1152 samples are compressed into a frame of approximately 450 bytes—418 bytes for data and 32 bytes for the header.

2. Use the Fourier transform to transform the time domain data to the frequency domain, sending the results to the psychoacoustical analyzer.

The fast Fourier transform changes the data to the frequency domain. The frequency domain data is then sent to a psychoacoustical analyzer. One purpose of this analysis is to identify masking tones and masked frequencies in a local neighborhood of frequencies over a small window of time. The psychoacoustical analyzer outputs a set of **signal-to-mask ratios (SMRs)** that can be used later in quantizing the data. The SMR is the ratio between the amplitude of a masking tone and the amplitude of the minimum masked frequency in the chosen vicinity. The compressor uses these values to choose scaling factors and quantization levels so that quantization error mostly falls below the masking threshold. Step 5 explains this process further.

Another purpose of the psychoacoustical analysis is to identify the presence of transients and temporal masking. When the MDCT is applied in a later step, transients have to be treated in smaller window sizes to achieve better time resolution in the encoding. If not, one transient sound can mask another that occurs close to it in time. Thus, in the presence of transients, windows are made one third their normal size in the MDCT.

3. Divide each frame into 32 frequency bands.

Steps 2 and 3 are independent and actually could be done in parallel. Dividing the frame into frequency bands is done with filter banks. Each filter bank is a bandpass filter that allows only a range of frequencies to pass through. (Chapter 7 gives more details on bandpass filters.) The complete range of frequencies that can appear in the original signal is 0 to ½ the sampling rate, as we know from the Nyquist theorem. For example, if the sampling rate of the signal is 44.1 kHz, then the highest frequency that can be present in the signal is 22.05 kHz. Thus, the filter banks yield 32 frequency bands between 0 and 22.05 kHz, each of width 22,050 / 32, or about 689 Hz.

The 32 resulting bands are still in the time domain. Note that dividing the audio signal into frequency bands increases the amount of data by a factor of 32 at this point. That is, there are 32 sets of 1152 time domain samples, each holding just the frequencies in its band. (You can understand this better if you imagine that the audio signal is a piece of music that you decompose into 32 frequency bands. After the decomposition, you could play each band separately and hear the musical piece, but only those frequencies in the band. The segments would need to be longer than 1152 samples for you to hear any music, however, since 1152 samples at a sampling rate of 44.1 kHz is only 0.026 seconds of sound.)

4. Use the MDCT to divide each of the 32 frequency bands into 18 subbands for a total of 576 frequency subbands.

The MDCT, like the Fourier transform, can be used to change audio data from the time domain to the frequency domain. Its distinction is that it is applied on overlapping windows in order to minimize the appearance of spurious frequencies that occur because of discontinuities at window boundaries. (*Spurious frequencies* are frequencies that aren't really in the audio, but that are yielded from the transform.) The overlap between successive MDCT windows varies depending on the information that the psychoacoustical analyzer provides about the nature of the audio in the frame and band. If there are transients involved, then the window size is shorter for greater temporal resolution. Otherwise, a larger window is used for greater frequency resolution.

5. Sort the subbands into 22 groups, called *scale factor bands*, and based on the SMR, determine a scaling factor for each scale factor band. Use nonuniform quantization combined with scaling factors to quantize.

Values are raised to the ¾ power before quantization. This yields nonuniform quantization, aimed at reducing quantization noise for lower amplitude signals, where it has a more harmful impact.

The psychoacoustical analyzer provides information that is the basis for sorting the subbands into **scale factor bands**. The scale factor bands cover several MDCT coefficients and more closely match the critical bands of the human ear. This is one of the ways in which MP3 is an improvement over MPEG-1 layers 1 and 2.

All bands are quantized by dividing by the same value. However, the values in the scale factor bands can be scaled up or down based on their SMR. Bands that have a lower SMR are multiplied by larger scaling factors because the quantization error for these bands has less impact, falling below the masking threshold.

Consider this example. Say that an uncompressed band value is 20,000 and values from all bands are quantized by dividing by 128 and rounding down. Thus the quantized value would be 156. When the value is restored by multiplying by 128, it is 19,968, for an error of 32 / 20,000 = 0.0016. Now suppose the psychoacoustical analyzer reveals that this band requires less precision because of a strong masking tone. Thus, it determines that the band should be scaled by a factor of 0.1. Now we have $floor((20{,}000 \times 0.1) / 128) = 15$. Restoring the original value, we get $15 \times 128 = 19{,}200$, for an error of 800 / 20000 = 0.04.

An appropriate psychoacoustical analysis provides scaling factors that increase the quantization error where it doesn't matter in the presence of masking tones. Scale factor bands effectively allow less precision (i.e., fewer bits) to store values if the resulting quantization error falls below the audible level. This is one way to reduce the amount of data in the compressed signal.

6. Encode side information.

Side information is the information needed to decode the rest of the data, including where the main data begins, whether granule pairs can share scale factors, where scale factors and Huffman encodings begin, the Huffman table to use, the quantization step, and so forth.

7. Use Huffman encoding on the resulting 576 quantized MDCT coefficients.

The result of the MDCT is 576 coefficients representing the amplitudes of 576 frequency subbands. Huffman encoding is applied at this point to further compress the signal.

Huffman encoding is a compression method that assigns shorter codes to symbols that appear more often in the signal or file being encoded, and longer codes for symbols that appear infrequently. Here's a sketch of how it works. Imagine that you are encoding 88 notes from a piano keyboard. You can use 7 bits for each note. (Six bits would be too few, since with six bits you can represent only $2^6 = 64$ different notes.) In a particular music file, you have 100 instances of notes. The number of instances of each is recorded in the table below. Not all 88 notes are used, but this is not important to the example. (This is just a contrived example, so don't try to make sense of it musically.)

Note	Instances of Note
C4	31
B4	20
F3	16
D4	11
G4	8
E4	5
A3	4
B3	3
F4	2

There are 100 notes to be encoded here. If each requires 7 bits, that's 700 bits for the encoded file. It's possible to reduce the size of this encoded file if we use fewer than seven bits for the notes that appear most often. We can choose a different encoding by building what's called a *Huffman tree*. We begin by creating a node (just a circle in a graph) for each of the notes in the file and the number of instances of that note, like this:

The initial placement of the nodes isn't important, although a good placement can make the tree look neater after you've finished joining nodes. Now the idea is to combine the two nodes that have the smallest value, making a node above, marking it with the sum of the chosen nodes' values, and joining the new node with lines to the nodes below. (The lines connecting the nodes are called **arcs**.) B3/3 and F4/2 have the smallest values, so we join them, like this:

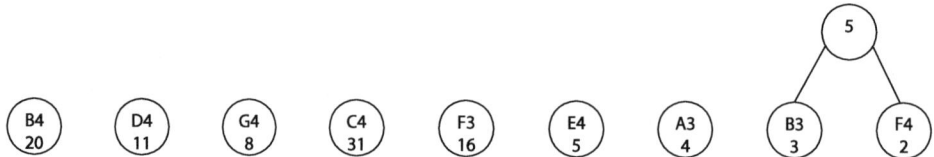

At the next step, A3/4 and the 5 node just created can be combined. (We could also combine A3/4 with E4/5. The choice between the two is arbitrary.) The sum of the instances is 9.

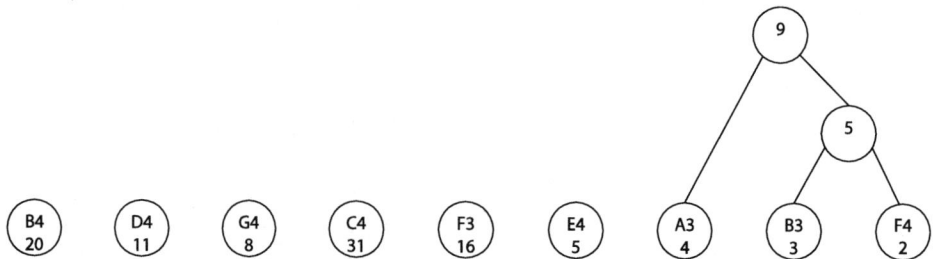

In the next two steps, we combine E4/5 with 9 and then D4 with G4, as shown.

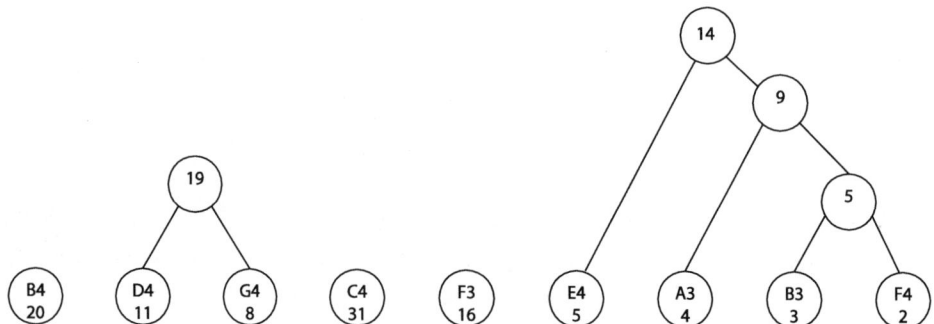

Continuing in this manner, the final tree becomes this:

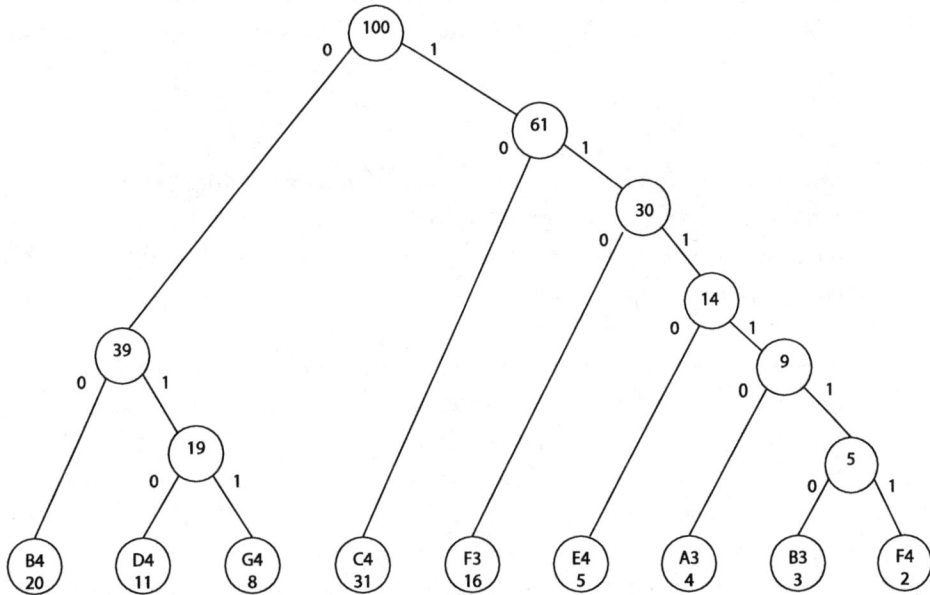

Notice that the left arc from each node has been labeled with a 0 and the right with a 1. The nodes at the bottom represent the notes to be encoded. You can get the code for a note by reading the 0s and 1s on the arcs that take you from the top node to one of the notes at the bottom. For example, to get to B4, you follow the arcs labeled 0 0. Thus, the new encoding for B4 is 0 0, which requires only two bits. To get to B3, you follow the arcs labeled 1 1 1 1 1 0. The new encoding for B3 is 1 1 1 1 1 0, which requires six bits. All the new encodings are given in the table below:

Note	Instances of Note	Code in Binary	Number of Bits
C4	31	10	2
B4	20	00	2
F3	16	110	3
D4	11	010	3
G4	8	011	3
E4	5	1110	4
A3	4	11110	5
B3	3	111110	6
F4	2	111111	6

Note that not all notes are encoded in the same number of bits. This is not a problem to the decoder because no code is a prefix of any other. (This way, the decoder can figure out where a code ends without knowing its length.) With the encoding that we just derived, which uses fewer bits for notes that occur frequently, we need only $31\times2 + 20\times2 + 16\times3 + 11\times3 + 8\times3 + 5\times4 + 4\times5 + 3\times6 + 2\times6 = 277$ bits as opposed to the 700 needed previously.

This illustrates the basic concept of Huffman encoding. However, it is realized in a different manner in the context of MP3 compression. Rather than generate a Huffman table based on the data in a frame, MP3 uses a number of predefined Huffman tables defined in the MPEG standard. A variable in the header of each frame indicates which of these tables is to be used.

Steps 5, 6, and 7 can be done iteratively. After an iteration, the compressor checks that the noise level is acceptable and that the proper bit rate has been maintained. If there are more bits that could be used, the quantizer can be reduced. If the bit limit has been exceeded, quantization must be done more coarsely. The level of distortion in each band is also analyzed. If the distortion is not below the masking threshold, then the scale factor for the band can be adjusted.

8. Put the encoded data into a properly formatted frame in the bit stream.
The header of each frame is as shown in Table 5.4. The data part of each frame consists of the scaled, quantized MDCT values.

AAC compression, the successor to MP3, uses similar encoding techniques but improves on MP3 by offering more sampling rates (8 to 96 kHz), more channels (up to 48), and arbitrary bit rates. Filtering is done solely with the MDCT, with improved frequency resolution for signals without transients and improved time resolution for signals with transients. Frequencies over 16 kHz are better preserved. The overall result is that many listeners find AAC files to have better sound quality than MP3 for files compressed at the same bit rate.

5.3.8.4 Lossless Audio Compression

Lossless audio codecs include FLAC, Apple Lossless, MPEG-4 ALS, and Windows Media Audio Lossless, among others. All of these codecs compress audio in a way that retains all the original information. The audio, upon decompression, is identical to the original signal (disregarding insignificant computation precision errors). Lossless compression generally reduces an audio signal to about half its original size. Let's look at FLAC as an example of how it's done.

Like a number of other lossless codecs, FLAC is based on **linear predictive coding**. The main idea is as follows:

⟩ Consider the audio signal in the time domain.

) Come up with a function that reasonably predicts what an audio sample is likely to be based on the values of previous samples.

) Using that formula on n successive samples, calculate what $n + 1$ "should" be. This value is called the *approximation*.

) Subtract the approximation from the actual value. The result is called the **residual** (or **residue** or **error**, depending on your source).

) Save the residual rather than the actual value in the compressed signal. Since the residual is likely to be less than the actual value, this saves space.

) The decoder knows the formula that was used for approximating a sample based on previous samples, so with only the residual, it is able to recover the original sample value.

The formula for approximating a sample could be as simple as the following:

$$\sum_{i=1}^{p} \hat{x}(n) = a_i x(n - i)$$

where $\hat{x}(n)$ is the approximation for the nth sample and a_i is the predictor coefficient. The residual $e(n)$ is then

$$e(n) = x(n) - \hat{x}(n)$$

The compression ratio is of course affected by the way in which the predictor coefficient is chosen.

Another source of compression in FLAC is **inter-channel decorrelation**. For stereo input, the left and right channels can be converted to mid and side channels with the following equations:

$$mid = \frac{left + right}{2}$$

$$side = left - right$$

Values for *mid* and *side* are generally smaller than *left* and *right*, and *left* and *right* can be retrieved from *mid* and *side* as follows:

$$right = mid - \frac{side}{2}$$

$$right + side = left$$

A third source of compression is a version of Huffman encoding called **Rice encoding**. Rice codes are special Huffman codes that can be used in this context. A parameter is dynamically set and changed based on the signal's distribution, and this parameter is used to generate the Rice codes. Then the table does not need to be stored with the compressed signal.

FLAC is unpatented and open source. The FLAC website is a good source for details and documentation about the implementation of the codec.

5.4 REFERENCES

In addition to references cited in previous chapters:

Advanced Linux Sound Architecture (ALSA) project homepage, http: // www.alsa-project.org/main/index.php/Main_Page.

FLAC. Free Lossless Audio Codec, https://xiph.org/flac/.

G.711zz: 1988. "Pulse Code Modulation (PCM) of Voice Frequencies." https://www.itu.int/rec/T-REC-G.711-198811-I/en.

Hacker, Scot. *MP3: The Definitive Guide.* Sebastopol , CA: O'Reilly, 2000.

ISO/IEC 11172-3: 1993. "Information technology -- Coding of Moving Pictures and Associated Audio for Digital Storage Media at up to about 1,5 MBit/s -- Part 3: Audio," http://www.iso.org/iso/catalogue_detail .htm?csnumber=22412.

Li, Ze-Nian and Mark S. Drew. *Fundamentals of Multimedia.* Upper Saddle River, NJ: Prentice Hall, 2004.

libsndfile. http://www.mega-nerd.com/libsndfile/.

Rossing, Thomas D., F. Richard Moore, and Paul A. Wheeler. *The Science of Sound,* 3rd ed. San Francisco: Addison-Wesley, 2002.

4Front Technologies, http://www.opensound.com/.

CHAPTER SIX

MIDI and Sound Synthesis

6.1 CONCEPTS

6.1.1 THE BEGINNINGS OF SOUND SYNTHESIS

Sound synthesis has an interesting history in both the analog and digital realms. Precursors to today's sound synthesizers include a colorful variety of instruments and devices that generated sound electrically rather than mechanically. One of the earliest examples was Thaddeus Cahill's telharmonium (also called the dynamophone), patented in 1897. The telharmonium was a gigantic 200-ton contraption built of "dynamos" that were intended to broadcast musical frequencies over telephone lines. The dynamos, precursors of the tonewheels to be used later in the Hammond organ, were specially geared shafts and inductors that produced alternating currents of different audio frequencies controlled by velocity-sensitive keyboards. Although the telharmonium was mostly unworkable, generating too strong a signal for telephone lines, it opened people's minds to the possibilities of electrically-generated sound.

The 1920s through the 1950s saw the development of various electrical instruments, most notably the theremin, the ondes Martenot, and the Hammond organ. The theremin, patented in 1928, consisted of two sensors allowing the player to control frequency and amplitude with hand gestures. The Martenot, invented in the same year, was similar to the theremin in that it used vacuum tubes and produced continuous frequencies, even those lying between conventional note pitches. It could be played in one of two ways: either by sliding a metal ring worn on the right-hand index finger in front of the keyboard or by depressing keys on the six-octave keyboard, making it easier to master than the theremin. The Hammond organ was invented in 1938 as an electric alternative to wind-driven pipe organs. Like the telharmonium, it used tonewheels, in this case producing harmonic combinations of frequencies that could be mixed by sliding drawbars mounted on two keyboards.

As sound synthesis evolved, researchers broke even farther from tradition, experimenting with new kinds of sound apart from music. Sound synthesis in this context was a process of recording, creating, and compiling sounds in novel ways. The **musique concrète** movement of the 1940s, for example, was described by founder Pierre Schaeffer as "no longer dependent upon preconceived sound abstractions, but now using fragments of sound existing concretely as sound objects (Schaeffer 1952). "Sound objects" were to be found not in conventional music but directly in nature and the environment—train engines rumbling, cookware rattling, birds singing, etc. Although it relied mostly on naturally occurring sounds, musique concrète could be considered part of the electronic music movement in the way in which the sound montages were constructed, by means of microphones, tape recorders, varying tape speeds, mechanical reverberation effects, filters, and the cutting and resplicing of tape.

In contrast, the contemporaneous **Elektronische Musik** movement sought to synthesize sound primarily from electronically produced signals. The movement was defined in a series of lectures given in Darmstadt, Germany, by Werner Meyer-Eppler and Robert Beyer and entitled "The World of Sound of Electronic Music." Shortly thereafter, West German Radio (WDR) opened a studio dedicated to research in electronic music, and the first *Elektronische Musik* production, *Musica su due dimensioni*, appeared in 1952. This composition featured a live flute player, a taped portion manipulated by a technician, and artistic freedom for either one of them to manipulate the composition during the performance. Other innovative compositions followed, and the movement spread throughout Europe, the United States, and Japan.

There were two big problems in early sound synthesis systems. First, they required a great deal of space, consisting of a variety of microphones, signal generators, keyboards, tape recorders, amplifiers, filters, and mixers. Second, they were difficult to communicate with. Live performances might require instant reconnection of patch cables and a wide range of setting changes. "Composed" pieces entailed tedious recording, re-recording, cutting, and splicing of tape. These problems spurred the development of automated systems. The Electronic Music Synthesizer, developed at RCA in 1955, was a step in the direction of programmed music synthesis. Its second incarnation in 1959, the Mark II, used binary code punched into paper to represent pitch and timing changes. While it was still a large and complex system, it made advances in the way humans communicate with a synthesizer, overcoming the limitations of what can be controlled by hand in real time.

Technological advances in the form of transistors and voltage controllers made it possible to reduce the size of synthesizers. Voltage controllers could be used to control the oscillation (frequency) and amplitude of a sound wave. Transistors replaced bulky vacuum tubes as a means of amplifying and switching electronic signals. Among the first to take advantage of the new technology in the building of analog synthesizers were Don Buchla and Robert Moog. The Buchla Electric Music Box and the Moog synthesizer, developed in the 1960s, both used voltage controllers and transistors. One main difference was that the Moog synthesizer allowed standard keyboard input, while the Electric Music Box used touch-sensitive metal pads housed in wooden boxes. Both, however, were analog devices, and as such, they were difficult to set up and operate. The much smaller Minimoog, released in 1970, was more affordable and user-friendly, but the digital revolution in synthesizers was already underway.

When increasingly inexpensive microprocessors and integrated circuits became available in the 1970s, digital synthesizers began to appear. Where analog synthesizers were programmed by rearranging a tangle of patch cords, digital synthesizers could be adjusted with easy-to-use knobs, buttons, and dials. Synthesizers took the form of electronic keyboards like the one shown in Figure 6.1, with companies like Sequential Circuits, Electronics, Roland, Korg, Yamaha, and Kawai taking the lead in their development. They were certainly easier to play and program than their analog counterparts. A limitation to their use, however, was that the control surface was not standardized, and it was difficult to get multiple synthesizers to work together.

FIGURE 6.1: PROPHET-5 SYNTHESIZER

In parallel with the development of synthesizers, researchers were creating languages to describe the types of sounds and music they wished to synthesize. One of the earliest digital sound synthesis systems was developed by Max V. Mathews at Bell Labs. In its first version, created in 1957, Mathews' MUSIC I program could synthesize sounds with just basic control over frequency. By 1968, Mathews had developed a fairly complete sound synthesis language in MUSIC V. Other sound and music languages that were developed around the same time or shortly thereafter include Csound (created by Barry Vercoe, MIT, in the 1980s), Structured Audio Orchestras Language (SAOL, part of MPEG-4 standard), Music 10 (created by John Chowning and James Moorer, Stanford, in 1966), cmusic (created by F. Richard Moore, University of California San Diego in the 1990s), and pcmusic (also created by F. Richard Moore).

In the early 1980s, led by Dave Smith from Sequential Circuits and Ikutaro Kakehashi from Roland, a group of the major synthesizer manufacturers decided that it was in their mutual interest to find a common language for their devices. Their collaboration resulted in the 1983 release of the MIDI 1.0 Detailed Specification. The original document defined only basic instructions, things like how to play notes and control volume. Later revisions added messages for greater control of synthesizers and branched out to messages controlling stage lighting. General MIDI (1991) attempted to standardize the association between program numbers and instruments synthesized. It also added new connection types (e.g., USB, FireWire, and wireless), and new platforms such as mobile phones and video games.

This short history lays the groundwork for the two main topics to be covered in this chapter: symbolic encoding of music and sound information—in particular, MIDI—and how this encoding is translated into sound by digital sound synthesis. We begin with a definition of MIDI and an explanation of how it differs from digital audio, after which we can take a closer look at how MIDI commands are interpreted via sound synthesis.

6.1.2   MIDI COMPONENTS

MIDI (Musical Instrument Digital Interface) is a term that actually refers to a number of things:

> A symbolic language of event-based messages frequently used to represent music.

> A standard interpretation of messages, including what instrument sounds and notes are intended upon playback (although the messages can be interpreted to mean other things, at the user's discretion).

> A type of physical connection between one digital device and another.

> input and output ports that accommodate the MIDI connections, translating back and forth between digital data to electrical voltages according to the MIDI protocol.

> A transmission protocol that specifies the order and type of data to be transferred from one digital device to another.

Let's look at all of these associations in the context of a simple real-world example. (Refer to the Chapter 1 for an overview of your DAW and MIDI setup.) A setup for recording and editing MIDI on a computer commonly has these five components:

> *A means to input MIDI messages:* a MIDI input device, such as a **MIDI keyboard** or **MIDI controller.** This could be something that looks like a piano keyboard, only it doesn't generate sound itself. Often MIDI keyboards have controller functions as well, such as knobs, faders, and buttons, as shown in Figure 1.5 in Chapter 1. It's also possible to use your computer keyboard as an

input device if you don't have any other controller. The MIDI input program on your computer may give you an interface on the computer screen that looks like a piano keyboard, as shown in Figure 6.2.

FIGURE 6.2: SOFTWARE INTERFACE FOR MIDI CONTROLLER FROM APPLE LOGIC

》 *A means to transmit MIDI messages:* a cable connecting your computer and the MIDI controller via MIDI ports or another data connection such as USB or FireWire.

》 *A means to receive, record, and process MIDI messages:* a **MIDI sequencer**, which is software on your computer providing a user interface to capture, arrange, and manipulate the MIDI data. The interfaces of two commonly used software sequencers—Logic (Mac-based) and Cakewalk Sonar (Windows-based) are shown in Figures 1.49 and 1.50 of Chapter 1. The interface of Reason (Mac or Windows) is shown in Figure 6.3.

》 *A means to interpret MIDI messages and create sound:* either a hardware or a software synthesizer. All three of the sequencers pictured in the aforementioned figures give you access to a variety of software synthesizers (**soft synths**, for short) and instrument plug-ins (soft synths often created by third-party vendors). If you don't have a dedicated hardware or software synthesizer within your system, you may have to resort to the soft synth supplied by your operating system. For example, Figure 6.4 shows that the only choice of synthesizer for that system setup is the Microsoft GS Wavetable Synth. Some sound cards have hardware support for sound synthesis, so this may be another option.

》 *A means to do digital-to-analog conversion and listen to the sound:* a sound card in the computer or external audio interface connected to a set of loudspeakers or headphones.

> **ASIDE:** We use the term *synthesizer* in a broad sense here, including samplers that produce sound from memory banks of recorded samples. We'll explain the distinction between synthesizers and samplers in more detail in Section 6.1.6.

FIGURE 6.3: REASON'S SEQUENCER

FIGURE 6.4: USING THE OPERATING SYSTEM'S SOFT SYNTH

The basic setup for your audio/MIDI processing was described in Chapter 1 and is illustrated again here in Figure 6.5. This setup shows the computer handling the audio and MIDI processing. These functions are generally handled by audio/MIDI processing programs like Apple Logic, Cakewalk Sonar, Ableton Live, Steinberg Nuendo, or Digidesign Pro Tools, all of which provide a software interface for connecting the microphone, MIDI controller, sequencer, and output. All of these software systems handle both digital audio and MIDI processing, with samplers and synthesizers embedded. Details about particular configurations of hardware and software are given in Section 6.2.1.

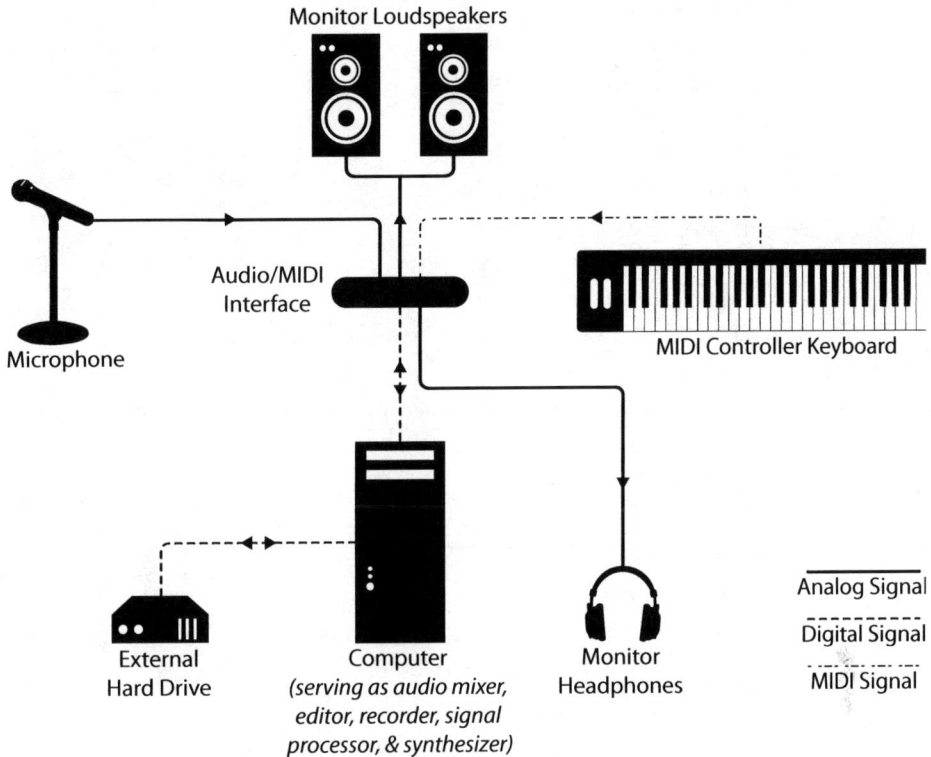

FIGURE 6.5: SETUP FOR AUDIO/MIDI PROCESSING

When you have your system properly connected and configured, you're ready to go. Now you can "arm" the sequencer for recording, press a key on the controller, and record that note in the sequencer. Most likely pressing that key doesn't even make a sound, since we haven't yet told the sound where to go. Your controller may look like a piano, but it's really just an input device sending a digital message to your computer in some agreed upon format. This is the purpose of the MIDI transmission protocol. In order for the two devices to communicate, the connection between them must be designed to transmit MIDI messages. For example, the cable could be USB at the computer end and have dual 5-pin DIN connectors at the keyboard end, as shown in Figure 6.6. The message that is received by your MIDI sequencer is in a prescribed MIDI format. In the sequencer, you can save this and any subsequent messages into a file. You can also play the messages back and, depending on your settings, the notes upon playback can sound like any instrument you choose from a wide variety of choices. It is the synthesizer that turns the symbolic MIDI message into digital audio data and sends the data to the sound card to be played.

6.1.3 MIDI DATA COMPARED TO DIGITAL AUDIO

Consider how MIDI data differs from digital audio as described in Chapter 5. You aren't recording something through a microphone. MIDI keyboards don't necessarily make a sound when you strike a key on a piano keyboard-like

FIGURE 6.6: 5-PIN DIN CONNECTOR FOR MIDI

controller, and they don't function as stand-alone instruments. There's no sampling or quantization going on at all. Instead, the controller is engineered to know that when a certain key is played, a symbolic message should be sent detailing the performance information.

In the case of a key press, the MIDI message would convey the occurrence of a Note On, followed by the note pitch played (e.g., middle C) and the velocity with which it was struck. The MIDI message generated by this action is only three bytes long. It's essentially just three numbers, as shown in Figure 6.7. The

> **ASIDE:** Many systems interpret a Note On message with velocity 0 as "note off" and use this as an alternative to the Note Off message.

first byte is a value between 144 and 159. The second and third bytes are values between 0 and 127. The fact that the first value is between 144 and 159 is what makes it identifiable by the receiver as a Note On message, and the fact that it is a Note On message is what identifies the next two bytes as the specific note and velocity. A Note Off message is handled similarly, with the first byte identifying the message as Note Off and the second and third giving note and velocity information (which can be used to control note decay).

first byte (status byte)	second byte (data byte)	third byte (data byte)
144	65	91

FIGURE 6.7: NOTE ON MESSAGE WITH DATA BYTES

Let's say that the key is pressed and a second later it is released. Thus, the playing of a note for one second requires six bytes. (We can set aside the issue of how the time between the notes is stored symbolically, since it's handled at a lower level of abstraction.) How does this compare to the number of bytes required for digital audio? One second of 16-bit mono audio at a sampling rate of 44,100 Hz requires 44,100 samples/s × 2 bytes/sample = 88,200 bytes/s. Clearly, MIDI can provide a more concise encoding of sound than digital audio.

MIDI differs from digital audio in other significant ways as well. A digital audio recording of sound tries to capture the sound exactly as it occurs by sampling the sound pressure amplitude over time. A MIDI file, on the other hand, records only symbolic messages. These messages make no sound unless they are interpreted to do so by a synthesizer. When we speak of a MIDI "recording," we mean it only in the sense that MIDI data has been captured and stored—not in the sense that *sound* has actually been recorded. While MIDI messages are most frequently interpreted and synthesized into musical sounds, they can be interpreted in other ways (as we'll illustrate in Section 6.2.8.5). The messages mean only what the receiver interprets them to mean.

With this caveat in mind, we'll continue from here under the assumption that you're using MIDI primarily for music production since this is MIDI's most common application. When you "record" MIDI music via a keyboard controller, you're saving information about what notes to play, how hard or fast to play them, how to modulate them with pitch bend or with a sustain pedal, and what instrument the notes should sound like upon playback. If you already know how to read music and play the piano, you can enjoy the direct relationship between your input device—which is essentially a piano keyboard—and the way it saves your performance—the notes, the timing, even the way you strike the keys if you have a velocity-sensitive controller. Many MIDI sequencers have multiple ways of viewing your file, including a track view, a piano roll view, an event list view, and even a staff view, which shows the notes that you played in standard music notation. These are shown in Figure 6.8 through Figure 6.11.

FIGURE 6.8: TRACK VIEW IN CAKEWALK SONAR

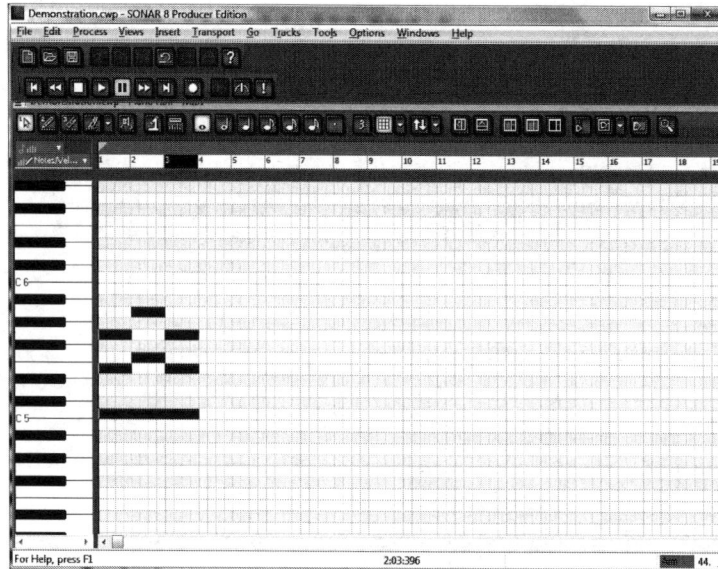

FIGURE 6.9: PIANO ROLL VIEW IN CAKEWALK SONAR

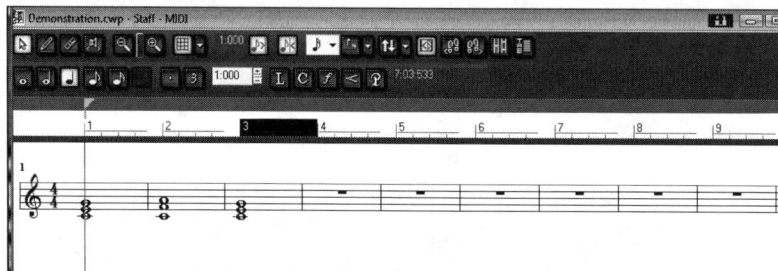

FIGURE 6.10: STAFF VIEW IN CAKEWALK SONAR

FIGURE 6.11: EVENT LIST VIEW IN CAKEWALK SONAR

Another significant difference between digital audio and MIDI is the way in which you edit them. You can edit uncompressed digital audio down to the sample level, changing the values of individual samples if you like. You can requantize or resample the values, or process them with mathematical operations. But they are always values representing changing air pressure amplitude over time. With MIDI, you have no access to individual samples, because that's not what MIDI files contain. Instead, MIDI files contain symbolic representations of notes, key signatures, durations of notes, tempo, instruments, and so forth, making it possible for you to edit these features with a simple menu selection or an editing tool.

For example, if you play a piece of music and hit a few extra notes, you can get rid of them later with an eraser tool. If your timing is a little off, you can move notes over or shorten them with the selection tool in the piano roll view. If you change your mind about the instrument sound you want or the key you'd like the piece played in, you can change these with a click of the mouse. Because the sound has not actually been synthesized yet, it's possible to edit its properties at this high level of abstraction.

> **ASIDE:** The word sample has different meanings in digital audio and MIDI. In MIDI, a sample is a small sound file representing a single instance of sound made by some instrument, like a note played on a flute.

MIDI and digital audio are simply two different ways of recording and editing sound—with an actual real-time recording or with a symbolic notation. They serve different purposes. You can actually work with both digital audio and MIDI in the same context, if both are supported by the software. Let's look more closely now at how this all happens.

6.1.4 CHANNELS, TRACKS, AND PATCHES IN MIDI SEQUENCERS

A software MIDI sequencer serves as an interface between the input and output. A **track** is an editable area on your sequencer interface. You can have dozens or even hundreds of tracks in your sequencer. Tracks are associated with areas in memory where data is stored. In a multitrack editor, you can edit multiple tracks separately, indicating input, output, amplitude, special effects, and so forth separately for each.

Some sequencers accommodate three types of tracks: audio, MIDI, and instrument. An audio track is a place to record and edit digital audio. A MIDI track stores MIDI data and is output to a synthesizer, either a software device or to an external hardware synth through the MIDI output ports. An instrument track is essentially a MIDI track combined with an internal soft synth, which in turn sends its output to the sound card. It may seem like there isn't much difference between a MIDI track and an instrument track. The main difference is that the MIDI track has to be more explicitly linked to a hardware or software synthesizer that produces its sound, whereas an instrument track has the synth, in a sense, "embedded" in it. Figure 6.12 shows each of these types of tracks.

FIGURE 6.12: THREE TYPES OF TRACKS IN LOGIC

A **channel** is a communication path. According to the MIDI standard, a single MIDI cable can transmit up to 16 channels. Without knowing the details of how this is engineered, you can just think of it abstractly as 16 separate lines of communication.

There are both input and output channels. An incoming message can tell what channel it is to be transmitted on, and this can route the message to a particular device. In the sequencer pictured in Figure 6.13, track 1 is listening on all channels, indicated by the word OMNI. Track 2 is listening only on channel 2.

The output channels are pointed out in the figure, also. When the message is sent out to the synthesizer, different channels can correspond to different instrument sounds. The parameter setting marked with a patch cord icon is the **patch**. A patch is a message to the synthesizer—just a number that indicates how the synthesizer is to operate as it creates sounds. The synthesizer can be programmed in different ways to respond to the patch setting. Sometimes the patch refers to a setting you've stored in the synthesizer that tells it what kinds of waveforms to combine or what kind of special effects to apply. In the example shown in Figure 6.13, however, the patch is simply interpreted as the choice of instrument that the user has chosen for the track. Track 1 is outputting on channel 1 with the patch set to Acoustic Grand Piano. Track 2 is outputting on channel 2 with the patch set to Cello.

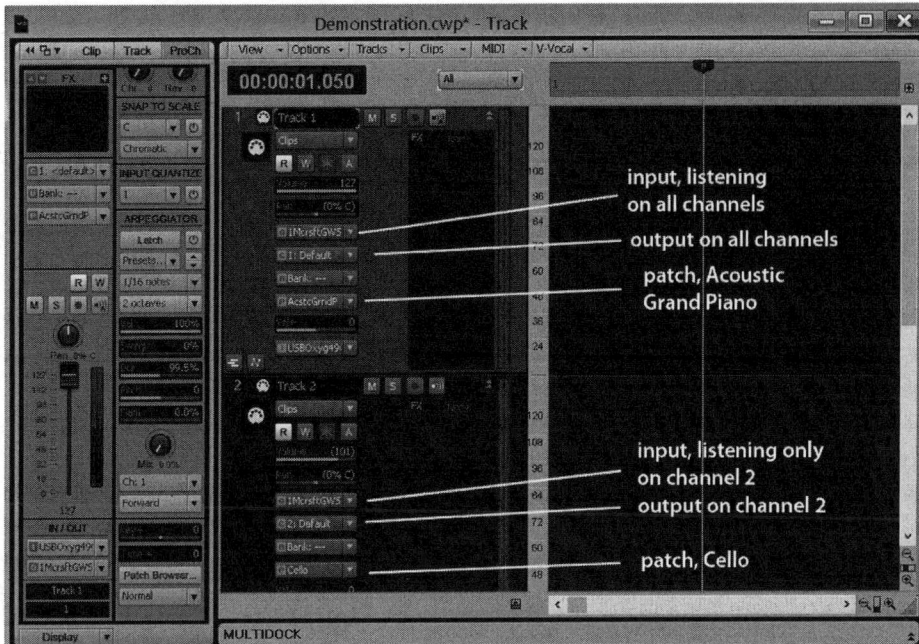

**FIGURE 6.13: PARAMETER SETTINGS IN CAKEWALK SONAR—
INPUT AND OUTPUT CHANNELS AND PATCH**

It's possible to call for a patch change by means of the Program Change MIDI message. This message sends a number to the synthesizer corresponding to the index of the patch to load. A Program Change message is inserted into track 1 in Figure 6.13. You can see a little box with *p14* in it at the bottom of the track indicating that the synth should be changed to patch 14 at that point in time. This is interpreted as changing the instrument patch from a piano to tubular bells. In the setup pictured, we're just using the Microsoft GS Wavetable Synth as opposed to a more refined synth. For the computer's built-in synth, the patch number is interpreted according to the General MIDI standard. The choices of patches in this standard can be seen when you click on the drop-down arrow on the patch parameter, as shown in Figure 6.14. You can see that the fifteenth patch down the list is tubular bells. (The Program Change message is still 14 because the numbering starts at 0.)

In a later section in this chapter, we'll look at other ways that the Program Change message can be interpreted by a synthesizer.

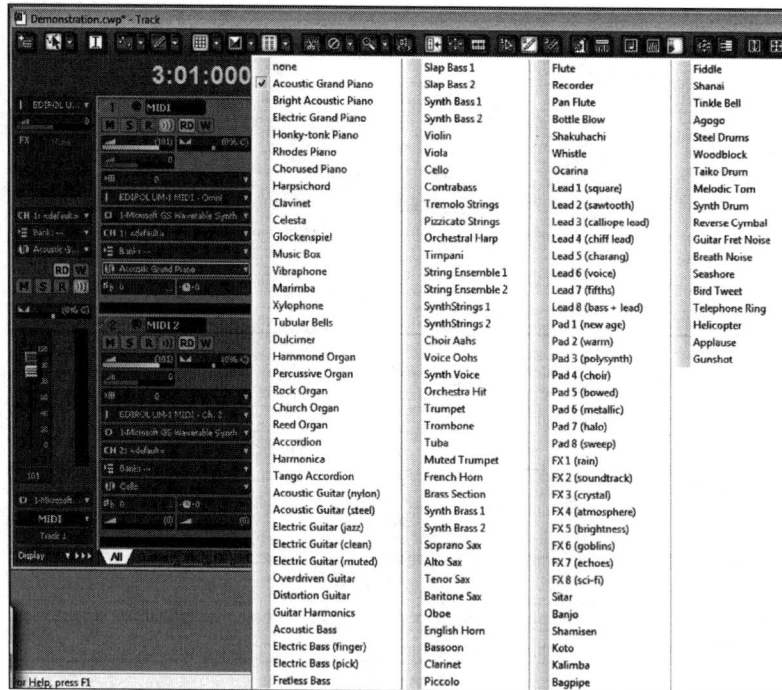

FIGURE 6.14: PATCH ASSIGNMENTS IN THE GENERAL MIDI STANDARD, AS SHOWN IN CAKEWALK SONAR

6.1.5 A CLOSER LOOK AT MIDI MESSAGES

6.1.5.1 Binary, Decimal, and Hexadecimal Numbers

When you read about MIDI message formats or see them in software interfaces, you'll find that they are sometimes represented as binary numbers, sometimes as decimal numbers, and sometimes as hexadecimal numbers (hex, for short), so you should get comfortable moving from one base to another. Binary is base 2, decimal is base 10, and hex is base 16. You can indicate the base of a number with a subscript, as in 01111100_2, $7C_{16}$, and 124_{10}. Often, *0x* is placed in front of hex numbers, as in 0x7C. Some sources use an *H* after a hex number, as in 7CH. Usually, you can tell by context what base is intended, and we'll omit the subscript unless the context is not clear. We assume that you understand number bases and can convert from one to another. If not, you should easily be able to find a resource on this for a quick crash course.

Binary and hexadecimal are useful ways to represent MIDI messages because they allow us to divide the messages in to meaningful groups. A **byte** is eight bits. Half a byte is four bits, called a **nibble**. The two nibbles of a MIDI message can encode two separate pieces of information. This fact becomes important in interpreting MIDI messages, as we'll show in the next section. In both the binary and hexadecimal representations, we can see the two nibbles as two separate pieces of information, which isn't possible in decimal notation.

A convenient way to move from hexadecimal to binary is to translate each nibble into four bits and concatenate them into a byte. For example, in the case of 0x7C, the *7* in hexadecimal becomes 0111 in binary. The *C* in hexadecimal becomes 1100 in binary. Thus 0x7C is 01111100 in binary. (Note that the symbols A through F correspond to decimal values 10 through 15, respectively, in hexadecimal notation.)

6.1.5.2 MIDI Messages, Types, and Formats

In Section 6.1.3, we showed you an example of a commonly used MIDI message, Note On, but now let's look at the general protocol.

MIDI messages consist of one or more bytes. The first byte of each message is a **status byte**, identifying the type of message being sent. This is followed by 0 or more **data bytes**, depending on the type of message. Data bytes give more information related to the type of message, like note pitch and velocity related to Note On.

All status bytes have a 1 as their most significant bit, and all data bytes have a 0. A byte with a 1 in its most significant bit has a value of at least 128. That is, 10000000 in binary is equal to 128 in decimal, and the maximum value that an 8-bit binary number can have (11111111) is the decimal value 255. Thus, status bytes always have a decimal value between 128 and 255. This is 10000000 through 11111111 in binary and 80 through FF in hex.

MIDI messages can be divided into two main categories: Channel messages and System messages. Channel messages contain the channel number. They can be further subdivided into Voice and Mode messages. Voice messages include Note On, Note Off, Polyphonic Key Pressure, Control Change, Program Change, Channel Pressure/ Aftertouch, and Pitch Bend. A mode indicates how a device is to respond to messages on a certain channel. A device might be set to respond to all MIDI channels (called Omni mode), or it might be instructed to respond to polyphonic messages or only monophonic ones. **Polyphony** involves playing more than one note at the same time.

System messages are sent to the whole system rather than a particular channel. They can be subdivided into Real-Time, Common, and System-Exclusive messages (SysEx). The System Common messages include Tune Request, Song Select, and Song Position Pointer. The System Real-Time messages include Timing Clock, Start, Stop, Continue, Active Sensing, and System Reset. SysEx messages can be defined by manufacturers in their own way to communicate things that are not part of the MIDI standard. The types of messages are diagrammed in Figure 6.15. A few of these messages are shown in Table 6.1.

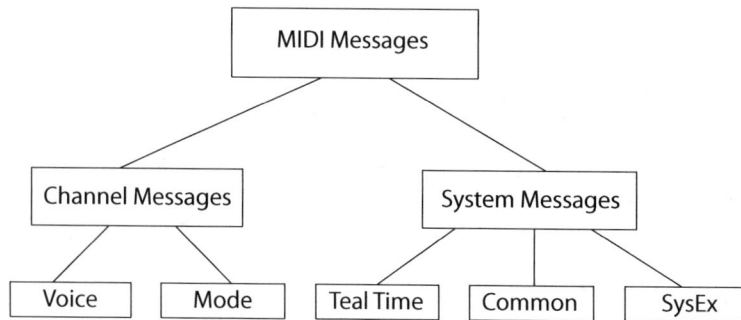

FIGURE 6.15: TYPES OF MIDI MESSAGES

Hexadecimal*	Binary**	Number of data bytes	Description
Channel Voice Messages			
8n	1000mmmm	2	Note Off
9n	1001mmmm	2	Note On
An	1010mmmm	2	Polyphonic Key Pressure/Aftertouch
Bn	1011mmmm	2	Control Change***
Cn	1100mmmm	1	Program Change
Dn	1101mmmm	1	Channel Pressure/ Aftertouch
En	1110mmmm	2	Pitch Bend Change
Channel Mode Messages			
Bn	1101mmmm	2	Selects Channel Mode
System Messages			
F3	11110011	1	Song Select
F8	11111000	0	Timing Clock
F0	11110000	variable	System Exclusive

*Each *n* is a hex digit between 0 and F.

**Each *m* is a binary digit between 0 and 1.

***Channel Mode messages are a special case of Control Change messages. The difference is in the first data byte. Data byte values 0x79 through 0x7F have been reserved in the Control Change message for information about mode changes.

TABLE 6.1: EXAMPLES OF MIDI MESSAGES

Consider the MIDI message shown in all three numerical bases in Figure 6.16. In the first byte, the most significant bit is 1, identifying this as a status byte. This a Note On message. Since it is a Channel message, it has the channel in its least significant four bits. These four bits can range from 0000 to 1111, corresponding to channels 1 through 16. (Notice that the binary value is one less than the channel number as it appears on our sequencer interface. A Note On message with 0000 in the least significant nibble indicates channel 1, one with 0001 indicates channel 2, and so forth.)

MAX DEMO:
MIDI Messages
http://bit.ly/29g3FCN

A Note On message is always followed by two data bytes. Data bytes always have a most significant bit of 0. The note to be played is 0x41, which translates to 65 in decimal. By the MIDI standard, note 60 on the keyboard is middle C, C4. Thus, 65 is five semitones above middle C, which is F4. The second data byte gives the velocity of 0x5B, which in decimal translates to 91 (out of a maximum 127).

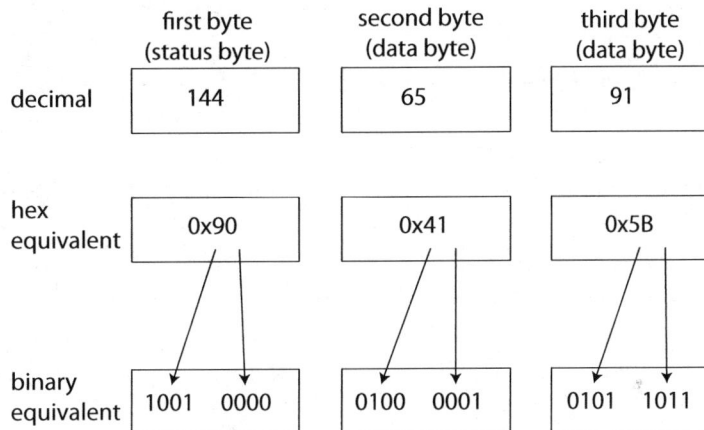

FIGURE 6.16: NOTE ON MESSAGE WITH DATA BYTES

6.1.6 SYNTHESIZERS VS. SAMPLERS

As we've emphasized from the beginning, MIDI is a symbolic encoding of messages. These messages have a standard way of being interpreted, so you have some assurance that your MIDI file generates a similar performance no matter where it's played in the sense that the instruments played are standardized. How "good" or "authentic" those instruments sound all comes down to the synthesizer and the way it creates sounds in response to the messages you've recorded.

FLASH TUTORIAL:
MiDI Defense
http://bit.ly/29liBUm

We find it convenient to define **synthesizer** as any hardware or software system that generates sound electronically based on user input. Some sources distinguish between samplers and synthesizers, defining the latter as devices that use additive, subtractive, FM, AM, or some other method of synthesis as opposed to having recourse to stored "banks" of samples. Our usage of the term is diagrammed in Figure 6.17.

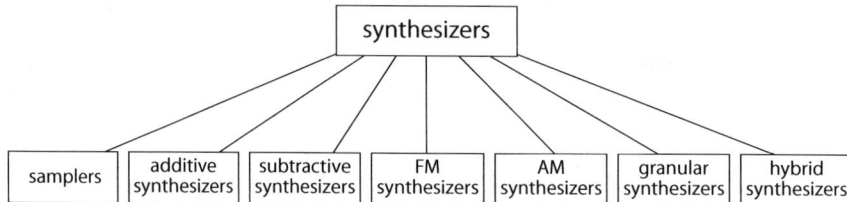

FIGURE 6.17: TYPES OF SYNTHESIZERS

A **sampler** is a hardware or software device that can store large numbers of sound clips for different notes played on different instruments. These clips are called **samples** (a different use from this term, to be distinguished from individual digital audio samples). A repertoire of samples stored in memory is called a **sample bank**. When you play a MIDI data stream via a sampler, these samples are pulled out of memory and played—a C on a piano, an F on a cello, or whatever is asked for in the MIDI messages. Because the sounds played are actual recordings of musical instruments, they sound realistic.

The NN-XT sampler from Reason is pictured in Figure 6.18. You can see that there are WAV files for piano notes, but there isn't a WAV file for every single note on the keyboard. In a method called **multisampling**, one audio sample can be used to create the sound of a number of neighboring ones. The notes covered by a single audio sample constitute a **zone**. The sampler is able to use a single sample for multiple notes by pitch shifting the sample up or down by an appropriate number of semitones. The pitch can't be stretched too far, however, without eventually distorting the timbre and amplitude envelope of the note so that the note no longer sounds like the instrument and frequency it's supposed to be. Higher and lower notes can be stretched more without our minding it, since our ears are less sensitive in these areas.

There can be more than one audio sample associated with a single note, also. For example, a single note can be represented by three samples where notes are played at three different velocities—high, medium, and low. The same note has a different timbre and amplitude envelope depending on the velocity with which it is played, so having more than one sample for a note results in more realistic sounds.

Samplers can also be used for sounds that aren't necessarily recreations of traditional instruments. It's possible to assign whatever sound file you want to the notes on the keyboard. You can create your own entirely new sound bank, or you can purchase additional sound libraries and install them (depending on the features offered by your sampler). Sample libraries come in a variety of formats. Some contain raw audio WAV or AIFF files which have to be mapped individually to keys. Others are in special sampler file formats that are compressed and automatically installable.

FIGURE 6.18: THE NN-XT SAMPLER FROM REASON

A synthesizer, if you use this word in the strictest sense, doesn't have a huge memory bank of samples. Instead, it creates sound more dynamically. It could do this by beginning with basic waveforms like sawtooth, triangle, or square waves and performing mathematical operations on them to alter their shapes. The user controls this process by knobs, dials, sliders, and other input controls on the control surface of the synthesizer—whether this is a hardware synthesizer or a soft synth. Under the hood, a synthesizer could be using a variety of mathematical methods, including additive, subtractive, FM, AM, wavetable synthesis, or physical modeling. We'll examine some of these

ASIDE: Even the term *analog synthesizer* can be deceiving. In some sources, an analog synthesizer is a device that uses analog circuits to generate sound electronically. But in other sources, an analog synthesizer is a digital device that emulates good old fashioned analog synthesis in an attempt to get some of the "warm" sounds that analog synthesis provides. The Subtractor polyphonic synthesizer (Figure 6.19) from Reason is described as an analog synthesizer, although it processes sound digitally.

methods in more detail in Section 6.3.3. This method of creating sounds may not result in making the exact sounds of a musical instrument. Musical instruments are complex structures, and it's difficult to model their timbre and amplitude envelopes exactly. However, synthesizers can create novel sounds that we don't often, if ever, encounter in nature or music, offering creative possibilities to innovative composers. The Subtractor polyphonic synthesizer from Reason is pictured in Figure 6.19.

FIGURE 6.19: SUBTRACTOR POLYPHONIC SYNTHESIZER FROM REASON

In reality, there's a good deal of overlap between these two ways of handling sound synthesis. Many samplers allow you to manipulate the samples with methods and parameter settings similar to those in a synthesizer. And, like a sampler, a synthesizer doesn't necessarily start from nothing. It generally has basic patches (settings) that serve as a starting point, prescribing, for example, the initial waveform and how it should be shaped. That patch is loaded in, and the user can make changes from there. You can see that both devices pictured in Figures 6.18 and 6.19 allow the user to manipulate the amplitude envelope (the **ADSR**—Attack-Decay-Sustain-Release—settings), apply modulation, use low-frequency oscillators (LFOs), and so forth. The possibilities seem endless with both types of sound synthesis devices.

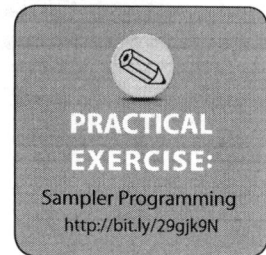

PRACTICAL EXERCISE:

Sampler Programming
http://bit.ly/29gjk9N

6.1.7 SYNTHESIS METHODS

There are several different methods for synthesizing a sound. The most common method is called **subtractive synthesis**. Subtractive synthesizers, such as the one shown in Figure 6.19, use one or more oscillators to generate a sound with lots of harmonic content. Typically this is a sawtooth, triangle, or square wave. The idea here is that the sound you're looking for is hiding somewhere in all those harmonics. All you need to do is subtract the harmonics you don't want, and you'll expose the properties of the sound you're trying to synthesize. The actual subtraction is done using a filter. Further shaping of the sound is accomplished by modifying the filter parameters over time using envelopes or low-frequency oscillators. If you can learn all the components of a subtractive synthesizer, you're well on your way to understanding the other synthesis methods because they all use similar components.

The opposite of subtractive synthesis is **additive synthesis**. This method involves building the sound you're looking for using multiple sine waves. The theory here is that all sounds are made of individual sine waves that come together to make a complex tone. While you can theoretically create any sound you want using additive synthesis, this is a very cumbersome method of synthesis and is not commonly used.

Another common synthesis method is called **frequency modulation (FM) synthesis**. This method of synthesis works by using two oscillators with one oscillator modulating the signal from the other. These two oscillators are called the **modulator** and the **carrier**. With this synthesis method some really interesting sounds can be created that would be difficult to achieve with subtractive synthesis. The Yamaha DX7 synthesizer is probably the most popular FM synthesizer and also was the first commercially available digital synthesizer. Figure 6.20 shows an example of an FM synthesizer from Logic Pro.

Wavetable synthesis is a synthesis method where several different single-cycle waveforms are strung together in what's called a wavetable. When you play a note on the keyboard, you're triggering a predetermined sequence of waves that transition smoothly between each other. This synthesis method is not very good at mimicking acoustic instruments, but it's very good at creating artificial sounds that are constantly in motion.

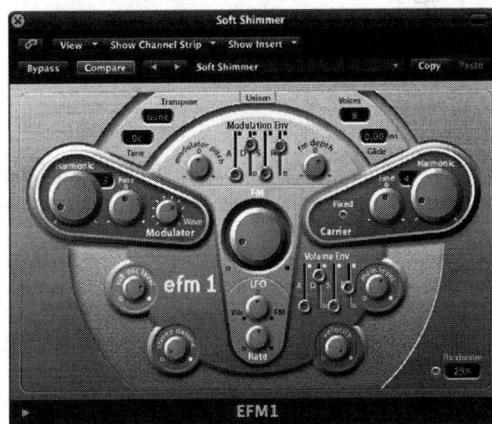

FIGURE 6.20: FM SYNTHESIZER FROM LOGIC PRO

Other synthesis methods include granular synthesis, physical modeling synthesis, and phase distortion synthesis. If you're just starting out with synthesizers, begin with a simple subtractive synthesizer and then move on to an FM synthesizer. Once you've run out of sounds you can create using those two synthesis methods, you'll be ready to start experimenting with some of these other synthesis methods.

6.1.8 SYNTHESIZER COMPONENTS

6.1.8.1 Presets

Now let's take a closer look at synthesizers. In this section, we're referring to synthesizers in the strict sense of the word—those that can be programmed to create sounds dynamically, as opposed to using recorded samples of real instruments. Synthesizer programming entails selecting an initial patch or waveform, filtering it, amplifying it, applying envelopes, applying low-frequency oscillators to shape the amplitude or frequency changes, and so forth, as we'll describe below.

There are many different forms of sound synthesis, but they all use the same basic tools to generate the sounds. The difference is how the tools are used and connected together. In most cases, the software synthesizer comes with a large library of pre-built patches that configure the synthesizer to make various sounds. In your own work, you'll probably use the presets as a starting point and modify the patches to your liking. Once you learn to master the tools, you can start building your own patches from scratch to create any sound you can imagine.

6.1.8.2 Sound Generator

The first object in the audio path of any synthesizer is the **sound generator**. Regardless of the synthesis method being used, you have to start by creating some sort of sound that is then shaped into the specific sound you're looking for. In most cases, the sound generator is made up of one or more oscillators that create simple sounds like sine, sawtooth, triangle, and square waves. The sound generator might also consist of a noise generator that plays pink noise or white noise. You might also see a **wavetable oscillator** that can play a pre-recorded complex shape. If your synthesizer has multiple sound generators, there is also some sort of mixer that merges all the sounds together. Depending on the synthesis method being used, you may also have an option to decide how the sounds are combined (through addition, multiplication, modulation, etc.).

Because synthesizers are most commonly used as musical instruments, there typically is a control on the oscillator that adjusts the frequency of the sound that is generated. This frequency can usually be changed remotely over time, but typically you choose some sort of starting point and any pitch changes are applied relative to the starting frequency.

Figure 6.21 shows an example of a sound generator. In this case we have two oscillators and a noise generator. For the oscillators you can select the type of waveform to be generated. Instead of your being allowed to control the pitch of the oscillator in actual frequency values, the default frequency is defined by the note A (according to the manual). You get to choose which octave you want the A to start in and can further tune up or down from there in semitones and cents (hundredths of semitones).

An option included in a number of synthesizer components is **keyboard tracking**, which allows you to control how a parameter is set, or how a feature is applied depending on which key on the keyboard is pressed. The keyboard tracking (Kbd. Track) button in our example sound generator defines whether you want the oscillator's frequency to change relative to the MIDI note number coming in from the MIDI controller. If this button is off, the synthesizer plays the same frequency regardless of the note played on the MIDI controller. The Phase, FM, Mix, and Mode controls determine the way these two oscillators interact with each other.

FIGURE 6.21: EXAMPLE OF A SOUND GENERATOR IN A SYNTHESIZER
[IMAGE COURTESY OF MIKKO NIIRANEN / NIRUDE]

6.1.8.3 Filters

A **filter** is another object that is often found in the audio path. A filter is an object that modifies the amplitude of specified frequencies in the audio signal. There are several types of filters. In this section, we describe the basic features of filters most commonly found in synthesizers. For more detailed information on filters, see Chapter 7.

Low-pass filters attempt to remove all frequencies above a certain point defined by the filter **cutoff frequency**. There is always a slope to the filter that defines the rate at which the frequencies are attenuated above the cutoff frequency. This is often called the **filter order**. A first-order filter attenuates frequencies above the cutoff frequency at the rate of 6 dB per octave. If your cutoff frequency is 1 kHz, a first-order filter attenuates 2 kHz by –6dB below the cutoff frequency; 4 kHz by –12 dB; 8 kHz by –18 dB; and so on. A second-order filter attenuates 12 dB per octave, a third-order filter is 18 dB per octave, and a fourth-order filter is 24 dB per octave. In some cases, the filter order is fixed, but more sophisticated filters allow you to choose the filter order that is the best fit for the sound you're looking for. The cutoff frequency is typically the frequency that has been attenuated –6 dB from the level of the frequencies that are unaffected by the filter. The space between the cutoff frequency and frequencies that are not affected by the filter is called the filter **typography.** The typography can be shaped by the filter's **resonance** control. Increasing the filter resonance creates a boost in the frequencies near the cutoff frequency.

High-pass filters are the opposite of low-pass. Instead of removing all the frequencies above a certain point, a high-pass filter removes all the frequencies below a certain point. A high-pass filter has a cutoff frequency, filter order, and resonance control just like the low-pass filter.

Bandpass filters are a combination of a high-pass and low-pass filter. A bandpass filter has a low cutoff frequency and a high cutoff frequency with filter order and resonance controls for each. In some cases, a bandpass filter is implemented with a fixed bandwidth or range of frequencies between the two cutoff frequencies. This simplifies the number of controls needed because you simply need to define a center frequency that positions the bandpass at the desired location in the frequency spectrum.

Bandstop filters (also called **notch** filters) creates a boost or cut of a defined range of frequencies. In this case the filter frequency defines the center of the notch. You might also have a bandwidth control that adjusts the range of frequencies to be boosted or cut. Finally, you have a control that adjusts the amount of change applied to the center frequency.

Figure 6.22 shows the filter controls in our example synthesizer. In this case we have two filters. Filter 1 has frequency and resonance controls and allows you to select the type of filter. The filter type selected in the example is a low-pass second order (12 dB per octave) filter. This filter also has a keyboard tracking knob where you can define the extent to which the filter cutoff frequency is changed relative to different frequencies. When you set the filter cutoff frequency using a specific key on the keyboard, the filter is affecting harmonic frequencies relative to the fundamental frequency of the key you pressed. If you play a key one octave higher, the new fundamental frequency generated by the oscillator is the same as the first harmonic of the key you were pressing when you set the filter. Consequently, the timbre of the sound changes as you move to higher and lower frequencies because the filter frequency is not changing when the oscillator frequency changes. The filter keyboard tracking allows you to change the cutoff frequency of the filter relative to the key being pressed on the keyboard. As you move to lower notes, the cutoff frequency also lowers. The knob allows you to decide how dramatically the cutoff frequency gets shifted relative to the note being pressed. The second filter is a fixed filter type (second order low-pass) with its own frequency and resonance controls and has no keyboard tracking option.

We'll discuss the mathematics of filters in Chapter 7.

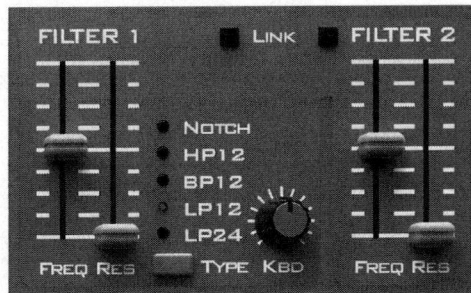

FIGURE 6.22: EXAMPLE OF FILTER SETTINGS IN A SYNTHESIZER
[IMAGE COURTESY OF MIKKO NIIRANEN / NIRUDE]

6.1.8.4 Signal Amplifier

The last object in the audio path of a synthesizer is a **signal amplifier**. The amplifier typically has a master volume control, like the one shown in Figure 6.23, that sets the final output level for the sound. In the analog days this was a **VCA (Voltage Controlled Amplifier)** that allowed the amplitude of the synthesized sound to be controlled externally over time. This is still possible in the digital world, and it is common to have the amplifier controlled by several external modulators to help shape the amplitude of the sound as it is played. For example, you could control the amplifier in a way that lets the sound fade in slowly instead of cutting in quickly.

6.1.8.5 Modulation

Modulation is the process of changing a shape of a waveform over time. This is done by continuously changing one of the parameters that defines the waveform by multiplying it by some coefficient. All the major parameters that define a waveform can be modulated, including its frequency, amplitude, and phase. A graph of the coefficients by which the waveform is modified shows us the shape of the modulation over

FIGURE 6.23: MASTER VOLUME CONTROLLER FOR THE SIGNAL AMPLIFIER IN A SYNTHESIZER
[IMAGE COURTESY OF MIKKO NIIRANEN / NIRUDE]

time. This graph is sometimes referred to as an **envelope** that is imposed over the chosen parameter, giving it a continuously changing shape. The graph might correspond to a continuous function, like a sine, triangle, square, or sawtooth. Alternatively, the graph might represent a more complex function, like the ADSR (**Attack-Delay-Sustain-Release**) envelope illustrated in Figure 6.25.

We'll look at mathematics of amplitude, phase, and frequency modulation in Section 6.3. For now, we'll focus on LFOs and ADSR envelopes, commonly used tools in synthesizers.

6.1.8.6 LFO

LFO stands for **low frequency oscillator**. An LFO is simply an oscillator just like the ones found in the sound generator section of the synthesizer. The difference here is that the LFO is not part of the audio path of the synthesizer. In other words, you can't hear the frequency generated by the LFO. Even if the LFO was put into the audio path, it oscillates at frequencies well below the range of human hearing so it isn't heard anyway. An LFO oscillates anywhere from 10 Hz down to a fraction of a Hertz.

LFO's are used like envelopes to modulate parameters of the synthesizer over time. Typically you can choose from several different waveforms. For example, you can use an LFO with a sinusoidal shape to change the pitch of the oscillator over time, creating a vibrato effect. As the wave moves up and down, the pitch of the oscillator follows. You can also use an LFO to control the sound amplitude over time to create a pulsing effect.

Figure 6.24 shows the LFO controls on a synthesizer. The Waveform button toggles the LFO between one of six different waveforms. The Dest button toggles through a list of destination parameters for the LFO. Currently, the LFO is set to create a triangle wave and apply it to the pitch of Oscillators 1 and 2. The Rate knob defines the frequency of the LFO, and the Amount knob defines the amplitude of the wave or the amount of modulation that is applied. A higher amount creates a more dramatic change to the destination parameter. When the Sync button is engaged, the LFO frequency is synchronized to the incoming tempo for your song based on a division defined by the Rate knob such as a quarter note or a half note.

FIGURE 6.24: LFO CONTROLS ON A SYNTHESIZER
[IMAGE COURTESY OF MIKKO NIIRANEN / NIRUDE]

6.1.8.7 Envelopes

Most synthesizers have at least one envelope object. An envelope is an object that controls a synthesizer parameter over time. The most common application of an envelope is an **amplitude envelope**. An amplitude envelope gets applied to the signal amplifier for the synthesizer. Envelopes have four parameters: attack time, decay time, sustain level, and release time (ADSR). The sustain level defines the amplitude of the sound while the note is held down on the keyboard. If the sustain level is at the maximum value, the sound is played at the amplitude defined by the master volume controller. Consequently, the sustain level is typically an attenuator that reduces rather than amplifies the level. If the other three envelope parameters are set to zero time, the sound is simply played at the amplitude defined by the sustain level relative to the master volume level.

The attack and decay values control how the sound begins. If the attack is set to a positive value, the sound fades in to the level defined by the master volume level over the period of time indicated in the attack. When the attack fade-in time completes, the amplitude moves to the sustain level. The decay value defines how quickly that move happens. If the decay is set to the lowest level, the sound jumps instantly to the sustain level once the attack completes. If the decay time has a positive value, the sound slowly fades down to the sustain level over the period of time defined by the decay after the attack completes.

The release time defines the amount of time it takes for the sound level to drop to silence after the note is released. You might also call this a fade-out time. Figure 6.25 is a graph showing these parameters relative to amplitude and time. Figure 6.26 shows the amplitude envelope controls on a synthesizer. In this case, the envelope is bypassed because the sustain is set to the highest level and everything else is at the lowest value.

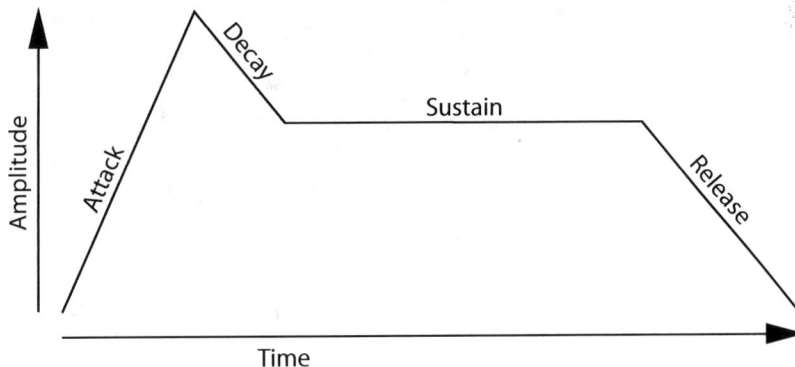

MAX DEMO:
ADSR Envelopes
http://bit.ly/29wo1KB

FIGURE 6.25: GRAPH OF ADSR ENVELOPE

Envelopes can be used to control almost any synthesizer parameter over time. You might use an envelope to change the cutoff frequency of a filter or the pitch of the oscillator over time. Generally speaking, if you can change a parameter with a slider or a knob, you can modulate it over time with an envelope.

FIGURE 6.26: ENVELOPE CONTROLS ON A SYNTHESIZER
[IMAGE COURTESY OF MIKKO NIIRANEN / NIRUDE]

6.1.8.8 MIDI Modulation

You can also use incoming MIDI commands to modulate parameters on the synthesizer. Most synthesizers have a predefined set of MIDI commands it can respond to. More powerful synthesizers allow you to define any MIDI command and apply it to any synthesizer parameter. Using MIDI commands to modulate the synthesizer puts more power in the hands of the performer.

Here's an example of how MIDI modulation can work. Piano players are used to getting a different sound from the piano depending on how hard they press the key. To recreate this touch sensitivity, most MIDI keyboards change the velocity value of the Note On command depending on how hard the key is pressed. However, MIDI messages can be interpreted in whatever way the receiver chooses. Figure 6.27 shows how you might use velocity to modulate the sound in the synthesizer. In most cases, you would expect the sound to get louder when the key is pressed harder. If you increase the Amp knob in the velocity section of the synthesizer, the signal amplifier level increases or decreases with the incoming velocity information. In some cases, you might also expect to hear more harmonics with the sound if the key is pressed harder. Increasing the value for the F.Env knob adjusts the depth at which the filter envelope is applied to the filter cutoff frequency. A higher velocity means that the filter envelope makes a more dramatic change to the filter cutoff frequency over time.

FIGURE 6.27: VELOCITY MODULATION CONTROLS ON A SYNTHESIZER
[IMAGE COURTESY OF MIKKO NIIRANEN / NIRUDE]

Some MIDI keyboards can send After Touch or Channel Pressure commands if the pressure at which the key is held down changes. You can use this pressure information to modulate a synthesizer parameter. For example, if you have an LFO applied to the pitch of the oscillator to create a vibrato effect, you can apply incoming key pressure data to adjust the LFO amount. This way, the vibrato is only applied when the performer desires it by increasing the pressure at which he or she is holding down the keys. Figure 6.28 shows some controls on a synthesizer to apply After Touch and other incoming MIDI data to four different synthesizer parameters.

6.2 APPLICATIONS

6.2.1 LINKING CONTROLLERS, SEQUENCERS, AND SYNTHESIZERS

In this section, we'll look at how MIDI is handled in practice.

First, let's consider a very simple scenario in which you're generating electronic music in a live performance. In this situation, you need only a MIDI controller and a synthesizer. The controller collects the performance information from the musician and transmits that data

FIGURE 6.28: AFTER TOUCH MODULATION CONTROLS ON A SYNTHESIZER
[IMAGE COURTESY OF MIKKO NIIRANEN / NIRUDE]

to the synthesizer. The synthesizer in turn generates sound based on the incoming control data. This all happens in real time, the assumption being that there is no need to record the performance.

Now suppose you also want to capture the musician's performance. In this situation, you have two options. The first option involves setting up a microphone and making an audio recording of the sounds produced by the synthesizer during the performance. This option is fine assuming you don't ever need to change the performance, and you have the resources to deal with the large file size of the digital audio recording.

The second option is simply to capture the MIDI performance data coming from the controller. The advantage here is that the MIDI control messages constitute much less data than the data that would be generated if a synthesizer were to transform the performance into digital audio. Another advantage to storing in MIDI format is that you can go back later and easily change the MIDI messages, which generally is a much easier process than digital audio processing. If the musician played a wrong note, all you need to do is change the data byte representing that note number, and when the stored MIDI control data is played back into the synthesizer, the synthesizer generates the correct sound. In contrast, there's no easy way to change individual notes in a digital audio recording. Pitch correction plug-ins can be applied to digital audio, but they potentially distort your sound, and sometimes can't fix the error at all.

So let's say you go with option two. For this, you need a MIDI sequencer between the controller and the synthesizer. The sequencer captures the MIDI data from the controller and sends it on to the synthesizer. This MIDI data is stored in the computer. Later, the sequencer can recall the stored MIDI data and send it again to the synthesizer, thereby perfectly recreating the original performance.

The next questions to consider are these: Which parts of this setup are hardware and which are software? And how do these components communicate with each other? Four different configurations for linking controllers, sequencers, and synthesizers are diagrammed in Figure 6.29. We'll describe each of these in turn.

Option 1: All hardware

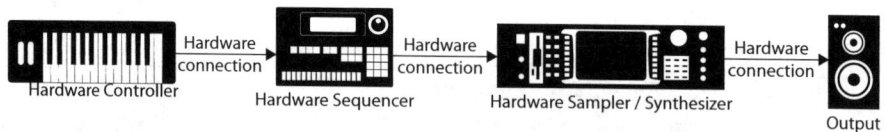

Option 2: Audio processing program has both sequencer and soft synths

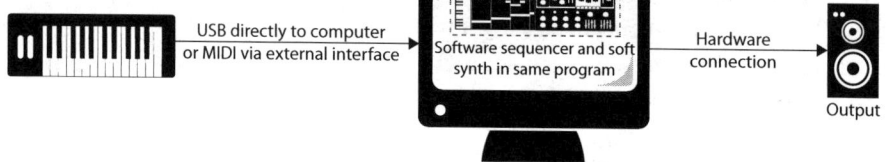

Option 3: Third party provides soft synth in audio wrapper

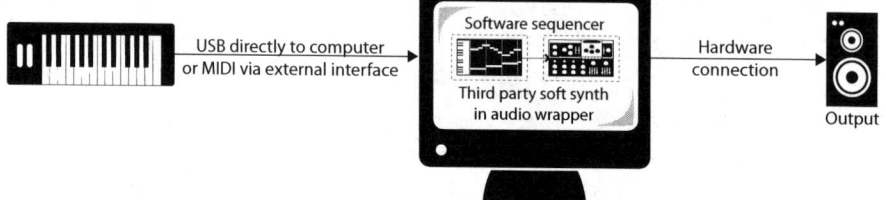

Option 4: Software sequencer in one program is rewired to soft synth in another

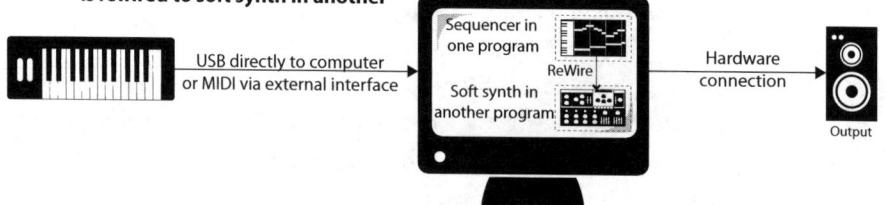

FIGURE 6.29: CONFIGURATIONS LINKING CONTROLLERS, SEQUENCERS, AND SYNTHESIZERS

In the early days of MIDI, hardware synthesizers were the norm, and dedicated hardware sequencers existed, like the one shown in Figure 6.30. Thus, an entire MIDI setup could be accomplished through hardware, as diagrammed in option 1 of Figure 6.28.

FIGURE 6.30: A DEDICATED MIDI SEQUENCER

Now that personal computers have ample memory and large external drives, software solutions are more common. A standard setup is to have a MIDI controller keyboard connected to your computer via USB or through a USB MIDI interface like the one shown in Figure 6.31. Software on the computer serves the role of sequencer and synthesizer. Sometimes one program can serve both roles, as diagrammed in option 2 of Figure 6.29. This is the case, for example, with both Cakewalk Sonar and Apple Logic, which provide a sequencer and built-in soft synths. Sonar's sample-based soft synth is called the TTS, shown in Figure 6.32. Because samplers and synthesizers are often made by third party companies and then incorporated into software sequencers, they can be referred to as **plug-ins**. Logic and Sonar have numerous plug-ins that are automatically installed—for example, the EXS24 sampler (Figure 6.33) and the EFM1 FM synthesizer (Figure 6.34).

FIGURE 6.31: A USB MIDI INTERFACE FOR A PERSONAL COMPUTER

FIGURE 6.32: TTS SOFT SYNTH IN CAKEWALK SONAR

FIGURE 6.33: EXS24 SAMPLER IN LOGIC

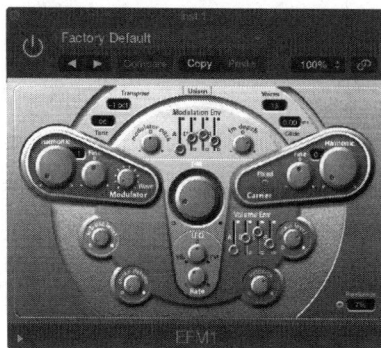

FIGURE 6.34: EFM1 SYNTHESIZER IN LOGIC

Some third-party vendor samplers and synthesizers are not automatically installed with a software sequencer, but they can be added by means of a **software wrapper**. The software wrapper makes it possible for the plug-in to run natively inside the sequencer software. This way, you can use the sequencer's native audio and MIDI engine and avoid the problem of having several programs running at once and having to save your work in multiple formats. Typically what happens is a developer creates a standalone soft synth like the one shown in Figure 6.35. He can then create an Audio Unit wrapper that allows his program to be inserted as an Audio Unit instrument, as shown for Logic in

ASIDE: As you work with MIDI and digital audio, you'll develop a large vocabulary of abbreviations and acronyms. In the area of plug-ins, the abbreviations relate to standardized formats that allow various software components to communicate with each other. **VSTi** stands for **virtual studio technology instrument**, created and licensed by Steinberg. This is one of the most widely used formats. **DXi** is a plug-in format based on Microsoft DirectX, and is a Windows-based format. **AU**, standing for **audio unit**, is a Mac-based format. **MAS** refers to plug-ins that work with Digital Performer, an audio/MIDI processing system created by the MOTU company. **RTAS (Real-Time AudioSuite)** is the protocol developed by Digidesign for Pro Tools. You need to know which formats are compatible on which platforms. You can find the most recent information through the documentation of your software or through online sources.

Figure 6.36. He can also create a VSTi wrapper for his synthesizer that allows the program to be inserted as a VSTi instrument in a program like Cakewalk, an MAS wrapper for MOTU Digital Performer, and so forth. A setup like this is shown in option 3 of Figure 6.29.

FIGURE 6.35: SOFT SYNTH RUNNING AS A STANDALONE APPLICATION

**FIGURE 6.36: SOFT SYNTH RUNNING IN LOGIC THROUGH
AN AUDIO UNIT INSTRUMENT WRAPPER**

An alternative to built-in synths or installed plug-ins is to have more than one program running on your computer, each serving a different function to create the music. An example of such a configuration would be to use Sonar or Logic as your sequencer, and then use Reason to provide a wide array of samplers and synthesizers. This setup introduces a new question: How do the different software programs communicate with each other?

One strategy is to create little software objects that pretend to be MIDI or audio inputs and outputs on the computer. Instead of linking directly to input and output hardware on the computer, you use these software objects as virtual cables. That is, the output from the MIDI sequencer program goes to the input of the software object, and the output of the software object goes to the input of the MIDI synthesis program. The software object functions as a virtual wire between the sequencer and synthesizer. The audio signal output by the soft synth can be routed directly to a physical audio output on your hardware audio interface, to a separate audio recording program, or back into the sequencer program to be stored as sampled audio data. This configuration is diagrammed in option 4 of Figure 6.29.

An example of this virtual wire strategy is the ReWire technology developed by Propellerhead and used with its sampler/synthesizer program, Reason. Figure 6.37 shows how a track in Sonar can connect to a sampler in Reason. The track labeled "MIDI to Reason" has the MIDI controller as its input and Reason as its output. The NN-XT sampler in Reason translates the MIDI commands into digital audio and sends the audio back to the track labeled "Reason to Audio." This track sends the audio output to the sound card.

FIGURE 6.37: REWIRING BETWEEN SONAR AND REASON

Other virtual wiring technologies are available. **Soundflower** is another program for Mac OS X developed by Cycling '74 that creates virtual audio wires that can be routed between programs. **CoreMIDI Virtual Ports** are integrated into Apple's CoreMIDI framework on Mac OS X. A similar technology called **MIDI Yoke** (developed by a third party) works in the Windows operating systems. **JACK** is an open source tool that runs on Windows, Mac OS X, and various UNIX platforms to create virtual MIDI and audio objects.

6.2.2   CREATING YOUR OWN SYNTHESIZER SOUNDS

Section 6.1.8 covered the various components of a synthesizer. Now that you've read about the common objects and parameters available on a synthesizer, you should have an idea of what can be done with one. So how do you know which knobs to turn and when? There's not an easy answer to that question. The thing to remember is that there are no rules. Use your imagination and don't be afraid to experiment. In time, you'll develop an instinct for programming the sounds you can hear in your head. Even if you don't feel like you can create a new sound from scratch, you can easily modify existing patches to your liking, learning to use the controls along the way. For example, if you load up a synthesizer patch and you think the notes cut off too quickly, just increase the release value on the amplitude envelope until it sounds right.

PRACTICAL EXERCISE:

Subtractive Synthesis
http://bit.ly/29uyKZ1

Most synthesizers use obscure values for the various controls, in the sense that it isn't easy to relate numerical settings to real-world units or phenomena. Reason uses control values from 0 to 127. While this nicely correlates to MIDI data values, it doesn't tell you much about the actual parameter. For example, how long is an attack time of 87? The answer is that it doesn't really matter. What matters is what it sounds like. Does an attack time of 87 sound too short or too long? While it's useful to understand what the controller affects, don't get too caught up in trying to figure out what exact value you're dialing in when you adjust a certain parameter. Just listen to the sound that comes out of the synthesizer. If it sounds good, it doesn't matter what number is hiding under the surface. Just remember to save the settings so you don't lose them.

6.2.3   MAKING AND LOADING YOUR OWN SAMPLES

Sometimes you may find that you want a certain sound that isn't available in your sampler. In that case, you may want to create your own sample.

If you want to create a sampler patch that sounds like a real instrument, the first thing to do is find someone who has the instrument you're interested in and get them to play different notes one at a time while you record them. To make sure you don't have to stretch the pitch too far for any one sample, make sure you get a recording for at least three notes per octave within the instrument's range.

Some instruments can sound different depending on how they are played. For example, a trumpet sounds very different with a mute inserted on the horn. If you want your sampler to be able to create the muted sound, you might be able to mimic it using filters in the sampler, but you'll get better results by just recording the real trumpet with the mute inserted. Then you can program the sampler to play the muted samples instead of the unmuted ones when it receives a certain MIDI command.

Keep in mind that the more samples you have, the more RAM space the sampler requires. If you have 500 MB worth

MAX DEMO:
Subtractonaut Synthesizer
http://bit.ly/29ItNQS

PRACTICAL EXERCISE:
Programming Sampler Instruments
http://bit.ly/29gjLB7

VIDEO TUTORIAL:
Guitar Sampler Demo
http://bit.ly/29gIJkO

of recorded samples and you want to use them all, the sampler is going to use up 500 MB of RAM on your computer. The trick is finding the right balance between having enough samples so that none of them get stretched unnaturally, but not so many that you use up all the RAM in your computer. As long as you have a real person and a real instrument to record, go ahead and get as many samples as you can. It's much easier to delete the ones you don't need than to schedule another recording session to get the two notes you forgot to record.

Once you have all your samples recorded, you need to edit them and add all the metadata required by the sampler. In order for the sampler to do what it needs to do with the audio files, the files need to be in an uncompressed file format. Usually this is WAV or AIF format. Some samplers have a limit on the sampling rate they can work with. Make sure you convert the samples to the rate required by the sampler before you try to use them.

The first bit of metadata you need to add to each sample is a loop start and loop end marker. Because you're working with prerecorded sounds, the sound doesn't necessarily keep playing just because you're still holding the key down on the keyboard. You could just record your samples so they hold on for a long time, but that would use up an unnecessary amount of RAM. Instead, you can tell the sampler to play the file from the beginning and stop playing the file when the key on the keyboard is released. If the key is still down when the sampler reaches the end of the file, the sampler can start playing a small portion of the sample over and over in an endless loop until the note is released. The challenge here is finding a portion of the sample that loops naturally without any clicks or other swells in amplitude or harmonics.

Figure 6.38 shows a loop defined in a sample editing program. On the left side of the screen you can see the overall waveform of the sample, in this case a violin. In the time ruler above the waveform you can see a bar labeled Sustaining Loop. This is the portion of the sample that is looped. On the right side of the screen you can see a close-up view of the loop point. The left half of the wave is the end of the sample, and the right part of the wave is the start of the loop point. The trick here is to line up the loop points so the two parts intersect with the zero amplitude cross point. This way you avoid any clicks or pops that might be introduced when the sampler starts looping the playback.

VIDEO TUTORIAL:
Recorder Sampler
Demo
http://bit.ly/29g79Fq

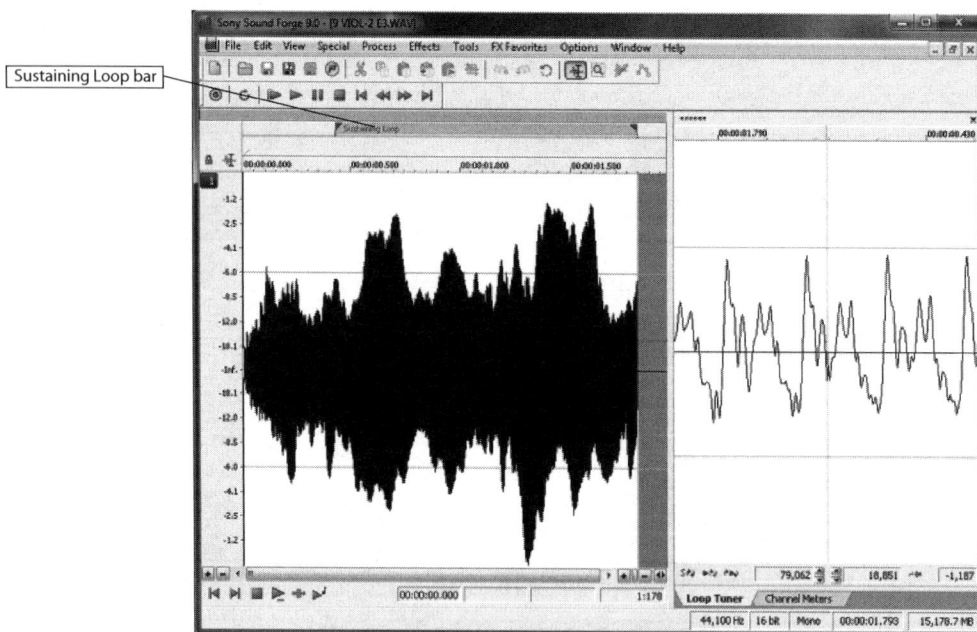

FIGURE 6.38: EDITING SAMPLE LOOP POINTS

In some sample editors you can also add other metadata that saves you programming time later; an example of this is shown in Figure 6.39. For WAV and AIF files, you can add information about the root pitch of the sample and the range of notes this sample should cover. You can also add information about the loop behavior. For example, do you want the sample to continue to loop during the release of the amplitude envelope, or do you want it to start playing through to the end of the file? You could set the sample not to loop at all and instead play as a "one shot" sample. This means the sample ignores Note Off events and plays the sample from beginning to end every time. Some samplers can read that metadata and do some preprogramming for you on the sampler when you load the sample.

Once the samples are ready, you can load them into the sampler. If you weren't able to add the metadata about root key and loop type, you'll have to add that manually into the sampler for each sample. You'll also need to decide which notes trigger each sample and which velocities each sample responds to. This process of assigning root keys and key ranges to all your samples is a time consuming but essential process. Figure 6.40 shows a list of sample WAV files loaded in a software sampler. In the figure we have the sample "PianoC43.wav" selected. In the center of the screen you can see the span of keys that have been assigned to that sample. Along the bottom row of the screen you can see the root key, loop, and velocity assignments for that sample.

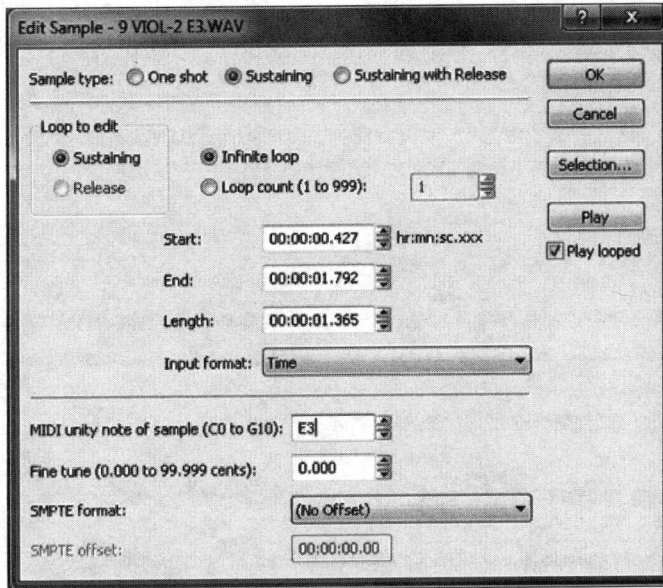

FIGURE 6.39: ADDING SAMPLE METADATA SUCH AS ROOT PITCH AND LOOP TYPE

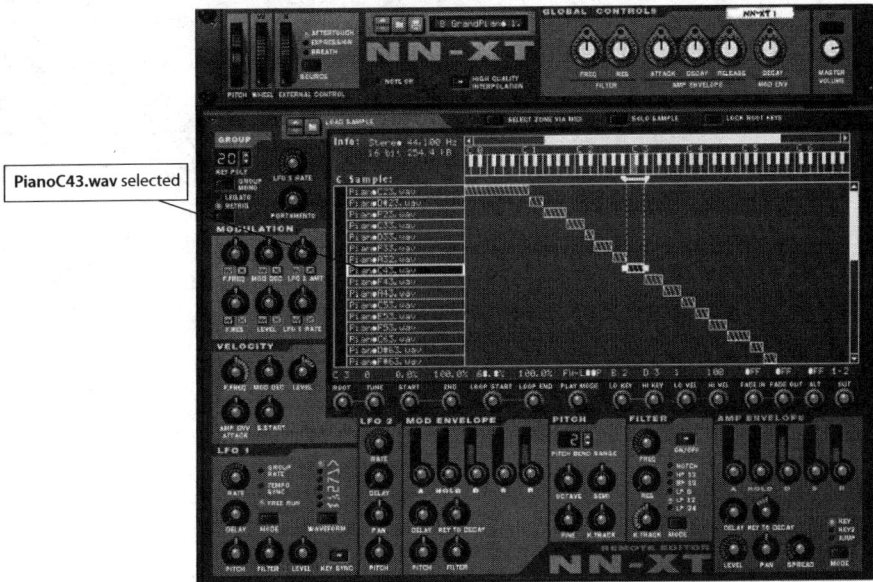

PianoC43.wav selected

FIGURE 6.40: LOADING AND ASSIGNING SAMPLES IN A SOFTWARE SAMPLER

Once you have all your samples loaded and assigned, each sample can be passed through a filter and amplifier which can in turn be modulated using envelopes, LFO, and MIDI controller commands. Most samplers let you group samples together into zones or keygroups, allowing you to apply a single set of filters, envelopes, etc. This feature can save a lot of time in programming. Imagine programming all of those settings on each of 100 samples without losing track of how far you are in the process. Figure 6.41 shows all the common synthesizer objects being applied to the "PianoC43.wav" sample.

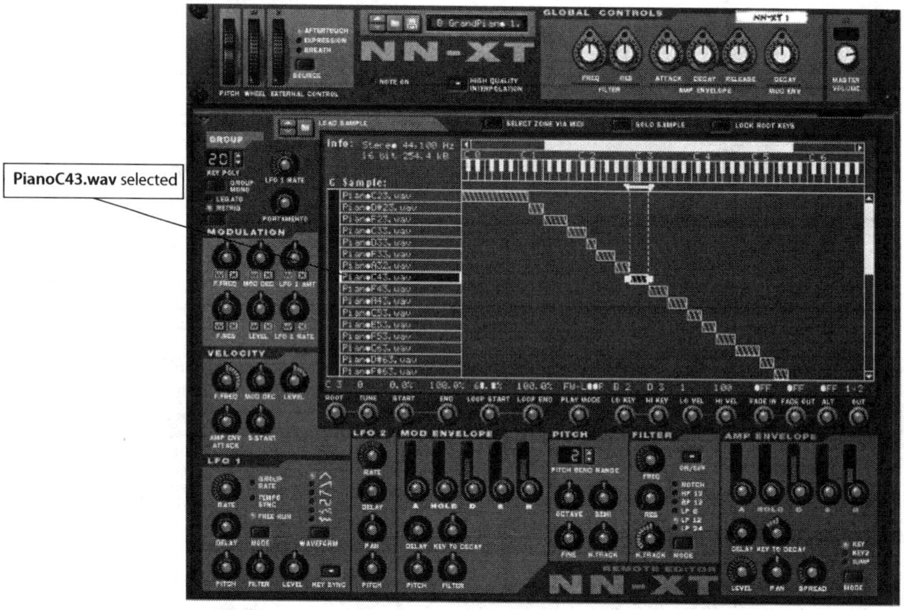

FIGURE 6.41: SYNTHESIZER FUNCTIONS THAT CAN BE APPLIED TO SAMPLES ONCE THEY HAVE BEEN LOADED AND ASSIGNED

6.2.4 DATA FLOW AND PERFORMANCE ISSUES IN AUDIO/MIDI RECORDING

Combined audio/MIDI recording can place high demands on a system, requiring a fast CPU and hard drive, an appropriate choice of audio driver, and a careful setting of the audio buffer size. These components affect your ability to record, process, and play sound, particularly in real time.

In Chapter 5, we introduced the subject of latency in digital audio systems. The problem of latency is compounded when MIDI data is added to the mix. A common frustration in MIDI recording sessions is that there can be an audible difference between the moment when you press a key on a MIDI controller keyboard and the moment when you hear the sound coming out of the headphones or monitors. In this case, the latency is the result of your buffer size. The MIDI signal generated by the key press must be transformed into digital audio by a synthesizer or sampler, and the digital data is then placed in the output buffer. This sound is not heard until the buffer is filled up. When the buffer is full, it undergoes analog-to-digital conversion and is sent to the headphones or monitors. Playback latency results when the buffer is too large. As discussed in Chapter 5, you can reduce the playback latency by using a low-latency audio driver like ASIO or reducing the buffer size if this option is available in your driver. However, if you make the buffer size too low, you'll have breaks in the sound when the CPU cannot keep up with the number of times it has to empty the buffer.

Another potential bottleneck in digital audio playback is the hard drive. Fast hard drives are a must when working with digital audio, and it is also important to use a dedicated hard drive for your audio files. If you're storing your audio files on the same hard drive as your operating system, you'll need a larger playback buffer to accommodate all the times the hard drive is busy delivering system data instead of your audio. If you get a second hard drive and use it only for audio files, you can usually get away with a much smaller playback buffer, thereby reducing the playback latency.

When you use software instruments, there are other system resources besides the hard drive that also become a factor to consider. Software samplers require a lot of system RAM because all the audio samples have to be loaded completely in RAM in order for them to be instantly accessible. On the other hand, software synthesizers that generate the sound dynamically can be particularly hard on the CPU. The CPU has to mathematically create the audio stream in real time, which is a more computationally intense process than simply playing an audio stream that already exists. Synthesizers with multiple oscillators can be particularly problematic. Some programs let you offload individual audio or instrument tracks to another CPU. This could be a networked computer running a processing node program or some sort of dedicated processing hardware connected to the host computer. If you're having problems with playback dropouts due to CPU overload and you can't add more CPU power, another strategy is to render the instrument audio signal to an audio file that is played back instead of generated live (often called *freezing* a track). However, this effectively disables the MIDI signal and the software instrument, so if you need to make any changes to the rendered track, you need to go back to the MIDI data and re-render the audio.

6.2.5   NON-MUSICAL APPLICATIONS FOR MIDI

6.2.5.1 MIDI Show Control

MIDI is not limited to use for digital music. There have been many additions to the MIDI specification to allow MIDI to be used in other areas. One addition is the MIDI Show Control Specification. MIDI Show Control (MSC) is used in live entertainment to control sound, lighting, projection, and other automated features in theatre, theme parks, concerts, and more.

MSC is a subset of the MIDI Systems Exclusive (SysEx) status byte. MIDI SysEx commands are typically specific to each manufacturer of MIDI devices. Each manufacturer gets a SysEx ID number. MSC has a SysEx sub-ID number of 0x02. The syntax, in hexadecimal, for a MSC message is:

```
F0 7F <device_ID> 02 <command_format> <command> <data> F7
```

-)) `F0` is the status byte indicating the start of a SysEx message.
-)) `7F` indicates the use of a SysEx sub-ID. This is technically a manufacturer ID that has been reserved to indicate extensions to the MIDI specification.
-)) `<device_ID>` can be any number between 0x00 and 0x7F, indicating the device ID of the thing you want to control. These device ID numbers have to be set on the receiving end as well, so each device knows which messages to respond to and which messages to ignore. 0x7F is a universal device ID. All devices respond to this ID regardless of their individual ID numbers.
-)) `02` is the sub-ID number for MIDI Show Control. This tells the receiving device that the bytes that follow are MIDI Show Control syntax as opposed to MIDI Machine Control, MIDI Time Code, or other commands.
-)) `<command_format>` is a number indicating the type of device being controlled. For example, 0x01 indicates a lighting device, 0x40 indicates a projection device, and 0x60 indicates a pyrotechnics device. A complete list of command format numbers can be found in the MIDI Show Control 1.1 specification.
-)) `<command>` is a number indicating the type of command being sent. For example, 0x01 is Go, 0x02 is Stop, 0x03 is Resume, 0x0A is Reset.
-)) `<data>` represents a variable number of data bytes that are required for the type of command being sent. A Go command might need some data bytes to indicate the cue number that needs to be executed from a list of cues on the device. If no cue number is specified, the device simply executes the next cue in the list. Two data bytes (0x00, 0x00) are still needed in this case as delimiters for the cue number syntax. Some MSC devices are able to interpret the message without these delimiters, but they're technically required in the MSC specification.
-)) `F7` is the End of Systems Exclusive byte indicating the end of the message.

Most lighting consoles, projection systems, and computer sound playback systems used in live entertainment are able to generate and respond to MSC messages. Typically, you don't have to create the commands manually in hex. You have a graphical interface that lets you choose the command you want from a list of menus. Figure 6.42 shows some MSC Fire commands for a lighting console generated as part of a list of sound cues. In this case, the sound effect of a firecracker is synchronized with the flash of a strobe light using MSC.

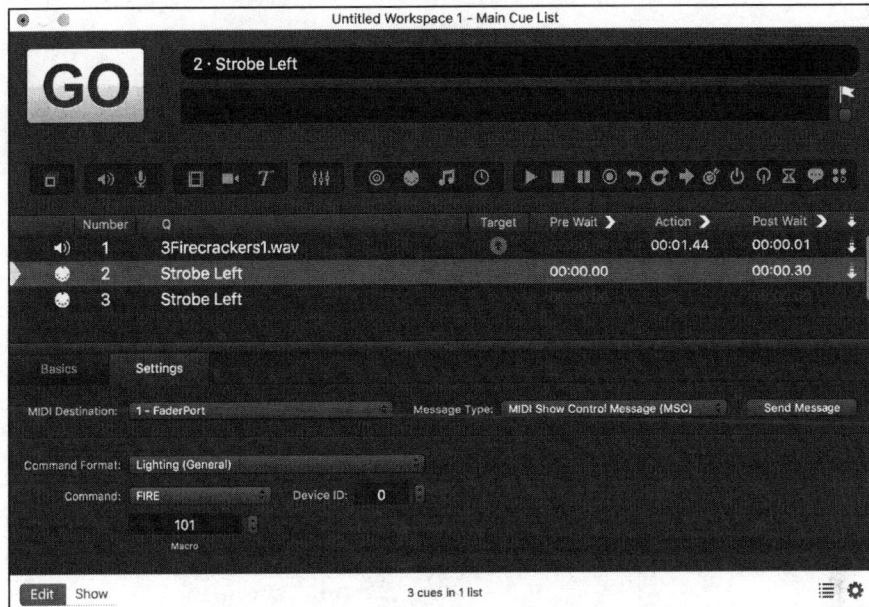

FIGURE 6.42: A LIST OF SOUND AND MIDI SHOW CONTROL CUES IN A SOUND PLAYBACK SYSTEM FOR LIVE ENTERTAINMENT

6.2.5.2   MIDI Relays and Footswitches

You may not always have a device that knows how to respond to MIDI commands. For example, although there is a MIDI Show Control command format for motorized scenery, the motor that moves a unit on or off the stage doesn't understand MIDI commands. However, it does understand a switch. There are many options available for MIDI-controlled relays that respond to a MIDI command by making or breaking an electrical contact closure. This makes it possible for you to connect the wires for the control switch of a motor to the relay output, and then when you send the appropriate MIDI command to the relay, it closes the connection and the motor starts turning.

Another possibility is that you may want to use MIDI commands without a traditional MIDI controller. For example, maybe you want a sound effect to play each time a door is opened or closed. Using a MIDI footswitch device, you could wire up a magnetic door sensor to the footswitch input and have a MIDI command sent to the computer each time the door is opened or closed. The computer could then be programmed to respond by playing a sound file. Figure 6.43 shows an example of a MIDI relay device.

6.2.5.3   MIDI Time Code

MIDI sequencers, audio editors, and audio playback systems often need to synchronize their timeline with other systems. Synchronization could be needed
for working with sound for video, lighting systems in live performance, and even
automated theme park attractions. The
world of filmmaking has been dealing
with synchronization issues for decades,
and the Society of Motion Picture and

FIGURE 6.43: A MIDI-CONTROLLABLE RELAY

Television Engineers (SMPTE) has developed a standard format for a time code that
can be used to keep video and audio in sync. Typically this is accomplished using
an audio signal called **linear time code** that has the synchronization data encoded
in SMPTE format. The format is Hours:Minutes:Seconds:Frames. The number of
frames per second varies, but the standard allows for 24, 25, 29.97 (also known as
30-Drop), and 30 frames per second.

MIDI Time Code (MTC) uses this same time code format, but instead of being
encoded into an analog audio signal, the time information is transmitted in digital
format via MIDI. A full MIDI Time Code message has the following syntax:

```
F0 7F <device_ID> <sub-ID 1> <sub-ID 2> <hr> <mn> <sc> <fr> F7
```

)) `F0` is the status byte indicating the start of a SysEx message.

)) `7F` indicates the use of a SysEx sub-ID. This is technically a manufacturer ID
that has been reserved to indicate extensions to the MIDI specification.

)) `<device_ID>` can be any number between 0x00 and 0x7F indicating the device ID of the thing you want to control. These device ID numbers have to
be set on the receiving end as well so each device knows which messages to
respond to and which messages to ignore. 0x7F is a universal device ID. All
devices respond to this ID regardless of their individual ID numbers.

)) `<sub-ID 1>` is the sub-ID number for MIDI Time Code. This tells the receiving device that the bytes that follow are MIDI Time Code syntax as opposed
to MIDI Machine Control, MIDI Show Control, or other commands. There
are a few different MIDI Time Code sub ID numbers. `01` is used for full
SMPTE messages and for SMPTE user bits messages. `04` is used for a MIDI
Cueing message that includes a SMPTE time along with values for markers
such as Punch In/Out and Start/Stop points. `05` is used for real-time cueing
messages. These messages have all the marker values but use the quarter-frame
format for the time code.

❯ `<sub-ID 2>` is a number used to define the type of message within the `sub-ID 1` families. For example, there are two types of full messages that use `01` for `sub-ID 1`. A value of `01` for `sub-ID 2` in a full message would indicate a full time code message whereas `02` would indicate a user bits message.

❯ `<hr>` is a byte that carries both the hours value as well as the frame rate. Since there are only 24 hours in a day, the hours value can be encoded using the five least significant bits, while the next two greater significant bits are used for the frame rate. With those two bits you can indicate four different frame rates (24, 25, 29.97, 30). As this is a data byte, the most significant bit stays at `0`.

❯ `<mn>` represents the minutes value 00–59.

❯ `<sc>` represents the seconds value 00–59.

❯ `<fr>` represents the frame value 00–29.

❯ F7 is the End of Systems Exclusive byte indicating the end of the message.

For example, to send a message that sets the current timeline location of every device in the system to 01:30:35:20 in 30 frames/second format, the hexadecimal message would be:

F0 7F 7F 01 01 61 1E 23 14 F7

Once the full message has been transmitted, the time code is sent in quarter-frame format. Quarter-frame messages are much smaller than full messages. This is less demanding of the system since only two bytes rather than ten bytes have to be parsed at a time. Quarter-frame messages use the 0xF1 status byte and one data byte with the high nibble indicating the message type and the low nibble indicating the value of the given time field. There are eight message types, two for each time field. Each field is separated into a least-significant (LS) nibble and a most-significant (MS) nibble:

> 0 = Frame count LS
> 1 = Frame count MS
> 2 = Seconds count LS
> 3 = Seconds count MS
> 4 = Minutes count LS
> 5 = Minutes count MS
> 6 = Hours count LS
> 7 = Hours count MS and SMPTE frame rate

As the name indicates, quarter-frame messages are transmitted in increments of four messages per frame. Messages are transmitted in the order listed above. Consequently, the entire SMPTE time is completed every two frames. Let's break down the same 01:30:35:20 time value into quarter-frame messages in hexadecimal. This time value would be broken up into eight messages:

F1 04   (Frame LS)
F1 11   (Frame MS)

F1 23   (Seconds LS)
F1 32   (Seconds MS)

F1 4E   (Minutes LS)
F1 51   (Minutes MS)

F1 61   (Hours LS)
F1 76   (Hours MS and Frame Rate)

When synchronizing systems with MIDI Time Code, one device needs to be the master time code generator and all other devices need to be configured to follow the time code from this master clock. Figure 6.44 shows Logic Pro configured to synchronize to an incoming MIDI Time Code signal. If you have a mix of devices in your system that follow LTC or MTC, you can also put a dedicated time code device in your system that collects the time code signal in LTC or MTC format and then relays that time code to all the devices in your system in the various formats required, as shown in Figure 6.45.

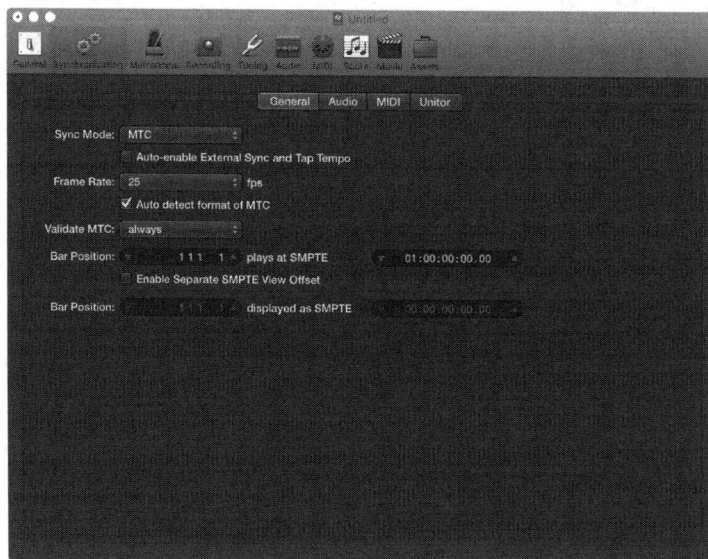

FIGURE 6.44: MIDI TIME CODE SYNCHRONIZED FOR LOGIC PRO

FIGURE 6.45: A DEDICATED SMPTE SYNCHRONIZATION DEVICE CAPABLE OF DISTRIBUTING LINEAR TIME CODE AND MIDI TIME CODE

6.2.5.4 MIDI Machine Control

Another subset of the MIDI specification is a set of commands that can control the transport system of various recording and playback systems. Transport controls are things like play, stop, rewind, record, etc. This command set is called MIDI Machine Control. The specification is quite comprehensive and includes options for SMPTE time code values, as well as confirmation response messages from the devices being controlled. A simple MMC message has the following syntax:

MAX
DEMO:
MTC MMC
http://bit.ly/29nThLv

```
F0 7F <device_ID> 06 <command> F7
```

⟩ `F0` is the status byte indicating the start of a SysEx message.
⟩ `7F` indicates the use of a SysEx sub-ID. This is technically a manufacturer ID that has been reserved to indicate extensions to the MIDI specification.
⟩ `<device_ID>` can be any number between 0x00 and 0x7F indicating the device ID of the thing you want to control. These device ID numbers have to be set on the receiving end as well so each device knows which messages to respond to and which messages to ignore. 0x7F is a universal device ID. All devices respond to this ID regardless of their individual ID numbers.
⟩ `06` is the sub-ID number for MIDI Machine Control. This tells the receiving device that the bytes that follow are MIDI Machine Control syntax as opposed to MIDI Show Control, MIDI Time Code, or other commands.
⟩ `<command>` can be a set of bytes as small as one byte and can include several bytes communicating various commands in great detail. A simple play (0x02) or stop (0x01) command only requires a single data byte.
⟩ `F7` is the End of Systems Exclusive byte indicating the end of the message.

A MMC command for PLAY would look like this:

```
F0 7F 7F 06 02 F7
```

MIDI Machine Control was really a necessity when most studio recording systems were made up of several different magnetic tape-based systems or dedicated hard disc recorders. In these situations, a single transport control would make sure all the devices were doing the same thing. In today's software-based systems, MIDI Machine Control is primarily used with MIDI control surfaces, like the one shown in Figure 6.46, that connect to a computer so you can control the transport of your DAW software without having to manipulate a mouse.

FIGURE 6.46: A DEDICATED MIDI MACHINE CONTROL DEVICE

6.3 SCIENCE, MATHEMATICS, AND ALGORITHMS

6.3.1 MIDI SMF FILES

If you'd like to dig into the MIDI specification more deeply—perhaps writing a program that can either generate a MIDI file in the correct format or interpret one and turn it into digital audio—you need to know more about how the files are formatted.

Standard MIDI Files (**SMF**), with the *.mid* or *.smf* suffix, encode MIDI data in a prescribed format for the header, timing information, and events. Format 0 files are for single tracks, Format 1 files are for multiple tracks, and Format 2 files are for multiple tracks where a separate song performance can be represented. (Format 2 is not widely used.) SMF files are platform-independent, interpretable on PCs, Mac, and Linux machines.

Blocks of information in SMF files are called **chunks**. The first chunk is the **header chunk**, followed by one or more **data chunks**. The header and data chunks begin with four bytes (a four-character string) identifying the type of chunk they are. The header chunk then has four bytes giving the length of the remaining fields of the chunk (which is always six for the header), two bytes telling the format (MIDI 0, 1, or 2), two bytes telling the number of tracks, and two bytes with information about how timing is handled.

Data are stored in **track chunks.** A track chunk also begins with four bytes telling the type of chunk, followed by four bytes telling how much data is in the chunk. The data then follow. The bytes which constitute the data are track events: either regular MIDI events like Note On; meta-events like changes of tempo, key, or time signature; or SysEx events. The events begin with a timestamp telling when they are to happen. Then the rest of the data are MIDI events with the format described in Section 6.1. The structure of an SMF file is illustrated in Figure 6.47, where "MThd" is the abbreviation used to indicate that it's a header chunk, and "MTrk" indicates that it's a track chunk.

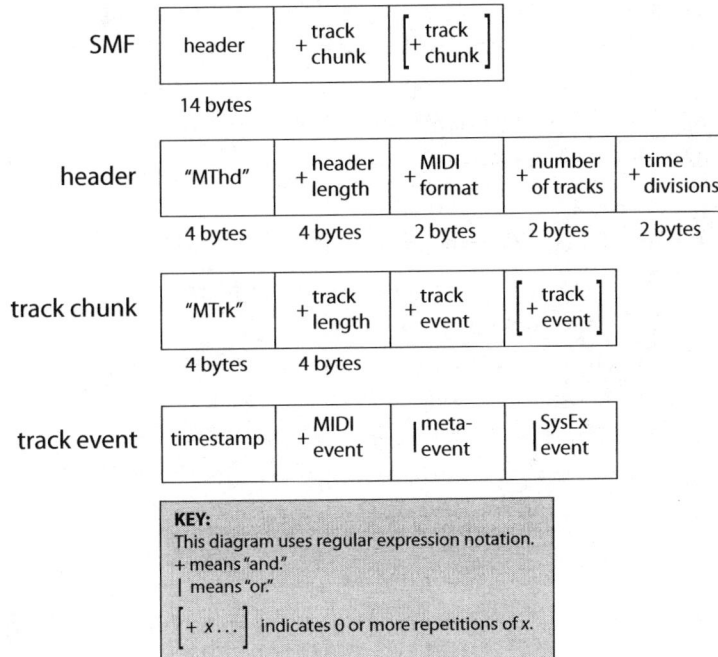

FIGURE 6.47: SMF FILE STRUCTURE

MIDI event **timestamps** tell the change in time between the previous event and the current one, using the tick-per-beat, frame rate in frames/s, and tick/frame defined in the header. The timestamp itself is given in a variable-length field. To accomplish this, the first bit of each byte in the timestamp indicates how many bytes are to follow in the timestamp. If the bit is a 0, then the value in the following seven bits of the byte make up the full value of the timestamp. If the bit is a 1, then the next byte is also to be considered part of the timestamp value. This ultimately saves space. It would be wasteful to dedicate four bytes to the timestamp just to take care of the few cases where there is a long pause between one MIDI event and the next one.

An important consideration in writing or reading SMF files is the issue of whether bytes are stored in little-endian or big-endian format. In **big-endian format**, the most significant byte is stored first in a sequence of bytes that make up one value. In **little-endian**, the least significant byte is stored first. SMF files store bytes in big-endian format. If you're writing an SMF-interpreting program, you need to check the endianness of the processor and operating system on which you'll be running the program. A PC/Windows combination is generally little-endian, so a program running on that platform has to swap the byte-order when determining the value of a multiple-byte timestamp.

More details about SMF files can be found at *www.midi.org*. To see the full MIDI specification, you have to order and pay for the documentation. Paul Messick's *Maximum MIDI: Music Applications in C++* is a good source to help you write a C++ program that reads and interprets SMF files.

6.3.2   SHAPING SYNTHESIZER PARAMETERS WITH ENVELOPES AND LFOS

Let's make a sharp turn now from MIDI specifications to the mathematics and algorithms under the hood of synthesizers.

In Section 6.1.8.7, envelopes were discussed as a way of modifying the parameters of some synthesizer functions—for example, the cutoff frequency of a low- or high-pass filter or the amplitude of a waveform. The mathematics of envelopes is easy to understand. The graph of the envelope shows time on the horizontal axis and a "multiplier" or coefficient on the vertical axis. The parameter in question is simply multiplied by the coefficient over time.

Envelopes can be generated by simple or complex functions. The envelope could be a simple sinusoidal, triangle, square, or sawtooth function that causes the parameter to go up and down in a regular pattern. In such cases, the envelope is called an *oscillator*. The term low-frequency oscillator (LFO) is used in synthesizers because the rate at which the parameter is caused to change is low compared to audible frequencies.

>>

MATLAB EXERCISE:

Creating LFOs

in MATLAB
http://bit.ly/2ba3dwP

An ADSR envelope has a shape like the one shown in Figure 6.25. Such an envelope can be defined by the attack, decay, sustain, and release points, between which

straight (or evenly curved) lines are drawn. Again, the values in the graph represent multipliers to be applied to a chosen parameter.

The exercises associated with this section invite you to modulate one or more of the parameters of an audio signal with an LFO and also with an ASDR envelope that you define yourself.

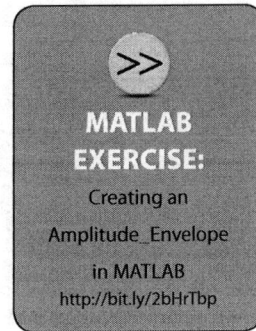

> **>>**
>
> **MATLAB EXERCISE:**
>
> Creating an
> Amplitude_Envelope
> in MATLAB
> http://bit.ly/2bHrTbp

6.3.3   TYPES OF SYNTHESIS

6.3.3.1 Table-lookup Oscillators and Wavetable Synthesis

We have seen how single-frequency sound waves are easily generated by means of sinusoidal functions. In our example exercises, we've done this through computation, evaluating sine functions over time. In contrast, **table-lookup oscillators** generate waveforms by means of a set of lookup wavetables stored in contiguous memory locations. Each **wavetable** contains a list of sample values constituting one cycle of a sinusoidal wave, as illustrated in Figure 6.48. Multiple wavetables are stored so that waveforms in a wide range of frequencies can be generated.

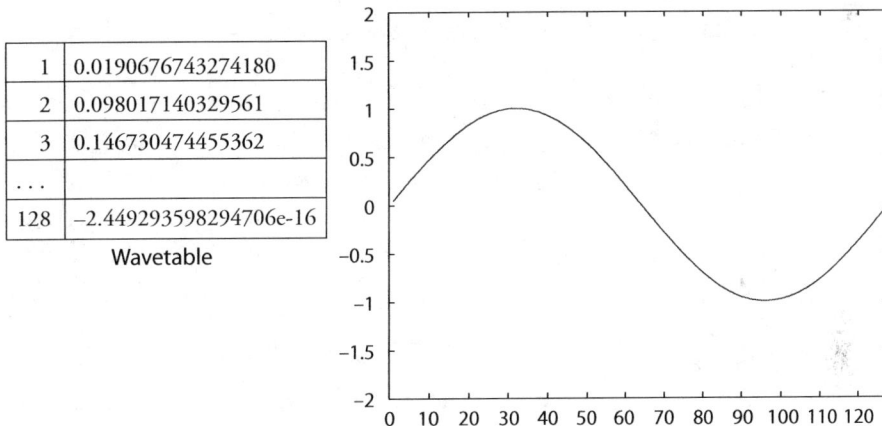

1	0.0190676743274180
2	0.098017140329561
3	0.146730474455362
. . .	
128	−2.449293598294706e-16

Wavetable

FIGURE 6.48: A WAVETABLE IN A TABLE-LOOKUP OSCILLATOR

With a table-lookup oscillator, a waveform is created by advancing a pointer through a wavetable, reading the values, cycling back to the beginning of the table as necessary, and outputting the sound wave accordingly.

With a table of N samples representing one cycle of a waveform and an assumed sampling rate of r samples/s, you can generate a fundamental frequency of r/N Hz simply by reading the values out of the table at the sampling rate. This entails stepping through the indexes of the consecutive memory locations of the table. The wavetable in Figure 6.48 corresponds to a fundamental frequency of $48{,}000/128 = 375$ Hz.

>>

MATLAB EXERCISE:

Creating and Using a

Wavetable in MATLAB
http://bit.ly/29f2qn9

Harmonics of the fundamental frequency of the wavetable can be created by skipping values or inserting extra values in between those in the table. For example, you can output a waveform with twice the frequency of the fundamental by reading out every other value in the table. You can output a waveform with half the frequency of the fundamental by reading each value twice, or by inserting values in between those in the table by interpolation.

The phase of the waveform can be varied by starting at an offset from the beginning of the wavetable. To start at a phase offset of $p\pi$ radians, you would start reading at index $(pN)/2$. For example, to start at an offset of $\pi/2$ in the wavetable of Figure 6.48, you would start at index $((1/2) \times 128)/2 = 32$.

To generate a waveform that is not a harmonic of the fundamental frequency, it's necessary to add an increment to the consecutive indexes that are read out from the table. This increment i depends on the desired frequency f, the table length N, and the sampling rate r, defined by $i = (f \times N)/r$. For example, to generate a waveform with frequency 750 Hz using the wavetable of Figure 6.48 and assuming a sampling rate of 48,000 Hz, you would need an increment of $i = (750 \times 128)/48{,}000 = 2$. We've chosen an example where the increment is an integer, which is good because the indexes into the table have to be integers.

What if you wanted a frequency of 390 Hz? Then the increment would be $i = (390 \times 128)/48{,}000 = 1.04$, which is not an integer. In cases where the increment is not an integer, interpolation must be used. For example, if you want to go an increment of 1.04 from index 1, that would take you to index 2.04. Assuming that our wavetable is called *table*, you want a value equal to *table*[2] + 0.04 × (*table*[3] − *table*[2]). This is a rough way to do interpolation. Cubic spline interpolation can also be used as a better way of shaping the curve of the waveform. The exercise associated with this section suggests that you experiment with table-lookup oscillators in MATLAB.

An extension of the use of table-lookup oscillators is wavetable synthesis. Wavetable synthesis was introduced in digital synthesizers in the 1970s by Wolfgang Palm in Germany. This was the era when the transition was being made from the analog to the digital realm. **Wavetable synthesis** uses multiple wavetables, combining them with additive synthesis and crossfading and shaping them with modulators, filters, and amplitude envelopes. The wavetables don't necessarily have to represent simple sinusoidals but can be more complex waveforms. Wavetable synthesis was

> **ASIDE:** The term "wavetable" is sometimes used to refer a memory bank of samples used by sound cards for MIDI sound generation. This can be misleading terminology, as wavetable synthesis is a different thing entirely.

innovative in the 1970s in allowing for the creation of sounds not realizable by solely analog means. This synthesis method has now evolved to the Waldorf Nave synthesizer for the iPad.

6.3.3.2 Additive Synthesis

In Chapter 2, we introduced the concept of frequency components of complex waves. This is one of the most fundamental concepts in audio processing, dating back to the groundbreaking work of Jean-Baptiste Joseph Fourier in the early 1800s. Fourier was able to prove that any periodic waveform is composed of an infinite sum of single-frequency waveforms of varying frequencies and amplitudes. The single-frequency waveforms that are summed to make the more complex one are called the **frequency components**.

The implications of Fourier's discovery are far-reaching. It means that, theoretically, we can build whatever complex sounds we want just by adding sine waves. This is the basis of additive synthesis. We demonstrated how it works in Chapter 2, illustrated by the production of square, sawtooth, and triangle waveforms. Additive synthesis of each of these waveforms begins with a sine wave of some fundamental frequency, f. As you recall, a square wave is constructed from an infinite sum of odd-numbered harmonics of f of diminishing amplitude, as in

$$A\sin(2\pi ft) + \frac{A}{3}\sin(6\pi ft) + \frac{A}{5}\sin(10\pi ft) + \frac{A}{7}\sin(14\pi ft) + \frac{A}{9}\sin(18\pi ft) + \cdots$$

A sawtooth waveform can be constructed from an infinite sum of all harmonics of f of diminishing amplitude, as in

$$\frac{2}{\pi}\left(A\sin(2\pi ft) + \frac{A}{2}\sin(4\pi ft) + \frac{A}{3}\sin(6\pi ft) + \frac{A}{4}\sin(8\pi ft) + \frac{A}{5}\sin(10\pi ft) + \cdots\right)$$

A triangle waveform can be constructed from an infinite sum of odd-numbered harmonics of f that diminish in amplitude and vary in their sign, as in

$$\frac{8}{\pi^2}\left(A\sin(2\pi ft) - \frac{A}{3^2}\sin(6\pi ft) + \frac{A}{5^2}\sin(10\pi ft)\right.$$
$$\left. - \frac{A}{7^2}\sin(14\pi ft) + \frac{A}{9^2}\sin(18\pi ft) - \frac{A}{11^2}\sin(22\pi ft) + \cdots\right)$$

These basic waveforms turn out to be very important in subtractive synthesis, as they serve as a starting point from which other, more complex sounds can be created.

To be able to create a sound by additive synthesis, you need to know the frequency components to add together. It's usually difficult to get the sound you want by adding waveforms from the ground up. It turns out that subtractive synthesis is often an easier way to proceed.

6.3.3.3 Subtractive Synthesis

The first synthesizers, including the Moog and the Buchla Music Box, were analog synthesizers that made distinctive electronic sounds different from what is produced by traditional instruments. This was part of the fascination that listeners had for them. They did this by **subtractive synthesis**, a process that begins with a basic sound and then selectively removes frequency components. The first digital synthesizers imitated their analog precursors. Thus, when people speak of analog synthesizers today, they often mean digital subtractive synthesizers. The Subtractor Polyphonic Synthesizer shown in Figure 6.19 is an example of one of these.

The development of subtractive synthesis arose from an analysis of musical instruments and the way they create their sound, the human voice being among those instruments. Such sounds can be divided into two components: a source of excitation and a resonator. For a violin, the source is the bow being drawn across the string, and the resonator is the body of the violin. For the human voice, the source results from air movement and muscle contractions of the vocal cords, and the resonator is the mouth. In a subtractive synthesizer, the source could be a pulse, sawtooth, or triangle wave or random noise of different colors (colors corresponding to how the noise is spread out over the frequency spectrum). Frequently, preset patches are provided, which are basic waveforms with certain settings like amplitude envelopes already applied (another usage of the term *patch*). Filters are provided that allow you to remove selected frequency components. For example, you could start with a sawtooth wave and filter out some of the higher harmonic frequencies, creating something that sounds fairly similar to a stringed instrument. An amplitude envelope could be applied also to shape the attack, decay, sustain, and release of the sound.

6.3.3.4 Amplitude Modulation (AM)

Amplitude, phase, and frequency modulation are three types of modulation that can be applied to synthesize sounds in a digital synthesizer. We explain the mathematical operations below. In Section 6.1.8.5, we defined **modulation** as the process of changing the shape of a waveform over time. Modulation has long been used in analog telecommunication systems as a way to transmit a signal on a fixed frequency channel. The frequency on which a television or radio station is broadcast is referred to as the **carrier signal** and the message "written on" the carrier is called the **modulator signal**. The message can be encoded on the carrier signal in one of three ways: **AM (amplitude modulation)**, **PM (phase modulation)**, or **FM (frequency modulation)**.

Amplitude modulation (AM) is commonly used in radio transmissions. It entails sending a message by modulating the amplitude of a carrier signal with a modulator signal.

In the realm of digital sound as created by synthesizers, AM can be used to generate a digital audio signal of N samples by application of the following equation:

$$a(n) = \sin\left(\frac{\omega_c n}{r}\right) \times \left(1.0 + A\cos\left(\frac{\omega_m n}{r}\right)\right)$$

$$for\ 0 \leq n \leq N-1$$

*where N is the number of samples,
ω_c is the angular frequency of the carrier signal,
ω_m is the angular frequency of the modulator signal,
r is the sampling rate, and A is the amplitude*

EQUATION 6.1: AMPLITUDE MODULATION FOR DIGITAL SYNTHESIS

The process is expressed algorithmically in Algorithm 6.1. The algorithm shows that the AM synthesis equation must be applied to generate each of the samples for $1 \leq t \leq N$.

```
algorithm amplitude_modulation
/*
Input:
f_c, the frequency of the carrier signal
f_m, the frequency of a low frequency modulator signal
N, the number of samples you want to create
r, the sampling rate
A, to adjust the amplitude of the
Output:
y, an array of audio samples where the carrier has been amplitude modulated
        by the modulator */
{
```

```
        for (n = 1 to N)
            y[n] = sin(2*pi*f_c*n/r) * (1.0 + A*cos(2*pi*f_m*n/r));
}
```

ALGORITHM 6.1: AMPLITUDE MODULATION FOR DIGITAL SYNTHESIS

Algorithm 6.1 can be executed at the MATLAB command line with the statements below, generating the graphs in Figure 6.49. Because MATLAB executes the statements as vector operations, a loop is not required. (Alternatively, a MATLAB program could be written using a loop.) For simplicity, we'll assume $A = 1$ in what follows.

```
N = 44100;
r = 44100;
n = [1:N];
f_m = 10;
f_c = 440;
m = cos(2*pi*f_m*n/r);
c = sin(2*pi*f_c*n/r);
figure;
AM = c.*(1.0 + m);
plot(m(1:10000));
axis([0 10000 -2 2]);
figure;
plot(c(1:10000));
axis([0 10000 -2 2]);
figure;
plot(AM(1:10000));
axis([0 10000 -2 2]);
wavplay(c, 44100);
wavplay(m, 44100);
wavplay(AM, 44100);
```

This yields the following graphs:

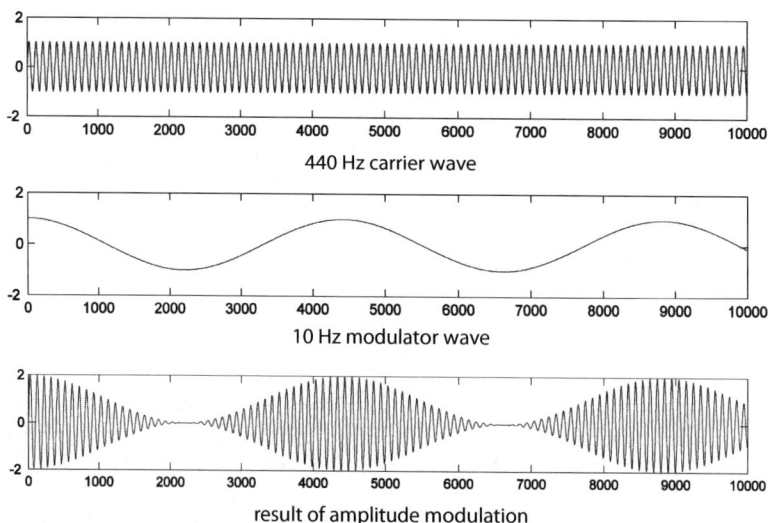

440 Hz carrier wave

10 Hz modulator wave

result of amplitude modulation

FIGURE 6.49: AMPLITUDE MODULATION USING TWO SINUSOIDALS

If you listen to the result, you'll see that amplitude modulation creates a kind of tremolo effect.

The same process can be accomplished with more complex waveforms. *HornsE04.wav* is a 132,300-sample audio clip of horns playing at a sampling rate of 44,100 Hz. Below, we shape it with a 440 Hz cosine wave (Figure 6.50). This same process would work on any *.wav* file.

```
N = 132300;
r = 44100;
c = wavread('HornsE04.wav');
n = [1:N];
m = sin(2*pi*10*n/r);
m = transpose(m);
AM2 = c .* (1.0 + m);
figure;
plot(c);
axis([0 132300 -2 2]);
figure;
plot(m);
axis([0 132300 -2 2]);
figure;
plot(AM2);
axis([0 132300 -2 2]);
wavplay(c, 44100);
wavplay(m, 44100);
wavplay(AM2, 44100);
```

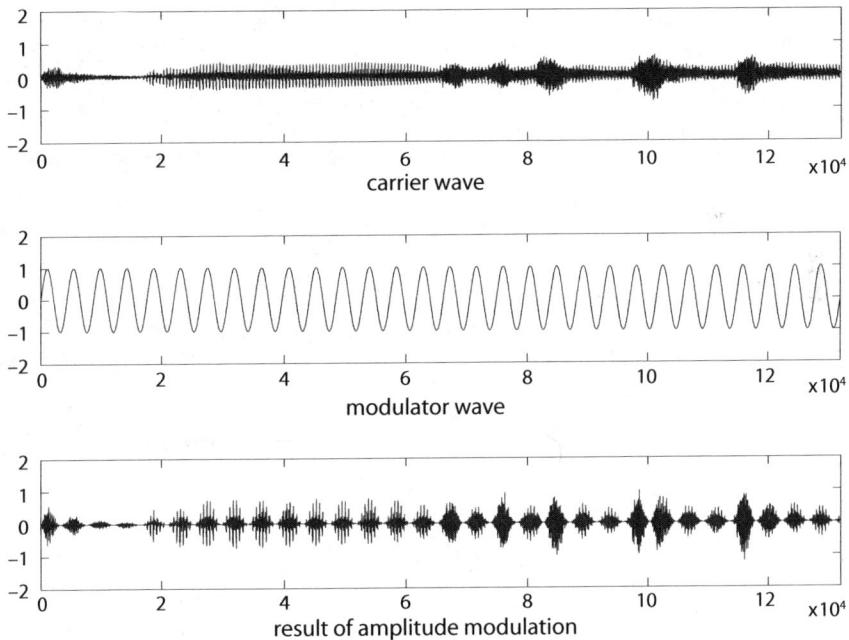

carrier wave

modulator wave

result of amplitude modulation

FIGURE 6.50: AMPLITUDE MODULATION OF A COMPLEX AUDIO SIGNAL

The audio effect is different, depending on which signal is chosen as the carrier and which as the modulator. Below, the carrier and modulator are reversed from the previous example, generating the graphs in Figure 6.51.

```
N = 132300;
r = 44100;
m = wavread('HornsE04.wav')
n = [1:N];
c = sin(2*pi*10*n/r);
c = transpose(c);
AM3 = c .* (1.0 + m);
figure;
plot(c);
axis([0 132300 -2 2]);
figure;
plot(m);
axis([0 132300 -2 2]);
figure;
plot(AM3);
axis([0 132300 -2 2]);
wavplay(c, 44100);
wavplay(m, 44100);
wavplay(AM3, 44100);
```

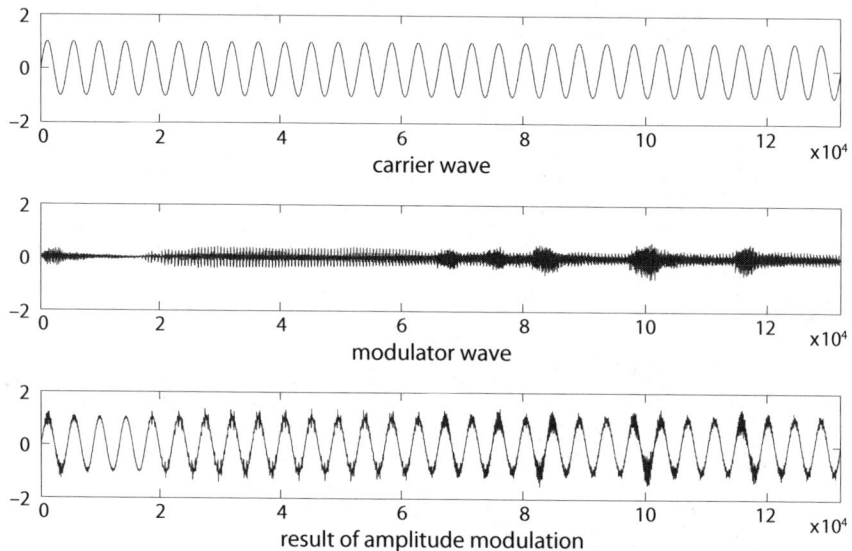

carrier wave

modulator wave

result of amplitude modulation

FIGURE 6.51: AMPLITUDE MODULATION OF A COMPLEX AUDIO SIGNAL
WITH CARRIER AND MODULATOR WAVES REVERSED

Amplitude modulation produces new frequency components in the resulting waveform at $f_c + f_m$ and $f_c - f_m$, where f_c is the frequency of the carrier and f_m is the frequency of the modulator. These are called **sidebands**. You can verify that the sidebands are at $f_c + f_m$ and $f_c - f_m$ with a little math based on the properties of sines and cosines. (The third step comes from the cosine product rule.)

$$\cos(2\pi f_c n)(1.0 + \cos(2\pi f_m n)) =$$
$$\cos(2\pi f_c n) + \cos(2\pi f_c n)\cos(2\pi f_m n) =$$
$$\cos(2\pi f_c n) + \frac{1}{2}\cos(2\pi(f_c + f_m)n) + \frac{1}{2}\cos(2\pi(f_c - f_m)n)$$

This derivation shows that there are three frequency components: one with frequency f_c, a second with frequency $f_c + f_m$, and a third with frequency $f_c - f_m$.

To verify this with an example, you can generate a graph of the sidebands in MATLAB by doing a Fourier transform of the waveform generated by AM and plotting the magnitudes of the frequency components. MATLAB's *fft* function does a Fourier transform of a vector of audio data, returning a vector of complex numbers. The *abs* function turns the complex numbers into a vector of magnitudes of frequency components. Then these values can be plotted with the *plot* function. We show the graph only from frequencies 1 through 600 Hz, since the only frequency components for this example lie in this range. Figure 6.52 shows the sidebands corresponding to the AM performed in Figure 6.49. The sidebands are at 450 Hz and 460 Hz, as predicted.

```
figure;
fftmag = abs(fft(AM));
plot(fftmag(1:600));
```

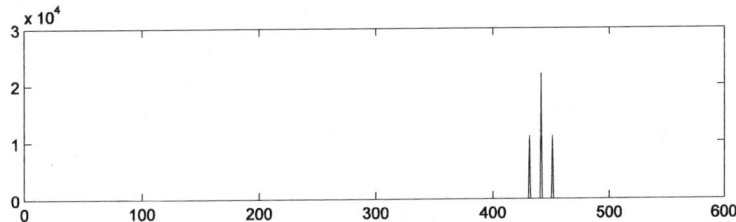

FIGURE 6.52: FREQUENCY COMPONENTS AFTER AMPLITUDE MODULATION IN FIGURE 6.49

6.3.3.5 Ring Modulation

Ring modulation entails multiplying two signals. To create a digital signal using ring modulation, Equation 6.2 can be applied.

$$r(n) = A_1 \sin\left(\frac{\omega_1 n}{r}\right) \times A_2 \sin\left(\frac{\omega_2 n}{r}\right)$$

$$for\ 0 \le n \le N - 1$$

*where N is the number of samples, r is the sampling rate,
where ω_1 and ω_2 are the angular frequencies of two signals,
and A_1 and A_2 are their respective amplitudes*

EQUATION 6.2: RING MODULATION FOR DIGITAL SYNTHESIS

Since multiplication is commutative, there's no sense in which one signal is the carrier and the other the modulator. Ring modulation is illustrated with two simple sine waves in Figure 6.53. The ring-modulated waveform is generated with the MATLAB commands below. Again, we set amplitudes to 1.

```
N = 44100;
r = 44100;
n = [1:N];
w1 = 440;
w2 = 10;
rm = sin(2*pi*w1*n/r) .* cos(2*pi*w2*n/r);
plot(rm(1:10000));
axis([1 10000 -2 2]);
```

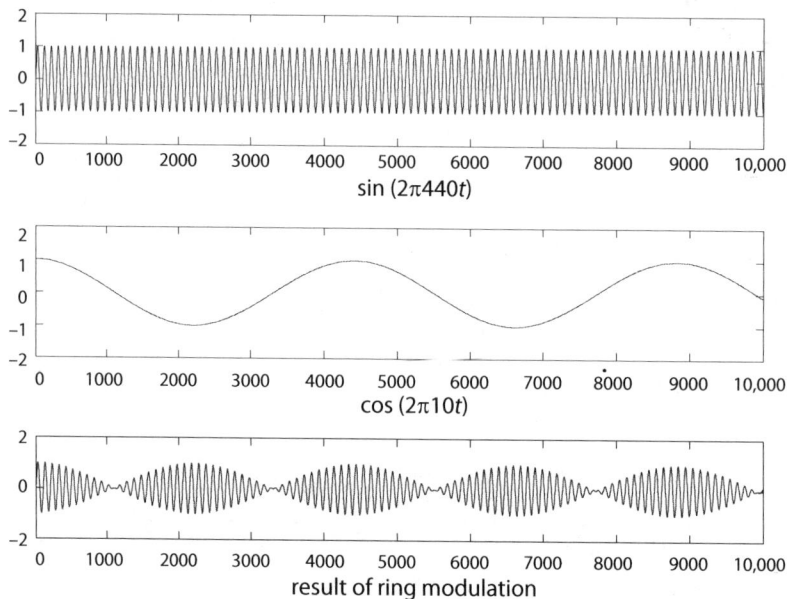

$\sin(2\pi 440t)$

$\cos(2\pi 10t)$

result of ring modulation

FIGURE 6.53: RING MODULATION USING TWO SINUSOIDALS

6.3.3.6 Phase Modulation (PM)

Even more interesting audio effects can be created with phase modulation (PM) and frequency modulation (FM). We're all familiar with FM radio, which is based on sending a signal by frequency modulation. Phase modulation is not used extensively in radio transmissions because it can be ambiguous to interpret at the receiving end, but it turns out to be fairly easy to implement PM in digital synthesizers. Some hardware-based synthesizers that are commonly referred to as FM actually use PM synthesis internally—the Yamaha DX series, for example.

Recall that the general equation for a cosine waveform is $A\cos(2\pi fn + \phi)$ where f is the frequency and ϕ is the phase. Phase modulation involves changing the phase over time. Equation 6.3 uses phase modulation to generate a digital signal.

$$p(t) = A\cos\left(\frac{\omega_c n}{r} + I\sin\left(\frac{\omega_m n}{r}\right)\right)$$

$$for\ 0 \leq n \leq N - 1$$

where N is the number of samples,
ω_c is the angular frequency of the carrier signal,
ω_m is the angular frequency of the modulator signal,
r is the sampling rate, I is the index of modulation,
and A is amplitude

EQUATION 6.3: PHASE MODULATION FOR DIGITAL SYNTHESIS

Phase modulation is demonstrated in MATLAB with the following statements:

```
N = 44100;
r = 44100;
n = [1:N];
f_m = 10;
f_c = 440;
w_m = 2 * pi * f_m;
w_c = 2 * pi * f_c;
A = 1;
I = 1;
p = A*cos(w_c * n/r + I*sin(w_m * n/r));
plot(p);
axis([1 30000 -2 2]);
wavplay(p, 44100);
```

The result is graphed in Figure 6.54.

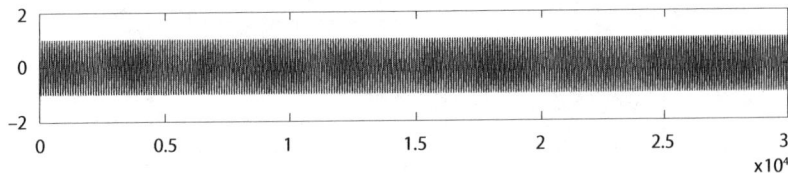

FIGURE 6.54: PHASE MODULATION USING TWO SINUSOIDALS,
WHERE ω_c=2π440 AND ω_m=2π10

The frequency components shown in Figure 6.55 are plotted in MATLAB with

```
fp = fft2(p);
figure;
plot(abs(fp));
axis([400 480 0 18000]);
```

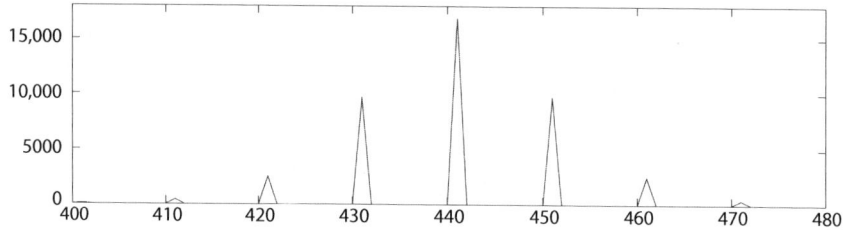

FIGURE 6.55: FREQUENCY COMPONENTS FROM PHASE MODULATION IN FIGURE 6.54

Phase modulation produces an infinite number of sidebands (many of whose amplitudes are too small to be detected). This fact is expressed in Equation 6.4.

$$cos\left(\omega_c n + I\sin\left(\omega_m n\right)\right) = \sum_{k=-\infty}^{\infty} J_k(I)cos\left(\left[\omega_c + k\omega_m\right]n\right)$$

EQUATION 6.4: PHASE MODULATION EQUIVALENCE WITH ADDITIVE SYNTHESIS

$J_k(I)$ gives the amplitude of the frequency component for each kth component in the phase-modulated signal. These scaling functions $J_k(I)$ are called *Bessel functions of the first kind*. It's beyond the scope of the book to define these functions further. You can experiment for yourself to see that the frequency components have amplitudes that depend on I. If you listen to the sounds created, you'll find that the timbres of the sounds can also be caused to change over time by changing I. The frequencies of the components, on the other hand, depend on the ratio of ω_c/ω_m. You can try varying the MATLAB commands above to experience the wide variety of sounds that can be created with phase modulation. You should also consider the possibilities of applying additive or subtractive synthesis to multiple phase-modulated waveforms.

The solution to the exercise associated with the next section gives a MATLAB .*m* program for phase modulation.

6.3.3.7 Frequency Modulation (FM)

We have seen in the previous section that phase modulation can be applied to the digital synthesis of a wide variety of waveforms. Frequency modulation is equally versatile and frequently used in digital synthesizers. Frequency modulation is defined recursively as follows:

$$f(n) = A \cos \left(p(n) \right) \ \text{ and}$$

$$p(n) = p(n-1) + \frac{\omega_c}{r} + \left(\frac{I\omega_m}{r} \times \cos \left(\frac{n \times \omega_m}{r} \right) \right)$$

$$\text{for } 0 \le n \le N - 1 \text{ and } p(0) = \frac{\omega_c}{r} + \frac{I\omega_m}{r}$$

where N is the number of samples,
ω_c is the angular frequency of the carrier signal,
ω_m is the angular frequency of the modulator signal,
r is the sampling rate,
I is the index of modulation,
and A is amplitude

EQUATION 6.5: FREQUENCY MODULATION FOR DIGITAL SYNTHESIS

Frequency modulation can yield results identical to phase modulation, depending on how input parameters are handled in the implementation. A difference between phase and frequency modulation is the perspective from which the modulation is handled. Obviously, the former is shaping a waveform by modulating the phase, while the latter is modulating the frequency. In frequency modulation, the change in the frequency can be handled by a parameter d, an absolute change in carrier signal frequency, which is defined by $d = If_m$. The input parameters $N = 44{,}100$, $r = 44{,}100$, $f_c = 880$, $f_m = 10$, $A = 1$, and $d = 100$ yield the graphs shown in Figure 6.56 and Figure 6.57. We suggest that you try to replicate these results by writing a MATLAB program based on Equation 6.5 defining frequency modulation.

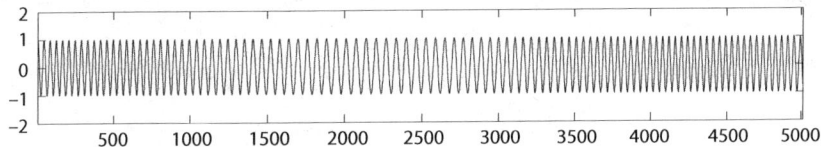

>>

MATLAB EXERCISE:

Frequency Modulation

for Digital Synthesis in

MATLAB

http://bit.ly/29kDca9

FIGURE 6.56: FREQUENCY MODULATION USING TWO SINUSOIDALS, WHERE $\omega_c = 2\pi880$ and $\omega_m = 2\pi10$

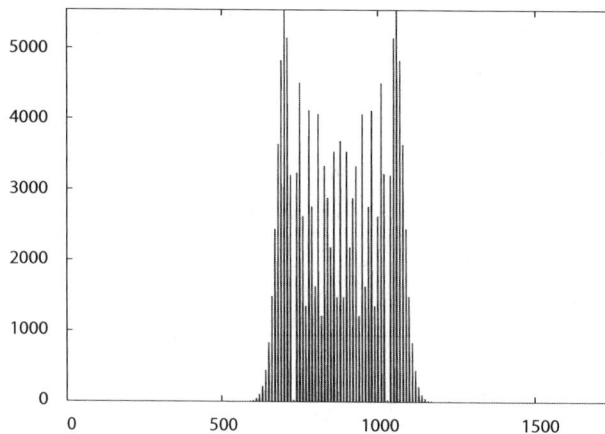

FIGURE 6.57: FREQUENCY COMPONENTS AFTER FREQUENCY MODULATION IN FIGURE 6.56

6.3.4   CREATING A BLOCK SYNTHESIZER IN MAX

Earlier in this chapter, we discussed the fundamentals of synthesizers and the types of controls and processing components you might find built in to their function. In Section 6.1 and in several of the practical exercises and demonstrations, we took you through these components and features one by one. Breaking apart a synthesizer into these individual blocks makes it easier to understand the signal flow and steps behind audio synthesis. In this book, we generally look at software synthesizers in the examples due to their flexibility and availability. Most of them come with a full feature set of oscillators, amplifiers, filters, envelopes, and other synthesis objects. Back in the early days of audio synthesis, however, most of this functionality was delegated to separate, dedicated devices. The oscillator device only generated tones. If you also needed a noise signal, that might require you to find a separate piece of hardware. If you wanted to filter the signal, you would need to acquire a separate audio filtering device. These devices were all connected by a myriad of audio patch cables, which could quickly become a complete jumble of wires. The beauty of hardware synthesis was its modularity. There were no strict rules on what wire must plug into what jack. Where a software synth today might have one or two filters at specific locations in the signal path, there was nothing to stop someone back then from connecting a dozen filters in a row if they wanted to and had the available resources. While the modularity and expanse of these setups may seem daunting, it allowed for maximum flexibility and creativity, and could result in some interesting, unique, and possibly unexpected synthesized sounds.

MAX
DEMO:

Block Synthesizer
http://bit.ly/29nTIed

Wouldn't it be fun to recreate this in the digital world as software? Certainly there are some advantages in this, such as reduced cost, potentially greater flexibility and control, a less-cluttered tabletop, not to mention less risk of electrocuting yourself or frying a circuit board. The remainder of this section takes you through the creation of several of these synthesis blocks in Max, which lends itself quite well to the concept of a creating and using a modular synthesizer. At the end of this example, we'll see how we can then combine and connect these blocks in any imaginable configuration to create some possibly never-before-heard sounds.

It is assumed that you're proficient in the basics of Max. If you're not familiar with an object we use or discuss, please refer to the Max help and reference files for that object (**Help > Open [ObjectName] Help** in the file menu, or **Right-click > Open [ObjectName] Help**). Every object in Max has a help file that explains and demonstrates how the object works. Additionally, if you hover the mouse over an inlet or outlet of an object, Max often shows you a tooltip with information on its format or use. We also try to include helpful comments and hints within the solution itself.

At this point in the chapter, you should be familiar with a good number of these synthesis blocks and how they are utilized. We'll look at how you might create an audio oscillator, an amplification stage, and an envelope block to control some of our synth parameters. Before we get into the guts of the synth blocks, let's take a moment to think about how we might want to use these blocks together and consider some of the features of Max that lend themselves to this modular approach.

It would be ideal to have a single window where you could add blocks and arrange and connect them in any way you want. The blocks themselves would need to have inputs and outputs for audio and control values. The blocks should have the relevant and necessary controls (knobs, sliders, etc.) and displays. We also don't necessarily need to see the inner workings of the completed blocks, and because screen space is at a premium, the blocks should be as compact and simply packaged as possible. From a programming point of view, the blocks should be easily copied and pasted, and if we had to change the internal components of one type of block, it would be nice if the change reflected across all the other blocks of that type. In this way, if we wanted, say, to add another waveform type to our oscillator blocks later on and we had already created and connected dozens of oscillator blocks, we wouldn't have to go through and reprogram each one individually.

There is an object in Max called the *bpatcher*. It is similar to a typical *subpatcher* object in that it provides a means to create multiple elements and a complex functionality inside of one single object. However, where the *subpatcher* physically contains the additional objects within it, the *bpatcher* essentially allows you to embed an entire other patcher file inside your current one. It also provides a "window" into the patcher file itself, showing a customizable area of the embedded patcher contents. Additionally, like the *subpatcher*, the *bpatcher* allows for connection to and from custom inlets and outlets in the patcher file. Using the *bpatcher* object, we're able to create each synth block in its own separate patcher file. We can configure the customizable viewing window to maximize display potential while keeping screen real estate to a minimum. Creating another block is as simple as duplicating the one *bpatcher* object (no multiple objects to deal with), and as the *bpatcher* links to the one external file, updating the block file updates all of the instances in our main synthesizer file. To tell a *bpatcher* which file to link, you open the *bpatcher* Inspector window (**Object > Inspector** in the file menu, or select the object and **Right-click > Inspector**) and click the **Choose** button on the **Patcher File** line to browse for the patcher file, as shown in Figure 6.58.

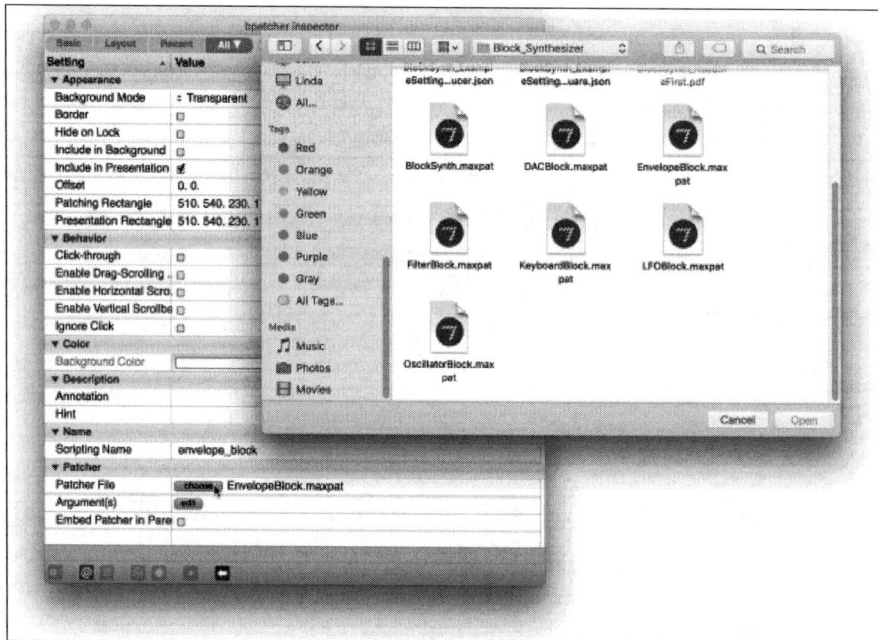

FIGURE 6.58: BPATCHER OBJECT INSPECTOR

Of course, before we can embed our synth block files, we need to actually create them. Let's start with the oscillator block, as that's the initial source for our sound synthesis. Figure 6.59 shows you the oscillator block file in programming mode.

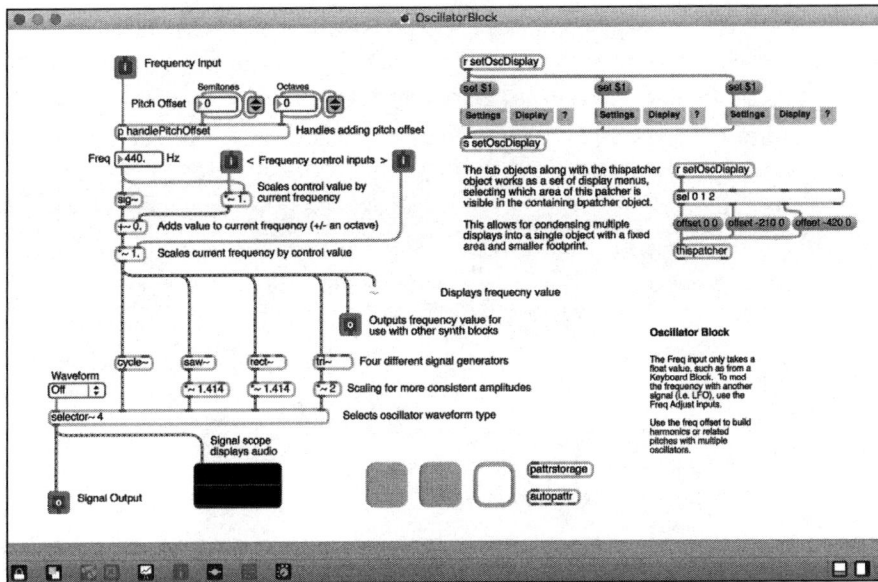

FIGURE 6.59: OSCILLATOR BLOCK IN PROGRAMMING MODE

While the oscillator block may appear complex at first, there is a good bit of content that we added to improve the handling and display of the block for demonstrative and educational purposes. The objects grouped at the top-right side of the patcher enable multiple display views for use within the *bpatcher* object. This is a useful and interesting feature of the *bpatcher* object, but we're not going to focus on the nuts and bolts of it in this section. There is a simple example of this kind of implementation in the built-in *bpatcher* help file (**Help > Open [ObjectName] Help** in the file menu, or **Right-click > Open [ObjectName] Help**), so feel free to explore this further on your own. There are some additional objects and connections that are added to give additional display and informational feedback, such as the *scope~* object that displays the audio waveform and a *number~* object as a numerical display of the frequency, but these are relatively straightforward and non-essential to the design of this block. If we were to strip out all the objects and connections that don't deal with audio or aren't absolutely necessary for our synth block to work, it would look more like the file in Figure 6.60.

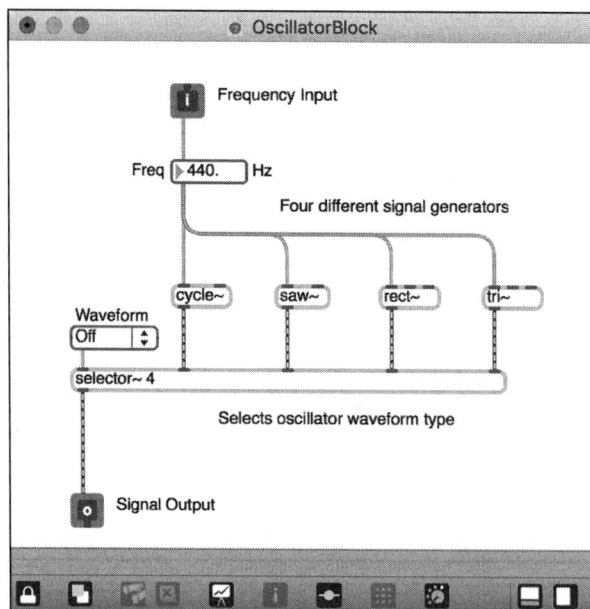

FIGURE 6.60: OSCILLATOR BLOCK STRIPPED DOWN

In its most basic functionality, the oscillator block simply generates an audio signal of some kind. In this case, we chose to provide several different options for the audio signal, including an object for generating basic sine waves (*cycle~*), sawtooth waves (*saw~*), square waves (*rect~*) and triangle waves (*tri~*). Each of these objects takes a number in to its leftmost inlet to set its frequency. The *selector~* object is used to select between multiple signals, and the desired signal is passed through based on the waveform selected in the connected user interface dropdown menu (umenu). The inlets and outlets may seem strange when used in a standalone patcher file, and at this stage they aren't really useful. However, when the file is linked into the *bpatcher* object, these inlets and outlets appear on the *bpatcher* and allow you access to these signals and control values in the main synth patcher.

While this module alone would enable you to begin synthesizing simple sounds, one of the purposes of the modular synthesizer blocks is to be able to wire them together to control each other in interesting ways. In this respect, we may want to consider ways to control or manipulate our oscillator block. The primary parameter in the case of the oscillator is the oscillator frequency, so we should incorporate some control elements for it. Perhaps we would want to increase or decrease the oscillator frequency, or even scale it by an external factor. Consider the way some of the software or hardware synths previously discussed in this chapter have manipulated the oscillator frequency. Looking back at the programming mode for this block, you may recall seeing several inlets labeled "frequency control" and some additional connected objects. A close view of these can be seen in Figure 6.61.

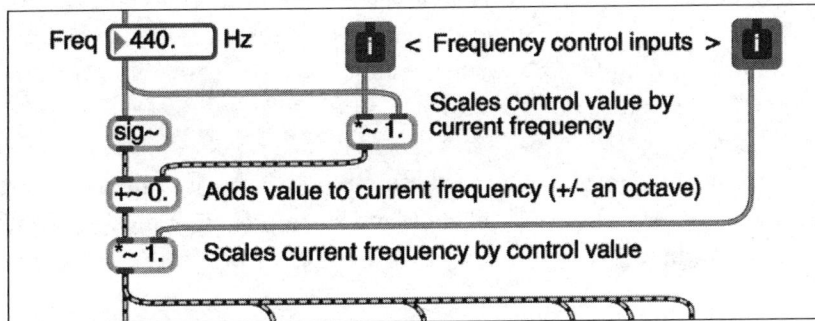

FIGURE 6.61: OSCILLATOR BLOCK FREQUENCY CONTROL INPUTS

These control inputs in Figure 6.61 are attached to several arithmetic objects, including addition and multiplication. The "~" following the mathematical operator simply means that this version of the object is used for processing signal rate (audio) values. This is the sole purpose of the *sig~* object also seen here; it takes the static numerical value of the frequency (shown at 440 Hz) and outputs it as a signal rate value, meaning it is constantly streaming its output. In the case of these two control inputs, we set one of them up as an additive control, and the other a multiplicative control. The inlet on the left is the additive control. It adds to the oscillator frequency an amount equal to some portion of the current oscillator frequency value. For example, if for the frequency value shown it receives a control value of 1, it adds 440 Hz to the oscillator frequency. If it receives a control value of 0.5, it adds 220 Hz to the oscillator frequency. If it receives a control value of 0, it adds nothing to the oscillator frequency, resulting in no change.

At this point we should take a step back and ask ourselves, "What kind of control values should we be expecting?" There is really no one answer to this, but as the designers of these synth blocks we should perhaps establish a convention that is meaningful across all of our different synthesizer elements. For our purposes, a floating-point range between 0.0 and 1.0 seems simple and manageable. Of course, we can't stop someone from connecting a control value outside of this range to our block if they really wanted. That's just what makes modular synthesis so fun.

Going back to the second control input (multiplicative) in Figure 6.61, you can see that it scales the output of the oscillator directly by this control value. If it receives a control value of 0, the oscillator's frequency is 0 and it outputs silence. If it receives a control value of 1, the signal is multiplied by 1, resulting in no change. Notice that the multiplication object has been set to a default value of 1, so that the initial oscillator without any control input behaves normally. The addition object has been initialized for that behavior as well. It is also very important to include the decimal (.) with these initial values, as that tells the object to expect a floating-point value rather than an integer (default). Without the decimal, the object may round or truncate the floating-point value to the nearest integer, resulting in our case to a control value of either 0 or 1, which would be rather limiting.

Let's now take a look at what goes into an amplification block. The amplification block is simply used to control the amplitude, or level, of the synthesized audio. Figure 6.62 shows you our amplifier block file in programming mode. There isn't much need to strip down the non-essentials from this block, as there's just not much to it.

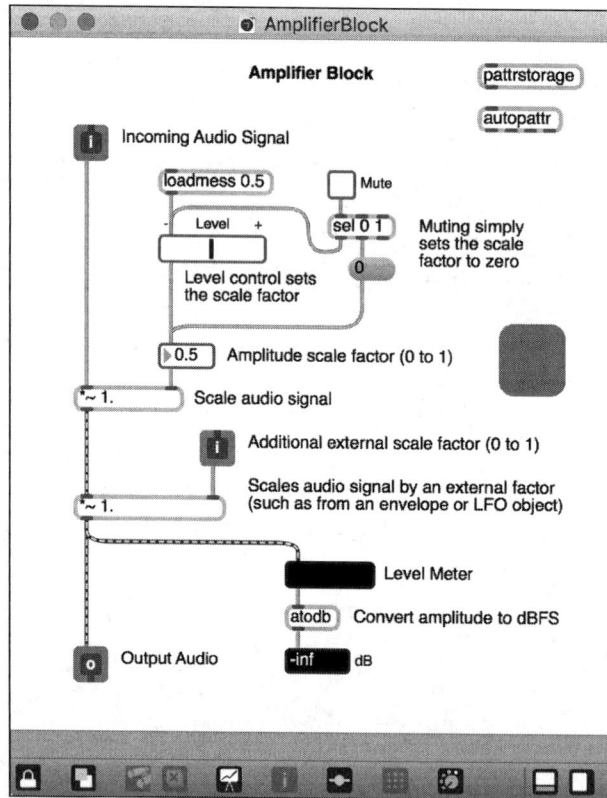

FIGURE 6.62: AMPLIFIER BLOCK IN PROGRAMMING MODE

Tracing the audio signal path straight down the left side of the patcher, you can see that there are two stages of multiplication, which essentially is amplification in the digital realm. The first stage of amplification is controlled by a level slider and a mute toggle switch. These interface objects allow the overall amplification to be set graphically by the user. The second stage of amplification is set by an external control value. Again, this is another good fit for the standard range we decided on of 0.0 to 1.0. A control value of 0 causes the signal amplitude to be scaled to 0, outputting silence. A control value of 1 results in no change in amplification. On the other hand, could you think of a reason we might want to increase the amplitude of the signal, and input a control value greater than 1.0? Perhaps a future synth block may have good reason to do this. Now that we have these control inputs available, we should start thinking of how we might actually control these blocks, such as with an envelope.

Figure 6.63 shows our envelope block in programming mode. Like the oscillator block, there are quite a few objects that we included to deal with additional display and presentational aspects that aren't necessary to the block's basic functionality. It too has a group of objects in the top-right corner dedicated to enabling alternate views when embedded in the *bpatcher* object. If we were again to strip out all the objects and connections that don't deal with audio or aren't absolutely necessary for our synth block to work, it would look more like the file in Figure 6.64.

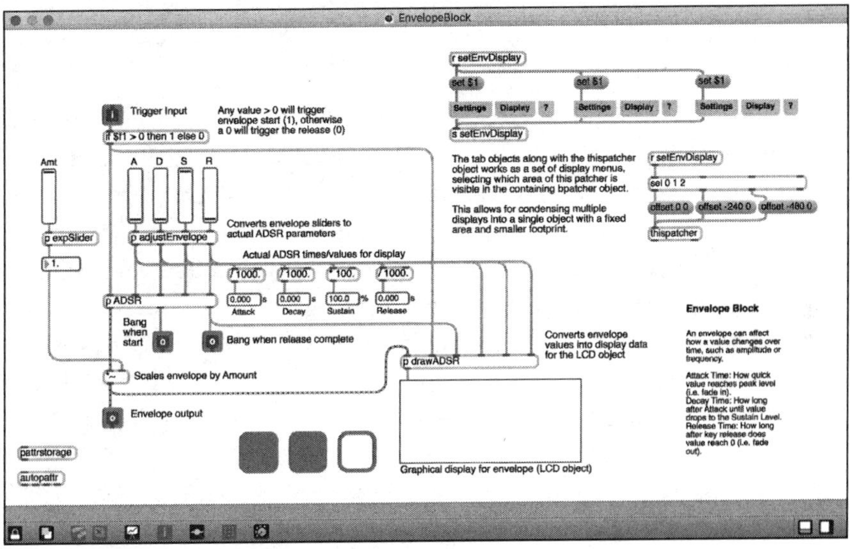

FIGURE 6.63: ENVELOPE BLOCK IN PROGRAMMING MODE

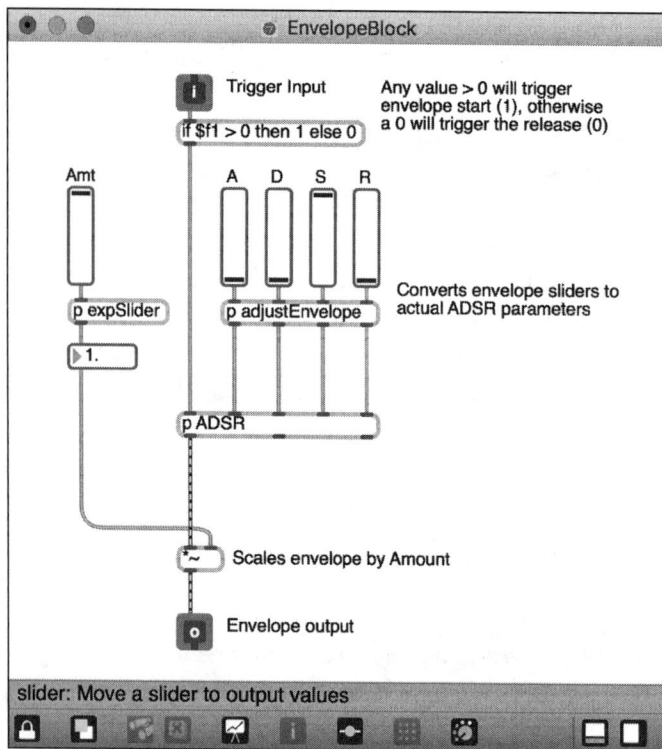

FIGURE 6.64: ENVELOPE BLOCK STRIPPED DOWN

While it incorporates signal rate objects, the envelope doesn't actually involve the audio signal. Its output is used purely for control. Then again, it's possible for the user to connect the envelope block output to the audio signal path, but it probably won't sound very good if it even makes a sound at all. Let's start with the inlet at the top. In order for an envelope to function properly, it has to know when to start and when to stop. Typically it starts when someone triggers a note, such as by playing a key on a keyboard, and it releases when the key is let go. Thinking back to MIDI and how MIDI keyboards work, we know that when a key is pressed, it sends a Note On command accompanied by a velocity value between 1 and 127. When the key is released, it often sends a Note On command with a velocity value of zero. In our case, we don't really care what the value is between 1 and 127; we need to start the envelope regardless of how hard the key is pressed.

This velocity value lends itself to being a good way to tell when to trigger and release an envelope. It would be useful to condition the input to give us only the two cases we care about: start and release. There are certainly multiple ways to implement this in Max, but a simple *if…then* object is an easy way to check this logic using one object. The *if…then* object checks if the value at inlet 1 ($f1) is greater than 0 (as is the case for 1 to 127), and if so it outputs the value 1. Otherwise (if the inlet value is less than or equal to 0), it outputs 0. Since there are no negative velocity values, we've just lumped them into the release outcome to cover our bases. Now our input value results in a 1 or a 0 relating to a start or release envelope trigger.

As is often the case, it just so happens that Max has a built-in *adsr~* object that generates a standard ADSR envelope. We opted to create our own custom ADSR *subpatcher*. However, its purpose and inlets/outlets are essentially identical, and it's meant to be easily interchangeable with the *adsr~* object. You can find more about our custom ADSR *subpatcher* and the reason for its existence in the Max Demo "ADSR Envelopes" back in section 6.1.8.7. For the moment, we'll refer to it as the standard *adsr~* object.

Now, it just so happens that the *adsr~* object's first inlet triggers the envelope start when it sees any non-zero number, and it triggers the release when it receives a 0. Our input is thus already primed to be plugged straight into this object. It may also seem that our conditioning is now somewhat moot, since any typical velocity value, being a positive number, triggers the envelope start of the *adsr~* object just as well as the number 1. However, it is still important to consider that perhaps the user may (for creative reasons) connect a different type of control value other than note velocity to the envelope trigger input. The conditioning *if…then* object thereby ensures a more widely successful operation with potentially unexpected input formats.

The *adsr~* object also takes four other values as input. These are, as you might imagine, the attack time, decay time, sustain value, and release time. For simple controls, we've provided the user with four sliders to manipulate these parameters. In between the sliders and the *adsr~* inlets, we need to condition the slider values to relate to usable ADSR values. The *subpatcher adjustEnvelope* does just that, and its contents can be seen in Figure 6.65. The four slider values (default 0 to 127) are converted to time values of appropriate scale, and—in the case of sustain—a factor ranging from 0.0 to 1.0. The *expSlider subpatchers* as seen in earlier Max demos give the sliders an exponential curve, allowing for greater precision at lower values.

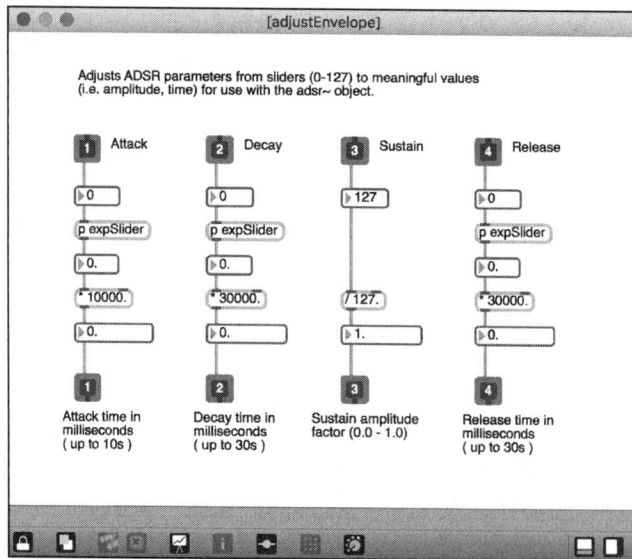

FIGURE 6.65: ADJUSTENVELOPE SUBPATCHER CONTENTS

The generated ADSR envelope ranges from 0.0 to 1.0, rising and falling according to the ADSR input parameters. Before reaching the final outlet, the envelope is scaled by a user-definable amount also ranging from 0.0 to 1.0, which essentially controls the impact the envelope has on the controllable parameter it is affecting.

It would too time-consuming to go through all of the modular synth blocks that we have created or that could potentially be created as part of this Max example. However, these and other modular blocks can be downloaded and explored from the "Block Synthesizer" Max demo presented at the start of this section. The blocks include the oscillator, amplifier, and envelope blocks discussed here, as well as a keyboard input block, LFO (low-frequency oscillation) block, filter block, and a DAC (digital-to-analog) block. Each individual block file is fully commented to assist you in understanding how it was put together. These blocks are all incorporated as *bpatcher* objects into a main *BlockSynth. maxpat* patcher, shown in Figure 6.66, where they can all be arranged, duplicated, and connected in various configurations to create a great number of synthesis possibilities. You can also check out the additional included *BlockSynth_Example.maxpat* and example settings files to see a few configurations and settings we came up with to create some unique

MAX EXERCISE:
Modulation Wheel
http://bit.ly/29LTW90

MAX EXERCISE:
Low-Frequency Oscillator
http://bit.ly/29h7WHd

synth sounds. Feel free to come up with your own synth blocks and implement them as well. Some possible ideas might be a metering block to provide additional displays and meters for the audio signal, a noise generator block for an alternative signal source or modulator, or perhaps a polyphony block to manage several instances of oscillator blocks and allow multiple simultaneous notes to be played.

FIGURE 6.66: MAIN BLOCK SYNTH PATCHER WITH EMBEDDED BPATCHER BLOCKS

Software synthesis is really the bedrock of the Max program, and you can learn a lot about Max through programming synthesizers. To that end, we have also created two Max programming exercises using our Subtractonaut synthesizer. These programming assignments challenge you to add some features to the existing synthesizer. Solution files are available on this book's website showing how these features might be programmed.

6.4 REFERENCES

In addition to references cited in previous chapters:

Boulanger, Richard, and Victor Lazzarini, eds. *The Audio Programming Book.* Cambridge, MA: The MIT Press, 2011.

Huntington, John. *Control Systems for Live Entertainment.* Boston: Focal Press, 1994.

Messick, Paul. *Maximum MIDI: Music Applications in C++.* Greenwich, CT: Manning Publications, 1998.

Schaeffer, Pierre. *A la recherche d'une musique concrète.* Paris, Éditions du Seuil, 1952.

CHAPTER SEVEN
Audio Processing

7.1 CONCEPTS

7.1.1 IT'S *ALL* AUDIO PROCESSING

We've entitled this chapter "Audio Processing" as if this were a separate topic within the realm of sound. But actually, everything we do to audio is a form of processing. Every tool, plug-in, software application, and piece of gear is essentially an audio processor of some sort. What we set out to do in this chapter is to focus on particular kinds of audio processing, covering the basic concepts, applications, and underlying mathematics of these. For the sake of organization, we divide the chapter into processing related to frequency adjustments and processing related to amplitude adjustment, but in practice these two areas are interrelated.

7.1.2 FILTERS

You have seen in previous chapters how sounds are generally composed of multiple frequency components. Sometimes it's desirable to increase the level of some frequencies or decrease others. To deal with frequencies or bands of frequencies selectively, we have to separate them out. This is done by means of filters. The frequency processing tools in the following sections are all implemented with one type of filter or another.

There are a number of ways to categorize filters. If we classify them according to what frequencies they attenuate, then we have these types of band filters:

- ⟩ **low-pass filter**—retains only frequencies below a given threshold.
- ⟩ **high-pass filter**—retains only frequencies above a given threshold.
- ⟩ **bandpass filter**—retains only frequencies within a given frequency band.
- ⟩ **bandstop filter**—eliminates frequencies within a given frequency band.
- ⟩ **comb filter**—attenuates frequencies in a manner that, when graphed in the frequency domain, has a "comb" shape. That is, multiples of some fundamental frequency are attenuated across the audible spectrum.

)) **peaking filter**—boosts or attenuates frequencies in a band.
)) **shelving filters**
)) **low-shelf filter**—boosts or attenuates low frequencies.
)) **high-shelf filter**—boosts or attenuates high frequencies.

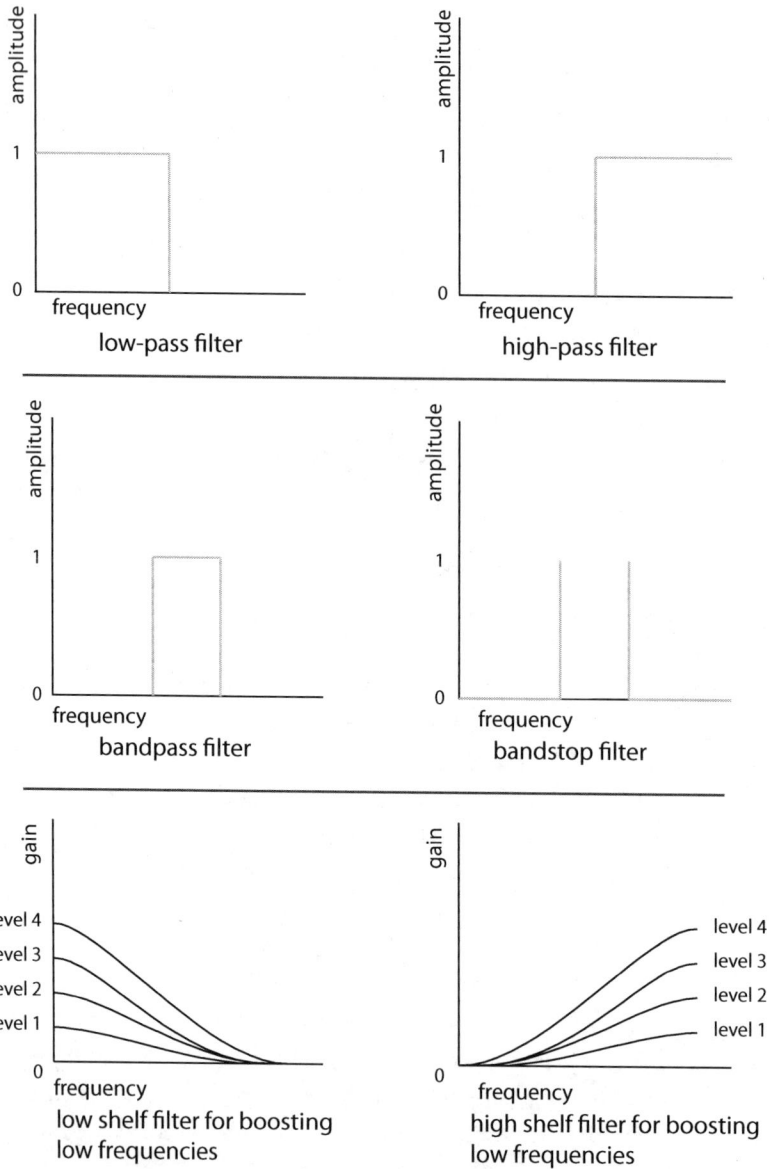

FIGURE 7.1: FREQUENCY RESPONSES OF DIFFERENT FILTER TYPES

Figure 7.1 gives rough pictures of the frequency responses of these filters. The frequency response graph has frequencies across the horizontal axis and either gain or amplitude on the vertical axis. You see these frequency response "shapes" as icons in EQ plug-ins and other frequency adjustment tools. For example, the icons in the Filter column of the parametric EQ in Figure 7.4 represent, respectively, a peaking filter, low shelf filters, high shelf filters, low-pass filter, high pass filter, and another peaking filter.

Filters that have a known mathematical basis for their frequency response graphs and whose behavior is therefore predictable at a finer level of detail are sometimes called **scientific filters**. This is the term Adobe Audition uses for Bessel, Butterworth, Chebyshev, and elliptical filters. The Bessel filter's frequency response graph is shown in Figure 7.2.

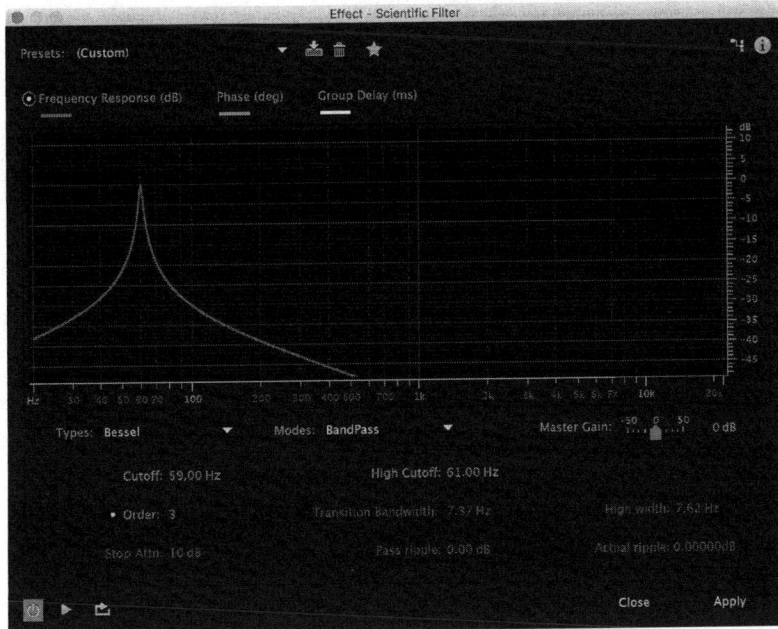

FIGURE 7.2: BESSEL SCIENTIFIC FILTER FROM ADOBE AUDITION

If we classify filters according to the way in which they are designed and implemented, then we have these types:

> **IIR filters**—infinite impulse response filters.

> **FIR filters**—finite impulse response filters.

Adobe Audition uses FIR filters for its graphic equalizer but IIR filters for its parametric equalizer (described below). This is because FIR filters give more consistent phase response, while IIR filters give better control over the cutoff points between attenuated and non-attenuated frequencies. The mathematical and algorithmic differences of FIR and IIR filters are discussed in Section 7.3. The difference between designing and implementing filters in the time domain vs. the frequency domain is also explained in Section 7.3.

Convolution filters are a type of FIR filter that can apply reverberation effects so as to mimic an acoustical space. The way this is done is to record a short loud burst of sound in the chosen acoustical space and use the resulting sound samples as a filter on the sound to which you want to apply reverb. This is described in more detail in Section 7.1.6.

7.1.3 EQUALIZATION

Audio **equalization**, more commonly referred to as **EQ**, is the process of altering the frequency response of an audio signal. The purpose of equalization is to increase or decrease the amplitude of chosen frequency components in the signal. This is achieved by applying an audio filter.

EQ can be applied in a variety of situations and for a variety of reasons. Sometimes, the frequencies of the original audio signal may have been affected by the physical response of the microphones or loudspeakers, and the audio engineer wishes to adjust for these factors. Other times, the listener or audio engineer might want to boost the low end for a certain effect, "even out" the frequencies of the instruments, or adjust frequencies of a particular instrument to change its timbre, to name just a few of the many possible reasons for applying EQ.

Equalization can be achieved by either hardware or software. Two commonly-used types of equalization tools are **graphic** and **parametric EQs**. Within these EQ devices, low-pass, high-pass, bandpass, bandstop, low-shelf, high-shelf, and peak-notch filters can be applied.

7.1.4 GRAPHIC EQ

A graphic equalizer is one of the most basic types of EQ. It consists of a number of fixed, individual frequency bands spread out across the audible spectrum, with the ability to adjust the amplitudes of these bands up or down. To match our non-linear perception of sound, the center frequencies of the bands are spaced logarithmically. A graphic EQ is shown in Figure 7.3. This equalizer has 31 frequency bands, with center frequencies at 20 Hz, 25 Hz, 31 Hz, 40 Hz, 50 Hz, 63 Hz, 80 Hz, and so forth in a logarithmic progression up to 20 kHz. Each of these bands can be raised or lowered in amplitude individually to achieve an overall EQ shape.

While graphic equalizers are fairly simple to understand, they are not very efficient to use since they often require that you manipulate several controls to accomplish a single EQ effect. In an analog graphic EQ, each slider represents a separate filter circuit that also introduces noise and manipulates phase independently of the other filters. These problems have given graphic equalizers a reputation for being noisy and rather messy in their phase response. The interface for a graphic EQ can also be misleading because it gives the impression that you're being more precise in your frequency processing than you actually are. That single slider for 1000 Hz can affect anywhere from one third of an octave to a full octave of frequencies around the center frequency itself, and consequently each actual filter overlaps neighboring ones in the range of frequencies it affects. In short, graphic EQs are generally not preferred by experienced professionals.

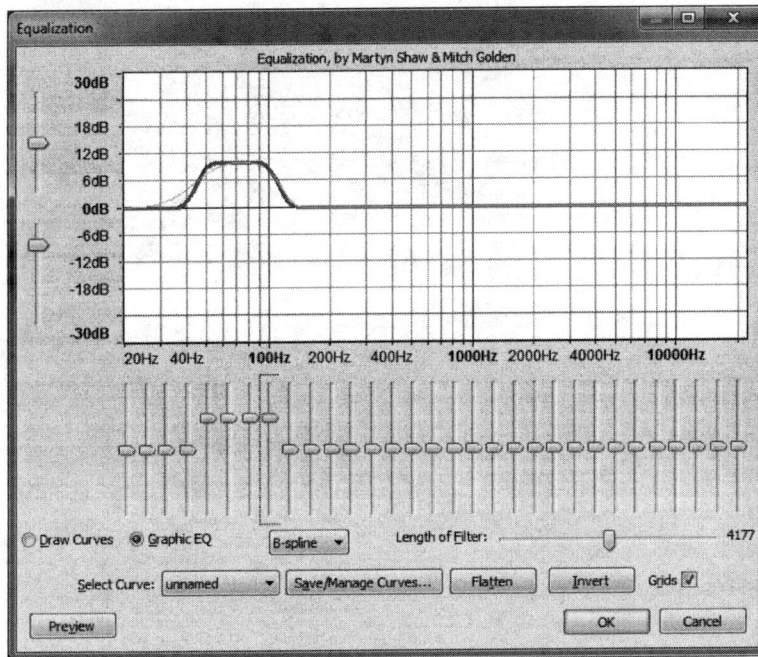

FIGURE 7.3: GRAPHIC EQ IN AUDACITY

7.1.5 PARAMETRIC EQ

A parametric equalizer, as the name implies, has more parameters than the graphic equalizer, making it more flexible and useful for professional audio engineering. Figure 7.4 shows a parametric equalizer. The different icons on the filter column show the types of filters that can be applied. They are, from top to bottom, peak-notch (also called *bell*), low-pass, high-pass, low-shelf, and high-shelf filters. The available parameters vary according to the filter type. This particular filter is applying a low-pass filter on the fourth band and a high-pass filter on the fifth band.

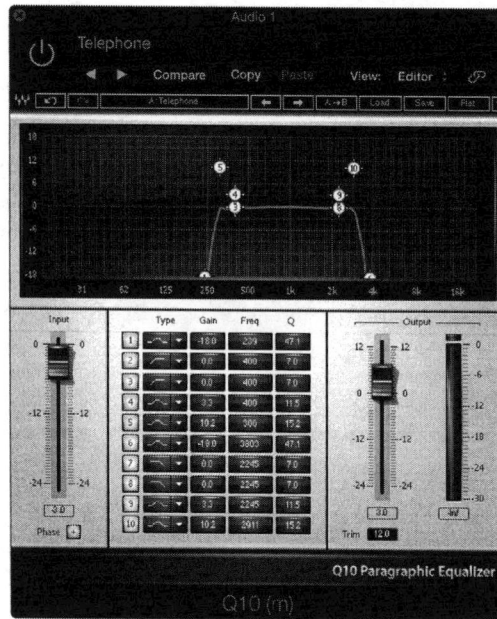

FIGURE 7.4: PARAMETRIC EQ IN CAKEWALK SONAR

For the peak-notch filter, the frequency parameter corresponds to the center frequency of the band to which the filter is applied. For the low-pass, high-pass, low-shelf, and high-shelf filters, none of which have an actual "center," the frequency parameter represents the cut-off frequency. The numbered circles on the frequency response curve correspond to the filter bands. Figure 7.5 shows a low-pass filter in band 1 where the **6 dB down point**—the point at which the frequencies are attenuated by 6 dB—is set to 500 Hz.

> **ASIDE:** The term "paragraphic EQ" is used for a combination of a graphic and parametric EQ, with sliders to change amplitudes and parameters that can be set for Q, cutoff frequency, etc.

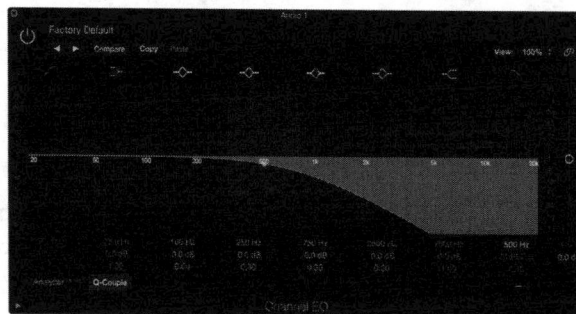

FIGURE 7.5: LOW-PASS FILTER IN A PARAMETRIC EQ WITH CUT-OFF FREQUENCY OF 500 HZ

The gain parameter is the amount by which the corresponding frequency band is boosted or attenuated. The gain cannot be set for low- or high-pass filters, as these types of filters are designed to eliminate all frequencies beyond or up to the cut-off frequency.

The Q parameter is a measure of the height versus the width of the frequency response curve. A higher Q value creates a steeper peak in the frequency response curve compared to a lower one, as shown in Figure 7.6.

Some parametric equalizers use a **bandwidth** parameter instead of Q to control the range of frequencies for a filter. Bandwidth works inversely from Q in that a larger bandwidth represents a larger range of frequencies. The unit of measurement for bandwidth is typically an octave. A bandwidth value of 1 represents a full octave of frequencies between the 6 dB down points of the filter.

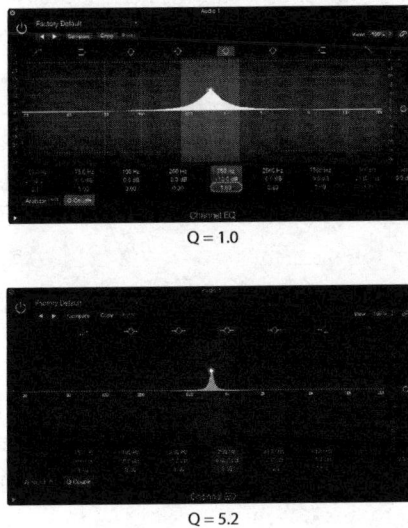

Q = 1.0

Q = 5.2

FIGURE 7.6: COMPARISON OF Q VALUES FOR TWO PEAK FILTERS

7.1.6   REVERB

When you work with sound either live or recorded, the sound is generally captured with the microphone very close to the source of the sound. With the microphone very close, and particularly in an acoustically treated studio with very little reflected sound, it is often desired or even necessary to artificially add a reverberation effect to create a more natural sound, or perhaps to give the sound a special effect. Usually a very dry initial recording is preferred, so that artificial reverberation can be applied more uniformly and with greater control.

MAX DEMO:
Reverb
http://bit.ly/29uF6as

There are several methods for adding reverberation. Before the days of digital processing, this was accomplished using a reverberation chamber. A reverberation chamber is simply a highly reflective, isolated room with very low background noise. A loudspeaker is placed at one end of the room, and a microphone is placed at the other end. The sound is played into the loudspeaker and captured back through the microphone with all the natural reverberation added by the room. This signal is then mixed back into the source signal, making it sound more reverberant. Reverberation chambers vary in size and construction, some larger than others, but even the smallest ones would be too large for a home, much less a portable studio.

Because of the impracticality of reverberation chambers, most artificial reverberation is added to audio signals using digital hardware processors or software plug-ins, commonly called **reverb processors**. Software digital reverb processors use software algorithms to add an effect that sounds like natural reverberation. These are essentially delay algorithms that create copies of the audio signal that get spread out over time and with varying amplitudes and frequency responses.

A sound that is fed into a reverb processor comes out of that processor with thousands of copies or virtual reflections. As described in Chapter 4, there are three components of a naturally reverberant field. A digital reverberation algorithm attempts to mimic these three components.

The first component of the reverberant field is the **direct sound**. This is the sound that arrives at the listener directly from the sound source without reflecting from any surface. In audio terms, this is known as the **dry** or **unprocessed sound**. The dry sound is simply the original, unprocessed signal that is passed through the reverb processor. The opposite of the dry sound is the **wet** or **processed sound**. Most reverb processors include a wet/dry mix that allows you to balance the direct and reverberant sound. Removing all of the dry signal leaves you with a very ambient effect, as if the actual sound source was not in the room at all.

The second component of the reverberant field is the **early reflections**. Early reflections are sounds that arrive at the listener after reflecting from the first one or two surfaces. The number of early reflections and their spacing vary as a function of the size and shape of the room. The early reflections are the most important factor contributing to the perception of room size. In a larger room, the early reflections take longer to hit a wall and travel to the listener. In a reverberation processor, this parameter is controlled by a **pre-delay** variable. The longer the pre-delay, the longer time you have between the direct sound and the reflected sound, giving the effect of a larger room. In addition to pre-delay, controls are sometimes available for determining the number of early reflections, their spacing, and their amplitude. The spacing of the early reflections indicates the location of the listener in the room. Early reflections that are spaced tightly together give the effect of a listener who is closer to a side or corner of the room. The amplitude of the early reflections suggests the distance from the wall. On the other hand, low-amplitude reflections indicate that the listener is far away from the walls of the room.

The third component of the reverberant field is the **reverberant sound**. The reverberant sound is made of up of all the remaining reflections that have bounced around many surfaces before arriving at the listener. These reflections are so numerous and close together that they are perceived as a continuous sound. Each time the sound reflects off a surface, some of the energy is absorbed. Consequently, the reflected sound is quieter than the sound that arrives at the surface before being reflected. Eventually all the energy is absorbed by the surfaces and the reverberation ceases. Reverberation time is the length of time it takes for the reverberant sound to decay by 60 dB, effectively a level so quiet it ceases to be heard. This is sometimes referred to as the **RT60**, or also the **decay time**. A longer decay time indicates a more reflective room.

Because most surfaces absorb high frequencies more efficiently than low frequencies, the frequency response of natural reverberation is typically weighted toward the low frequencies. In reverberation processors, there is a parameter for reverberation dampening. This applies a high-shelf filter to the reverberant sound that reduces the level of the high frequencies. This dampening variable can suggest to the listener the type of reflective material on the surfaces of the room.

Figure 7.7 shows a popular reverberation plug-in. The three sliders at the bottom-right of the window control the balance between the direct, early reflection, and reverberant sound. The other controls adjust the setting for each of these three components of the reverberant field.

The reverb processor pictured in Figure 7.8 is based on a complex computation of delays and filters that achieve the effects requested by its control settings. Reverbs such as these are

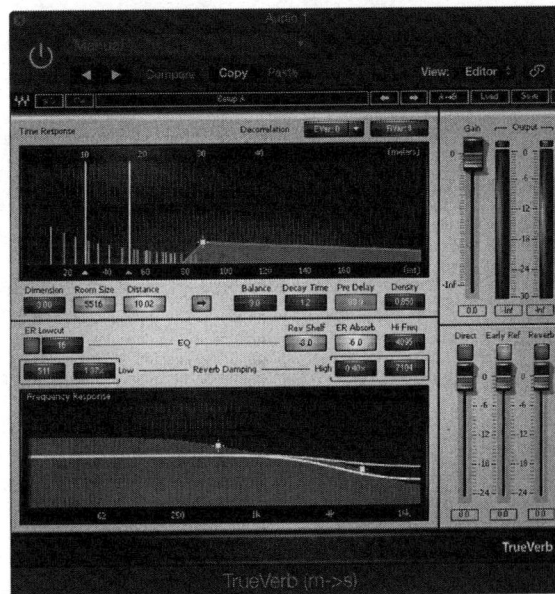

FIGURE 7.7: THE TRUEVERB REVERBERATION PLUG-IN FROM WAVES

often referred to as **algorithmic reverbs**, after their unique mathematical designs.

There is another type of reverb processor called a **convolution reverb**, which creates its effect using an entirely different process. A convolution reverb processor uses an **impulse response** (**IR**) captured from a real acoustic space, such as the one shown in Figure 7.8. An impulse response is essentially the recorded capture of a sudden burst of sound as it occurs in a particular acoustical space. If you were to listen to the IR, which in its raw form is simply an audio file, it would sound like a short "pop" with a somewhat unique timbre and decay tail. The impulse response is applied to an audio signal by a process known as **convolution**, which is where this reverb effect gets its name. Applying convolution reverb as a filter is like passing

ASIDE: Convolution is a mathematical process that operates in the time domain, which means that the input to the operation consists of the amplitudes of the audio signal as they change over time. Convolution in the time domain has the same effect as mathematical filtering in the frequency domain, where the input consists of the magnitudes of frequency components over the frequency range of human hearing. Filtering can be done in either the time domain or the frequency domain, as will be explained in Section 7.3.

the audio signal through a representation of the original room itself. This makes the audio sound as if it were propagating in the same acoustical space as the one in which the impulse response was originally captured, adding its reverberant characteristics.

With convolution reverb processors, you lose the extra control provided by the traditional pre-delay, early reflections, and RT60 parameters, but you often gain a much more natural reverberant effect. Convolution reverb processors are generally

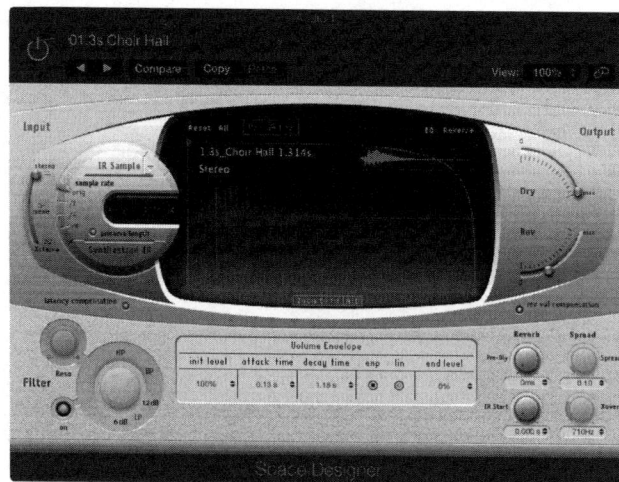

FIGURE 7.8: A CONVOLUTION REVERB PROCESSOR FROM LOGIC

more CPU-intensive than their more traditional counterparts, but with the speed of modern CPUs, this is not a big concern. Figure 7.8 shows an example of a convolution reverb plug-in.

7.1.7 FLANGE

Flange is the effect of combing out frequencies in a continuously changing frequency range. The flange effect is created by adding two identical audio signals, with one slightly delayed relative to the other, usually on the order of milliseconds. The effect involves continuous changes in the amount of delay, causing the combed frequencies to sweep back and forth through the audible spectrum.

In the days of analog equipment like tape decks, flange was created mechanically in the following manner: Two identical copies of an audio signal (usually music) were played, simultaneously and initially in sync, on two separate tape decks. A finger was pressed slightly against the edge (called the *flange*) of one of the tapes, slowing down its rpms. This delay in one of the copies of the identical waveforms being summed resulted in the combing out of a corresponding fundamental frequency and its harmonics. If the pressure increased continuously, the combed frequencies swept continuously through some range. When the finger was removed, the slowed tape would still be playing behind the other. However, pressing a finger against the other tape could sweep backward through the same range of combed frequencies and finally put the two tapes in sync again.

Artificial flange can be created through mathematical manipulation of the digital audio signal. However, to get a classic-sounding flanger, you need to do more than simply delay a copy of the audio. This is because tape decks used in analog flanging had inherent variability that caused additional phase shifts and frequency combing, and thus they created a more complex sound. This fact hasn't stopped clever software developers, however. The flange processor shown in Figure 7.9 from Waves is one that includes a tape emulation mode and includes presets that emulate several kinds of vintage tape decks and other analog equipment.

FIGURE 7.9: A DIGITAL FLANGE PROCESSOR

7.1.8 VOCODERS

A **vocoder** (voice encoder) is a device that was originally developed for low-bandwidth transmission of voice messages, but is now used for special voice effects in music production.

The original idea behind the vocoder was to encode the essence of the human voice by extracting just the most basic elements—the consonant sounds made by the vocal cords and the vowel sounds made by the modulating effect of the mouth. The consonants serve as the carrier signal and the vowels (also called *formants*) serve as the modulator signal. By focusing on the most important elements of speech necessary for understanding, the early vocoder encoded speech efficiently, yielding a low bandwidth for transmission. The resulting voice heard at the other end of the transmission didn't have the complex frequency components of a real human voice, but enough information was there for the words to be intelligible.

Today's vocoders, used in popular music, combine voice and instruments to make the instrument sound as if it's speaking, or conversely, to make a voice have a robotic or "techno" sound. The concept is still the same, however. Harmonically-rich instrumental music serves as the carrier, and a singer's voice serves as the modulator. An example of a software vocoder plug-in is shown in Figure 7.10.

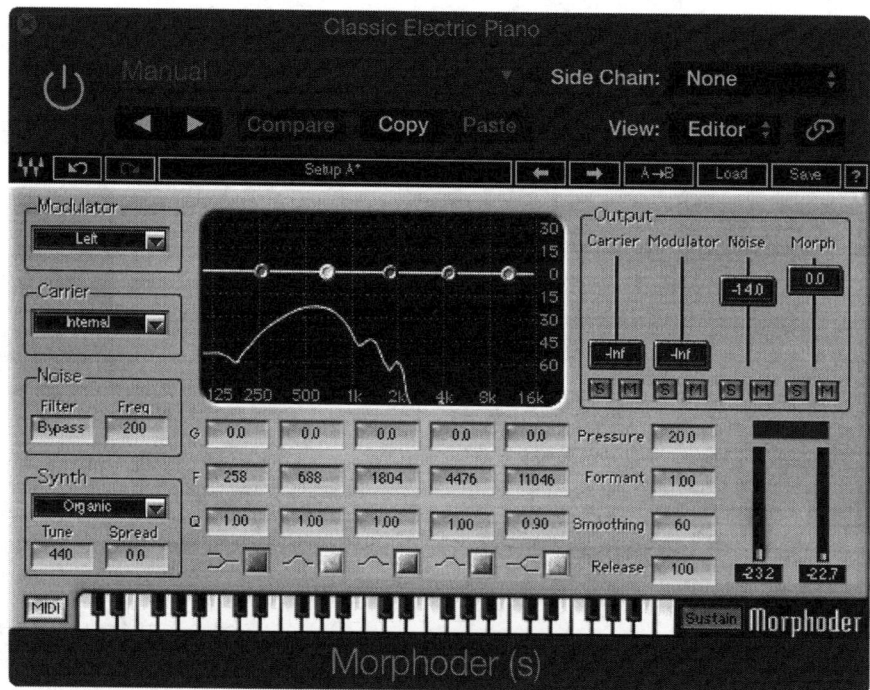

FIGURE 7.10: A VOCODER PROCESSOR

7.1.9 AUTOTUNERS

An **autotuner** is a software or hardware processor that is able to move a pitch of the human
voice to the frequency of the nearest desired
semitone. The original idea was that if the singer was slightly off-pitch, the autotuner could
correct the pitch. For example, if the singer was
supposed to be on the note A at a frequency of
440 Hz and she was actually singing the note
at 435 Hz, the autotuner would detect the dis-
crepancy and make the correction.

ASIDE: Autotuners have also been
used in popular music as an effect rather than a pitch correction. Snapping
a pitch to set semitones can create a
robotic or artificial sound that adds a
new complexion to a song. Cher used
this effect in her 1998 *Believe* album. In
the 2000s, T-Pain further popularized
its use in R&B and rap music.

If you think about how an autotuner might
be implemented, you'll realize the complexities
involved. Suppose you record a singer singing
just the note A, which she holds for a few seconds. Even if she does this nearly perfectly, her voice contains not just the note A, but also harmonic overtones that are positive integer multiples of the fundamental frequency. Your algorithm for the software
autotuner first must detect the fundamental frequency—call it f—from among all the
harmonics in the singer's voice. It then must determine the actual semitone nearest to
f. Finally, it has to move f and all of its harmonics by the appropriate adjustment. All
of this sounds possible when a single clear note is steady and sustained long enough for
your algorithm to analyze it. But what if your algorithm has to deal with a constantly-
changing audio signal, which is the nature of music? Also, consider the dynamic pitch
modulation inherent in a singer's vibrato, a commonly used vocal technique. Detect-
ing individual notes, separating them one from the next, and snapping each note sung
and all its harmonics to appropriate semitones is no trivial task. An example of an
autotune processor is shown in Figure 7.11.

7.1.10 DYNAMICS PROCESSING

7.1.10.1 Amplitude Adjustment and Normalization

One of the most straightforward types of audio processing is amplitude adjustment—
something as simple as turning up or down a volume control. In the analog world, a
change of volume is achieved by changing the voltage of the audio signal. In the digital
world, it's achieved by adding to or subtracting from the sample values in the audio
stream—just simple arithmetic.

An important form of amplitude processing is **normalization**, which entails increasing the amplitude of the entire signal by a uniform proportion (Figure 7.12).

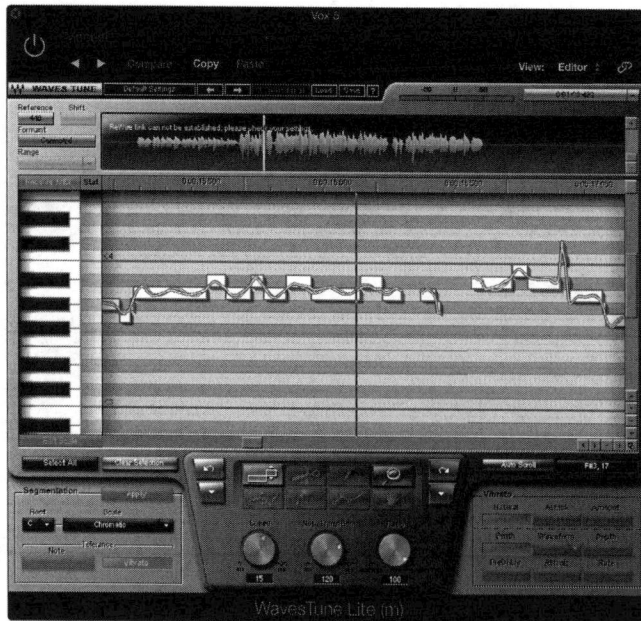

FIGURE 7.11: AN AUTOTUNE PROCESSOR

Normalizers achieve this by allowing you to specify the maximum level you want for the signal, in percentages or dB, and increasing each sample's amplitude by an identical proportion so that the loudest existing sample is adjusted up or down to the desired level. This is helpful in maximizing the use of available bits in your audio signal, as well as matching amplitude levels across different sounds. Keep in mind that this will increase the level of everything in your audio signal, including the noise floor.

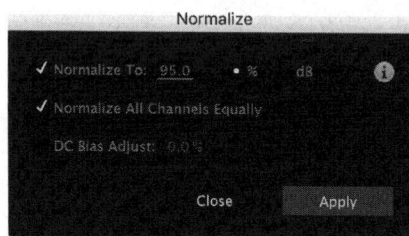

FIGURE 7.12: NORMALIZER FROM ADOBE AUDITION

7.1.10.2 Dynamics Compression and Expansion

Dynamics processing refers to any kind of processing that alters the dynamic range of an audio signal, whether by compressing or expanding it. As explained in Chapter 5, the dynamic range is a measurement of the perceived difference between the loudest and quietest parts of an audio signal. In the case of an audio signal digitized in n bits per sample, the maximum possible dynamic range is computed as the logarithm of the ratio between the loudest and the quietest measurable samples—that is, $20\log_{10}(2^{n-1}/(1/2))$. We saw in Chapter 5 that we can estimate the dynamic range as $6n$ dB. For example, the maximum possible dynamic range of a 16-bit audio signal is about 96 dB, while that of an 8-bit audio signal is about 48 dB.

MAX DEMO: Compression http://bit.ly/29uxEw5

The value of $20\log_{10}(2^{n-1}/(1/2))$ dB gives you an upper limit on the dynamic range of a digital audio signal, but a particular signal may not occupy that full range. You might have a signal that doesn't have much difference between the loudest and quietest parts, like a conversation between two people speaking at about the same level. On the other hand, you might have at a recording of a Rachmaninoff symphony with a very wide dynamic range. Or you might be preparing a background sound ambience for a live production. In the final analysis, you may find that you want to alter the dynamic range to better fit the purposes of the recording or live performance. For example, if you want the sound to be less obtrusive, you may want to compress the dynamic range so that there isn't such a jarring effect from a sudden difference between a quiet and a loud part.

In dynamics processing, the two general possibilities are compression and expansion, each of which can be done in the upward or downward direction (Figure 7.13). Generally, compression attenuates the higher amplitudes and boosts the lower ones, the result of which is less difference in level between the loud and quiet parts, reducing the dynamic range. Expansion generally boosts the high amplitudes and attenuates the lower ones, resulting in an increase in dynamic range. To be precise:

- » **Downward compression** attenuates signals that are above a given threshold, not changing signals below the threshold. This reduces the dynamic range.
- » **Upward expansion** boosts signals that are above a given threshold, not changing signals below the threshold. This increases the dynamic range.
- » **Upward compression** boosts signals that are below a given threshold, not changing signals above the threshold. This reduces the dynamic range.
- » **Downward expansion** attenuates signals that are below a given threshold, not changing signals above the threshold. This increases the dynamic range.

The common parameters that can be set in dynamics processing are the threshold, attack time, and release time. The **threshold** is an amplitude limit on the input signal that triggers compression or expansion. (The same threshold triggers the deactivation of compression or expansion when it is passed in the other direction.) The **attack time** is the amount of time allotted for the total amplitude increase or reduction to be achieved after compression or expansion is triggered. The **release time** is the amount

of time allotted for the dynamics processing to be "turned off," reaching a level where a boost or attenuation is no longer being applied to the input signal.

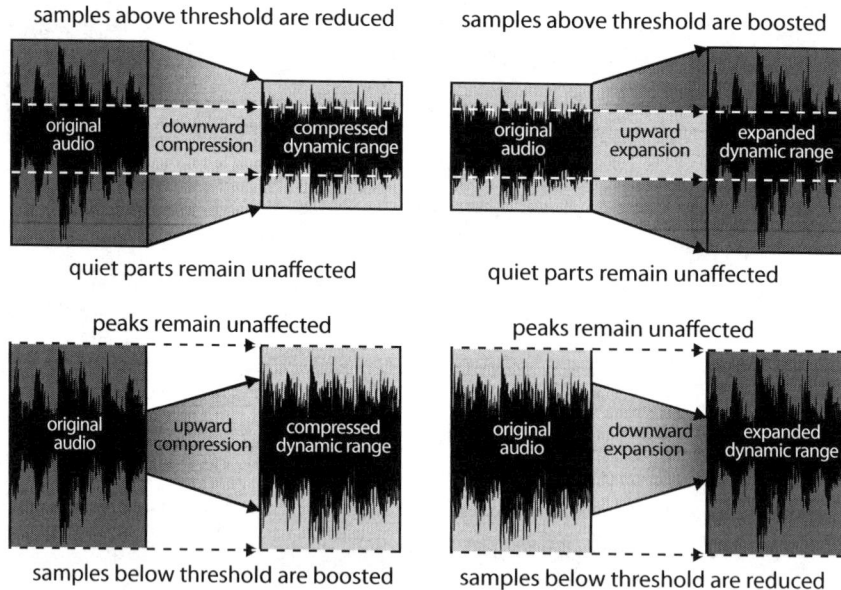

FIGURE 7.13: DYNAMICS COMPRESSION AND EXPANSION

Adobe Audition has a dynamics processor with a large amount of control. The control of most dynamics processors are simpler than this—allowing only compression, for example, with the threshold setting applying only to downward compression. Audition's processor allows settings for compression and expansion and has a graphical view, and thus it's a good one to illustrate all of the dynamics possibilities.

Figure 7.14 shows two views of Audition's dynamics processor, the graphic and the traditional, with settings for downward and upward compression. The two views give the same information but in a different form.

In the graphic view, the unprocessed input signal is on the horizontal axis, and the processed input signal is on the vertical axis. The traditional view shows that anything above –35 dBFS should be compressed at a 2:1 ratio. This means that the level of the signal above –35 dBFS should be reduced by ½ . Notice that in the graphical view, the slope of the portion of the line above an input value of –35 dBFS is ½. This slope gives the same information as the 2:1 setting in the traditional view. On the other hand, the 3:1 ratio associated with the –55 dBFS threshold indicates that for any input signal below –55 dBFS, the difference between the signal and –55 dBFS should be reduced to one-third the original amount. When either threshold is passed (–35 or –55 dBFS), the attack time (given on a separate panel not shown) determines how long the compressor takes to achieve its target attenuation or boost. When the input signal moves back between the values of –35 dBFS and –55 dBFS, the release time determines how long it takes for the processor to stop applying the compression.

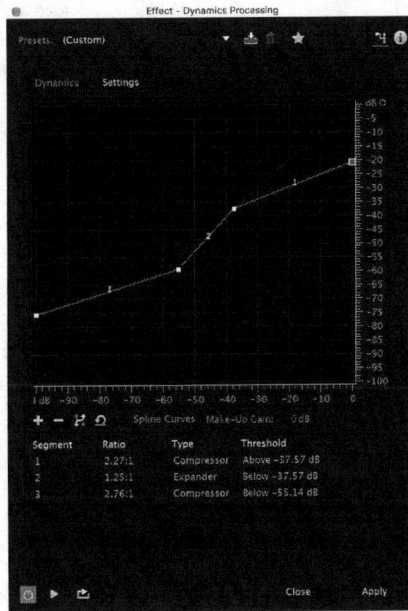

FIGURE 7.14: DYNAMICS PROCESSING IN ADOBE AUDITION, DOWNWARD AND UPWARD COMPRESSION

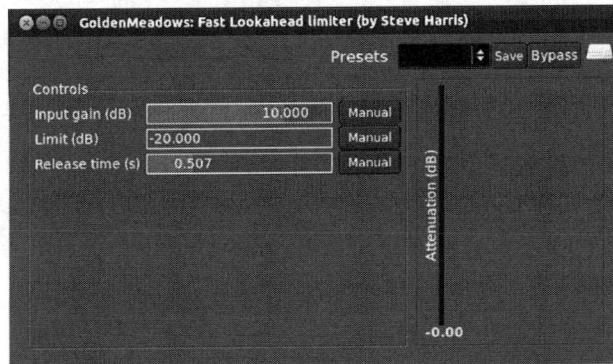

FIGURE 7.15: SC1 COMPRESSOR PLUG-IN FOR ARDOUR

A simpler compressor, one of the Ardour LADSPA plug-ins, is shown in Figure 7.15. In addition to attack, release, threshold, and ratio controls, this compressor has knee radius and makeup gain settings. The **knee radius** allows you to shape the attack of the compression to something other than linear, giving a potentially smoother transition when it kicks in. The **makeup gain** setting (often called simply **gain**) allows you to boost the entire output signal after all other processing has been applied.

7.1.10.3 Limiting and Gating

A **limiter** is a tool that prevents the amplitude of a signal from going over a given level. Limiters are often applied on the master bus, usually post-fader. Figure 7.16 shows the LADSPA Fast Lookahead Limiter plug-in. The input gain control allows you to increase the input signal before it is checked by the limiter. This limiter

> **ASIDE:** A limiter could be thought of as a compressor with a compression ratio of infinity to 1. See the next section on dynamics compression.

looks ahead in the input signal to determine if it is about to go above the limit, in which case the signal is attenuated by the amount necessary to bring it back within the limit. The lookahead allows the attenuation to happen almost instantly, and thus there is no attack time. The release time indicates how long it takes to go back to 0 attenuation when limiting the current signal amplitude is no longer necessary. You can watch this work in realtime by looking at the attenuation slider on the right, which bounces up and down as the limiting is put into effect.

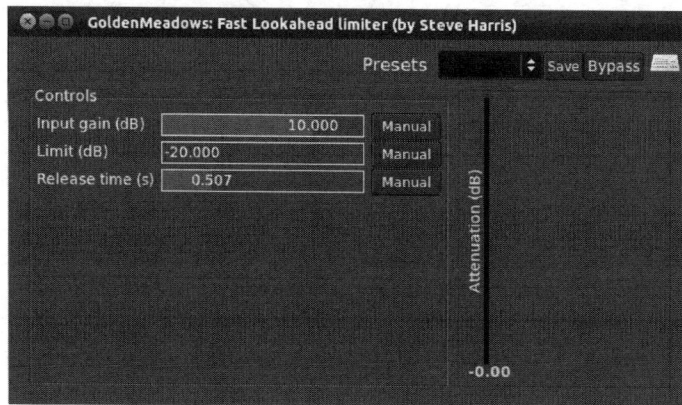

FIGURE 7.16: LADSPA LIMITER PLUG-IN

A **gate** allows an input signal to pass through only if it is above a certain threshold. A **hard gate** has only a threshold setting, typically a level in dB above or below which the effect is engaged. Other gates allow you to set an attack, hold, and release time to affect the opening, holding, and closing of the gate (Figure 7.17). Gates are sometimes used for drums or other instruments to make their attacks appear sharper and reduce the bleed from other instruments unintentionally captured in that audio signal.

A **noise gate** is a specially designed gate that is
intended to reduce the extraneous noise in a signal. If
the noise floor is estimated
to be, say, –80 dBFS, then a
threshold can be set so that
anything quieter than this
level is blocked out, effectively transmitted as silence.

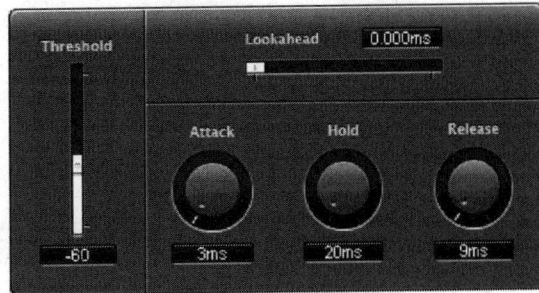

FIGURE 7.17: GATE

A **hysteresis control** on a noise gate indicates that there is a threshold difference between opening and closing the gate. In the noise gate in Figure 7.18, the threshold of
–50 dB and the hysteresis setting of –3 dB indicate that the gate closes at –50 dBFS
and opens again at –47 dBFS. The side chain controls allow some signal other than the
main input signal to determine when the input signal is gated. The side chain signal
could cause the gate to close based on the amplitudes of only the high frequencies
(high cut) or low frequencies (low cut).

In a practical sense, there is no real difference between a gate and a noise gate. A
common misconception is that noise gates can be used to remove noise in a recording. In reality, all they can really do is mute or reduce the level of the noise when only
the noise is present. Once any part of the signal exceeds the gate threshold, the entire
signal is allowed through
the gate, including the
noise. Still, it can be very
effective at clearing up the
audio in between words or
phrases on a vocal track,
or reducing the overall
noise floor when you have
multiple tracks with active
regions but no real signal,
perhaps during an instru-
mental solo.

FIGURE 7.18: NOISE GATE (LOGIC PRO)

7.2 APPLICATIONS

7.2.1 MIXING

7.2.1.1 Mixing Contexts and Devices

A **mixing console**, or **mixer**, is a device that takes several different audio signals and mixes them together, to be sent to another device in a more consolidated or organized manner. Mixing can be done in a variety of contexts. Mixing during a live performance requires that an audio engineer balance the sounds from a number of sources. Mixing is also done in the sound studio, as the recordings from multiple channels or on multiple tracks are combined.

Mixing can also be done with a variety of tools. An audio engineer doing the mixing of a live performance could use a hardware device like the one shown in Figure 7.19, an analog mixing console. Digital mixers have now become more common (Figure 7.20), and as you can see, they look pretty much the same as their analog counterparts. Software mixers, with user interfaces modeled after equivalent hardware, are a standard part of audio processing programs like Pro Tools, Apple Logic, Ableton Live, and Cakewalk Sonar. The mixing view for a software mixer is sometimes called the **console view**, as is the case with Cakewalk Sonar, pictured in Figure 7.21.

ASIDE: The fact that digital consoles often follow analog models of control and layout is somewhat of a hot topic. On one hand, this similarity provides some standardization and ease of transition between the two types of consoles. Yet with all of the innovations in user interface technology, you might wonder why these implementations have remained so "old fashioned." Many people are beginning to use high-tech UI devices like the iPad along with wireless control protocols like OSC to reinvent the way mixing and audio manipulation is done. While it may take some time for these new techniques to emerge and catch on, the possibilities they provide are both fascinating and seemingly limitless.

FIGURE 7.19: AN ANALOG MIXING CONSOLE

FIGURE 7.20: A DIGITAL MIXING CONSOLE

In the following section, we introduce the different components and functions of mixers. Whether a mixer is analog or digital, or hardware or software, is not the point. The controls and functions of mixers are generally the same no matter what type you're dealing with or the context in which you're doing the mixing.

FIGURE 7.21: CONSOLE VIEW (MIXING VIEW) IN CAKEWALK SONAR

7.2.1.2 Inputs and Outputs

The original concept behind a mixer was to take the signals from multiple sources and combine them into a single audio signal that could be sent to a recording device or to an amplification system in a performance space. These so-called "mix down" consoles would have several audio input connections, but very few output connections. With the advent of surround sound, distributed sound reinforcement systems, multitrack recorders, and dedicated in-ear monitors, most modern mixing consoles have just as many, if not more, outputs than inputs, allowing the operator to create many different mixes that are delivered to different destinations.

Consider the situation of a recording session of a small rock band. You could easily have more than twenty-four microphones spread out across the drums, guitars, vocalists, and so on. Each microphone connects to the mixing console on a separate audio input port and is fed into an **input channel** on the mixing console. Each channel has a set of controls that allows you to optimize and adjust the volume level and frequency response of the signal and send that signal to several **output channels** on the mixing console. Each output channel represents a different mix of the signals from the various microphones. The **main mix** output channel likely contains a mix of all the different microphones and is sent to a pair (or more) of monitor loudspeakers in the control room for the recording engineer and other participants to listen to the performance from the band. This main mix may also represent the artistic arrangement of the various inputs, decided upon by the engineer, producer, and band members, eventually intended for mixed-down distribution as a stereo or surround master audio file. Each performer in the band is also often fed a separate **auxiliary output** mix into her headphones. Each auxiliary mix contains a custom blend of the various instruments that each musician needs to hear in order to play her part in time and in tune with the rest of the band. Ideally, the actual recording is not a mix at all. Instead, each input channel has a **direct output** connection that sends the microphone signal into a dedicated channel on a multitrack recording device, which in the digital age is often a dedicated computer DAW. This way the raw, isolated performances are captured in their original state, and the artistic manipulation of the signals can be accomplished incrementally and non-destructively during the mixing process.

7.2.1.3 Channel Strips

Configuring all the knobs, buttons, and faders on a suitably sized mixing console makes all of the above functions possible. When you see a large mixing console like the one pictured in Figure 7.19, you might feel intimidated by all the knobs and buttons. It's important to realize that most of the controls are simply duplicates. Each input channel is represented by a vertical column, or **channel strip**, of controls as shown in Figure 7.22.

MAX
DEMO:
Mixing Consoles
http://bit.ly/29lujy8

It's good to realize that the audio signal typically travels through the channel strip and its various controls from top to bottom. This makes it easy to visualize the audio signal path and understand how and when the audio signal is being affected. For example, you'll usually find the preamp gain control at the top of the channel strip, as this is the first circuit the audio signal encounters, while the level fader at the bottom is the last component the signal hits as it leaves the channel strip to be mixed with the rest of the individual signals.

7.2.1.4 Input Connectors

Each input channel has at least one input connector, as shown in Figure 7.23. Typically this is an XLR connector. Some mixing consoles also have a ¼″ TRS connector on each input channel. The idea for including both is to use the XLR connector for microphone signals and the ¼″ connector for line level or high impedance instrument signals, though you can't use both at the same time. In some cases, both connectors feed into the same input circuitry, allowing you to use the XLR connector for line level signals as well as microphone signals. This is often desirable, and whenever possible you should use the XLR connector rather than the ¼″ because of its benefits such as a locking connection. In some cases, the ¼″ connector feeds into the channel strip on a separate path from the XLR connector, bypassing the microphone preamplifier or encountering a −20 dB attenuation before entering the preamplifier. In this situation, running a line level signal through the XLR connector may result in a clipped signal because there is no gain adjustment to compensate for the increased voltage level of the line level signal. Each mixing console implements these connectors differently, so you'll need to read the manual to find out the specific configuration and input specifications for your mixing console.

7.2.1.5 Gain Section

The gain section of the channel strip includes several controls. The most important is the **gain knob**. Sometimes labeled **trim**, this knob controls the preamplifier for the input channel. The preamplifier is an electrical circuit that can amplify the incoming audio signal to the optimal line level voltage suitable for use within the rest of the console. The preamplifier is often designed for high quality and very low noise, so that it can boost the audio signal without adding a lot of noise or distortion.

FIGURE 7.22: A SINGLE CHANNEL STRIP FROM AN ANALOG MIXING CONSOLE

Because of the sheer number of electrical circuits an audio signal can pass through in a mixing console, the signal can pick up a lot of noise as it travels around in the console. The best way to minimize the effects of this noise is to increase the **signal-to-noise ratio** from the very start. Since the preamplifier is able to increase the level of the incoming audio signal without increasing the noise level in the console, you can use the preamplifier to increase the ratio between the noise floor of the mixing console and the level of your audio signal. Therefore, the goal of the gain knob is to achieve the highest value possible without clipping the signal. (Chapter 8 has more details on gain setting.) The gain section of the channel strip includes several controls as shown in Figure 7.24.

This is the only place in the console (and likely your entire sound system) where you can increase the level of the signal without also increasing the noise. Thus, you should get all the gain you can at this stage. You can always turn the level down later in the signal chain. Don't succumb to the temptation to turn down the mixing console preamplifier as a convenient way to fix problems caused downstream by power amplifiers and loudspeakers that are too powerful or too sensitive for your application. Also, you should not turn down the preamplifier in an effort to get all the channel faders to line up in a straight row. These are excellent ways to create a noisy sound system because you're decreasing the signal-to-noise ratio for the incoming audio signal. Once you've set that gain knob to the highest level you can without clipping the signal, the only reason you should ever touch it again is if the signal coming into the console gets louder and starts clipping the input.

If you're feeding a line level signal into the channel, you might find that you're clipping the signal even though the gain knob is turned all the way down. Most mixing consoles have a **pad** button next to the gain knob. This pad button (sometimes labeled "–20

FIGURE 7.23: INPUT CONNECTORS FOR A SINGLE CHANNEL ON A MIXING CONSOLE

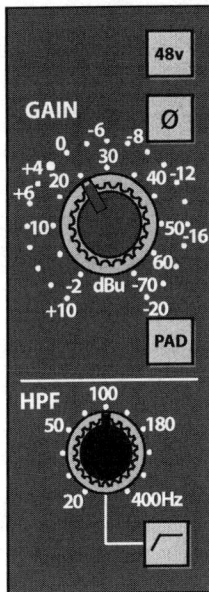

FIGURE 7.24: GAIN SECTION OF AN INPUT CHANNEL STRIP

dB," "Line," "range," or "Mic/Line") attenuates the signal by –20 dB, which should allow you to find a setting on your gain knob that doesn't clip. Using the pad button shouldn't necessarily be something you do automatically when using line level signals, as you're essentially undoing 20 dB of built-in signal-to-noise ratio. Don't use it unless you have to. Be aware that sometimes this button also serves to reroute the input signal using the ¼" input instead of the XLR. On some consoles that have both ¼" and XLR inputs yet don't have a pad button, it's because the –20 dB attenuation is already built into the signal chain of the ¼" input. These are all factors to consider when deciding how to connect your equipment to the mixing console. (A Max demo in Chapter 8 provides more information on gain setting.)

Another button you'll commonly find next to the gain knob is labeled **Ø**. This is probably the most misunderstood button in the world of sound. Unfortunately, the mixing console manufacturers contribute to the confusion by labeling this button with the universal symbol for **phase**. In reality, this button has nothing to do with phase. This is a **polarity button**. Pressing this button simply inverts the polarity of your signal.

The badly-chosen symbol for the polarity button is inherited from the general confusion among sound practitioners about the difference between phase and polarity. It's true that for pure sine waves, a 180-degree phase shift is essentially identical to a polarity inversion. But that's the only case where these two concepts intersect. In the real world of sound, pure sine waves are hardly ever encountered. For complex sounds that you deal with in practice, phase and polarity are fundamentally different. Phase changes in complex sounds are typically the result of an offset in time. The phase changes as a result of timing offsets are not consistent across the frequency spectrum. A shift in time that would create a 180-degree phase offset for a 1 kHz sound would create a 360-degree phase offset for 2 kHz. This inconsistent phase shift across the frequency spectrum for complex sounds is the cause of comb filtering when two identical sounds are mixed together with an offset in time. Given that a mixing console is all about mixing sounds, it is very easy to cause comb filtering when mixing two microphones that are picking up the same sound at two different distances, resulting in a time offset.

If you think the button in question adjusts the phase of your signal (as the symbol on the button suggests), you might come to the conclusion that pressing this button manipulates the timing of your signal and compensates for comb filter problems. Nothing could be further from the truth. In a comb filter situation, pressing the polarity button for one of the two signals in question simply converts all cancelled frequencies into frequencies that reinforce each other. All the frequencies that were reinforcing each other will now cancel out. Once you've pressed this button, you still have a comb filter. It's just an inverted comb filter. When you encounter two channels on your console that cause a comb filter when mixed together, a better strategy is to simply eliminate one of the two signals. After all, if these two signals are identical enough to cause a comb filter, you don't really need both of them in your mix, do you? Simply ducking (lowering) the fader on one of the two channels will solve your comb filter problem much more efficiently, and certainly more so than using the polarity button.

If this button has nothing to do with phase, what reason could you possibly have to push it? There are many situations where you might run into a polarity problem with one of your input signals. The most common is the dreaded "pin 3 hot" problem. In Chapter 1, we talked about the pinout for an XLR connector. We said that pin 2 carries the positive or "hot" signal, and pin 3 carries the negative or "cold" signal. This is a standard from the Audio Engineering Society that was ratified in 1982. Prior to that, each manufacturer did things differently. Some used pin 2 as hot, and some used pin 3 as hot. This isn't really a problem until you start mixing and matching equipment from different manufacturers. Let's assume your microphone uses pin 2 as hot, but your mixing console uses pin 3 as hot. In that situation, the polarity of the signal coming into the mixing console is inverted. Now if you connect another microphone to a second channel on your mixing console and that microphone also uses pin 3 as hot, you have two signals in your mixing console that are running in opposite polarity. In these situations, having a polarity button on each channel strip is an easy way to solve this problem. Despite the "pin 2 hot" standard being now thirty years old, there are still some manufacturers making pin-3-hot equipment.

Even if all your equipment is running pin 2 hot, you could still have a polarity inversion happening in your cables. If one end of your cable is accidentally wired up incorrectly (which happens more often than you might think), you could have a polarity inversion when you use that cable. You could take the time to re-solder that connector (which you should ultimately take care of), but if time is short or the cable is hard to get to, you could simply press the polarity button on the mixing console and instantly solve the problem.

There could be artistic reasons you would want to press the polarity button. Consider the situation where you are trying to capture the sound of a drum. If you put the microphone over the top of the drum, when the drum is hit, the diaphragm of the microphone pulls down towards the drum. When this signal passes through your mixing console on to your loudspeakers, the loudspeaker driver also pulls back away from you. Wouldn't it make more sense for the loudspeaker driver to jump out towards you when the drum is hit? To solve this problem you could go back to the drummer and move the microphone so it sits underneath the drum, or you could save yourself the trip and just press the polarity button. The audible difference here might be subtle, but when you put enough subtle differences together, you can often get a significant difference in audio quality.

Another control commonly found in the gain section is the **phantom power** button. Phantom power is a 48-volt electrical signal that is sent down the shield of the microphone cable to power condenser microphones. In our example, there is a dedicated 48-volt phantom power button for each input channel strip. In some consoles, there's a global phantom power button that turns on phantom power for all inputs.

The last control that is commonly found in the gain section of the console is a high-pass filter. Pressing this button filters out frequencies below the cutoff frequency for the filter. Sometimes this button has a fixed cutoff frequency of 80 Hz, 100 Hz, or 125 Hz. Some mixing consoles give you a knob along with the button that allows you to set a custom cutoff frequency for the high-pass filter. When working with microphones, it's very easy to pick up unwanted sounds that have nothing to do with the sound you're trying to capture. Footsteps, pops, wind, and handling noise from people touching and moving the microphone are all examples of unwanted sounds that can show up in your microphone. The majority of these sounds fall in very low frequencies. Most musical instruments and voices do not generate frequencies below 125 Hz, so you can safely use a high-pass to filter out frequencies lower than that. Engaging this filter removes most of these unwanted sounds before they enter the signal chain in your system without affecting the good sounds you're trying to capture. Still, all filters have an effect on the phase of the frequencies surrounding the cutoff frequency, and they can introduce a small amount of additional noise into the signal. For this reason, you should leave the high-pass filter disengaged unless you need it.

7.2.1.6 Insert

Next to the channel input connectors there is typically a set of **insert** connections. Insert connections consist of an output and input that allow you to connect some kind of external processing device in line with the signal chain in the channel strip. The insert output takes the audio signal from the channel directly after it exits the preamplifier, though some consoles let you choose at what point in the signal path the insert path lies. Thinking back to the top-down signal flow, the insert connections are essentially "inserting" an extra component at that point on the channel strip. In this case, the component isn't built into the channel strip like the EQ or pan controls. Rather, the device is external and can be whatever the engineer wishes to use. If, for example, you want to compress the dynamics of the audio on input channel 1, you can connect the insert output from channel 1 to the input of an external compressor. Then the output of the compressor can be connected to the insert input on channel 1 of the mixing console. The compressed signal is then fed back into the channel strip and continues down the rest of the signal chain for channel 1. If nothing is connected to the insert ports, they are bypassed and the signal is fed directly through the internal signal chain for that input channel. When you connect a cable to the insert output, the signal is almost always automatically rerouted away from the channel strip. You'll need to feed something back into the insert input in order to continue using that channel strip on the mixing console.

There are two different connection designs for inserts on a mixing console. The ideal design is to have a separate ¼" or XLR connection for both the insert output and input. This allows you to use standard patch cables to connect the external processing equipment, and may also employ a balanced audio signal. If the company making the mixing console needs to save space or cut down on the cost of the console, they might decide to integrate both the insert output and input on a single ¼" TRS connector. In this case, the input and output are handled as unbalanced signals using the tip for one signal, the ring for the other signal, and a shared neutral on the sleeve. There is no standard for whether the input or output is carried on the tip vs. the ring. To use this kind of insert requires a special cable with three connectors. On one end is a ¼" TRS connector. This connector has two cables coming out of the end. One cable feeds an XLR male or a ¼" TS connector for the insert output, and an XLR female or a ¼" TS connector for the insert input.

7.2.1.7 Equalizer Section

After the gain section of the channel strip, the next section your audio signal encounters is the **equalizer section (EQ)**, as shown in Figure 7.25. The number of controls you see in this section of the channel strip varies greatly across the various models of mixing consoles. Very basic consoles may not include an EQ section at all. Generally speaking, the more money you pay for the console, the more knobs and buttons you find in the EQ section. We discussed the equalization process in depth in Chapter 7.

Even the simplest of mixing consoles typically has two channels of EQ in each channel strip. These are usually a high-shelf and a low-shelf filter. These simple EQ sections consist of two knobs. One controls the gain for the high-shelf, and the other for the low-shelf. The shelving frequency is a fixed value. If you pay a little more for your mixing console, you can get a third filter—a mid-frequency peak-notch filter. Again, the single knob is a gain knob with a fixed center frequency and bandwidth.

The next controllable parameter you'll get with a nicer console is a frequency knob. Sometimes only the mid-frequency notch filter gets the extra variable

FIGURE 7.25: EQ SECTION OF AN INPUT CHANNEL STRIP

center frequency knob, but the high- and low-shelf filters may get a variable filter frequency using a second knob as well. With this additional control, you now have a semi-parametric filter. If you are given a third knob to control the filter **Q** or **bandwidth**, the filter becomes fully parametric. From there you simply get more bands of fully parametric filters per channel strip as the cost of the console increases.

Depending on your needs, you may not require five bands of EQ per channel strip. The option that is absolutely worth paying for is an EQ bypass button. This button routes the audio signal in the channel around the EQ circuit. This way, the audio signal doesn't have to be processed by the EQ if you don't need any adjustments to the frequency response of the signal.

Routing around the EQ solves two potential problems. The first is the problem of inheriting someone else's solution. There are a lot of knobs on a mixing console, and they aren't always reset when you start working on a new project. If the EQ settings from a previous project are still dialed in, you could be inheriting a frequency adjustment that's not appropriate for your project. Having an EQ bypass button is a quick way to turn off all the EQ circuits so you're starting with a clean slate. The bypass button can also help you quickly do an A/B comparison without having to readjust all of the filter controls. The second problem is related to noise floor. Even if you have all the EQ gain knobs flattened out (no boost or cut), your signal is still passing though all those circuits and potentially collecting some noise along the way. Bypassing the EQ allows you to avoid that unnecessary noise.

7.2.1.8 Auxiliaries

The **Auxiliary** controls in the channel strip are shown in Figure 7.26. Each auxiliary send knob represents an additional physical audio path/output on the mixing console. As you increase the value of an auxiliary send knob, you're setting a certain level of that channel's signal to be sent into that auxiliary bus. As each channel is added into the bus to some degree, a mix of those sounds is created and sent to a physical audio output connected to that bus. You can liken the function of the auxiliary busses to an actual bus transportation system. Each bus, or bus line, travels to a unique destination, and the send knob controls how much of that signal is getting on the bus to go there. In most cases, the mixing console will also have a master volume control to further adjust the combined signal for each auxiliary output. This master control can be a fader or a knob, and is usually located in the central control section of the mixing console.

An auxiliary control is used whenever you need to send a unique mix of the various audio signals in the console to a specific device or person. For example, when you record a band, the lead singer wears headphones to hear the rest of the band as well as her own voice. Perhaps the guitar is the most important instrument for the singer to hear because the guitar contains the information about the right pitch the singer needs to use with her voice. In this situation, you would connect her headphones to a cable that is fed from an auxiliary output, which we'll call "Aux 1," on the mixing console. You might dial in a bit of sound to Aux 1 across each input channel of the mixing console, but on the channels containing the guitar and the singer's own vocals, the Aux 1 controls would be set to a higher value so they're louder in the mix being sent to the singer's headphones.

The auxiliary send knobs on an input channel strip come in two configurations. **Pre-fader** aux sends a signal level into the aux bus independent of the position of the channel fader. In our example of the singer in the band, a pre-fade aux would be desirable because once you've dialed in an aux mix that works for the singer, you don't want that mix changing every time you adjust the channel fader. When you adjust the channel fader, it's in response to the main mix that is heard in the control room, which has no bearing on what the singer needs to hear.

The other configuration for an aux send is **post-fader**. In this case, dialing in the level on the aux send knob represents a level relative to the fader position for that input channel. So when the main mix is changed via the fader, the level in that aux send is changed as well. This is particularly useful

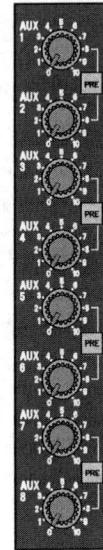

FIGURE 7.26: AUXILIARY SECTION
OF INPUT CHANNEL STRIP

when you're using an aux bus for some kind of effect processing. In our same recording session example, you might want to add some reverberation to the mix. Instead of inserting a separate reverb processor on each input channel, requiring multiple processors, it's much simpler to connect an aux output on the mixing console to the input of a single reverb processor. The output of the reverb processor then comes back into an unused input channel on the mixing console. This way, you can use the aux sends to dial in the desired amount of reverb for each input channel. The reverb processor then returns a reverberant mix of all of the sounds that get added into the main mix.

Once you get a good balance of reverb dialed in on an aux send for a particular input channel, you don't want that balance to change. If the aux send to the reverb is pre-fader, when the fader is used to adjust the channel level within the main mix, the reverb level remains the same, disrupting the balance you achieve. Instead, when you turn up or down the channel fader, the level of the reverb should also increase or decrease respectively so the balance between the dry and the reverberant (wet) sound stays consistent. Using a post-fader aux send accomplishes this goal.

Some mixing consoles give you a switch to change the behavior of an aux bus between pre-fader and post-fader, while in other consoles this behavior may be fixed. Sometimes this switch is located next to the aux master volume control and changes the pre-fader or post-fader mode for all of the channel aux sends that feed into that bus. More expensive consoles allow you to select pre- or post-fader behavior in a channel-specific way. In other words, each individual aux send dial on an input channel strip has its own pre- or post-fade button. With this flexibility, Aux 1 can be set as a pre-fade aux for input channel 1 and a post-fade aux for input channel 2.

7.2.1.9 Fader and Routing Section

The fader and routing section shown in Figure 7.27 is where you usually spend most of your time working with the console in an iterative fashion during the artistic process of mixing. The fader is a vertical slider control that adjusts the level of the audio signal sent to the various mixes you've routed on that channel. There are two common fader lengths: 60 mm and 100 mm. The 100 mm faders give your fingers greater range and control and are easier to work with. The fader is primarily an attenuator. It reduces the level of the signal on the channel. Once you've set the optimal level for the incoming signal with the preamplifier, you use the fader to reduce that level to something that fits well in the mix with the other sounds. The fader is a very low-noise circuit, so you can really set it to any level without having adverse effects on signal-to-noise ratio. One way to think about it is that the preamplifier is where the science happens; the fader is where the art happens. The fader can reduce the signal level all the way to nothing ($-\infty$ or $-$inf), but typically has only five to ten dB on the amplification end of the level adjustment scale. When the fader is set to 0 dB, also referred to as *unity*, the audio signal passes through with no change in level. You should set the fader level to whatever sounds best, and don't be afraid to move it around as the levels change over time.

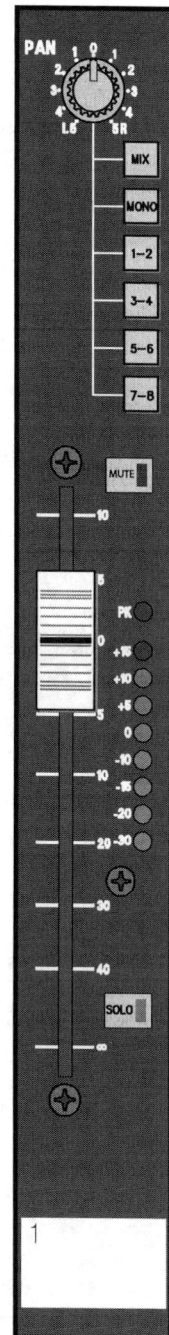

FIGURE 7.27: FADER AND ROUTING SECTION OF AN INPUT CHANNEL STRIP

Near the fader there is usually a set of signal routing buttons. These buttons route the audio signal at a fixed level relative to the fader position to various output channels on the mixing console. There is almost always a main left and right stereo output (labeled "MIX" in Figure 7.27), and sometimes a mono or center output. Additionally, you may also be able to route the signal to one or more group outputs or subgroup mixes. A **subgroup** (sometimes, as with auxiliaries, also called a **bus**) represents a mixing channel where input signals can be grouped together under a master volume control before being passed on to the main stereo or mono output, as shown in Figure 7.28. An example of subgroup routing would be to route all the drum microphones to a subgroup so you can mix the overall level of the drums in the main mix using only one fader. A **group** is essentially the same thing, except it also has a dedicated physical output channel on the mixing console. The terms **bus**, **group**, and **subgroup** are often used interchangeably. Group busses are almost always post-fader, and unlike auxiliary busses don't have variable sends—it's all or nothing. Group routing buttons are often linked in stereo pairs, where you can use the pan knob to pan the signal between the paired groups, in addition to panning between the main stereo left and right bus.

FIGURE 7.28: MASTER CONTROL SECTION OF AN ANALOG MIXING CONSOLE

Also near the fader you usually have a **mute button**. The mute button mimics the behavior of pulling the input fader all the way down. In this case, pre-fade auxiliaries would continue to function. The mute button comes in handy when you want to stop hearing a particular signal in the main mix, but you don't want to lose the level you have set on the fader or lose any auxiliary functionality, like a signal being sent to a headphone or monitor mix. Instead of a mute button, you may see an on/off button. This button shuts down the entire channel strip. In that situation, all signals stop on the channel, including groups, auxiliaries, and direct outs. Just to confuse you, manufacturers may use the terms **mute** and **on/off** interchangeably, so in some cases a mute button may behave like an on/off button and vice versa. Check the user manual for the mixing console to find out the exact function of your button.

Next to the fader there is typically a **pre-fade listen** (**PFL**) or a **solo** button. Pressing the PFL button routes the signal in that channel strip to a set of headphones or studio monitor outputs. Since it is pre-fade, you can hear the signal in your headphones even if the fader is down or the mute button is pressed. This is useful when you want to preview the sound on that channel before you allow it to be heard via your main or group outputs. If you have a solo button, when pressed it will also mute all the other channels, allowing you to hear only the solo-enabled channels. Solo is found in recording studio consoles or audio recording software. Sometimes the terms *PFL* and *solo* are used interchangeably, so again, check the user manual for your mixing console to be sure of the function for this button.

Similar to PFL is **after-fade listen** (**AFL**). AFL is found on output faders, allowing you to preview in your headphones the signal that is passing through a subgroup, group, aux, or main output. The after-fade feature is important because it allows you to hear exactly what is passing through the output, including the level of the fader. For example, if a musician says that he can't hear a given instrument in his monitor, you can use the AFL feature for the aux that feeds that monitor to see if the instrument can be heard. If you can hear it in your headphones, then you know that the aux is functioning properly. In this case, you may need to adjust the mix in that aux to allow the desired instrument to be heard more easily. If you can't hear the desired instrument in your headphones, then you know that you have a routing problem in the mixing console that's preventing the signal from sending out from that aux output.

Depending on the type of mixing console you're using, you may also have some sort of **PPM (Peak Program Meter)** near the fader. In some cases, this will be at the top of the console on a meter bridge. Cheaper consoles will just give you two LED indicators, one for when an audio signal is present and another for when the signal clips. More expensive consoles will give you high-resolution PPMs with several different level indicators. A PPM is more commonly found in digital systems, but it is also used in analog equipment. A PPM is typically a long column of several LED indicators in three different colors, as shown in Figure 7.29. The green area represents signal levels below the nominal operating level, the yellow area represents signals at or above nominal level, and the red area represents a signal that is clipping or very near to clipping. A PPM is very useful for measuring peak values in an audio signal because it responds very quickly to the audio signal. If you're trying to find the right position for a preamplifier, a PPM will show you exactly when the signal clips. Most meters in audio software are programmed to behave like a PPM.

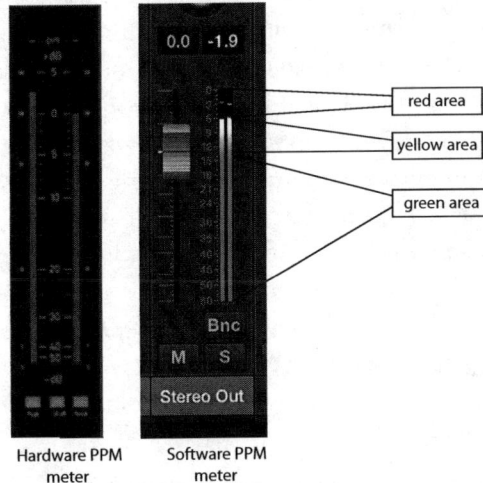

Hardware PPM meter   Software PPM meter

FIGURE 7.29: PPM METERS

7.2.2 APPLYING EQ

An equalizer can be incredibly useful when used appropriately, and incredibly danger-ous when used inappropriately. Knowing when to use an EQ is just as important as knowing how to use it to accomplish the effect you are look-ing for. Every time you think you want to use an EQ you should evaluate the situation against this rule of thumb: EQ should be used to create an effect, not to solve a problem. Using an EQ as a problem solver can cause new problems when you should really just figure out what's causing the original problem and fix that instead. Only if the problem can't be solved in any other way should you pull up the EQ—for example, if you're working post-production on a recording captured earlier during a film shoot, or you've run into an acoustical issue in a space that can't be treated or physically modified. Rather than solving problems, you should try to use an EQ as a tool to achieve a certain kind of sound. Do you like your

MAX DEMO:
Equalization
http://bit.ly/29jQ43c

music to be heavy on the bass? An EQ can help you achieve this. Do you really like to hear the shimmer of the cymbals in a drum set? An EQ can help.

Let's examine some common problems you may encounter where you might be tempted to use an EQ inappropriately. As you listen to the recording you're making of a singer, you notice that the recorded audio has a lot more low frequency than high frequency content, leading to a decreased intelligibility. You go over and stand next to the performer to hear what he actually sounds like, and notice that he sounds quite different than what you're hearing from the microphone. Standing next to him, you can hear all those high frequencies quite well. In this situation you may be tempted to pull out your EQ and insert a high-shelf filter to boost all those high frequencies. This should be your last resort. Instead, you might notice that the singer is singing into the side of the microphone instead of the front. Because microphones are more directional at high frequencies than low frequencies, singing into the side of the microphone would mean that the microphone picks up the low frequency content very easily but the high frequencies are not being captured very well. In this case you would be using an EQ to boost something that isn't being picked up very well in the first place. You will get much better results by simply rotating the microphone so it is pointed directly at the singer so the singer is singing into the part of the microphone that is more sensitive to high frequencies.

Another situation you may encounter would be when mixing the sound from multiple microphones either for a live performance or a recording. You notice as you start mixing everything together that a certain instrument has a huge dip at around 250 Hz. You might be tempted to use an EQ to increase 250 Hz. The important thing to keep in mind here is that most microphones are able to pick up 250 Hz quite well from every direction, and it is unlikely that the instrument itself is somehow not generating the frequencies in the 250 Hz range while still generating all the other frequencies reasonably well. So before you turn on that EQ, you should mute all the other channels on the mixer and listen to the instrument alone. If the problem goes away, you know that whatever is causing the problem has nothing to do with EQ. In this situation, comb filtering is the likely culprit. There's another microphone in your mix that was nearby and happened to be picking up this same instrument at a slightly longer distance of about two feet. When you mix these two microphones together, 250 Hz is one of the frequencies that cancels out. If comb filtering is the issue, you should try to better isolate the signals either by moving the microphones farther apart or by preventing them from being summed together in the mix. A gate might come in handy here, too. If you gate both signals you can minimize the times when both microphones are mixed together, since the signals won't be let through when the instruments they are being used for aren't actually playing.

If comb filtering isn't the issue, try moving a foot or two closer to or farther away from the loudspeakers. If the 250 Hz dip goes away in this case, there's likely a standing wave resonance in your studio at the mix position that is cancelling out this frequency. Using an EQ in this case will not solve the problem since you're trying to boost something that is actively being cancelled out. A better solution for the standing wave would be to consider rearranging your room or applying acoustical treatment to the offending surfaces that are causing this reflective buildup.

Suppose you are operating a sound reinforcement system for a live performance and you start getting feedback through the sound system. When you hear that single frequency start its endless loop through the system, you might be tempted to use an EQ to pull that frequency out of the mix. This will certainly stop the feedback, but all you really get is the ability to turn the system up another decibel or so before another frequency will inevitably start to feed back. Repeat the process a few times and in no time at all you will have completely obliterated the frequency response of your sound system. You won't have feedback, but the entire system will sound horrible. A better strategy for solving this problem would be to get the microphone closer to the performer and move the performer and the microphone farther away from the loudspeakers. You'll get more gain this way, and you can maintain the frequency response of your system. (Chapter 4 has more on potential acoustic gain. Chapter 8 has an exercise on gain setting.)

We could examine many more examples of an inappropriate use of an EQ, but they all go back to the rule of thumb regarding the use of an EQ as a problem solver. In most cases, an EQ is a very ineffective problem solver. It is, however, a very effective tool for shaping the tonal quality of a sound. This is an artistic effect that has little to do with problems of a given sound recording or reinforcement system. Instead you are using the EQ to satisfy a certain tonal preference for the listener. These effects could be as subtle as reducing an octave band of frequencies around 500 Hz by –3 dB to achieve more intelligibility for the human voice by allowing the higher frequencies to be more prominent. The effect could be as dramatic as using a bandpass filter to mimic the effect of a small, cheap loudspeaker in a speakerphone. When using an EQ as an effect, keep in mind another rule of thumb. When using an EQ, you should reduce the frequencies that are too loud instead of increasing the frequencies that are too quiet. Every sound system, whether in a recording studio or a live performance, has an amplitude ceiling—the point at which the system clips and distorts. If you've done your job right, you will be running the sound system at an optimal gain, and a 3 dB boost of a given frequency on an EQ could be enough to cause a clipped signal. Reducing frequencies is always safer than boosting them, since reducing them will not blow the gain structure in your signal path.

7.2.3   APPLYING REVERB

Almost every audio project you do will likely benefit from some reverb processing. In a practical sense, most of the isolation strategies we use when recording sounds will have a side effect of stripping the sound of natural reverberation. So anything recorded in a controlled environment such as a recording studio will probably need some reverb added to make it sound more natural. There are varying opinions on this among audio professionals. Some argue that artificial reverberation processers sound quite good now, and since it is impossible to remove natural reverberation from a recording, it makes more sense to capture your recorded audio as dry as possible. This way, you're able to artificially add back whatever reverberation you need in a way that you can control. Others argue that having musicians perform in an acoustically dry and isolated environment will negatively impact the quality of their performance. Think about how much more confident you feel when singing in the shower. The tiled surfaces in the shower create a natural reverberation that makes your voice sound better to you than normal. That gives you the confidence to sing in a way that you probably don't in public.

> **ASIDE:** In an attempt to reconcile these two schools of thought on reverberation in the recording studio, some have resorted to installing active acoustic systems in the recording studio. These systems involve placing microphones throughout the room that feed into live digital signal processors that generate thousands of delayed sounds that are then sent into several loudspeakers throughout the room. This creates a natural-sounding artificial reverb that is captured in the recording the same as natural reverb. The advantage here is that you can change the reverb by adjusting the parameters of the DSP for different recording situations. To hear an example of this kind of system in action, see the video at http://tinyurl.com/grsv645 from TRI Studios, where Bob Weir from the Grateful Dead has installed an active acoustic system in his recording studio.

So some recording engineers would prefer to have some natural reverberation in the recording room to help the musicians to deliver a better performance. If that natural reverberation is acoustically well controlled, you could even end up with a recording that sounds pretty good already and might require minimal additional processing.

Regardless of the amount of reverb you already have in your recording, you will likely still want to add some artificial reverb to the mix. There are three places you can apply the reverb in your signal chain. You can set it up as an insert for a specific channel in a multi-channel mix. In this case the reverb only gets applied to the one specific channel, and the other channels are left unchanged. You have to adjust the wet/dry mix in the reverb processor to create an appropriate balance. This technique can be useful for a special effect you want to put on a specific sound, but using this technique on every channel in a large, multi-channel mix costs you a lot in CPU performance because of the multiple reverb processors that are running simultaneously. If you have a different reverb setting on each channel, you could also have a rather confusing mix since every sound will seem to be in a different acoustic environment. Maybe that's what you want if you're creating a dream sequence or something abstract for a play or film, but for a music recording it usually makes more sense to have every instrument sound like it is in the same room.

The second reverb technique can solve both the problem of CPU performance and varying acoustic signatures. In this case you would set up a mix bus that has a reverb inserted. You would set the reverb processor to 100% wet. This basically becomes the sound of your virtual room. Then you can set up each individual channel in your mix to have a variable aux send that dials in a certain amount of the signal into the reverb bus. In other words, the individual sends decide how much that instrument interacts with your virtual room. The individual channel will deliver the dry sound to the mix, and the reverb bus will deliver the wet. The amount of sound that is sent on the variable aux send determines the balance of wet to dry. This strategy allows you to send many different signals into the reverb processor at different levels, and therefore to have a separate wet/dry balance for each signal while using only one reverberation processor. The overall wet mix can also be easily adjusted using the fader on the aux reverb bus channel. This technique is illustrated in Figure 7.30.

The third strategy for applying reverberation is to simply apply a single reverb process to an entire mix output. This technique is usually not preferred because you have no control over the reverb balance between

FIGURE 7.30: ROUTING EACH CHANNEL THROUGH A SINGLE REVERB BUS

the different sounds in the mix. You would use this technique if you don't have access to the raw tracks or if you are trying to apply a special reverb effect to a single audio file. In this case, just pick a reverb setting and adjust the wet/dry mix until you achieve the sound you are looking for.

The most difficult task in using reverb is to find the right balance. It is very easy to overdo the effect. The sound of reverberation is so intoxicating that you have to constantly fight the urge to apply the effect more dramatically. Before you commit to any reverb effect, listen to it through a few different speakers or headphones and in a few different listening environments. A reverb effect that sounds like a good balance in one environment might sound over the top in another. Listen to other mixes of similar music or sound to compare your work with the work of seasoned professionals. Before long you'll develop a sixth sense for the kind of reverb to apply in a given situation.

7.2.4 APPLYING DYNAMICS PROCESSING

When deciding whether to use dynamics processing you should keep in mind that a dynamics processor is simply an automatic volume knob. Any time you find yourself constantly adjusting the level of a sound, you may want to consider using some sort of dynamics processor to handle that for you. Most dynamics processors are in the form of downwards compressors. These compressors work by reducing the level of sounds that are too loud while letting quieter sounds pass without any change in level.

One example compression being helpful is when mixing multiple sounds together from a multitrack recording. The human voice singing with other instruments is usually a much more dynamic sound than the other instruments. Guitars and basses, for example, are not known as particularly dynamic instruments, while a singer is constantly changing volume throughout a song. This is one of the tools a singer uses to produce an interesting performance. When mixing a singer along with the instruments from a band, the band essentially creates a fairly stable noise floor. The word *noise* is not used here in a negative context; rather, it is used to describe a sound that is different from the vocal and has the potential of masking the vocal if there is not enough difference in level between the two. As a rule of thumb, for adequate intelligibility of the human voice, the peaks of the voice signal need to be approximately 25 dB louder than the noise floor, which in this case is the band. It is quite possible for a singer to perform with a 30 dB dynamic range. In other words, the quietest parts of the vocal performance are 30 dB quieter than the loudest parts of the vocal performance.

If the level of the band is more or less static and the voice is moving all around, how are you going to maintain that 25 dB ratio between the peaks of the voice and the level of the band? In this situation, you will never find a single level for the vocal fader that will allow it to be heard and understood consistently throughout the song. You could painstakingly draw in a volume automation curve in your DAW software, or you could use a compressor to do it for you. If you can set the threshold somewhere in the middle of the dynamic range of the vocal signal and use a 2:1 or 4:1 compression ratio, you can easily turn that 30 dB of dynamic range into a 20 dB range or less. Since the compressor is turning down all the loud parts, the compressed signal will sound much quieter than the uncompressed signal, but if you turn the signal up using either the output gain of the compressor or the channel fader, you can bring it back to a better level. With the compressed signal, you can now much more easily find a level for the voice that allows it to sit well in the mix. Depending on how aggressive you are about the compression, you may still need to automate a few volume changes, but the compressor has helped turn a very difficult-to-solve problem into something more manageable.

ASIDE: There is some disagreement among audio professionals about the use of compressors. There are some who consider using a compressor as a form of cheating. Their argument is that no compressor can match the level of artistry that can be accomplished by a skilled mixer with their fingers on the faders. In fact, if you ask some audio mix engineers which compressors they use, they will respond by saying that they have ten compressors and will show them to you by holding up both hands and wiggling their fingers!

Rather than using a compressor to allow a sound to more easily take focus over a background sound, you can also use compression as a tool for getting a sound to sit in the mix in a way that allows other sounds to take focus. This technique is used often in theatre and film for background music and sound effects. The common scenario is when a sound designer or composer tries to put some underscore music or background sounds into a scene for a play or a film and the director inevitably says, "turn it down, it's too loud." You turn it down by 6 dB or so, and the director still thinks it's too loud. By the time you turn it down enough to satisfy the director, you can hardly hear the sound and before long, you'll be told to simply cut it because it isn't contributing to the scene in any meaningful way.

The secret to solving this problem is often compression. When the director says the sound is too loud, what he really means is that the sound is too interesting. More interesting than the actor, in fact, and consequently the audience is more likely to pay attention to the music or the background sound than they are to the actor. One common culprit when a sound is distracting is that it is too dynamic. If the music is constantly jumping up and down in level, it will draw your focus. Using a compressor to make the underscore music or background sounds less dynamic allows them to sit in the mix and enhance the scene without distracting from the performance of the actor.

Compression can be a useful tool, but like any good thing, if it's overused compression can be detrimental to the quality of your sound. Dynamics is one quality of sound and music that makes it exciting, interesting, and evocative. A song with dynamics that have been completely squashed will not be very interesting to listen to, and can cause great fatigue on the ears. Also, if you apply compression inappropriately, it may cause audible artifacts in the sound, where you can hear when the sound is being attenuated and released. This is referred to as *pumping* or *breathing*, and it usually means you've taken the compression too far or in the wrong direction. So you have to be very strategic about the use of compression and go easy on the compression ratio. Often, a mild compression ratio is enough to tame an overly dynamic sound without completely stripping it of all its character.

7.2.5   APPLYING SPECIAL EFFECTS

One of the most common special effects is using delay to create an echo effect. This is used often in popular music. The challenge with a delay effect is to synchronize the timing of the echoes with the beat of the music. If you're using a delay plug-in with a DAW program, the plug-in will try to use the metronome of your project file to create the delay timing. This works if you recorded the music to the system's metronome, but if you just recorded everything freestyle, you have to synchronize the delay manually. Typically this is done with a tap pad. Also called **tap-delay**, this plug-in uses a pad or button that you can tap along with the beat of the music to keep the echoes synchronized. The echoes usually get in sync with the music after eight taps, but as the performance from the musician changes, you need to periodically re-tap the plug-in. Figure 7.31 shows a tap delay processor with the mouse pointer on the tap pad.

FIGURE 7.31: A TAP DELAY PLUG-IN

Other special effects including flangers, pitch shifting/autotune, and so on. may be applied in several different situations. There are really no rules with special effects. Just make sure you have a real reason for using the effect and don't overdo it.

7.3 SCIENCE, MATHEMATICS, AND ALGORITHMS

7.3.1 CONVOLUTION AND TIME-DOMAIN FILTERING

In earlier chapters, we showed how audio signals can be represented in either the time domain or the frequency domain. In this section, you'll see how mathematical operations are applied in these domains to implement filters, delays, reverberation, and so on. Let's start with the time domain.

Filtering in the time domain is done by a convolution operation. Convolution uses a **convolution filter**, which is an array of N values that, when graphed, takes the basic shape shown in Figure 7.32. A convolution filter is also referred to as a **convolution mask**, an **impulse response (IR)**, or a **convolution kernel**. There are two commonly-used time-domain convolution filters that are applied to digital audio. They are **FIR filters (finite impulse response)** and **IIR filters (infinite impulse response)**.

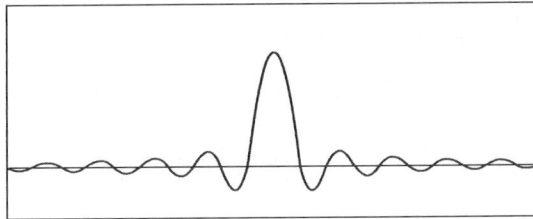

FIGURE 7.32: GRAPH OF TIME-DOMAIN CONVOLUTION FILTER

Equation 7.1 describes FIR filtering mathematically.

$$\boldsymbol{y}(n) = \boldsymbol{h}(n) \otimes \boldsymbol{x}(n) = \sum_{k=0}^{N-1} \boldsymbol{h}(k)\boldsymbol{x}(n-k) = \sum_{k=0}^{N-1} \boldsymbol{a}_k \boldsymbol{x}(n-k)$$

where N is the size of the filter and $x(n-k) = 0$ if $n - k < 0$

EQUATION 7.1: FIR FILTER

By our convention, boldface variables refer to vectors (arrays). In this equation, $\boldsymbol{h} = [a_0,\ a_1, a_2 \ldots, a_{N-1}]$ is the convolution filter, which is a vector of multipliers to be applied successively to audio samples. The number of multipliers is the order of a filter, N in this case. N is sometimes also referred to as the number of **taps** in the filter.

It's helpful to think of Equation 7.1 algorithmically, as described Algorithm 7.1. The notation $y(n)$ indicates that the nth output sample is created from a convolution of input values from the audio signal x and the filter multipliers in h, as given in the summation. The equation is repeated in a loop for every sample in the audio input.

ASIDE: You can actually think of equations such as Equation 7.1 in one of two ways. x and y could be understood as vectors of audio samples in the time domain, x being the input and y being the output. The equation must be executed N times to get each nth output sample. Alternatively, y could be understood as a function with input n. The function is executed N times to yield all N output samples.

```
/*Input:
x, an array of digitized audio samples (i.e., in the time domain) of size M
h, a convolution filter of size N (Specifically, a finite-impulse-
response filter, FIR
Output:
y, the audio samples, filtered
*/

for (n=0 to N-1) {
        y(n) = h(n)⊗x(n) = ∑ᴺ⁻¹ₖ₌₀h(k)x(n-k)
        where x(n-k) = 0 if n-k<0
}
```

ALGORITHM 7.1: CONVOLUTION WITH A FINITE IMPULSE RESPONSE (FIR) FILTER

The FIR convolution process is described diagrammatically in Figure 7.33.

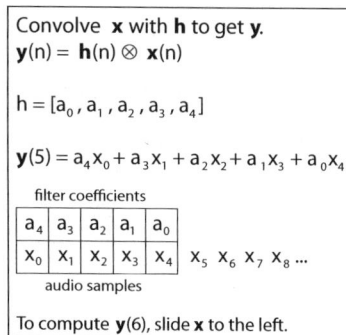

Convolve **x** with **h** to get **y**.
$y(n) = h(n) \otimes x(n)$

$h = [a_0, a_1, a_2, a_3, a_4]$

$y(5) = a_4 x_0 + a_3 x_1 + a_2 x_2 + a_1 x_3 + a_0 x_4$

filter coefficients

a_4	a_3	a_2	a_1	a_0				
x_0	x_1	x_2	x_3	x_4	x_5	x_6	x_7	x_8 ...

audio samples

To compute $y(6)$, slide **x** to the left.

FIGURE 7.33: FILTERING IN THE TIME DOMAIN BY CONVOLVING WITH AN FIR FILTER

You can implement convolution yourself as a function, or you can use MATLAB's *conv* function. The *conv* function requires two arguments. The first is an array containing the coefficients of the filter, and the second is the array of time domain audio samples to be convolved. Say that we have an FIR filter of size 3 defined as:

$$y(n) = 0.4x(n) + 0.3x(n-1) + 0.3x(n-2)$$

EQUATION 7.2: EQUATION FOR AN EXAMPLE FIR FILTER

In MATLAB, the coefficients of the filter can be stored in an array h like this:

```
h = [0.4 0.3 0.3];
```

Then we can read in a sound file and convolve it and listen to the results.

```
x = wavread('ToccataAndFugue.wav');
y = conv(h,x);
sound(y, 44100);
```

(This is just an arbitrary example with a random filter to demonstrate how you convolve in MATLAB. We haven't yet considered how the filter itself is constructed.)

IIR filters are also time domain filters, but the process by which they work is a little different. An IIR filter has an infinite length, given by this equation:

$$\boldsymbol{y}(n) = \boldsymbol{h}(n) \otimes \boldsymbol{x}(n) = \sum_{k=0}^{\infty} \boldsymbol{h}(k)\boldsymbol{x}(n-k)$$

where $x(n-k) = 0$ if $n-k < 0$

and k is theoretically infinite

EQUATION 7.3: IIR FILTER, INFINITE FORM

We can't deal with an infinite summation in practice, but Equation 7.3 can be transformed to a *difference equation* form which gives us something we can work with.

$$\boldsymbol{y}(n) = \boldsymbol{h}(n) \otimes \boldsymbol{x}(n) = \sum_{k=0}^{N-1} \boldsymbol{a}_k \boldsymbol{x}(n-k) - \sum_{k=1}^{M} \boldsymbol{b}_k \boldsymbol{y}(n-k)$$

where N is the size of the forward filter, M is the size of the feedback filter,
and $x(n-k) = 0$ if $n-k < 0$

EQUATION 7.4: IIR FILTER, DIFFERENCE EQUATION FORM

In Equation 7.4, N is the size (also called *order*) of the **forward filter** and M is the size of the **feedback filter**. The output from an IIR filter is determined by convolving the input and combining it with the feedback of previous output. In contrast, the output from an FIR filter is determined solely by convolving the input.

FIR and IIR filters each have their advantages and disadvantages. In general, FIR filters require more memory and processor time. IIR filters can more efficiently create a sharp cutoff between frequencies that are filtered out and those that are not. An FIR filter requires a larger filter size to accomplish the same sharp cutoff as an IIR filter. IIR filters also have the advantage of having analog equivalents, which facilitates their design. An advantage of FIR filters is that they can be constrained to have **linear phase response**, which means that phase shifts for frequency components are proportional to the frequencies. This is good for filtering music because harmonic frequencies are phase-shifted by the same proportions, preserving their harmonic relationship. Another advantage of FIR filters is that they're not as sensitive to the noise that results from low bit depth and round-off error.

The exercise associated with this section shows you how to make a convolution filter by recording an impulse response in an acoustical space. Also, in Section 7.3.9, we'll show a way to apply an IIR filter in MATLAB.

PRACTICAL EXERCISE:
Creating Your Own
Convolution Reverb
http://bit.ly/29wrWXI

7.3.2 LOW-PASS, HIGH-PASS, BANDPASS, AND BANDSTOP FILTERS

You may have noticed that in our discussion of frequency domain and time domain filters, we didn't mention *how* we got the filters—we just *had* them and applied them. In the case of an FIR filter, the filter is represented in the coefficients $[a_0, a_1, a_2, \ldots, a_{N-1}]$. In the case of the IIR filter, the filter resides in coefficients $[a_0, a_1, a_2, \ldots, a_{N-1}]$ and $[b_1, b_2, b_2, \ldots, b_M]$.

Without explaining in detail the mathematics of filter creation, we can show you algorithms for creating low-pass, high-pass, bandpass, and bandstop filters when they are given the appropriate parameters as input. **Low-pass filters** allow only frequencies below a cutoff frequency f_c to pass through. Thus, Algorithm 7.2 takes f_c as input and outputs an N-element array constituting a low-pass filter. Similarly, Algorithm 7.3 takes f_c as input and yields a high-pass filter, and Algorithm 7.4 and Algorithm 7.5 take f_1 and f_2 as input to yield bandpass and bandstop filters. These algorithms yield

MATLAB EXERCISE:
Creating FIR Filters
in MATLAB
http://bit.ly/29ohB0T

C++ PROGRAMMING EXERCISE:
Creating FIR
Filters in C++
http://bit.ly/29onefu

time-domain filters. If you're interested in how these algorithms were derived (see Ifeachor and Jervis 1993, Steiglitz 1996, or Burg 2008.

```
algorithm FIR_low_pass filter
/*
Input:
f_c, the cutoff frequency for the low-pass filter, in Hz
f_samp, sampling frequency of the audio signal to be filtered, in Hz
N, the order of the filter; assume N is odd
Output:
h, a low-pass FIR filter in the form of an N-element array */
{
//Normalize f_c and ω_c so that π is equal to the Nyquist angular frequency
  f_c = f_c/f_samp
  ω_c = 2*π*f_c
  middle = N/2          /*Integer division, dropping remainder*/
  for i = -N/2 to N/2
   if (i == 0) h(middle) = 2*f_c
   else h(i + middle) = sin(ω_c*i)/(π*i)
}
```

ALGORITHM 7.2: LOW-PASS FILTER

```
algorithm FIR_high_pass filter
/*
Input:
f_c, the cutoff frequency for the high pass filter, in Hz
f_samp, sampling frequency of the audio signal to be filtered, in Hz
N, the order of the filter; assume N is odd
Output:
h, a high-pass FIR filter in the form of an N-element array */
{
//Normalize f_c and ω_c so that π is equal to the Nyquist angular frequency
  f_c = f_c/f_samp
  ω_c = 2*π*f_c
  middle = N/2          /*Integer division, dropping remainder*/
  for i = -N/2 to N/2
   if (i == 0)  h(middle) = 1 - 2*f_c
   else h(i + middle) = -sin(ω_c*i)/(π*i)
 }
```

ALGORITHM 7.3: HIGH-PASS FILTER

```
algorithm FIR_bandpass filter
/*
Input:
f1, the lowest frequency to be included, in Hz
f2, the highest frequency to be included, in Hz
f_samp, sampling frequency of the audio signal to be filtered, in Hz
N, the order of the filter; assume N is odd
```

```
Output:
h, a bandpass FIR filter in the form of an N-element array */
{
//Normalize f_c and ω_c so that π is equal to the Nyquist angular frequency
  f1_c = f1/f_samp
  f2_c = f2/f_samp
  ω1_c = 2*π*f1_c
  ω2_c = 2*π*f2_c
  middle = N/2          /*Integer division, dropping remainder*/
  for i = -N/2 to N/2
   if (i == 0) h(middle) = 2*(f2_c - f1_c)
   else
   h(i + middle) = sin(ω2_c*i)/(π*i) - sin(ω1_c*i)/(π*i)
  }
```

ALGORITHM 7.4: BANDPASS FILTER

```
algorithm FIR_bandstop filter
/*
Input:
f1, the highest frequency to be included in the bottom band, in Hz
f2, the lowest frequency to be included in the top band, in Hz
Everything from f1 to f2 will be filtered out
f_samp, sampling frequency of the audio signal to be filtered, in Hz
N, the order of the filter; assume N is odd
Output:
h, a bandstop FIR filter in the form of an N-element array */
{
//Normalize f_c and ω _c so that π is equal to the Nyquist angular fre-
quency
  f1_c = f1/f_samp
  f2_c = f2/f_samp
  ω1_c = 2*π*f1_c
  ω2_c = 2*π*f2_c
  middle = N/2          /*Integer division, dropping remainder*/
  for i = -N/2 to N/2
   if (i == 0) h(middle) = 1 - 2*(f2_c - f1_c)
   else
   h(i + middle) = sin(ω1_c*i)/(π*i) - sin(ω2_c*i)/(π*i)
}
```

ALGORITHM 7.5: BANDSTOP FILTER

As an exercise, you can try implementing these algorithms in C++, Java, or MAT-LAB and see if they actually work. In Section 7.3.9, we'll show you some higher level tools in MATLAB's digital signal processing toolkit that create these types of filters for you.

7.3.3   THE Z-TRANSFORM

If you continue to work in digital signal processing, you need to be familiar with the **z-transform**, a mathematical operation that converts a discrete time domain signal into a frequency domain signal represented as real or complex numbers. The formal definition is below.

Let $x(n)$ be a sequence of discrete values for $n = 0,1,\ldots$. The **one-sided z-transform** of $x(n)$, $X(z)$, is a function that maps from complex numbers to complex numbers as follows:

$$X(z) = \sum_{n=0}^{\infty} x(n)z^{-n}$$

where z is a complex number.

EQUATION 7.5: THE ONE-SIDED Z-TRANSFORM

A full z-transform sums from $-\infty$ to ∞, but the one-sided transform suffices for us because n is an index into an array of audio samples and will never be negative.

In practice, our sector of time domain audio samples has a finite length N. Thus, if we assume that $x(n) = 0$ for $n \geq N$, then we can redefine the transform as:

$$X(z) = \sum_{n=0}^{N-1} x(n)z^{-n}$$

$X(z)$ is a discrete function from complex variables to complex variables. Now, look at what results if we set $z = e^{i2\pi k/N}$ and apply the z-transform to a vector of length N (applying the equation N times for $0 \leq k < N$). This yields the following:

$$for\ 0 \leq k < N,\ X(z_k) = \sum_{n=0}^{N-1} x(n)\left(e^{\frac{i2\pi k}{N}}\right)^{-n} = \sum_{n=0}^{N-1} x(n)e^{\frac{-i2\pi kn}{N}}$$

$$= \sum_{n=0}^{N-1} x(n)\cos\left(\frac{2\pi kn}{N}\right) - ix(n)\sin\left(\frac{2\pi kn}{N}\right)$$

EQUATION 7.6: THE DISCRETE FOURIER TRANSFORM AS A SPECIAL CASE OF THE Z-TRANSFORM

The idea of Equation 7.6 is that we are evaluating the equation for each kth frequency component ($2\pi k/N$) to determine N frequency components in the audio data. You can see that this equation is equivalent to the definition of the discrete Fourier transform given in Chapter 2. The Fourier transform transforms from the time domain (real numbers) to the frequency domain (complex numbers), but since real numbers are a subset of the complex numbers, the Fourier transform is an instance of a z-transform.

7.3.4   FILTERING IN THE TIME AND THE FREQUENCY DOMAINS

In Chapter 2, we showed how the Fourier transform can be applied to transform audio data from the time to the frequency domain. The Fourier transform is a function that maps from real numbers (audio samples in the time domain) to complex numbers (frequencies, which have magnitude and phase). We showed in the previous section that the Fourier transform is a special case of the z-transform, a function that maps from complex numbers to complex numbers. Now let's consider the equivalence of filtering in the time and frequency domains. We begin with some standard notation.

Say that you have a convolution filter as follows:

$$y(n) = h(n) \otimes x(n)$$

By convention, the z-transform of $x(n)$ is called $X(z)$, the z-transform of $y(n)$ is called $Y(z)$, and the z-transform of $h(n)$ is called $H(z)$, as shown in Table 7.1.

	Time domain	Frequency domain
input audio	$x(n)$	$X(z)$
output, filtered audio	$y(n)$	$Y(z)$
filter	$h(n)$	$H(z)$
filter operation	$y(n) = h(n) \otimes x(n)$	$X(z) = H(z) \times Y(z)$

TABLE 7.1: CONVENTIONAL NOTATION FOR TIME AND FREQUENCY-DOMAIN FILTERS

The convolution theorem is an important finding in digital signal processing that shows us the equivalence of filtering in the time domain vs. the frequency domain. By this theorem, instead of filtering by a convolution, as expressed in $y(n) = h(n) \otimes x(n)$, we can filter by multiplication, as expressed in $Y(z) = H(z) \times X(z)$. (Note that $H(z) \times X(z)$ is an element-by-element multiplication of order N.) That is, if you take a time domain filter, transform it to the frequency domain, transform your audio data to the frequency domain, multiply the frequency domain filter and the frequency domain audio data, and do the inverse Fourier transform on the result, you get the same result as you would get by convolving the time domain filter with the time domain audio data. This is in essence the **convolution theorem**, explained diagrammatically in Figure 7.34. In fact, with a fast implementation of the Fourier transform, known as the **fast Fourier transform** (**FFT**), filtering in the frequency domain is more computationally efficient than filtering in the time domain. That is, it takes less time to do the operations.

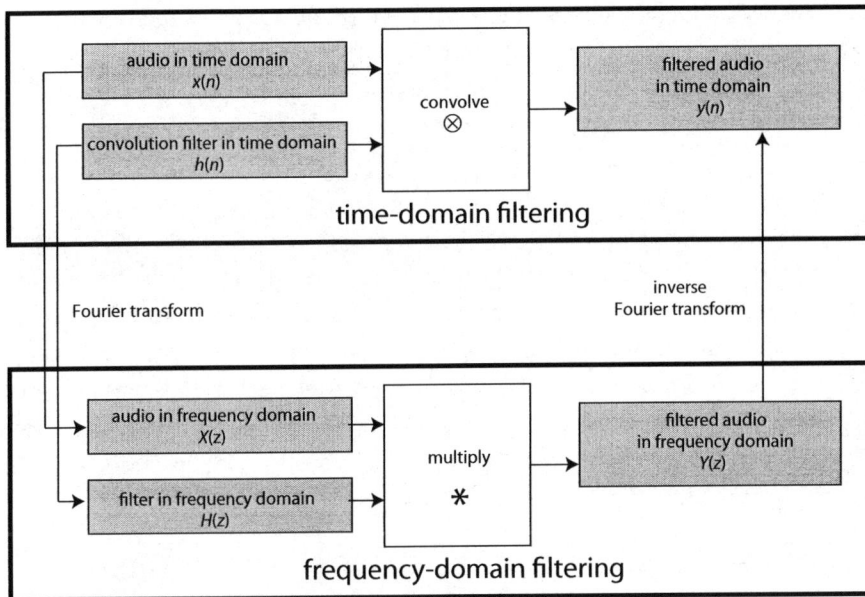

FIGURE 7.34: THE CONVOLUTION THEOREM

MATLAB has a function called *fft* for performing the Fourier transform on a vector of audio data and a function called *conv* for doing convolutions. However, to get a closer view of these operations, it may be enlightening to try implementing these functions yourself. You can implement the Fourier transform either directly from Equation 7.6, or you can try the more efficient algorithm, the fast Fourier transform. To check your accuracy, you can compare your results with MATLAB's functions. You can also compare the run times of programs that filter in the time vs. the frequency domain. We leave this as an activity for you to try.

In Chapter 2, we discussed the necessity of applying the Fourier transform over relatively small segments of audio data at a time. These segments, called **windows**, are on the order of about 1024 to 4096 samples. If you use the fast Fourier transform, the window size must be a power of 2. It's not hard to get an intuitive understanding of why the window has to be relatively small. The purpose of the Fourier transform is to determine the frequency components of a segment of sound. Frequency components relate to pitches that we hear. In most sounds, these pitches change over time, so the frequency components change over time. If you do the Fourier transform on, say, five seconds of audio, you'll get an imprecise view of the frequency components in that time window, called **time slurring**. However, what if you choose a very small window size, say just one sample? You couldn't possibly determine any frequencies in one sample, which at a sampling rate of 44.1 kHz is just 1/44,100 second. Frequencies are determined by how a sound wave's amplitude goes up and down as time passes, so some time must pass for there to be such a thing as frequency.

The upshot of this observation is that the discrete Fourier transform has to be applied over windows of samples where the windows are neither too large nor too small. Note that the window size has a direct relationship with the number of frequency components you detect. If your window has a size of N, then you get an output telling you the magnitudes of $N/2$ frequency bands from the discrete Fourier transform, ranging in frequency from 0 to the Nyquist frequency (half the sampling rate). An overly small window in the Fourier transform gives you very high time resolution, but tells you the magnitudes of only a small number of discrete, wide bands of frequencies. An overly large window yields many frequency bands, but with poor time resolution that leads to slurring. You want to have good enough time resolution to be able to reconstruct the resulting audio signal, but also enough frequency information to apply the filters with proper effect. Choosing the right window size is a balancing act.

7.3.5 DEFINING FIR AND IIR FILTERS WITH Z-TRANSFORMS, FILTER DIAGRAMS, AND TRANSFER FUNCTIONS

Now let's look at how the z-transform can be useful in describing, designing, and analyzing audio filters. We know that we can do filtering in the frequency domain with the operation

$$Y(z) = H(z) \times X(z)$$

EQUATION 7.7: FILTERING IN THE FREQUENCY DOMAIN

If we have the coefficients defining an FIR filter, $[a_0, a_1, a_2 \ldots, a_{N-1}]$, then $H(z)$ is derived directly from the definition of the z-transform.

$$H(z) = \sum_{n=0}^{N-1} h(n) z^{-n} = a_0 + a_1 z^{-1} + a_2 z^{-2} + \cdots + a^{N-1} z^{-(N-1)}$$

EQUATION 7.8: H(Z), AN FIR FILTER IN THE FREQUENCY DOMAIN

Consider our previous example of an FIR filter,

$$y(n) = 0.4x(n) + 0.3x(n-1) + 0.3x(n-2)$$

where $h = [a_0, a_1, a_2] = [0.4, 0.3, 0.3]$. This filter can be transformed to the frequency domain by applying the z-transform.

$$H(z) = \sum_{n=0}^{N-1} h(n)z^{-n} = a_0 + a_1 z^{-1} + a_2 z^{-2} + \cdots + a^{N-1} z^{-(N-1)}$$

$$0.4 + 0.3z^{-1} + 0.3z^{-2}$$

Filters can be expressed diagrammatically in terms of the z-transform, as illustrated in Figure 7.35. The z^{-m} elements are **delay elements**.

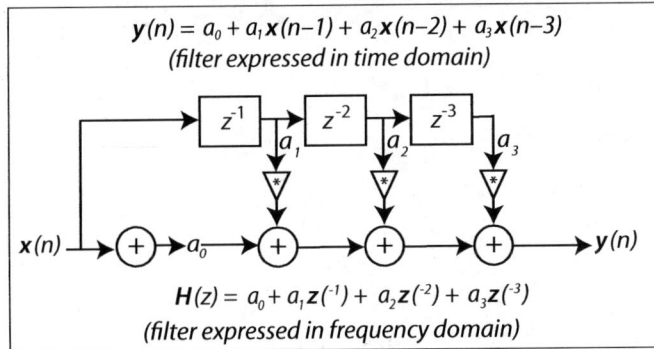

$y(n) = a_0 + a_1 x(n-1) + a_2 x(n-2) + a_3 x(n-3)$
(filter expressed in time domain)

$H(z) = a_0 + a_1 z^{(-1)} + a_2 z^{(-2)} + a_3 z^{(-3)}$
(filter expressed in frequency domain)

FIGURE 7.35: EXAMPLE FIR FILTER DIAGRAM

To derive $H(z)$ for an IIR filter, we rearrange Equation 7.7 as a ratio of the output to the input:

$$H(z) = \frac{Y(z)}{X(z)}$$

EQUATION 7.9: FILTER IN THE FREQUENCY DOMAIN AS A RATIO OF OUTPUT TO INPUT

This form of the filter is called the **transfer function**. Using the definition of the IIR filter, $y(n) = h(n) \otimes x(n) = \sum_{k=0}^{N-1} a_k\, x(n-k) - \sum_{k=1}^{M} b_k\, y(n-k)$, we can express the IIR filter in terms of its coefficients $[a_0, a_1, a_2, \ldots, a_{N-1}]$ and $[b_1, b_2, b_3, \ldots, b_M]$, which yields the following transfer function defining the IIR filter:

$$H(z) = \frac{Y(z)}{X(z)} = \frac{a_0 + a_1 z^{-1} + a_2 z^{-2} + \cdots + a_{N-1} z^{N-1}}{1 + b_1 z^{-1} + b_2 z^{-2} + \cdots + b_M z^{N-M}}$$

$$= \frac{a_0 z^N + a_1 z^{N-1} + \cdots + a_{N-1} z^{2N-1}}{z^N + b_1 z^{N-1} + \cdots + b_m z^{2N-M}}$$

EQUATION 7.10: TRANSFER FUNCTION FOR AN IIR FILTER

(The usefulness of transfer functions will become apparent in the next section.) An IIR filter in the frequency domain can be represented with a filter diagram as shown in Figure 7.36.

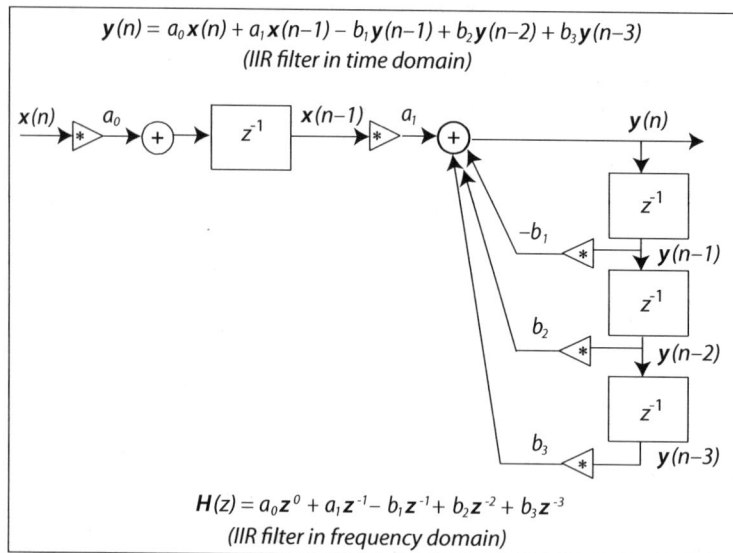

FIGURE 7.36: EXAMPLE IIR FILTER DIAGRAM

7.3.6 GRAPHING FILTERS AND PLOTTING ZERO-POLE DIAGRAMS

The function $H(z)$ defining a filter has a complex number z as its input parameter. Complex numbers are expressed as $a + bi$, where a is the real number component, b is the coefficient of the imaginary component, and i is $\sqrt{-1}$. The complex number plane can be graphed as shown in Figure 7.37, with the real component on the horizontal axis and the coefficient of the imaginary component on the vertical axis. Let's look at how this works.

With regard to Figure 7.37, let x, y, and r denote the lengths of line segments $\overline{AB}$, $\overline{BC}$, and $\overline{AC}$, respectively. Since the circle is a unit circle, $r = 1$. From trigonometric relations, we get:

$$x = \cos\theta$$
$$y = \sin\theta$$

Point C represents the number $\cos\theta + i\sin\theta$ on the complex number plane. By Euler's identity, $\cos\theta + i\sin\theta = e^{i\theta}$. $H(z)$ is a function that is evaluated around the unit circle and graphed on the complex number plane. Since we are working with discrete values, we are evaluating the filter's response at N discrete points evenly distributed around the unit circle. Specifically, the response for the kth frequency component is found by evaluating $\boldsymbol{H(z_k)}$ at $z = e^{i\theta} = e^{i2\pi k/N}$ where N is the number of frequency components. The output, $\boldsymbol{H(z_k)}$, is a complex number, but if you want to picture the output in the graph, you can consider only the magnitude of $\boldsymbol{H(z_k)}$, which would be a real number coming out of the complex number plane (as we'll show in Figure 7.41). This helps you to visualize how the filter attenuates or boosts the magnitudes of different frequency components.

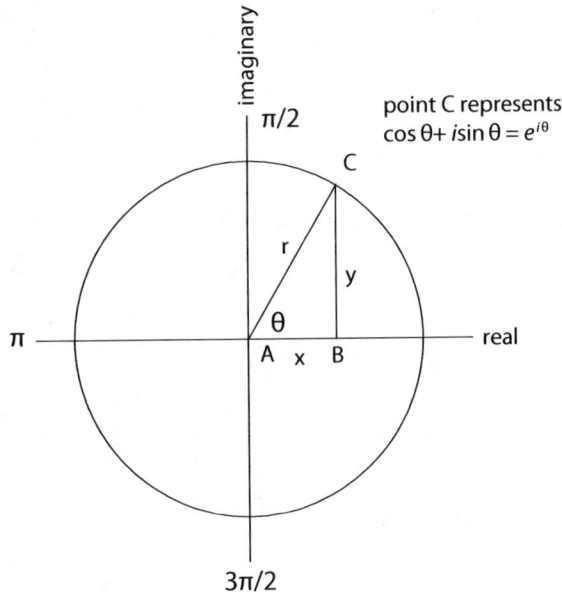

The magnitude of $H(z)$ can be visualized coming out of the complex number plane in the z direction.

FIGURE 7.37: A CIRCLE WITH RADIUS 1 ON THE COMPLEX NUMBER PLANE, WITH $\theta = 2\pi k/N$

This leads us to a description of the zero-pole diagram, a graph of a filter's transfer function that marks places where the filter does the most or least attenuation (the zeroes and poles, as shown in Figure 7.38). As the numerator of $Y(z)/X(z)$ goes to 0, the output frequency is getting smaller relative to the input frequency. This is called a *zero*. As the denominator goes to 0, the output frequency is getting larger relative to the input frequency. This is called a *pole*.

To see the behavior of the filter, we can move around the unit circle looking at each frequency component at point $e^{i\theta}$ where $\theta = 2\pi k/N$ for $0 \le k < N-1$. Let d_{zero} be the point's distance from a zero and d_{pole} be the point's distance from a pole. If, as you move from point P_k to point P_{k+1} (these points representing input frequencies $e^{i2\pi k/N}$

and $e^{i2\pi(k+1)/N}$, respectively), the ratio d_zero/d_pole gets larger, and the filter progressively allows more of the frequency $e^{i2\pi k/N}$ to "pass through" as opposed to $e^{i2\pi(k+1)/N}$.

Let's try this mathematically with a couple of examples. These examples will get you started in your understanding of zero-pole diagrams and the graphing of filters, but the subject is complex. MATLAB's Help has more examples and more explanations, and you can find more details in the books on digital signal processing listed in our references.

First let's try a simple FIR filter. The coefficients for this filter are [1,-0.5]. In the time domain, this filter can be seen as a convolution represented as follows:

$$y(n) = \sum_{k=0}^{1} h(k)x(n-k) = x(n) - 0.5x(n-1)$$

EQUATION 7.11: CONVOLUTION FOR A SIMPLE FILTER IN THE TIME DOMAIN

Converting the filter to the frequency domain by the z-transform, we get:

$$H(z) = 1 - 0.5z^{-1} = \frac{z(1 - 0.5z^{-1})}{z} = \frac{z - 0.5}{z}$$

EQUATION 7.12: DELAY FILTER REPRESENTED AS A TRANSFER FUNCTION

In the case of this simple filter, it's easy to see where the zeroes and poles are. At $z = 0.5$, the numerator is 0. Thus, a zero is at point (0.5, 0). At $z = 0$, the denominator is 0. Thus, a pole is at (0,0). There is no imaginary component to either the zero or the pole, so the coefficient of the imaginary part of the complex number is 0 in both cases.

Once we have the zeroes and poles, we can plot them on the graph representing the filter, $H(z)$, as shown in Figure 7.38. To analyze the filter's effect on frequency components, consider the kth discrete point on the unit circle, point P_k, and the behavior of filter $H(z)$ at that point. Point P_0 is at the origin, and the angle formed between the x-axis and the line between P_0 and P_k is $\theta = 2\pi k/N$. Each such point P_k at angle $\theta = 2\pi k/N$ corresponds to a frequency component $e^{i2\pi k/N}$ in the audio that is being filtered. Assume that the Nyquist frequency has been normalized to π. Thus, by the Nyquist theorem, the only valid frequency components to consider are between 0 and π. Let d_{zero} be the distance between P_k and a zero of the filter, and let d_{pole} be the distance between P_k and a pole. The magnitude of the frequency response, $H(z)$, will be smaller in proportion to d_{zero}/d_{pole}. For this example the pole is at the origin, so for all points P_k, d_{pole} is 1. Thus the magnitude of d_{zero}/d_{pole} depends entirely on d_{zero}. As d_{zero} gets larger, the frequency response gets larger. d_{zero} increases as you move from $\theta = 0$

to $\theta = \pi$. Since the frequency response increases as frequency increases, this filter is a high-pass filter, attenuating low frequencies more than high ones.

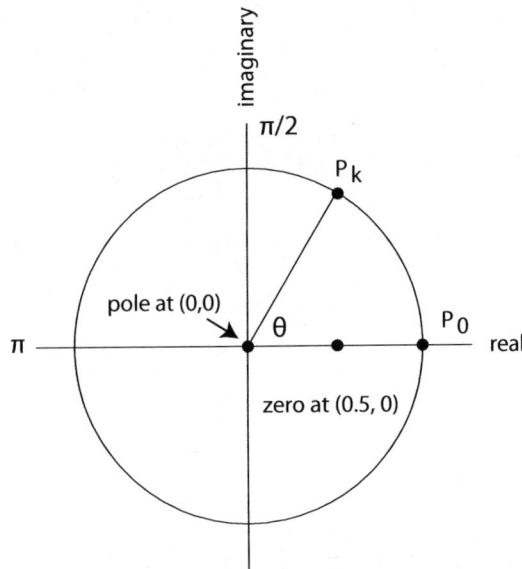

FIGURE 7.38: ZERO-POLE GRAPH OF SIMPLE DELAY FILTER

Now let's try a simple IIR filter. Say that the equation for the filter is this:

$$y(n) = x(n) - x(n-2) - 0.49y(n-2)$$

EQUATION 7.13: EQUATION FOR AN IIR FILTER

The coefficients for the forward filter are [1,0,-1], and the coefficients for the feedback filter are [0,-0.49]. Applying the transfer function form of the filter, we get:

$$H(z) = \frac{1 - z^{-2}}{1 - 0.49z^{-2}} = \frac{z - 1}{z^2 - 0.49} = \frac{(z+1)(z-1)}{(z+0.7i)(z-0.7i)}$$

EQUATION 7.14: EQUATION FOR IIR FILTER, VERSION 2

From Equation 7.14, we can see that there are zeroes at $z = 1$ and $z = -1$, and poles at $z = 0.7i$ and $z = -0.7i$. The zeroes and poles are plotted in Figure 7.39. This diagram is harder to analyze by inspection because there are two zeroes and two poles.

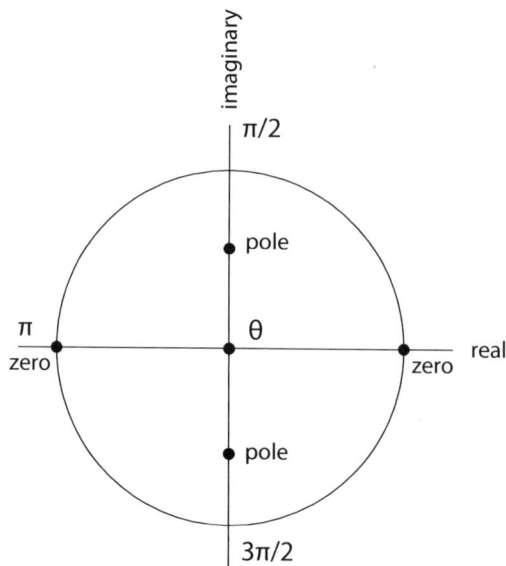

FIGURE 7.39: A ZERO-POLE DIAGRAM FOR AN IIR FILTER WITH TWO ZEROES AND TWO POLES

If we graph the frequency response of the filter, we can see that it's a bandpass filter. We can do this with MATLAB's *FVTool* (Filter Visualization Tool). The *FVTool* expects the coefficients of the transfer function (Equation 7.10) as arguments. The first argument of *FVTool* should be the coeffients of the numerator ($a_0, a_1, a_2, \ldots$), and the second should be the coefficients of the denominator ($b_1, b_2, b_3, \ldots$). Thus, the following MATLAB commands produce the graph of the frequency response, which shows that we have a bandpass filter with a rather wide band (Figure 7.40).

```
a = [1 0 -1];
b = [1 0 -0.49];
fvtool(a,b);
```

(You have to include the constant **1** as the first element of *b*.) MATLAB's *FVTool* is discussed further in Section 7.3.9.

We can also graph the frequency response on the complex number plane, as we did with the zero-pole diagram, but this time we show the magnitude of the frequency response in the third dimension by means of a surface plot. This plot is shown in Figure 7.41. Writing a MATLAB function to create a graph such as this is left as an exercise.

>>

MATLAB EXERCISE:

Graphing a Filter on the Complex Number Plane
http://bit.ly/29lrl7D

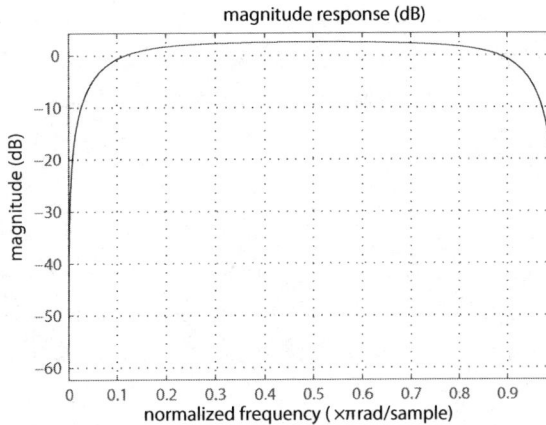

FIGURE 7.40: FREQUENCY RESPONSE OF BANDPASS FILTER

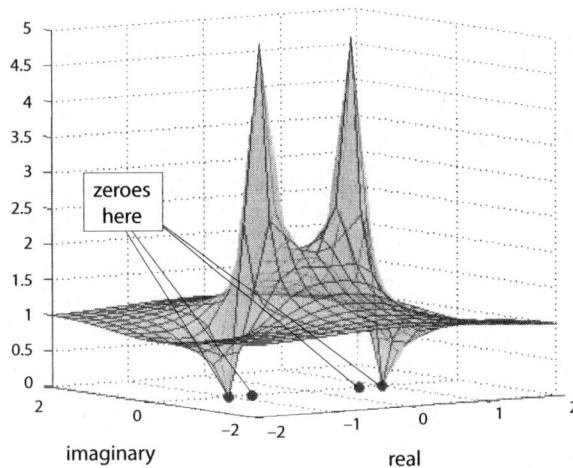

FIGURE 7.41: SURFACE PLOT OF FILTER ON COMPLEX
NUMBER PLANE, WITH ZEROES MARKED IN GRAY

7.3.7 COMB FILTERS AND DELAYS

In Chapter 4, we discussed comb filtering in the context of acoustics and showed how comb filters can be made by means of delays. Let's review comb filtering now.

A comb filter is created when two identical copies of a sound are summed (in the air or by means of computer processing, for example), with one copy being offset in time from the other. The amount of offset determines which frequencies are combed out. The equation that predicts the combed frequency is given below.

Given a delay of t seconds between two identical copies of a sound,
then the frequencies f_i that will be combed are
$$f_i = \frac{2i + 1}{2t} \text{ for all integers } i \geq 0$$

EQUATION 7.15: COMB FILTERING

For a sampling rate of 44.1 kHz, 0.01 is equivalent to 441 samples. This delay is demonstrated in the MATLAB code below, which applies a delay of 0.01 seconds to white noise and graphs the resulting frequencies. (The white noise was created in Audition and saved in a raw PCM file.)

```
fid = fopen('WhiteNoise.pcm', 'r');
y = fread(fid, 'int16');
y = y(1:44100);
first = y(442:44100);
second = y(1:441);
y2 = cat(1, first, second);
y3 = y + y2;
plot(abs(fft(y3)));
```

You can see in Figure 7.42 that with a delay of 0.01 seconds, the frequencies that are combed out are 50 Hz, 150 Hz, 250 Hz, and so forth, while frequencies of 100 Hz, 200 Hz, 300 Hz, and so forth are boosted.

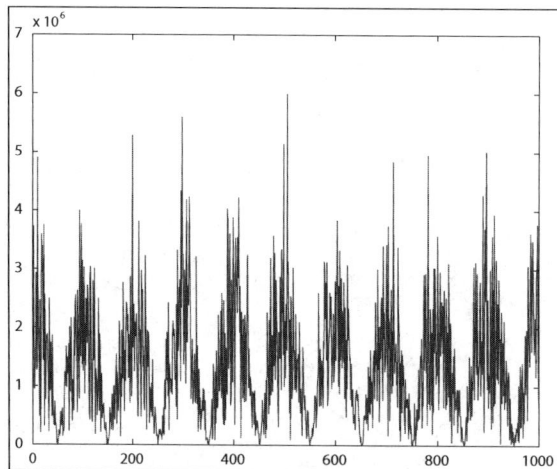

FIGURE 7.42: COMB FILTERING

We created the comb filter above "by hand" by shifting the sample values and summing them. We can also use MATLAB's *FVTool*.

```
a = [1  zeroes(1,440) 0.5];
b = [1];
fvtool(a,b);
axis([0 .008 -8 6]);
```

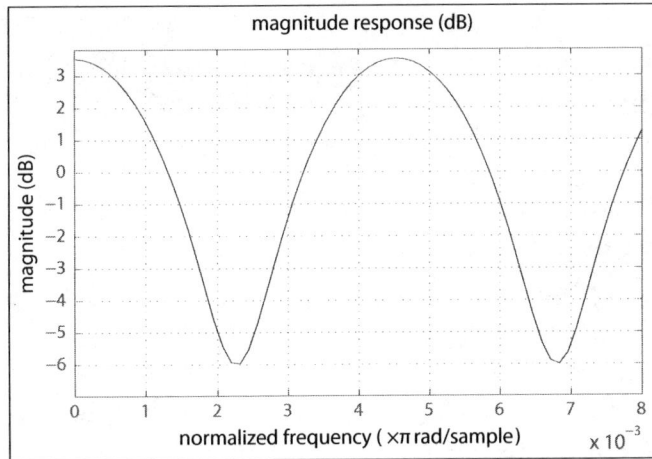

FIGURE 7.43: COMB FILTERING THROUGH *FVTool*

The *x*-axis in Figure 7.43 is normalized to the Nyquist frequency. That is, for a sampling rate of 44.1 kHz, the Nyquist frequency of 22,050 Hz is normalized to 1. Thus, 50 Hz falls at position 0.002 and 100 Hz at about 0.0045, and so on.

Comb filters can be expressed as either non-recursive FIR filters or recursive IIR filters. A simple non-recursive comb filter is expressed by the following equation:

$$y(n) = x(n) + g \times x(n - m)$$

where y is the filtered audio in the time domain,
x is the original audio in the time domain,
m is the amount of delay in samples, and $|g| \leq 1$

EQUATION 7.16: EQUATION FOR AN FIR COMB FILTER

In an FIR comb filter, a fraction of an earlier sample is added to a later one, creating a repetition of the original sound. The distance between the two copies of the sound is controlled by *m*.

A simple recursive comb filter is expressed by the following equation:

$$y(n) = x(n) + g \times y(n - m)$$

where y is the filtered audio in the time domain,
x is the original audio in the time domain,
m is the amount of delay in samples, and $|g| \leq 1$

EQUATION 7.17: EQUATION FOR AN IIR COMB FILTER

You can see that Equation 7.17 represents a recursive filter because the output $y(n-m)$ is fed back in to create later output. With this feedback term, an earlier sound continues to have an effect on later sounds, but with decreasing intensity each time it is fed back in (because of the multiplier $|g| < 1$).

7.3.8   FLANGING

Flanging is defined as a time-varying comb filter effect. It results from the application of a delay between two identical copies of audio where the amount of delay varies over time. This time-varying delay results in different frequencies and their harmonics being combed out at different moments in time. The time delay can be controlled by an LFO.

Flanging originated in the analog world as a trick performed with two tape machines playing identical copies of audio. The sound engineer was able to delay one of the two copies of the recording by pressing his finger on the rim or "flange" of the tape deck. Varying the pressure would vary the amount of delay, creating a "swooshing" sound.

Flanging effects have many variations. In basic flanging, the frequencies combed out are in a harmonic series at any moment in time. Flanging by means of phase-shifting can result in the combing of non-harmonic frequencies, so that the space between combed frequencies is not regular. The amount of feedback in flanging can also be varied. Flanging with a relatively long delay between copies of the audio is sometimes referred to a **chorusing**.

Guitars are a favorite instrument for flanging. The rock song "Barracuda" by Heart is good example of guitar flanging, but there are many others throughout rock history.

We leave flanging as an exercise for the reader, referring you to *The Audio Programming Book* cited in the references for an example implementation.

7.3.9   THE DIGITAL SIGNAL PROCESSING TOOLKIT IN MATLAB

Section 7.3.2 gives you algorithms for creating a variety of FIR filters. MATLAB also provides built-in functions for creating FIR and IIR filters. Let's look at the IIR filters first.

MATLAB's *butter* function creates an IIR filter called a Butterworth filter, named for its creator. Consider this sequence of commands:

```
N = 10;
f = 0.5;
[a,b] = butter(N, f);
```

The *butter* function call sends in two arguments: the order of the desired filter, N; and the cutoff frequency, f. The cutoff frequency is normalized so that the Nyquist frequency (½ the sampling rate) is 1, and all valid frequencies lie between 0 and 1. The function call returns two vectors, a and b, corresponding to the vectors a and b in Equation 7.4. (For a simple low-pass filter, an order of 6 is fine. The order is the number of coeffients.)

Now with the filter in hand, you can apply it using MATLAB's *filter* function. The *filter* function takes the coefficients and the vector of audio samples as arguments:

```
output = filter(a,b,audio);
```

You can analyze the filter with the *FVTool*.

```
FVTool(a,b)
```

The *FVTool* provides a GUI through which you can see multiple views of the filter, including those in Figure 7.44. In the first figure, the blue line is the magnitude frequency response and the green line is phase.

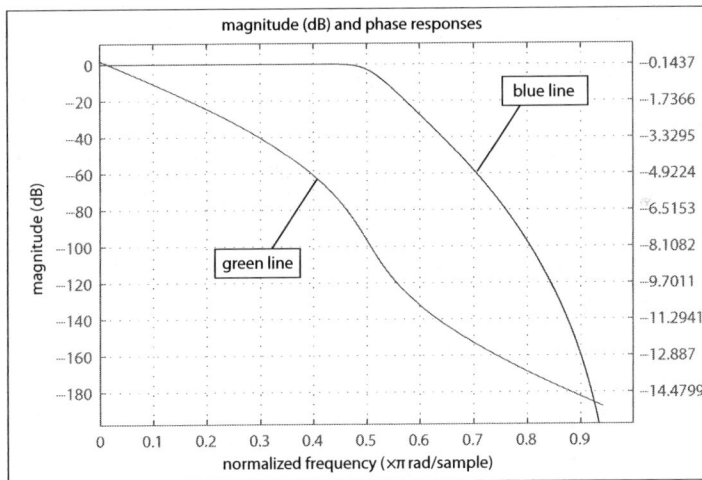

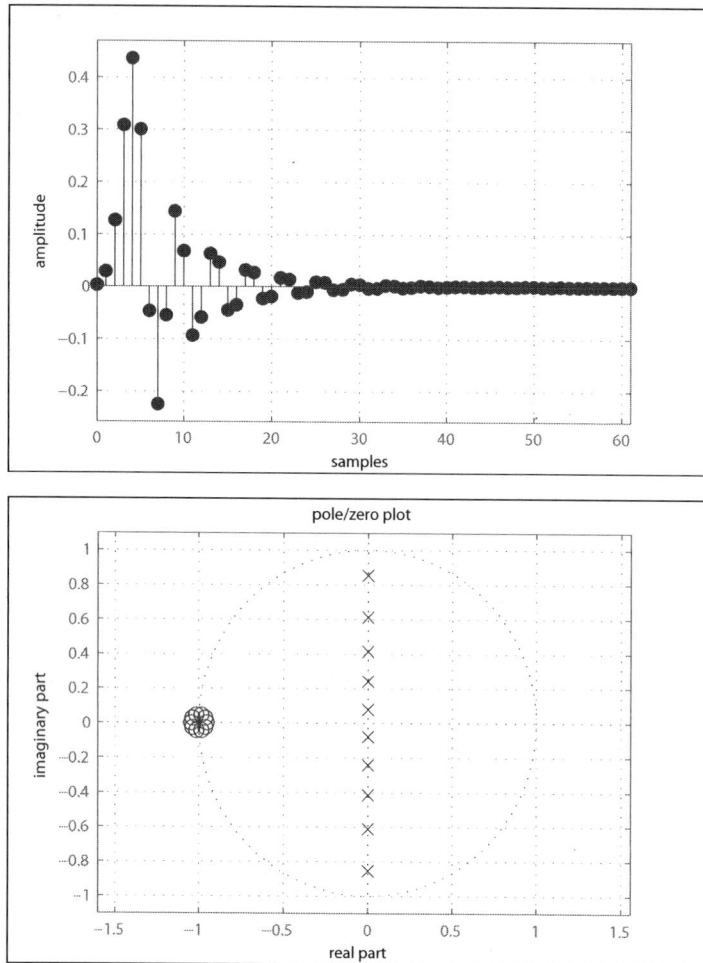

FIGURE 7.44: FILTER VISUALIZATION TOOL IN MATLAB

Another way to create and apply an IIR filter in MATLAB is by means of the function *yulewalk*. Let's try a low-pass filter as a simple example. Figure 7.45 shows the idealized frequency response of a low-pass filter. The *x*-axis represents normalized frequencies, and f_c is the cutoff frequency. This particular filter allows frequencies that are up to ¼ the sampling rate to pass through, but it filters out all the rest.

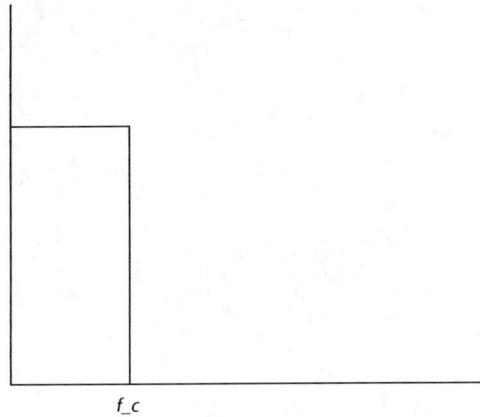

FIGURE 7.45: FREQUENCY RESPONSE OF AN IDEAL LOW-PASS FILTER

The first step in creating this filter is to store its "shape." This information is stored in a pair of parallel vectors, which we'll call f and m. For the four points on the graph in Figure 7.46, f stores the frequencies, and m stores the corresponding magnitudes. That is, $f = [f1\ f2\ f3\ f4]$ and $m = [m1\ m2\ m3\ m4]$, as illustrated in the figure. For the example filter we have:

```
f = [0 0.25 0.25 1];
m = [1 1 0 0];
```

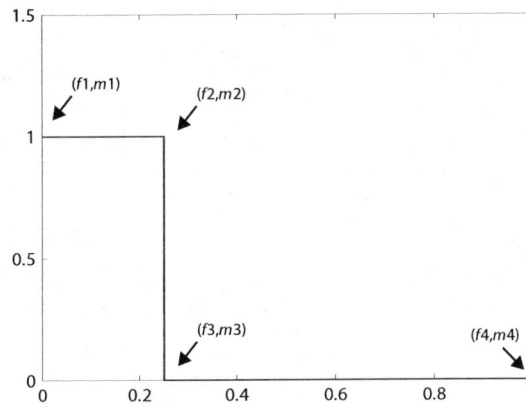

FIGURE 7.46: POINTS CORRESPONDING TO INPUT PARAMETERS IN *YULEWALK* FUNCTION

Now that you have an ideal response, you use the *yulewalk* function in MATLAB to determine what coefficients to use to approximate the ideal response.

```
[a,b] = yulewalk(N,f,m);
```

Again, an order $N = 6$ filter is sufficient for the low-pass filter. You can use the same *filter* function as above to apply the filter. The resulting filter is given in Figure 7.47. Clearly, the filter cannot be created perfectly, as you can see from the large ripple after the cutoff point.

ASIDE: The *yulewalk* function in MATLAB is named for the Yule-Walker equations, a set of linear equations used in auto-regression modeling.

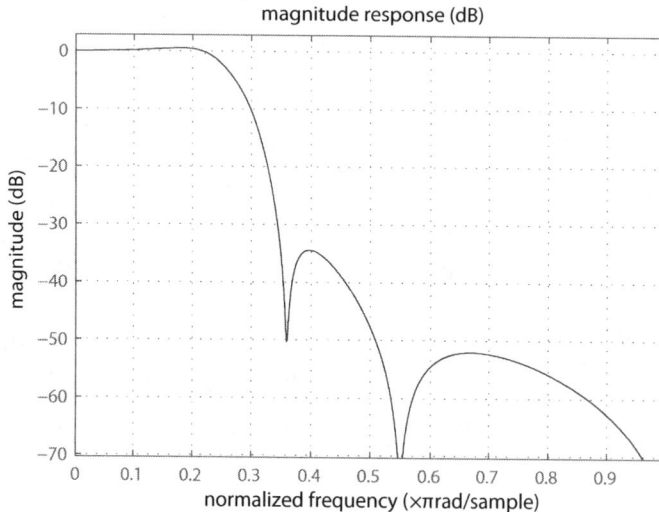

FIGURE 7.47: FREQUENCY RESPONSE OF A *YULEWALK* FILTER

The finite counterpart to the *yulewalk* function is the *fir2* function. Like *butter*, *fir2* takes as input the order of the filter and two vectors corresponding to the shape of the filter's frequency response. Thus, we can use the same *f* and *m* as before. *fir2* returns the vector *b* constituting the filter.

```
h = fir2(N,f,m);
```

We need to use a higher order filter because this is an FIR. $N = 30$ is probably high enough.

MATLAB's extensive signal processing toolkit includes a Filter Design and Analysis Tool (FDATool) with an easy-to-use graphical user interface that allows you to design the types of filters discussed in this chapter. A Butterworth filter is shown in Figure 7.48. You can adjust the parameters in the tool and see how the roll-off and ripples change accordingly. Experimenting with this tool helps you know what to expect from filters designed by different algorithms.

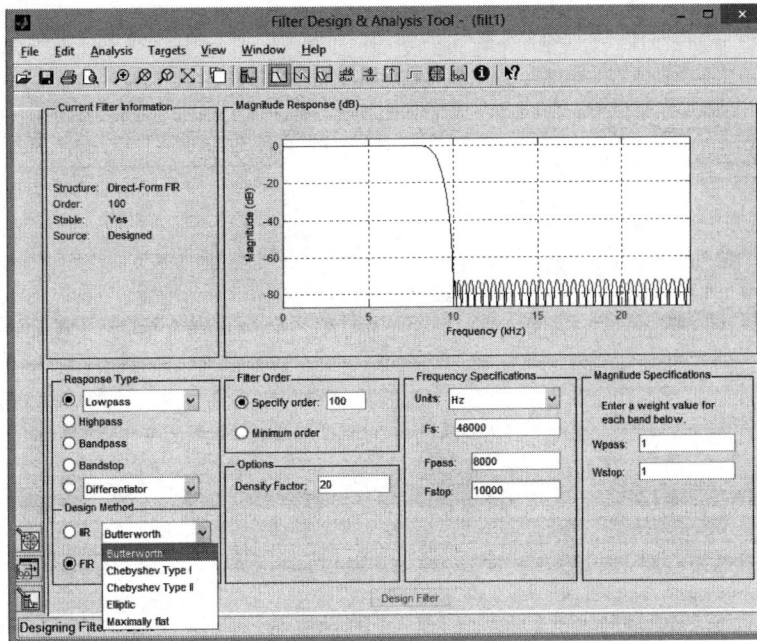

FIGURE 7.48: BUTTERWORTH FILTER DESIGNED IN MATLAB'S FILTER DESIGN AND ANALYSIS TOOL

7.3.10 EXPERIMENTS WITH FILTERING: VOCODERS AND PITCH GLIDES

Vocoders were introduced in Section 7.1.8. The implementation of a vocoder is sketched in Algorithm 7.6 and diagrammed in Figure 7.49. The MATLAB and C++ exercises associated with this section encourage you to try your hand at the implementation.

```
algorithm vocoder
/*
Input:
        c, an array of audio samples constituting the carrier signal
        m, n array of audio samples constituting the modulator signal
Output:
        v, the carrier wave modulated with the modulator wave */
{
        Initialize v with 0s
        Divide the carrier into octave-separated frequency bands with
          bandpass filters
        Divide the modulator into the same octave-separated
          frequency bands with bandpass filters
        for each band
                use the modulator as an amplitude envelope for the carrier
}
```

ALGORITHM 7.6: SKETCH OF AN IMPLEMENTATION OF A VOCODER

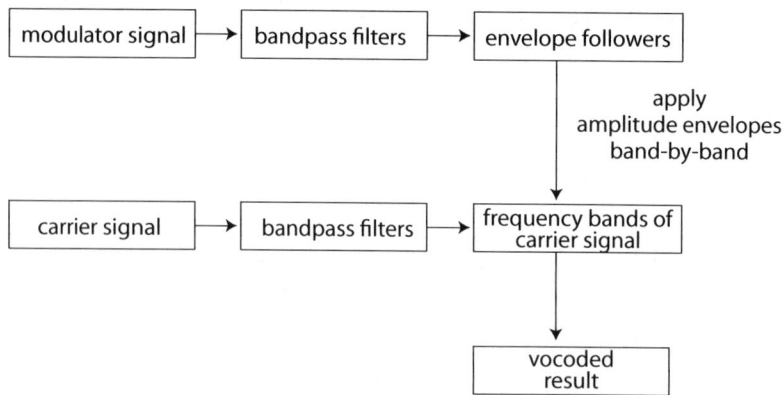

```
modulator signal → bandpass filters → envelope followers
                                              │
                                              │ apply
                                              │ amplitude envelopes
                                              │ band-by-band
                                              ▼
carrier signal → bandpass filters → frequency bands of
                                    carrier signal
                                              │
                                              ▼
                                         vocoded
                                         result
```

FIGURE 7.49: OVERVIEW OF VOCODER IMPLEMENTATION

Another interesting programming exercise is the implementation of a pitch glide. A **Risset pitch glide** is an audio illusion that sounds like a constantly rising pitch. It is the aural equivalent of the visual image of a stripe on a barber pole that seems to be rising constantly. Implementing the pitch glide is suggested as an exercise for this section.

7.3.11 REAL-TIME VS. OFF-LINE PROCESSING

Up to this point, we've primarily considered off-line processing of audio data in the programs that we've asked you to write in the exercises. This makes the concepts easier to grasp, but hides the very important issue of real-time processing, where operations have to keep pace with the rate at which sound is played.

Chapter 2 introduces the idea of audio streams. In Chapter 2, we give a simple program that evaluates a sine function at the frequency of desired notes and writes the output directly to the audio device so that notes are played when the program runs. Chapter 5 gives a program that reads a raw audio

>> **MATLAB EXERCISE:** Creating a Vocoder in MATLAB http://bit.ly/29rOOnP

{} **C++ PROGRAMMING EXERCISE:** Creating a Vocoder in C++ http://bit.ly/29LYUCv

>> **MATLAB EXERCISE:** Creating a Pitch Glide in MATLAB http://bit.ly/29lrAop

{} **C++ PROGRAMMING EXERCISE:** Creating a Pitch Glide in C++ http://bit.ly/29uA7ab

file and writes that to the audio device to play it as the program runs. The program from Chapter 5 with a few modifications is given here for review.

```
/*Use option -lasound on compile line. Send in number of samples and raw
sound file name.*/

#include </usr/include/alsa/asoundlib.h>
#include <math.h>
#include <iostream>
using namespace std;

static char *device = "default";     /*default playback device */
snd_output_t *output = NULL;
#define PI 3.14159

int main(int argc, char *argv[])
{
        int err, numRead;
        snd_pcm_t *handle;
        snd_pcm_sframes_t frames;
        int numSamples = atoi(argv[1]);

        char* buffer = (char*) malloc((size_t) numSamples);
        FILE *inFile = fopen(argv[2], "rb");
        numRead = fread(buffer, 1, numSamples, inFile);
        fclose(inFile);

        if ((err = snd_pcm_open(&handle, device, SND_PCM_STREAM_PLAYBACK,
0)) < 0){
                printf("Playback open error: %s\n", snd_strerror(err));
                exit(EXIT_FAILURE);
        }
        if ((err = snd_pcm_set_params(handle,
                SND_PCM_FORMAT_U8,
                SND_PCM_ACCESS_RW_INTERLEAVED,
                1,
                44100, 1, 400000) ) < 0 ){
                printf("Playback open error: %s\n", snd_strerror(err));
                exit(EXIT_FAILURE);
        }

        frames = snd_pcm_writei(handle, buffer, numSamples);
        if (frames < 0)
          frames = snd_pcm_recover(handle, frames, 0);
        if (frames < 0) {
          printf("snd_pcm_writei failed: %s\n", snd_strerror(err));
        }
}
```

PROGRAM 7.1: READING AND WRITING RAW AUDIO DATA

This program uses the library function *send_pcm_writei* to send samples to the audio device to be played. The audio samples are read from an input file into a buffer and transmitted to the audio device without modification The variable *buffer* indicates where the samples are stored, and *sizeof(buffer)/8* gives the number of samples given that this is 8-bit audio.

Consider what happens when you have a much larger stream of audio coming in and you want to process it in real time before writing it to the audio device. This entails continuously filling up and emptying the buffer at a rate that keeps up with the sampling rate.

Let's do some analysis to determine how much time is available for processing based on a given buffer size. For a buffer size of N and a sampling rate of r, then N/r seconds pass before additional audio data will be required for playing. For $N = 4096$ and $r = 44,100$, this would be $4096/44,100 = 0.0929$ ms. (This scheme implies that there will be latency between the input and output, at most N/r seconds.)

What if you wanted to filter the input audio before sending it to the output? We've seen that filtering is more efficient in the frequency domain using the FFT. Assuming the input is in the time domain, our program has to do the following:

》 Convert data to the frequency domain with inverse FFT.

》 Multiply the filter and the audio data.

》 Convert data back to the time domain with inverse FFT.

》 Write the data to the audio device.

The computational complexity of the FFT and IFFT is $O(N \log N)$, on the order of $4096 \times 12 = 49,152$ operations (times 2). Multiplying the filter and the audio data is $O(N)$, and writing the data to the audio devices is also $O(N)$, adding on the order of 2×4096 operations. This yields on the order of 106,496 operations to be done in 0.0929 ms, or about 0.9 μs per operation. Considering that today's computers can do more than 100,000 MIPS (millions of instructions per second), this is not unreasonable.

We refer the reader to Boulanger and Lazzarini's *The Audio Programming Book* for more examples of real-time audio processing.

7.4 REFERENCES

Boulanger, Richard, and Victor Lazzarini, eds. *The Audio Programming Book*. Cambridge, MA: The MIT Press, 2011.

Flanagan, J.L., and R. M. Golden. "Phase Vocoder," *The Bell System Technical Journal* 45, no.9 (1966): 1493–1509.

Ifeachor, Emmanuel C., and Barrie W. Jervis. *Digital Signal Processing: A Practical Approach*. Addison-Wesley, 1993.

CHAPTER EIGHT

Getting to Work

8.1 SOUND FOR ALL OCCASIONS

This book is intended to be useful to sound designers and technicians in theatre, film, and music production. It is also aimed at computer scientists who would like to collaborate with such artists and practitioners or design the next generation of sound hardware and software for them.

We've provided a lot of information in previous chapters moving through the concepts, applications, and underlying science of audio processing. In the end, we realize that most of our readers want to do something creative, whether designing and setting up the sound backdrop for a theatre performance, creating a soundtrack for film, producing music, or writing programs for innovative sound processing. It's doubtful and not even necessary that you have mastered all the material in the previous chapters, but it serves as a foundation and a reference for your practical and artistic work. In this chapter, we pull things together by going into more detail on the artists' and practitioners' hands-on work.

8.2 WORKFLOW IN SOUND AND MUSIC PRODUCTION

There are three main stages in the workflow for sound and music creation: **pre-production**, when you design your project and choose your basic equipment; **production**, when you record and edit the sound; and **post-production**, when you mix and master the sound (for CDs and DVDs) and deliver it, either live or on a permanent storage medium. In this chapter we examine these three steps as they apply to sound, regardless of the ultimate purpose, including music destined for CD, DVD, or the web; sound scores for film or video; or music and sound effects for live theatre performances. The three main stages of workflow can be further divided into a number of steps, with some variations depending on the purpose and delivery method of the sound.

》 **Pre-production**
　　》 Designing and composing sound and music.

》 Analyzing recording needs (choosing microphones, hardware and software, recording environment, etc.), making a schedule, and preparing for recording.

•**Production**

》 Recording, finding, and/or synthesizing sound and music.

》 Creating sound effects.

》 Synchronizing.

•**Post-production**

》 Audio processing individual tracks and mixing tracks (applying EQ, dynamics processing, special effects, stereo separation, etc.).

》 Overdubbing.

》 Mastering (for CD and DVD music production).

》 Finishing the synchronization of sound and visual elements (for production of sound scores for film or video).

》 Channeling output.

Clearly, all of this work is based on the first important, creative step—sound design and/or music composition. Design and composition are very big topics in and of themselves and are beyond the scope of this book. In what follows, we assume that for the most part the sound that is to be created has been designed or the music to be recorded has been composed, and you're ready to make the designs and compositions come alive.

8.2.1 PRE-PRODUCTION

8.2.1.1 Making a Schedule

A logical place to begin as you initiate a project is by making a schedule for the creation of the different audio artifacts that make up the entire system. Your project could be comprised of many different types of sounds, including live recordings (often on different tracks at different moments), existing recordings, Foley sound effects, MIDI-synthesized music or sound, or algorithmically-generated music or sound. Some sounds may need to be recorded in the presence of others that have already been created, and these interdependencies determine your scheduling. For example, if you're going to record singers against a MIDI-sequenced backing track, the backing track will have to be created ahead of time—at least enough of the backing track so that that the singers are able to sing on pitch and in time with the music.

You also need to consider where and how the artifacts will be made. Recording sessions may need to be scheduled and musicians hired. Also, you'll need to get the proper equipment ready for on-location or outdoor recording sessions.

To some extent you can't plan out the entire process ahead of time. The creative process is messy and somewhat unpredictable. But the last thing you want is to run into some technical roadblock when the creative juices start flowing. So plan ahead as best you can to make sure that you have all the necessary elements in the right place at the right time as you work through the project.

8.2.1.2 Setting Up for Recording

In Chapter 1, we introduced a wide variety of audio hardware and software. We'll now give an overview of different recording situations you might encounter and the equipment appropriate for each.

The ideal recording situation would be a professional recording studio. These studios typically have a large stage area where the performance can be recorded. Ideally, the stage has very meticulously controlled acoustics along with separate isolation booths, high-quality microphones, a control room that is isolated acoustically from the stage, and a professional recording engineer to conduct the recording. If you have enough money, you can rent time in these studios and get very good results. If you have a lot of money, you can build one yourself! Figure 8.1 shows an example of a world-class professional recording studio.

FIGURE 8.1: MANIFOLD RECORDING STUDIO NEAR CHAPEL HILL, NC

While you can get some really amazing recordings in a professional recording studio, you can still get respectable results by setting up your own recording environment using off-the-shelf tools. The first thing to do is find a place to record. This needs to be a quiet room without a lot of noise from the air handling and a fairly neutral acoustic environment. In other words, you usually don't want to hear the room in your recordings. Examples of isolation rooms and techniques can be found in Chapter 4.

Once you have a room in which to make your recording, you need a way to get some cables run into the room for your microphones as well as any headphones or other monitors required for the performer. These cables ultimately run back to wherever you are setting up your computer and recording interface. One thing to keep in mind is that, depending on how well your recording room is isolated from your control room, you may need to have a **talkback microphone** at your computer routed to the performer's headphones. Some mixing consoles include a talkback microphone. A simple way to set up your own is to just connect a microphone to your audio interface and set up an extra recording track in your recording software. If that track is record-enabled, the performer will hear it along with his or her own microphone. You can also get a dedicated monitor management device that includes a talkback microphone and the ability to control and route the recording signal to all the various headphones and monitors for both you and the performer. An example of a monitor management device is shown in Figure 8.2.

FIGURE 8.2: THE MACKIE BIG KNOB MONITOR MANAGEMENT DEVICE

You might find yourself in the situation where you need to record a live performance happening in a theatre, concert hall, or other live venue. The trick here is to get your recording without impacting the live performance. The simplest solution is to set up a couple of area microphones on the stage and run them back to your recording equipment. If there are already microphones in place for live sound reinforcement, you can sometimes use those to get your recording. One way to do that is to work with the live sound engineer to get a mix of all the microphones using an auxiliary output of the live mixing console. Assuming extra aux outputs are available, this is typically a simple thing to implement. Just make sure you speak with the engineer ahead of time about it. You won't make any friends if you show up 15 minutes before the show starts and ask the engineer for a feed from the mixing console. The disadvantage to this is that you're pretty much stuck with the mix that the live engineer gives you. Everything is already mixed. If you ask nicely, you might be able to get two aux feeds with vocals on one and musical instruments on the other. This gives you a little more flexibility, but you are still limited to the mix that is happening on each aux feed. A better solution that requires more planning is to split the microphone signals to go to your recording equipment as well as the live mixing console. It is important to use a transformer-isolated splitter so it doesn't negatively impact the live sound. These isolated splitters will essentially make your feed invisible to the live mixing console. You can get splitters with multiple channels, or just single-channel splitters like the one shown in Figure 8.3. With this strategy you can get a separate track for each microphone on the stage, allowing you to create your own mix later when the live performance is over.

Sometimes you need to record something that is not practical to bring into a controlled environment like a recording studio. For example, if you want to record the sound of an airplane taking off, you're going to have to go stand next to a runway at the airport with a microphone. This is called recording **on location**. In these situations, the goal is to find a balance between fidelity, isolation, cost, and convenience. It's very difficult to get all four of these things in every scenario, so compromises have to be made. The solution that offers the best isolation

FIGURE 8.3: A TRANSFORMER ISOLATED MICROPHONE SPLITTER

is not likely to be convenient, and may be fairly expensive. For example, if you want to record thunder without picking up the sounds of rain, dog barks, cars, birds, and other environmental sounds, you need to find an outdoor location that is far from roads, houses, and trees, but that also offers shelter from the rain for your equipment. Once you find that place, you need to predict when a thunderstorm will happen and get there in time to set up your equipment before the storm begins. Since this is not a very practical plan, you may have to make some compromises and be prepared to spend a long time recording storms in order to get a few moments where you manage to get the sound of thunder when nothing else is happening. Every recording situation is different, but if you understand the options that are available, you can be better prepared to make a good decision.

There are some unique equipment considerations you need to keep in mind when recording on location. You may not have access to electricity, so all your equipment may need to be battery-powered. We described some handheld, battery-powered recording devices in Chapter 1. Another common problem when recording on location is wind. Wind blowing across a microphone will destroy your recording. Even a light breeze can be problematic. Most microphones come with a simple windscreen that can go over the microphone, but in particularly windy conditions, such as the one shown in Figure 8.4, a more robust windscreen may be necessary.

FIGURE 8.4: A RYCOTE WINDJAMMER MICROPHONE WIND SCREEN

8.2.2   PRODUCTION

8.2.2.1 Capturing the Four-dimensional Sound Field

When listening to sound (such as at a live orchestral concert) in an acoustic space, you hear different sounds arriving from many directions. The various instruments are spread out on a stage, and their sound arrives at your ears somewhat spread out in time and direction according to the physical location of the instruments. You also hear subtly nuanced copies of the instrument sounds as they're reflected from the room surfaces at even more varying times and directions. The audience makes their own sound in applause, conversation, shuffling in seats, cell phones going off, and so on. These sounds arrive from different directions as well. Our ability to perceive this four-dimensional effect is the result of the physical characteristics of our hearing system. With two ears, the differences in arrival time and intensity between them allow us to perceive sounds coming from many different directions. Capturing this effect with audio equipment and then either reinforcing the live audio or recreating the effect upon playback is quite challenging.

The biggest challenge is the microphone. A traditional microphone records the sound pressure amplitude at a single point in space. All the various sound waves arriving from different directions at different times are merged into a single electrical voltage wave on a wire. With all the data merged into a single audio signal, much of the four-dimensional acoustic information is lost. When you play that recorded sound out of a loudspeaker, all the reproduced sounds are now coming from a single direction as well. Adding more loudspeakers doesn't solve the problem because then you just have every sound repeated identically from every direction, and the precedence effect will simply kick in and tell our brains that the sound is only coming from the lone source that hits our ears first.

The first step in addressing some of these problems is to start using more than one microphone. Stereo is the most common recording and playback technique. Stereo is an entirely man-made effect, but produces a more dynamic effect upon playback of the recorded material with only one additional loudspeaker. The basic idea is that since we have two ears, two loudspeakers should be sufficient to reproduce some of the four-dimensional effects of acoustic sound. It's important to understand that there is no such thing as stereo sound in an acoustic space. You can't make a stereo recording of a natural sound. When recording sound that will be played back in stereo, the most common strategy is recording each sound source with a dedicated microphone that is as acoustically isolated as possible from the other sound sources and microphones. For example, if you were trying to record a simple rock band, you would put a microphone on each drum in the drum kit as close to the drum as possible. For the electric bass, you would put a microphone as close as possible to the amplifier and probably use a hardwired cable from the instrument itself. This gives you two signals to work with for that instrument. You would do the same for the guitar. If possible, you might even isolate the bass amplifier and the guitar amplifier inside acoustically sealed boxes or rooms to

> **ASIDE:** If the instruments are all acoustically isolated, the musicians may have a hard time hearing themselves and each other. This poses a significant obstacle, as they will have a difficult time trying to play together. To address this problem, you have to set up a complicated monitoring system. Typically each musician has a set of headphones that feeds him or her a custom mix of the sounds from each microphone/instrument.

keep their sound from bleeding into the other microphones. The singer would also be isolated in a separate room with a dedicated microphone.

During the recording process, the signal from each microphone is recorded on a separate track in the DAW software and written to a separate audio file on the hard drive. With an isolated recording of each instrument, a mix can be created that distributes the sound of each instrument between two channels of audio that are routed to the left and right stereo loudspeaker. To the listener sitting between the two loudspeakers, a sound that is found only on the left channel sounds like it comes from the left of the listener and vice versa for the right channel. A sound mixed equally into both channels seems to the listener to be coming from an invisible loudspeaker directly in the middle. This is called the **phantom center channel**. By adjusting the balance between the two channels, you can place sounds at various locations in the phantom image between the two loudspeakers. This flexibility in mixing is possible only because each instrument was recorded in isolation. This stereo mixing effect is very popular and produces acceptable results for most listeners.

When recording in a situation where it's not practical to use multiple microphones in isolation, such as for a live performance or a location recording where you're capturing an environmental sound, it's still possible to capture the sound in a way that creates a stereo-like effect. This is typically done using two microphones and manipulating the way the pickup patterns of the microphones overlap. Figure 8.5 shows a polar plot for a cardioid microphone. Recall that a cardioid microphone is a directional microphone that picks up the sound very well on-axis with the front of the microphone, but doesn't pick up the sound as well off-axis. This polar plot shows only one plotted line, representing the pickup pattern for a specific frequency (usually 1 kHz), but keep in mind that the directivity of the microphone changes slightly for different frequencies. Lower frequencies are less directional and higher frequencies are more directional than what is shown in Figure 8.5. With that in mind, we can examine the plot for this frequency to get an idea of how the microphone responds to sounds from varying directions. Our reference level is taken at 0° (directly on-axis). The dark black line representing the relative pickup level of the microphone intersects with the 0 dB line at 0°. As you move off-axis, the sensitivity of the microphone changes. At around 75°, the line intersects with the −5 dB point on the graph, meaning that at that angle, the microphone picks up the sound 5 dB quieter than it does on-axis. As you move to around 120°, the microphone now picks up the

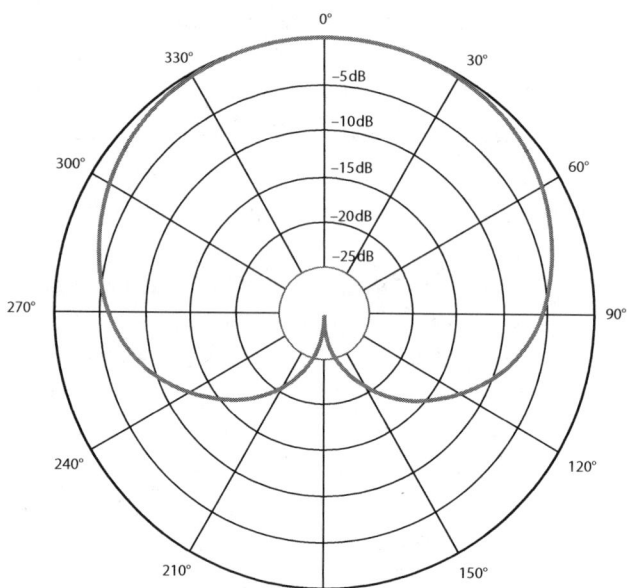

FIGURE 8.5: POLAR PATTERN FOR
A CARDIOID MICROPHONE

sound 15 dB quieter than the on-axis level. At 180° the level is null.

One strategy for recording sound with a stereo effect is to use an X-Y cross-pair. The technique works by taking two matched cardioid microphones and positioning them so the microphone capsules line up horizontally at 45° angles that cross over the on-axis point of the opposite microphone. Getting the capsules to line up horizontally is very important because you want the sound from every direction to arrive at both microphones at the same time, and therefore in the same phase.

Figure 8.6 shows a recording device with integrated X-Y cross-pair microphones, and Figure 8.7 shows the polar patterns of both microphones when used in this configuration. The signals of these two microphones are recorded onto separate tracks and then routed to separate loudspeakers for playback. The stereo effect happens when these two signals combine in the air from the loudspeakers.

Let's first examine the audio signals that are unique to the left and right channels. For a sound that arrives at the microphones 90° off-axis, there is an approximately 15 dB difference in level for that sound captured between the two microphones. As a rule of thumb, whenever you have a level difference that is 10 dB or greater between two similar sounds, the louder sound takes precedence. Consequently, when that sound is played back through the two loudspeakers, it is per-

FIGURE 8.6: A PORTABLE RECORDING DEVICE USING INTEGRATED MICROPHONES IN AN X-Y CROSS-PAIR

ceived as though it's located entirely at the right loudspeaker. Likewise, a sound arriving 270° off-axis sounds as though it's located entirely at the left loudspeaker. At 0°, the sound arrives at both microphones at the same level. Because the sound is at an equal level in both microphones, and therefore is played back equally loud through both loudspeakers, it sounds to the listener as if it's coming from the phantom center image of the stereo field. At 45°, the polar plots tell us that the sound arrives at the right microphone approximately 7 dB louder than at the left. Since this is within the 10 dB range for perception, the level in the left channel causes the stereo image of the sound to be

ASIDE: At 0° on-axis to the X-Y pair, the individual microphone elements are still tilted 45°, making the microphone's pickup a few dB quieter than its own on-axis level would be. Yet because the sound arrives at both microphones at the same level and the same phase, the sound is perfectly reinforced, causing a boost in amplitude. In this case the result is actually slightly louder than the on-axis level of either individual microphone.

pulled slightly over from the right channel, now seeming to come from somewhere between the right speaker and the phantom center location. If the microphones are placed appropriately relative to the sound being recorded, this technique can provide a fairly effective stereo image without requiring any additional mixing or panning.

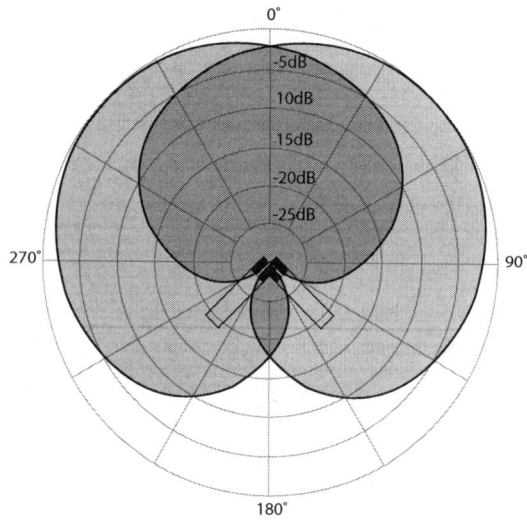

FIGURE 8.7: POLAR PATTERNS FOR TWO CARDIOID MICROPHONES IN AN X-Y CROSS-PAIR

Another technique for recording a live sound for a stereo effect is called **mid-side**. Mid-side also uses two microphones, but unlike X-Y, one microphone is a cardioid microphone and the other is a bidirectional or figure-eight microphone. The cardioid microphone is called the **mid microphone** and is pointed forward (on-axis), and the figure-eight microphone is called the **side microphone** and is pointed perpendicular to the mid microphone. Figure 8.8 shows the polar patterns of these two microphones in a mid-side configuration.

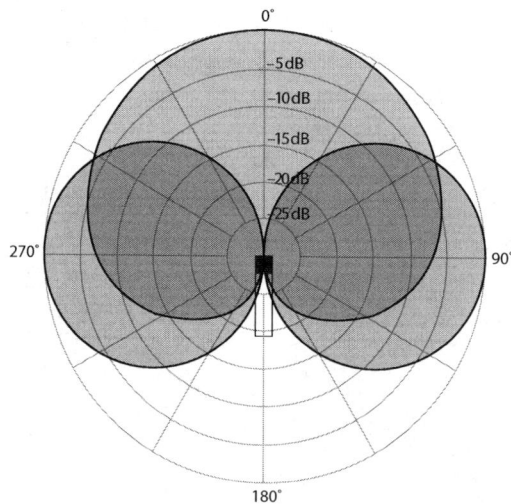

FIGURE 8.8: POLAR PATTERNS FOR TWO MICROPHONES IN A MID-SIDE SETUP

The side microphone has a single diaphragm that responds to pressure changes on either side of the microphone. The important thing to understand here is that because of the single diaphragm, the sounds on either side of the microphone are captured in opposite polarity. That is, a sound that causes a positive impulse on the right of the microphone causes a negative impulse on the left of the microphone. It is this polarity effect of the figure-eight microphone that allows the mid-side technique to work. After you've recorded the signal from these two microphones onto separate channels, you have to set up a mid-side matrix decoder in your mixing console or DAW software in order to create the stereo mix. To create a mid-side matrix, you take the audio from the mid microphone and route it to both left and right output channels (pan center). The audio from the side microphone gets split two ways. First it gets sent to the left channel (pan left). Then it gets sent also to the right channel (pan right) with the polarity inverted. Figure 8.9 shows a mid-side matrix setup in Logic. The "Gain" plugin inserted on the "Side -" track is being used only to invert the polarity (erroneously labeled "Phase Invert" in the plug-in interface).

FIGURE 8.9: MID-SIDE MATRIX IN LOGIC

Through the constructive and destructive combinations of the mid and side signals at varying angles, this matrix creates a stereo effect at its output. The center image is essentially derived from the on-axis response of the mid microphone, which by design happens also to be the off-axis point of the side microphone. Any sound that arrives at 0° to the mid microphone is added to both the left and right channels without any interaction from the signal from the side microphone, since at 0° to the mid-side setup the side microphone pickup is null. If you look at the polar plot in Figure 8.8, you can see that the mid microphone picks up every sound within a 120° spread with only 6 dB or so of variation in level. Aside from this slight level difference, the mid microphone doesn't contain any information that can alone be used to determine a sound's placement in the stereo field. However, approaching the 300° point (arriving more from the left of the mid-side setup), you can see that the sound arriving at the mid microphone is also picked up by the side microphone at the same level and the same polarity. Similarly, a sound that arrives at 60° also arrives at the side microphone at the same level as the mid, but this time it is inverted in polarity from the signal at the mid microphone. If you look at how these two signals combine, you can see that the mid sound at 300° mixes together with the "Side +" track and, because it is the same polarity, it reinforces in level. That same sound mixes together with the "Side −" track and cancels out because of the polarity inversion. The sound that arrives from the left of the mid-side setup therefore is louder on the left channel, and accordingly appears to come from the left side of the stereo field upon playback. Conversely, a sound coming from the right side at 60° reinforces when mixed with the "Side −" track but cancels out when mixed with the "Side +" track, and the matrixed result is louder in the right channel and accordingly appears to come from the right of the stereo field. Sounds that arrive between 0° and 300° or 0° and 60° have a more moderate reinforcing and canceling effect, and the resulting sound appears at some varying degree between left, right, and center depending on the specific angle. This creates the perception of sound that is spread between the two channels in the stereo image.

The result here is quite similar to the X-Y cross-pair technique with one significant difference. Adjusting the relative level of the "Mid" track alters the spread of the stereo image. Figure 8.10 shows a mid-side polar pattern with the mid microphone attenuated −10 dB. Notice that the angle where the two microphones pick up the sound at equal levels has narrowed to 45° and 315°. This means that when they are mixed together in the mid-side matrix, a smaller range of sounds are mixed equally into both left and right channels. This effectively widens the stereo image. Conversely, increasing the level of the mid microphone relative to the side microphone causes more sounds to be mixed into the left and right channels equally, thereby narrowing the stereo image. Unlike the X-Y cross-pair, with mid-side the stereo image can be easily manipulated after the recording has already been made.

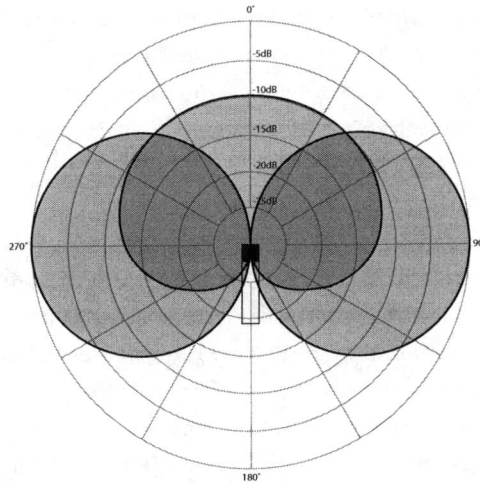

FIGURE 8.10: POLAR PATTERNS FOR TWO MICROPHONES IN MID-SIDE SETUP WITH THE MID MICROPHONE ATTENUATED −10 DB (WIDE MODE)

The concept behind mid-side recording can be expanded in a number of ways to allow recordings to capture sound in many directions while still maintaining the ability to recreate the desired directional information on playback. One example is shown in Figure 8.11. This microphone from the Soundfield company has four microphone capsules in a tetrahedral arrangement, each pointing a different direction. Using proprietary matrix processing, the four audio signals captured from this microphone can be combined to generate a mono, stereo, mid-side, four-channel surround, five-channel surround, or even a seven-channel surround signal.

The counterpart to setting up microphones for stereo recording is setting up loudspeakers for stereo listening. Thus, we touch on the mid-side technique in the context of loudspeakers in Section 8.2.4.5.

The most simplistic (and arguably the most effective) method for capturing four-dimensional sound is binaural recording. It's quite phenomenal that despite having only two transducers in our hearing system (our ears), we are somehow able to hear and perceive sounds from all directions. So instead of using complicated setups with multiple

FIGURE 8.11 SOUNDFIELD MICROPHONE

microphones, just by putting two microphones inside the ears of a real human, you can capture exactly what the two ears are hearing. This method of capture inherently includes all of the complex interaural time and intensity difference information caused by the physical location of the ears and the human head that allows the brain to decode and perceive the direction of the sound. If this recorded sound is then played back through headphones, the listener perceives the sound almost exactly as it was perceived by the listener in the original recording. While wearable headphone-style binaural microphone setups exist, sticking small microphones inside the ears of a real human is not always practical, and an acceptable compromise is to use a binaural dummy head microphone. A dummy head microphone is essentially the plastic head of a mannequin with molds of a real human ears on either side of the head. Inside each of these prosthetic ears is a small microphone, the two together capturing a binaural recording. Figure 8.12 shows a commercially available dummy head microphone from Neumann.

With binaural recording, the results are quite effective. All the level, phase, and frequency response information of the sound arriving at both ears individually that allows us to perceive sound is maintained in the recording. The real limitation here is that the effect is largely lost when the sound is played through loudspeakers. The interaural isolation provided by headphones is required when listening to binaural recordings in order to get the full effect.

A few algorithms have been developed that mimic the binaural localization effect. These algorithms have been implemented into binaural panning

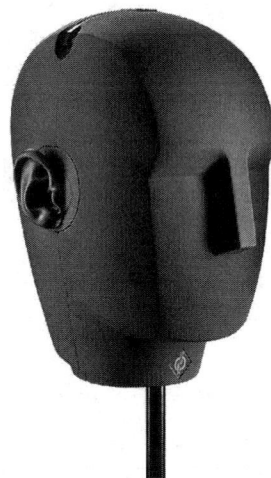

FIGURE 8.12: A BINAURAL RECORDING DUMMY HEAD WITH BUILT-IN MICROPHONES

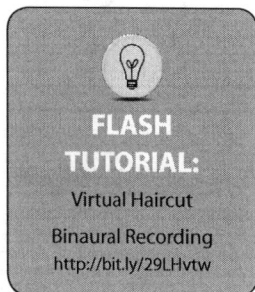

FLASH TUTORIAL:

Virtual Haircut

Binaural Recording

http://bit.ly/29LHvtw

plug-ins that are available for use in many DAW software programs, allowing you to artificially create binaural effects without requiring the dummy head recordings. An example of a binaural panning plug-in is shown in Figure 8.13. One algorithm is called the Cetera algorithm and is owned by the Starkey Hearing Technologies company. They use the algorithm in their hearing aids to help the reinforced sound from a hearing aid sound more like the natural response of the ear. Starkey created a demo of their algorithm called the

Starkey Virtual Barbershop. Although this recording sounds like it was captured with a binaural recording system, the binaural localization effects are actually rendered on a computer using the Cetera algorithm.

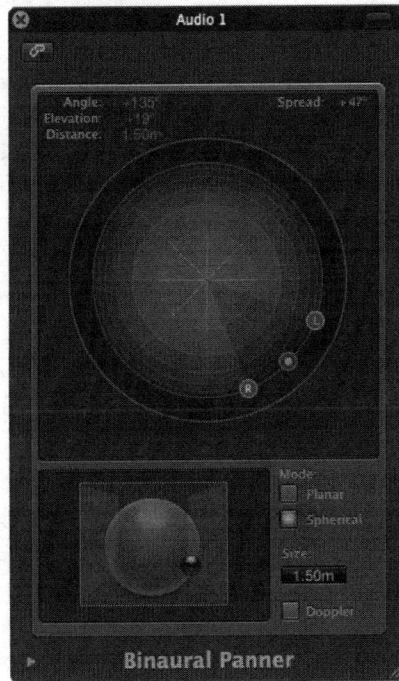

FIGURE 8.13: THE BINAURAL PANNING INTERFACE IN LOGIC

8.2.2.2 Setting Levels for Recording

Before you actually hit the "record" button, you'll want to verify that all your input levels are correct. The goal is to adjust the microphone preamplifiers so the signal from each microphone is coming into the digital converters at the highest voltage possible without clipping. Start by record-enabling the track in your software, and then have the performer do the loudest part of his or her performance. Adjust the preamplifier so that this level is at least 6 dB below clipping. This way when the performer sings or speaks louder, you can avoid a clip. While recording, keep an eye on the input meters for each track and make sure nothing clips. If you do get a clip, at the very least you need to reduce the input gain on the preamplifier. You may also need to redo that part of the recording if the clip was bad enough to cause audible distortion.

8.2.2.3 Multitrack Recording

As you learned in previous chapters, today's recording studios are equipped with powerful multitrack recording software that allows you to record different voices and instruments on different tracks. This environment requires that you make choices about what elements should be recorded at the same time. For example, if you're recording music using real instruments, you need to decide whether to record everything at the same time or record each instrument separately. The advantage to recording everything at the same time is that the musicians can play together and feel their way through the song. Musicians usually prefer this, and you almost always get a better performance when they play together. The downside to this method is that with all the musicians playing in the same room, it's difficult to get good isolation between the instruments in the recording. Unless you're very careful, you'll pick up the sound of the drums on the vocalist's microphone. This is hard to fix in post-production, because if you want the vocals louder in the mix, the drums get louder, also.

If you decide to record each track separately, your biggest problem is going to be synchronization. If all the various voices and instruments are not playing together, they will not be very well synchronized. They will start and end their notes at slightly different times, they may not blend very well, and they may not all play at the same tempo. The first thing you need to do to combat this problem is to make sure the performer can hear the other tracks that have already been recorded. Usually this can be accomplished by giving the performer a set of headphones to wear that are connected to your audio interface. The first track you record will set the standard for tempo, duration, and so on. If the subsequent tracks can be recorded while the performer listens to the previous ones, the original track can set the tempo. Depending on what you are recording, you may also be able to provide a metronome or click track for the performers to hear while they perform their tracks. Most recording software includes a metronome or click track feature. Even if you use good monitoring and have the performers follow a metronome, there will still be synchronization issues. You may need to have them do certain parts several times until you get one that times out correctly. You may also have to manipulate the timing after the fact in the editing process.

Figure 8.14 shows a view from the mixing console during a recording session for a film score. You can see through the window into the stage where the orchestra is playing. Notice that the conductor and other musicians are wearing headphones to allow them to hear each other and possibly even the metronome associated with the beat map indicated by the timing view on the overhead screen. These are all strategies for avoiding synchronization issues with large multitrack recordings.

Another issue you will encounter in nearly every recording is that performers will make mistakes. Often the performer will need to make several attempts at a given performance before an acceptable performance is recorded. These multiple attempts are called **takes**, and each take represents a separate recording of the performer attempting the same performance. In some cases a given take may be mostly acceptable, but there

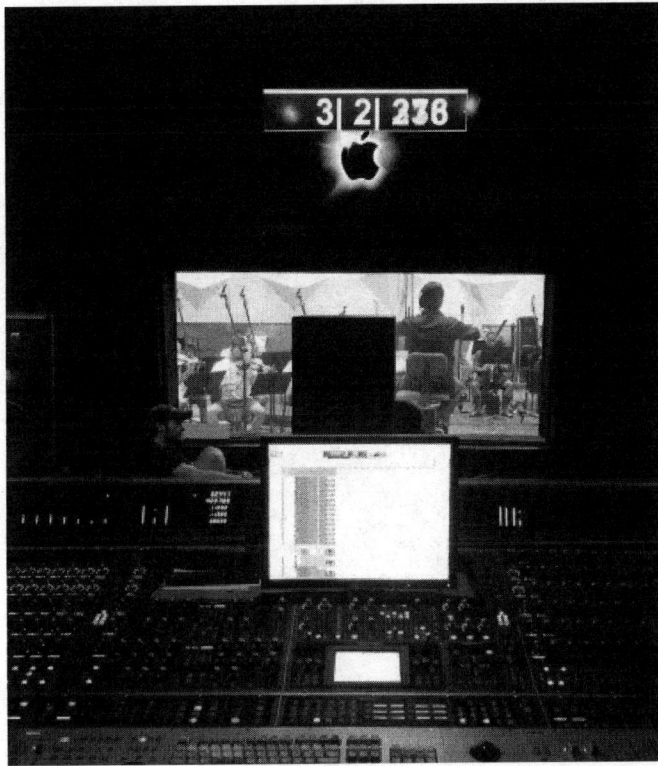

FIGURE 8.14: A VIEW FROM THE MIXING CONSOLE DURING A RECORDING SESSION FOR A FILM SCORE

was one small mistake. Instead of doing an entirely new take, you can just re-record that short period of the performance that contained the mistake. This is called **punch-in** recording.

To make a punch-in recording, you set up a start and stop time marker and start playback on the session. The performer hears the preceding several seconds and starts singing along with the recording. When the timeline encounters the start marker, the software starts writing the recording to the track and then reverts back to playback mode when the stop marker is reached. In the end you will have several takes and punch-ins folded into a single track. This is called a **composite track**, usually abbreviated to **comp**. A comp track allows you to unfold the track to see all the various takes. You can then go through them and select all the parts you want to keep from each take. A composite single version is created from all the takes you select. Figure 8.15 shows a multitrack recording session in Logic that uses a composite track that has been unfolded to show each take. The comp track is at the top and is color-coded to indicate which take was used for each period of time on the track.

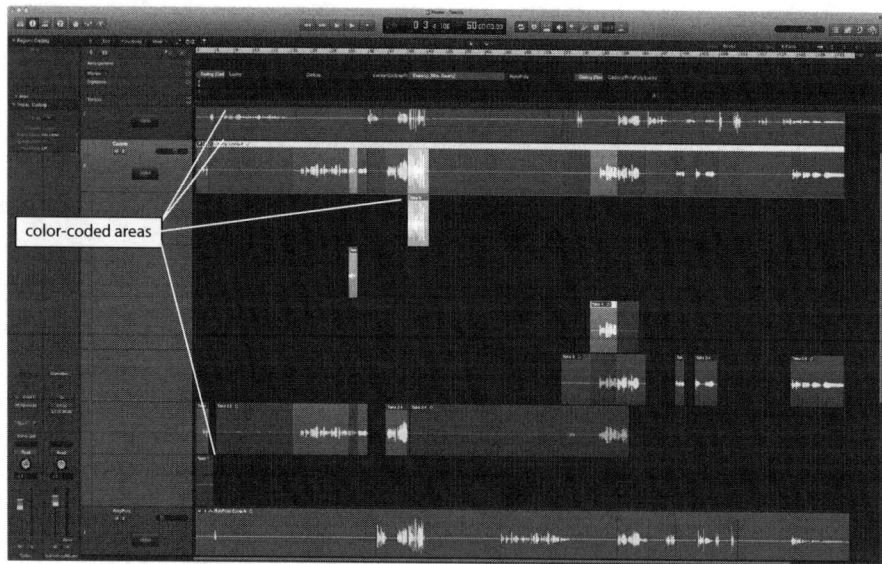

color-coded areas

**FIGURE 8.15: A MULTITRACK RECORDING SESSION IN LOGIC
WITH A COMPOSITE TRACK MADE UP FROM MULTIPLE TAKES**

8.2.2.4 Recording Sound for Film or Video

Production audio for film or video refers to the sound captured during the production process—when the film or video is actually being shot. In production, there may be various sounds you're trying to capture—the voices of the actors, environmental sounds, sounds of props, or other scenic elements. When recording in a controlled sound stage studio you generally can capture the production audio with reasonably good quality, but when recording on location you constantly have to battle background noise. The challenge in either situation is to capture the sounds you need without capturing the sounds you don't need.

All the same rules apply in this situation as in other recording situations. You need good quality microphones, and you need to get them as close as possible to the thing you're trying to record. Microphone placement can be challenging in a production environment where high definition cameras are close up on actors, capturing a lot of detail. Typically the microphone needs to be invisible or out of the camera shot. Actors can wear wireless lavaliere microphones as long as they can be hidden under some clothing. This placement affects the quality of the sound being picked up by the microphone, but in the production environment compromises are a necessity. The primary emphasis is of course on capturing the things that would be impossible or expensive to change in post-production, like performances or action sequences. For example, if you don't get the perfect performance from the actors, or the scenery falls down, it's very difficult to fix the problem without completely repeating the entire production process. On the other hand, if the production audio is not captured with a high enough quality, the actor can be brought back in alone to re-record the audio without having to reshoot the video. The bottom line is that in the production environment, the picture and the performance are the most important things. Capturing the production audio is ultimately of less importance because it's easier to fix in post-production.

With this in mind, most production audio engineers are willing to make some compromises by putting microphones under clothing. The other option is to mount a small directional microphone to a long pole called a **boom pole**. Someone outside the camera shot holds the pole, and he or she can get the microphone fairly close to actors or objects without getting the microphone in the shot. Because reshooting is so expensive, the most important job of the boom pole operator is to keep the microphone out of the shot. Picking up usable production audio is secondary.

Musical scores are another major element in film and video. Composers typically work first on developing a few musical themes to be used throughout the film while the editing process is still happening. Once a full edit is completed, the composer takes the themes and creates versions of various lengths to fit with the timing of the edited scenes. Sometimes this is done entirely with electronic instruments directly in the DAW with the video imported to the project file for a visual reference. Other times, a recording session is conducted where an orchestra is brought into a recording studio called a **scoring stage**. The film is projected in the studio and the composer, along with a conductor performs the musical passages for the film using clicks and streamers to help synchronize the important moments.

A final challenge to be mentioned in the context of film and video is the synchronization of sound and picture. The audio is typically captured on a completely different recording medium than the video or film, and the two are put back together in post-production. In the analog domain this can be a very tricky process. The early attempt at facilitating synchronization was the clapboard slate. The slate has an area where you can write the name of the show, the scene number, and the take number. There is also a block of wood connected to the slate with a hinge. This block of wood can be raised and lowered quickly onto the slate to make a loud clap sound. The person holding the slate reads the information written on the slate out loud while holding the slate in front of the camera and then drops the clapper. In post-production, the slate information can be seen on the film and heard on the audio recording. This way, you know that you have the correct audio recording with the correct video. The clap sound can easily be heard on the audio recording, and on the video you can easily see the moment that the clapper closes. The editor can line up the sound of the clap with the image of the clapper closing, and then everything after that is in sync. This simple and low-tech solution has proven to be quite effective and is still used in modern film-making along with other improvements in synchronization technology.

A time code format called SMPTE (Society of Motion Picture and Television Engineering) has been developed to address the issue of synchronization. The format of SMPTE time code is described in Chapter 6. The idea behind time code synchronization is that the film has a built-in measuring system. There are 24 frames or still pictures every second in traditional motion picture film, with each frame being easily identified. The problem is that on an audiotape there is no inherent way to know which part of audio goes with which frame of video. Part of the SMPTE time code specification includes a method of encoding the time code into an audio signal that can be recorded on a separate track of audio on the tape recorder. This way, the entire audio recording is linked to each frame of the video. In the digital domain, this time code can be encoded into the video signal as well as the audio signal, and the computer can keep everything in sync. The slate clapper has even been updated to display the current time code value to facilitate synchronization in post-production.

8.2.2.5 Sound Effects

Sound effects are important components in film, video, and theatre productions. Sound effects are sometimes referred to as **Foley sound**, named after Jack Foley, who did the original work on sound effect techniques in the early days of silent films. Foley artists are a special breed of filmmaker who create all the sound effects for a film manually in a recording session. Foley stages are recording studios with all kinds of toys, floor surfaces, and other gadgets that make various sounds. The Foley artists go into the stage and watch the film while performing all the sounds required, ranging from footsteps and turning doorknobs to guns, rain, and other environmental sounds. The process is a lot of fun, and some people build entire careers as Foley artists.

The first step in the creation of sound effects is acquiring some source material to work with. Commercial sound effect libraries are available for purchase, and there are some online sources for free sound effects, but the free sources are often of inconsistent quality. Sometimes you may need to go out and record your own source material. The goal here is not necessarily to find the exact sound you are looking for. Instead, you can try to find source material that has some of the characteristics of the sound. Then you can edit, mix and process the source material to achieve a more exact result.

VIDEO TUTORIAL:
Creating a
Sound Effect
http://bit.ly/29uL5vC

There are a few common tools used to transform your source sound. One of the most useful is pitch shifting. For example, spaghetti noodles breaking can sound like a tree falling when pitched down an octave or two. When using pitch shift, you will get the most dramatic transformative results when using a pitch shifter that does not attempt to maintain the original timing. In other words, when a sound is pitched up, it should also speed up. Pitch shifting in sound effect creation is demonstrated in the video associated with this section.

Another strategy is to mix several sounds together in a way that creates an entirely new sound. If you can break down the sound you are looking for into descriptive layers, you can then find source material for each of those layers and mix them all together. For example, you would never be able to record the roar of a Tyrannosaurus Rex, but if you can describe the sound you're looking for, perhaps as something between an elephant trumpeting and a lion roaring, you're well on your way to finding that source material and creating that new, hybrid sound.

Sometimes reverb or EQ can help achieve the sound you are looking for. If you have a vocal recording that you want to sound like it is coming from an old answering machine, using an EQ to filter out the low and high frequencies but enhance the mid frequencies can mimic the sound of the small loudspeakers in those machines. Making something sound farther away can be accomplished by reducing the high frequencies with an EQ to mimic the effect of the high frequency loss over distance, and some reverb can mimic the effect of the sound reflecting from several surfaces during its long trip.

8.2.2.6 MIDI and Other Digital Tools for Sound and Music Composition

In this section, we introduce some of the possibilities for sound and music creation that today's software tools offer, even to someone not formally educated as a composer. We include this section not to suggest that MIDI-generated music is a perfectly good substitute for music composed by classically trained musicians. However, computer-generated music can sometimes be appropriate for a project for reasons having to do with time, budget, resources, or style. Sound designers for film or theatre frequently take advantage of MIDI synthesizers and samplers as they create their soundscapes. Sometimes, a segment of music can be "sketched in" by the sound designer with MIDI sequencers, and this "rough draft" can serve as scratch or temporary music in a production or film. In this section, we'll demonstrate the functionality of digital music tools and show you how to get the most out of them for music composition.

Traditionally, composing is a process of conceiving melodies and harmonies and putting them down on paper, called a **musical score**. Many new MIDI and other digital tools have been created to help streamline and improve the scoring process—Finale, Sibelius, or the open source MuseScore, to name a few. Written musical scores can be played by live musicians either as part of a performance or during a recording session. But today's scoring software gives you even more options, allowing you to play back the score directly from the computer, interpreting the score as MIDI messages and generating the music through samplers and synthesizers. Scoring software also allows you to create audio data from the MIDI score and save it to a permanent file. Most software also lets you export your musical score as individual MIDI tracks, which can then be imported, arranged, and mixed in your DAW.

The musical quality of the audio that is generated from scoring software is dependent not only on the quality samplers and synthesizers used, but also on the scoring performance data that you include—marking for dynamics, articulation, and so forth. Although the amount of musical control and intuitiveness within scoring software continues to improve, we can't really expect the software to interpret *allegro con moto*, or even a *crescendo* or *fermata*, the way an actual musician would. If not handled carefully, computer-generated music can sound very "canned" and mechanical. Still, it's possible to use your digital tools to create scratch or temporary music for a production or film, providing a pretty good sense of the composition to collaborators, musicians, and audiences until the final score is ready to be produced. There are also a number of ways to tweak and improve computer-generated music. If you learn to use your tools well, you can achieve surprisingly good results.

As mentioned, the quality of the sound you generate depends in large part on your sample playback system. The system could be the firmware on a hardware device, a standalone software application, or a software plug-in that runs within your DAW. A basic sampler plays back a specific sound according to a received trigger, such as a key pressed on the MIDI keyboard or note data received from a music scoring application. Basic samplers may not even play a unique sound for each different key, but instead mathematically shape one sample file to produce multiple notes (as described in Chapter 6), where multiple variations of a sample or note are played back depending, for example, on how hard/loud a note is played. These samplers may also utilize other performance parameters and data to manipulate the sound for a more dynamic, realistic feel. For instance, the modulation wheel (or *mod wheel*) can be linked to an LFO that imparts a controllable vibrato characteristic to the sound sample. While these sampler features greatly improve the realism of sample playback, the most powerful samplers go far beyond this.

Another potent feature provided by some samplers is the **round robin**. Suppose you play two equivalent notes on a real instrument. Although both notes may have the same instrument and pitch and essentially the same force, in "real life" the two notes never sound exactly the same. With round robin, more than one version of a note is available for each instrument and velocity. The sampler automatically cycles playback through this set of similar samples so that no two consecutive "identical" notes sound exactly the same. In order to have round robin capability, the sampler has to have multiple takes of the audio samples for every note, and for multisampled sounds, this means multiple takes for every velocity as well. The number of round robin sound samples included varies from two to five, depending on the system. This duplication of samples obviously increases the memory requirements for the sampler. Some sampler systems instead use subtle processing to vary the way a sample sounds each time it is played back, simulating the round robin effect without the need for additional samples, but this may not achieve quite the same realism.

Another feature of high-end sampler instruments and sampler systems is **multiple articulations**. Consider the sound of a guitar, which has a different timbre depending whether it's played with a pick, plucked with a finger, palm-muted, or hammered on. Classical stringed instruments have even more articulations than do guitars. Rather than having a separate sampler instrument for each articulation, all of these articulations can be layered into one instrument, yet with the ability for you to maintain individual control. Typically the sampler has a number of **keyswitches** that switch between the articulations. These keyswitches are keys on the keyboard that are above or below the instrument's musical range. Pressing the key sets the articulation for notes to be played subsequently.

VIDEO TUTORIAL: Keyswitching http://bit.ly/29lxDcH

An example of keyswitches on a sampler can be seen in Figure 8.16. Some sampler systems even have intelligent playback that switch articulations automatically depending on how notes overlap or are played in relation to each other. The more articulations the system has, the better for getting realistic sound and range from an instrument. However, knowing how and when to employ those articulations is often limited by your familiarity with the particular instrument, so musical experience plays an important role here.

FIGURE 8.16 : SAMPLER WITH KEYSWITCHES

As you can see, realistic computer-generated music depends not only on the quality, but also the quantity and diversity of the content to play back. Realistic virtual instruments demand powerful and intelligent sampler playback systems, not to mention the computer hardware specs to support them. One company's upright bass instrument alone contains over 21,000 samples. For optimum performance, some of these larger sampler systems even allow networked playback, out-sourcing the CPU and memory load of samples to other dedicated computers.

> **ASIDE:** In addition to the round-robin and multiple articulation samples, some instruments also include release samples, such as the subtle sound of a string being released or muted, which are played back when a note is released to help give it a natural and realistic ending. Even these release samples could have round-robin variations of their own!

With the power and scope of the virtual instruments emerging today, it's possible to produce full orchestral scores from your DAW. As nice as these virtual instruments are, they will only get you so far without additional production skills that help you get the most out of your digital compositions.

With the complexity and diversity of the instruments that you'll attempt to perform on a simple MIDI keyboard, it may take several passes at individual parts and sections to capture a performance you're happy with. With MIDI, of course, merging performances and editing out mistakes is a simple task. It doesn't require dozens of layers of audio files, messy crossfades, and the inherent issues of recorded audio. You can do as many takes as necessary and break down the parts in whatever way that helps to improve the performance.

> **ASIDE:** **Quantization** means different things in the context of digital audio vs. MIDI. As explained in Chapter 5, quantization of digital audio refers to forcing audio samples to a fixed amplitude level in accordance with the chosen bit depth. Quantization in MIDI refers to adjusting the timing of notes to a chosen level of detail—whole notes, half notes, quarter notes, and so on.

If your timing is inconsistent between performances, you can always **quantize** the notes. **Quantization** in MIDI refers to adjusting the performance data to the nearest selectable time value, be it whole note, half note, quarter note, and so on. While quantizing can help tighten up your performance, it is also a main contributor to your composition sounding mechanical and unnatural. While you don't want to be off by a whole beat, tiny imperfections in timing are natural with human performance and can help your music sound more convincing. Some DAW sequencers will let you choose a degree of quantization, in addition to a unit of timing; in other words, you may choose how forceful you want to be when pushing your note data toward that fixed value. This will let you maintain some of the feel of your actual performance.

Most sequencers also have a collection of other MIDI processing functions; for example, with **randomization** you can select a group of notes that you've quantized and randomize the starting position and duration of the note (as well as other parameters such as note velocity) by some small amount, introducing some of these timing imperfections back into the performance. These processes are ironically sometimes known as **humanization** functions, which nevertheless can come in handy when polishing up a digital music composition.

When actual musicians play their instruments, particularly longer sustained notes, they typically don't play them at a constant level and timbre. They could be doing this in response to a marking of dynamics in the score (such as a crescendo), or they may simply be expressing their own style and interpretation of the music. Differences in the way notes are played also result from simple human factors. One trumpet player pushes the air a little harder than another to get a note started or to end a long note when he's running out of breath. The bowing motion on a stringed instrument varies slightly as the bow moves back and forth, and differs from one musician to another. Only a machine can produce a note in exactly the same way every time. These nuances aren't captured in timing or note velocity information, but some samplers can respond to MIDI control data in order to achieve these more dynamic performances. As the name might imply, an important one of these is MIDI controller 11, **expression**. Manipulating the expression value is a great way to add a natural, continuous arc to longer sustained notes, and it's a great way to simulate dynamic swells as well as variations in string bowing. In many cases, controller 11 simply affects the volume of the playback, although some samplers are programmed to respond to it in a more dynamic way. Many MIDI keyboards have an expression pedal input, allowing you to control the expression with a variable foot pedal. If your keyboard has knobs or faders, you can also set these to write expression data, or you can always draw it into your sequencer software by hand with a mouse or track pad.

An example of expression data captured into a MIDI sequencer region can be seen in Figure 8.17. MIDI controller 1, the **modulation wheel**, is also often linked to a variable element of the sampler instrument. In many cases, it will default as a vibrato control for the sound, either by applying a simple LFO to the pitch, or even dynamically crossfading with a recorded vibrato sample. When long sustained notes are played or sung live, a note pitch may start out normally, but as the note goes on, an increasing amount of vibrato may be applied, giving it a nice fullness. Taking another pass over your music performance with the modulation wheel in hand, you can bring in varying levels of vibrato at appropriate times, enhancing the character and natural feel of your composition.

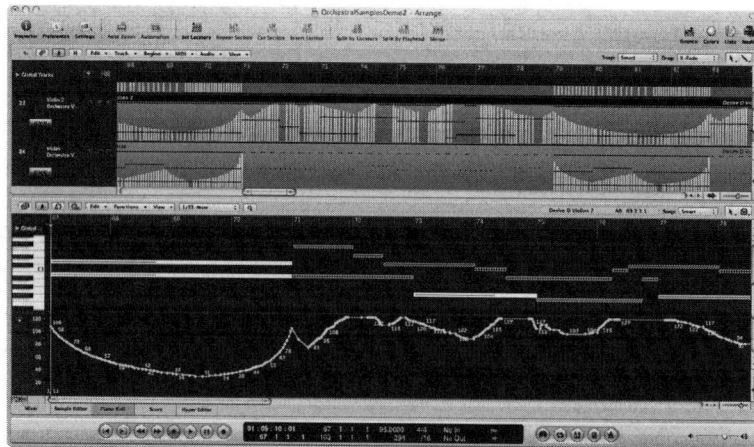

FIGURE 8.17: EXPRESSION DATA CAPTURED INSIDE A MIDI SEQUENCER REGION

As you can see, getting a great piece of music out of your digital composition isn't always as simple as playing a few notes on your MIDI keyboard. With all of the nuanced control available in today's sampler systems, crafting even a single instrument part can require careful attention to detail and is often an exercise in patience. Perhaps hiring a live musician sounds much better at the moment? Certainly, when you have access to the real deal, it is often a simpler and more effective way to create a piece of music. Yet if you enjoy total control over their production and are deeply familiar and experienced with your digital music production toolset, virtual instruments can be a fast and powerful means of bringing your music to life.

MAX DEMO:
Digital Music
Manipulation
http://bit.ly/29kHIL2

8.2.3 POST-PRODUCTION

8.2.3.1 Overdubbing

Post-production for film and video often requires a process of overdubbing. Overdubbing production audio is referred to as **ADR**, which stands for **Automated Dialog Replacement** or **Additional Dialogue Recording** (depending on who you ask). During this process, an actor is brought into a recording studio, looks at the scene that was filmed during the production process, and listens to the performance she gave. The actor then attempts to recreate that performance vocally. Overdubbing is typically done in small chunks in a loop so the actor has multiple attempts to get it right. She's trying to recreate not only the sound but also the speed of the original performance, so that the new recording is synchronized with the movement of the lips on the screen. System clicks and streamers can be used to help the actor. *Clicks* (sometimes called *beeps*) are a rhythmic sound, like a metronome, that counts down to a certain point when the actor needs to start or hit a particular word. *Streamers* are a visual reference that follows the same speed of the clicks. The streamer is a solid line across the screen that moves in time with the clicks, so you can see when important synchronization events occur.

Clicks and streamers are also used in other post-production audio tasks for synchronizing sound effects and music during recording sessions. A *click* refers to a metronome that the conductor and musicians listen to do keep the music in time with the picture. A *streamer* is a colored vertical line that moves across the screen over a period of 2 to 4 seconds. When the streamer reaches the end of the screen, the music is meant to have reached a certain point. For example, the beginning of each measure might need to synchronize with the switch in the camera shot.

FIGURE 8.18: A BLUE STREAMER (SHOWN HERE AS A GRAY BAR) USED TO HELP A MUSICIANS TIME OUT THEIR PERFORMANCE WITH THE PICTURE

8.2.3.2 Mixing

Mixing is the process in which multiple sounds recorded on different tracks in a DAW are combined, with adjustments made to their relative levels, frequency components, dynamics, and special effects. Then the resulting mix is channeled to different speakers appropriately. The mixing process, hardware, and software were covered in detail in Chapter 7. Thus, we focus here on practical and design considerations that direct the mixing process.

When you sit down to mix a recording, you go through a process of trying to balance how you want the recording to sound against the quality of the recording. Often you will be limited in what you're able to achieve with the mix because the source recording does not allow you sufficient manipulation. For example, if your recording of a band playing a song was recorded using a single overhead microphone, your ability to mix that recording is severely limited because all the instruments, room acoustics, and background noise are on the same track. You can turn the whole thing up or down, EQ and compress the overall recording, and add some reverb, but you have no control over the balance between the different instruments. On the other end of the spectrum, you could have a recording with each instrument, voices, and other elements on separate tracks, each recorded with separate microphones well-isolated from one another. In this scenario you have quite a bit of control over the mix, but mixing down 48 or more tracks is very time-consuming. If you don't have the time or expertise to harness all of that data, you may be forced to settle for something less than what you envision for the mix. Ultimately, you could work on a mix for the rest of your life and never be completely satisfied. So make sure you have clear goals and priorities for what you want to achieve with the mix, and work through each priority until you run out of time or run out of parameters to manipulate.

Mixing sound for film or video can be particularly challenging because there are often quite a few different sounds happening at once. One way of taming the mix is to use surround sound. Mixing the various elements to different loudspeakers separates the sounds such that each can be heard in the mix. Voices are typically mixed to the center channel, while music and sound effects are mixed to the four different surround channels.

Loudness and dynamics are also an issue that gets close attention in the mixing process. In some cases, you may need to meet a specific average loudness level over the course of the entire video. In other cases, you might need to compress the voices but leave the rest of the mix unchanged. The mix engineer will typically create **stems** (similar to busses or groups) to help with the process, such as a vocal stem, a music stem, and a sound effects stem. These stems can then be manipulated for various delivery mediums. You can see the usefulness of stems in situations where the sound being mixed is destined for one medium—for television broadcast or DVD distribution, for example. The audio needs of a television broadcast are very different from the needs of a DVD. If the mix is ultimately going to be adjusted for both of these media, it is much easier to use stems rather than returning to the original multitrack source, which may involve several hundred tracks.

> PRACTICAL EXERCISE:
> Mixing Multitrack Audio
> http://bit.ly/29uGycO

8.2.3.3 Mastering

When you've completed the mixing process for a recording project, the next step is mastering the mixed-down audio. **Mastering** is the process of adjusting the dynamics and frequency response of a mix in order to optimize it for listening in various environments and prepare it for storage on the chosen medium. The term *mastering* comes from the idea of a master copy from which all other copies are made. Mastering is a particularly important step for music destined for CD or DVD, ensuring consistent levels and dynamics from one song to the next in an album.

In some ways you could describe the mastering process as making the mix sound louder. When mixing a multitrack recording, one thing you watch for is clipped signals. Once the mix is completed, you may have a well-balanced mix, but overall the mix sounds quieter than other mixes you hear on commercial recordings. What is typically happening is that you have one instrument in your mix that is a bit more dynamic than the others, and in order to keep the mix from clipping, you have to turn everything down because of this one instrument. One step in the mastering process is to use a multiband compressor to address this problem.

A multiband compressor is a set of compressors, each of which operates on a limited frequency band without affecting others. A traditional compressor attenuates the entire mix when one frequency exceeds the threshold. A multiband compressor, on the other hand, attenuates an instrument that is dynamic in one frequency band without attenuating other bands. This is often much more effective than using a simple EQ because the processing is only applied when needed, whereas an EQ will boost or cut a certain range of frequencies all the time. This allows you to let the less-dynamic frequencies take a more prominent role in the mix, resulting in the entire mix sounding louder.

Figure 8.19 shows an example of a multiband compressor with five separate bands of compression centered on the frequency indicated by the gray dots. You can set a separate threshold, gain, and compression range. In this case, a range is taking place of a ratio. The idea is that you want to compress the frequency band to stay within a given range. As you adjust the gain for each band, that range gets shifted up or down. This has the effect of manipulating the overall frequency response of the track in a way that is responsive to the changing amplitudes of the various frequencies. For example, if the frequency band centered at 1.5 kHz gets suddenly very loud, it can be attenuated for that period of time but then restored when the sound in that band drops back down to a more regular level.

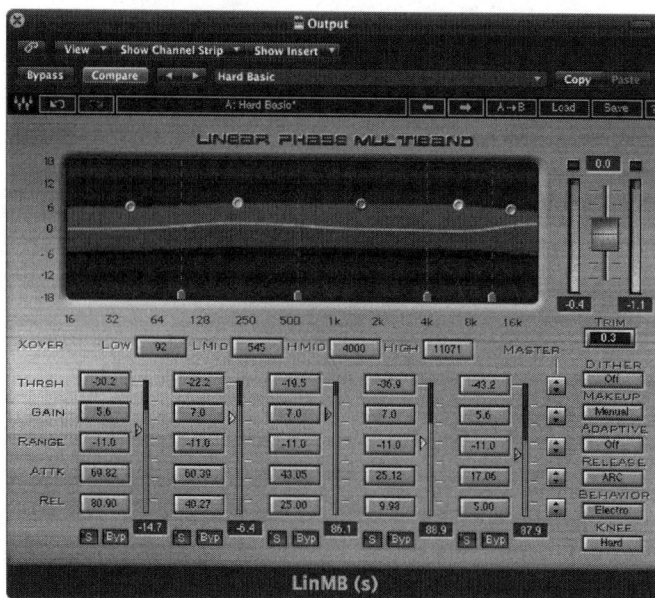

FIGURE 8.19: A MULTIBAND COMPRESSOR USED FOR MASTERING

You may also choose to apply some overall EQ in the mastering process to suit your taste. In some cases you may also manipulate the stereo image a bit to widen or narrow the overall stereo effect. You may also want to add a multiband limiter at the end of the processing chain to catch any stray clipped signals that may have resulted from your other processes. If you're converting to a lower bit depth, you should also apply a dither process to the mix to account for any quantization errors. For example, CDs require 16-bit samples, but most recording systems use 24 bits. Even if you are not converting bit depth you may still want to use dither, since most DAW programs process the audio internally at 32 or 64 bits before returning back the original 24 bits. A 24-bit dither could help you avoid any quantization errors that would occur in that process. Figure 8.20 shows an example of a multiband limiter that includes a dither processor.

8.2.4 LIVE SOUND

8.2.4.1 Designing a Sound Delivery System

Theatre and concert performances introduce unique challenges in pre-production not present in sound for CD, DVD, film, or video, due to the fact that the sound is delivered live. One of the most important parts of the process in this context is the design of a sound delivery system. The purpose of the design is to ensure clarity of sound and a uniform experience among audience members.

FIGURE 8.20: A MULTIBAND LIMITER WITH DITHER

In a live performance, it's quite possible that when the performers on the stage create their sound, that sound does not arrive at the audience loudly or clearly enough to be intelligible. A sound designer or sound engineer is hired to design a sound reinforcement system to address this problem. The basic process is to use microphones near the performers to pick up whatever sound they're making, and then play that sound out of strategically-located loudspeakers.

There are several things to consider when designing and operating a sound reinforcement system:

» The loudspeakers must faithfully generate a loud-enough sound.
» The microphones must pick up the source sound as faithfully as possible without getting in the way.
» The loudspeakers must be positioned in a way that will direct the sound to the listeners without sending too much sound to the walls or back to the microphones. This is because reflections and reverberations affect intelligibility and gain.
» Ideally, the sound system will deliver a similar listening experience to all the listeners regardless of where they sit.

Many of these considerations can be analyzed before you purchase the sound equipment so that you can spend your money wisely. Also, once the equipment is installed, the system can be tested and adjusted for better performance. These adjustments include repositioning microphones and loudspeakers to improve gain and frequency response, replacing equipment with something else that performs better, and adjusting the settings on equalizers, compressors, crossovers, and power amplifiers.

Most loudspeakers have a certain amount of directivity. Loudspeaker directivity is described in terms of the **6 dB down point**—a horizontal and vertical angle off-axis corresponding to the location where the sound is reduced by 6 dB. The 6 dB down point is significant because, as a rule of thumb, you want the loudness at any two points in the audience to differ by no more than 6 dB. In other words, the seat on the end of the aisle shouldn't sound more than 6 dB quieter or louder than the seat in the middle of the row or anywhere else in the audience.

The issue of loudspeaker directivity is complicated by the fact that loudspeakers naturally have a different directivity for each frequency. A single circular loudspeaker driver is more directional as the frequency increases because the loudspeaker diameter gets larger relative to the wavelength of the frequency. This high-frequency directivity effect is illustrated in Figure 8.21. Each of the six plots in the figure represents a different frequency produced by the same circular loudspeaker driver. In the figures, λ is the wavelength of the sound. (Recall that the higher the frequency, the smaller the wavelength. See Chapter 2 for the definition of wavelength, and see Chapter 1 for an explanation of how to read a polar plot.)

Going from top to bottom, left to right in Figure 8.21, the frequencies being depicted get smaller. Notice that frequencies having a wavelength that is longer than the diameter of the loudspeaker are dispersed very widely, as shown in the first two polar plots. Once the frequency has a wavelength that is equal to the diameter of the loudspeaker, the loudspeaker begins to exercise some directional control over the sound. This directivity gets narrower as the frequency increases and the wavelength decreases.

This varying directivity per frequency for a single loudspeaker driver partially explains why most full-range loudspeakers have multiple drivers. The problem is not that a single loudspeaker can't produce the entire audible spectrum. Any set of headphones uses a single driver for the entire spectrum. The problem with using one loudspeaker driver for the entire spectrum is that you can't distribute all the frequencies uniformly across the listening area. The listeners sitting right in front of the loudspeaker will hear everything fine, but for the listeners sitting to the side of the loudspeaker, the low frequencies will be much louder than the high ones. To distribute frequencies more uniformly, a second loudspeaker driver, considerably smaller than the first, can be added. Then an electronic unit called a **crossover** directs the high frequencies to

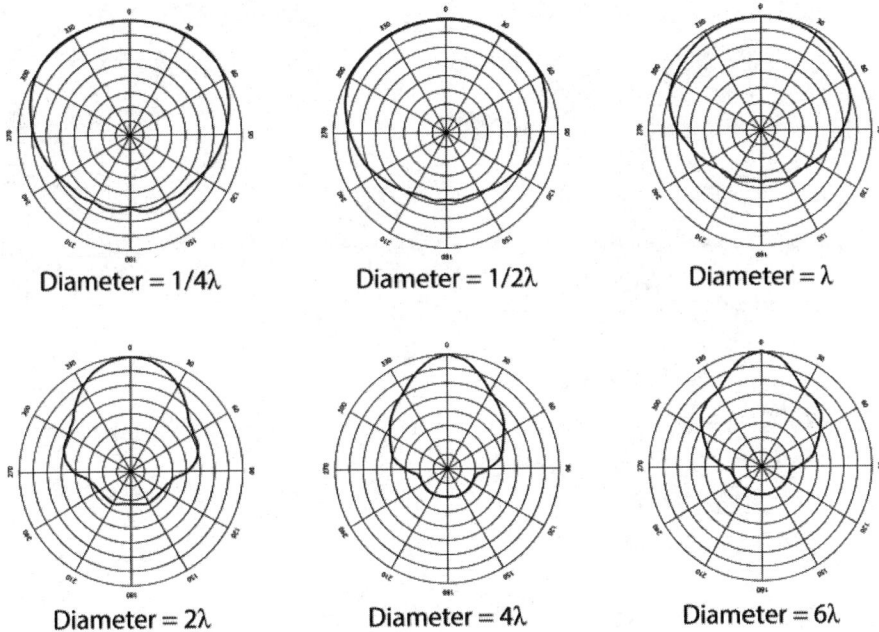

| Diameter = 1/4λ | Diameter = 1/2λ | Diameter = λ |

| Diameter = 2λ | Diameter = 4λ | Diameter = 6λ |

**FIGURE 8.21: DIRECTIVITY OF CIRCULAR RADIATORS—
DIAGRAMS CREATED FROM ACTUAL MEASURED SOUND**

the small driver and the low frequencies to the large driver. With two different-sized drivers, you can achieve a much more uniform directional dispersion, as shown in Figure 8.22. In this case, the larger driver is 5″ in diameter and the smaller one is 1″ in diameter. Wavelengths corresponding to frequencies of 500 Hz and 1000 Hz have larger wavelengths than 5″, so they are fairly omnidirectional. The reason that frequencies of 2000 Hz and above have consistent directivity is that the frequencies are distributed to the two loudspeaker drivers in a way that keeps the relationship consistent between the wavelength and the diameter of the driver. The 2000 Hz and 4000 Hz frequencies would be directed through the 5″ diameter driver because their wavelengths are between 6″ and 3″. The 8000 Hz and 16,000 Hz frequencies would be distributed to the 1″ diameter driver because their wavelengths are between 2″ and 1″. This way, the two different-sized drivers are able to exercise directional control over the frequencies that are radiating.

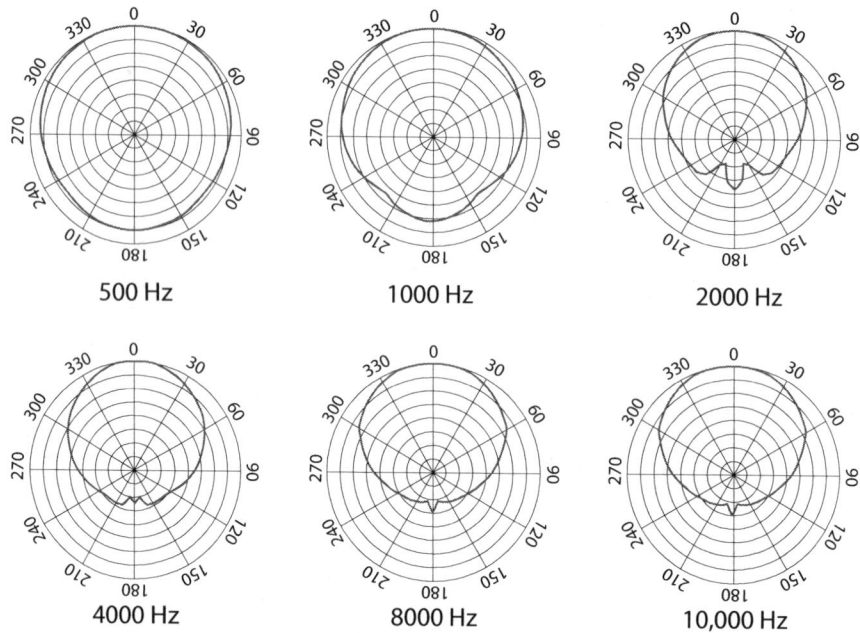

FIGURE 8.22: DIRECTIVITY OF 2-WAY LOUDSPEAKER SYSTEM WITH 5" AND 1" DIAMETER DRIVERS

There are many other strategies used by loudspeaker designers to get consistent pattern control, but all must take into account the size of the loudspeaker drivers and the way in which they affect frequencies. You can simply look at any loudspeaker and easily determine the lowest possible directional frequency based on the loudspeaker's size.

Understanding how a loudspeaker exercises directional control over the sound it radiates can also help you decide where to install and aim a loudspeaker to provide consistent sound levels across the area of your audience. Using the inverse square law in conjunction with the loudspeaker directivity information, you can find a solution that provides even sound coverage over a large audience area using a single loudspeaker. (The inverse square law is introduced in Chapter 4.)

Consider the example 1000 Hz vertical polar plot for a loudspeaker shown in Figure 8.23. If you're going to use that loudspeaker in the theatre shown in Figure 8.24, where do you aim the loudspeaker?

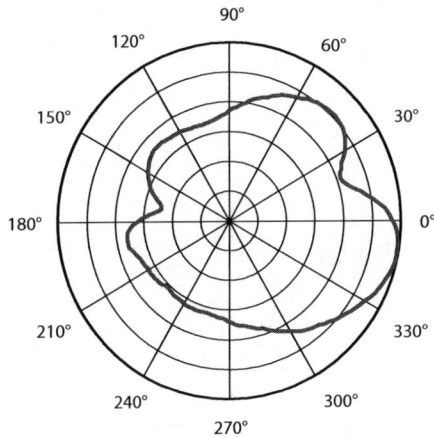

FIGURE 8.23: VERTICAL 1000 HZ POLAR PLOT FOR A LOUDSPEAKER

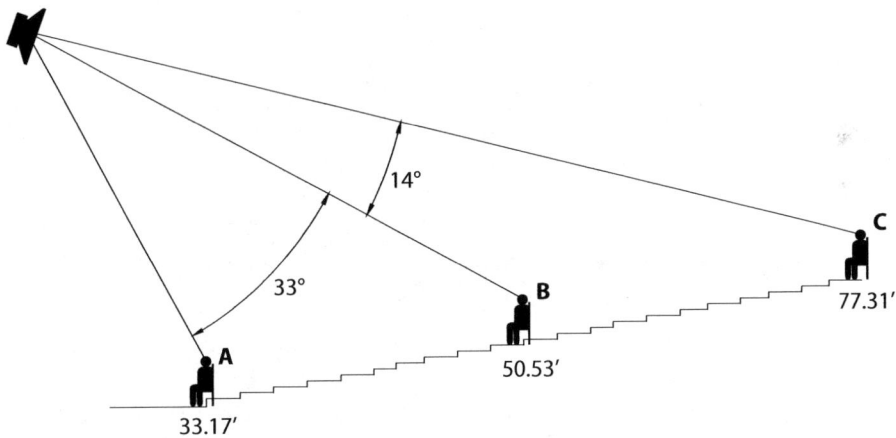

**FIGURE 8.24: SECTION VIEW OF AUDIENCE AREA WITH
DISTANCES AND ANGLES FOR A LOUDSPEAKER**

Most beginning sound system designers will choose to aim the loudspeaker at seat B, thinking that it will keep the entire audience as close as possible to the on-axis point of the loudspeaker. To test the idea, we can calculate the dB loss over distance using the inverse square law for each seat, and then subtract any additional dB loss incurred by going off-axis from the loudspeaker. Seat B is directly on axis with the loudspeaker, and according to the polar plot there is a loss of approximately 2 dB at 0 degrees. Seat A is 33 degrees down from the on-axis point of the loudspeaker, corresponding to 327 degrees on the polar plot, which shows an approximate loss of 3 dB. Seat C is 14 degrees off-axis from the loudspeaker, resulting in a loss of 6 dB according to the polar plot. Assuming that the loudspeaker is outputting 100 dBSPL at 1 meter (3.28 feet), we can calculate the dBSPL level for each seat as shown in Table 8.1.

A	Seat A dBSPL = 100 dB + 20log$_{10}$(3.28'/33.17') – 3 dB Seat A dBSPL = 100 dB + 20log$_{10}$(0.1) – 3 dB Seat A dBSPL = 100 dB + (20 × (– 1)) – 3 dB Seat A dBSPL = 100 dB + (–20) – 3 dB **Seat A dBSPL = 77 dBSPL**
B	Seat B dBSPL = 100 dB + 20log$_{10}$(3.28'/50.53') – 2 dB Seat B dBSPL = 100 dB + 20log$_{10}$(0.06) – 2 dB Seat B dBSPL = 100 dB + (20 × (– 1.19)) – 2 dB Seat B dBSPL = 100 dB + (–23.75) – 2 dB **Seat B dBSPL = 74.25 dBSPL**
C	Seat C dBSPL = 100 dB + 20log$_{10}$(3.28'/77.31') – 6 dB Seat C dBSPL = 100 dB + 20log$_{10}$(0.04) – 6 dB Seat C dBSPL = 100 dB + (20 × (– 1.37)) – 6 dB Seat C dBSPL = 100 dB + (–27.45) – 6 dB **Seat C dBSPL = 66.55 dBSPL**

TABLE 8.1: CALCULATING DBSPL OF A GIVEN LOUDSPEAKER AIMED ON-AXIS WITH SEAT B

In this case the loudest seat is seat A at 77 dBSPL, and seat C is the quietest at 66.55 dBSPL, with a 10.45 dB difference. As discussed, we want all the audience locations to be within a 6 dB range. But before we throw this loudspeaker away and try to find one that works better, let's take a moment to examine the reasons why we have such a poor result. The reason seat C is so much quieter than the other seats is that it is the farthest away from the loudspeaker and is receiving the largest reduction due to directivity. By comparison, A is the closest to the loudspeaker, resulting in the lowest loss over distance and only a 3 dB reduction due to directivity. To even this out, let's try having the farthest seat away have the least directivity loss and the closest seat to the loudspeaker have the most directivity loss.

The angle with the least directivity loss is around 350 degrees, so if we aim the loudspeaker so that seat C lines up with that 350 degree point, that seat will have no directivity loss. With that aim point, seat B will then have a directivity loss of 3 dB, and seat A will have a directivity loss of 10 dB. Now we can recalculate the dBSPL for each seat as shown in Table 8.2.

A	Seat A dBSPL = 100 dB + $20\log_{10}(3.28'/33.17') - 10$ dB Seat A dBSPL = 100 dB + $20\log_{10}(0.1) - 10$ dB Seat A dBSPL = 100 dB + $(20 \times (-1)) - 10$ dB Seat A dBSPL = 100 dB + $(-20) - 10$ dB **Seat A dBSPL = 70 dBSPL**
B	Seat B dBSPL = 100 dB + $20\log_{10}(3.28'/50.53') - 3$ dB Seat B dBSPL = 100 dB + $20\log_{10}(0.06) - 3$ dB Seat B dBSPL = 100 dB + $(20 \times (-1.19)) - 3$ dB Seat B dBSPL = 100 dB + $(-23.75) - 3$ dB **Seat B dBSPL = 73.25 dBSPL**
C	Seat C dBSPL = 100 dB + $20\log_{10}(3.28'/77.31') - 0$ dB Seat C dBSPL = 100 dB + $20\log_{10}(0.04) - 0$ dB Seat C dBSPL = 100 dB + $(20 \times (-1.37)) - 0$ dB Seat C dBSPL = 100 dB + $(-27.45) - 0$ dB **Seat C dBSPL = 72.55 dBSPL**

TABLE 8.2: CALCULATING DBSPL OF A GIVEN LOUDSPEAKER AIMED ON-AXIS WITH SEAT C

In this case our loudest seat is seat B at 73.25 dB SPL, and our quietest seat is seat A at 70 dBSPL, for a difference of 3.25 dB. Compared with the previous difference of 10.55 dB, we now have a much more even distribution of sound to the point where most listeners will hardly notice the difference. Before we fully commit to this plan we have to test these angles at several different frequencies, but this example serves to illustrate an important rule of thumb when aiming loudspeakers. In most cases, the best course of action is to aim the loudspeaker at the farthest seat, and have the closest seat be the farthest off-axis to the loudspeaker. This way, as you move from the closest seat to the farthest seat, while you're losing dB over the extra distance you're also gaining dB by moving more directly on-axis with the loudspeaker.

Fortunately there are software tools that can help you determine the best loudspeakers to use and the best way to deploy them in your space. These tools range in price from free solutions, such as MAPP Online Pro from Meyer Sound shown in Figure 8.25, to relatively expensive commercial products, like EASE from the Ahnert Feistel Media Group shown in Figure 8.26. These programs allow you to create a 2-D or 3-D drawing of the room and place virtual loudspeakers in the drawing to see how they disperse the sound. The virtual loudspeaker files come in several formats. The most common is the EASE format. EASE is the most expensive and comprehensive solution out there, and fortunately most other programs have the ability to import EASE loudspeaker files. Another format is the Common Loudspeaker Format (CLF). CLF files use an open format, and many manufacturers are starting to publish their loudspeaker data in CLF. Information on loudspeaker modeling software that uses CLF can be found at the website for the Common Loudspeaker Format Group http://www.clfgroup.org.

> **ASIDE:** EASE was developed by German engineers at ADA (Acoustic Design Ahnert) in 1990 and introduced at the 88th AES (Audio Engineering Society) Convention. That's also the same year that Microsoft announced Windows 3.0.

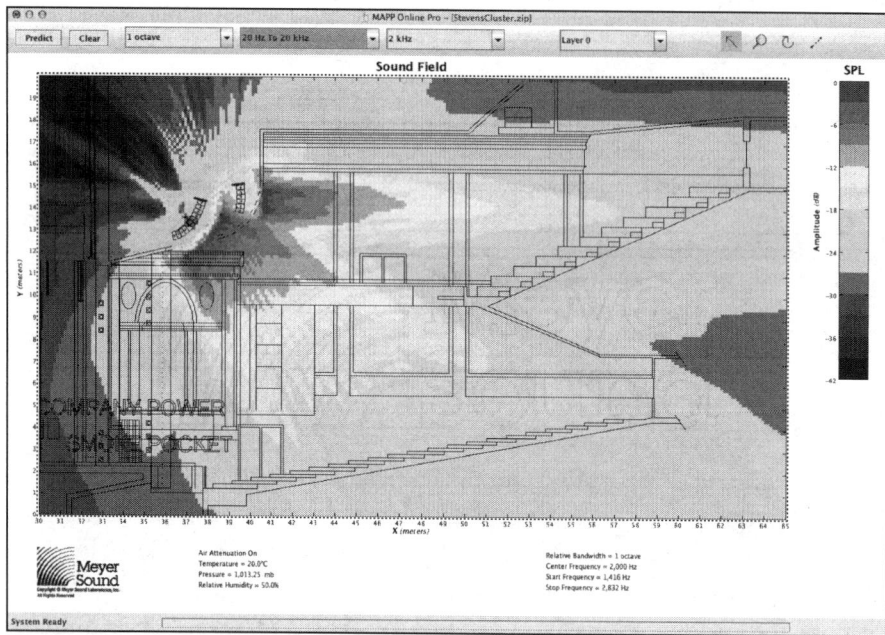

FIGURE 8.25: MAPP ONLINE PRO SOFTWARE FROM MEYER SOUND

8.2.4.2 System Documentation

Once you've decided on a loudspeaker system that distributes the sound the way you want, you need to begin the process of designing the systems that capture the sound of the performance and feed it into the loudspeaker system. Typically this involves creating a set of drawings that give you the opportunity to think through the entire sound system and explain to others—installers, contractors, or operators, for example—how the system will function.

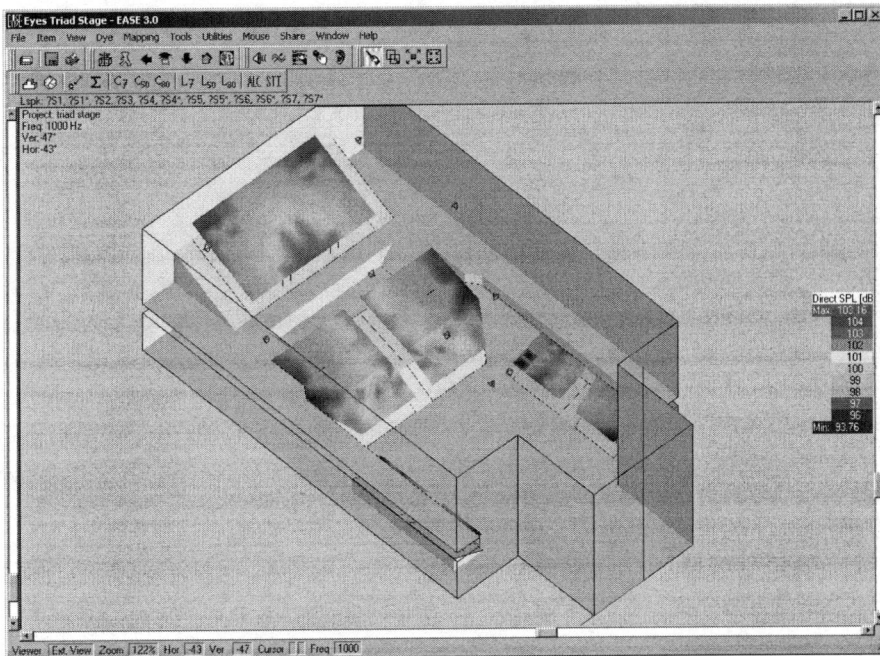

FIGURE 8.26: EASE SOFTWARE FROM AHNERT FEISTEL MEDIA GROUP

The first diagram to create is the system diagram. This is similar in function to an electrical circuit diagram, showing you which parts are used and how they're wired up. The sound system diagram shows how all the components of a sound system connect together in the audio signal chain, starting from the microphones and other input devices all the way through to the loudspeakers that reproduce that sound. These diagrams can be created digitally with vector drawing programs such as AutoCAD and Vectororks, or diagramming programs such as Visio and OmniGraffle.

The United States Institute for Theatre Technology (USITT) has published some guidelines for creating system diagrams. The most common symbol or block used in system diagrams is the generic device block shown in Figure 8.27. The "EQUIPMENT TYPE" label should be replaced with a descriptive term such a "CD PLAYER" or "MIXING CONSOLE." You can also specify the exact make and model of the equipment in the label above the block.

> **ASIDE:** You can read the entire USITT document on system diagram guidelines by visiting the USITT website: www.usitt.org/assets/1/27/Sound_Guildelines_2008.pdf

MAKE/MODEL_optional

EQUIPMENT TYPE

INPUT	OUTPUT
1	1
2	2

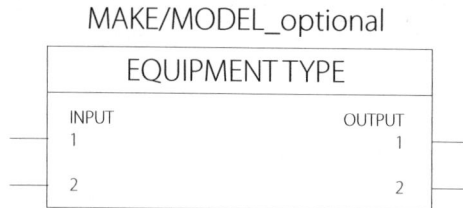

FIGURE 8.27: A GENERIC DEVICE BLOCK FOR SYSTEM DIAGRAMS

There are also symbols to represent microphones, power amplifiers, and loud-speakers. You can connect all the various symbols to represent an entire sound system. Figure 8.28 shows a very small sound system, and Figure 8.29 shows a full system diagram for a small musical theatre production.

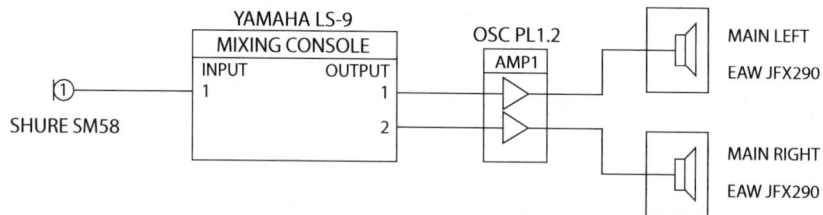

FIGURE 8.28: A SMALL SYSTEM DIAGRAM

While the system diagram shows the basic signal flow for the entire sound system, there is a lot of detail missing about the specific interconnections between devices. This is where a patch plot can be helpful. A **patch plot** is essentially a spreadsheet that shows every connection point in the sound system. You should be able to use the patch plot to determine which and how many cables you'll need for the sound system. It can also be a useful tool in troubleshooting a sound system that isn't behaving properly. When things go wrong with your sound system or something isn't working, the majority of the time it's because it isn't connected properly or one of the cables has been damaged. A good patch plot can help you find the problem by showing you where all the connections are located in the signal path. There is no industry standard for creating a patch plot, but the rule of thumb is to err on the side of too much information. You want every possible detail about every audio connection made in the sound system. Sometimes color coding can help make the patch plot easier to understand. Figure 8.30 shows an example patch plot for the sound system in Figure 8.28.

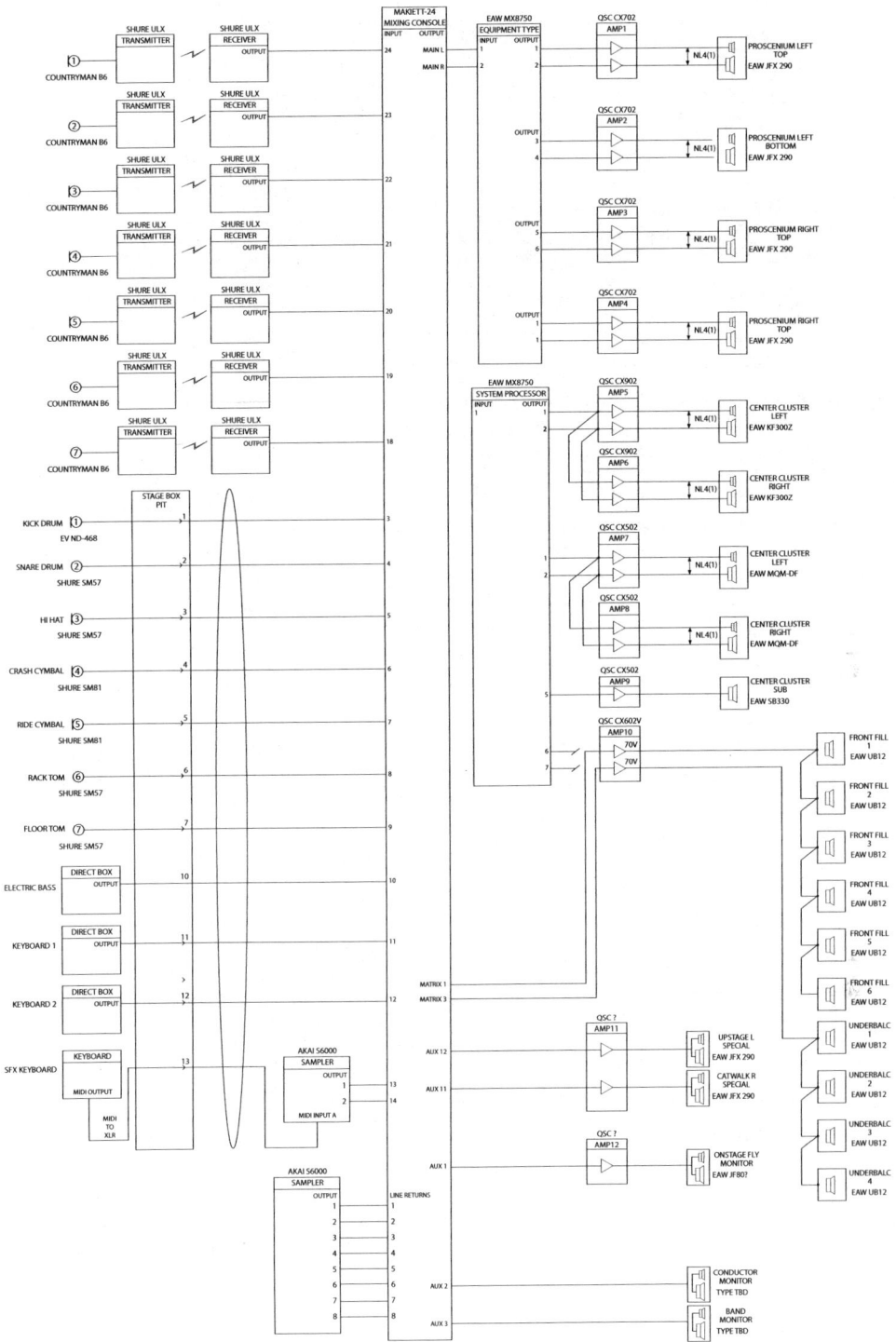

FIGURE 8.29: SYSTEM DIAGRAM FOR A FULL SOUND SYSTEM (EXPANDED VIEW ON THE FOLLOWING TWO PAGES)

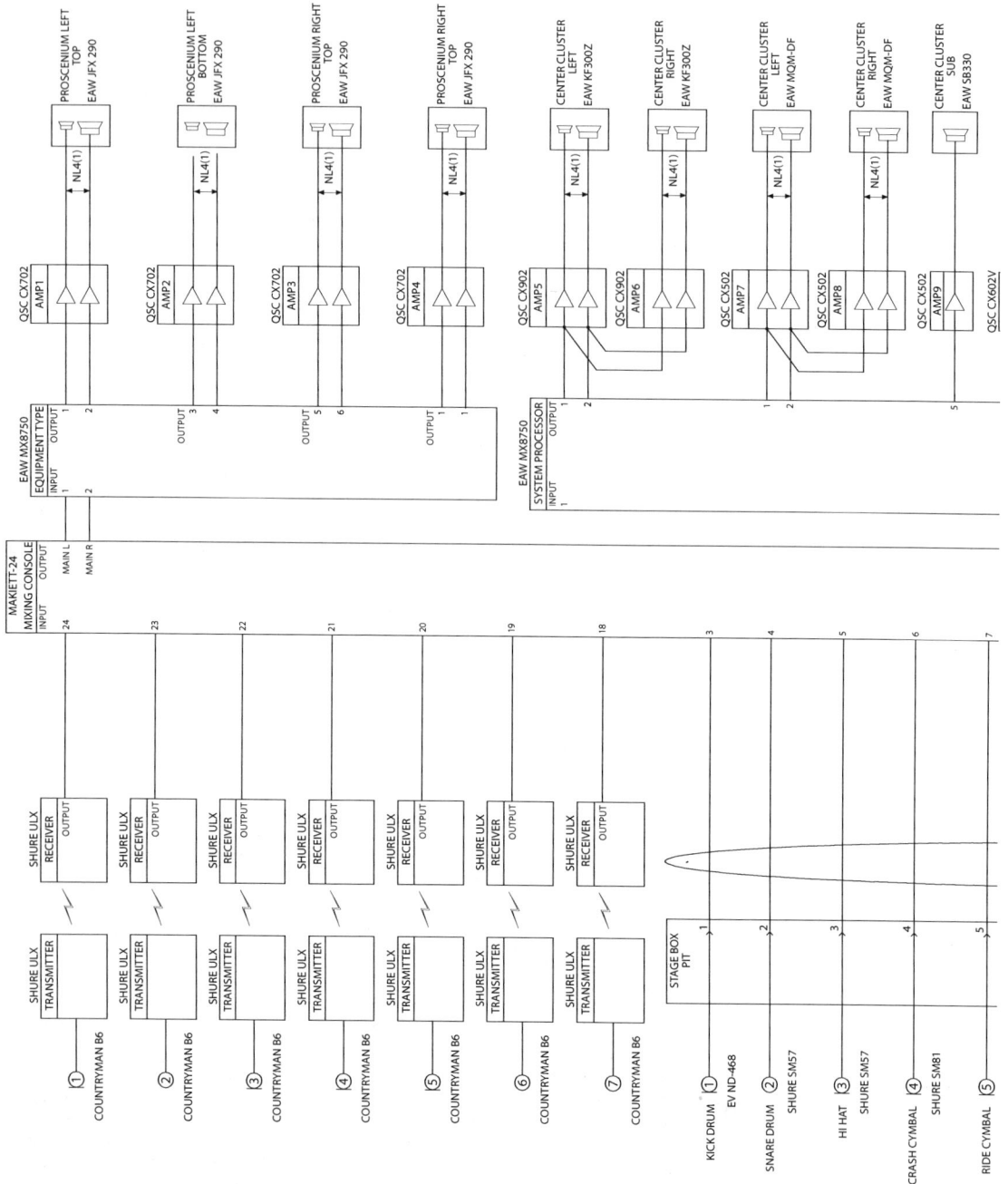

EXPANDED VIEW OF FIGURE 8.29: SYSTEM DIAGRAM FOR A FULL SOUND SYSTEM (PART 1, ROTATED VIEW)

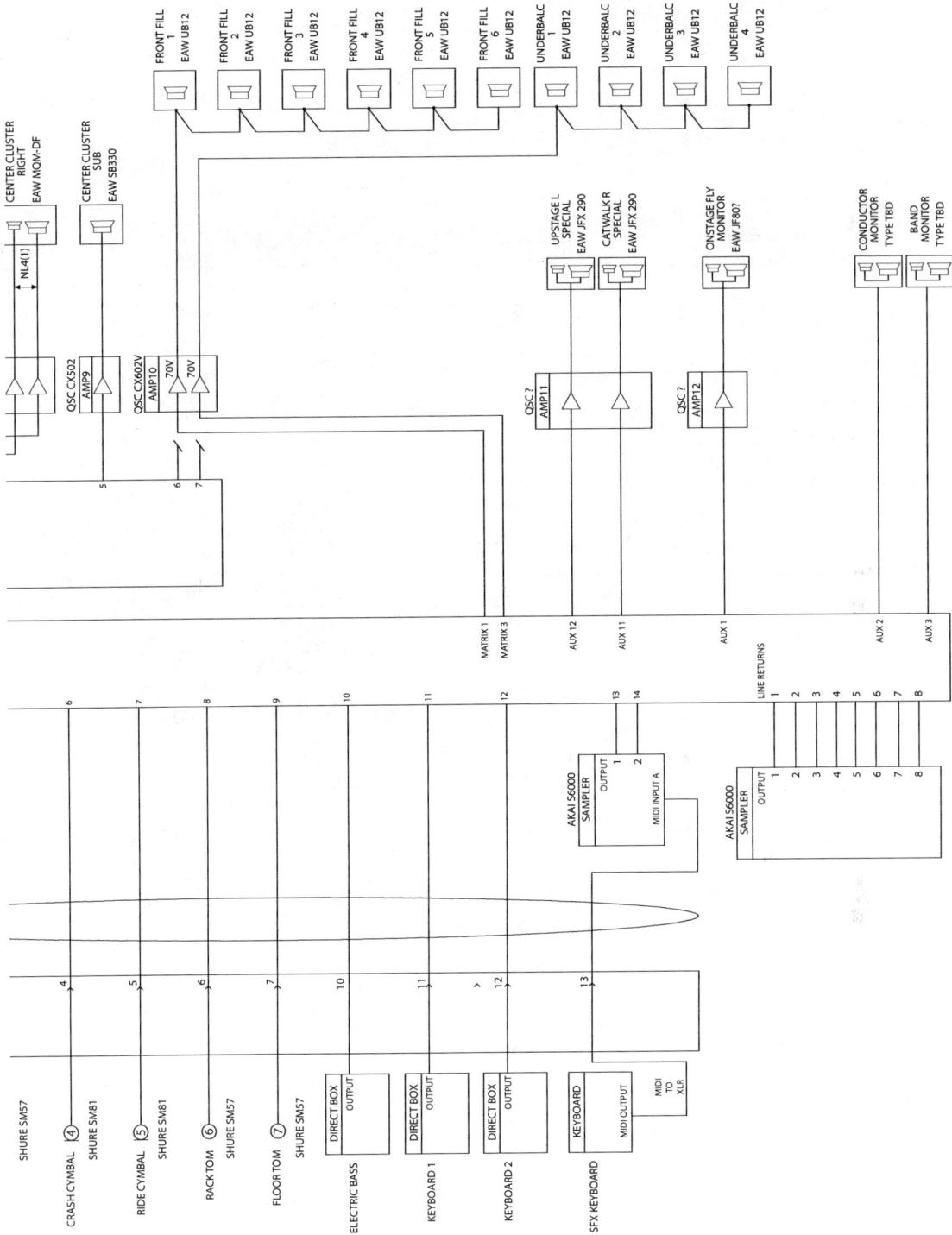

EXPANDED VIEW OF FIGURE 8.29: SYSTEM DIAGRAM FOR A FULL SOUND SYSTEM (PART 2, ROTATED VIEW)

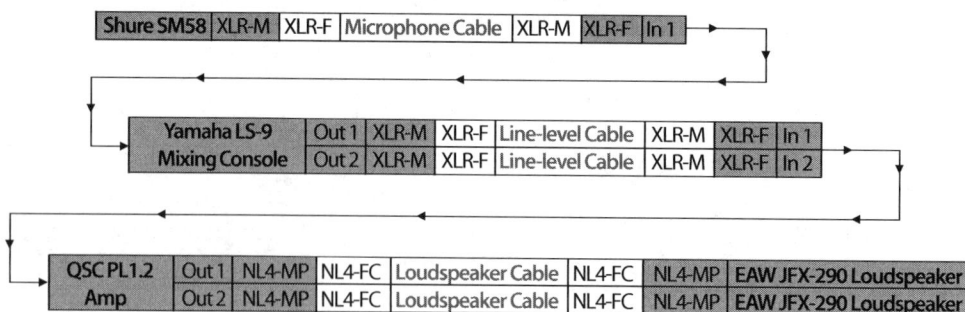

FIGURE 8.30: PATCH PLOT FOR A SIMPLE SOUND SYSTEM

8.2.4.3 Sound Analysis Systems

Section 8.2.4.1 discussed mathematical methods and tools that help you to determine were loudspeakers should be placed to maximize clarity and minimize the differences in what is heard in different locations in an auditorium. However, even with good loudspeaker placement, you'll find there are differences between the original sound signal and how it sounds when it arrives at the listener. Different frequency components respond differently to their environment, and frequency components interact with each other as sounds from multiple sources combine in the air. The question is, how are these frequencies heard by the audience once they pass through loudspeakers and travel through space encountering obstructions, varying air temperatures, comb filtering, and so forth? Is each frequency arriving at the audience's ears at the desired amplitude? Are certain frequencies too loud or too quiet? If the high frequencies are too quiet, you could sacrifice the brightness or clarity in the sound. Low frequencies that are too quiet could result in muffled voices.

ASIDE: *Acoustic* systems are systems in which the sounds produced depend on the shape and material of the sound-producing instruments. *Electroacoustic* systems produce sound through electronic technology such as amplifiers and loudspeakers.

There are no clear guidelines on what the "right" frequency response is because it usually boils down to personal preference, artistic considerations, performance styles, and so forth. In any case, before you can decide if you have a problem, the first step is to analyze the frequency response in your environment. With practice you can hear and identify frequencies, but sometimes being able to *see* the frequencies can help you to diagnose and solve problems. This is especially true when you're setting up the sound system for a live performance in a theatre.

A **sound analysis system** is one of the fundamental tools for ensuring that frequencies are being received at proper levels. The system consists of a computer running the analysis software, an audio interface with inputs and outputs, and a special **analysis microphone**. An analysis microphone is different from a traditional recording microphone. Most recording microphones have a varying response or sensitivity at different frequencies across the spectrum. This is often a desired result of their manufacturing and design, and part of what gives each microphone its unique sound. For analyzing acoustic or electroacoustic systems, you need a microphone that measures all frequencies equally. This is often referred to as having a **flat response**. In addition, most microphones are directional. They pick up sound better in the front than in the back. A good analysis microphone should be omnidirectional so it can pick up the sound coming at it from all directions. Figure 8.31 shows a popular analysis microphone from Earthworks.

FIGURE 8.31: EARTHWORKS M30 ANALYSIS MICROPHONE

There are many choices for analysis software, but they all fall into two main categories: signal-dependent and signal-independent. **Signal-dependent sound analysis systems** rely on a known stimulus signal that the software generates—e.g., a sine wave **sweep**. A **sine wave sweep** is a sound that begins at a low frequency sine wave and smoothly moves up in frequency to some given high frequency limit. The sweep, lasting a few seconds or less, is sent by a direct cable connection to the loudspeaker. You then place your analysis microphone at the listening location you want to analyze. The microphone picks up the sound radiated by the loudspeaker so that you can compare what the microphone picks up with what was actually sent out.

The analysis software records and stores the information in a file called an **impulse response**, a graph of the sound wave with time on the x-axis and the amplitude of the sound wave on the y-axis. This same information can be displayed in a frequency response graph, which has frequencies on the x-axis and the amplitude of each frequency on the y-axis. (In Section 2.3.6, we explained the mathematics that transforms the impulse response graph to the frequency response graph, and vice versa.) Figure 8.32 shows an example frequency response graph created by the procedure just described.

frequency response

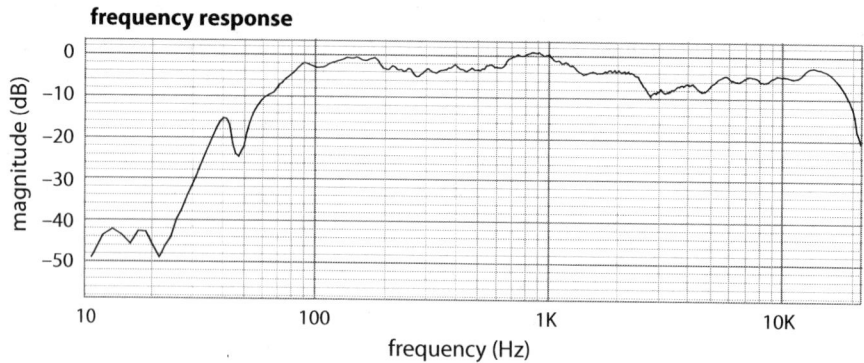

FIGURE 8.32: FREQUENCY RESPONSE GRAPH CREATED FROM
A SIGNAL-DEPENDENT SOUND ANALYSIS SYSTEM

Figure 8.33 shows a screenshot from FuzzMeasure Pro, a signal-dependent analysis program that runs on the Mac operating system. The frequency response is on the top, and the impulse response is at the bottom. As you recall from Chapter 2, the frequency response has frequencies on the horizontal axis and amplitudes of these frequency components on the vertical axis. It shows how the frequencies "respond" to their environment as they move from the loudspeaker to the microphone. We know that the sine wave emits frequencies distributed evenly across the audible spectrum, so if the sound is not affected in passage, the frequency response graph should be flat. But notice in the graph that the frequencies between 30 Hz and 500 Hz are 6 to 10 dB louder than the rest, which is their response to the environment.

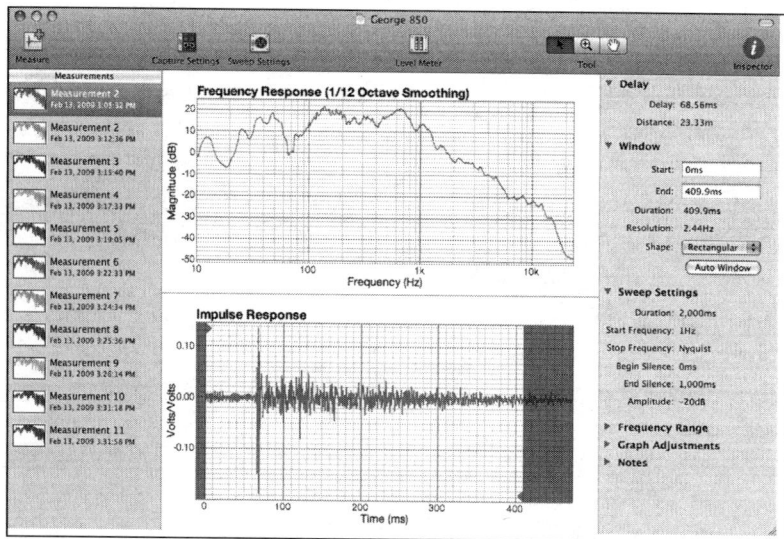

FIGURE 8.33: FUZZMEASURE PRO SOUND ANALYSIS SOFTWARE

When you look at an analysis such as this, it's up to you to decide if you've identified a problem that you want to solve. Keep in mind that the goal isn't necessarily to make the frequency response graph be a straight line, indicating all frequencies are of equal amplitude. The goal is to make the right kind of sound. Before you can decide what to do, you need to determine why the frequency response sounds like this. There are many possible reasons. It could be that you're too far off-axis from the loudspeaker generating the sound. That's not a problem you can really solve when you're analyzing a listening space for a large audience, since not everyone can sit in the prime location. You could move the analysis microphone so that you're on-axis with the loudspeaker, but you can't fix the off-axis frequency response for the loudspeaker itself. In the example shown in Figure 8.34, the loudspeaker system that is generating the sound uses two sets of sound radiators. One set of loudspeakers generates the frequencies above 500 Hz. The other set generates the frequencies below 500 Hz. Given that information, you could conclude that the low-frequency loudspeakers are simply louder than the high-frequency ones. If this is causing a sound that you don't want, you could fix it by reducing the level of the low-frequency loudspeakers.

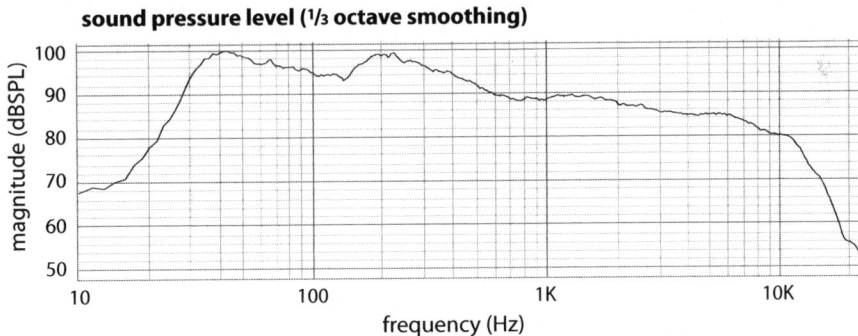

FIGURE 8.34: FREQUENCY RESPONSE GRAPH SHOWING A LOW FREQUENCY BOOST

Figure 8.35 shows the result after this correction. The gray line shows the original frequency response, and the black line shows the frequency response after reducing the amplitude of the low-frequency loudspeakers by 6 dB.

sound pressure level (¹/₃ octave smoothing)

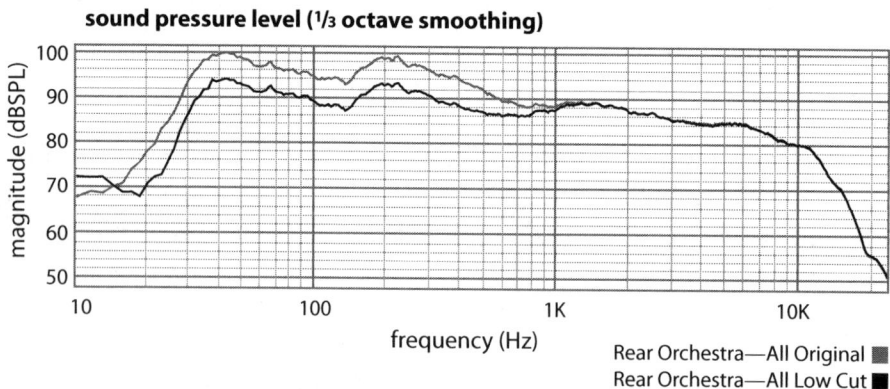

Rear Orchestra—All Original ■
Rear Orchestra—All Low Cut ■

FIGURE 8.35: ORIGINAL FREQUENCY RESPONSE (GRAY LINE) GRAPHED
WITH CORRECTED FREQUENCY RESPONSE (BLACK LINE)

The previous example gives you a sketch of how a sound analysis system might be used. You place yourself in a chosen position in a room where sound is to be performed or played, generate sound that is played through loudspeakers, and then measure the sound as it is received at your chosen position. The frequencies that are actually detected may not be precisely the frequency components of the original sound that was generated or played. By looking at the difference between what you played and what you are able to measure, you can analyze the frequency response of your loudspeakers, the acoustics of your room, or a combination of the two. The frequencies that are measured by the sound analysis system are dependent not only on the sound originally produced, but also on the loudspeaker types and positions, the location of the listener in the room, and the acoustics of the room. Thus, in addition to measuring the frequency response of your loudspeakers, the sound analysis system can help you to determine if different locations in the room vary significantly in their frequency response, leaving it to you to decide if this is a problem and what factor might be the source.

The advantage of a signal-dependent system is that it's easy to use, and with it you can get a good general picture of how frequencies will sound in a given acoustic space with certain loudspeakers. You also can save the frequency response graphs to refer to and analyze later. The disadvantage of a signal-dependent analysis system is that it uses only artificially-generated signals like sine sweeps, not real music or performances.

If you want to analyze actual music or performances, you need to use a **signal-independent analysis system**. These systems allow you to analyze the frequency response of recorded music, voice, sound effects, or even live performances as they sound in your acoustic space. In contrast to systems like FuzzMeasure, which know the precise sweep of frequencies they're generating, signal-independent systems must be given a direct copy of the sound being played so that the original sound can be compared with the sound that passes through the air and is received by the analysis microphone. This is accomplished by taking the original sound and sending one copy of it to the loudspeakers while a second copy is sent directly, via cable, to the sound analysis software. The software presumably is running on a computer that has a sound card attached with two sound inputs. One of the inputs is the analysis microphone, and one is a direct feed from the sound source. The software compares the two signals in real time—as the music or sound is played—and tells you what is different about them.

The advantage of the signal-independent system is that it can analyze "real" sound as it is being played or performed. However, real sound has frequency components that constantly change, as we can tell from the constantly changing pitches that we hear. Thus, there isn't one fixed frequency response graph that gives you a picture of how your loudspeakers and room are dealing with the frequencies of the sound. The graph changes dynamically over the entire time that the sound is played. For this reason, you can't simply save one graph and carry it off with you for analysis. Instead, your analysis consists of observing the constantly-changing frequency response graph in real time, as the sound is played. If you wanted to save a single frequency response graph, you'd have to do what we did to generate Figure 8.36—that is, get a screen capture of the frequency response graph at a specific moment in time—and the information you'd have is about only that moment. Another disadvantage of signal-independent systems is that they analyze the noise in the environment along with the desired sound.

Figure 8.36 was produced from a popular signal-independent analysis program called SmaartLive, which runs on Windows and Mac operating systems. The graph shows the difference, in decibels, between the amplitudes of the frequencies played versus those received by the analysis microphone. Because this is only a snapshot in time, coupled with the fact that noise is measured as well, it isn't very informative to look at just one graph like this. Being able to glean useful information from a signal-independent sound analysis system comes from experience in working with real sound—learning how to compare what you want, what you see, what you understand is going on mathematically, and—most importantly—what you hear.

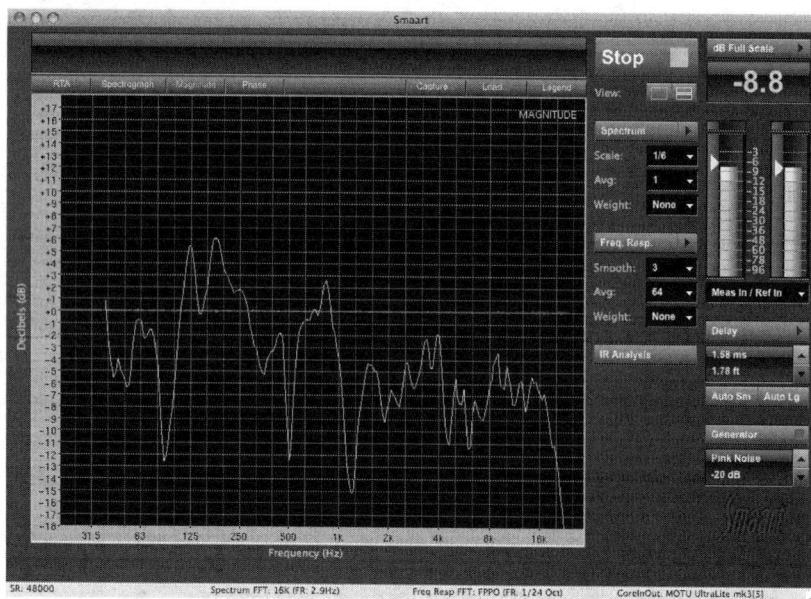

FIGURE 8.36: SMAARTLIVE SOUND ANALYSIS SOFTWARE

8.2.4.4 System Optimization

Once you have the sound system installed and everything is functioning, the system needs to be optimized. System optimization is a process of tuning and adjusting the various components of the sound system so that:

》 They're operating at the proper volume levels.

》 The frequency response of the sound system is consistent and desirable.

》 Destructive interactions between system components and the acoustical environment have been minimized.

》 The timing of the various system components has been adjusted so the audience hears the sounds at the right time.

The first optimization you should perform applies to the gain structure of the sound system. When working with sound systems in either live performance or a recording situation, gain structure is a big concern. In a live performance situation, the goal is to amplify sound. In order to achieve the highest potential for loudness, you need to get each device in your system operating at the highest level possible so you don't lose any volume as the sound travels through the system. In a recording situation, you're primarily concerned with signal-to-noise ratio. In both of these cases, good gain structure is the solution.

In order to understand gain structure, you first need to understand that all sound equipment makes noise. All sound devices also contain amplifiers. What you want to do is amplify the sound without amplifying the noise. In a sound system with good gain structure, every device is receiving and sending sound at the highest level possible without clipping. Lining up the gain for each device involves lining up the clip points. You can do this by starting with the first device in your signal chain, typically a microphone or some sort of playback device. It's easier to set up gain structure using a playback source because you can control the output volume. Start by playing something on the CD, synthesizer, computer, iPod or whatever your playback device is in a way that outputs the highest volume possible. This is usually done with either normalized pink noise or a normalized sine wave. Turn up the gain preamplifier on the mixing console or sound card input so that the level coming from the playback source clips the input. Then back off the gain until that sound is just below clipping. If you're recording this sound, your gain structure is now complete. Just repeat this process for each input. If it's a live performer on a microphone, ask him to perform at the highest volume they expect to generate and adjust the input gain accordingly.

If you're in a live situation, the mixing console will likely feed its sound into another device such as a processor or power amplifier. With the normalized audio from your playback source still running, adjust the output level of the mixing console so it's also just below clipping. Then adjust the input level of the next device in the signal chain so that it's receiving this signal at just below its clipping point. Repeat this process until you've adjusted every input and output in your sound system. At this point, everything should clip at the same time. If you increase the level of the playback source or input preamplifier on the mixing console, you should see every meter in your system register a clipped signal. If you've done this correctly, you should now have plenty of sound coming from your sound system without any hiss or other noise. If the sound system is too loud, simply turn down the last device in the signal chain. Usually this is the power amplifier.

MAX DEMO:
Gain Setting
http://bit.ly/29LWbZG

Setting up proper gain structure in a sound system is fairly simple once you're familiar with the process. The Max demo on gain structure associated with this section gives you an opportunity to practice the technique. Then you should be ready to line up the gain for your own systems.

Once you have the gain structure optimized, the next thing you need to do is try to minimize destructive interactions between loudspeakers. One reason that loudspeaker directivity is important is due to the potential for multiple loudspeakers to interact destructively if their coverage overlaps in physical space. Most loudspeakers can exercise some directional control over frequencies higher than 1 kHz, but frequencies lower than 1 kHz tend to be fairly omnidirectional, which means they will more easily run into each other in the air. The basic strategy to avoid destructive interactions

Single loudspeaker with 90° horizontal
coverage between –6dB downpoints

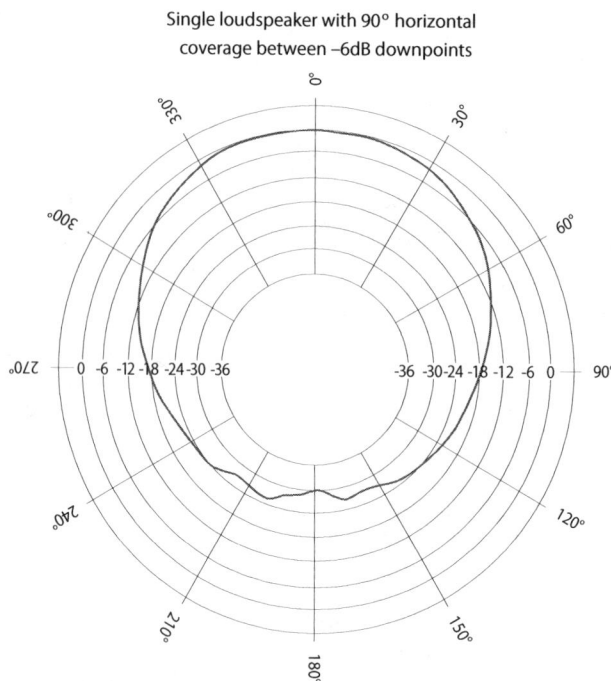

FIGURE 8.37: MINIMIZING COMB FILTERING BETWEEN TWO LOUDSPEAKERS (PART 1)

is to adjust the angle between two loudspeakers so their coverage zone intersects at the same dBSPL, and at the point in the coverage pattern where they are 6 dB quieter than the on-axis level, as shown in Figure 8.37. This overlap point is the only place where the two loudspeakers combine at the same level. If you can pull that off, you can then adjust the timing of the loudspeakers so they're perfectly in phase at that overlap point. Destructive interaction is eliminated because the waves reinforce each other, creating a 6 dB boost that eliminates the dip in sound level at high frequencies. The result is that there is even sound across the covered area. The small number of listeners who happen to be sitting in an area of overlap between two loudspeakers will effectively be covered by a virtual coherent loudspeaker.

When you move away from that perfect overlap point, one loudspeaker gets louder as you move closer to it, while the other gets quieter as you move farther away. This is handy for two reasons. First, the overall combined level should remain pretty consistent at any angle as you move through the perfect overlap point. Second, for any angle outside of that perfect overlap point, while the timing relationship between the two loudspeaker arrivals begins to differ, the loudspeakers also differ more and more in level. As pure comb filtering requires both of the interacting signals to be at the same amplitude, the level difference greatly reduces the effect of the comb filtering

Two loudspeakers with 90° horizontal coverage between –6dB that
are rotated so the –6dB downpoints that are rotated so the –6dB downpoints
intersect, creating a combined coherent coverage of 180°

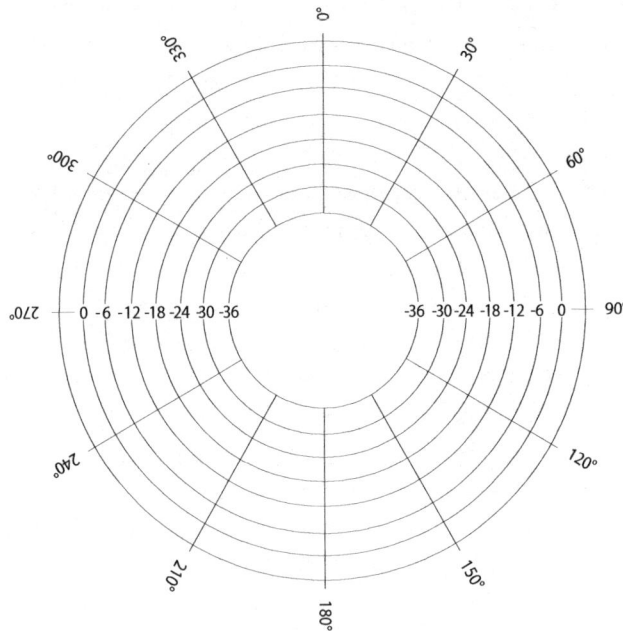

FIGURE 8.37: MINIMIZING COMB FILTERING BETWEEN TWO LOUDSPEAKERS (PART 2)

introduced by the shift in timing. The place where the sound from the two loudspeakers arrives at the same amplitude and comb filters the most is at center of the overlap, but this is the place where we aligned the timing perfectly to prevent comb filtering in the first place. With this technique, not only do you get the wider coverage that comes with multiple loudspeakers, but you also get to avoid the comb filtering!

What about the low frequencies in this example? Well, they're going to run into each other at similar amplitudes all around the room because they're more omnidirectional than the high frequencies. However, they also have longer wavelengths, which means they require much larger offsets in time to cause destructive interaction. Consequently, they largely reinforce each other, giving an overall low-frequency boost. Sometimes this free bass boost sounds good. If not, you can easily fix it with a system EQ adjustment by adding a low shelf filter that reduces the low frequencies by a certain amount to flatten out the frequency response of the system. This process is demonstrated in our video on loudspeaker interaction.

VIDEO TUTORIAL:
Loudspeaker
Interaction
http://bit.ly/29f9WhX

You should work with your loudspeakers in smaller groups, sometimes called *systems*. A center cluster of loudspeakers being used to cover the entire listening area from a single point source would be considered a system. You need to work with all the loudspeakers in that cluster to ensure they are working well together. A row of front-fill loudspeakers at the edge of the stage being used to cover the front few rows will also need to be optimized as an individual system.

Once you have each loudspeaker system optimized, you need to work with all the systems together to ensure they don't destructively interact with each other. This typically involves manipulating the timing of each system. There are two main strategies for time aligning loudspeaker systems. You can line the system up for coherence, or you can line the system up for precedence imaging. The coherence strategy involves working with each loudspeaker system to ensure that their coverage areas are as isolated as possible. This process is very similar to the process we described above for aligning the splay angles of two loudspeakers. In this case, you're doing the same thing for two loudspeaker systems. If you can line up two different systems so that the 6 dB down point of each system lands in the same point in space, you can then apply delay to the system arriving first so that both systems arrive at the same time, causing a perfect reinforcement. If you can pull this off for the entire sound system and the entire listening area, the listeners will effectively be listening to a single, giant loudspeaker with optimal coherence.

The natural propagation of sound in an acoustic space is not inherently very coherent due to the reflection and absorption of sound, resulting in destructive and constructive interactions that vary across the listening area. This lack of natural coherence is often the reason that a sound reinforcement system is installed in the first place. A sound system that has been optimized for coherence has the characteristic of sounding very clear and very consistent across the listening area. These can be very desirable qualities in a sound system where clarity and intelligibility are important. The downside to this optimization strategy is that it sometimes does not sound very natural. This is because with coherence optimized sound systems, the direct sound from the original source (such as a singer/performer on stage) typically has little to no impact on the audience, and so the audience perceives the sound as coming directly from the loudspeakers. If you're close to the stage and the singer, and the loudspeakers are way off to the side or far overhead, it can be strange to see the actual source yet hear the sound come from somewhere else. In an arena or stadium setting, or at a rock concert where you likely wouldn't hear much direct sound in the first place, this isn't as big a problem. Sound designers are sometimes willing to accept a slightly unnatural sound if it means that they can solve the clarity and intelligibility problems that occur in the acoustic space.

Optimizing the sound system for precedence imaging is completely opposite to the coherence strategy. In this case, the goal is to increase the clarity and loudness of the sound system while maintaining a natural sound as much as possible. In other words, you want the audience to be able to hear and understand everything in the performance, but you want them to think that what they are hearing is coming naturally from the performer instead of coming from loudspeakers in a sound system. In a precedence imaging sound system, each loudspeaker system behaves like an early reflection in an acoustic space. For this strategy to work, you want to maximize the overlap between the various loudspeaker systems. Each listener should be able to hear two or three loudspeaker systems from a single seat. The danger here is that these overlapping loudspeaker systems can easily comb filter in a way that will make the sound unpleasant or completely unintelligible. Using the precedence effect described in Chapter 4, you can manipulate the delay of each loudspeaker system so they arrive at the listener at least five milliseconds apart but no more than 30 milliseconds apart. The signals still comb filter, but in a way that our hearing system naturally compensates for. Once all of the loudspeakers are lined up, you'll also want to delay the entire sound system back to the performer position on stage. As long as the natural sound from the performer arrives first, followed by a succession of similar sounds from the various loudspeaker systems, each within this precedence timing window, you can get an increased volume and clarity as perceived by the listener while still maintaining the effect of a natural acoustic sound. If that natural sound is a priority, you can achieve acceptable results with this method, but you will sacrifice some of the additional clarity and intelligibility that comes with a coherent sound system.

Both of these optimization strategies are valid, and you'll need to evaluate in each case to decide which kind of optimized system best addresses the priorities of your situation. In either case, you need some sort of system processor to perform the EQ and delay functions for the loudspeaker systems. These processors usually take the form of a dedicated digital signal-processing unit with multiple audio inputs and outputs. These system processors typically require a separate computer for programming, but once the system has been programmed, the units perform quite reliably without any external control. Figure 8.38 shows an example of a programming interface for a system processor.

ASIDE: Your loudspeakers might sit still for the whole show, but the performers usually don't. Out Board's TiMax Tracker and Soundhub delay matrix system use radar technology to track actors and performers around a stage in three dimensions, automating and adjusting the delay times to maintain precedence and deliver natural, realistic sound throughout the performance.

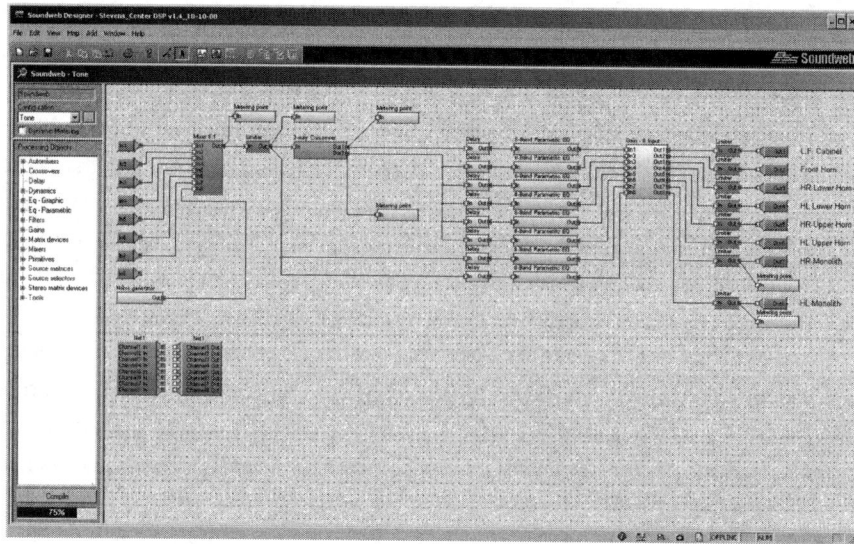

FIGURE 8.38: PROGRAMMING INTERFACE FOR A DIGITAL SYSTEM PROCESSOR

8.2.4.5 Multi-channel Playback

Mid-side can also be effective as a playback technique for delivering stereo sound to a large listening area. One of the limitations to stereo sound is that the effect relies on having the listener perfectly centered between the two loudspeakers. This is usually not a problem for a single person listening in a small living room. If you have more than one listener, such as in a public performance space, it can be difficult if not impossible to get all the listeners perfectly centered between the two loudspeakers. The listeners who are positioned to the left or right of the center line will not hear a stereo effect. Instead, they will perceive most of the sound to be coming from whichever loudspeaker they are closest to. A more effective strategy would be to set up three loudspeakers. One would be your mid loudspeaker and would be positioned in front of the listeners. The other two loudspeakers would be positioned directly on either side of the listeners, as shown in Figure 8.39.

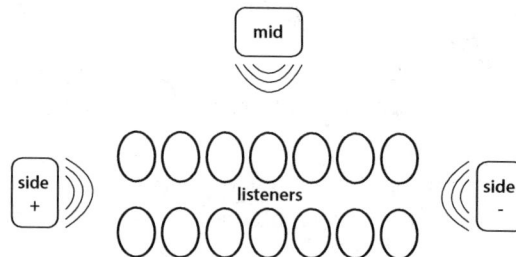

FIGURE 8.39: MID-SIDE LOUDSPEAKER SETUP

If you have an existing audio track that has been mixed in stereo, you can create a reverse mid-side matrix to convert the stereo information to a mid-side format. The mid loudspeaker gets an L+R audio signal equivalent to summing the two stereo tracks to a single mono signal. The side+ loudspeaker gets an L-R audio signal, equivalent to inverting the right channel polarity and summing the two channels to a mono signal. This will cancel out anything that is equal in the two channels, essentially removing all the mid information. The side- loudspeaker gets an R-L audio signal. Inverting the left channel polarity and summing to mono or simply inverting the side+ signal can achieve this effect. The listeners in this scenario will all hear something similar to a stereo effect. The right channel stereo audio will cancel out in the air between the mid and side+ loudspeakers, and the left channel stereo audio will cancel out in the air between the mid and side- loudspeakers. Because the side+/- loudspeakers are directly to the side of the listeners, they will all hear this stereo effect regardless of whether they are directly in front of the mid loudspeaker. Just like mid side recording, the stereo image can be widened or narrowed as the balance between the mid loudspeaker and side loudspeakers is adjusted.

You don't need to stop at just three loudspeakers. As long as you have more outputs on your playback system, you can continue to add loudspeakers to your system to help you create more interesting soundscapes. The concept of mid-side playback illustrates an important concept. Having multiple loudspeakers doesn't mean you have surround sound. If you play the same sound out of each loudspeaker, the precedence effect takes over and each listener will source the sound to the closest loudspeaker. To create surround-sound effects, you need to have different sounds in each loudspeaker. The concept of mid-side playback demonstrates how you can modify a single sound to have different properties in three loudspeakers, but you could also have completely different sounds playing from each loudspeaker. For example, instead of having a single track of raindrops playing out of ten loudspeakers, you could have ten different recordings of water dripping onto various surfaces. This will create a much more realistic and immersive rain effect. You could also mimic acoustic effects using multiple loudspeakers. You could have the dry sound of a recorded musical instrument playing out of the loudspeakers closest to the stage and then play various reverberant or wet versions of the recording out of the loudspeakers near the walls. With multiple playback channels and multiple loudspeakers, you could also create the effect of a sound moving around the room by automating volume changes over time.

8.2.4.6 Playback and Control

Sound playback has evolved greatly in the past decades, and it's safe to say tape decks with multiple operators and reel changes are a thing of history. While some small productions may still use CD players, MiniDiscs, or even MP3 players to play back their sound, it's also safe to say that computer-based playback is the system of choice, especially in any professional production. Already an integral part of the digital audio workflow, computers offer flexibility, scalability, predictability, and unprecedented control over audio playback. Being able to consistently run a performance and reduce operator error is a huge advantage that computer playback provides. Yet as simple as it may be to operate on the surface, the potential complexity behind a single click of a button can be enormous.

Popular computer sound playback software systems include SFX by Stage Research for Windows operating systems, and QLab by Figure 53 for a Mac. These playback tools allow for many methods of control and automation, including sending and receiving MIDI commands, scripting, Telnet, and more, allowing them to communicate with almost any other application or device. These playback systems also allow you to use multiple audio outputs, sending sound out anywhere you want, be it a few specific locations or the entire sound system. This is essential for creating immersive and dynamic surround effects. You'll need a separate physical output channel from your computer audio interface for each loudspeaker location (or group of loudspeakers, depending on your routing) in your system that you want to control individually.

Controlling these systems can be as simple as using the mouse pointer on your computer to click a "GO" button. Yet that single click could trigger layers and layers of sound and control cues, with specifically timed sequences that execute an entire automated scene change or special effect. Theme parks use these kinds of playback systems to automatically control an entire show or environment, including sound playback, lighting effects, mechanical automation, and any other special effects. Sometimes the simple "GO" isn't even triggered by a human operator, but by a timed script, making the entire playback and control a consistent and self-reliant process. Using MIDI or Open Sound Control, you can get into very complex control systems. Other possible examples include using sensors built into scenery or costumes for actor control, as well as synchronizing sound, lighting, and projection systems to keep precisely timed sequences operating together and exactly on cue, such as a simulated lightning strike.

Outside of an actual performance, these control systems can benefit you as a designer by providing a means of wireless remote control from a laptop or tablet, allowing you to make changes to cues while listening from various locations in the theatre.

>>

MATLAB EXERCISE:
Sculpting Sound
in MATLAB
http://bit.ly/29wlAYw

Using tools such as Max or Pd, you can capture input from all kinds of sources such as cameras, mobile devices, or even video game controllers, and use that control data to generate MIDI commands to control sound playback. You'll always learn more by actually doing it than simply reading about it, so included in this section are several exercises to get you going in making your own custom control and sound playback systems.

8.3 CREATIVE PROJECTS AND FINAL NOTE

Regardless of the path you've taken through this book's material, at some point you'll probably want to do something with the information. The book has looked at many concepts separa tely, but in a real project you'll apply a number of these concepts at the same time. The projects linked here are a sampling of the creative work possible when concepts, applications, and science are brought together.

This has been the ultimate purpose of our book: to encourage and provide resources for imaginative, innovative work in digital sound and music. We would love to hear from you, our readers—students, teachers, artists, self-taught hobbyists, professional sound designers and engineers. We're open to suggestions and corrections, and most of all we'd like to know about your own creative work.

Now go out and make a joyful noise!

8.4 REFERENCES

Davis, Gary and Ralph Jones. *Sound Reinforcement Handbook*, 2nd ed. Milwaukee, WI: Hal Leonard Publishing Corporation, 1990.

Huber, David and Robert Runstein. *Modern Recording Techniques*, 8th ed. New York: Focal Press, 2013.

Leonard, John. *Theatre Sound*. New York: Theatre Arts Books/Routledge, 2001.

McCarthy, Bob. *Sound Systems: Design and Optimization: Modern Techniques and Tools for Sound System Design and Alignment*, 3rd ed. New York: Focal Press, 2016

Slaton, Shannon. *Mixing a Musical: Broadway Theatrical Sound Techniques*. New York: Focal Press, 2001.

Yewdall, David. *Practical Art of Motion Picture Sound*, 4th ed. New York: Focal Press, 2011.

PRACTICAL EXERCISES:

Creating Your Own Digital Mixing Console
http://bit.ly/29lvM7L

Algorithmic Composition of Contrapuntal Music
http://bit.ly/2bxbWsc

Modeling and Printing 3D Objects That Make Sound
http://bit.ly/2bbZvjc

Programming and Composing with a Synthesizer
http://bit.ly/2bxbWsc

Synchronizing the Frequencies of Music and Image Computation in Real Time
http://bit.ly/2ba3PCl

APPENDIX A

Instructions for Using the Learning Supplements

Instructions for using the learning supplements are straightforward, as follows:

» **Practical Exercises:** Download the PDF. In some cases, there may be multiple files zipped together, in which case you'll have to unzip them. Solutions available upon request for instructors.

» **Flash Tutorials:** Be sure to have the Flash player installed in your browser, which is freely available online.

» **MAX Demos:** Download the Max Runtime environment from the Cycling '74 website, free of charge. Once you have Max Runtime on your computer, you can download the zip files for the MAX Demos. Unzip the zip file and look at the README pdf first to see a description of the MAX patcher. When you click on the PAT file, the Max Runtime will run it for you. If you want to program in MAX/MSP, you'll have to purchase the full version. We have provided a few MAX programming assignments that involve adding functionality to our pre-built demos. Alternatively, you could download the free equivalent of MAX, called PD (for Pure Data). The languages are very similar, although PD's Help is not as extensive as MAX's.

» **MATLAB Exercises:** Download the PDF. In some cases, there may be multiple files zipped together, in which case you'll have to unzip them. Solutions available upon request for instructors. If you don't have MATLAB, you can get Octave, its freeware equivalent, and try the examples in that environment.

» **Programming Exercises:** Download the PDF. In some cases, there may be multiple files zipped together, in which case you'll have to unzip them. Solutions available upon request for instructors.

APPENDIX B

List of Figures & Tables

***

Chapter 1 Figures & Tables

Chapter 3 Figures & Tables

Chapter 4 Figures & Tables

Chapter 5 Figures & Tables

Chapter 6 Figures & Tables

Chapter 7 Figures & Tables

Chapter 8 Figures & Tables

Index

About the Authors

Jennifer Burg and Jason Romney met as members of a committee helping to develop curriculum for a technology-target high school in Winston-Salem. They quickly recognized their complementary backgrounds and their shared interests in digital sound. Jennifer provided the mathematics and computer science perspective, and Jason added his considerable experience in sound design and his ability to give context and meaning to the book by relating science to applications. Thus a partnership was struck, with Eric Schwartz soon to be added as the third author.

Jennifer Burg began her career as a community college instructor of French and English. After "starting all over" and re-educating herself in computer science, she joined the Wake Forest University faculty in 1993, where she is now a professor of computer science. As co-initiator of the Humanitech Lab (formerly the STEM Incubator Program) and author of the textbook *The Science of Digital Media*, she has continued to build bridges between the humanities and computer science and to give relevance to science through hands-on, art-related applications. She wrote the music theory, mathematics, and algorithms sections of *Digital Sound and Music* and employed her English-major background in the overall editing of the book.

Jason Romney grew up acting in plays, learning to play various musical instruments, and taking things apart to figure out how they worked. As a theatre major in college he was introduced to theatre sound design, which seemed the perfect combination of these three interests. After graduating with a BFA in theatre design and technology, he received an MFA in sound design. Jason now works as a sound designer for live theatre and teaches sound design at the University of North Carolina School of the Arts. As a graduate student he quickly became frustrated with the lack of appropriate digital tools for theatre sound. Even the tools available from other disciplines came with no instructions on how to use them for theatre. This led Jason to search for his own solutions, which naturally led to researching the underlying science and technology behind these tools. His first computer program, written in REALBasic, was an emulator and remote editor for the popular Peavey PC1600x MIDI controller that is now used by professionals in the theatre, film, and music industries, as well as in educational institutions around the world. His master's thesis, "Computer Applications for Sound Design," included tutorials for using popular software tools from the recording and digital music industries to create sound content for live theatre. *Digital Sound and Music* is a natural extension of that work. Jason wrote the application sections of this book as well as the practical exercises. He also collaborated with Eric Schwartz on the design and programming of the video, Flash, and Max Demos.

Eric Schwartz earned his bachelor of science in electrical engineering with a concentration in audio engineering and a minor in computer engineering from the University of Miami, providing him with the technical expertise to help with the scientific and conceptual portions of the book. After spending some time working for an acoustical consulting firm, Eric's artistic side drew him back to earn a master's degree in sound design and production from the University of North Carolina School of the Arts, where Jason Romney advised on his master's thesis, "Achieving Acoustical Character In Sound." The thesis investigated scientific principles in acoustics and psychoacoustics aimed at practical techniques for manipulating sounds for an intended acoustical perspective. Eric's multidisciplinary interests in audio and multimedia led him to join the book-writing team as the creator and developer of many of the Flash and MAX/MSP tutorials and as co-author of the applications portions of the book. He also created the book's website at http://digitalsoundandmusic.com, where the learning supplements and tutorials are hosted. After several years building his own freelancing business—designing sound, composing music, and engineering audio for various mobile games, apps, films, videos, podcasts, live performances, and more—Eric has found himself shifting gears once more and is now busy applying his practical problem-solving, analytical, and creative skills and experience toward the growth and strategic success of Envato, a leading online marketplace for creative assets and people.